THE SACRED BOOKS OF THE EAST

F. MAX MULLER (ED.)

LIST OF THE 50 VOLUMES

1. Upanishads.
2. Sacred Laws of Aryas.
3. Texts of Confucianism.
4. Zend-Avesta.
5. Pahlavi Texts.
6. Qur'an.
7. Institutes of Vishnu.
8. Bhagavadgita, & c.
9. Qur'an.
10. (i) Dhammapada.
10. (ii) Sutta-Nipata.
11. Buddhist Suttas.
12. Satapatha-Brahmana.
13. Vinaya Texts.
14. Sacred Laws of Aryas.
15. Upanishads.
16. Texts of Confucianism.
17. Vinaya Texts.
18. Pahlavi Texts.
19. Fo-sho-hing-tsanking.
20. Vinaya Texts.
21. Saddharma Pundarika.
22. Gaina-Sutras.
23. Zend-Avesta.
24. Pahlavi Texts.
25. Laws of Manu.
26. Satapatha-Brahmana.
27. Texts of Confucianism (Li Ki).
28. Texts of Confucianism (Li Ki).
29. Grihya-Sutras.
30 Grihya-Sutras.
31. Zend-Avesta.
32. Vedic Hymns.
33. Minor Law-Books.
34. Vedanta-Sutras.
35. Milinda.
36. Milinda.
37. Pahlavi Texts.
38. Vedanta-Sutras.
39. Texts of Taoism
40. Texts of Taoism
41. Satapatha-Brahmana
42. Atharva-veda.
43. Satapatha-Brahmana.
44. Satapatha-Brahmana.
45. Gaina-Sutras.
46. Vedic Hymns.
47. Pahlavi Texts.
48. Vedanta-Sutras.
49. (i) Buddhakarita.
49. (ii) Mahayana Texts.
50. A General Index

The Sacred Books of the East, Vol. 25

THE LAWS OF MANU

Edited by

F. MAX. MULLER

Translated with Extracts from Seven Commentaries

by

G. BUHLER

GYAN

Published by

GYAN

Gyan Publishing House
5, Ansari Road
Daryaganj, New Delhi-110002
Phone: 011-47034999, 9811692060
E-mail: books@gyanbooks.com

Distribution Network
gyanbooks.com
India, USA, Canada, UK, Australia, France

ISBN : 978-81-212-2937-1 (Set)
ISBN : 978-81-212-2824-4 (PB)
First Published, 1886

2nd Impression 2021

Printed at: Gyan Press, Delhi.

The Sacred Books of the East, Vol. 25

The Laws of Manu
Edited by: F. Max. Muller, Translated by: G. Buhler

THE

SACRED BOOKS OF THE EAST

TRANSLATED

BY VARIOUS ORIENTAL SCHOLARS

AND EDITED BY

F. MAX MÜLLER

VOL. XXV

Oxford

AT THE CLARENDON PRESS

1886

THE LAWS OF MANU

TRANSLATED

WITH EXTRACTS FROM SEVEN COMMENTARIES

BY

G. BÜHLER

Oxford

AT THE CLARENDON PRESS

1886

CONTENTS.

INTRODUCTION.

THE LAWS OF MANU.

INTRODUCTION.

I.

DIFFICULT as the historical problems are which the Dharma-sûtras translated in vols. ii and xiv of this Series offer, they are infinitely less complicated than those connected with the metrical law-books and especially with the Manu-smr*i*ti, or, to speak more exactly, with Bhr*i*gu's version of the Institutes of the Sacred Law proclaimed by Manu. Though mostly the materials available for the inquiry into the history of the Dharma-sûtras are scanty, and in part at least belong to the floating traditions which are generally current among the learned, but of uncertain origin, they not only exhibit no extravagancies, but agree fully with the facts known from strictly historical sources. Moreover, and this is the most important point, though the text of the Dharma-sûtras has not always been preserved with perfect purity, they have evidently retained their original character. They do not pretend to be anything more than the compositions of ordinary mortals, based on the teaching of the Vedas, on the decisions of those who are acquainted with the law, and on the customs of virtuous Âryas. In some cases their authors say as much in plain words. Thus Âpastamba repeatedly laments the sinfulness and the weakness of 'the men of later times,' and Gautama warns against an imitation of the irregular conduct of the ancients whose great 'lustre' preserved them from falling. It is, further, still possible to recognise, even on a superficial examination, for what purpose the Dharma-sûtras were originally composed. Nobody can doubt for a moment that they are manuals written by the teachers of the Vedic schools for the guidance of their pupils, that at first they were held to be authoritative in restricted circles, and that they were later only acknowledged as sources of the sacred law applicable to all Âryas. This fact is fully acknowledged by the Hindu tradition, even in cases where the Dharma-sûtras no longer are the property of particular Vedic schools.

The metrical Smritis, on the other hand, are surrounded by clearly fictitious traditions, by mythological legends which either may have grown up spontaneously, because the real origin had been forgotten, or may have been fabricated intentionally in order to show that these works possess divine authority and, hence, have a claim to implicit obedience on the part of all Âryas. Nay, what is more, such legends or portions of them have been introduced into the text, and obscure the real character of the Smritis. These peculiarities are particularly marked in the Mânava Dharmasâstra, where the whole first chapter is devoted to the purpose of showing the mighty scope of the book, and of setting forth its divine origin as well as the manner in which it was revealed to mankind. Its opening verses narrate how the great sages approached Manu, the descendant of self-existent Brahman, and asked him to explain the sacred law. Manu agrees to their request, and gives to them an account of the creation as well as of his own origin from Brahman. After mentioning that he learnt 'these Institutes of the Sacred Law' from the creator who himself produced them, and that he taught them to the ten sages whom he created in the beginning, he transfers the work of expounding them to Bhrigu, one of his ten mind-born sons. The latter begins his task by completing, as the commentators call it, Manu's account of the creation. First he gives the theory of the seven Manvantaras, the Yugas, and other divisions of time, as well as an incidental description of the order of the creation. Next he briefly describes the duties of the four principal castes, passes then to an encomium of the Brâhmanas and of the Institutes of Manu, and winds up with an enumeration of the contents of all the twelve chapters of the work, which he promises to expound 'exactly as it was revealed to him.' In the following chapters we find frequent allusions to the situation which the first describes. In about forty passages a new topic is introduced by a prefatory verse which contains phrases like 'such and such a matter has been explained to you, now listen to,' &c., or 'I will next declare,' &c.

Twice (V, 1–3 and XII, 1–2) the sages are represented as interrupting Bh*ri*gu's discourse and expressing their desire to be instructed on particular points, and on both occasions Bh*ri*gu is again named as the narrator. Moreover in a number of verses[1] Manu is particularly mentioned as the author of certain rules, and II, 7 the authoritativeness of Manu's teaching is emphatically asserted, 'because he was omniscient.' In two other passages Manu appears, however, in different characters. VII, 42 he is enumerated among the kings who gained sovereignty by their humility, and XII, 123 he is identified with the supreme Brahman.

This account of the origin of our Manu-sm*ri*ti would have to be slightly modified by those who accept as genuine the verse[2] which stands at the beginning of the Sm*ri*ti according to the commentators Govindarâ*g*a, Nârâya*n*a, and Râghavânanda, as well as according to the Ka*s*mîr copy and other MSS. As this verse contains an invocation of the self-existent Brahman, and a promise to explain the laws which Manu taught, it indicates, as Govindarâ*g*a says[3], that 'some pupil of Bh*ri*gu recites the work which had descended to him through an unbroken line of teachers.' According to this version we have, therefore, a triple exordium instead of a double one, and our Manu-sm*ri*ti does not contain the original words of Bh*ri*gu, but a recension of his recension such as it had been handed down among his pupils. The additional verse is apparently intended to make the story more plausible.

The remarks which the commentators make on this narrative are scanty, and, though they are meant to support its credibility, they are, partly at least, calculated to discredit it. Medhâtithi states in his remarks on Manu I, 1, that the Pra*g*âpati Manu was 'a particular individual, perfect

[1] See the index s. v. Manu. [2] See note on Manu I, 1.

[3] इह भृगुशिष्यः कश्चिदविच्छिन्नपरंपरायातस्मृत्यर्थप्रबन्धमिदमाह ॥

in the study of many branches of the Veda, in the knowledge (of its meaning) and in the performance (of its precepts), and known through the sacred tradition which has been handed down in regular succession[1].' Govindarâ*g*a closely agrees, and says that Manu is 'a great sage, who received his name on account of his acquaintance with the meaning of the whole Veda, who is known to all learned men through the tradition handed down in regular succession, and who is entrusted with causing the creation, preservation, and destruction (of the world)[2].' Kullûka, on the other hand, though he agrees with respect to the etymology and explanation of Manu's name, deriving it from man, 'to know (the meaning of the Veda),' and though he admits the human character of his *S*âstra, somewhat differs in the description of the person. Referring to XII, 123, he declares Manu to be a manifestation or incarnation of the supreme Soul. Further, Medhâtithi and Kullûka adduce in their remarks on the same verse various passages from the *S*ruti and the Sm*ri*ti, tending to prove the authoritativeness of the Manu-sm*ri*ti. Both quote slightly varying versions of the famous Vedic passage which declares that 'All Manu said is medicine.' Medhâtithi adds only one more anonymous verse, to the effect that 'the Vedas were proclaimed by the great sages, but the Smârta or traditional lore by Manu[3].' Kullûka gives two other passages, one from the B*ri*haspati-sm*ri*ti which places Manu's *S*âstra at the head of all works of the same class, and another from the Mahâbhârata which declares that 'the Purâ*n*as, Manu's laws, the Vedas, and the medical works must not be opposed by (adverse) reasoning.' Both commentators mention also that the pre-eminence of Manu's teaching is admitted in other passages of the Vedas, the Purâ*n*as, the

---

[1] मनुर्नाम कश्चित्पुरुषविशेषोनेकवेदशाखाध्ययनविज्ञानानुष्ठानसंपन्नः स्मृतिपरंपराप्रसिद्धः ॥

[2] मनुर्नाम महर्षिरशेषवेदार्थज्ञानेन प्राप्तमनुसंज्ञ आगमपरंपरया सकलविद्वज्जनकर्णगोचरीभूतः सर्गस्थितिप्रलयकारणेधिकृतः ॥

[3] ऋचो यजूंषि सामानि मन्त्रा आथर्वणाश्च ये। महर्षिभिस्तु तत्प्रोक्तं स्मार्तं तु मनुरब्रवीत् ॥

Itihâsas, and the Sm*ri*tis. Finally, in the notes on Manu I, 58, they discuss the question, how the Sm*ri*ti can be called the Mânava Dharma*s*âstra, though, as is admitted in the work itself, Brahman was its real author. Medhâtithi offers two explanations. First he contends that Brahman produced only 'the multitude of injunctions and prohibitions,' while the work itself was composed by Manu. Next he says that, according to others, the *S*âstra may be called Manu's, even if it were first composed by Brahman. In proof of this assertion he points to the analogous case of the river Ganges, which, though originating elsewhere, i.e. in heaven, is called Haimavatî, because it is first seen in the Himavat or Himâlaya, and to that of the Kâ*th*aka *S*âkhâ, which, though studied and taught by many others, is named after Ka*th*a. In conclusion, he adds, 'Nârada also records, "This work, consisting of one hundred thousand verses, was composed by Pra*g*âpati (Brahman); it was successively abridged by Manu and others[1]."' Kullûka, who gives a somewhat insufficient abstract of Medhâtithi's discussion, refers to the same passage of Nârada, and bases on it his own explanation of I, 58, according to which it means that Brahman first composed the law-book, and that Manu condensed its contents in his own language and taught it in that form to his pupils.

This is, as far as I know, all that the commentaries say about Manu and the history of the Mânava Dharma*s*âstra, and their remarks contain also the substance of all that has been brought forward in other discussions on the same subject, with which we meet elsewhere[2]. Important as they may appear to a Hindu who views the question of the origin of the Manu-sm*ri*ti with the eye of faith, they are of little value for the historical student who stands outside the circle of the Brâhmanical doctrines. The statements regarding the person of Manu can, at the best, only furnish materials

[1] नारदश्च स्मरति । शतसाहस्रो ग्रन्थः प्रजापतिना कृतः स मन्वादिभिः क्रमेण संक्षिप्त इति ॥

[2] See e. g. the passages translated in Professor Max Müller's Ancient Sanskrit Literature, pp. 87–94.

for mythological research. The arguments in support of the authenticity and authoritativeness of the Manu-sm*ri*ti are extremely weak. For the Vedic passage which the commentators adduce is, strictly speaking, a misquotation. It occurs in four slightly differing versions in three Sa*m*hitâs and in one Brâhma*n*a [1]. But in all the four places it refers, in the first instance, to Vedic Mantras which Manu is said to have revealed or seen. As, however, the assertion of the wholesomeness of Manu's teaching is couched in general terms, it may probably be inferred that many sayings, attributed to the father of mankind, were known to the authors of the four Vedic works, and it is not improbable that legal maxims were included amongst them [2]. But Medhâtithi's and Kullûka's assumption that our Manu-sm*ri*ti is meant in the passages quoted would require very strong special proof, as its language and part of its doctrines by no means agree with those of the Vedic times. Of course, no such proof is offered, and it is not probable that it ever will be offered. The quotations made by the commentators from the Mahâbhârata and from the B*ri*haspati-sm*ri*ti, as well as their well-founded assertion that in the Purâ*n*as and in many Sm*ri*tis Manu is frequently referred to as an authority on the sacred law, are of greater importance. It is undoubtedly true that the two works mentioned by Kullûka refer to a particular Dharma*s*âstra attributed to Manu, and the same remark holds good with respect to those passages of the Purâ*n*as and of the Sm*ri*tis where, in enumerations of the authors of Dharma*s*âstras, Manu is placed at the head of the list. Yet even this evidence is of little use, because on the one hand the antiquity of many of the works in which Manu's name occurs is extremely doubtful, and on the other hand the existence of several recensions of Manu's laws is admitted, and can be shown to have been a fact. Hence a reference to a Manu-sm*ri*ti in a

[1] Kâ*th*aka XI, 5 (apparently quoted by Medhâtithi); Maitrâya*n*îyâ Sa*m*hitâ I, 1, 5; Taittirîyâ Sa*m*hitâ II, 2, 10, 2; and Tâ*n*dya Brâhma*n*a XXIII, 16, 7 (quoted by Kullûka).

[2] I would not infer with Professor Max Müller, India, what can it teach us? p. 364, that a legal work ascribed to a Manu was known to the authors of the four works; see also below, p. lx.

Purâ*n*a or a Sm*ri*ti does not prove much for Bh*ri*gu's Sa*m*hitâ, if, at the same time, it is not made evident that the latter is really meant, and that the work in which it is contained really has a claim to be considered ancient. In illustration of this point it may suffice to remark here that the B*ri*haspati-sm*ri*ti, which Kullûka adduces as a witness, is by no means an ancient work, but considerably later than the beginning of our era, because it gives a definition of golden dînâras, an Indian coin struck in imitation of and called after the Roman denarii [1]. Regarding Manu and the Mahâbhârata more will be said below. Medhâtithi's quotation from Nârada is very unlucky; for it is inexact, and worded in such a manner as to veil the serious discrepancy which exists between the stories told in the Mânava Dharma*s*âstra and in the Nârada-sm*ri*ti. The introduction to the latter, as read in the MSS. of the vulgata, does not state that the original law-book of one hundred thousand verses was composed by Pra*g*âpati and abridged by Manu and others, but alleges that its author was Manu Pra*g*âpati, and that Nârada and Sumati the son of Bh*ri*gu summarised it [2]. The text of Nârada, which is accompanied by Kalyâ*n*abha*tt*a's edition of Asahâya's commentary, names one more sage, Mârka*nd*eya, who also tried his hand at Manu Pra*g*âpati's enormous work. Whichever of the two versions may be the original one, it is evident that Medhâtithi's representation of Nârada's statement is inexact, and that the latter differs considerably from the story in our Manu-sm*ri*ti, which asserts that it is the original work composed by Brahman, and revealed by Manu to Bh*ri*gu, who explains it to the great sages 'exactly as he received it.' Hence Nârada's story discredits the details of the account given in the Mânava Dharma*s*âstra. It might, at the best, be only quoted to prove the existence of the general belief that Manu was the first lawgiver of India. These remarks will

[1] West and Bühler, Digest, p. 48, third edition.

[2] See Jolly, Nârada, p. 2, and Tagore Lectures of 1883, p. 46. My conjecture that the introduction to Nârada belongs to Asahâya, not to the Sm*ri*ti itself (West and Bühler, Digest, p. 49), is not tenable.

suffice to show that the explanatory notes offered by the Indian commentators on the origin and history of the Manu-smriti are not suited to furnish a basis for a critical discussion of these questions, and that hence they have been deservedly set aside by most modern Sanskritists who have written on the subject. As regards the theories of the latter, it would be useless to enumerate those preceding Professor Max Müller's now generally accepted view, according to which our Manu-smriti is based on, or is in fact a recast of an ancient Dharma-sûtra. But, well known as are his hypotheses and the later discoveries confirming them, an introduction to the laws of Manu would, I think, be incomplete without a full restatement of his arguments and of their additional supports furnished by others.

The considerations on which Professor Max Müller based his explanation of the origin of the Manu-smriti may be briefly stated as follows [1]. The systematic cultivation of the sacred sciences of the Brâhmans began and for a long time had its centre in the ancient Sûtrakaranas, the schools which first collected the fragmentary doctrines, scattered in the older Vedic works, and arranged them for the convenience of oral instruction in Sûtras or strings of aphorisms. To the subjects which these schools chiefly cultivated, belongs besides the ritual, grammar, phonetics, and the other so-called Aṅgas of the Veda, the sacred law also. The latter includes not only the precepts for the moral duties of all Âryas, but also the special rules regarding the conduct of kings and the administration of justice. The Sûtra treatises on law thus cover the whole range of topics, contained in the metrical Smritis attributed to Manu, Yâgñavalkya, and other sages. Though only one Dharma-sûtra, that of the Âpastambîyas, actually remains connected with the aphorisms on the ritual and other sacred subjects, the existence of the Dharmasâstras of Gautama, Vasishtha, and Vishnu, which are likewise composed in Sûtras, proves that formerly

[1] See his letter to Mr. Morley, reprinted in Sacred Books of the East, vol. ii, pp. ix-xi, and Hist. Anc. Sansk. Lit. pp. 132-134. Compare also the analogous views formed independently by Professors Weber and Stenzler, Indische Studien, vol. i, pp. 69, 143, 243-4.

they were more numerous. The perfectly credible tradition of the Mîmâmsâ school, which declares that originally each Vedic school or Karana possessed a peculiar work on Dharma, confirms this assumption. While the Dharma-sûtras possess a considerable antiquity, dating between 600–200 B.C., the metrical Smritis cannot be equally ancient, because there is much in their form that is modern, and especially because the epic Anushtubh Sloka, in which they are written, was not used for continuous composition during the Sûtra period. As the metrical Smritis are later than the Dharma-sûtras, it is, under the circumstances stated, very probable that each of them is based on a particular Dharma-sûtra. The Mânava Dharmasâstra in particular may be considered as a recast and versification of the Dharma-sûtra of the Mânava Sûtrakarana, a subdivision of the Maitrâyanîya school, which adheres to a redaction of the Black Yagur-veda.

Considering the state of our knowledge of Vedic literature thirty years ago, the enunciation of this hypothesis was certainly a bold step. The facts on which it rested were few, and the want of important links in the premises laid it open to weighty objections. No proof was or could be furnished that the Sûtras of Gautama, Vasishtha, and Vishnu originally were manuals of Vedic schools, not codes promulgated for the guidance of all Âryas, as the Hindu tradition, then known, asserted. The assumption that it was so, rested solely on the resemblance of their form and contents to those of the Âpastambîya Dharma-sûtra. No trace of a Mânava Dharma-sûtra could be shown, nor could any connexion between the Mânava Dharmasâstra and the school of the Mânavas, except through their titles, be established. The assertion that the Brâhmans had turned older Sûtras, and especially Dharma-sûtras, into metrical works, written in epic Slokas, had to be left without any illustration, and no cause was assigned which would explain this remarkable change. As a set off against these undeniable weaknesses, Professor Max Müller's hypothesis possessed two strong points which secured for it from the outset a favourable reception on the part of all Sanskritists of the historical school. First, it substituted a rational theory of historical development for the fantastic fables of the Hindu tradition and for the hopeless uncertainty which characterised the earlier speculations of European scholars concerning the origin of the so-called Indian codes of law. Secondly, it fully agreed with many facts which the beginning exploration of Vedic literature had brought to light, and which, taken as a whole, forced on all serious students the conviction that the systematic cultivation of all the Indian *S*âstras had begun in the Vedic schools. Subsequent events have shown that Professor Max Müller was right to rely on these two leading ideas, and that his fellow Sanskritists did well to follow him, instead of taking umbrage at the minor flaws. Slowly but steadily a great number of the missing links in the chain of evidence has been brought to light by subsequent investigations. We now know that the Sûtra works of other schools than the Âpastambîyas included or still include treatises on the sacred law. The Dharma-sûtra of the Baudhâyanîyas, the oldest Sûtra-*k*ara*n*a of the Taittirîya Veda, has been recovered. Though the connexion between the several parts of the great body of Sûtras has been severed, it is yet possible to recognise that it once was closely joined to the G*ri*hya-sûtra[1]. The recovery of the entire collection of Hira*n*yake*s*i-sûtras has proved that these too include a Dharma-sûtra, which in this instance has been borrowed from the earlier Âpastambîyas[2]. The mystery which surrounded the position of the Dharma*s*âstras of Gautama, Vish*n*u, and Vasish*th*a has been cleared up. To the assertion that they were composed by ancient *Ri*shis for the welfare of mankind, we can at present oppose another tradition according to which they were at first studied and recognised as authoritative by particular schools only, adhering respectively to the Sâma-veda, Black Yagur-veda, and the Rig-veda[3]. Internal evidence confirming this tradition has been found in the case of Gautama's Dharma*s*âstra and of the Vish*n*u-sm*ri*ti, or, more correctly,

[1] Sacred Books of the East, vol. xiv, p. xxxi.
[2] Sacred Books of the East, vol. ii, p. xxiii.
[3] Sacred Books of the East, vol. ii, pp. xlv–xlviii; vol. vii, pp. x–xvi; vol. xiv, pp. xl–xlv.

of the Kâ*th*aka Sûtras. These latter discoveries are of particularly great importance, because they fully establish the truth of the assumption, underlying Professor Max Müller's theory, that in post-Vedic times the Brâhmans did not hesitate to change the character of ancient school-books and to convert them into generally binding law-codes, either by simply taking them out of their connexion with the *S*rauta and G*ri*hya-sûtras or by adding besides matter which, in the eyes of orthodox Hindus, must greatly increase the sentiment of reverence felt for them. It is especially the case of the so-called Vish*n*u-sm*ri*ti, which deserves the most careful attention. The beginning and the end of the work distinctly characterise it as a revelation of the god Vish*n*u. Vish*n*u, Vaish*n*ava worship and philosophy are on various occasions praised and recommended in the course of the discussions. Yet the difference in the style of the introductory and concluding chapters leaves no doubt that they are later additions, and the perfectly credible tradition of the Pa*nd*its of Pu*n*a and Benares, the occurrence of particular sacred texts known to the Kâ*th*akas alone, as well as the special resemblance of its contents to those of the Kâ*th*aka G*ri*hya-sûtra, make it perfectly certain that the work is only a Vaish*n*ava recast of the Kâ*th*aka Dharma-sûtra[1]. We thus obtain in this case the confirmation of almost every fact which the conversion of the Dharma-sûtra of the Mânavas into the revealed code of the Pra*g*âpati Manu presupposes, with the sole exception of the substitution of epic *S*lokas for aphoristic prose. With respect to the last point, the further exploration of the Smriti literature has furnished numerous analogies. As an instance to the point we can now cite the fragments of the so-called B*ri*hat Sañkha Dharma*s*âstra, which, as the quotations show, must

---

[1] A quotation in Govindarâ*g*a's Sm*ri*tima*ñg*arî, fol. 12[b], l. 8 (India Office Collection, No. 1736), contains a very small portion of this work. When explaining the penance for the murder of a Brâhma*n*a, mentioned Manu XI, 74, Govindarâ*g*a says, अवस्थानं कठसूत्रकृता व्याख्यानं [तं]। त्वक्त्यागो भक्तत्यागो वस्त्रत्याग इति॥ त्वग् [त्वक्त्यागः] क्षुरादिना देहतक्षणम्॥ The quotation shows that the Dharma-sûtra of the Ka*th*as mentioned the fanciful expiations ending in death, which are given in all the ancient law-books, but omitted in the Vish*n*u-sm*ri*ti.

formerly have consisted of prose and verse, while the available MSS. show Sûtras and Anushtubhs in one chapter only, and Slokas alone in the remainder[1]. There are, further, such works like the two Âsvalâyana Smritis and the Saunaka-smriti, evidently versifications of the corresponding Grihya-sûtras, with or without the additions of extraneous matter[2]. In short, among all the general propositions concerning the origin of the metrical Smritis, which Professor Max Müller advanced, only one, the assertion that during the Sûtra period of 600–200 B.C. works written in continuous epic verse were unknown, has proved untenable in its full extent. It seems no longer advisable to limit the production of Sûtras to so short and so late a period as 600–200 B.C., and the existence of metrical school-manuals at a much earlier date has been clearly demonstrated[3]. It is now evident that the use of the heroic metre for such works did not begin all of a sudden and at a certain given date. But it seems, nevertheless, indisputable that the use of aphoristic prose was adopted earlier than that of verse. For in all known cases a Sûtra, not a metrical Samgraha, Vârttika, or Kârikâ, stands at the head of each series of school-books, and some of the most salient peculiarities of the Sûtra style reappear in that of the metrical manuals[4]. With respect to the conjectures specially affecting the Mânava Dharmasâstra, the former existence of a Mânava Dharma-sûtra, consisting of prose mixed with verses in several metres, has been established by the discovery of some quotations in the Vâsishtha Dharma-sûtra, and their contents show that the work known to the author of the latter Sâstra was closely related to our Manu-smriti. As regards the connexion of this Dharma-sûtra, and consequently of our Manu-smriti with the Sûtrakarana of the Mânavas, the results of the late researches have not been equally satisfactory. The recovery of the writings of the Mânavas has not only not furnished any facts in support of the supposed connexion, but, on the contrary, has raised difficulties, as it

[1] West and Bühler, Digest of H. L. p. 40, third edition.
[2] West and Bühler, loc. cit. p. 51.
[3] Goldstücker, Mânavakalpa-sûtra, p. 78.
[4] West and Bühler, loc. cit. pp. 42, 44.

appears that the doctrines of the Mânava Grihya-sûtra differ very considerably from those of our Mânava Dharmasâstra. All that has been brought forward in substantiation of this portion of Professor Max Müller's hypothesis is that as close an affinity exists between the Vishnusmriti, the modern recension of the Kâthaka Dharma-sûtra, and our Manu-smriti, as is found between the Kâthaka and Mânava Grihya-sûtras and between the Kâthaka and Mânava Samhitâs, and that hence the Vedic original of the Manu-smriti may be supposed to have belonged to the Mânava school[1]. The conclusive force of this argument is no doubt somewhat weakened, as Dr. von Bradke has pointed out, by the fact that the Vishnu-smriti is not the original Kâthaka Dharma-sûtra. But to reject it altogether on account of this circumstance would be going too far. For the agreement between the Smritis of Manu and Vishnu extends to many subjects where the latter shows no traces of recasting, and may be reasonably supposed to faithfully represent the original Dharma-sûtra. Nevertheless a full reconsideration of this point is indispensable. Before we proceed to that, it will, however, be advisable first to supplement Professor Max Müller's arguments against the antiquity of our Manu-smriti by the discussion of some of its passages which clearly admit an acquaintance with a large body of older legal literature and particularly with Dharma-sûtras, and, secondly, to re-examine and complete the proof for the former existence of a Mânava Dharma-sûtra and for its having been the precursor of the metrical law-book.

Among the passages of the Manu-smriti which disprove the claim, set up by its author, to be the first legislator, and which show that he had many predecessors, the first place must be allotted to its statements regarding controversies and conflicting decisions on certain points of the ritual and of the law. Such cases are by no means rare. Thus the observances of 'some,' with respect to the order of the several ceremonies at a Srâddha[2] and to the disposal

[1] Professor Jolly, Sacred Books of the East, vol. vii, pp. xxvi-xxvii; and Dr. von Bradke, Jour. Germ. Or. Soc. vol. xxxii, pp. 438-441.

[2] The same difference of opinion is mentioned in Sâṅkhâyana Grihya-sûtra IV, 1, 10.

of the funeral cakes, are mentioned Manu III, 261. Discussions of the ancient sages, exactly resembling those met with in the Dharma-sûtras[1], are given IX, 31–55 regarding the long-disputed question whether a son begotten on a wife by a stranger, but with the husband's consent, belongs to the natural parent or to 'the owner of the soil.' In the same chapter it is stated, just as in Gautama's Dharma-sûtra[2], that 'some' permit the procreation of a second son with an appointed widow. Manu X, 70–71, we find a decision on the question whether, as 'some' assert, the seed be more important, or, as 'others' state, the soil, or, as 'again others' maintain, the seed and the soil have equal importance, and, XI, 45, we are told that the sages, i. e. all sages, are convinced of the efficacy of penances for atoning unintentional offences, while 'some' declare that they even destroy the guilt of him who sinned intentionally. The latter point is discussed in exactly the same manner Gaut. XIX, 3–6. In other cases the author is less explicit. He merely places conflicting opinions side by side without indicating that they belong to different authorities, and hence he has mostly succeeded in misleading the commentators as to his real meaning. Thus we read Manu II, 145, that the teacher is less venerable than the father and the mother, while the next following verses teach exactly the contrary doctrine. The commentators are much perplexed by this contradiction. But if we turn to Gautama II, 50–51, where it is said, 'The teacher is chief among all Gurus; some say (that) the mother (holds the first place),' it is not doubtful that the Manu-smriti gives in the first verse the opinion of Gautama's 'some' as the pûrvapaksha, and adduces the following one in order to prove its incorrectness. A similar case occurs Manu III, 23–25, where three opinions regarding the permissibility of certain marriage-rites are enumerated, the last of which is the siddhânta or the author's own view.

It might be contended that these passages, the list of

[1] See especially Vas. XVII, 6–9, where one of the verses of the Manu-smriti occurs.

[2] Gaut. XVIII, 8.

which might be considerably enlarged, do not necessarily force on us the conviction that they refer to actual law-books which preceded our Manu-sm*ri*ti. If they stood by themselves, they might possibly be explained as showing nothing more than that legal and ritual questions had long engaged the attention of the learned. But this subterfuge becomes impossible, as we find in other verses the explicit confession that the author of the Manu-sm*ri*ti knew Dharma*s*âstras. Three passages allude to their existence in general terms. The first occurs in the definition of the terms *S*ruti and Sm*ri*ti, Manu II, 10, 'But by *S*ruti (revelation) is meant the Veda, and by Sm*ri*ti (tradition) the Institutes of the sacred law.' In the text the last word, dharma*s*âstram, stands in the singular. But it must doubtlessly be taken, as Kullûka[1] and Nârâya*n*a[2] indicate, in a collective sense. Another mention of law-books is found Manu XII, 111, where a dharmapâ*th*aka*h*, 'one who recites (the Institutes of) the sacred law,' is named among the members of a parishad or assembly entitled to decide difficult points of law. The commentators are unanimous in explaining dharma, literally 'the sacred law,' by 'the Institutes of the sacred law' or 'the Sm*ri*tis of Manu and others,' and it is indeed impossible to take the word in any other sense than that of 'law-books[3].' The third passage is perfectly explicit, as the word Dharma*s*âstra is used in the plural. It occurs in the section on funeral sacrifices, Manu III, 232, 'At a (sacrifice in honour) of the manes he must let (his guests) hear the Veda, the Institutes of the sacred law (dharma*s*âstrâ*n*i),' &c.[4] Here the existence of many earlier law-books is plainly acknowledged. The character of the Institutes of the sacred law, known to the author of our Manu, may be inferred

---

[1] मन्वादिशास्त्रं स्मृतिः ॥

[2] धर्मशास्त्रं प्राधान्येन । यत्रानुशासनीयं तद्धर्मशास्त्रम् ॥

[3] Medh. धर्मपाठको मन्वादिस्मृतिशास्त्राणामध्येता ॥ Gov. मानवादिधर्माध्येता ॥ Kull. मानवादिधर्मशास्त्रवेदी ॥ Nand. धर्मशास्त्रपाठकः ॥ The full significance of this passage will be shown below, p. lii.

[4] See also Professor Stenzler in the Indische Studien, vol. i, p. 245; Dr. Johänntgen, Das Gesetzbuch des Manu, p. 76.

from some other passages which reveal an acquaintance with the Aṅgas of the Veda[1]. Manu II, 141, and IV, 98, these auxiliary sciences are mentioned in a general way. From Manu III, 185, where it is said that a Brâhma*n*a who knows the six Aṅgas sanctifies the company at a *S*râddha dinner, we learn that their number, as known to our author, did not differ from that mentioned in all Vedic works. Further, the name of the first Aṅga, the Kalpa, occurs III, 185, and the mention of a Nairukta among the members of a parishad shows that the fourth, the Nirukta, was also known. With the latter and the remaining four, which the author of the Manu-sm*ri*ti in all probability also knew, we are not immediately concerned. But the first, the Kalpa, possesses a very great interest for our purposes. This term, as is well known, denotes collectively those Sûtras of the Vedic schools which teach the performance of the *S*rauta sacrifices, the rites especially described in the *S*ruti. Hence both *S*rauta-sûtras and, of course, also Sûtra-*k*ara*n*as must have preceded the Manu-sm*ri*ti. If it is now borne in mind that according to the Hindu tradition, mentioned above, all Sûtra*k*ara*n*as formerly possessed Dharma-sûtras, and that in some existing Kalpas the Dharma-sûtras are closely connected with the *S*rauta-sûtras, it becomes exceedingly probable, nay, certain, that our Mânava Dharma*s*âstra is later than some of the Dharma-sûtras. This conclusion is further corroborated by those passages of the Manu-sm*ri*ti where the author quotes the opinions of individual predecessors. Manu III, 16 we read, 'According to Atri and (Gautama) the son of Utathya[2] he who weds a *S*ûdra woman becomes an outcast, according to *S*aunaka on the birth of a son, and according to Bh*ri*gu he who has (male) offspring from a (*S*ûdra female alone).' Under the above explanation, which is adopted by the majority of the commentators,

[1] See also Professor Stenzler, loc. cit.; Dr. Johänntgen, loc. cit. p. 74.

[2] The form Utathya is a corruption of the Vedic U*k*athya, and shows the substitution of a dental for a palatal, which is not uncommon in the Prâkrit dialects. Hence it possesses a certain value as an additional proof for the post-Vedic origin of the Manu-sm*ri*ti.

and is confirmed by an analogous passage of the aphoristic Dharmasâstra of Usanas[1], the author adduces there the opinions of four older authorities, all of which are credited by the Hindu tradition with the revelation of law-books. We still possess several Smritis attributed to Atri, Saunaka, and to Gautama, as well as one said to belong to Bhrigu. With the exception of the aphoristic Gautamîya Dharmasâstra all these works are modern, some being metrical recensions of older Sûtras, and some of very doubtful origin. It is, therefore, impossible that any of the existing Dharmasâstras, Atri, Saunaka, and Bhrigu, can be referred to by Manu, and, as a matter of fact, the opinions quoted cannot be traced in them. But if we turn to Gautama's Sûtra we find among those persons who defile the company at a Srâddha dinner, and who are thus excluded from the community of the virtuous, the sûdrâpati, literally 'the husband of a Sûdra female[2].' The real signification of the compound seems, however, to be, as Haradatta suggests, 'he whose only wife or dharmapatnî is a Sûdrâ.' As it appears from Manu III, 17–19, that the opinion attributed to the son Utathya was the same, it is not at all unlikely that the Manu-smriti actually quotes the still existing Sûtra of Gautama. Another reference to a lost Sûtra occurs at Manu VI, 21, where it is said of the hermit in the forest, 'Or he may constantly subsist on flowers, roots, and fruit alone . . . . . . , following the rule of the (Institutes) of Vikhanas.' The original Sanskrit of the participial clause is 'vaikhânasamate sthitah,' and means literally 'abiding by the Vaikhânasa opinion.' The commentators, with the exception of Nârâyana, are unanimous in declaring that

[1] Us. Dharmasâstra, chap. III, पतितो वृपलीपतिः । न पततीत्येके । ब्राह्मणस्य कल्पविहिताश्चतस्रोनुपूर्वेण भार्या भवन्तीति वसिष्ठ आह । पतति न पततीति संशयः । वृपल्यां पततीति हारीतः । जननात्पततीति शौनकः । तदपत्यः पततीति गौतमः ॥ Though Usanas' statements regarding the opinions of the ancient lawyers do not agree with those of the Manu-smriti, except in the case of Saunaka, they are yet important, because they show that differences of opinion regarding the effects of a marriage with a Sûdrâ did occur. See also Jolly, Tagore Lectures, p. 53.

[2] Gautama XV, 18; Sacred Books of the East, vol. ii, p. 255.

the word Vaikhânasa here denotes a *S*âstra or Sûtra promulgated by Vikhanas, in which the duties of hermits were described at length[1]. The correctness of this opinion seems to me indisputable. For the word mata, 'opinion,' in Manu's verse, requires that the preceding part of the compound should denote either a person, or a school, or a work. If we take vaikhânasa in the sense of hermit in the forest, we obtain the meaningless translation, 'a hermit may subsist on flowers, &c., following the opinion of hermits.' It is, therefore, necessary to interpret vaikhânasa with the commentators in the sense of vaikhânasa *s*âstra, and to refer it to a particular work which taught the duties of hermits. The existence of such a book is attested not only by Manu's commentators, but also by other ancient and modern authors. Baudhâyana mentions it explicitly[2], and seems to give a short summary of its contents in the third chapter of the third Prasna of his Dharma*s*âstra. Haradatta, the commentator of Âpastamba and Gautama, also appears to have known it. In his notes on Gautama III, 2, he gives the derivation of vaikhânasa, a hermit in the forest, saying, 'The vânaprastha is called vaikhânasa, because he lives according to the rule promulgated by Vikhanas,' and adds, 'For that (sage) chiefly taught that order[3].' If the statements made to me by Indian Pa*nd*its are to be trusted, we may even hope to recover the work in course of time. It must be an exceedingly ancient book, as the secondary meaning of vaikhânasa, a hermit, which can have arisen only in the manner suggested by Haradatta[4], occurs in the

---

[1] Medh. वैखानसं नाम शास्त्रं यत्र वानप्रस्थस्य धर्मा विहितास्तेषां मते स्थितः॥ Gov. वैखानसाख्ये वानप्रस्थशास्त्रदर्शने स्थितः॥ Kull. वैखानसो वानप्रस्थः। तद्धर्मप्रतिपादकशास्त्रदर्शने .स्थितः॥ Nand. वैघा[खा]नसमतं विघ[ख]नसा प्रोक्तं सूक्तं[चं] तत्र हि वानप्रस्थधर्मस्य पूर्णोपदेशः क्रियते॥ Nâr. वैखानसमते वानप्रस्थमते॥

[2] Baudh. Dharma. II, 11, 14; Sacred Books of the East, vol. xiv, p. 259.

[3] वैखानसो वानप्रस्थः। विखनसा प्रोक्तेन मार्गेण वर्तत इति। तेन हि स आश्रमः प्राधान्येन प्रतिपादितः॥

[4] The double v*ri*ddhi in vaikhânasa is according to the analogy of the words enumerated in the âk*ri*ti-ga*n*a anu*s*atikâdi, Pâ*n*. VII, 3, 20.

oldest known Dharma-sûtra. Under these circumstances it is not advisable to assume that it had any connexion with the Vaikhânasa Sûtra*k*ara*n*a, a subdivision of the Taittirîyas, which seems to have been one of the youngest schools adhering to the Black Ya*g*ur-veda[1]. But it is evident that the ancient Vaikhânasa Sûtra, which treated of an important portion of the sacred law, preceded our Manu-sm*r*iti.

Another reference to the opinion of a person who is the reputed author of a still existing Dharma-sûtra is found at Manu VIII, 140, where the rate of legal interest on secured loans is thus described: 'A money-lender may stipulate, as an increase on his capital, for the interest allowed by Vasish*th*a, and take monthly the eightieth part of a hundred.' If we turn to the Vâsish*th*a Dharma*s*âstra, we read, III, 51[2], 'Hear the interest for a money-lender, declared by Vasish*th*a, five mâshas (may be taken every month) for twenty (kârshâpa*n*as).' Though the wording of the Manu-sm*r*iti differs from that adopted in the Vâsish*th*a Dharma*s*âstra, the meaning of both passages is the same. The eightieth part of one hundred is one and a quarter per cent, and the same rate is obtained if five mâshas are charged for twenty kârshâpa*n*as, i. e. for four hundred mâshas[3]. Both law-books, therefore, evidently refer to the same rule of Vasish*th*a. But the correctness of the further inference that the author of the Manu-sm*r*iti used the Vâsish*th*a Dharma*s*âstra is not so easily demonstrable as might seem from the extracts given above. For Vas. III, 51 itself is a quotation, marked as such by its final iti (left untranslated) and the phrase, 'Now they quote also,' which is prefixed to Sûtra 48. Hence it might be argued that the agreement of the

---

[1] See Professor Max Müller, Anc. Sansk. Lit. p. 199; Professor Weber, Indische Studien, vol. i, p. 83. A portion of the Vaikhânasa *S*rauta-sûtra is preserved in the modern transcripts, belonging to the Bombay University and the Munich Royal Libraries, which Professor Haug had made from a Baro*d*â MS.

[2] Sacred Books of the East, vol. xiv, p. 16; according to Dr. Führer's edition, Vas. III, 50.

[3] *G*agannâtha, in Col. Dig. I, 25, gives a somewhat different calculation. But the general sense remains the same. I follow K*r*ish*n*apa*nd*ita and Haradatta on Gautama XII, 29.

two passages furnishes no stringent proof for the posteriority of the Manu-smriti to that which bears Vasishtha's name, that, on the contrary, it perhaps merely indicates the dependence of both works on a common source, be it on some older work or on the tradition current in the Brâhmanical schools. Such an objection would in most similar cases be perfectly legitimate, but in the present one it is, I think, barred by some peculiar circumstances. From the above-mentioned Hindu tradition, preserved by Govindasvâmin[1], we learn that the Vâsishtha Dharmasâstra originally belonged to a school of *Ri*g-vedins who ascribed the settlement of their laws to the famous Vedic *Ri*shi Vasishtha. The rule limiting the monthly interest on secured loans to one and a quarter per cent is found also in Gautama's Dharma-sûtra XII, 29, a work which, as has been shown elsewhere[2], is older than the Vasishtha-smriti. But neither there nor in any other work where it occurs[3] is its enunciation attributed to Vasishtha. Hence it is most probable that this addition was made by those who attributed their laws to Vasishtha, and who, therefore, had an interest in vindicating the invention of an important legal maxim for their spiritual head. If their law-book gives the rule in the form of a quotation, they probably do not mean to indicate that an older verse ascribing it to Vasishtha existed, but that the rule itself was an ancient one, and had been taken from a law-book or from the tradition of the Brâhmanical schools. With this explanation the mention of Vasishtha's name, made in Manu VIII, 140, still remains an indication that its author knew and referred to the existing Vâsishtha Dharmasâstra.

These passages are far too numerous to be set aside as possibly later interpolations, and there is, indeed, no circumstance connected with any of them which could lead to such a supposition. We must, therefore, admit that they clearly disprove the claim of the Manu-smriti to the first

[1] See above, p. xx.
[2] Sacred Books of the East, vol. ii, pp. liii, liv.
[3] See e. g. Yâgñ. II, 37, and the texts of Brihaspati and Vyâsa quoted in Col. Dig. I, 26–27.

place among Indian law-books which the first chapter sets up, and that they furnish a strong support to the view according to which the Manu-smr*i*ti belongs to a later stage of literary development than the Dharma-sûtras.

In turning to the second point of our supplement, it will be advisable to reconsider in detail the passages of the Vasish*th*a-smr*i*ti, which prove the former existence of a Mânava Dharma-sûtra, and which, as the preceding discussion has established the priority of the Vasish*th*a-smr*i*ti to our Manu, possess a particularly great importance. The chief passage occurs Vasish*th*a IV, 5–8[1], where we read:

5. The Mânava (Sûtra states), 'Only when worshipping the manes and the gods, or when honouring guests, he may certainly do injury to animals.'

6. 'On offering the honey-mixture (to a guest), at a sacrifice and at the rites in honour of the manes, but on these occasions only, may an animal be slain; that (rule) Manu proclaimed.'

7. 'Meat can never be obtained without injury to living beings, and injury to living beings does not procure heavenly bliss: hence (the sages declare) the slaughter (of beasts) at a sacrifice not (to be) slaughter (in the ordinary sense of the word).'

8. 'Now he may also cook a full-grown ox or a full-grown he-goat for a Brâhma*n*a or a Kshatriya guest; in this manner they offer hospitality to such (a man).'

As has been stated in the introduction to Vasish*th*a[2], all the four Sûtras must be taken as a quotation, because the particle iti, 'thus,' occurs at the end of IV, 8, and because the identity of Sûtra 6 with Manu V, 41, as well as the close resemblance of Sûtra 7 to Manu V, 48, shows that the quotation is not finished with Sûtra 5. If we accept this explanation

[1] पितृदेवातिथिपूजायामप्येव पशुं हिंस्यादिति मानवम् ॥५॥ मधुपर्के च यज्ञे च पितृदैवतकर्मणि । अत्रैव च पशुं हिंस्यान्नान्यथेत्य ब्रवीन्मनुः ॥६॥ नाकृत्वा प्राणिनां हिंसां मांसमुत्पद्यते क्वचित् । न च प्राणिवधः स्वर्ग्यस्तस्माद्यागे वधोऽवधः ॥७॥ अथापि ब्राह्मणाय वा राजन्याय वाभ्यागताय महोक्षाणं वा महाजं वा पचेदेवमस्मा आतिथ्यं कुर्वन्तीति ॥८॥

[2] Sacred Books of the East, vol. xiv, pp. xviii–xix.

we have in our passage the usual arrangement followed in the Dharma-sûtras. First comes the prose rule, next the verses which confirm it, and finally a Vedic passage on which both the rule and the verses rest. It may be added that the explanation of the passage given by K*ri*sh*n*a-pa*nd*ita Dharmâdhikârin in his commentary on Vasish*th*a, according to which the word Mânavam, explained above by 'the Mânava (Sûtra),' is to mean 'the (opinion) of Manu' (manumatam), cannot be upheld, for several reasons. First, the wording of the text of Sûtra 5 looks like a real quotation, not like a summary of Manu's views by Vasish-*th*a. This becomes quite clear, if we compare Vasish*th*a I, 17, where undoubtedly a rule of Manu, corresponding to Mânava Dh. VII, 203, and VIII, 41, is given in Vasish*th*a's words, 'Manu has declared (that) the (peculiar) laws of countries, castes, and families (may be followed) in the absence of (rules of) the revealed texts[1].' Secondly, the great differences between several other passages, quoted by Vasish*th*a as Manu's, and the corresponding passages of the text of our Manu-sm*ri*ti, as well as the fact that the latter, as we have seen, refers to the Vâsish*th*a Dharma*s*âstra, do not permit us to assume, with K*ri*sh*n*apa*nd*ita, that Vasish*th*a knew and referred to our Manu.

If it is thus necessary to admit that Vasish*th*a's quotation is taken from a Mânava Dharma-sûtra, the agreement of the doctrine taught in the quotation and of a portion of the text with those of our Manu-sm*ri*ti show further that this Dharma-sûtra must have been the forerunner of our metrical law-book. An examination of the other quotations from Manu, which occur in the Vasish*th*a-sm*ri*ti, will show that this agreement was, though pretty close, not complete. The identity of the view, ascribed to Manu by Vasish*th*a I, 17, with the contents of Manu VII, 203, and VIII, 41, has already been mentioned. Vasish*th*a III, 2, a Mânava *S*loka is quoted which agrees literally with Manu II, 168. The same remark applies to the quotation at Vasish*th*a XX, 18, which is found Manu XI, 152. Another passage,

[1] देशधर्मजातिधर्मकुलधर्मान्श्रुत्यभावादब्रवीन्मनुः ॥

Vas. XIII, 16, shows considerable verbal differences. According to Vasish*th*a, Manu's verse is: 'Be it fruit, or water, or sesamum, or food, or whatever be (the gift) at a *S*râddha, let him not, having just accepted it, recite the Veda; for it is declared in the Sm*ri*ti that the hands of Brâhma*n*as are their mouths,' while we read Manu IV, 117, 'Be it an animal or a thing inanimate, whatever be the (gift) at a *S*râddha, let him not, having just accepted it, recite the Veda; for it is declared in the Sm*ri*ti that the hand of a Brâhma*n*a is his mouth[1].' The last quotation which occurs Vas. XIX, 37, and refers to the *s*ulka, (exemptions from) taxes and duties[2], is in the Trish*t*ubh metre, and, hence, cannot have a place in our Manu-sm*ri*ti. But it is remarkable that the latter does not even show a corresponding Anush*t*ubh verse, and that the contents of the quotation do not quite agree with the teaching of our Manu. The latter mentions the exemption of a sum less than a kârshâpa*n*a incidentally X, 120. It agrees also with Manu's doctrines that *S*rotriyas, ascetics, alms, and sacrifices should not be taxed. But there are no indications that infants, messengers, and ambassadors, or the remnant left to a plundered trader, should go free. With respect to those living by arts (*s*ilpa), our Manu teaches, VII, 138, and X, 120, just like most other ancient authors, that artisans are to do monthly one piece of work for the king. Though this corvée amounts to a pretty severe tax, it is, of course, possible to contend that Manu's rule does not exactly contradict that quoted by Vasish*th*a. Besides these passages, there are some other verses[3] which contain the well-known phrase, 'manur abravît, thus Manu spoke,'

[1] Vas. मानवं चात्र श्लोकमुदाहरन्ति । फलान्यापस्तिलान्भक्ष्यान्यच्चान्यच्छ्राद्धिकं भवेत् । प्रतिगृह्याप्यनध्यायः पाण्यास्या ब्राह्मणाः स्मृता इति ॥ Manu, प्राणि वा यदि वाप्राणि यत्किंचिच्छ्राद्धिकं भवेत् । तदालभ्याप्यनध्यायः पाण्यास्यो हि द्विजः स्मृतः ॥

[2] 'No duty (is paid) on a sum less than a kârshâpa*n*a, there is no tax on a livelihood gained by arts, nor on an infant, nor on a messenger, nor on what has been received as alms, nor on the remnants of property left after a robbery, nor on a *S*rotriya, nor on an ascetic, nor on a sacrifice.'

[3] Vas. XI, 23; XII, 16; XXIII, 43; XXVI, 8.

and mention Manu as the authority for the rule taught. With respect to these references it seems to me not probable that they have been taken from the Mânava Dharma-sûtra. We shall see below[1] that from the earliest times the mythical Manu, the father of mankind, was considered as the founder of the social and moral order, and that he was considered to have first taught or revealed religious rites and legal maxims. Hence I believe that these four verses give nothing more than an expression of the belief that their doctrines go back to the first progenitor of men[2]. The first three among them either contradict or find no counterpart in our Manu-sm*ri*ti. The fourth agrees in substance with Manu XI, 260–261. But it occurs in a chapter which is probably spurious, or, at least, full of interpolations. Whatever view may be taken concerning these passages, the allegation that the Mânava Dharma-sûtra, known to Vasish*th*a, closely resembled, but was not identical with our Manu, need not be modified.

If we look for other traces of the Sûtra, quoted by Vasish*th*a, it is possible that Gautama, who mentions an opinion of Manu, XXI, 7, refers to it. His Dharma-sûtra is even older than Vasish*th*a's, and long anterior to our Manu-sm*ri*ti. But the possibility that Gautama refers not to a rule of the Mânava Dharma-sûtra, but to a maxim generally attributed to the mythical Manu, is not altogether excluded. Gautama says, 'Manu (declares that) the first three (crimes, the intentional murder of a Brâhma*n*a, drinking Surâ, and the violation of a Guru's bed) cannot be expiated[3].' The wording of the Sûtra shows that it is not a quotation, but a summary of Manu's opinion. Our Manu-sm*ri*ti explicitly teaches, XI, 90, the same doctrine with respect to the intentional murder of a Brâhma*n*a, and, if my explanation of XI, 147 is accepted, also with respect to the intentional drinking of Surâ. As regards the third offence, there is no

[1] See p. lviii.

[2] The meaning of the phrase in the verse, occurring in the quotation from the Mânava Dharma-sûtra, is probably the same.

[3] त्रीणि प्रथमान्यनिर्देश्यानि मनुः ॥ The same opinion is expressed in the Mahâbhârata XII, 165, 34, but not attributed to Manu.

direct statement. But the expiations, prescribed XI, 104–105, amount to a sentence of death. Hence our Manu-smriti, too, practically declares the crime to be inexpiable during the offender's lifetime. Its original, the Dharma-sûtra, may, therefore, be supposed to have had the rule which Gautama attributes to Manu. Nevertheless, owing to the circumstances mentioned above, Gautama's passage cannot be adduced as a perfectly certain proof of the early existence of the Mânava Dharma-sûtra.

Among the remaining Dharma-sûtras[1] there is only the fragment attributed to Usanas which seems to quote a Sûtra of Manu. At the beginning of the first chapter[2] we find a very corrupt passage containing a prose-quotation which according to two of my MSS. belongs to Manu, but according to a third to Sumantu. As the latter copy is, however, clearly more incorrect than the other two, and as a Sûtra by Sumantu is not known from other sources, the reading of the first two seems to be preferable. The contents of the quotation which apparently prescribes that on the death of an infant, of an emigrant, of one who keeps no sacred fires, of one who kills himself by starvation or by self-cremation, and of one slain in battle, no period of impurity need be kept, agree with the teaching of our Manu-smriti, V, 78, 89, 94, 98.

There is, further, one among the Vedic books on the ritual, the *S*âṅkhâyana G*ri*hya-sûtra, which possibly refers to the Mânava Dharma-sûtra. This work quotes the verse, Manu V, 41, which, as has been shown above, occurred also in the Dharma-sûtra as well as several other *S*lokas of

---

[1] Regarding the passage of Âpastamba II, 16, 1, which ascribes the revelation of the *S*râddhas to Manu, see below, p. lix.

[2] I transcribe the whole beginning of the work, तत्र जन्ममरणयोः काले देशान्तरयोः शौचं दशरात्रं मातापितृभ्यः सूतकं मातुरित्येके ॥ उपस्पृश्य ---- मनुराह ॥ बाले देशान्तरस्थे चानग्निके चोराध्वाने (?) अनाशकेग्निप्रवेशे युद्धहते च सद्यः ॥ शौचानष्ट पतिताभितनिन्दिताचारैर्न सह संवसेत् ॥ Thus two MSS.; the third reads, उपस्पृश्य तु सुमन्तुराह । and further on, सौचानष्टाति ताभित्त° । It is impossible to restore the whole passage. The end of the quotation may have been सद्यः शौचमिष्टमिति ॥

C 2

our Manu-smriti, partly in better versions[1]. As the Grihya-sûtra agrees also in a number of its rules very characteristically with Manu, it is not improbable that its author may have drawn on the original of the latter. But before one can be perfectly confident on this point, it is necessary that some difficult questions regarding the critical condition of Sâṅkhâyana's text should be cleared up more fully than has been done hitherto. More important than the passages from the last work is the evidence which the Kâmandakîya Nîtisâra furnishes, where twice opinions of the Mânavâh and once an opinion of Manu are quoted, but rejected in favour of the views of the author's teacher, Kânakya Kautilya. In one case the doctrine, attributed to the Mânavâh, agrees with the teaching of our Manu-smriti. We read in the discussion on the number of the prakritis, the constituent elements of the mandala or political circle to which a king must pay attention, Kâm. Nît. VII, 24–25, 'With respect to this (question) the Mânavas record that five constituent elements, the ministers and the rest, belong severally to each of the twelve kings. But those original twelve (kings) and those (others), the ministers and the rest, (are) seventy-two (in number, and form) the whole circle of constituent elements[2].' Our Manu-smriti states, VII, 155–156, that twelve kings belong to the mandala, and adds ver. 157, 'The minister, the kingdom, the fortress, the treasury, and the army are five other (constituent elements of the circle); for these are mentioned in connexion with each (of the first twelve); thus the whole circle (consists), briefly (speaking, of) seventy-two (constituent parts).' The other two passages differ. According to Kâmandaki II, 3, the Mânavas teach that the sciences, which a king must study, are three only, the threefold (Veda), the theory of professions and trades, and the

[1] Oldenberg, Sâṅkh. Gri. S. in the Indische Studien, vol. xv, p. 11.

[2] द्वादशानां नरेन्द्राणां पञ्च पञ्च पृथक्पृथक्। ह्यमात्याद्याश्च प्रकृतीरामनन्तीह मानवाः ॥२४॥ मौला द्वादश यास्त्वेता ह्यमात्याद्यास्तथा च याः। सप्ततिर्द्व्यधिका ह्येताः सर्वं प्रकृतिमण्डलम् ॥२५॥ I read according to the commentary सप्ततिर्द्व्यधिका instead of the senseless सप्ततिश्चाधिका of the text.

science of government, 'because the science of dialectics or reasoning is a subdivision of the threefold (Vedic lore[1]),' while Manu VII, 43 enumerates five branches of learning, or at least four, if either Medhâtithi's or Nârâya*n*a's explanation of the term âtmavidyâ, rendered in the translation by 'the knowledge of the (supreme) Soul,' is accepted[2]. Again, we hear, Kâmandaki XI, 67, that Manu fixed the number of ministers (amâtya), which the king must appoint, at twelve. But according to Manu VII, 54, no more than seven or eight are required. These quotations show that Kâmandaki knew a work, attributed to Manu, which contained rules on the duties of kings, and in some respects agreed with the seventh chapter of our Manu-sm*ri*ti. If I conclude that this must have been the old Mânava Dharma-sûtra, it is because Kâmandaki twice alludes to it by the title Mânavâ*h*, literally 'those who study a work proclaimed by Manu,' or, more freely rendered, 'the Mânava school.' It is a very common practice of Indian authors to refer in this manner to the books restricted to special schools. But I know of no case where the doctrines of the Mânava Dharma*s*âstra, or of any other work which is destined for all Âryans and acknowledged as authoritative by all, are cited in the same or in a similar way. Nor is it usual to contrast, as Kâmandaki does, the rules taught by Manu with those of other teachers and afterwards to reject them[3]. If a Hindu writer on law finds it necessary to set aside an opinion of Manu, he either passes by it in silence or he interprets the passage where it occurs in accordance with the principles of some other Sm*ri*ti with

[1] त्रयी वार्त्ता दण्डनीतिरिति विद्या हि मानवाः । त्रय्या एव विभागोयं सेयमान्वीक्षिकी मता ॥ ३ ॥

[2] With respect to Medhâtithi's and Nârâya*n*a's explanations, see the note to the translation. I will add that Kâm. Nît. II, 7, आन्वीक्षिक्यात्मविज्ञानम् 'The science of dialectics (is) a means of fully recognising the Soul or Self,' speaks in favour of Nârâya*n*a's explanation, and that it would perhaps have been better if I had placed the latter in the text.

[3] As the learned editor of the Nîtisâra (Preface, p. 2) asserts that its author was a Buddhist, it might be conjectured that the latter treated Manu with small respect, because he belonged to a heterodox sect. But it ought to be noted that no proof is offered for the above assertion, and that the work contains no trace of Buddhism.

which he himself agrees. Hence it is not doubtful that Kâmandaki's references point to a work of Manu which, though highly esteemed, did not hold the same paramount position as Bh*ri*gu's version of Manu's laws. In other words, Kâmandaki's Manu must have been the property of a particular school, and that was just the case with the Mânava Dharma-sûtra. The fact that all the known Dharma-sûtras contain a more or less detailed description of the duties of kings agrees well with this supposition, and so does the circumstance that Kâmandaki's Nîtisâra is either really an ancient work, composed long before the beginning of our era, or at least a later recension of such an old book[1]. These are all the certain indications of the former existence of a Mânava Dharma-sûtra which I have been able to find. It is possible that the same work is also alluded to in some verses of the twelfth and thirteenth Parvans of the Mahâbhârata. But this question is, as we shall see below, surrounded with great difficulties, and its solution somewhat doubtful. Among the passages, discussed above, none are so important as Vasish*th*a's quotations. The remainder contribute, however, to give a more definite idea of the range of subjects included in the lost work, and they confirm the conclusion, drawn from the former, that the Mânava Dharma-sûtra closely resembled our Manu-sm*ri*ti.

The investigations concerning the last point, the question if any traces of a connexion of our Manu-sm*ri*ti with the writings of the Mânava school are discoverable, have hitherto led, as stated above, to a negative result. They were, of course, directed to a comparison of the Mânava G*ri*hya-sûtra with the Dharma*s*âstra, as both works of

[1] The work claims to be the composition of a pupil of *K*andragupta's famous minister, *K*â*n*akya Kau*t*ilya or Kau*t*alya, to whom a portion of the Mangalâ*k*ara*n*a is dedicated, and who is frequently referred to as the Guru or teacher. Though there is no clear evidence corroborating this statement, there is also none to rebut it. In favour of this claim speaks the fact that the name of the author is a nomen gentile. For among the ancient writers the practice of signing their books with the family-name is almost universal. Later it seems to have fallen into disuse. The Nîtisâra is quoted by the oldest commentator of Manu, Medhâtithi.

necessity frequently treat of the same subjects. On comparing the corresponding portions of the two works, Professor Jolly[1] found no special agreement with respect to the ages prescribed for the performance of the Sa*m*skâras, with respect to the marriage-rites and to the rules for the conduct of students and of Snâtakas. Nor was he able to discover in the Manu-sm*ri*ti any of the curious technical terms and phrases used in the G*ri*hya-sûtra, while the somewhat closer resemblance in the Mantras of the Vai*s*vadeva ceremony and in a few other points turned out to be without conclusiveness on account of the concurrent agreement of other G*ri*hya-sûtras. Dr. von Bradke's re-examination of the question[2] did not yield any other result. I can only bear witness to the general correctness of these remarks. Though it is possible to adduce some passages, not mentioned by Professor Jolly[3], in which the G*ri*hya-sûtra shows a special affinity with the Sm*ri*ti, the very great differences which occur in other sections[4], the absence of an agreement in particularly characteristic rules[5], and the

[1] On the Vish*n*u Dharma-sûtra and the Kâ*th*aka; Transactions of the Royal Bavarian Academy, 1879, ii, p. 82 seq.

[2] Journal of the German Oriental Society, vol. xxxii, p. 438.

[3] Among the rules which specially agree, I may mention one from the section on the Initiation, Mân. G*ri*. Sû. I, 22 (end), अथ भैक्षं चरते [चरेत्] । मातरमेवाग्रे । याश्चान्याः सुहृदो यावत्यो वा संनिहिताः स्युः ॥ 'Next he shall go out to beg, first, to his mother and to other females who are friendly, or to as many as may be near.' These Sûtras correspond to Manu II, 50, 'Let him first beg food of his mother, or of his sister, or of his own maternal aunt, or of (some other) female who will not disgrace him (by a refusal).' I am not aware that this rule occurs in any other Sm*ri*ti.

[4] Among the very great discrepancies I would point to such as those occurring in the section on the marriage-rites. The Manu-sm*ri*ti III, 20–34, describes the well-known eight modes by which a woman may be obtained from her family. But the Mânava G*ri*hya-sûtra I, 7–8, knows two only, the Brâhma and the *S*aulka rites, the latter of which corresponds to the Âsura or Mânusha rite of the other Sm*ri*tis, and sanctions the purchase of the bride from her parents.

[5] The absence of agreement in characteristic rules is particularly noticeable in the chapter on the study of the Veda and the stoppages of the Veda study. There the general rules, e.g. regarding the beginning, length, and ending of the school-term, which are found also in other Sm*ri*tis, agree in both works. But none of those special prescriptions which the Mânava G*ri*hya-sûtra gives for the time when and the ceremonies with which particular portions of the Maitrâya*n*î Sa*m*hitâ are to be learnt can be traced in the Manu-sm*ri*ti.

non-occurrence of Mantras, peculiar to the Maitrâyanîya-Mânava school in the Manu-smriti, do not permit us to consider them as decisive for the settlement of the question. On the other hand, this negative result does not preclude the possibility that the supposed connexion between the original of the Manu-smriti and the Mânava school may nevertheless have existed. For the examples of the Hairanyakesas and Mâdhyamdinas show that the Sûtras, adopted by a school, are not always composed by one and the same teacher, but sometimes are made up of fragments originally belonging to different authors. In the case of the Mâdhyamdinas the author of the Srauta-sûtra is a Kâtyâyana, while the Grihya-sûtra bears the name of a Pâraskara. In the case of the Hairanyakesas the Dharma-sûtra, though it is ascribed to Hiranyakesin Satyâshâdha, is in reality the work of Âpastamba, and differs both in its language and in its contents very much from the Grihya-sûtra [1]. Moreover, the Hairanyakesa Kayana-sûtra has been taken over, as its colophon clearly proves, from the Bhâradvâgas. It is, therefore, still possible that the ancient Mânava Dharma-sûtra was considered as the special property of the Mânavas, but was not composed by the same teacher as the Grihya-sûtra, or that, though both works had the same author, the materials for their composition were borrowed from different sources. Either supposition would explain the discrepancies between the two works. If we now could show that some other work belonging to the Mânava Karana shows a special affinity to the Manu-smriti, the view that the original of the latter was first the property of that school might be still upheld. A renewed examination of the various treatises, studied and claimed as their own by the Mânavas, has convinced me that such a connecting link is actually found among them. This is the Srâddhakalpa, a description of the ordinary funeral sacrifices which the Mânava Grihya-sûtra does not treat in detail, but barely touches in the sections on the Ashtakâ rites (II, 8–9). If this treatise has not been taken into consideration by Professor Jolly and

[1] Sacred Books of the East, vol. ii, p. xxiii.

Dr. von Bradke, the reason is that it is not contained in Professor Haug's collection of the Mânava Sûtras, the only one which has hitherto been accessible to European students. In my copy of the works of the Mânava school it stands after the Pravarâdhyâya[1]. It consists of four short Kha*nd*as. The first begins with the words, 'Now we will explain the rules for the funeral sacrifices,' and treats of the following points: the invitation of qualified Brâhma*n*as, their hospitable reception with the Arghya in the house of the sacrificer, the invocations asking the Vi*s*vedevas and the manes to attend, and the burnt oblations offered to Soma, Yama, and Agni. The Mantras which are to be used seem, if not all, at least for the greater part, to have been taken from the Maitrâya*n*î Sa*m*hitâ. This section shows hardly any special agreement with the Manu-sm*ri*ti, except in the rule, known also from other Dharma-sûtras, which prescribes the entertainment of two guests at the rite in honour of the gods, and of three at the offering to the manes or of one on either occasion, as well as in the number and the deities of the burnt oblations which precede the *S*râddha (Manu III, 123, 211). But the second Kha*nd*a, which contains the description of the *S*râddha ceremony, opens with a couple of verses, the first of which corresponds almost literally[2] with Manu III, 274. The only important difference is that at the end the words 'in the rainy season and under (the constellation) Maghâ*h*' take the place of Manu's 'when the shadow of the elephant falls towards the east.' It must be noted that, though Vish*n*u LXXVIII, 52–53 and Vasish*th*a XI, 40 have passages which contain similar prayers of the manes, their wording differs very considerably from that of the *S*râddhakalpa and of

[1] My MS. of the writings of the Mânava *K*ara*n*a, which was copied in 1864–65 at Nâsik, includes, besides the Sa*m*hitâ and the Upanishad, counted as the fifth Kâ*nd*a, all the portions of the *S*rauta-sûtra, known from Professor Haug's MSS. together with the Kumâra or Kumârila Bhâshya and portions of a later v*ri*tti by Mi*s*ra Bâlak*ri*sh*n*a, as well as the G*ri*hya-sûtra with its Bhâshya, the Pûra*n*âkhya, by Bha*tt*a Ash*t*âvakra (not by Kumârila, as I conjectured in West and Bühler's Digest, p. 46, note a), and the *S*râddhakalpa.

[2] अपि नः स्वकुले भूयाद्यो नो दद्यात्त्रयोदशीम्। पायसं मधुसर्पिभ्यां वर्षासु च मघासु च॥

the Manu-smr*i*ti. The second verse[1] bears a faint resemblance to Manu III, 202, as it declares that water offered in vessels of gold, silver, or Udumbara 'becomes imperishable.' The following prose portion has little in common with Manu's rules. Curiously enough, it prescribes that the funeral cakes are to be offered after the guests have finished their meal, a custom which Manu III, 261 attributes to 'some.' The section closes with some *S*lokas[2], the last of which is nearly identical with Manu III, 283. The chief difference is, that in the first line the word *S*râddhe, 'at a *S*râddha,' occurs instead of snâtvâ, 'after his bath.' The second var. lect. samâhita*h*, 'with a concentrated mind,' instead of dvigottama*h*, 'a Brâhma*n*a,' is found in the Southern MSS. of Manu. The next section, which is not numbered in the colophon as Kha*nd*a 3, but separately, treats of the Abhyudaya, or V*ri*ddhi-*s*râddha, the funeral oblations which must be offered on all joyful occasions, such as the celebration of the birth of a son, a wedding, and so forth[3]. As Manu mentions this variety of the *S*râddha only incidentally, III, 254, the contents of this Kha*nd*a find no counterpart in the Sm*r*iti. But among its numerous *S*lokas one line agrees literally with Manu IX, 186 a[4]. The fourth and last section of the Kalpa, which is marked as the Pari*s*ishta, the addenda, gives miscellaneous rules regarding the times when *S*râddhas may be performed, the manner in which the fulfilment of certain special wishes may be secured, and the persons to be entertained on such occasions. It consists chiefly of

---

[1] सौवर्णेषु च पात्रेषु राजतौदुम्बरेषु च। दत्तमक्षय्यतां याति खड्गेनार्षकृतेन च (sic) ॥

[2] दश पूर्वान्दशापरानात्मनश्चैकवि॰शतिम् (sic)। श्राद्धकृन्मोचयेत्पापान्महतोप्येनसः पितॄन् ॥ श्राद्धं च यो न दद्यात्पितृभ्यश्च कदाचन (sic)। षष्टिवर्षसहस्राणि विष्ठायां जायते कृमिः ॥ यदेव तर्पयत्यद्भिः पितॄन्श्राद्धे समाहितः। तेनैव सर्वमाप्नोति पितृयज्ञक्रियाफलमिति ॥ इति मानवश्राद्धकल्पे द्वितीयः खण्डः समाप्तः ॥

[3] Beginning अथ वृद्धिश्राद्धं व्याख्यास्यामः ॥ Colophon, इति मानवसूत्रे अभ्युदयश्राद्धम् ॥

[4] त्रयाणामुदकं कार्यं त्रिषु पिंडः प्रवर्तते ॥

verses, seven[1] of which are either quite or nearly identical with passages of the Manu-sm*ri*ti III, 82, 125–126, 145, 185, 148, and 186, while another, which teaches that the invited Brâhma*n*as and the sacrificer must remain chaste 'because the manes dwell with them[2],' agrees in substance with Manu III, 189. Two among the seven *S*lokas, those corresponding to Manu III, 125–126, occur also in the Vâsish*th*a and Baudhâyana Dharma*s*âstras. The remainder are not traceable in the ancient Sûtras.

These remarks show that the Mânava *S*râddhakalpa consists, like many other handbooks of Vedic schools, of several pieces, which probably have been composed successively at different times. Even the whole treatise may be possibly later than the G*ri*hya-sûtra, and may have been added in order to supplement its too curt rules on funeral sacrifices. But in spite of these admissions, the fact that it contains so many verses partly or wholly agreeing with the Manu-sm*ri*ti, keeps its importance for the point under consideration. If an adherent of the Mânava school found it necessary to compose a treatise on a subject like the *S*râddhas, he would, as a matter of course, base it on the usage and the teaching of his school. Hence it may be assumed that the verses which he inserted were current in

---

[1] a. कुर्यादहरहः श्राद्धमन्नाद्येनोदकेन वा। पयोमूलफलैर्वापि पितृभ्यः प्रीतिमाहरेत्॥ In the corresponding verse of Manu, Medh. and Gov. read आहरन् instead of Kullûka's आवहन्॥ b. द्वौ दैवे त्रीन्पित्रै [त्र्य] एकैकमुभयत्र वा। भोजयेत्सुसमृद्धोपि न प्रसज्जेत विस्तरां [रे]॥ सत्क्रियां देशकालौ च द्रव्यं ब्राह्मणसंपदः। पंचैतांनि [तान्वि] स्तरो हन्ति तस्मान्नेहतु [न्नेहेत] विस्तरं [रे]॥ c. यत्नेन भोजयेच्छ्राद्धे बह्वृचं वेदपारगं। शाखांतगमध्वर्युं छंदोगं वा समाप्तिगम्॥ d. पञ्चाग्निं वि [ग्निस्त्रि] सुपर्णं च [श्च] त्रिणाचिकेतः षडंगवित्। ब्रह्मदेयानुसंतानो ज्येष्ठसामग एव च॥ e. मातामहं मातुलं च स्वस्रीयं श्वशुरं गुरुं। दौहित्रं विट्पतिं बंधु [धुम्] ऋत्विग्याज्यौ च भोजयेत्॥ f. वेदार्थी विप्रवक्ता च ब्रह्मचारि [चर्ये] सदा स्थिता: [त:]। शतायुश्चैव विज्ञेया ब्राह्मणाः पंक्तिपावनाः॥ The fifth and sixth verses have been transposed by a mistake of the copyist.

[2] पूर्वेद्युरामंत्रितो विप्रैः [तैर्वि॰] पितरः संवसंति वै। यजमानश्च ता रात्रिं वसेयुर्ब्रह्मचारिणः (sic)॥

the latter, and it is not improbable that they may have occurred in one of its written works. As, further, the Manu-smriti rests on a Mânava Dharma-sûtra, and has derived from the latter a number of its verses, the most natural explanation of the partial agreement between the *S*râddhakalpa and the Smriti is that both have drawn on the same source, the Mânava Dharma-sûtra. If that is so, the latter must have been considered as authoritative by the Mânavas, and have been their peculiar property. Though several links in this chain of arguments must unfortunately remain hypothetical, it seems to me, especially if taken together with Professor Jolly's and Dr. von Schröder's above-mentioned discoveries regarding the relation of the books of the Kâthaka school to those of the Maitrâyanîya-Mânavas and of the Vishnu-smriti to the Manu-smriti, sufficiently strong to show that also this part of Professor Max Müller's hypothesis is more than an ingenious conjecture.

In conclusion, I may mention that two other circumstances—a certain agreement between the Maitrâyana-brâhmanopanishad and the Manu-smriti, as well as the preference which the latter shows for North-western India in its description of the countries where pure Âryan customs prevail (II, 17–22)—may also point to a connexion of the Manu-smriti and of its original with the Mânava school. In the Upanishad VI, 37, we find quoted, as a generally known maxim, a verse which occurs Manu III, 76. Two other verses, Manu VI, 76–77, agree in substance with Maitr. Up. III, 4[1], and some of Manu's statements regarding the Âtman and the results of the gunas or qualities closely correspond to the doctrines taught in the Upanishad[2]. On a closer examination these resemblances lose, however, a good deal of their significance. For the ideas expressed in Manu III, 76 are likewise traceable in a Vedic passage quoted in Vasishtha's Dharma-sûtra. The comparison of the human body to an impure dwelling (Manu VI, 76–77) reappears even in Buddhistic works[3]. The corresponding philosophical tenets, finally,

[1] Sacred Books of the East, vol. xv, p. 298, note 1. [2] See below, p. lxxiii.
[3] Dhammapada, 147–150; Johänntgen, Das Gesetzbuch des Manu, p. 93.

occur in a portion of the Manu-smriti which probably is not ancient[1], and they are held by several of the special schools of philosophy. As regards the passages in Manu's second chapter which praise the holiness of the districts between the Drishadvatî and the Sarasvatî, and between the Yamunâ and the Gaṅgâ, they may indicate, as Dr. Johänntgen thinks[2], that the home of the school which produced the Mânava Dharma-sûtra lies in those districts. If that were certain, it would agree well enough with the facts known regarding the ancient seats of the Mânavas. The latter are a North-western sect, and extended, as the Mahârnava asserts[3], from the Mayûra hill to Gugarat. Unfortunately, however, the Dharma-sûtras of Vasishtha and Baudhâyana contain almost exactly the same statements as Manu, and hence the verses of the latter possibly mean nothing more than that the Mânavas, like many other Vedic schools, considered India north of the Vindhyas, and especially the districts adjoining the sacred rivers, as the true home of Brâhmanism and of Âryan purity.

II.

While the preceding discussion has shown that our Mânava Dharmasâstra is based on a Mânava Dharma-sûtra which probably was the exclusive property of the Maitrâyanîya-Mânava school, we have now to consider some questions connected with the conversion of the locally authoritative Sûtra into a law-book claiming the allegiance of all Âryans and generally acknowledged by them. The problems which now have to be solved, or at least to be attempted, are the following: 1. what circumstances led to the substitution of a universally binding Mânava Dharmasâstra for the manual of the Vedic school? 2. why was so prominent a position allotted to the remodelled Smriti?

[1] See below, p. lxix.

[2] Loc. cit. pp. 109–110.

[3] Sacred Books of the East, vol. ii, p. xxxi; and L. von Schröder, Maitrâyanî Samh. I, pp. xxiv–xxviii. The ancient inscriptions name Maitrâyana Brâhmanas as donees in the Central India Agency and Gugarat. The Mânava school still exists in the latter country and in Khândesh.

3. how was the conversion effected? and 4. when did it probably take place?

Though the absence of all historical information, and even of a trustworthy tradition, makes it impossible to give full and precise details in answering the first question, it is yet, I think, possible to recognise the general cause which led to the production of that class of secondary Sm*ri*tis to which the Mânava Dharma*s*âstra belongs [1]. This cause lies, it seems to me, in the establishment of special law schools which were independent of any particular *S*âkhâ of the Veda, and which supplanted the Vedic *K*ara*n*as as far as the teaching of the sacred law is concerned. Evident as it is that the Vedic schools first systematised and cultivated the six sciences which, on account of their close connexion with the Veda, are called its Aṅgas or limbs, it is no less apparent that, as the materials for each of these subjects accumulated and the method of their treatment was perfected, the enormous quantity of the matter to be learnt, and the difficulty of its acquisition depressed the Vedic schools from their high position as centres of the intellectual life of the Âryas, and caused the establishment of new special schools of science, which, while they restricted the range of their teaching, taught their curriculum thoroughly and intelligently. In the Vedic schools a full and accurate knowledge of the sacred texts was, of course, always the primary object. In order to gain that the pupils had to learn not only the Sa*m*hitâ text of the Mantras and Brâhma*n*as, but also their Pada, Krama, and perhaps still more difficult pâ*th*as or modes of recitation. This task no doubt required a considerable time, and must have fully occupied the twelve terms of four and a half or five and a half months which the Sm*ri*tis give as the average duration of the studentship for the acquisition of one Veda [2]. As long as the Aṅgas consisted of short simple treatises, it was also possible to

[1] Regarding the various classes of secondary Sm*ri*tis, see West and Bühler, Digest, p. 32, third edition.

[2] See Manu III, 1, and IV, 95, as well as the parallel passages quoted in the notes.

commit them to memory and to master their contents in the twelve terms, consisting of the seven or eight dark fortnights from the month Pausha to Vais*â*kha[1]. But when the Kalpa or ritual alone reached dimensions as in the Sûtras of the Baudhâyanîyas and Âpastambîyas, while the grammar developed into as artificial a system as that of Pâ*n*ini, it became a matter of sheer impossibility for one man to commit to memory and to fully understand the sacred texts together with the auxiliary sciences, especially as the number of the latter was increased in early times by the addition of the Nyâya or Pûrvâ Mîmâ*m*sâ, the art of interpreting the rules of the Veda[2]. The members of the Vedic schools were then placed before two alternatives. They might either commit to memory all the Vedic texts of their *S*âkhâs together with the Aṅgas, renouncing the attempt at understanding what they learnt, or they had to restrict the number of the treatises which they learnt by heart, while they thoroughly mastered those which they acquired. Those who adhered to the former course became living libraries, but were unable to make any real use of their learning. Those who adopted the second alternative might become great scholars in the science of the sacrifice, grammar, law or astronomy, but they could not rival with the others in the extent of the verbal knowledge of the sacred books. Thus the Vedic schools ceased to be the centres of intellectual, and were supplanted by the special, schools of science.

The present state of learning in India proves beyond doubt that this change actually took place in the manner described, and direct statements in the ancient text-books, as well as their condition, allow us to recognise the various stages which led up to it. The true modern representatives of the ancient *K*ara*n*as are the so-called Vaidiks, men who, mostly living on charity, devote their energy exclusively to the acquisition of a verbal knowledge of the

[1] See Manu IV, 98, and the parallel passages quoted in the note. According to some Sm*ri*tis the Aṅgas might be studied at any time out of term (Vas. XIII, 7).

[2] Regarding the early existence of the Pûrvâ Mîmâ*m*sâ, see Sacred Books of the East, vol. ii, p. xxvii; and the verse on the constitution of a Parishad, quoted Baudh. I, 1, 8; Vas. III, 20.

sacred texts and of the Aṅgas of their *S*âkhâs as well as of some other works, more or less closely connected with the Veda. A perfect Vaidik of the Â*s*valâyana school knows the Rig-veda according to the Sa*m*hitâ, Pada, Krama, *G*a*t*â and Ghana Pâ*th*as, the Aitareya Brâhma*n*a and Âra*n*yaka, the ritualistic Sûtras of Â*s*valâyana, *S*aunaka's Prâti*s*âkhya and the *S*ikshâ, Yâska's Nirukta, the grammar of Pâ*n*ini, the Vedic calendar or *G*yotisha, the metrical treatise called the *Kh*andas, Yâ*gñ*avalkya's Dharma*s*âstra, portions of the Mahâbhârata, and the philosophical Sûtras of Ka*n*âda, *G*aimini, and Bâdarâya*n*a. Similarly the Vaidiks of the Ya*g*us, Sâman, and Atharvan schools are able to recite, more or less perfectly, the whole of the works of their respective *S*âkhâs as well as some other non-Vedic books[1]. But it would be in vain to expect from such men an explanation of the literary treasures which they possess. It is not the professional Vaidik who can perform the great sacrifices according to the *S*rauta-sûtras, interpret the intricate system of Pâ*n*ini's grammar, or decide a knotty point of law according to the Dharma-sûtra or the secondary Sm*ri*ti which he knows by heart. For these purposes one must go to quite different classes of men. The performance of the great *S*rauta sacrifices lies in the hands of the *S*rotriya or *S*rautî, who unites with a thoroughly verbal knowledge of the sacred texts of his *S*âkhâ a full acquaintance with the meaning of the *S*rauta-sûtras and with the actual kriyâ or manual work, described in the Prayogas. The *S*rautî, as well as his humbler fellow-worker, the so-called Yâ*gñ*ika or Bha*tt*a*g*î, who knows the G*ri*hya-sûtras and performs the rites prescribed for domestic occurrences, likewise both belong to the representatives of the Vedic schools. They make, however, no pretence to a knowledge of the whole range of the Aṅgas, but content themselves with studying the Kalpa, or parts of it, and perhaps the *S*ikshâ[2]. Real

[1] Regarding the necessity for a Vaidik to learn non-Vedic books, see Vas. XXVII, 6.

[2] Regarding the present condition of the Vedic schools and of Vedic learning, see Haug, Brahma und die Brahmanen, p. 47; and R. G. Bhâ*nd*ârkar's careful paper, 'The Veda in India' (Ind. Ant. III, 132 sqq.) From personal observa-

proficiency in the other still surviving Aṅgas, grammar, law, and astronomy is to be found only with those Pandits who fulfil their duty of studying the Veda by committing to memory a few particularly important sections, such as the Pâvamânî-hymns of the Rig-veda or the Satarudriya of the Yagur-veda, or by confining themselves to the few verses which occur in the Brahmayagña and the Samdhyâvandana[1]. Their chief aim is to be perfect in one or more of the special sciences which they study, without reference to a particular Vedic school. Thus, though a Pandit who chiefly devotes himself to the sacred law may belong to the Vedic school of Baudhâyana or Âpastamba, he will not make Baudhâyana's or Âpastamba's Dharma-sûtra the starting-point of his studies. On the contrary, it will frequently happen that he possesses no knowledge of the Dharma-sûtra of his school, except a few passages quoted in the commentaries and digests. If he has read the whole work, he will consult it only as one of the many utterances of the ancient sages. He will not attribute to it a higher authority than to other Smritis, but interpret it in accordance with the rules of the secondary Dharmasâstras of Manu or Yâgñavalkya. A good illustration of this state of things is furnished by Sâyana-Mâdhava's treatment of Baudhâyana in his Vyavahâramâdhava, a treatise on civil and criminal law supplementing his commentary on Parâsara's Smriti. Though he himself tells us, in the introduction to the Parâsara-smriti-vyâkhyâ[2], that he belonged to the school of Baudhâyana, and though he seems to have written a commentary on Baudhâyana's Sûtras, he relies, e.g. for the law of Inheritance, not on Baudhâyana's Dharma-sûtra, but on Vigñânesvara's exposition of Yâgñavalkya. He quotes Baudhâyana only in three places[3]. As far as the law is concerned, Sâyana follows the theories of the

tion I can add to Professor Bhândârkar's statements that Vaidiks of the White Yagur-veda are found also in Northern India. I have also heard of Vaidiks of the Sâma-veda among the Parvatîyas in the Panjab, and of the Atharva-veda in the Central India Agency.

[1] Bhândârkar, loc. cit. p. 132 note.

[2] Parâsara-smriti-vyâkhyâ, p. 3, ver. 7 (Calcutta edition).

[3] Burnell, Dâyavibhâga, pp. 9, 39, 41.

special law school of his time and of his country, without particular reference to the teaching of his Vedic *K*ara*n*a.

This depression of the Vedic *K*ara*n*as through special schools, which took over the scientific cultivation of a most important portion of the Aṅgas, is not of modern date. It goes back to a time which lies long before the beginning of the historical period of India. We have various indications in the ancient books which force us towards this conclusion. Thus Yâska's Nirukta, a work which undoubtedly belongs to a very early period, quotes Vaiyâkara*n*as, grammarians; Nairuktas, etymological exegetes; and Yâ*gñ*ikas, ritualists; and contrasts their conflicting opinions[1]. If these schools were at issue with respect to grammatical or exegetical questions, it follows that the subjects which they taught were no longer cultivated by the same persons as auxiliary branches of the Vedic lore, but that each had received in a special school a separate development as an independent science. The actual condition in which the various Aṅgas have been preserved, fully agrees with this view. It shows that two at least, grammar and astronomy, slipped away from the control of the Vedic *K*ara*n*as in very early times. For not one of those schools, the text-books of which have survived, possesses a grammatical or an astronomical handbook of its own. Pâ*n*ini's Ash*t*âdhyâyî is the sole representative of the Vyâkara*n*a class of the Aṅgas, and is equally acknowledged by the followers of all Vedas. But grammar, as taught by Pâ*n*ini, is no longer a mere handmaiden of the Vedavidyâ. It is an independent science which lays down the laws, applicable to the whole Sanskrit language, and treats what we now call the classical Sanskrit as the standard of Âryan speech, the Vedic forms as anomalies. As the numerous quotations of older schools and older teachers in Pâ*n*ini's own work, in the Prâti*s*âkhyas, and in Yâska's Nirukta clearly show, a very considerable number of more ancient works did precede the Ash*t*âdhyâyî, and the latter is undoubtedly the final outgrowth of a long scientific development[2]. A good many of the lost

[1] Nirukta I, 12; V, 11; VII, 4; XIII, 9.

[2] See Max Müller, History of Ancient Sanskrit Literature, p. 150, who says

works seem to have treated grammar from the same standpoint as Pâ*n*ini's book. But it may be reasonably supposed that the earliest among them mainly or even exclusively taught the rules applicable to the Vedic texts, studied by the several *K*ara*n*as to which the authors belonged. This stage of grammatical research belongs, however, to a remote past. Indian grammar, as it first becomes known to us, is no longer entirely subservient to the wants of the Veda-study, but works, though it still takes account of the Veda, for its own ends.

The science of astronomy is still more loosely connected with the Vedic schools. All the traces of its really having been an Aṅga consist in the small treatise, entitled *G*yotisha, of which two slightly different recensions are extant, one belonging to the Rig-veda and one to the Ya*g*ur-veda. All the other works on this subject, even the ancient ones such as the Gârgî Sa*m*hitâ, as well as the Vâsish*th*a Sa*m*hitâ and Siddhânta, show no connexion with the Veda or Vedic schools, except that their authorship is ascribed to *R*ishis or descendants of the families of *R*ishis.

As regards the sacred law, the fact that such late offshoots of the Vedic tree, as the Âpastambîyas and the Haira*n*yake*s*as, possess Dharma-sûtras, proves that this subject much longer formed part of the curriculum of the Vedic schools. But already one of the most ancient grammarians of the historical period of India, Pata*ñg*ali, hints that in his times the Dharma was taught not only in the Vedic but also in special schools. For on the one hand he refers to the Dharma-sûtras[1], on the other he teaches the formation of a special word, dhârmavidya, which denotes 'a person who studies or knows the dharmavidyâ, the science of the sacred law[2].' Possibly the word dharma*s*âstra, the Institutes of the sacred law, which occurs

most appropriately that the Hindus ought to speak not of the Pâ*n*inyâdyâ vaiyâkara*n*â*h*, but of the Pâ*n*inyantâ*h*.

[1] See the remarks on Pâ*n*ini I, 1, 47.

[2] See the remarks on Pâ*n*ini IV, 2, 60 (vol. ii, p. 248, Kielhorn). I follow Dr. Kielhorn, who prints the words 'vidyâ *k*ânaṅgakshatradharmatripûrvâ' as a remark of Pata*ñg*ali, not as a Vârttika of Kâtyâyana.

d 2

occasionally in his Bhâshya[1], may also point to manuals, studied by the special schools, which differed from the Dharma-sûtras. But it is not absolutely conclusive, as a Dharma-sûtra too may be called a Dharmasâstra, because it teaches the sacred law. If we go back to still earlier times we find the existence of special law schools clearly indicated even in some of the Dharma-sûtras. The passages which are most explicit on this point are those which describe the constitution of a Parishad or an assembly of learned men, entitled to decide doubtful law cases. For we read, Vasishtha III, 20, and Baudhâyana I, 1, 8, 'Four men who each know one of the four Vedas, a student of the Mîmâmsâ, one who knows the Angas, one who recites (the works on) the sacred law (dharmapâthaka), and three Brâhmanas belonging to (three different) orders (constitute) an assembly consisting of, at least, ten (members)[2].' Here the reciter or teacher of the sacred law is named side by side with him who knows the Angas. As the two works in which the verse occurs are Dharma-sûtras belonging to the Kalpa section of the Angas, it is evident that the teacher of the sacred law must be a person who specially devotes himself to the study of that subject, and knows more than one Dharma-sûtra. Hence it follows that special law schools must have existed at the time when these two Dharma-sûtras were composed[3]. It may also be that already then these special schools had elaborated

[1] See Kâtyâyana's Vârttika 39 on Pânini I, 2, 64, and Patañgali's remarks thereon (Kielhorn, Mah. vol. i, p. 242).

[2] See also Manu XII, 111; and above, p. xxv.

[3] The significance of the passage quoted comes out still stronger, if we compare Gautama's rule (XXVIII, 49), which differs very considerably: 'They declare that an assembly (parishad, shall consist) at least (of) the ten following (members, viz.) four men who have completely studied the four Vedas, three men belonging to the (three) orders enumerated first, (and) three men who know (three) different (institutes of) law.' Gautama says nothing of men specially devoted to the study of the sacred law. He requires three persons, knowing three different Dharma-sûtras. He and Âpastamba are perfectly aware of the fragmentary character of their rules, and particularly refer their pupils (Gaut. XVI, 49; Âp. I, 3, 11, 38) in certain cases to the teaching of other schools, which, being comprised under the general term Smriti, have authority, provided the teachers were orthodox Sishtas (Gaut. I, 2; Âp. I, 1, 1, 2; Vas. I, 4; Baudh. I, 1, 1, 3).

manuals of their own which differed from the Dharma-sûtras. In favour of this opinion the metrical quotation at Baudhâyana II, 4, 14–15 may be adduced, as it seems to have been taken from a work in Anush*t*ubh-*S*lokas[1]. Though the unsatisfactory state of the text of Baudhâyana does not allow us to insist too strongly on this passage, it is undeniable that the formation of special law schools must inevitably lead after a short time to the composition of manuals for their use. It is, no doubt, true that their founders possessed in the Dharma-sûtras, the number of which, to judge from the quotations, must have been very great, plentiful materials on which they could base their investigations. But the treatment of a science from a new point of view was in itself an incentive to the production of new manuals, and there were in the case of the special law schools also other reasons which made such a course desirable. Minute as the Dharma-sûtras generally are on the majority of the topics connected with the moral duties of Âryas, their arrangement of the rules is frequently unsystematic, and their treatment of the legal procedure, the civil and the criminal law, with the exception of one single title, the dâyavibhâga, i. e. the law of inheritance and partition, extremely unsatisfactory. With respect to the other titles, the Dharma-sûtras give nothing more than a few hints, intended to indicate the general principles, but they never proceed systematically, and always show most embarrassing omissions. From the standpoint of the Vedic schools, a more detailed and orderly treatment of these matters was, of course, irrelevant, as their chief aim was to point out the road to the acquisition of spiritual merit, and to guard their pupils against committing sin. Though some of their members might be called upon, and no doubt actually were destined in later life, to become practical lawyers, as Dharmâdhikârins, i. e. legal advisers of kings and chiefs, or as judges, and to settle the law between man and man, the few general principles which they had learnt during their course of instruction would suffice for their wants. For the details

[1] Sacred Books of the East, vol. xiv, p. xli.

were settled according to the law of custom, which, as the Dharma-sûtras themselves indicate, was in ancient times even a greater power in India than it is in our days. When the sacred law became a separate science to which men devoted all or the best part of their energy, the case became different. However much the specialists might be convinced of the supreme importance of the moral side of the Dharma, they could not possibly shut their eyes against the glaring deficiencies of the old text-books, and they were, of a necessity, driven to remedy them. In order to effect this, two courses were open to them. They might either remodel the old existing works or compose entirely new ones. As might be expected from the universal tendency, observable throughout the whole of the sacred literature of India, they gave preference to the former alternative, and the result of their work was that class of the secondary Sm*ri*tis, the chief surviving representatives of which are the Dharma*s*âstras of Manu and Yâ*gñ*avalkya. These works reveal their origin by the following marks. They are the exclusive property of the special law schools, and they show a fuller and more systematic treatment of all legal topics, while, at the same time, more or less clear traces of older redactions, connected with the Vedic schools, are to be found. They are free from all signs of sectarian influence, or of having been composed, like many of the later Digests, at royal command. They, finally, exhibit unmistakable marks of being school-books. If we examine our Manu-sm*ri*ti with respect to these points, its connexion with an older Vedic work has been shown above, and the fact that it is, and has been ever since we have any information regarding its existence, in the keeping of the Pa*nd*its, who especially devote themselves to the study of law, will be patent to every student of the Dharma*s*âstras. That it treats all legal topics more fully and more systematically than the Dharma-sûtras, and especially devotes much more space to those subjects which are briefly noticed in the latter works, is no less evident. It will suffice here to point out the fact that the description of the duties of the king, including the administration of justice and the civil and criminal law, occupies considerably more than one-third of the whole. For chapters vii–ix contain no less than 982 verses, while the total number amounts to 2,684 [1]. None of the older law-books devotes more than one-fifth of its text to such matters [2]. The freedom of the Manu-smriti from all sectarian influence is perfect. It nowhere teaches the performance of other rites than those prescribed in the Vedic writings, and it nowhere inculcates the exclusive worship of one of the deities of the Paurânik sects as we find it recommended, for instance, in the Vishnu-smriti. Nor is there any hint that it was written by order of some king or chief with the purpose of serving as a Digest of the sacred law. Finally, the marks of its being a school-book, intended for the instruction of all Âryas, are unmistakable. We are told, Manu I, 103, that 'a learned Brâhmana must carefully study these (Institutes), and must duly instruct his pupils in them,' but that 'nobody else (shall do it).' Who the pupils, entitled to learn the work, are, is explained II, 16. There it is said that 'he for whom (the performance of) the rites, beginning with the Garbhâdhâna and ending with the Antyeshti, is ordained together with recitation of sacred formulas, is entitled to study it, but no other man whatsoever.' Hence Brâhmans are to teach the Sâstra, and all Âryas may learn it. It further agrees with its character as a school-book, if the phalasruti or statement of the rewards to be gained by its study, Manu XII, 126, asserts that a twice-born man, who is able to recite 'these Institutes, will be always virtuous in conduct, and will reach (i. e. after death) whatever condition he desires.' The first object which the student may gain is self-improvement, and the second happiness after death [3].

[1] About the same ratio, 367 : 1009 is found in Yâgñavalkya's Smriti.

[2] Thus in the Gautamîya, seven pages of the text out of thirty-four are filled with legal matters; in the Vâsishtha, twelve pages out of eighty-one; in the Âpastambîya, ten out of ninety-eight; and in the Baudhâyanîya, about seven out of a hundred and fifteen.

[3] Other secondary Smritis, e.g. Yâgñavalkya's (III, 330–334). give much more detailed statements regarding the rewards to be obtained. But in substance they always agree with Manu.

If we accept the conclusion which the preceding discussion tends to establish, that the special law schools produced the first and the most ancient division of the secondary Smritis on the basis of older Dharma-sûtras, and that one among these schools, which, however, cannot be further specified, turned the Mânava Dharma-sûtra into our metrical Smriti[1], we obtain also satisfactory answers to two other questions. First, it becomes explicable why the latter work shows so little connexion with the special doctrines and usages of the Mânavas. If adherents of the Vedic Mânava school, as Professor E. Hopkins conjectures[2], had undertaken the revision of their Dharma-sûtra, they would not have forgotten to mention such ceremonies as those which, according to their Grihya-sûtra, must be performed on beginning the study of particular portions of their Samhitâ[3], and, above all, they would have allowed Mantras belonging to the Maitrâyanî Sâkhâ to stand. Again, if the task had fallen to the share of the members of some other Vedic school, we should find some points mentioned which were of special interest to them. The entire absence of all distinctive marks of any Vedic school which the Manu-smriti exhibits can only be explained on the hypothesis that it was remodelled by persons for whom such minute distinctions had no interest, and who concentrated their attention on those rules which they considered essential for all Âryas. Secondly, the view expressed above furnishes us with an answer to the question why the Manu-smriti, like all other works of its class, emphatically claims the allegiance of all Hindus. It is obvious that every special law school must assert, if its labour is not to be in vain, the general applicability of its doctrines and rules to all mankind.

If we now turn to the second point, what reasons induced the special law schools to select just the Mânava Dharma-sûtra among the large number of similar works

[1] This view, which I first taught in my lectures on the Hindu law, delivered in the Vienna University during the winter, 1881–82, has been accepted by Professor J. Jolly, Tagore Lectures, p. 41, and Lecture II passim, as well as p. 347 (end).

[2] Proceedings of the American Oriental Society, October, 1883, p. xix.

[3] See above, p. xxxix, note 5.

for the basis of their studies and to recast it, the answer is not difficult to find. The reason for this selection, and for the high veneration in which the Manu-smriti has been held and is still held by Hindus, lies, without doubt, in the myths which, since very early times, have clustered round the name of Manu, and in progress of time have been more and more developed and brought into a system.

In Vedic mythology, Manu, or Manus, as he is also called in the Rig-veda, is the heros eponymos of the human race, and by his nature belongs both to gods and to men. As a divine being he is described as the son of the Âditya Vivasvat and of 'the female of equal colour,' whom Vivasvat's wife, Saranyû, made to take her place[1], or as the offspring of Svayambhû, self-existent Brahman[2]. In the same quality he is invoked at the sacrifices as pragâpati, the Lord of created beings[3], and in Kutsâyana's hymn of praise, which is quoted in the Maitrâyana Brâhmanopanishad (V, 1), he is identified with Brahman, the supreme Soul[4]. In the systematised theology of the Nairuktas he appears as one of the deities residing in heaven[5]. His human character comes out still more frequently. He is named in the Rig-veda together with other sages of a remote antiquity[6], the Taittirîya-samhitâ speaks of him as of the father of a family who divides his estate among his sons[7], and the Satapatha-brâhmana opens one of its legends regarding him with a passage which represents him as following the usual daily customs of men[8].

Manu's position as the progenitor of mankind is usually

[1] Vâlakhilya IV, 1; Atharva-veda VIII, 10, 24; Sat. Br. XIII, 4, 3, 3; and Nirukta XII, 10.

[2] See the Vedic sloka quoted Nirukta III, 4, about which more will be said below. A third account, Vâlakhilya III, 1, makes him the son of Samvarana, who possibly may be identical with the Rishi mentioned RV. V, 33, 10.

[3] Taitt. Samh. III, 2, 8, 1; IV, 1, 9, 1; Vâg. Samh. XI, 66; Maitr. Samh. II, 7, 7.

[4] The edition reads annam, food. But Professor Max Müller's MS. has correctly Manu (S. B. E. XV, p. 303 note). My copy has मनुः.

[5] Nirukta XII, 33-34.

[6] RV. I, 80, 16; I, 112, 16, &c.

[7] Taitt. Samh. III, 1, 9, 4.

[8] Sat. Br. I, 8, 1; Sacred Books of the East, vol. xii, p. 216, 'In the morning they brought to Manu water for washing, just as they (are wont to) bring (water) for washing the hands.'

indicated in general terms only. In the Rig-veda he is repeatedly called 'Father Manu[1].' In other passages we meet frequently with the assertion that 'the five tribes,' or 'these created beings,' or 'the races of men' are his offspring[2]. But in the famous legend of the flood, given by the *S*atapatha-brâhma*n*a[3], we have a circumstantial account of the manner in which he produced the human race. According to that Brâhma*n*a, Manu alone was saved by the advice of a fish from a great flood which destroyed all created beings. Being desirous of offspring he engaged in worshipping and in performing austerities. During this time he offered a Pâka-ya*g*ña. His oblations produced a woman, I*d*â or I*l*â, a personification of the i*d*â ceremony and of 'the blessing of the sacrifice.' Though solicited by Mitra and Varu*n*a to become theirs, she acknowledged herself Manu's daughter, and stayed with him. 'With her,' the Brâhma*n*a concludes in somewhat ambiguous terms, 'he went on worshipping and performing austerities. Through her he generated this race, which is called the race of Manu.' Though this legend is alluded to in another Brâhma*n*a[4], and repeated in later Sanskrit works, it may be reasonably doubted whether it contains the original version of the production of mankind through Manu. It seems more probable that an older myth ascribed to him not a reproduction, but the first creation or procreation of the human race.

Being the father of mankind, Manu is naturally considered as the founder of social and moral order, as a ruler of men, and as a *R*ishi to whom sacred texts were revealed, as the inventor of sacrificial rites, and the author of legal maxims. We find, therefore, passages which assert that he was a king[5], which speak of his coronation, or make him

[1] RV. I, 80, 16; I, 124, 2; II, 33, 13, &c.

[2] RV. III, 24, 3; Taitt. Sa*m*h. I, 5, 1, 3; I, 5, 6, 1; III, 4, 22; III, 4, 3, 7; VI, 1, 5, 6, &c.; *S*at. Br. XIII, 4, 3, 3.

[3] Sacred Books of the East, vol. xii, pp. 216-219.

[4] Weber, Indische Streifen, vol. i, p. 11, note 3.

[5] See e.g. *S*atapatha-brâhma*n*a XIII, 4, 3, 3, and RV. I, 112, 8. In the latter passage the epithet *s*ûra, the hero, characterises Manu as a royal personage.

the ancestor of kings. Thus a Mantra, recited at the Abhisheka of a king[1], asserts that Pragâpati formerly anointed Indra, Soma, Varuna, Yama, and Manu, and among the mythical kings Saryâta is called Manu's son[2], while Purûravas is the offspring of Manu's daughter, Idâ or Ilâ[3]. In later times this ancient idea, which makes Manu the first king of men and the ancestor of kings, has led to his being placed at the head of mythical and of partly historical genealogies. From him springs Ikshvâku, the first king of the solar dynasty and the historical Kalukya, and Kola kings name Manu as the founder of their families.

Much more frequently the Veda alludes to, or explicitly mentions, Manu as the inventor of sacrificial rites. The Rig-veda contains a very large number of passages[4] which speak of Manu's sacrifices, and of his having kindled the sacred fire, or invoked the gods to accept the offerings of the Rishis just as they accepted those of Manu. The same assertions are repeated in the Yagur-veda[5], and the Satapatha-brâhmana (I, 5, 1–7) says very explicitly, 'Manu, indeed, worshipped with sacrifices in the beginning; imitating that, this progeny (of his now) sacrifices.' In addition to the fire-worship, Manu is also said to have invented the Srâddhas or funeral sacrifices. The chief passage bearing on this point occurs in Âpastamba's Dharma-sûtra II, 18, 1, where it is stated that the gods went to heaven in reward of their sacrifices, and that Manu, seeing men left behind, 'revealed this ceremony, which is designated by the word Srâddha.' Though this passage is not marked as a quotation, its style clearly shows that it has either been borrowed from a Brâhmana, or that it gives a summary of

[1] Ait. Br. VIII, 8, 1.

[2] Sat. Br. IV, 1, 5, 2; compare also Ait. Br. IV, 32; VIII, 21, where the name is Sâryâta.

[3] RV. I, 31, 4; X, 95; and Sat. Br. XI, 5, 1, 1. In the first passage I take manave in the sense of mânavâya.

[4] See Bergaigne, Religion Védique, I, 62–70, where, it seems to me, a great many difficult passages have been explained more successfully than in the translations of other Vedists, who take the word manu too freely in the sense of man.

[5] See e.g. Taitt. Samh. I, 7, 1, 3; II, 5, 9, 1; III, 3, 2, 1; V, 4, 10, 5.

a longer story contained in such a work[1]. It is probably on account of this legend that 'Manu, the offspring of the Sun,' receives in the Mahâbhârata[2] the epithet *S*râddha-deva, which may be rendered either 'the deity of the *S*râddha,' or, perhaps better, 'he whose deity is the *S*râddha, i. e. the *S*râddha-worshipper.' Closely connected with Manu's position as inventor of sacrifices is the ancient myth, mentioned above, which makes him the father of I*d*â; and from the same idea spring probably the legends regarding his bull, whose voice destroyed the demons, and regarding the sacrifice of his wife, Manâvî[3].

That Manu was credited with the revelation of Mantras has been stated above[4] in the remarks on the passages from the three redactions of the Ya*g*ur-veda and of the Tâ*n*dya-brâhma*n*a. The older works, however, nowhere attribute to him entire hymns, but mostly small numbers of verses only. The same is the case in the Index of the *Ri*shis of the White Ya*g*ur-veda, while the Sarvânukrama*n*î of the Rig-veda ascribes five entire Sûktas, VIII, 27–31, to Manu Vaivasvata, as well as a few verses to Manu Âpsava and to Manu Sâ*m*vara*n*a. An interesting passage in the beginning of the last section of the *Kh*ândogyopanishad[5] informs us that that work was revealed by Brahmâ (Hira*n*yagarbha) to Pra*g*âpati (Ka*s*yapa), by Pra*g*âpati to Manu, and by Manu to mankind. This legend proves that the ancient Vedic schools believed Manu to have taught more than a few verses and hymns. It also helps us to understand better the phrase of the four Vedic books quoted, 'All

[1] If Professor Max Müller, India, What can it teach us? pp. 234–235 and 365, thinks that Âpastamba's passage betrays a consciousness of the later origin of the *S*râddha rites, I am unable to follow him. It seems to me more probable that it is only intended to explain the holiness and efficacy of the funeral sacrifices, and why they secure heaven for the worshipper and the worshipped ancestor. In the Brâhma*n*as similar introductions, in which the Devas play the part of Manu, are prefixed to the descriptions of most sacrifices. As the *S*râddhas specially concern men, the father of mankind is very appropriately represented as their inventor.

[2] Mah. XII, 121, 29.

[3] Sacred Books of the East, vol. xii, pp. 29-30; see also the passages and essays quoted there in note 1.

[4] See p. xvi.

[5] Sacred Books of the East, vol. i, p. 144.

Manu said is medicine.' As has been pointed out above, the assertion contained in this sentence is so general that it makes us suspect the existence of many sayings of Manu on religious subjects. Though the *Kh*ândogya is probably not as ancient as the Sa*m*hitâs of the Yagur-veda, or even as the Tâ*nd*ya, and though it hence would be more than hazardous to assume that this very passage is alluded to in the latter, the idea that Manu acted as mediator between Brahman and mankind, and that he taught the way to final liberation, may yet belong to very early times, and may have been one of the causes which led to the sweeping generalisation. The same passages probably testify also to the early existence of the belief that Manu first settled the Dharma, which, as the preceding discussion shows, is but a natural outgrowth from the conceptions which make him the founder of the moral and social order of the world. The published Sa*m*hitâs and Brâhma*n*as contain, as far as I know, no explicit statement on this subject. But an allusion to it seems to occur in the passage of the Taittirîya-sa*m*hitâ which declares that Manu divided his estate among his sons. Baudhâyana [1], at least, has taken it in this sense, as he places it at the head of his rules on inheritance. The oldest direct testimony on this point is the *S*loka quoted in Yâska's Nirukta III, 4, which says, 'According to the sacred law the inheritance goes without a distinction to the children of both sexes, (that) Manu, the offspring of the Self-existent (Svâyambhuva), has declared at the beginning of the creation [2].' The text shows the Vedic accents, the use of which appears to be confined to the Sa*m*hitâs and Brâhma*n*as. As the verse is emphatically called a *S*loka, it cannot have been taken

[1] Sacred Books of the East, vol. xiv, p. 224.

[2] I do not share Professor von Roth's misgivings (Nirukta, Notes, pp. 24-26) regarding the genuineness of this verse, and of the whole legal discussion in sections 4-6 of the third book of the Nirukta. We know now that the views of the ancient authors on the succession of daughters differed very considerably. Hence the incidental discussion of this vexed question in the Nirukta need not raise any suspicion. Similar digressions are not uncommon in other Vedic works. The difficulty with respect to the compound *rik*s*lokâbhyâm, in the words introducing the verse, disappears if it is taken as a Dvandva, and not, as Professor von Roth seems to do, as a Karmadhâraya.

from a work of the former class. It probably belongs to one of the lost accented Brâhma*n*as. That it did not form part of the Mânava Dharma-sûtra follows, not only from the use of the accents, but also from its contents. Its doctrine does not agree with that of our Manu-sm*ri*ti, which, with respect to the greater part of the rules on inheritance, may be considered as a faithful representative of the original Dharma-sûtra. Though Manu IX, 131–139 strongly insists on the right of an appointed daughter, and, indeed, of every daughter who has no brothers, to succeed to the paternal estate, he nowhere lays down the rule, which, according to Yâska, is taught in our verse, that daughters under all circumstances share equally with sons. To daughters who have brothers Manu allots one-fourth of a share.

In the Dharma-sûtras the verses which contain the phrase 'manur abravît, thus Manu has said,' or equivalents thereof, become more frequent. The passages of Vasish*th*a and of *S*âṅkhâyana in which it occurs have been discussed above. Two verses of this description are found in Baudhâyana's Dharma-sûtra (IV, 1, 13; 2, 15), and a considerable number in U*s*anas' aphoristic Dharma*s*âstra[1]. In the Mahâbhârata[2], in our Manu-sm*ri*ti itself, in the Nârada-sm*ri*ti[3], and in other secondary law-books it is also of common occurrence. Its real meaning is, as Professor Hopkins (loc. cit.) has pointed out, no other than that the rule to which it is appended was thought to be ancient and indisputable. Hence it is sometimes used vicariously for appeals to the teaching of the Veda[4] and of Pra*g*âpati. That the cause of

[1] Instances of this kind occur, especially in the *S*râddhakalpa, chapter IV, भवति चात्र श्लोकः। दत्तानुयोगाद्धनहेतोः पतितान्मनुरब्रवीत् (sic) ॥ ---- असमानयाजकाश्च श्रुतिविक्रयिकाश्च ये। अस्य पूर्वप्रजातानां पतितान्मनुरब्रवीत् (sic) ॥ and in chapter VI, नद्यः कूपतडागास्तु सरांसि सरितस्तथा। असंपृक्तान्यदोषाणि मनुः स्वायंभुवोब्रवीत् ॥ अशृतान्नानि मूलानि धान्यकाः सक्तवश्च ताः। परपाकनिवृत्तानां भोज्यान्नं मनुरब्रवीत् ॥ ----स्त्रीमुखे च सुरागन्धमदोषमनुरब्रवीत् ॥

[2] Proceedings of the American Oriental Society, October, 1883, p. xix.

[3] J. Jolly, Tagore Lectures, p. 46.

[4] Compare e. g. Vas. XVII, 10–11, and Manu IX, 182–3.

its adoption was not the existence of a primeval Mânava Dharma-sûtra or *S*âstra, but the belief in the revelation of the law by Manu is proved also by the wide divergence of the doctrines attributed to the father of mankind from each other and from the teaching of the Manu-sm*ri*ti.

These legends and mythological conceptions are amply sufficient to show why the special law schools should have directed their attention to the Mânava Dharma-sûtra, and should have chosen that in preference to other similar works as the basis of one of their text-books. Even if the author of the Sûtra, who in the tradition of the Mânavas[1] is sometimes called Manvâ*k*ârya and sometimes Mânavâ*k*ârya, really was a historical personage named after the progenitor of men, and was considered as such by the adherents of his own school, yet a confusion between him and his mythical namesake was in course of time inevitable. Even Âpastamba, who himself claims to be no more than a common sinful mortal, has not escaped the fate of being turned into a half-divine being by the authors of the Mahâbhârata[2] and of the Purâ*n*as.

[1] All I can adduce regarding the tradition of the Mânavas is found in some not very clear verses of the Maṅgalâ*k*ara*n*as, prefixed to the two books of Ash*t*âvakra's commentary on the G*ri*hya-sûtra. In the beginning of the prathamapurushabhâshya he says, according to Professor Haug's MS. (Munich Roy. Lib. Sansk. MSS., No. 51), नमो भाष्यकारा[य] मानवाचार्याय नमः। यस्याः प्रसादान्मनुना शब्दशास्त्रमिदं (?) कृतम्। सरस्वत्युपनामानि (?) सा नः पातु सरस्वती॥ My MS. omits the invocation of the Bhâshyakâra and of Mânavâ*k*ârya and reads in the last line सरस्वत्पूनानि कल्पयतु सा°॥ The dvitîyapurushabhâshya begins, according to my MS., सरस्वत्याः प्रसादेन यथैतत्कृतवान्पुरा। भगवान्मानवाचार्यः पूरणाख्यं प्रयत्नतः॥१॥ अष्टावक्रेण देवेन तां तुष्ट्वा तु (?) सरस्वतीम्। शते पूर्णे तु वर्षाणामृतौ शिशिरसंज्ञिके॥२॥ नमस्करोमि तां देवीं यस्या एव प्रभावतः। प्राप्तं यत्तन्महात्पुरण्य [एतन्महापुरण्यं ?] वृहद्धर्माभिधायकम्॥३॥ In the first line of the second verse I propose to read अष्टावक्रेण देवेन कृतं तुष्ट्वा सरस्वतीम् and to translate, 'As the venerable Mânavâ*k*ârya composed this (Sûtra) by the favour of Sarasvatî, (even so) the (commentary) called Pûra*n*a was carefully written by Ash*t*âvakradeva after he had pleased Sarasvatî, when one hundred years (of the Lokakâla) were completed, in the season called the dewy one.' These verses seem to indicate that, according to the tradition of the Mânavas, a historical Mânavâ*k*ârya or Manvâ*k*ârya composed the G*ri*hya-sûtra, which was also called B*ri*haddharma, by the special favour of the goddess Sarasvatî.

[2] See Mah. XIII, 66, 12.

A Manu who composed a treatise on the sacred law which gained some notoriety was, therefore, sure of divine honours. As soon as the identification of the author of the Sûtra with the father of mankind was made, it was a matter of course that the Manu-sm*ri*ti obtained a particularly high position, and was accepted as the paramount authority on the sacred law.

The legends given above render us yet another service. They explain the origin of the seemingly contradictory statements of the Sm*ri*ti regarding Manu. When he is represented there as a descendant of self-existent Brahman and a Pra*g*âpati who takes a prominent part in the creation, or as identical with the supreme Brahman[1], and on the other hand as a *Ri*shi and as a king of the remotest antiquity, it is now patent that these conceptions have been taken over from Vedic literature and that, different as they are, they have all grown out of the one fundamental idea which makes the first man and progenitor a half-divine and half-human being, an assistant in the work of creation, and the founder of moral and social order among men. Some of the remaining elements of the myth of Manu, as told in the Sm*ri*ti, are likewise clearly developments of Vedic ideas. Thus the interposition of the androgynous Virâ*g* in Manu's genealogy (I, 32–33) is foreshadowed by a curious passage of the Atharva-veda, VIII, 10, where the female Virâ*g* is said to have been 'in the beginning this (whole world),' and to have yielded blessings to various classes of beings. According to verse 24, 'Manu, the son of Vivasvat, was her calf[2], when P*ri*thî Vainya milked from her agriculture and grain-bearing plants.' It would, therefore, seem that Virâ*g*, who repeatedly plays a part in Vedic cosmogony, was already there connected with Manu. Further, the substitution of seven or more Manus for one, has probably been caused, as the Petersburg Dictionary (s. v. manu) suggests, by the diversity of the genealogies found in the various Vedic passages. It is even not improbable that the Vedic schools believed, when Kâtyâ-

[1] The same identification occurs Mah. I, 1, 32.

[2] This statement alludes to the fact that Indian cows do not allow themselves to be milked, except when their calves stand by.

yana composed his Sarvânukramanikâ of the Rig-veda, in the existence of several distinct Manus. Finally, the association of the ten great sages whom Manu Svâyambhuva created, and who in turn created other Manus (I, 34-36), in the work of creation, rests on such passages as those quoted by Âpastamba II, 24, 3-6, 13, where successive destructions of the world are mentioned, and 'this creation is declared to be the work of Pragâpati and of the sages.' But the complete development of the myth of Manu belongs to the schools of the Paurânikas and Aitihâsikas, and we find in the Purânas and in the Mahâbhârata many legends which are partly identical with or closely related to that told in our Smriti [1].

The third problem, to say how the conversion of the Mânava Dharma-sûtra into our Manu-smriti was effected, presents very considerable difficulties, and admits of an approximative solution only. It involves the consideration of three questions. First, which portions of our Manu-smriti are ancient and which are later additions? secondly, whence have the additions been derived? and thirdly, whether they have been added at one time or successively? In our attempts to distinguish between the old and the modern elements in our Manu-samhitâ we must be guided, except where we have quotations from the old Dharma-sûtra, by the analogies which the other existing Dharma-sûtras furnish. For it may be assumed as a general maxim, that rules and other statements of our Manu, which find counterparts in the critically unsuspicious portions of the Sûtras of Gautama, Baudhâyana, Âpastamba, and Vasishtha, probably occurred also in the Mânava Dharma-sûtra. Single exceptions are, of course, possible, because, though the Dharma-sûtras show a very decided class-affinity, they yet differ in the details. The one devotes greater attention to one subject, and the other to others. Hence it may be, that occasionally a rule which is found in the Dharma-sûtras, nevertheless did not occur in the Mânava-sûtra, but was added on its

[1] See H. H. Wilson, Vishnu-purâna, vol. i, pp. 104-5 (ed. Hall); Professor Hopkins, Journal of the American Oriental Society, vol. xi, pp. 247-256.

revision. To a certain extent we may also avail ourselves of the Vishnu-smriti for the same purpose. But a greater degree of caution will be necessary, as this work, though in the main a representative of the Kâthaka Dharma-sûtra, contains also an admixture of modern elements. On the other hand, those rules and discussions which cannot be traced in one of the old Sûtras, are at least suspicious, and require careful consideration. The ultimate decision, if such passages have indeed to be considered as additions, must depend on various collateral circumstances. The safest criterion will always be the character of the ideas which they express. If these are entirely foreign to the Sûtras or to Vedic literature, they may be confidently rejected as interpolations. A good deal depends also on their position and on the manner in which they fit into the context. Numerous cases will, however, remain doubtful.

If we examine Manu's text according to these principles, the more important results will be as follows :—The whole first chapter must be considered as a later addition. No Dharma-sûtra begins with a description of its own origin, much less with an account of the creation. The former, which would be absurd in a Dharma-sûtra, has been added in order to give authority to a remodelled version. The latter has been dragged in, because the myths connected with Manu presented a good opportunity 'to show the greatness of the scope of the work,' as Medhâtithi says. The table of contents, given at the end of chapter I, was, of course, also foreign to the original Sûtra. Chapters II–VI, on the other hand, seem to represent with tolerable faithfulness the contents of the corresponding sections of the Mânava Dharma-sûtra. Nearly all the rules are found in the other Dharma-sûtras and in the Vishnu-smriti, and more than three-fourths of the verses find counterparts in the aphorisms and verses of the older law-books. Nevertheless, the hand of the remodeller is not rarely visible. There are, besides the verses which announce the transition from one subject to the other[1], a considerable number of smaller and some

[1] These verses probably mark the subdivisions of the Adhyâyas, the Kandikâs or Khandas of the ancient Sûtra.

larger interpolations. To the latter belong, in the second chapter, vv. 1–11 and vv. 88–100. The first passage gives a philosophical account of the origin of actions (1–5), such as is not found in any older law-book; further, a verse (v. 6) stating the sources of the sacred law, which is unnecessary on account of v. 12, and suspicious on account of the double description of the third source of the law, by the synonymous terms *s*îla and â*k*âra [1]. The contents of the remaining verses, the praise of the Manu-sm*ri*ti (v. 7), the advice how the different authorities are to be studied (v. 8), the declaration of the reward for obedience to the revealed texts (v. 9), the definition of the terms *S*ruti and Sm*ri*ti, and the declaration of their authoritativeness, are likewise superfluous, and clearly later enlargements. The second passage (vv. 88–100), which enumerates the organs of sensation and action and teaches the necessity of controlling them, interrupts the continuity of the text very needlessly, and has nothing whatsoever to do with the matter treated of. Among the smaller interpolations in this chapter, vv. 13, 16, 27, 28, 142, 143, 213–215, 221, and 239 must certainly be reckoned. It also seems probable that the passage on the importance of the syllable Om, of the Vyâh*ri*tis, and of the Sâvitrî (vv. 76–87), as well as that on the humility and meekness required of a Brâhma*n*a (vv. 160–163), and that on the worship due to parents and a teacher (vv. 225–237), have been enlarged, though in each case something of the kind may have occurred in the Dharma-sûtra. In the third chapter, there is one longer passage (vv. 192–201) which, beyond all doubt, has been added by a later hand. For the classification of the Manes, which it contains, is in this form foreign to Vedic literature. More doubtful are the discussions on the duty of conjugal intercourse (vv. 46–50), on the honour due to women (vv. 55–60), on the excellence of the order of householders (vv. 79–80), and on the results of inviting sinners and men of bad conduct to *S*râddhas (vv. 169–182). Possibly the ancient Sûtra contained hints on some of these subjects, but it is most improbable that it

[1] See note to the translation.

should have entered into all the details which our text gives. The passage on the householders has probably been placed wrongly. Most of its verses ought to stand in the discussion on the relative importance of the orders at the end of chapter VI. In the fourth chapter the first section on the means by which a Brâhma*n*a may subsist (vv. 1–24) is exceedingly suspicious. The Dharma-sûtras, e.g. Vasish*th*a XII, 2–4, no doubt sometimes prefix brief hints on the manner in which a Snâtaka may support himself, to the rules regarding his behaviour. But they do not mention the curious classification of the means of subsistence, *Ri*ta, Am*ri*ta, M*ri*ta, Pram*ri*ta, and *S*vav*ri*tti (vv. 5, 6), which, though common in the Purâ*n*as and other later works, is unknown in Vedic literature. As, moreover, Vasish*th*a's rules, which enumerate the persons by whom a Snâtaka may be supported, occur further on (IV, 33–34), it is not improbable that the whole section consisting of the first twenty-four verses is a later addition. With still greater certainty the same may be said of vv. 85–91, which describe the heinousness of the offence committed by him who accepts gifts from a royal usurper and other wicked persons, and enumerate the twenty-one hells which will be the offender's portion. For it is not doubtful that, even if the Sûtrakâras were acquainted with a classification of the regions of punishment, their enumeration ought not to stand here, but, as in the Vish*n*u-sm*ri*ti, at the beginning of the section on crimes and penances. Other probable interpolations are vv. 172–174 on the results of sin, vv. 180–185 on the reasons why quarrels with near relatives should be avoided, vv. 238–243 on the reasons why spiritual merit should be accumulated. Finally, the section on gifts and the acceptance of gifts (vv. 186–197) seems to be strongly mixed with modern elements. The next following two chapters present fewer suspicious passages. Nevertheless, the preamble to the section on forbidden food, V, 1–4, the verses 19–21, which prescribe the penances for eating mushrooms, onions, leeks, and so forth, must be certainly rejected. For the former belong to the artificial framework which has been placed round the old Sûtra, and the latter ought to stand in chapter XI. From the quotation in

Vasishtha IV, 5-8, it is further evident that the rules on the permissibility of meat have been much altered and enlarged in accordance with the growing repugnance against the slaughter of animals. The last section of the same chapter, on the duties of women, has probably had the same fate. The example of the Vâsishtha Dharmasâstra shows that some of the old Sûtrakâras treated the duties of women in two separate sections[1]. But it also proves that they did not, as our Manu-smriti does, go twice over the same matter. It is evident that either here or in the beginning of the ninth chapter the same verses have been needlessly repeated by the author of the remodelled version. In the sixth chapter there is only one passage, vv. 61-82, which goes beyond the range of the Dharma-sûtras. None of the latter enters into such details regarding the meditations to which an ascetic must give himself up in order to attain salvation. The subject naturally tempted the remodeller of the Smriti to expand the shorter notes of the original. Very different is the case of the next three chapters, VII-IX, which treat of the duties of a king, and of civil and criminal law. These sections probably bear only a faint resemblance to the corresponding portions of the original work. Among the 226 verses of the seventh chapter there are only fifty-four to which passages of the Dharma-sûtras and the Vishnu-smriti correspond. If one pays attention to the rules regarding the king's duties, given in the Dharma-sûtras of Gautama, Âpastamba, and Vasishtha, as well as to the references to the opinions of the Mânavas and of Manu, made in the Kâmandakîya Nîtisâra[2], it would seem probable that the contents of this section of the Mânava Dharma-sûtra cannot have differed very much from those of the third chapter of Vishnu, and that about two-thirds of the seventh Adhyâya of our Manu-smriti have been added when it was recast. With respect to the eighth chapter and the first 224 verses of the ninth, which give the rules regarding the eighteen titles of the law, the remodeller seems to have been equally active. We must ascribe to

[1] See Vas. V and XVII, 55-80.

[2] See above, p. xxxvi.

him the systematic arrangement of the legal rules, which is not found in any of the ancient Dharma-sûtras, and is even neglected in the Vish*n*u-sm*ri*ti. He is most probably also responsible for more than one-half of the verses of these chapters. In the eighth Adhyâya only three-sevenths of the rules of our Manu can be traced in the Dharma-sûtras or in the Vish*n*u-sm*ri*ti, which latter, as far as these topics are concerned, may be considered a faithful representative of the Kâ*th*aka Dharma-sûtra [1]. Two of Manu's titles, concerns among partners [2] and the resumption of gifts, are not mentioned in the older works; and the rules under a third, rescission of purchase and sale, have no resemblance to those of Vish*n*u. In the ninth chapter the chief topics, treated under the head, duties of husband and wife, are discussed or at least touched on in the Sûtras. But the latter place them differently, and give them much more concisely. The notes to the translation show that only one-fourth of Manu's verses corresponds to utterances of the ancient teachers. The section on inheritance has probably suffered much less, since upwards of eighty verses out of one hundred and seventeen agree with the teaching of the Sûtras, and since among those, the contents of which are not represented in the older works, only eleven, vv. 108–110, 128–129, 133, 138, 147, 184, 215, and 217, are really suspicious or clearly interpolated. Most of these latter contain clumsy repetitions of matters discussed in other places, and v. 217 gives a supplementary rule which but ill agrees with the spirit pervading the remainder of the section. Some of the other, apparently unsuspicious, verses may, of course, possibly be interpolations. But their contents are in harmony with the spirit of the Dharma-sûtras, and with the eliminations, proposed above, Manu's theory of inheritance and partition is self-consistent. The views, expressed under the eighteenth title, on gambling and betting, agree with those of Gautama and Baudhâyana, who both strongly disapprove of these prac-

[1] To this conclusion points the absence of systematic arrangement in Vish*n*u III–V.

[2] Manu's rules on this subject have probably been borrowed from a *S*rauta-sûtra, where the distribution of the sacrificial fees is usually explained.

tices. The former enumerates the gambler among the men who defile the company at a *S*râddha, and the latter names gambling among the crimes which render men impure. Though Âpastamba and Vish*n*u are less puritanical, and permit gambling under royal, i.e. police-supervision, or provide only punishments for cheating (Vish*n*u V, 134–135), the teaching of our Sm*ri*ti is, nevertheless, probably ancient. But the section has been enlarged by the addition of miscellaneous rules and by the allusion to the evil results of gambling 'in former ages,' i.e. to those exemplified by the fate of Yudhish*th*ira and Nala. The last 106 verses of the ninth chapter which, according to the table of contents in the first chapter, teach the removal of (men nocuous like) thorns (ka*nt*akoddhara*n*a), correspond to a part of the prakîr*n*aka or miscellaneous rules of Yâ*gñ*avalkya and Nârada. This section seems to have grown out of those legal rules in the Mânava Dharma-sûtra which did not fit into the system of the eighteen titles. But, as very few verses only correspond to rules of the Dharma-sûtras, its ancient portion is probably small. The greater part of its contents is made up of repetitions and additions inserted by the author of the remodelled version.

The rules on times of distress, given in chapter X, differ considerably from those of the Dharma-sûtras, as they include also the theory of the descent of the mixed castes. The older works treat this subject either in connexion with the law of marriage or with the rules of inheritance. Considering the great inequality which the Sûtras show in the arrangement of the various topics, it is, however, not impossible that the Mânava Dharma-sûtra placed the section on the mixed castes just before the âpaddharmas, and that the author of the metrical version combined both in one chapter and gave them a common title. But it is not in the least doubtful that the treatment of the subject in the former work must have been very different from that which it receives in vv. 1–74. The Dharma-sûtras enumerate either one or two sets of mixed castes, briefly indicating their origin, and, sometimes, their modes of life. They also add a few verses or rules regarding the changes to be attained in successive generations, as well as regarding the manner in which men of low descent may be detected. Our Manu-smriti, on the other hand, is much more minute in its details, and introduces a good many new names of which the Sûtras know nothing. These additions have probably expanded the section to three times its original extent. The immediately following rules, vv. 75–100, on the occupations of the castes and their manner of subsisting in times of distress, agree, in the main, with the Sûtras, and seem to have been changed very little. But the supplementary notes on the same subject, vv. 101–131, are probably additions made on the revision of the work. The few ancient rules which they contain are partly repetitions of matters already discussed (e. g. vv. 113–114) and partly misplaced (e. g. vv. 111, 115–117, 119)[1].

The eleventh chapter is again, like chapters II–VI, in all probability a faithful representative of the corresponding portion of the Mânava Dharma-sûtra. We find here again that the great majority of the rules corresponds to those of the Dharma-sûtras and of the Vishnu-smriti. The agreement with the latter is particularly close, and appears especially in the classification of crimes, the enumeration of the diseases caused by offences committed in a former life, and in many details referring to penances. Curious and against the practice of the older works is the combination of the rules on gifts and the performance of sacrifices, vv. 1–43, with the section on penances. The excuses which the commentators offer for this anomaly[2] are, I fear, insufficient to explain it. It seems more probable that here, as in the preceding chapter, two separate sections of the original work have been welded together into one Adhyâya. In favour of this view it may be pointed out that in Gautama's Dharma-sûtra, XVIII, 28–32, a number of rules, corresponding to Manu XI, 11–23, stand just before the Prâyaskittakânda. A passage of the Mahâbhârata, which will be

[1] A characteristic sign of the great changes which chapters VII–X have undergone consists in the allusions to legends famous in the Purânas and the Mahâbhârata; see also below, p. lxxix.

[2] See note on Manu XI, 1.

discussed below, shows exactly the same combination as our Smriti.

The twelfth chapter, finally, is certainly almost entirely due to the author of the metrical version. Its contents are partly foreign to the Dharma-sûtras and partly repetitions. The classification of actions and existences as sâttvika, râgasa, and tâmasa, i. e. as modified by the three qualities of Goodness, Activity, and Darkness, finds no place in the older law-books. It is based on the doctrines which are taught in the Sâmkhya, Yoga, and Vedânta systems, and some traces of which are found in the Maitrâyanabrâhmanopanishad[1]. Equally or similarly minute details are, however, to be met with only in the Purânas, the Mahâbhârata, and some of the metrical Smritis, which blend philosophical ideas with the sacred law. The next following discussion on the karmavipâka, the results of sinful acts in future births, vv. 51–81, is altogether wrongly placed. It evidently ought to stand in the beginning of the section on penances, where Vishnu and Yâgñavalkya have a number of corresponding Sûtras and verses. As it is found in the Manusmriti in a different position, it is most probably an addition made on the revision of the work. The section on the means of attaining supreme bliss, vv. 82–104, returns to the questions which have already been discussed in the fourth and sixth chapters, and adds nothing that is new. The long peroration at the end, vv. 116–126, cannot have formed part of the Dharma-sûtra, as it again refers to the myth concerning the origin of the Sâstra, narrated in the spurious first chapter. But the small piece on the manner of deciding doubtful legal questions, vv. 105–115, belonged probably to the original work. To this conclusion point its close agreement with the rules of the Dharma-sûtras, and the circumstance that Gautama also places the corresponding Sûtras just at the end of his work.

If thus it is extremely probable that the contents of more than half the verses in our Manu-smriti cannot have been derived from the ancient Mânava Dharma-sûtra, we

[1] Maitr. Up. III, 3, 5, 6; compare Manu XII, xii, 32–33.

have now to face the question whence this large amount of additional matter has been taken. A clue to the solution of this problem is furnished by the peculiar relation of the Manu-smriti to the Mahâbhârata, which undoubtedly is one of the most ancient metrical works of Indian literature, and the great storehouse of the earliest forms of post-Vedic mythology and doctrine. The connexion existing between these two works, and its importance for the history of the Institutes of Manu, has been recognised by most Sanskritists who have directed their attention to the investigation of the origin of the secondary Smritis. Many years ago Professor Weber[1] pointed out that the Mahâbhârata contains not only a number of quotations from Manu, some of which are found either with or without variations in the existing Smriti, while others are not traceable, but also a considerable number of verses, not attributed to Manu, which, nevertheless, are included in the Dharmasâstra. He inferred from these facts that the existing Manu-smriti cannot have been extant in its present shape even at the period to which the later portions of the Mahâbhârata belong, and that the author or authors of the latter work must have known and used an older redaction of Manu's law-book. Another conclusion, based on the agreement of numerous Slokas, especially in the twelfth and thirteenth Parvans of the great epic with verses of the Manu-smriti, has been drawn by Rao Saheb V. N. Mandlik[2], who is convinced that the editor of the latter has drawn, to a large extent, on the former work. Of late Professor Hopkins[3] has made a careful analysis of the quotations from Manu found in the Mahâbhârata. According to him, their number is thirty-three, among which seventeen are traceable, five being verbal quotations, the rest agreeing in doctrine only. His explanation for the untraceable quotations is not that they have been taken from an older recension of the Manu-smriti, but that a floating mass of

[1] History of Indian Literature, p. 279; compare also Professor Stenzler in the Indische Studien, vol. i, p. 245.

[2] The Mayûkha and Yâgñavalkya, introd. to Yâgñ. p. xlvii.

[3] Proceedings of the American Oriental Society, October, 1883, pp. xix–xx, and now Journal of the American Oriental Society, vol. xi, p. 257 seqq.

unwritten sayings of Manu existed, some of which were incorporated with the Dharma-sûtra of the Mânavas in its revision, while others were not. He also notices the fact that our Manu-smriti contains many verses which occur also in the Mahâbhârata without being attributed to Manu, as well as some which are ascribed to other authorities.

These somewhat divergent results of my predecessors show very clearly that the Mahâbhârata may be expected to render some assistance for the solution of our problem. But they indicate also that the utilisation of the facts which it offers requires some caution.

In resuming the enquiry into the relation of the two works and its bearing on the history of our Manu text, the first point to be ascertained is, whether the Mahâbhârata really mentions a law-book of Manu, and whether this work is identical either with the ancient Dharma-sûtra or with the existing Smriti, or if it differed from both. According to what has been said above[1] regarding the ancient belief ascribing the settlement of social and religious institutions to the Father of mankind, and the real meaning of the phrase 'thus Manu has spoken,' it is evident that Professor Hopkins has correctly distinguished between sayings of Manu on religious and legal matters, and law-books attributed to him, and that he is right in refusing to recognise in every mention of Manu's name a reference to a Smriti of his. Hence the number of passages useful for comparison is very much restricted. Those only which explicitly mention a Sâstra of Manu are really indisputable evidence. The estimation of the value of the remainder must depend on collateral circumstances. Quotations of the former kind are not numerous in the Mahâbhârata. Nevertheless, some do occur in the twelfth and thirteenth Parvans, and they clearly prove that the authors of these books knew a Mânava Dharmasâstra not identical but closely connected with our Smriti. Thus we read, Mah. XII, 56, 23-25, where the power of Brâhmanas is being described, 'High-minded Manu likewise, O king of kings, sang two Slokas in his Laws (sveshu dharmeshu), those, O descendant of Kuru,

[1] See p. lx.

thou shouldst keep in thy heart (23). Fire sprang from water, Kshatriyas from Brâhma*n*as, iron from stone, the all-penetrating power of these (three) has no effect on that whence they were produced (24). When iron strikes stone, when fire meets water, when a Kshatriya shows hostility to a Brâhma*n*a, then these (three assailants) perish.' Again, Mah. XIII, 46, 30–36, in a discussion on the prerogatives of a Brâhma*n*a's Brâhma*n*î wife who, we are told, is alone entitled to attend her husband and to assist him in the performance of his religious duties, the conclusion runs as follows: 'And in those Institutes which Manu proclaimed (manunâbhihita*m* *s*âstram), O great king, descended from Kuru, this same eternal law is found (35). Now if (a man) out of love acts differently, O Yudhish*th*ira, he is declared to be (as despicable as) a *K*â*nd*âla (sprung from the) Brâhma*n*a (caste 36).' Nothing can be clearer than these two passages. The second speaks plainly of a *S*âstra proclaimed by Manu, and the first of his Dharmâ*h*, a word in the plural, very commonly used to denote a book on the sacred law. Moreover, the second is clearly a paraphrase of Manu IX, 87, and reproduces its second line to the letter. Of the two verses quoted in the first, one agrees with Manu IX, 321, but the other one is not traceable. While these two quotations would seem to indicate a very close connexion between the Mânava *S*âstra of the Mahâbhârata and our Sm*ri*ti, a third from the Râ*g*adharmas of Manu Prâ*k*etasa—i. e. from the section on the duties of kings belonging to the Mânava[1]—reveals a greater dis-

[1] Though I will not deny that some show of argument might be made for the supposition that the Râ*g*adharmas of Manu Prâ*k*etasa were a separate work, different from the *S*âstra referred to in the preceding quotations, because the epithet Prâ*k*etasa is here added to Manu's name, and because at Mah. XII, 38, 2, we find Manu Prâ*k*etasa named as the author of a Râ*g*a*s*âstra in company with B*ri*haspati and U*s*anas, to whom separate Nîti*s*âstras were attributed, I yet hold this to be improbable. For the legends regarding the descent of the lawgiver Manu vary in the Mahâbhârata. He is in other passages sometimes called Svâyambhuva, and sometimes (e. g. XII, 349, 51) Vaivasvata. Further, a separate Nîti*s*âstra of Manu is not quoted elsewhere. On the other hand, the section on the duties of kings bears in every law-book the separate title Râ*g*adharmâ*h*, and the commentators of our Manu-sm*ri*ti call its seventh chapter expressly by this name.

crepancy. We read, Mah. XII, 57, 43–45, 'And the following two verses are pronounced[1] by Manu Prâketasa in the Law of kings, listen to them attentively, O lord of kings! (43.) A man should abandon, like a leaky ship in the ocean, the following six persons,—a teacher who does not instruct, a priest unable to recite the Veda, a king who affords no protection, a quarrelsome wife, a herdsman who loves to stay in the village, and a barber who seeks the forest.' Neither of these verses is found in our Manu, though the latter inveighs against kings who do not protect their subjects (VII, 143–144).

If we turn to the passages in which Manu—not his *S*âstra—is named as an authority, I know only of one that may be confidently considered to contain a reference to a law-book. In the *S*akuntalopâkhyâna, Mah. I, 73, 8–13, king Dushyanta tries to persuade the reluctant object of his affections to consent to a Gândharva union by a discussion of the law of marriage. He first briefly mentions the number of the marriage-rites (v. 8[a]) and their names (vv. 8[b]–9[a]) in the same order as Manu, and then goes on, 'Learn that among these (rites), as Manu Svâyambhuva has formerly declared, the first four are lawful and recommended for a Brâhma*n*a; know, O blameless one, that six, according to their order, are lawful for a Kshatriya (9[b]–10). But the Râkshasa rite also is ordained for men of the royal caste, and the Âsura rite is prescribed for Vai*s*yas and *S*ûdras. But among the (last) five, three are declared lawful and two unlawful (v. 11). The Pai*s*âka and Âsura (rites) must never be used. According to this rule (marriages) must be concluded, this is the path of duty (v. 12). Do not question the legality of the Gândharva and Râkshasa (rites) for Kshatriyas. Without a doubt they may be used, be it separate or mixed' (v. 13).

The close verbal agreement of this passage with Manu III, 20–26, on the one hand, and its serious discrepancy with respect to a portion of the doctrine, make it, I think, very probable that it is a paraphrase or adaptation of a part

[1] The original has udâh*ri*tau, which is ambiguous and may also mean 'quoted.'

of a Mânava Dharmaśâstra which closely resembled, but was not quite identical with, the existing text. Verse 8ᵇ–9ᵃ agrees literally with Manu III, 21; and vv. 11ᵇ–13 come close to Manu III, 25–26. But vv. 9ᵇ–11ᵃ, though they have a certain affinity to Manu III, 23–24, show, nevertheless, a considerable difference in doctrine. For Manu declares (v. 23) the first six rites to be lawful for a Brâhmaṇa, the four following ones for a Kshatriya, and the same four, with the exception of the Râkshasa rite, for Śûdras and Vaiśyas, while v. 24 says that the first four rites are recommended, and that the Râkshasa rite alone is permissible to Kshatriyas, and the Âsura to the two lowest classes. According to the Mahâbhârata, on the other hand, Manu approved of the first four rites in the case of Brâhmaṇas, and of the first six in case of Kshatriyas. To the latter he allowed also the seventh, the Râkshasa rite, and confined Vaiśyas and Śûdras to the purchase of their brides, the Âsura rite. The most probable explanation of this contradiction seems to me the assumption that the text of Manu, known to the author of the Upâkhyâna, slightly differed from that which we find at present.

Another passage is more doubtful. Mah. XIII, 61, 34–35, various opinions are enumerated with respect to the question how large a share of the guilt incurred by ill-protected and ill-governed subjects falls on the king[1]. The decision is that, according to the teaching of Manu, the negligent ruler is loaded with a fourth share. This doctrine, which is found also in other passages of the Mahâbhârata, contradicts that taught in our Manu-smṛiti as well as in the older Dharma-sûtras, where a sixth part of the sins committed by subjects is said to fall on their lord. The circumstance that several opinions are contrasted may be used as an argument for the opinion that here, too, an individual law-book of Manu's is referred to. If that were so, the passage would reveal another remarkable discrepancy between the older and the present texts. But to my mind

[1] चतुर्थं तस्य पापस्य राजा विन्दति भारत ॥३४॥ अपाहुः सर्वमेवेति भूयोऽर्धमिति निश्चयः। चतुर्थं मतमस्माकं मनोः श्रुत्वानुशासनम् ॥३५॥

it seems, just because the teaching of our Manu agrees with the Dharma-sûtras, more probable that the author of the Mahâbhârata makes here, as in other cases, a random appeal to Manu's name merely in order to give weight to his peculiar opinion.

There are two other longer pieces in the Mahâbhârata which are ascribed to Manu. In one case it is perfectly evident that there exists no connexion with our Sm*ri*ti. The philosophical conversation between Manu and B*ri*haspati, which fills chapters 200–206 of Mah. XII, has neither any distinctive doctrines nor any verses in common with the Mânava Dharma*s*âstra. On the contrary, it shows a leaning towards the Vaish*n*ava creed.

With respect to the second passage, Mah. XII, 36, 3–50, a doubt is at least possible. It contains an 'ancient legend' (purâ*n*a itihâsa), narrating how Manu revealed in the beginning to the sages the law regarding food, and some miscellaneous rules concerning worthy recipients, gifts, Veda-study, and penances. Manu's speech consists of forty-five verses, among which two agree fully and five partly with *S*lokas of our Sm*ri*ti[1]. But one of the fully agreeing verses (v. 46) occurs also in two Dharma-sûtras, and belongs, therefore, to the traditional lore of the Vedic schools. Though the remainder is not traceable in the older works, the faintness of the resemblance makes it, I think, more probable that the Mahâbhârata accidentally attributes to Manu verses now read in his Sm*ri*ti, than that its author extracted them and the whole piece from a Mânava *S*âstra.

But whatever may be the correct interpretation of the mention of Manu in these passages, it remains indisputable that the author or authors of the first, twelfth, and thirteenth Parvans of the Mahâbhârata knew a Mânava Dharma*s*âstra which was closely connected, but not identical with the existing text. The latter must, therefore, as Professor Weber has pointed out, be considered later than

[1] Mah. XII, 36, 27 = Manu IV, 218; first pâda of ver. 28^{a} = first pâda of Manu IV, 220; ver. 28^{b} = Manu IV, 217^{a}; first pâda of ver. 29^{a} = first pâda of Manu IV, 210^{b}; ver. 46 = Manu II, 157; ver. 47^{a} = Manu II, 158^{a}.

these 'latest portions of the epic.' The latter conclusion is, it seems to me, confirmed by some indications in the Sm*ri*ti which point to an acquaintance with the Mahâbhârata. The warning regarding the consequences of gambling, Manu IX, 227, certainly presupposes a knowledge of the legend of the Kurus and Pâ*nd*avas. When it is stated there that 'in a former Kalpa the vice of gambling has been seen to cause great enmity,' this assertion can only point in the first instance to the match played between Yudhish*th*ira and Duryodhana, which was the immediate cause of the great war. It may also contain, as some commentators think, an allusion to the fate of king Nala, but that can only be a secondary meaning, because war was not the result of his gambling. More significant than this passage is the fact that in chapters VII–X of the Manu-sm*ri*ti a number of legends are quoted in illustration or in support of rules which, as the commentators repeatedly assert[1], are taken from the Mahâbhârata, and that in one case just those which are mentioned in one verse of Manu (IX, 314) are found close together in the same chapter of the Mahâbhârata.

This relative position of the two works might induce us to assume with Rao Saheb V. N. Ma*nd*lik that the Mahâbhârata had a direct influence on the final redaction of the Manu-sm*ri*ti, and that the author of the latter appropriated from the former the very large number of identical verses which in the Mahâbhârata are not ascribed to Manu.

Tempting as the hypothesis of the dependence of the Sm*ri*ti on the epic is, because it would account for the adoption of the Anush*t*ubh metre in the latter, a careful examination of the corresponding passages leads to a very different result. On going over the third, twelfth, and thirteenth Parvans of the Mahâbhârata I have succeeded in identifying upwards of 260 verses or portions of verses, not attributed to Manu, with *S*lokas of the Manu-sm*ri*ti. This number, which corresponds to about one-tenth of the bulk of the latter work, would no doubt be considerably swelled by a comparison of the remaining portions of the epic, and

[1] See notes to VII, 41; VIII, 110; IX, 23, 129, 314–315, &c.

it may be that even in the Parvans examined some identical pieces have escaped my notice. The number of the verses which has to be compared is so enormous that mistakes are easily possible; but the identifications made are amply sufficient for the purpose of illustrating the relation between the two works. The corresponding passages vary considerably in extent, from a single pâda or a single line to sections of twenty to forty verses. Where larger sections agree, it is rare that more than half-a-dozen verses stand in the same order in both works, and it happens not rarely that a series of identical *S*lokas is interrupted by the expansion of one verse into two, or by a contraction of two into one. Further, the purpose which an identical line or verse is made to serve sometimes differs, and sometimes a various reading alters its sense entirely. The various readings are exceedingly numerous, and the better one is sometimes found in the Mahâbhârata and sometimes in Manu. If we enter on a more detailed analysis of the corresponding passages, there are three cases in which one or two consecutive chapters of the Mahâbhârata contain from twenty to forty verses which occur in our Manu. Mah. XII, 232–233 include the greater portion of Bh*ri*gu's account of the creation and some of the verses, said to have been enunciated by Manu himself on the same subject, i. e. Manu I, 18^b, 20, 28–29, 64–78, 81–86.

Further, Mah. XIII, 48, 14–44 gives a portion of Manu's definitions of and rules regarding the mixed castes, and contains the verses X, 27–32, 33^a, 34–37, 38^a, 39–40, 50, 52^b, 58–60, and 62, mostly with considerable variations, and *S*lokas resembling Manu X, 42–43 are found Mah. XIII, 33, 21–22, and 35, 17–18.

Finally, Mah. XII, 165, which treats of gifts, sacrifices, and penances much in the same manner as the eleventh chapter of Manu, exhibits, mostly in the beginning, the following verses, partly in somewhat different versions, XI, 2^b, 3^b, 4^a, 7, 11–17, 20, 22^b, 23^a, 27^a, 29–31, 34–40, 91^b, 105, 150, 177^b, 181, 207. The general sense of some other *S*lokas corresponds without a real agreement in words, and the same chapter of the Mah. contains also vv. 31^a and 32^a, three-quarters of Manu II, 238, and v. 68[a] the first half of Manu III, 172. Equivalents of Manu XI, 44, 74, 76[a], 77, 84 are found Mah. XII, 34, 2; 35, 4–6; 263, 45[b]–46[a]. Among other somewhat longer corresponding passages the following are the most noteworthy. Portions of the discussion on the reverence due to parents and teachers, Manu II, 229–234, occur Mah. XII, 108, 5–12. The rules regarding the disposal of the fee at an Ârsha wedding and the respect to be shown to females are found Mah. XIII, 45, 20; 46, 1–7, and some verses, Manu III, 134–135, 140–142, 158–159, 172, 180–181, 184–185, from the section on *S*râddhas, Mah. XIII, 90, as well as fragments of III, 267–274 in the beginning of Mah. XIII, 88. The warning against quarrels with relatives, Manu IV, 179–185, is repeated Mah. XII, 244, 14[b]–21[a]. A number of the rules applicable to the ascetic, Manu VI, 42–48, 57[b], 58[a], reappears in the beginning of Mah. XII, 246 and 279, while Manu VI, 49 is read Mah. XII, 331, 30. The sketch of the state administration, Manu VII, 115–122, is given mostly in the same words, Mah. XII, 87, 3–11[a], and the same chapter contains also closely agreeing precepts regarding taxation together with the verses Manu VII, 127 and 139[a]. The remainder of the corresponding passages ranges between triplets and single feet of *S*lokas, and is scattered over all the twelve chapters of Manu. The portions of the Mahâbhârata where we chiefly meet with them, are III, 94, 180; XII, 15, 244–245, 265; XIII, 44–46, 90, 104–105, 115, 152[1].

In order to complete this sketch of the relation in which the two works stand towards each other, it will be advisable to give one of the three longest corresponding passages in full, and to carefully note both the points of contact and of difference. The piece most suitable for such a comparison is that from the first book of Manu. For the latter doubtlessly belongs to the additions made by the editor of the metrical version, and its account of the creation presents numerous problems which have sorely puzzled the com-

[1] It is impossible to give here more than these general indications. A more complete list of the verses of the Manu-smr*i*ti occurring in the Mah. will be found in the Appendix.

mentators. The solution of some of these difficulties is furnished by the corresponding passage of the Mahâbhârata. This passage occurs in an account of the creation, communicated by Vyâsa-K*ri*sh*n*a-Dvaipâyana to his son *S*uka, which Bhîshma narrates to Yudhish*th*ira.

MAHÂBHÂRATA XII, 232.	MANU I.
11. Vyâsa said: In the commencement exists the Brahman without beginning or end, unborn, luminous, free from decay, immutable, eternal, unfathomable by reasoning, not to be fully known.	
12. Fifteen nimeshas (twinklings of the eye are) one kâsh*th*â[1], but thirty kâsh*th*âs one should reckon as one kalâ; moreover, thirty kalâs and that which may amount to the tenth part of a kalâ shall be one muhûrta; 13. Thirty muhûrtas shall make a day and a night—that number has been fixed by the sages; a month is declared (to consist of) thirty nights and days, and a year of twelve months.	64. Eighteen nimeshas (twinklings of the eye are one kâsh*th*â[1]), thirty kâsh*th*âs one kalâ, thirty kalâs one muhûrta, and as many (muhûrtas) one day and night.
14. But those acquainted with calculations call two progresses of the sun, the southern and the northern one, a year[2].	
15. The sun divides the days and nights of the world of men[3], the night (being intended)	65. The sun divides days and nights, both human and divine, the night (being intended)

[1] Regarding the difference between the two computations, see Wilson, Vish*n*u-purâ*n*a I, 47 (ed. Hall).

[2] The verse marked as 14 in the Bombay edition consists of a single line only.

[3] The reading of the Mahâbhârata, mânushalaukike for mânushadaivike, seems the better one.

f 2

for the repose of created beings and the day for exertion.

16. A month is a day and a night of the manes, but their division (is as follows): the bright (fortnight)[1] is their day for active exertion, the dark (fortnight) their night for sleep.

17. A year is a day and a night of the gods; the division is (as follows): the half year during which the sun progresses to the north will be the day, that during which it goes southwards the night.

18. Counting the sum of years (consisting) of those human days and nights which have been mentioned above, I will declare (the duration of) a day and night of Brahman.

19. I will declare severally and in due order the totals of the years in the Kṛita, Tretâ, Dvâpara, and Kali ages[2].

20. They declare that the Kṛita age (consists of) four thousand years (of the gods); the twilight preceding it consists of as many hundreds, and the twilight following it of the same number.

21. In the (other) three ages,

for the repose of created beings and the day for exertion.

66. A month is a day and a night of the manes, but the division is according to fortnights. The dark (fortnight) is their day for active exertion, the bright (fortnight) their night for sleep.

67. A year is a day and a night of the gods; the division is (as follows): the half year during which the sun progresses to the north will be the day, that during which it goes southwards the night.

68. But hear now the brief (description of) the duration of a night and day of Brahman and of the several ages (of the world) according to their order.

69. They declare that the Kṛita age (consists of) four thousand years of the gods; the twilight preceding it consists of as many hundreds, and the twilight following it of the same number.

70. In the (other) three ages,

[1] The reading of the Mahâbhârata is obviously faulty, as it is well known that the dark fortnight is, according to the Hindus, the day of the manes. The fault has probably arisen by an accidental transposition of the words suklah and krishnah. The second var. lect. of the Mah. tayoh punah for tu pakshayoh is less intelligible than Manu's, because a substantive is required to which suklah and krishnah can be referred.

[2] It is a particularly significant fact that in spite of the great difference between the two works, both show the intercalation of a fresh exordium.

with the preceding twilights and in the twilights following them, the thousands and hundreds are diminished by one-fourth (in each)[1].

22. These support the eternal, everlasting worlds; this is known as the eternal Brahman to those who know Brahman.

23. In the K*ri*ta age Dharma is four-footed and entire, and (so is) Truth; nor does any gain which is opposed to that (spirit of justice) accrue by unrighteousness[2].

24. In the other (three ages), by reason of (unjust) gains, Dharma is deprived successively of one foot, and unrighteousness increases through theft, falsehood, and fraud.

25. (Men are) free from disease, accomplish all their aims, and live four hundred years in the K*ri*ta (age); but in the Tretâ age (and the following ones) their life is lessened by one quarter in each[3];

26. And the doctrines of the Veda decrease, as we

with their twilights preceding and following, the thousands and hundreds are diminished by one (in each).

81. In the K*ri*ta age Dharma is four-footed and entire, and (so is) Truth; nor does any gain accrue to men by unrighteousness.

82. In the other (three ages), by reason of (unjust) gains, Dharma is deprived successively of one foot, and through (the prevalence of) theft, falsehood, and fraud the merit (gained by men) is diminished by one-fourth (in each).

83. (Men are) free from disease, accomplish all their aims, and live four hundred years in the K*ri*ta (age), but in the Tretâ and (in each of) the succeeding (ages) their life is lessened by one quarter.

84. The life of mortals, mentioned in the Veda, the de-

[1] The reading of Manu, sasa*m*dhyâ*m*seshu *k*a for sa*m*dhâ*m*seshu tata*h*, seems preferable, but his ekâpâyena is inferior to the ekapâdena of the Mahâbhârata.

[2] Nîlaka*nth*a explains âgama in this verse and the next by 'doctrine.' I translate it by 'gain,' in accordance with the rendering adopted for Manu, but willingly acknowledge that the other rendering is possible in both works, and that the meaning may be 'nor does any unrighteous doctrine, opposed to that (Dharma), prevail' (Mah.), 'nor is any unrighteous doctrine spread among men' (Manu).

[3] The reading k*ri*te tretâyuge tveshâm instead of Manu's k*ri*te tretâdishu hyeshâm is more archaic.

hear, in each successive age, as well as the lives (of men), their blessings (â*s*isha*h*), and the rewards which the Veda yields[1].

sired results (â*s*isha*h*) of sacrificial rites, and the (supernatural) power of embodied (spirits) are fruits proportioned among men according to (the character of) the age[1].

27. One set of duties (is prescribed) for men in the K*ri*ta age, different ones in the Tretâ and in the Dvâpara, and (again) another (set) in the Kali age, in proportion as (those) ages decrease in length.

28. In the K*ri*ta age the chief (virtue is the performance of) austerities, in the Tretâ (divine) knowledge is most excellent, in the Dvâpara they declare sacrifices (to be best), in the Kali liberality alone.

29. The wise know such (a period of) twelve thousand (divine) years (to be understood by) the term an age (of the gods); that (period) being multiplied by one thousand is called a day of Brahman.

30. (Know his) night to be as long[2]. At the beginning of that (day) the lord who is the Universe finally awakes, after having entered deep meditation

85. One set of duties (is prescribed) for men in the K*ri*ta age, different ones in the Tretâ and in the Dvâpara, and again another (set) in the Kali age, in proportion as (those) ages decrease in length.

86. In the K*ri*ta age the chief (virtue) is declared to be (the performance of) austerities, in the Tretâ (divine) knowledge, in the Dvâpara (the performance of) sacrifices, in the Kali liberality alone.

71–72. These twelve thousand (years), which thus have been mentioned above as the total of four (human) ages, are called one age of the gods. But know that the sum of one thousand ages of the gods (makes) one day of Brahman, and that his night has the same length[2].

[1] The Sanskrit text of the two *S*lokas agrees somewhat better than the translation. It looks as if neither of them was the original version, which probably declared that the age of men, their blessings, and the rewards of deeds, such as they are promised in the Veda, diminish in each successive age. Another version, which almost exactly agrees with Manu's, occurs Mah. III, 200, 115.

[2] Both the Mah. and Manu have the accusative case râtrim, which does not agree with the preceding verb *g*ñeyam (Manu) u*k*yate (Mah.) It would seem that both give adaptations of an older verse, where a word like âhu*h*, which governed the accusative, occurred. Though the verb was changed, the further alteration of the case was forgotten.

and having slept during the period of destruction.

31. Those (only) who know that Brahman's day ends after (the completion of) one thousand ages (of the gods) and that his night lasts a thousand ages, are (really) men acquainted with (the length of) days and nights.

73. Those (only) who know that the holy day of Brahman, indeed, ends after (the completion of) one thousand ages (of the gods), and that his night lasts as long, are (really) men acquainted with (the length of) days and nights.

32. When imperishable Brahman awakes at the end of his night, he modifies himself and creates the element (called) the Great One (and) from that mind which is discrete.

MAHÂBHÂRATA II, 233.

1. Luminous Brahman is the seed from which single element this whole twofold creation, the immovable and the movable, has been produced.

2. Awaking at the beginning of his day, he creates the world by means of Ignorance—even first the element, (called) the Great One, (next) speedily mind which is discrete;

3. And conquering here resplendent (mind) which goes far, enters many paths, and has the nature of desire and doubt, creates the seven mind-born ones.

4. Mind, impelled by the desire to create, performs the work of creation by modifying itself; thence ether is produced; they declare that sound is the quality of the latter.

75. Mind, impelled by the desire to create, performs the work of creation by modifying itself; thence ether is produced; they declare that sound is the quality of the latter.

5. But from ether, modifying itself, springs the pure, powerful wind, the vehicle of all perfumes; touch is considered to be its quality.

6. Next from wind, modifying itself, proceeds the brilliant light which illuminates and is white; that is declared to possess the quality of colour;

7. And from light, modifying itself, (comes) water which possesses taste; from water smell and earth; (such) is declared (to be) the creation of (them) all.

8. The qualities of each earlier-named (element) enter each of the later-named ones, and whatever place (in the sequence) each of them occupies, even so many qualities it is declared to possess[1].

9. If some, perceiving a smell in water through a want of care, attribute (that quality to water), one must know that it belongs to earth alone, (and that it is) adventitious in water and wind.

10. Those Âtmans of seven kinds[2], which possess various powers, were severally unable to create beings without fully uniting themselves.

11. These great Âtmans, uniting and mutually combining

76. But from ether, modifying itself, springs the pure, powerful wind, the vehicle of all perfumes; that is held to possess the quality of touch.

77. Next from wind, modifying itself, proceeds the brilliant light which illuminates and dispels darkness; that is declared to possess the quality of colour.

78. And from light, modifying itself, (is produced) water, declared to possess the quality of taste; from water earth, which has the quality of smell; such is the creation in the beginning.

20. Among them each succeeding (element) acquires the quality of the preceding one, and whatever place (in the sequence) each of them occupies, even so many qualities it is declared to possess.

[1] The position of this verse in the Mahâbhârata makes the conjecture, put forward in the note to the translation, that the correct position of Manu I, 20 is after verse 78, exceedingly probable.

[2] According to Nîlaka*nth*a, the seven Âtmans, called above, ver. 3, the seven mind-born ones, are Mahat, Aha*m*kâra, and the five subtile elements.

with each other, entered the body; hence one speaks of Purusha [i. e. him who resides (usha) in a fortress (pur)].

12. In consequence of that entering (*s*raya*n*a), the body (*s*arîra) becomes endowed with a (perceptible) form, and consists of sixteen[1] (constituent parts).

That the great elements[2] enter together with the karman (merit and demerit).

18b. That the great elements enter together with their functions (karman)[3].

13. Taking with him all the elements, that first creator of created beings (enters it) in order to perform austerities; him they call the lord of created beings.

14. He, indeed, creates the creatures, both the immovable and the movable; then that Brahmâ creates gods, sages, manes, and men,

15. The worlds, rivers, oceans, the quarters of the compass, mountains, trees, men, Kinnaras, Rakshas, birds, tame and wild beasts, and snakes, the imperishable and the perishable, both the immovable and the movable.

16. Whatever course of action they adopted in a former creation, even that

28. But to whatever course of action the Lord at first appointed each (kind of

[1] The sixteen constituent parts are, according to Nîlaka*nth*a, the five gross elements and the eleven organs.

[2] Nîlaka*nth*a takes mahânti bhûtâni, 'the great elements,' in the sense of 'the subtile elements, and the great ones, the mahattattvas' (bhûtâni sûkshmâ*n*i mahânti mahattatattvâni).

[3] This line is a good example, showing how the same words of the ancient school-tradition were made to serve different purposes.

alone they adopt in each succeeding creation.

17. They turn to noxiousness or harmlessness, gentleness or ferocity, virtue or sin, truth or falsehood, according to the disposition with which they were (first) created; hence that (particular course of action) pleases each.

beings), that alone it has spontaneously adopted in each succeeding creation.

29. Whatever he assigned to each at the (first) creation, noxiousness or harmlessness, gentleness or ferocity, virtue or sin, truth or falsehood, that clung (afterwards) spontaneously to it.

The remainder of Vyâsa's narrative, which continues through the following twenty-six verses, may be omitted, as, further on, it presents few points of contact with our Smriti. It must, however, be noticed that, according to verses 25–26, 'the Lord assigned to his creatures their names and conditions, in accordance with the words of the Veda.' This idea agrees with Manu I, 21, but the wording of the two passages differs very considerably.

The lesson which the facts, revealed by the above discussion, teach, is a double one. First, they clearly show that the editor of our metrical Manu-smriti has not drawn on the Mahâbhârata, but that the authors of both works have utilised the same materials. Secondly, they make it highly probable that the materials, on which both works are based, were not systematic treatises on law and philosophy, but the floating proverbial wisdom of the philosophical and legal schools which already existed in metrical form. The first point is so evident that it seems to me unnecessary to waste any more words on it. With respect to the second conclusion, I would point out that it is made unavoidable by the peculiar character of the differences found in closely connected *S*lokas, by the occurrence of identical lines and pâdas in verses whereof the general sense differs, and by the faint, shadowy resemblance in words and ideas, observable in other pieces. I may add, further, that the supposition that each special school possessed such a body of metrical maxims is perfectly well founded.

As has been repeatedly stated, the text-books of the ancient Vedic schools, the Sûtras and the Upanishads, contain already a not inconsiderable proportion of Anush*t*ubh verses which sometimes recur in identical or slightly varying forms. Hence it is no more than might be expected that the teachers of the special schools should have continued in the path of their predecessors, and should have gradually augmented the stock of their 'Spruchweisheit,' until it extended to all legal and philosophical topics, and the accumulation of these detached verses made it easy and tempting to convert the old aphoristic handbooks into metrical treatises[1]. The answer, which we are thus obliged to give to the question whence the editor of our Manu-sm*ri*ti took his additional materials, agrees very closely with Professor Hopkins' hypothesis, who, as mentioned above, considers the law-book to be a conglomerate of the Mânava Dharma-sûtra and of the floating sayings attributed to Manu, the father of mankind. The latter restriction seems to me unadvisable, because among the mass of corresponding pieces found in the Mahâbhârata comparatively few are attributed to the Pra*g*âpati, and because a Hindu who was

[1] The probability of the existence of such a body of metrical maxims would become still more apparent, if it were possible to enter here on a comparison of portions of the older Purâ*n*as with the Mahâbhârata and the metrical Sm*ri*tis, as well as on a detailed consideration of the ancient Buddhist literature. Though the difficulty and magnitude of such a task forbid its being attempted in this Introduction, I cannot refrain from inserting a few general hints. The Purâ*n*as contain a good deal that is identical with or similar to passages of the Mahâbhârata and Manu, and it is in many cases impossible to assume that the corresponding verses have been borrowed from the latter works. The Purâ*n*as, some of which, like the Vâyu, even in their present shape, go back to a very respectable antiquity, are popular sectarian compilations of mythology, philosophy, history, and the sacred law, intended, as they are now used, for the instruction of the unlettered classes, including the upper divisions of the *S*ûdra var*n*a, the so-called Sa*kkh*ûdras. It was only natural that their authors should have appropriated suitable portions of the floating metrical wisdom of the philosophical and legal schools.

The comparison of the ancient Buddhist literature is particularly instructive, because the Buddhists are a special philosophical school, and because their oldest works, though mostly consisting of prose, include a considerable number of *S*lokas, among which a certain number, as, for instance, in the Dhammapada, shows affinities to verses of the Mahâbhârata and even of Manu. They probably took over a certain stock of ancient metrical maxims, and added a great number of new ones.

thoroughly convinced of the truth of the dogma that Manu first taught the sacred law, would not hesitate to ascribe to that sage all the maxims which seemed to him to bear the stamp of authenticity, even if others attributed them to different authorities.

The answer to the next question, whether the conversion of the Mânava Dharma-sûtra was effected at one time or by degrees, and whether Bh*ri*gu's recension has to be considered as the immediate offspring or as a remoter descendant of the Sûtra, must, I think, be answered, as has been tacitly assumed in the preceding discussion, in the sense of the first alternative. Not long ago it seemed that the contrary opinion was the more probable one. But the closer one examines the facts which at first sight seem to lead up to the inference that Bh*ri*gu's Manu-sa*m*hitâ forms the last link in a long chain of metrical Manu-sm*ri*tis, the more one sees that they possess no, or very little, importance. On the other hand, those arguments which speak in favour of our text being, if not the first, at least one of the first attempts at a conversion of a Vedic school-book into a special law-book, gain by the same process in force and increase in number. The points which have been brought forward in order to prove that the existing text of Manu has suffered many recasts are, first, its numerous contradictory passages; secondly, the explicit statement of the Hindu tradition in the preface to the Nârada-sm*ri*ti; thirdly, the quotations from a B*ri*hat Manu and a V*ri*ddha Manu met with in the medieval Digests of law; and fourthly, the untraceable or partly traceable quotations from Manu's Dharma*s*âstra found in some of the older Sanskrit works. The existence of these facts is undeniable. But it is not difficult to show that they are partly useless as arguments, and partly, under a better interpretation, lead to quite other conclusions. Thus in weighing the value of the argument drawn from the occurrence of contradictory passages, two circumstances, which mostly have been left out of account, must be kept in mind: first, that it is a common habit of Indian authors to place conflicting opinions, supported by authorities of equal weight, side by side, and to allow an option, or to mention time-honoured rules, legal customs, and social institutions, and afterwards to disapprove of them; and secondly, that, as our Smriti is in any case a recast of an earlier Sûtra, that fact alone is sufficient to account for contradictions. It has been shown above[1], that some contradictory passages, such as those concerning the respective rank of the mother and the teacher, or regarding the permissibility of certain marriage-rites, express conflicting views, mentioned also in the Dharma-sûtras. The Manusmriti only reproduces the ancient opinions, but omits, possibly for metrical reasons, to mark them as belonging to different authors or schools. In other cases we may hesitate between two explanations. If we find, for instance, that our text in the third and ninth chapters[2] violently inveighs against Âsura marriages, and in the eighth and ninth[3] lays down rules which presuppose the legality of the sale or purchase of a bride, we may assume that the first utterance is due to the editor of the metrical version, and that the second represents the more archaic doctrine of the Dharma-sûtra. In favour of this supposition it may be urged that the Mânava Grihya-sûtra unhesitatingly admits the acquisition of a bride by purchase[4]. But it is also possible that the Dharma-sûtra itself contained both the condemnation of the custom and the rules regulating it. For similar contradictions occur also in other Sûtras. Thus Âpastamba expressly forbids, in his sections on Dharma, the sale and gift of children and the procreation of Kshetraga sons[5]. Yet, in his Srauta-sûtra I, 9, 7, he gives a rule showing how the Pindapitriyagña is to be performed by the son of two fathers (dvipitâ). Such a person can only be a Kshetraga, a Dvyâmushyâyana Dattaka, or a Putrikâputra. If it is borne in mind that Baudhâyana, on whose works Âpastamba's Sûtras are based, admits the affiliation which the later member of his vidyâvamsa rejects, the obvious explanation of the contradiction is that Âpastamba, in spite of his disapproval of other than Aurasa sons, did

[1] See p. xxiv. [2] Manu III, 25, 51-54; IX, 98-100.
[3] Manu VIII, 204, 224-225; IX, 97. [4] See above, p. xxxix.
[5] Âp. Dh. S II, 13, 11; 27, 2.

not venture to change the prescriptions which he found in the older *S*rauta-sûtra. Similarly, the supposition that the author of the Mânava Dharma-sûtra, though condemning Âsura marriages, was unwilling to expunge the rules regulating the sale, is not at all improbable. It seems to be even better than the explanation proposed first. For the prohibition of the Âsura rite occurs in the quotation found in the *S*akuntalopâkhyâna, and the latter, as we shall see presently, in all probability refers to the Mânava Dharma-sûtra. Hence I think that at least the remarks made Manu III, 26 did stand in the ancient text. The other repetitions of the same sentiments may have been added on the revision. Another famous instance of a contradiction, Manu IX, 58–70, where the appointment of a widow is first permitted and next forbidden, has probably to be explained in the same manner. If I here differ from Professor Jolly[1] and others, who ascribe the prohibition to the remodeller of the Dharma-sûtra, and if I adhere to the view expressed by B*ri*haspati and some Indian commentators, my reasons are that, as the conflicting statements of the Dharma-sûtras show, the propriety of the Niyoga was not generally acknowledged even in ancient times, and that the medieval Nibandhakâras frequently follow the strange method of teaching adopted by Manu. They, too, describe various antiquated customs, and afterwards add the remark that the matter taught is forbidden in the Kali age. Among the clear cases where a conflict of statements has been caused by additions of the editor, I may mention the rule, Manu IV, 222, prescribing a penance for an unlawful acceptance of food, which differs from that given XI, 153. Here the former must be considered spurious, because it occurs in a chapter which has nothing to do with penances. It is evident that neither the instances just mentioned, nor indeed any other, where our Sm*ri*ti exhibits either two ancient conflicting rules or a modern precept contradicting an ancient one, can be used as arguments showing that the Mânava Dharma-sûtra underwent more than one revision. Under these circumstances it might appear advisable to rely on those contradictions

[1] Tagore Lectures, pp. 48, 61.

which occur in the decidedly modern portions of our text, in the additions to the ancient Dharma-sûtra, and to maintain that e.g. the differences in the two accounts of the creation[1], Manu I, 7–58 and 62–86, indicate that the first chapter owes its present shape to two different authors. Such a mode of reasoning would, no doubt, be correct if the additions to the Dharma-sûtra were independent, original productions. But as the preceding discussion on the sources of this additional matter has shown that the first chapter is a compilation from older versus memoriales, which certainly contained portions and possibly even the whole of both accounts, it becomes inconclusive. The contradictory verses may either have been strung together, as Medhâtithi seems to suggest[2], merely because they really are or were considered paraphrases of Vedic passages, or they may have been reconciled with each other by one of those ingenious methods of interpretation of which the Indian schoolmen are such great masters.

As regards the second argument, the assertion of the Nârada-sm*ri*ti[3], that Manu composed a Dharma*s*âstra in 100,000 verses arranged in 1080 chapters, which was successively reduced by Nârada to 12,000, by Mârka*nd*eya to 8,000, and by Bh*ri*gu's son, Sumati, to 4,000 verses, is so circumstantial that, in spite of its obvious exaggerations, it might be considered to have a substratum of truth, and to be important for the history of Manu's law-book. Abridgments of larger works[4] are in literature as common as expansions of shorter ones. Yet the only assertion in the above account, which we can test, is certainly not true, that Nârada's version of Manu's laws is more ancient than that by Sumati Bhârgava or Bh*ri*gu. The actual position of the

---

[1] See also Dr. Johänntgen, Über das Gesetzbuch des Manu, p. 15.

[2] In his discussion on the aim of the first chapter Medhâtithi says (comm. on I, 6): – – – – निरतिशयैश्वर्यहेतुधर्माद्विपरीतश्चाधर्मः । तद्रूपपरिज्ञानार्थमिदं शास्त्रं महाप्रयोजनमध्येतव्यमित्यध्यायतात्पर्यम् । मूलं त्वत्र मन्त्रार्थवादाः सामान्यतो दृष्टं च । तथा च मन्त्रः । तम आसीदित्यादि ॥

[3] See above, p. xvii; and Jolly, Tagore Lectures, p. 57.

[4] The two versions of Nârada furnish an interesting instance; see Jolly, loc. cit. p. 57.

two works has been inverted. Nârada's Vyavahâramât*ri*kâ shows a far more advanced development of the judicial theories than Bh*ri*gu's Sa*m*hitâ, and contains matter which conclusively proves that it cannot date from an earlier time than the fourth or fifth century of our era [1]. As this test fails, Nârada's statement cannot be used for the determination of the order in which the various versions of Manu's laws were composed. It becomes more probable that it has been framed, with a view to enhance the importance of the Nârada-sm*ri*ti, on the model of such purely fictitious stories respecting the origin of the Dharma, as that given in the Mahâbhârata XII, 59, 22, and 80 seqq., where we are told that Brahman, assisted by the gods, first produced a Dharma*s*âstra in 100,000 chapters, which was successively abridged by *Sam*kara in 10,000, by Indra in 5,000, by B*ri*haspati in 3,000, and by Kâvya in 1,000 Adhyâyas. Against the genuineness of Nârada's story we may also adduce the Paurâ*n*ik statement, according to which Manu's laws were remodelled first by Bh*ri*gu, secondly by Nârada, thirdly by B*ri*haspati, and fourthly by Aṅgiras [2].

The third argument, drawn from the fact that the medieval Nibandhas and commentaries quote passages from a B*ri*hat (great) and V*ri*ddha (old) Manu, has still less value. Professor Jolly has of late asserted in his able discussion [3] of the quotations from these works that they are later, not earlier, than the existing text of Manu, because some of their rules resemble the advanced teaching of Yâg*ñ*avalkya and Nârada, while others contradict our Manu on points where he holds archaic views. Moreover, a passage of V*ri*ddha Manu, to which Professor Max Müller has first called attention [4], possibly indicates an acquaintance with Greek astrology. I can only agree with Professor Jolly's conclusions, and add that a comparison of the quotations from B*ri*hat and V*ri*ddha Manu with Bh*ri*gu's Sa*m*hitâ produces the impression that both works—if indeed the titles refer

[1] West and Bühler, Digest, pp. 48–50, third edition; Jolly, Tagore Lectures, p. 56: Preface to the Translation of Nârada, pp. xv–xvii.

[2] Ma*n*d*lik, the Vyavahâramayûkha and Yâg*ñ*., p. xlvii; Jolly, Tagore Lectures, p. 44.

[3] Tagore Lectures, pp. 65–66.

[4] India, what can it teach us? p. 366.

to two and not to one—must have been enlarged versions of the latter[1]. As it thus appears that there existed recensions posterior to our Manu-sm*ri*ti, the existence of untraceable or partly traceable quotations from Manu's Dharma*s*âstra in A*s*vaghosha's Vagrasû*k*î[2] and from Manu in Varâhamihira's B*ri*hat-sa*m*hitâ[3] possesses no great significance. With respect to Varâhamihira's reference, it must be noted that, according to Albîrûnî's Indica, two astrological Sa*m*hitâs, called after Manu, existed in the eleventh century A.D., the smaller of which was an abridgment made by a perfectly well-known human author[4]. Hence Varâhamihira may have taken his verses on the character of women from the latter. In both quotations the *S*lokas, not found in our Sm*ri*ti, have a very modern look. The case is, however, different with the quotations from Manu, which, as has been shown above, occur in the Mahâbhârata. We have been compelled to admit that the existing text of our Sm*ri*ti is younger than the epic. If, therefore, the law-book referred to in the latter is not the ancient Dharma-sûtra, we must also concede the existence of a secondary recension which preceded Bh*ri*gu's Sa*m*hitâ. The solution of this question is, owing to the

[1] In order to enable the reader to form his own judgment on this point, I add a list of the quotations which I have noted. Those from B*ri*hat Manu occur, 1. Col. Dig. II, 3, 26; 2. Col. Dig. V, 428 = *G*î. Dây. XI, 6, 34; 3. Datt. Mîm. II, 8; 4. May. IV, 5, 53;—those from V*ri*ddha Manu, 1. Col. Dig. III, 1, 69; 2. Col. Dig. III, 1, 83 = May. XI, 5 = Viv. *K*int. p. 99; 3. Col. Dig. III, 1, 86 = Viv. *K*int. p. 89; 4. Col. Dig. III, 1, 90 = May. XI, 5 = Viv. *K*int. p. 100; 5. Col. Dig. III, 1, 93 = Viv. *K*int. p. 103; 6. Col. Dig. V, 162 = Viv. *K*int. p. 272 = Varad. p. 21 = *G*î. Dây. IX, 17 (where attrib. to B*ri*hat M.); 7. Col. Dig. V, 408 = Sm*ri*. *K*and. XI, 1, 15 = Sar. Vil. 504 = Varad. pp. 33, 40 = Vîram. III, 1, 2 = *G*î. Dây. XI, 1, 7 and Viv. *K*int. p. 289 (where attrib. to B*ri*hat M.); 8. Mit. II, 5, 6 = Viv. *K*int. p. 289 and Varad. p. 37 (where attrib. to B*ri*hat M.) = Sar. Vil. 591 (where attrib. to M.); 9. Viv. *K*int. pp. 126–7; 10. Viv. *K*int. p. 180; 11. Varad. p. 50; 12. Varad. p. 28, where in reality Manu IX, 206 seems to be quoted.

[2] Weber, Indische Streifen, vol. i, pp. 190, 192, 198.

[3] Kern, B*ri*hat-sa*m*hitâ, chapter 74, vv. 7–15, and Preface, p. 43.

[4] Albîrûnî, Indica, chapter xiv; see also Kern, loc. cit. p. 42, where the probability of the existence of a Mânavî Sa*m*hitâ has been shown. Albîrûnî says that the title of the two works was Mânasa (Mânavî?), and that the shorter one had been composed by one PN*K*L, a native of Southern India. I owe these notes to the kindness of Professor Sachau, the learned editor and translator of Albîrûnî's important work.

shortness of the extracts, very difficult. But, considering all things, I feel inclined to assume that the author or authors of the Mahâbhârata knew only the Dharma-sûtra. The character of the four verses and a half, quoted verbally, as well as of the paraphrase in the *S*akuntalopâkhyâna agrees well enough with this assumption, because the Mânava Dharma-sûtra, as we have seen, certainly did contain numerous *S*lokas. It is further corroborated by the fact that the Mahâbhârata does not differ in its arrangement, or rather in its want of an arrangement of the civil and criminal law, from the Dharma-sûtras. Though the epic contains numerous verses on these topics, it nowhere shows an acquaintance with the eighteen titles of the law which are so characteristic of the secondary Sm*ri*tis, the handbooks of the special law schools. On the other side it may be urged that the Mahâbhârata says nothing of Dharma-sûtras, and that its general view of the origin of the sacred law coincides with that expressed in the later law-books. It holds that the moral and legal doctrines were revealed for the benefit of the human race, first by Brahman to various mythical *Ri*shis, and by them to mankind. This objection may, however, be met by the not unreasonable assumption that at the time when the Mahâbhârata was composed, the real origin of the old Sûtras had been forgotten, while the text had not yet been materially altered. What has been said above regarding the rise of the special law schools, and the facts known regarding the change in the tradition concerning the Sûtras of Gautama and Vasish*th*a, make the hypothesis of such a transitional period not at all improbable. Should, nevertheless, the possibility of the existence of a metrical redaction of the Mânava-sûtra, preceding that ascribed to Bh*ri*gu, be considered as not altogether excluded, it would at least be necessary to concede that it could not have contained the present arrangement of the Vyavahâra portion under titles.

While there is thus no proof for the opinion that the modern portions of the Manu-sm*ri*ti have been gradually added one to the other, or that the present text is one of the last links in a long chain of metrical recensions, there are several points which tend to show that our Manu-sa*m*hitâ is one of the first attempts at remodelling a Dharma-sûtra. The most important argument for its comparatively early date is furnished by the incompleteness and awkwardness of its rules on judicial procedure and on civil law[1]. If we compare these rules with those of the Dharma-sûtras and with those of the other metrical Sm*ri*tis, they are somewhat more explicit than the former, but very much inferior to the latter. As regards procedure, the Manu-sm*ri*ti pays more attention to the moral side of the duties, incumbent on the judge and the other persons concerned, than to the technicalities, which are much more clearly and minutely described in the Dharma*s*âstras of Yâ*g*ñavalkya and Nârada. In this respect it comes close to the Dharma-sûtras, with which it particularly agrees in the absence of all mention of written plaints and of documentary evidence, as well as in the shortness of its remarks on ordeals. Among the ancient law-books the Vâsish*th*a Dharma*s*âstra is the only one which has allusions to written documents, and names them, XVI, 10, 14–15, as one of the means of legal proof. In the other Dharma-sûtras there is no indication that their authors were acquainted with the art of writing. I have already pointed out in the Introduction to my translation of Vasish*th*a[2] that most probably this omission has to be explained not by the assumption that in the times of Gautama, Baudhâyana, and Âpastamba writing was unknown or little used in India, but by the consideration that the general character of the Dharma-sûtras, which principally pay attention to the moral side of the law, does not require the introduction of matters belonging more properly to the customs of the country or to the Artha*s*âstra. Whatever may be thought of the prevalence of writing during the earlier times and of the value of my explanation, it may be regarded as perfectly certain that

[1] See on this subject and the following discussion, Weber, History of Indian Literature, pp. 279–281; Stenzler, Yâ*g*ñavalkya, pp. vii–x; Journal of the German Or. Soc. vol. ix, on the Indian Ordeals; and Jolly, Tagore Lectures, pp. 45–49.

[2] Sacred Books of the East, vol. xvi, p. xxvi.

Bh*ri*gu's Manu-sa*m*hitâ belongs to a period when the art of writing was known and generally practised. For, first, we find two clear references to written documents, 'what has been caused to be written by force' (lekhita, VIII, 168) and royal edicts (*s*âsana, IX, 232). Secondly, we have the expression nibandh, 'to record,' in a passage (VIII, 255) where the context leaves no doubt that a written entry is referred to. When it is said there, that in a boundary-dispute the king shall record the boundary, according to the unanimous declaration of the witnesses, together with their names, it is impossible to imagine how he can do so without drawing up a written document, which, of a necessity, must have legal force for the future. This use of the verb nibandh makes it further probable that Medhâtithi is not altogether wrong, when he explains (VIII, 76) the compound anibaddha*h*, 'a person not appointed (to be a witness to a transaction),' by 'a person not entered (as a witness in the document),' and refers the rule to cases of loans and other commercial transactions. Thirdly, there is the term kara*n*a (VIII, 54 and 154), which, though less explicit, likewise points to the use of written bonds for loans. The former passage declares that 'a debt which is proved by kara*n*a' (kara*n*ena vibhâvitam) must be paid, and the commentators explain kara*n*a to mean 'written bonds, witnesses, and so forth.' Hence it has been rendered in the translation by 'good evidence.' Verse 154 prescribes that a debtor 'who, unable to pay a debt (at the fixed time), wishes to make a new contract, may renew (lit. change) the kara*n*am (kara*n*am parivartayet[1]).' Two commentators, Kullûka and Râghava, take the word here in the sense of 'a written bond,' while the older ones, Govinda. Nârâya*n*a, and probably also Medhâtithi, explain it by 'bonds and so forth,' and make it include agreements before witnesses. From these explanations and the use of the word kara*n*a in other legal works it would appear that kara*n*a may also be cited as a witness for the acquaintance of our author with the art of writing. To the conclusion that writing must have been extensively used in business-

[1] Nandana's reading kâra*n*am is clearly erroneous; see below, p. cxxxiv.

dealings points, finally, the whole state of civilisation to which Manu's rules are adapted. The highly developed trade by land and by sea [1], on which ad valorem duties were imposed [2], the existence of official lists of prices which were renewed periodically [3], the complicated system of calculations of interest, among which we find compound interest [4], and the occurrence of mortgages [5], would be impossible without written documents. These facts appear to me so eloquent that even though all the passages adduced above, which explicitly mention written documents, could be proved to be late interpolations, the general aspect of this question would remain unchanged. If, under these circumstances, Manu's rules on evidence contain nothing definite on the admissibility of documents, and if he agrees in this particular with the Dharma-sûtras and differs strongly from the Dharma*s*âstras of Yâ*gñ*avalkya and Nârada as well as other metrical Sm*ri*tis, this omission gains a great importance for the historical position of the Sa*m*hitâ. Whether we explain it by an oversight of the editor or by the assumption that he left the determination of the value of written documents to custom or to another *S*âstra, it shows that he was acquainted with the Dharma-sûtras alone or with Dharma-sûtras and such metrical Sm*ri*tis as excluded the section on documents. As he certainly was an adherent of a special law school, and bent on making his work as complete as possible, he would not have omitted so important a point if he had known law-books like the Yâ*gñ*avalkya-sm*ri*ti.

The omission of the details regarding ordeals is no less significant. Manu VIII, 109–116 describes only the administration of oaths more fully, and mentions the ordeals by fire and water in a cursory manner. Among the Dharma-sûtras there is only the Âpastambîya which (II, 29, 6) recommends the employment of divine proof (daiva) or ordeals in a general way without adding any particulars. The secondary law-books of Yâ*gñ*avalkya and Nârada describe five kinds of ordeals, and enter, the second more

[1] VIII, 156–157. [2] VII, 127–128; VIII, 348.
[3] VIII, 401–402. [4] VIII, 139–143, 151–153. [5] VIII, 165.

fully than the first, on descriptions of the manner in which they must be performed. Even the Vish*n*u-sm*ri*ti agrees with them, and the fragments of the lost metrical Sm*ri*tis show that most of the latter, too, contained sections resembling those of Yâ*gñ*avalkya and Nârada. It would be, in my opinion, a mistake to infer from the silence of Gautama, Baudhâyana, and Vasish*th*a that in ancient times ordeals were unknown in India. Traces of such practices. which were formerly prevalent in various forms also among other Indo-European races, are found, as might be expected, even in Vedic works. If the authors of the Dharma-sûtras ignore them or just indicate their existence, the correct explanation of this fact, too, is that they considered the subject not important enough for giving details, and left it to custom. The authors of the secondary Sm*ri*tis, as a matter of course, were anxious to fill up the blank left by their predecessors. But they probably did nothing more than bring the various local customs into a system which gradually was made more and more complete. Under these circumstances the fact that Manu's rules stand midway between those of the Dharma-sûtras and of the other metrical law-books is another argument for allotting the first place to his Sa*m*hitâ. In the treatment of the civil and criminal law the inferiority of the Manu-sm*ri*ti to the other Dharma*s*âstras of the same class, even to Yâ*gñ*avalkya's, which contains a much smaller number of verses on Vyavahâra, manifests itself in various ways. In spite of the attempt at a scientific classification of the rules under certain heads, the arrangement of these sections is cumbrous and disorderly. Twice, at the end of the eighth and ninth chapters, we find collections of miscellaneous rules, which, as a comparison of the works of Yâ*gñ*avalkya and Nârada shows, might for the greater part have been easily fitted in to the one or the other of the eighteen titles. Under the single titles the rules are sometimes badly arranged. This is particularly visible in the chapter on inheritance, where, to mention only one most conspicuous instance of this want of care, the verse asserting the right of the mother and grandmother to take the estate of a predeceased son or grandson, is placed so awkwardly that it is absolutely impossible to guess which place in the sequence of heirs the author meant to allot to them. As stated above, the verse most probably was inserted by the editor of the ancient Dharma-sûtra. If he had cared at all for order and intelligibility, he ought not to have contented himself with the enunciation of the maxim that these persons do inherit, but he ought to have indicated where the preceding close series of heirs has to be broken in order to admit them. Very significant, too, are the constant mingling of moral exhortations with the legal rules and the occasional recommendation of quaint judicial devices which are common in the earlier stages of the development of the law. Though the duty of kings to protect their subjects and to restrain the wicked has been fully explained in the seventh chapter, yet in the sections on theft (VIII, 302–311), on violence (VIII, 343–347), and on adultery (VIII, 386–387), the author expatiates again and again on the necessity of eradicating such offences. In the second case the specific rules, providing for the punishment of sâhasa crimes, are left out, the omission being repaired at the end of the ninth chapter. Both Yâ*gñ*avalkya and Nârada think it unnecessary to recur to the moral obligations of the king after pointing them out once. Both refrain also from mentioning the curious expedient which Manu recommends (VIII, 182–184) for the decision of doubtful disputes regarding deposits. Another important point is that Manu's rules on some titles are exceedingly incomplete, and touch one particular case only, from which it is not always easy to deduce the general principle. Thus, in treating of the subtraction or resumption of gifts, Manu (VIII, 212–213) confines his remarks to pious gifts which are not applied in the manner stipulated. Yâ*gñ*avalkya (II, 175–177) gives under this head at least some general principles, showing what is required for the validity of gifts; while Nârada[1] offers a fairly full and systematic treatment of the whole law of gifts. A similarly gradual development is visible under other heads, especially concerns among

[1] Professor Jolly's Translation, pp. 59–60.

partners and rescission of sale and purchase, the rules under which latter head Manu gives partly in their proper place and partly among the miscellaneous precepts at the end of the eighth chapter. A third point, finally, which deserves to be noted here, is the fact that legal definitions are almost entirely wanting in the Manu-smriti, become more frequent in Yâgñavalkya's work, and are regularly given by Nârada, as well as that many single rules which are common to Manu and Yâgñavalkya, or to Manu, Yâgñavalkya, and Nârada, are framed in the latter works with much greater precision than in the former[1]. The inferiority of the Manu-smriti in all these points can only be explained by the assumption that it was composed at a time when the systematic treatment of the law had been begun, but had not reached a high state of perfection, while the superiority of the other metrical Smritis permits us to infer that they belong to a much later period when the special law schools had made a considerable progress in the elaboration of their theories. This argument is, it seems to me, the strongest which can be brought forward as a firm basis for the universally prevalent belief of all European and Indian Sanskritists in the priority of our Manu to all other known secondary law-books. For wherever we are able to trace larger portions of the history of a special Brâhmanical science, as e.g. in the case of grammar, we find that the later authors, though belonging to different schools and creeds, and though differing in the actual doctrines, invariably avail themselves of the method of their predecessors, developing and refining it more and more. Retrogressive steps, examples of which seem to occur in the handbooks of the Vedic schools[2], have hitherto not been found[3]. All

[1] Compare e.g. the rules regarding lawful interest, Manu VIII, 140-142, and Yâgñ. II, 34.

[2] Compare e.g. the case of the Gautamîya and Baudhâyanîya Dharma-sûtras, where the second and later work is inferior in method to the earlier one.

[3] Should it be objected that the Vishnu-smriti, though certainly younger than Manu's and Yâgñavalkya's Dharmasâstras, is deficient in a systematic arrangement of the rules on civil and criminal law, the answer would be that the editor of this work appears to have been a Vaishnava sectarian, not an adherent of a school which made the law its special object of study.

the other arguments which have been or can be adduced to prove the antiquity of our Manu-smriti are less conclusive. If it has been said that this work contains some very archaic doctrines[1] which are not found in the other secondary law-books, that is perfectly true. But the inference regarding its age becomes doubtful, because on other subjects Manu is ahead of the other Smritis[2], and because in general the development of the actual doctrines seems to have been not quite steady and continuous. Still more precarious are the arguments, based on the language of the Manu-smriti, on its not mentioning the Greek astrology or Greek coinage and similar points. As we have to deal with a recast of a very ancient book, and as its editor has utilised a good many ancient verses in compiling his recension, it is only to be expected that a number of archaic forms and phrases should be found. But it is evident that they prove nothing with respect to the period when the compilation was made, because it is impossible to decide in each case to which of its component parts the archaism belongs. As regards the remaining argumenta a silentio, they are equally inconclusive. Even if we grant, for argument's sake, the correctness of the assertion that our Manu contains no allusion to the Greek order of the planets, to the zodiac, to judicial astrology, and to Greek or Scythian dînâras, drammas, and nânakas, while all the other secondary law-books mention one or the other of these foreign importations, the omission may be purely accidental. These and similar points can be used for no other purpose than to show that there is nothing in Manu's text that compels us to place it in or after the period between 300–500 A.D., during which Greek influence made itself strongly felt in India. They possess

[1] One of the clearest instances of this kind is Manu's doctrine with regard to the succession of females to the estate of males, where the exclusion of the wife agrees with the teaching of the Dharma-sûtras (Jolly, Tagore Lectures, p. 48). The assertion of Professor Hopkins (Castes according to the M. Dh. p. 108 seqq.), that the prerogatives of Brâhmanas are greater according to Yâgñ. than according to Manu, seems to me erroneous, and chiefly based on an inadmissible interpretation of some passages of Manu. In my opinion the mutual relations of the castes, as described in the two law-books, cannot be used to prove a priority of the one to the other.

[2] E.g. in the doctrine concerning the Niyoga.

a certain importance only as auxiliaries to the chief argument derived from the imperfect development of the method or formal treatment of the law. But considering all that has been said in the preceding discussion, it is, I think, not too much to say that there is no obstacle against, and some reason for, our accepting as true the assertion, which is made in the Manu-smriti itself and supported by the tradition preserved in the Skanda-purâna, that Bhrigu's[1] Samhitâ is the first and most ancient recast of a Dharmasâstra attributed to Manu, which latter, owing to the facts pointed out in the first part of this Introduction, must be identified with the Mânava Dharma-sûtra. Though this recast must be considered the work of one hand, the possibility that single verses may have been added later or altered, is of course not excluded. A perfectly intact preservation of an Indian work which has been much studied, is a priori improbable, and the divergence of the commentators with respect to certain verses shows that some of those contained in our text were suspected by the one or the other of them. But the number of Slokas with regard to which real doubts can be entertained is comparatively small, and hardly amounts to more than a dozen[2].

The above discussion has also to a certain extent defined the relative position of our Manu-smriti in Brâhmanical literature, and has thus opened the way for the consideration of the last remaining problem, the question when the conversion of the Mânava Dharma-sûtra into a metrical law-book

[1] A clear and definite explanation of the question why the Hindu tradition ascribes the promulgation of Manu's laws to Bhrigu has hitherto not been traced. Bhrigu's only connexion with Manu is that mentioned in the text, according to which he is one of the mind-born sons or creatures of the father of mankind. This version of the legend of his origin is, however, by no means common. In the Mahâbhârata XII, 182–192, we find 'a condensed Dharmasâstra,' which is said to have been revealed by Bhrigu to Bharadvâga. It includes an account of the creation, but makes no mention of Manu. As Bhrigu appears also elsewhere as the author of a Dharmasâstra, it is just possible that the legend may be based on Bhrigu's fame as a legislator and as the offspring of Manu.

[2] Many more verses are left out partly in Medhâtithi's Bhâshya and partly in Nandana's commentary. But see below, pp. cxxvi and cxxxv, where it has been shown that omissions in the accessible MSS. of these two works alone do not mean much.

may have taken place. The terminus a quo which has been gained for the composition of Bh*ri*gu's Sa*m*hitâ is the age of the Mahâbhârata, and the terminus ad quem the dates of the metrical Smr*i*tis of Yâ*g*ñavalkya and Nârada. Though we are at present not in a position to assert anything positive regarding the period when the Mahâbhârata and especially its twelfth and thirteenth Parvans were written, and though the date of Yâ*g*ñavalkya's Dharma*s*âstra is very doubtful, yet some facts known regarding the Nârada-sm*ri*ti are not without importance for framing our answer to the difficult question now proposed. Both Professor Jolly and myself[1] have lately discussed the significance of the mention of golden dînâras or denarii in the longer and more authentic version of Nârada and of the circumstance that Asahâya, a predecessor of Manu's earliest commentator, Medhâtithi, explained it and have arrived at a very similar conclusion, viz. that the Nârada-sm*ri*ti dates either shortly before or shortly after the middle of the first thousand years of our era. If that is so, Bh*ri*gu's Sa*m*hitâ must, in consideration of the arguments just stated, be placed not only earlier, but considerably earlier, and the assertion that it must have existed at least in the second century of our era is not unwarranted. This latter inference is also made inevitable by the discovery that we have to admit the former existence of very ancient commentaries, and of at least one ancient Vârttika or Kârikâ which referred to the text of Manu, known to us. With respect to the commentaries, Medhâtithi, the author of the Manubhâshya, is a most valuable and clear witness. This author, who probably wrote in the ninth century A.D.[2], very frequently quotes opinions and various readings, expressed or men-

---

[1] Jolly, Tagore Lectures, p. 56; West and Bühler, Digest, p. 48. To the arguments adduced there I would add that Bâ*n*a, the friend of *S*rîharsha-Harshavardhana (606-7–648 A.D.), makes a pretty clear allusion to the Nâradîya Dharma*s*âstra in the Kâdambarî, p. 91, l. 13 (Peterson's edition), where he calls a royal palace nâradîyam ivâvar*n*yamânarâ*g*adharmam, 'similar to the Nâradîya (Dharma*s*âstra), because there the duties of kings were taught (by the conduct of the ruler) just as they are taught (in the law-book).'

[2] For the details, see below, pp. cxxi–cxxiii.

tioned by his predecessors, and shows by the number of the conflicting explanations which he sometimes adduces for a passage of the text, that in his time a very large number of commentaries on the Manu-smriti existed. Among the persons thus quoted, he designates some by the terms Pûrva and *K*iramtana. Pûrva, which means both 'former' and 'ancient,' is an ambiguous word. It can be applied to all persons who wrote before the author, though it frequently is used in speaking of those who lived centuries ago. *K*iramtana, 'long previous or ancient,' is much stronger, and, according to the usage of Indian authors, denotes a predecessor belonging to a remote antiquity. As Medhâtithi, writing in the ninth century, knew of commentaries to which he was compelled to assign a remote antiquity, it is only a moderate estimate if we assume that the earliest among them were in his time from three to four hundred years old. But if in the sixth or even in the fifth century A.D. glosses on our text existed, its composition must go back to much earlier times. For the widely divergent and frequently very questionable explanations of the more difficult passages, which Medhâtithi adduces from his predecessors, indicate that even the earliest among them were separated by a considerable interval from the compilator of the Manu-samhitâ, an interval so great that the real meaning of the text had been forgotten.

The merit of the discovery that one of the lost metrical Dharmasâstras, the Brihaspati-smriti, was a Vârttika on our text of Manu, belongs to Professor Jolly, whose careful investigation of the fragments of the lost law-books, contained in the modern Digests, has contributed very materially to the elucidation of a difficult chapter in the history of Indian legal literature. He shows[1] that Brihaspati not only allots to Manu's Smriti the first place among all law-books, but that he explains, amplifies, and occasionally corrects its rules on various portions of the Vyavahâra. The particulars from Manu which Brihaspati mentions are such as to leave no doubt that the text which he knew in

[1] Tagore Lectures, pp. 60-62; see also above, p. xvi.

no way differed from that known to us. He explains, as Professor Jolly points out, the curious terms, used Manu VIII, 49, for the various modes by which a creditor may recover a debt, as well as the expression asvâmin, which occurs in the title of law, called Asvâmivikraya. He further mentions that Manu IX, 57–68 first teaches and afterwards forbids the practice of Niyoga, and gives, as it seems to me [1], the correct explanation of this contradiction. He also notes that Manu IX, 221–228 forbids gambling, which other writers on law permit under due supervision, and he corrects Manu's rules regarding the indivisibility of clothes and other objects enumerated IX, 219. An apparent contradiction in B*ri*haspati's rules with respect to subsidiary sons [2] proves that he knew and accepted Manu's teaching on this subject. He declares that the substitutes for a legitimate son of the body are forbidden in the Kaliyuga, and yet admits the rights of a Putrikâ or appointed daughter, who mostly is reckoned among the substitutes. This difficulty is easily solved, if it is borne in mind that Manu, differing from the other ancient law-books, does not reckon the Putrikâ among the subsidiary sons. He separates her, IX, 127–140, from the Gau*n*a Putras, IX, 158–181, and strongly insists on her rights, while he restricts those of the others very much. The list of instances where B*ri*haspati alludes to, annotates, or amplifies rules of Manu might, I think, be enlarged still further, and it seems to me that a comparison of those verses of his, which Colebrooke's Digest contains, with Manu gives one the impression that B*ri*haspati's work is throughout a revised and enlarged edition of the Bh*ri*gu-sa*m*hitâ, or, to use the Indian expression, a Manuvârttika or Manukârikâ. Professor Jolly, finally, has pointed out that this evidence concerning the relation between Manu and B*ri*haspati agrees with and gives some weight to the tradition preserved in the Skanda-purâ*n*a, according to which B*ri*haspati composed the third of the four versions of Manu's Dharma*s*âstra. The age of the B*ri*haspati-sm*ri*ti

[1] See also above, p. xciv.

[2] Jolly, Tagore Lectures, p. 158.

is circumscribed by its definition of the value of golden dînâras, and by the quotations from it which occur already in the oldest commentaries and Nibandhas from the ninth century A.D. downwards. Since the latter period it has been considered as a work of divine origin, revealed by the teacher of the gods. Hence Professor Jolly's supposition, that it must have existed some two or three hundred years earlier, places it not too early, but, in my opinion, rather too late. But even if the B*ri*haspati-sm*ri*ti dates only about 600 A.D., its statements regarding the high authority of Manu's teaching show that our version of the latter must have preceded it by many centuries.

The three points just discussed are, in my opinion, the only ones that are really useful for fixing the lower date of our Manu-sm*ri*ti. All the other facts known to me which bear on the question are made valueless by flaws of one kind or the other. Thus if we find that another metrical Dharma*s*âstra, the Kâtyâyana-sm*ri*ti, which probably belongs to the same period as the B*ri*haspati-sm*ri*ti, repeatedly quotes doctrines of Manu or Bh*ri*gu found in our text, it is nevertheless not permissible to assume confidently with Kullûka on Manu VIII, 350[1], that its author knew and explained our text. For, as Professor Jolly has shown[2], there are other cases in which the teaching attributed by Kâtyâyana to Bh*ri*gu or Manu differs from the opinion advanced in our Sm*ri*ti. It is, of course, possible that the author, who assumes the name of Kâtyâyana, may have made a slip, or may have known several Manu-sm*ri*tis or Bh*ri*gu-sm*ri*tis, and have referred in different places to different works. But, making every allowance for such possibilities, it cannot be said that his references furnish a really conclusive argument. Again, it has been pointed out[3] that the author of the Bhavishya-purâ*n*a has largely drawn on the first three chapters of our Manu, whom he also names, and nobody who carefully compares the two

[1] कात्यायनश्च भृगुशब्दोल्लेखनेन मनूक्तं श्लोकं व्यक्तं व्याख्यातवान् ॥

[2] Tagore Lectures, p. 62, ll. 22 and 24, B*ri*haspati has been printed twice by mistake for Kâtyâyana.

[3] Professor Aufrecht's Catal. Sansk. MSS. Bodl. Libr. p. 30.

texts can have any doubt who the borrower is, as the Purâna regularly substitutes easy readings for difficult ones, and adds numerous explanatory verses. Besides, Nârâyana, as well as Kullûka[1], quotes verses of the Bhavishya-purâna from a section on penances not found in the accessible MSS., which likewise are clearly intended to explain the text of our Samhitâ. All this is however useless, as for the present it is impossible to determine the date of the Purâna even approximatively. Professor H. H. Wilson[2], who has a very mean opinion of the book, declares that it cannot lay claim to a high antiquity, and seems to consider it a production of the ninth or tenth century A.D. Professor Aufrecht's discovery[3] that the Matsya-purâna, which mentions a Bhavishya-purâna in 14,500 verses, contains actually several sections which have been borrowed from the portions of the latter work preserved in the MSS., makes Professor Wilson's estimate improbable. For the Matsya-purâna was considered a canonical work about the year 1000 A. D., and used by Albîrûnî for his work on India[4]. Though it, therefore, becomes probable that the Bhavishya-purâna is much older than Professor Wilson was inclined to assume, the data thus gained are much too vague for inferences regarding the age of our Manu-smriti.

Equally unsatisfactory are the results which an examination of the quotations from the Manu-smriti, found in various Sanskrit works, yields us. Perfectly indisputable quotations are not very common, and they occur mostly in works of comparatively recent date, e. g. in the Yasastilaka of the Digambara-Gaina poet Somadeva, 959 A. D.[5], in Sankarâkârya's Sârîrakabhâshya, 804 A. D.[6], and in Kshî-

[1] See e. g. his remarks on Manu XI, 101, and Nârâyana's on XI, 131.

[2] Vishnu-purâna, vol. i, pp. lxii-lxiv, and Reinaud, Mémoire sur l'Inde, p. 396.

[3] Catalogue, p. 43.

[4] I owe the knowledge of this fact also to the kindness of Professor Sachau.

[5] See Professor Peterson's Report on the Search for Sanskrit MSS., 1883-84, pp. 42-43.

[6] Deussen, Vedânta, p. 36. With respect to the date of Sankarâkârya's work, I follow the Hindu tradition, which places the birth of the author in 788 A. D. According to the statement of the late Yagñesvara Sâstrî, with whom I discussed the passages which he adduces in the Âryavidyâsudhâkara, p. 226, the sampra-

rasvâmin's Amarakoshodghâ*t*ana[1]. Other cases, where we find verses from the Manu-sa*m*hitâ quoted in ancient works, are made inconclusive by the vagueness of the reference or by the circumstance that the same passages occur also in other works. Thus we find Manu VIII, 416, with a slight verbal difference at the end of the first line[2], in the *S*abara-bhâshya on Mîm. Sû. VI, 1, 12. Though the exact date of the latter work is uncertain, we know that it preceded Kumârilabha*tt*a's Tantravârttika, and its style, which closely resembles that of Pata*ñg*ali's Mahâbhâshya, makes it probable that its author lived not much later than the beginning of our era. Hence its testimony would be of the greatest interest, provided it were perfectly clear. Unfortunately the Bhâshya introduces the verse merely by the words eva*m k*a smarati, 'and thus he records or states in the Sm*ri*ti,' without specifying the author. As the doctrine of the verse which declares a wife, a son, and a slave to be incapable of holding and acquiring property is found, though expressed differently, also in the Nârada-sm*ri*ti, Vivâdapada V, 39, it may be that *S*abara took the passage from some other work than the Manu-sm*ri*ti. Again, though Pata*ñg*ali in the Vyâkara*n*amahâbhâshya on Pâ*n*ini VI, 1, 84 adduces Manu II, 120 without any variant[3], it would be extremely hazardous to conclude that he quotes from our text of Manu. For the Mahâbhârata (XIII, 104, 64[b]–65[a]) has exactly the same words.

dâya, referred to in his work, is that of *S*riṅgeri, where also documentary evidence for its correctness is said to exist. Hence I hesitate to accept Mr. Telang's conclusions, who places *S*aṅkara in the latter half of the sixth century, Mudrârâkshasa, Appendix, and Ind. Ant. vol. xiii, p. 95 seqq.

[1] Aufrecht, Journal of the Germ. Or. Soc. vol. xxviii, p. 107. The date of this author, who used to be identified with the teacher of *G*ayâpî*d*a of Ka*s*mîr (779–813 A. D.), seems, according to the latest researches, more recent.

[2] See the edition in the Bibl. Ind. vol. i, p. 611: भार्या दासश्च पुत्रश्च निर्धनाः सर्व एव ते। यत्ते समधिगच्छन्ति यस्य ते तस्य तद्धनम् ॥ At the end of the first line Manu has त्रय एवाधनाः स्मृताः ॥

[3] See vol. iii, p. 58 of Professor Kielhorn's edition. I may add that the same work on Pâ*n*ini II, 3, 35 (vol. i, p. 457, Kielhorn) quotes another verse, the first line of which agrees with Manu IV, 151[a], while the second entirely differs. In this case, too, the Mahâbhârata XIII, 104, 82 has a version closely resembling that of Manu.

More important are some allusions to the laws of Manu found in several works of considerable antiquity, and in inscriptions. Taken by themselves they would, indeed, not prove much. But considered in conjunction with the results of the three chief arguments, they certainly furnish a confirmation of the latter. The clearest case, perhaps, occurs in the Kirâtâr*g*unîya of Bhâravi, a poet, whose fame on the evidence of the Aihole inscription was well established in 634 A.D., and who, therefore, cannot possibly have lived later than in the beginning of the sixth century, but may be considerably older. He makes (Kir. I, 9) Yudhish*th*ira's spy say, 'He (Duryodhana), conquering the six (internal) foes, desiring to enter on the path, taught by Manu, that is difficult to tread, and casting off (all) sloth, since by day and by night he adheres to the (prescribed) division (of the royal duties), shows increased manly energy in accordance with the Nîti.' At first sight it might seem as if this passage contained nothing more than an expression of the ancient belief according to which Manu settled the duties of mankind, and among them also those of kings. But if we keep in mind the inferences made unavoidable by Medhâtithi's statements regarding the ancient commentaries and by the character of the B*ri*haspati-sm*ri*ti, it becomes more probable that Bhâravi alludes to the seventh chapter of Bh*ri*gu's version of the Manu-sm*ri*ti, which declares vinaya, humility or self-conquest, i. e. the conquest of the six internal foes, to be one of the chief qualities requisite for a king, and which carefully and minutely describes the employment of each watch of the day and the night. Other much less explicit allusions occur in the land-grants. It will suffice to adduce those found in the commencement of the Valabhî inscriptions of Dhruvasena I, Guhasena, and Dharasena II, to which I have called attention some time ago[1]. The oldest of them is dated Sa*m*vat 207, i. e. not later than 526 A. D.[2] There it is said in the description

[1] See West and Bühler, Digest, p. 46, and for the inscriptions, Indian Antiquary, vols. iv, p. 104; v, 28; vi, 11; vii, 67, 69, 71; viii, 302. For other passages, see Hopkins, Journal of the American Oriental Society, vol. xi, pp. 243-246.

[2] This is on the supposition that the era of the Valabhî plates began in 319 A. D., the latest date ever assigned to it.

of Dronasi*m*ha, the first Mahârâ*g*a of Valabhî and the immediate predecessor of Dhruvasena I, that 'like Dharmarâ*g*a (Yudhish*th*ira) he observed as his law the rules and ordinances taught by Manu and other (sages).' Strictly interpreted, the passage says nothing more than that in Dronasi*m*ha's times various law-books existed, one and the chief of which was attributed. But, considering what we know from other sources, it is not improbable that it refers to our Sa*m*hitâ, which is acknowledged by B*ri*haspati as the paramount authority. This is all I am able to bring forward in order to fix the lower limit of the Manu-sm*ri*ti. But the facts stated are, I think, sufficient to permit the inference that the work, such as we know it, existed in the second century A. D.

For an answer to the question whether our Manu-sm*ri*ti can go back to a higher antiquity, and how much older it may be, we have at present very scant data. Its posteriority to the twelfth and thirteenth Parvans of the Mahâbhârata teaches us, as already stated, nothing definite. But there is a passage in its tenth chapter, vv. 43–44, which has been frequently supposed to convey, and probably does contain, a hint regarding its lower limit. There the Kâmbo*g*as, Yavanas, *S*akas, and Pahlavas are enumerated among the races which, originally of Kshatriya descent, were degraded to the condition of *S*ûdras in consequence of their neglect of the Brâhma*n*as[1]. As the Yavanas are named together with the Kâmbo*g*as or Kâbulîs exactly in the same manner as in the edicts of A*s*oka[2], it is highly probable that Greek subjects of Alexander's successors, and especially the Bactrian Greeks, are meant. This point, as well as the mention of the *S*akas[3] or Scythians, would

[1] The verse contains also the name of the *K*înas, which formerly has been taken to be valuable as a chronological landmark. More modern researches have proved this view to be untenable; see A. von Gutschmid, Journal of the German Or. Soc. vol. xxxiv, pp. 202–208; Max Müller, India, what can it teach us? p. 131; Rig-veda, vol. iv, p. li.

[2] See e. g. the fifth rock-edict, where the Yona-Ka*m*boga-Ga*m*dhâra or Ga*m*dhâla are mentioned as A*s*oka's neighbours, the most distant being placed first.

[3] The earliest mention of the *S*akas probably occurs in a Vârttika of Kâtyâyana on Pâ*n*. VI, 1, 94, where *s*akandhu is explained by *s*aka + andhu. According to the traditional explanation the compound means 'the well of the *S*aka king.'

indicate that the *S*lokas could in no case have been written before the third century B. C. This limit would be still further and very considerably contracted if the mention of the Pahlavas were quite above suspicion, and if the deductions of my learned friend, Professor Nöldeke[1], regarding the age of this word were perfectly certain. Pahlava and its Iranian prototype Pahlav are, according to the concurrent testimony of the most distinguished Orientialists, corruptions of Parthava, the indigenous name of the Parthians[2]. Relying on the fact that the change of the Iranian *th* to *h* is first traceable in the name Meherdates, mentioned by Tacitus, and in the word Miiro, i. e. Mihira, on the coins of Kanishka or Kanerki[3], Professor Nöldeke concludes that the form Pahlav cannot have originated among the Iranians earlier than in the first century A. D., and that it cannot have been introduced into India before the second century of our era. If this inference were unassailable, the remoter limit of the Manu-sm*ri*ti would fall together with its lower one. But, with all due deference to the weight of Professor Nöldeke's name, I must confess that it appears to me very hazardous. For, first, the foundations of his theory are very narrow: secondly, one of his own facts is not quite in harmony with his assertions. However late we may place Kanishka, he cannot be later than the last quarter of the first century A. D. Kanishka was not a Parthian, and his coins probably were struck in the North of India. Hence it would appear that Iranian word-forms with the softening of *th* to *h* were known in India towards the end of the first century. Moreover, the word Pahlava occurs in the Girnâr inscription of Rudradâman[4], which was incised shortly before the year 72 of the era of the Western Kshatrapas. This era, as has been long ago conjectured, and is now incontestably proved by Mr. Fleet's important discoveries, is

[1] Weber, History of Indian Literature, pp. 187-8, note 201[a].

[2] Olshausen, Parthava und Pahlav, Mâda und Mâh (Monatsberichte der Berliner Akademie, 1877), and Nöldeke, Journal of the German Oriental Society, vol. xxxi, p. 557.

[3] Sallet, Die Nachfalger Alexanders des Gr. p. 197.

[4] Ind. Ant. vol. vii, p. 261. Rudradâman's lieutenant at Girnâr was the Pahlava Kulaipa (Khoraib?), son of Suvi*s*âkha.

the so-called Vikramasa*m*vat or, more correctly, the Sa*m*vat of the Mâlave*s*as, the lords of Mâlava, which began in 57 B.C. Rudradâman's inscription consequently dates from the year 21–22 A.D., and it is thus certain that the word Pahlava was used in India at the beginning of the first century A.D. These circumstances make it impossible to accept Professor Nöldeke's inferences from the occurrence of the softened Iranian forms. But the mere mention of the Pahlavas would show that Manu's verse cannot have been composed before the beginning of the first century B.C. The Parthian dynasty of the Arsacides was founded in the middle of the third century B.C., and its sixth ruler, Mithradates I, according to some classical authors, invaded India about the middle of the second century [1]. Coins of an Arsaces Theos and of an Arsaces Dikaios, who uses also the Prakrit language and the North-Indian alphabet, have been found in the Panjâb, and belong to the same or a little later times [2]. As the Brâhmans are ever ready to give foreign nations, with which they come into contact, a place in their ethnological system, it is quite possible that about the beginning of the first century B.C. an Indian origin might have been invented for the Pahlavas. But even this reduction of the remoter limit of the Manu-sm*ri*ti is, in my opinion, not quite safe. For though the evidence for the genuineness of Manu X, 43–44 is as complete as possible, and though the varia lectio for Pahlava, which Govinda offers, probably deserves no credit [3], there is yet a circumstance which raises a suspicion against the latter reading. Parallel passages, closely resembling Manu's two verses, are found in the Mahâbhârata XIII, 33, 21–23[a] and XIII, 35, 17–18, where the names of the degraded Kshatriya races are likewise enumerated, and the cause of their degradation is stated

[1] Lassen, Indische Alterthumskunde, II[2], 334.

[2] Sallet, Die Nachfalger Alexanders des Gr. pp. 51, 156-157.

[3] The commentators and MSS. all give the two verses. If some MSS. of Medhâtithi read Pahnava for Pahlava, that is a clerical mistake caused by the similarity of the subscribed Devanâgarî la and na. Govinda's var. lect. Pallava is improbable, because the other races mentioned in the second line of verse 44 all belong to the North of India, while the Pallavas are, as far as we know, confined to the South.

in exactly the same or similar words. Both passages name the Yavanas, and one also the *S*akas. But neither mentions the Pahlavas. Hence it becomes doubtful if the original version of these *S*lokas really did contain the latter name. It is further not impossible that its insertion is not due to the first remodeller of the Mânava Dharma-sûtra, but has crept in later accidentally, in the place of some other name. The Indian Pa*nd*its are not strong in ethnology and history, and habitually careless with respect to the names of peoples and countries, which they frequently alter, or substitute in their works one for the other. I have, therefore, not the courage to reduce the terminus a quo by more than a hundred years on the strength of this single word, which occurs in a verse that evidently has had originally a different form. I think it safer to rely more on the mention of the Yavanas, Kâmbo*g*as, and *S*akas, and to fix the remoter limit of the work about the beginning of the second century A. D., or somewhat earlier.

This estimate of the age of the Bh*ri*gu Sa*m*hitâ, according to which it certainly existed in the second century A. D., and seems to have been composed between that date and the second century B. C., agrees very closely with the views of Professor Cowell [1] and Mr. Talboys Wheeler [2]. It differs considerably from that lately expressed by Professor Max Müller, who considers our Manu to be later than the fourth century [3], apparently because a passage quoted from V*ri*ddha Manu, which he takes to be a predecessor of our Sa*m*hitâ, mentions the twelve signs of the zodiac. I do not think that it has been proved that every work which enumerates the râ*s*is must be later than the period when Ptolemy's astronomy and astrology were introduced into India. But irrespective of this objection, Professor Max Müller's opinion seems to me untenable, because, according to Professor Jolly's and my own researches [4], the V*ri*ddha or B*ri*hat Manu, quoted in the digests and commentaries, is not earlier, but later than Bh*ri*gu's Sa*m*hitâ. Whatever may be thought

[1] Elphinstone, History of India, p. 249 (edition of 1874).
[2] History of India, vol. ii, p. 422.
[3] India, what can it teach us? p. 366.
[4] See above, p. xcvii.

of the details of my inferences and conclusions, I believe that the rudimentary state of the legal theories in our Sa*m*hitâ, as compared with Yâg*ñ*avalkya and Nârada (fourth or fifth century A. D.), the fact that the B*ri*haspati-sm*ri*ti of the sixth or seventh century A. D. was a Vârttika on our text, and the assertion of Medhâtithi, that he knew in the ninth century commentaries belonging to a remote antiquity, force us to place it considerably before the term mentioned by Professor Max Müller.

III.

It now remains to give an account of the materials on which my translation is based, and of the manner in which they have been used. Among Sanskrit works the commentaries of Medhâtithi, Govindarâ*g*a, Sarva*gñ*a-Nârâya*n*a, Kullûkabha*tt*a, Râghavânanda, and Nandanâ*k*ârya, as well as an anonymous *T*ippa*n*a, contained in a Ka*s*mîr MS. of the Manu-sa*m*hitâ, are the sources on which I have chiefly relied. Among the earlier translations, Sir William Jones' famous versio princeps and Professor J. Jolly's annotated German translation[1] of chapter VIII and chapter IX, 1–102 have been carefully used. Occasionally Mr. Loiscleur Deslongchamps' well-known edition of the text, the English translation of chapters I–III, 33 by Târâ*k*and *K*akravartî (*K*uckerbutty)[2], and the Mârâ*th*î translation of *G*anârdan Vâsudev Gur*g*ar[3] have been consulted. Sir G. C. Haughton's edition and various Indian reprints of the text have been left aside, because they mostly repeat Kullûka's readings or give variae lectiones for which no sufficient authority is shown.

Among the Sanskrit commentaries on the Manu-sm*ri*ti the oldest extant is the voluminous Manubhâshya of Bha*tt*a

[1] Published in the Zeitschrift für vergleichende Rechtswissenschaft, vol. iii.

[2] I have used the copy of the India Office Library, 19–27, 17. The name of the author is given by Professor Goldstücker, On the Deficiencies, &c., p. 5, note.

[3] Published with the text of Manu, at the Nir*n*ayasâgar Press, Bombay, 1877.

Medhâtithi, the son of Bha*tt*a Vîrasvâmin. As its title, bhâshya, indicates, it is not a gloss which paraphrases every word of the text. Its aim is to show the general sense of Manu's dicta, to elucidate all really difficult passages, and to settle all doubtful points by a full discussion of the various possible interpretations, and of the opinions advanced by others. In carrying out this plan Medhâtithi displays a great amount of learning and not inconsiderable ability. He carefully uses a number of more ancient commentaries on Manu, and shows a full acquaintance with the *S*âstras requisite for the successful explanation of his text, with Vedic literature, grammar, Mîmâ*m*sâ, the Dharma-sûtras[1] and other Sm*ri*tis, Vedânta, and the Mahâbhârata. At the same time he avoids the common fault of Sanskrit commentators,—an undue copiousness in quotations which bear only remotely on the subject under consideration. Moreover, he frequently enhances the value of his explanations by illustrating Manu's rules by instances taken from every-day life, a point which most Hindu writers on law and on kindred subjects entirely neglect. Finally, he frequently takes up a much more independent position towards his author than the other commentators dare to assume. Thus he does not shrink from declaring that many verses are arthavâdas, without legal force, and that many single words have been inserted merely v*ri*ttapûra*n*ârtham, 'in order to make up the verse.' His chief weakness, on the other hand, which is not unfrequently observable, and which has drawn on him Kullûka's stricture[2] that he brings forward 'both valuable and valueless' remarks, consists in a disinclination to decide between conflicting interpretations and in his sometimes placing side

[1] Medhâtithi quotes the Dharma-sûtras in general, and Gautama, Baudhâyana, Âpastamba, and Vasish*th*a, as well as some other lost works, in particular. Among the lost Dharma-sûtras which he used, is a Kâtyâyanîya-sûtra, quoted on Manu VIII, 215, which seems to have treated the civil law in detail, and probably is the original of the metrical Kâtyâyana-sm*ri*ti, from which the digests give so numerous extracts.

[2] See the concluding verses of Kullûka's commentary. Sir W. Jones' statement that Medhâtithi's work is reckoned 'prolix and unequal' (Preface to the Translation, p. xvii, St. Grady) is probably based on this remark of Kullûka.

by side, as equally admissible, widely divergent opinions. This vacillation is perhaps justified in a restricted number of passages, where the text is really ambiguous or very obscure. But more commonly it seems to be due solely to an excessive veneration for the views of his predecessors [1], whose commentaries, in part at least, possessed a high antiquity and a great reputation, or whom he had personal reasons to respect. On several occasions he mentions certain explanations as those of the Pûrvas or *K*ira*m*tanas, i. e. of the ancient commentators. Thus he remarks on Manu IV, 223, 'But the exposition given above is the view of the Ancients; hence it has also been given by us [2].' In another case, when explaining Manu IX, 141 and 147, he notes that his interpretation is that of upâdhyâya, i. e. of his own teacher from whom he learnt the Manu-sa*m*hitâ. Disagreeable as this want of decision may be to those who look to a commentary for a concise and authoritative explanation of its text, yet it is not without advantages. His copiousness in quoting the opinions of his predecessors makes his work extremely important for the student of the history of the Manu-sm*ri*ti and of the Hindu law. The Bhâshya clearly proves that Manu's text had been made for centuries an object of deep research, and that many of its verses had given rise to widely different interpretations. It shows, further, that a good many various readings existed. Finally, a comparison of the later still extant commentaries leaves no doubt that these in general are based on the Manubhâshya, and that even their divergent opinions and readings are frequently derived from the earlier work. Under these circumstances the question of

[1] Though the opinions of 'others' are mentioned very frequently, and though sometimes those of three or four predecessors are contrasted, Medhâtithi gives only once the name of an earlier commentator, Manu IX, 253, अथ यावती काचित्फलश्रुतिः सा सर्वार्थवाद इति कावर (?) [v. l. कार (?)] विष्णुस्वामी । यदत्र तत्त्वं तद्दर्शितमधस्तात् ॥ The name seems to be Vish*n*usvâmin. But it is uncertain what the corrupt word, preceding it, may hide.

[2] यत्तु प्राग्व्याख्यातं तत्पूर्वेषां दर्शनमित्यस्माभिरपि वर्णितम् ॥ Compare also the remark on Manu V, 128, तत्र चिरंतनैर्व्याख्यातम् ॥

Medhâtithi's date acquires great importance. It is a matter of regret that in this, as in so many other cases, we do not possess any trustworthy historical information, but have to depend on such circumstantial evidence as can be collected from Medhâtithi's own quotations and from the quotations made by other authors from the Bhâshya. If we begin with the latter, the lower limit for the composition of Medhâtithi's work is fixed by Vi*g*ñânes*v*ara's reference to his explanation of Manu IX, 118[1]. Vi*g*ñânes*v*ara wrote his commentary on Yâ*g*ñavalkya in the reign of the *K*âlukya king, Vikramâditya VI, who ruled at Kalyâ*n*a from *S*akasa*m*vat 997–1048, or 1073–1126-7 A.D.[2] The manner in which Vi*g*ñânes*v*ara's reference is made, shows that in his times the Bhâshya possessed an established reputation. Hence it may be inferred that it was then not of recent date. To the same conclusion points also a passage in Kullûka's commentary on Manu VIII, 184[3], where, in a remark on the arrangement of verses 181–184, Medhâtithi's name is placed before that of Bho*g*arâ*g*a. As in enumerating their predecessors the commentators usually adhere to the natural order, and place the oldest name first, it is very probable that Kullûka means to indicate that Medhâtithi preceded Bho*g*arâ*g*a. If, as again is most likely, the latter is identical with the royal polyhistor who reigned at Dhârâ during the first half of the eleventh century A. D., it follows that Medhâtithi cannot have written later than in the tenth century. With respect to the remoter limit for the composition of the Bhâshya, I have formerly stated[4] that Medhâtithi quotes Kumârila and *S*añkarâ*k*ârya, the great authorities on Mîmâ*m*sâ and Vedânta. The former is mentioned by name in the remarks on Manu I, 3, and by his usual title Bha*tt*apâdâ*h*,

[1] Colebrooke, Mit. I, 7, 13.

[2] See Journ. Bo. Br. Roy. As. Soc. vol. ix, pp. 134–138, and West and Bühler, Digest of Hindu Law, pp. 15–17, third edition.

[3] यो निक्षेपमित्यादिश्लोकचतुष्टयस्य चेदृश एव पाठक्रमो मेधातिथिभोजराजादिभिर्निश्चितः ॥ See also Jolly, Tagore Lectures, p. 8.

[4] West and Bühler, Digest, p. v, first edition.

'the venerable Bha*tt*a,' in the commentary on Manu II, 18[1]. As regards *S*aṅkarâ*k*ârya, I find that Medhâtithi's acquaintance with his writings is by no means as certain as I formerly thought. For in the passage where my own copy, a transcript of a Pu*n*a MS., makes Medhâtithi quote the *S*ârîrakabhâshya, the older and better MSS. of the India Office read *S*ârîraka, which probably implies a reference to the *S*ârîraka-sûtras[2]. Under these circumstances it is no longer possible to assert that the Bhâshya is later than the works of the great Vedântist, who wrote in the beginning of the ninth century A. D. We have now only the quotations from Kumârila to fall back upon, whose date is much less certain. We know that Kumârila preceded *S*aṅkarâ*k*ârya[3], but the length of time which lies between them has hitherto not been exactly ascertained. Mr. Colebrooke, Dr. Burnell, and Professor Max Müller believe, for various reasons, that he lived in the seventh century or not later than 700 A.D.[4] Though, as far as his quotations go, Medhâtithi might have written earlier than the ninth century A. D., I still feel inclined to adhere to my former opinion. For a closer examination of the Bhâshya has revealed some other points which speak in favour of my view. Medhâtithi repeatedly quotes the metrical law-books of Yâg*ñ*avalkya, Nârada, and Parâ*s*ara, as well as the version of the Kâ*th*aka Dharma-sûtra, known as the Vish*n*u-sm*ri*ti, and considers all as canonical. None of these works has, however, a claim to a high antiquity; and the Vish*n*u-sm*ri*ti, in particular, which mentions the Greek name of a week-day, cannot be older than the fifth or sixth century A.D.

---

[1] I, 5, इति कुमारिलपक्षः ॥ II, 18, उक्तं च भट्टपादैः। विरुद्धा च विगीता च दृष्टार्था दृष्टकारणे [णा?]। स्मृतिर्न श्रुतिमूला द्यास्या [स्याद्या] चैषा [या] संभवश्रुतिः ॥

[2] Manu XII, 19, ननु च धर्माधर्मयोरिच्छां प्रति नियन्त्रित्वे [त्व] ऐश्वर्यं हीयते। तथा दर्शितं शारीरके [v. l. of my MS. शारीरकभाष्ये] यथेह राजा सेवानुरूपं ददाति न च तस्येश्वरत्वमपैति। यतो महापरमात्मानौ पश्यत इति व्यपदिश्यते ॥

[3] See Professor Cowell's note to Colebrooke's Essays, I, p. 323.

[4] See Professor Max Müller, India, what can it teach us? p. 308, note.

If Medhâtithi, nevertheless, considers it to be an inspired work, revealed by the god Vish*n*u, it is only reasonable to assume that a very considerable interval lies between the date of its composition and his own times. This is so much more probable, as the Vish*n*u-sm*ri*ti was probably written in Ka*s*mîr, which, as will be shown presently, was also Medhâtithi's home. A more definite result with respect to Medhâtithi's date is, I fear, at present not obtainable. His references to other works, such as a Vâkyapradîpa by one—rimi*s*ra[1], an Abhidhânakosha[2], Piṅgala's treatise on metrics[3], a work of the ancient writer on Sâ*m*khya, Vindhyavâsin, and so forth, are, in the present state of our knowledge of the history of Sanskrit literature, not particularly useful. The Bhâshya furnishes, however, two interesting details regarding Medhâtithi's personal history. First, we hear that he wrote a metrical treatise on the sacred law, called Sm*ri*tiviveka. Secondly, it appears that the valley of Kasmîr, which has produced so many Indian men of letters, was his native country. The Sm*ri*tiviveka is mentioned repeatedly in the Bhâshya as a comprehensive work in which difficult legal questions were fully discussed[4]. As regards the other point, there is no direct statement in the Bhâshya which mentions Medhâtithi's birthplace. But the author refers so frequently to Ka*s*mîr, its laws, its Vedic *S*âkhâ, and even to its language, that the inference that it was his native country becomes unavoidable. Thus in explaining the word svarâsh*t*re, 'in his own kingdom' (Manu VII, 32), and the term *g*anapada*h*, 'country or province' (Manu VIII, 41), he introduces the

[1] Manu XII, 118, प्रमाणान्तरमप्येकत्वप्रतिपादनपरत्वादेव ग्राह्यिणः प्रत्यग्वास्य—रिमिश्रैः कृत एव क्लेशः। उक्तं च वाक्यप्रदीपे। न तदस्ति च तत्राम्नीत्यादि॥ Professor Kielhorn informs me that the verse does not occur in Hari's Vâkyapadîya, which sometimes is called Vâkyapradîpa.

[2] Manu IX, 185–6; the words quoted are, दायाद्यं धनमिष्यते॥

[3] Manu IX, 42, यथोक्तं पिङ्गलेन। छन्दासिद्धिं [द्धं] गायेति॥ Piṅgala VIII, 1; see Weber, Indische Studien, VIII, 147.

[4] See e.g. comm. on II, 6, निपुणतश्चैव तन्निर्णीतमस्माभिः स्मृतिविवेके। and ibidem, तदेतद्विशतोस्माभिरुक्तम्। विस्तरस्तु स्मृतिविवेके द्रष्टव्यः॥

name of Kasmîr as an illustration [1]. Again, in giving examples of royal monopolies in the remarks on Manu VIII, 399, he states correctly that the sale of saffron is a prerogative of the king of Kasmîr. Further, he repeatedly refers to the Kâthaka Sâkhâ of the Black Yagur-veda, which for a long time has been confined to Kasmîr alone; and, when trying to prove in the notes on Manu I, 58, that the Mânava Dharmasâstra may be called Manu's, though it was first taught by Hiranyagarbha, he adduces as an analogous instance the Kâthaka, which, though studied and taught by many others, is named after Katha. Such an illustration would hardly occur to anybody but a student of the Kâthaka Sâkhâ. Still more decisive, finally, is his remark in the commentary on Manu IV, 59, where he says that the rainbow is called in Kasmîr vinakhâyâ [2].

As regards the history of the text of Medhâtithi's commentary, Mr. Colebrooke states in the preface to the Digest, p. xv (Madras edition), that 'the Bhâshya' having been partly lost, has been completed by other hands at the court of Madanapâla, a prince of Dîgh. This assertion probably rests on the authority of a stanza in the Sârdûla-vikrîdita measure, found in a number of copies at the end of a good many chapters, which says that 'the Bhâshya being mutilated, prince Madanapâla, the son of Sahârana, brought a MS. from another country and made a gîrnoddhâra, or restoration of the ruin, by causing copies to be taken from that [3].' Considering the wording of the verse,

[1] VII, 22, पितृपितामहादिक्रमागतो देशो व्यपदेशहेतुः। काश्मीरकस्य कश्मीराः पंचालानां पंचालाः॥ VIII, 41, कुरुकाशिकाश्मीरादिदेशनियमावधिर्जनपदः॥

[2] इन्द्रायुधं शरधनुर्विनच्छायेति या कश्मीरेषु कथ्यते॥ I must note that Professor Jolly, Tagore Lectures, p. 6, offers a different opinion, and takes Medhâtithi to be a southerner. His reasons—the termination svâmin in the name of Medhâtithi's father's name, Vîrasvâmin, and the attention paid by the ancient southern authors to the Bhâshya—do not seem to me sufficiently strong. For, as the Kasmirian name Kshîrasvâmin and scores of Svâmins in the northern inscriptions show, the title was, at least, formerly not confined to the south. Further, the intercourse between Kasmîr and southern India in the time of Bilhana and of Harshadeva accounts for the introduction of a Kasmîrian work to the notice of the southern Pandits.

[3] Professor Jolly states, Tagore Lectures, p. 7, that he has found the verse,

I can only agree with Professor Jolly (loc. cit.) that Madanapâla did not cause portions of the Bhâshya to be recomposed, but merely completed the defective MS. of his library from a copy purchased in some other part of India. The place where this *g*îr*n*oddhâra was made, was Kâsh*th*â, near Delhi. For as the verse says that Madana was the son of Sahâra*n*a, it is not doubtful that this person is identical with Madana or Madanapâla, the patron of Vi*s*ve*s*varabha*tt*a, who wrote the Subodhinî on the Mitâksharâ and the Prayoga- or Madanapâri*g*âta. Vi*s*ve*s*vara gives, in the introduction to the latter work, a portion of his patron's genealogy[1], and states that Madana belonged to the family of the chiefs of Kâsh*th*â, and was the second son of one Sâdhâra*n*a. It is easy to see that in the verse quoted above the Prakritic form Sahâra*n*a has been used instead of Sâdhâra*n*a for metrical reasons. This Madana has been identified by Mr. Colebrooke with the homonymous author of the Madanavinoda, which is dated in Vikramasa*m*vat 1431 or 1375 A.D., and Mr. Sarvâdhikâri[2] confirms this identification, by telling us that the Madanavinoda contains the same pedigree of Madana as the Pâri*g*âta. Hence 'the restoration' of the Bhâshya must have occurred about five hundred years ago.

---

more or less correctly given, in seven old MSS. from various parts of India. In my opinion it should be read as follows: मान्या कापि मनुस्मृतिस्तदुचिता व्याख्या मेधातिथेः सा लुप्तैव विधिवशात्क्वचिदपि प्राप्यानयत्पुस्तकम्। क्षोणीन्द्रो मदनः सहारणसुतो देशान्तरादाहृतं जीर्णोद्धारमचीकरत्तत इतस्तत्पुस्तकैर्लेखितैः ॥ I differ from Professor Jolly at the end of the second pâda, where he reads with a Benares MS. प्राप्यं न यत्पुस्तकम्, and at the end of the third pâda, where he changes the reading of the MSS. आहृते or आहृतो to आहृतैः.

[1] Aufrecht, Cat. Sansk. MSS. of the Bodleian Library, p. 274.

[2] Tagore Lectures of 1880, p. 389. Mr. Sarvâdhikâri wishes to read the date brahma (1) *g*agat (3) yuga (4) indu (1), (Mâgha sudi 6, Monday,) as 1231. He thinks that yuga may also denote the figure 2, and that the reading Vikramasa*m*vat 1231 is necessary, because the Pâri*g*âta is quoted by *Kande*s*vara*, who wrote in the thirteenth century. He is, however, mistaken, as the astronomical calculation shows that Mâgha sudi 6 of Vikramasa*m*vat 1431 did fall on a Monday (Jan. 8, 1375), while the same day in V.S. 1231 was a Thursday. The Pâri*g*âta quoted by *Kande*s*vara* must, therefore, be some other work on law. The title is a not uncommon one.

It would, however, seem that it either was not thorough, or that its effects were not lasting. For all the copies of Medhâtithi's commentary which I have seen or used are throughout more or less corrupt, and in some parts, especially in chapters VIII and IX, as well as at the end of chapter XII, in a desperate condition. The latter portion is in great confusion, some pieces being missing, and others being given twice over. In chapters VIII and IX many verses are left out, though it is evident from cross-references, or from remarks made by Kullûka, that they must have been explained by Medhâtithi. In the parts of the commentary still extant, the corruptions are often very bad, and the sense frequently doubtful or only to be made out conjecturally. Under these circumstances I believe that it would be unwise to attach too much weight to the omission of verses with respect to which the Bhâshya stands alone. Before we can attempt to come to a decision regarding the exact state of the Manu-sm*ri*ti in Medhâtithi's times, we require, I think, better MSS. of his work. The officers in charge of the search for Sanskrit MSS. in India could render a very great service to the history of the Indian law, if they would direct their efforts to the acquisition of really good MSS. of the Bhâshya, and if thus a competent scholar were enabled to publish a trustworthy edition. The MSS. used for the notes to my translation are, my own apograph of chapters I–VI and X–XII, made in 1864 from a Pu*n*a MS., and the copies of the India Office Library, Nos. 934–935, 1407–1409, 1414, 1551–1552. All of them go back to one codex archetypus, derived from Madana's restored copy, and the best is that contained in the Indian Office Library, Nos. 1551–1552, which is dated Sa*m*vat 1648, mârgas*i*rsha sudi 3, somavâsare, or Monday, November 18, 1591 A.D.[1]

Next, after the Manubhâshya, but probably at a considerable interval, follows the Manu*t*îkâ of Govindarâ*g*a,

[1] For this and some other calculations of dates I have to thank Dr. Schram, Privat-Docent of astronomical chronology in the University of Vienna.

the son of Bha*tt*a Mâdhava. The exact date of this author is likewise not ascertainable. He is extremely reticent about himself and his predecessors, and quotes, with the exception of Sm*ri*tis, not a single work on law except his own Sm*ri*ti-ma*ñg*arî or Sm*ri*ti-ma*ñg*arîpa*ñg*ikâ, a compilation of rules on penances[1], derived from various Dharma*s*âstras. The remoter limit of his age can, however, be deduced from Kullûka's remarks on Manu VIII, 184, whence it appears that Govindarâ*g*a was later than Bho*g*a of Dhârâ (first half of the eleventh century). The lower limit is fixed by the mention of his name in *G*îmûtavâhana's Dâyabhâga[2] and in *S*ûlapâ*n*i's work on penances[3]. I can only agree with Professor Jolly, who thinks that he lived in the twelfth or thirteenth century[4]. The termination of Govindarâ*g*a's name has induced several scholars (see Jolly, loc. cit.) to assume that he was a prince, and it has been proposed to identify him with a Govinda*k*andra of Benares or with a homonymous king of Kâno*g*. But the son of a Bha*tt*a can only be a Brâhma*n*a, and it must not be forgotten that Govindarâ*g*a is the equivalent of Govindrâo, a name very common among the Marâ*th*â Brâhma*n*as.

The Manu*t*ikâ is a very concise, but by no means obscure[5]

---

[1] Commentary on Manu III, 247 and 248; see also Kullûka on Manu IV, 212. A copy of this work, written at Vasurâvî in Sa*m*vat 1467, â*s*vina badi -- *s*anau, during the reign of Mahârâ*n*a Udayasi*m*ha, is preserved in the India Office Library, No. 1736. Colebrooke thought that the date had to be referred to the Vikrama era, and the editors of the series of facsimiles issued by the Palaeographical Society, No. III, have followed him. But it is not doubtful that the prince mentioned in the colophon is Mahârâ*n*a Udayasi*m*ha of Mevâ*d*, who ascended the throne in 1541 A. D. Hence the date of the MS. refers to the *S*aka era, and corresponds to 1545 A. D. The Sm*ri*ti-ma*ñg*arî contains no quotations from other law-books than Sm*ri*tis. The name of Govindarâ*g*a's father, Bha*tt*a Mâdhava, occurs frequently in the colophons of the several sections.

[2] Colebrooke, Dây. XI, 2, 31, where Govinda's name is also placed after Bho*g*arâ*g*a's.

[3] Aufrecht, Cat. Sansk. MSS. of the Bodleian Library, p. 283a.

[4] Jolly, Tagore Lectures, p. 9.

[5] 'Obscure' is the epithet applied to it by Sir W. Jones, Pref. to the transl. of Manu, p. xvii. (St. Grady). This estimate is probably derived from Kullûka's utterance in the concluding verses of his commentary, स्तोकं वस्तु निगूढमल्पवचनाद्गोवि-न्दराजो जगौ. It is only what might be expected from a plagiary who bitterly hated the man whose work he wished to supersede.

verbal paraphrase of Manu's text. In the main it is an abstract of Medhâtithi's Bhâshya from which Govinda has appropriated whatever seemed to him most valuable. He has discarded the greater number of his predecessor's optional explanations, as well as his lengthy controversial disquisitions on difficult points of law, while he has greatly condensed others. He has added explanations of those words on which Medhâtithi does not comment, and he sometimes also puts forward opinions, not traceable in the earlier work, which may be either his own or derived from sources inaccessible to us. But in such cases he is occasionally unlucky, and arrives at results which his successor Kullûka ridicules, not without reason. Thus in his remarks on Manu III, 50, where the text says that a man who restricts conjugal intercourse to a minimum, is equal in chastity to a student 'in whichever order he may live,' Govinda takes the last words in too literal a sense and enunciates the, for a Hindu, monstrous doctrine that Manu intends to permit ascetics, whose children have all died, to return to conjugal life and to repair the loss which they have suffered. Some other strange errors have been pointed out by Professor Jolly in his Tagore Lectures, p. 9, note 1. These occasional eccentricities do not, however, seriously diminish the usefulness of the Manu*t*ikâ. It remains not only the earliest, but the best complete explanation of Manu's text. It frequently assists the student to find his way through the tangled forest of the Bhâshya, and it contains many valuable interpretations of words left unexplained by Medhâtithi. The MS. used for the notes is the unique copy, acquired by myself for the Government of Bombay (Deccan College Library, Coll. of 1879–1880, No. 239). It is in a very fair condition, and contains the whole text and the commentary, excepting that on IX, 71–336. It was written at Stambhatîrtha or Cambay, probably about 250–300 years ago.

The chronological position of the next commentary on our list, Sarvag*ñ*a-Nârâya*n*a's Manvarthaviv*ri*ti or Manvarthanibandha, is fixed, as Professor Jolly has first pointed out, by a passage in the introduction to Râghavânanda's commentary[1]. The latter author says there that 'he has taken cognisance of (the opinions) approved by Kullûka and Nârâyana, and of those entertained in their hearts by Govinda and Medhâtithi.' As it is evident that in the second group the later author has been placed first, the assumption that the same order has been observed with respect to the first pair, and that Râghavânanda, applying the principle of uttarottaragarîyastva, i. e. naming the more important persons later, intends the whole series to be read backwards[2], is not unreasonable. In its favour speaks also the fact that Nârâyana quotes Govindarâga on Manu VIII, 123. In order to fix the date when Nârâyana wrote, we have to rely chiefly on some quotations. His opinions on law are first quoted by Kamalâkara, who wrote in the beginning of the seventeenth century[3]. But a Nâmanidhâna by Nârâyana Sarvagña is mentioned by Râyamukuta in his commentary on the Amarakosha, which was composed in 1431 A.D.[4] The only MS. of the Manvarthavivriti[5] hitherto found (Deccan College Collection of 1879–1880, No. 238) bears at the end of Adhyâya VIII, the date Sam. 1544 kaitra badi 9 ravau, which corresponds to Sunday, March 27, 1497 A.D. Hence it follows that Nârâyana cannot have written later than in the last half of the fourteenth century. Possibly he may be somewhat older.

The Manvarthavivriti is not a running commentary which explains every word of the text. It confines itself to the elucidation of selected difficult passages and words. It was written with the avowed intention of undoing the work of the author's predecessors. At the end of chapters

[1] Jolly, Tagore Lectures, p. 11; the passage has been printed in Dr. Burnell's Tanjore Catalogue, p. 126.

[2] This manner of enumerating a series of persons or of arguments is also found occasionally in older Sanskrit works; see e.g. Vasishtha XIII, 58.

[3] Aufrecht, Catalogue Sansk. MSS. Bodl. Libr. p. 279.

[4] See Professor Aufrecht's Analysis in the Journal of the German Oriental Society, vol. xxviii, p. 114.

[5] This MS., which has been used for the notes to the translation, is a very fair copy, containing the commentary alone. Fols. 1–8 have been half eaten by rats. Fols. 192–3 have been lost.

I, VI, and VIII we find a verse, apparently belonging to Nârâya*n*a, which says, 'This commentary of the Manu-sm*ri*ti, composed by the illustrious Nârâya*n*a Sarva*gñ*a, thrusts far away the exposition given in contemptible compilations [1].' Again, at the end of chapter IV we read, 'Direct your attention to the good words of Nârâya*n*a Sarva*gñ*a, which propound the real meaning of Manu and repel the exposition given in contemptible compilations [2].' As might be expected from these utterances, Nârâya*n*a shows a great anxiety to find explanations differing from those of Medhâtithi and Govinda. Sometimes he attains this aim by returning to views which Medhâtithi mentions and rejects; but more frequently his explanations have been either taken from commentaries inaccessible to us, or represent opinions formed by him independently. All his peculiar interpretations deserve careful attention. In many cases they are decidedly preferable to those of the other commentators, and have therefore been not rarely followed in the translation. Nârâya*n*a seems to have been not only deeply versed in the sacred law, but to have possessed also a knowledge of various other *S*âstras. As we learn from his commentary on Manu V, 56, 80, 104, XI, 72, he also wrote two other works on Dharma, a Kâmadhenudîpikâ and a *S*uddhidîpikâ. His Kosha has been mentioned above. Commentaries of his on parts of the Mahâbhârata, e.g. on the Udyogaparvan, on the Svargâroha*n*aparvan [3], and on the Sanatsu*g*âtîya, are still extant [4].

---

[1] श्रीनारायणसर्वज्ञकृता वृत्तिः मनुस्मृतेः । कुनिबन्धकृतव्याख्यामियं दूरे निरस्यति ॥ Thus at the end of chapter I; in the other two passages the MS. has the faulty form निरस्यते.

[2] व्याहृतमनुतात्पर्यप्रतिहतकुनिबन्धदर्शितव्याख्याम् । नारायणस्य सूक्तिं सर्वज्ञस्यानुसंधत्त ॥ Three other boastful verses occur at the end, 1. of chapter III, श्रीनारायणसर्वज्ञवृत्तिसंदर्शितानयाः । मनुस्मृतिगिराचार्य [र] मधिगच्छत सूरयः ॥ 2. of chapter V, श्रीनारायणसर्वज्ञनिर्मितां वीक्ष्य भारतीम् । धर्मस्य निर्णयं ब्रूत पदवाक्यसुनिश्चितम् ॥ 3. of chapter IX, श्रीनारायणसर्वज्ञोक्तं मन्वर्थनिबन्धनम् । वीक्ष्य धर्मं त्वरा ब्रूत वे[वि]त्य सर्वं कृते [ता] कृतम् ॥

[3] Weber, Berlin Catalogue, Nos. 304, 399: Aufrecht, Catalogue, Bodl. Libr. p. 2.

[4] Telang, Sacred Books of the East, vol. viii, p. 148.

The fourth work on our list, the well-known Manvarthamuktâvali of Kullûkabha*tt*a, the son of Divâkarabha*tt*a, was considered until lately the most trustworthy guide for the exposition of Manu. In the introductory verses to his commentary Kullûka informs us that he was a Gau*d*a or Bengali by birth, his father residing in Nandana in Varendrî[1], and that he wrote his work at Benares with the assistance of other Pa*nd*its. As regards his times, we only know that Nârâya*n*a Sarva*g*ña and another commentator, Dhara*n*îdhara[2], stood between him and Govindarâ*g*a, and that Raghunandana, who wrote in the beginning of the sixteenth century, is the earliest author who quotes him[3]. He, therefore, lived probably in the fifteenth century.

The Manvarthamuktâvali is, as Professor Jolly has been the first to recognise[4], little more than an improved edition of Govindarâ*g*a's Manu*t*îkâ. In spite of the asperity with which Kullûka repeatedly inveighs against his predecessor, he has not disdained to copy very large portions of the Manu*t*îkâ, sometimes verbatim and sometimes in very insufficient extracts, where the omissions make the meaning obscure. Moreover, even where the wording of the two commentaries differs, the influence of Govinda is distinctly visible. Under these circumstances the value of the Muktâvali is, since the recovery of the Manu*t*îkâ, not very great, though it is undeniable that in certain cases Kullûka's independent remarks or criticisms of the earlier works are useful. Its great fame in India and its frequent occurrence in the libraries of native lawyers in all parts of the Peninsula may be explained by the fact that it was written and approved at Benares, which town has, since remote times, been a most important literary centre and the chief source from which the Pa*nd*its draw their supplies of books. For the notes I

[1] In the colophon of chapter XII, the place is called Vârendranandana. The district of Varendra lies between Dinâjpur and the Ganges, Cunningham, Arch. Reports, XV, Plate 1, and p. 40.

[2] See concluding verses at the end of chapter XII.

[3] Aufrecht, loc. cit. p. 292.

[4] Die Juristischen Abschnitte aus dem Gesetzbuche des Manu, p. 3, des Separatabdrucks; Tagore Lectures, p. 10.

have used no MSS. of the Muktâvali; but two editions, *G*îbânand's reprint of the earlier Calcutta edition[1] and the Bombay lithographed edition of *S*akasa*m*vat 1780. The latter is by far the better one, but leaves, like all other editions which I have seen, much to desire from a critical point of view. There are a good many passages in which the text does not agree with the commentary.

On the Manvarthamuktâvali rests the Manvartha*k*andrikâ, written by Râghavânanda Sarasvatî, an ascetic of *S*aṅkarâ*k*ârya's school[2], and a pupil of one Vi*s*ve*s*vara-bhagavatpâda. Though the author asserts, as stated above, that he used four older commentaries, he mostly adheres to Kullûka's opinions. It is only rarely that he prefers Nârâya*n*a's interpretations or recurs to views of Govindarâ*g*a and Medhâtithi, which Kullûka refuted or left unnoticed. His exposition of the philosophical portions of the text is, however, mostly independent, and he interprets them throughout in such a manner as to agree with the Vedânta doctrines of his school. The *K*andrikâ is not a running commentary which paraphrases every word of Manu, but gives mostly, besides a short summary of the general meaning, merely remarks on difficult words and passages. It is probably a modern work, dating from the sixteenth or the beginning of the seventeenth century[3]. I have not met with any quotations from it in other law-books. The oldest known MS. is that brought by Anquetil from Gu*g*arât and deposited in the Bibliothèque Nationale at Paris (Devanâgarî 49, fonds d'Anquetil, No. 16). Its date, Sa*m*vat 1706 varshe kârttika badi 10 somadine, corresponds, according to Dr. Schram's

---

[1] The reason why I used this very incorrect text, was that Professor Jolly kindly lent me his copy in which he has entered the various readings of Medh., Gov., Nâr., Râgh., of the Ka*s*mîr copy and other MSS.

[2] According to H. H. Wilson, Works, I, pp. 202-3 (ed. Rost), the ascetics, bearing the title Sarasvatî, follow the sa*m*pradâya of *S*aṅkarâ*k*ârya. See also Aufrecht, Catalogue Sansk. MSS. Bodl. Libr. p. 227.

[3] Mr. Loiseleur Deslongchamps' attempt (Lois de Manou, p. xvi) to identify Râghavânanda with Raghunandana, the bha*tt*â*k*ârya of the sixteenth century, is an unlucky guess. It seems to me that the author of the *K*andrikâ is identical with the ascetic Râghavânanda, pupil of Advayânanda, pupil of Vi*s*ve*s*vara, who is mentioned as an author on Sâ*m*khya and Vedânta philosophy by Dr. F. E. Hall, Catalogue, pp. 6, 91, &c.

calculation, to Monday, November 29, 1649. Another old MS. of about the same date is mentioned by Dr. Burnell, Tanjore Catalogue, p. 126. For the notes I have used the Paris MS., which was kindly lent to me by the French Government, as far as Manu IX, 187. It contains both the commentary and the text, the former being, however, left out on I, 45–78. For the remaining portion I have consulted a very old, but much damaged copy of the Deccan College Collection of 1882–1883, acquired by Professor Bhâ*nd*ârkar for the Government of Bombay.

The name of the sixth commentary is, according to the MS., the loan of which I owe to the courtesy of Divân Bahâdur Raghunâthrâo of Madras, Manuvyâkhyâna, but according to Dr. Burnell, Tanjore Catalogue, p. 126, Nandinî. Its author calls himself Nandana (Nandanâ*k*ârya according to Dr. Burnell), the son of Lakshma*n*a, a member of the Bhâradvâ*g*a gotra, and the dear friend of the illustrious Vîramalla[1]. In all probability he was a native of Southern India. For his work is, as far as I am aware, known in Southern India alone; its MSS. are met with only in the Madras Presidency, and Professor Jolly (loc. cit., p. 12) has found that many of his peculiar readings agree with those found in Southern MSS. of the Manu-sm*ri*ti. As his name is not quoted in any commentary on Manu or in any work on law, known to me, it would seem that he is either of very modern date or that his opinions were not held in any great esteem. Mr. Raghunâthrâo's MS. is dated *S*akasa*m*vat 1724, Mâgha sudi pratipad, or 1803 A.D. The Manuvyâkhyâna is a very short commentary, which mostly repeats and explains only a few words or phrases of the text. It dismisses many verses which stand in need of elucidation with the curt remark spash*t*a*h*, 'clear,' and

[1] The colophon of chapter XII runs as follows: इति श्रीभारद्वाजगोत्रेण श्रीलक्ष्मणात्मजेन श्रीवीरमल्लप्रियसखेन श्रीनन्दनेन विरचिते मनुव्याख्याने भृगुप्रोक्तायां संहितायां द्वादशोध्यायः ॥ Vîramalla was probably a prince or chief, and the mention of his name will eventually aid to ascertain Nandana's time. A third variety of the latter's name occurs in the Madras edition of Colebrooke's Digest, p. xv, note 6, where the editor speaks of a commentary on Manu, Nandara*g*krit (?) by Nandarâ*g*a.

passes by others without any note. Though no names are ever quoted, most of the explanations have been taken on purely eclectic principles from the earlier commentaries, among which the first four of our list must certainly be reckoned. The favourite among them is the Manvartha-viv*ri*ti. The notes to the translation show a considerable number of cases where 'Nâr. and Nand.' form a separate group, and on important points advocate opinions opposed to those of Medhâtithi, Govinda, and Kullûka. But there are also other passages, concerning which Nandana agrees either with Medhâtithi alone, or with 'others,' quoted by Medhâtithi, with Kullûka or even with Govinda. Finally, he offers in a certain number of cases expositions not traceable elsewhere, some of which, especially those on the philosophical pieces, deserve attention. The text which Nandana follows, differs not inconsiderably from the vulgata. It shows, besides very numerous, more or less important variae lectiones, some omissions, additions, and transpositions of entire verses. Many of Nandana's various readings are derived from Medhâtithi, Nârâya*n*a, and other older commentators, who either themselves follow them or at least mention their existence. As regards those which Nandana alone offers, the majority seem to be either corruptelae or conjectures, and sometimes very unlucky ones[1]. The transpositions, which partly occur in passages regarding the order of which the other commentators agree, appear to have sometimes at least no better authority than guesses made by Nandana. Thus if he places Manu I, 27 after verse 19, and X, 14 after verse 6, and adds in each case that, 'if some read the verses further on, that must be due to an error of the copyists,' I can only see in this remark a

[1] To the first class belongs स्ववासिनीः for सुवासिनीः M. III, 114, the senseless कारणम् for करणम् M. VIII, 154 (not given in the notes), अभ्युक्रम् for अत्यन्तम् IX, 202, and so forth; to the second, दारकर्मण्यमैथुनी for दारकर्मणि मैथुने M. III, 5, परीक्षकान् for परीक्षितान् M. VII, 54, अलक्षितः for अलंधनः M. VIII, 162, नासिकायाः for दाढिकायाः M. VIII, 283 (not given in the notes), यमयोश्चैकगर्भेऽपि for यमयोश्चैव गर्भेषु M. IX, 126, अनन्तयाम् (loc. sing. of अनन्तरी!) for आनन्तर्यात् M. X, 28, and so forth.

confession of his having done violence to the traditional text. The verses which Nandana adds are, I think, all interpolations, some of which perhaps go back to early times, as they occur also in the Southern MSS. and in the Kasmîr copy. With respect to the omissions, Nandana sometimes follows one or several of the other commentators. In other cases he agrees with the Southern MSS. alone, and again in others he stands quite by himself. One of the omissions of the last class, Manu V, 61, is, as has been pointed out in the notes, purely due to an accidental lacuna in the MS. which Nandana used. With respect to numerous other cases it must be noted that the two copies of the Manuvyâkhyâna which European scholars have examined, Mr. Raghunâthrâo's and Dr. Burnell's (chapters VIII–IX, now in the India Office Library), differ very considerably. Thus in chapter VIII, Dr. Burnell's copy omits, according to Professor Jolly's collation [1], verses 8, 11, 14, 74, 81, 103, 227–228, 231, 332, while Mr. Raghunâthrâo's MS. has them all excepting verses 8, 228, and 231, and gives even notes on 11, 14, 81, 103, 227. These differences between the two copies seem to extend also to readings in Manu's text and to explanations. But it is not rarely difficult to give a definite opinion on these points, because Mr. Raghunâthrâo's MS. sometimes gives only the Pratîkas of the verses, and is often so corrupt that the sense can be made out only by means of conjectural emendations.

Under these circumstances it will not be advisable to attach too much weight to variae lectiones, derived from the Manuvyâkhyâna, which are not supported by the authority of other commentaries.

The anonymous *Tippana*, or collection of detached explanatory remarks, in the Kasmîr birch bark MS.[2] is of very small importance. It looks as if it owed its origin to the marginal notes of some learned Pandit, which, later, were copied with the text and placed after the verses to

[1] Compare also Professor Hopkins, Notes on the Nandinî, Proceedings of the American Oriental Society, October, 1883, p. xviii, where, however, only verses 8, 11, 74, 81, and 332 are enumerated as missing.

[2] Deccan College Collection of 1876–1877, No. 355.

which they refer. Professor Jolly [1] has pointed out that in one case it characteristically agrees with Govindarâ*g*a; and other instances, e.g. the remarks on Manu I, 52, may be added. There are also some cases (see e.g. the explanation of *d*imbha, Manu V, 91) where the Ka*s*mîr commentary agrees with curious explanations given by Nandana. The text also agrees occasionally with peculiar readings adopted by Nandana or by Nârâya*n*a and Nandana [2]. But I should consider it hazardous to draw from these instances any conclusions regarding the sources of the *T*ippa*n*a. The Ka*s*mîr MS., which has been very carefully written and corrected, is mutilated at the end, about one-third of each of the last dozen leaves being torn off. The loss falls on Manu XI, 218–XII, 126.

The above remarks on the materials which I had at my disposal show that, in spite of their undeniable importance, they were insufficient for a radical change in the treatment of Manu's text. As the recension, given by Kullûka, was the only one accessible in its entirety and in tolerably trustworthy copies, I could not do anything else than take that for the basis of my translation. Practical reasons, too, especially the consideration that the Indian public has been accustomed to Kullûka's text, and that the numerous references in the translations of Hindu law-books point to the Manu of Kullûka, made the adoption of this principle highly desirable. I have, therefore, retained every verse which Kullûka explains, though the weight of the authorities might be against its genuineness, and I have refrained from receiving into the text any verse which he omits. In cases of the former kind the names of the dissenting commentators have been given in the notes, where also translations of the best accredited and more important additional verses, given by other commentators, will be found [3]. I have, moreover,

[1] Tagore Lectures, p. 11.
[2] See e.g. notes on Manu I, 2; III, 59, 73, 195.
[3] I may add that I have paid no attention to those verses which the medieval Nibandhas on law quote as Manu's, but which are not traceable in the recension approved of by the commentators. These verses are in my opinion all spurious. In most cases we have simply to deal with misquotations caused by the careless-

adhered to Kullûka's order of the verses, except in some cases where he is evidently in the wrong, and the transposition causes no great inconvenience. On the other hand, I have tried to remove the numerous palpable blunders in the readings of the editions, which are mostly due, not to Kullûka himself, but to the editors of his text. The notes show what has been changed, and on whose authority it has been done. I have, finally, added a selection of the more important various readings given in the other commentaries.

With respect to the translation, my proceeding has been somewhat different. Though I should have liked to follow in the text Kullûka's commentary alone, and to give the renderings of the other commentators in the notes, I found that to be impracticable. The bulk of my volume would have become enormous, and in very many passages I should have been compelled to declare the rendering placed in the text to be utterly erroneous. In order to escape these difficulties I have generally, except in very doubtful passages, translated in accordance with that exposition which seemed to me most reasonable, and have placed some of the other particularly noteworthy explanations in the notes. In a certain number of verses where the real meaning of the text is very doubtful, I have not gone beyond a literal rendering of Manu's words, which, like the original, may be interpreted in different ways. In such cases the notes exhibit all the various interpretations found in the commentaries. In a very small number of verses the explanations of the commentators have been set aside altogether for reasons duly stated in the notes. The length of my notes varies very much, according to the interest or difficulty of the subject treated in the text. Thus the summary of the opinions of the commentators on the practically important titles of the Hindu law, Manu IX, 1–219, is as complete as the state of the MSS. allowed me to make it. Almost all the explanations of the difficult philosophical portions of chapters I and XII have likewise

ness of the Nibandhakâras, who are as little to be depended upon for accuracy as Indian writers on other scientific subjects or as the European medieval writers on classical philology. They quoted mostly, if not invariably, from memory.

been given. But the extracts from the commentaries on the easier sections referring to the duties of students, householders, Snâtakas, and so forth, have been made very short, as for the right understanding of the greater part of their verses little more is wanted than the parallel passages of the other ancient Sm*ri*tis. Among the latter, those translated in vols. ii, vii, and xiv of this series have been quoted everywhere. If Nârada has been excluded, the reason is that the new translation, which Professor Jolly will soon publish according to recently discovered materials, would have made the references useless. The quotations from Manu, which occur in the translated Nibandhas on Hindu law, have been collected, for the convenience of practical lawyers, in the Appendix. As regards the relation of my version to those of earlier translators, it will be evident to everybody how much I am indebted to Sir William Jones' great work, which, in spite of the progress made by Sanskrit philology during the last hundred years, still possesses a very high value. I have also to acknowledge my obligation to the German translation of chapter VIII and of vv. 1–102 of chapter IX by Professor Jolly, which is based on the materials used by myself. If no reference has been made to the translation lately published by Drs. Burnell and Hopkins, the reason is that the printing of mine was complete some time before its appearance.

In conclusion, I must express my thanks to several colleagues, especially to Professors Jolly and Kielhorn, for assistance rendered in various ways, as well as to Dr. R. Rost, Chief Librarian at the India Office; to K. M. Chatfield, Esq., Director of Public Instruction, Bombay; to the Director of the Bibliothèque Nationale of France; and to Divân Bahâdur Raghunâth Râo of Mylapur, Madras, for liberal loans of MSS.

LAWS OF MANU.

LAWS OF MANU.

CHAPTER I.

1. THE great sages approached Manu, who was seated with a collected mind, and, having duly worshipped him, spoke as follows:

2. 'Deign, divine one, to declare to us precisely and in due order the sacred laws of each of the (four chief) castes (var*n*a) and of the intermediate ones.

3. 'For thou, O Lord, alone knowest the purport, (i. e.) the rites, and the knowledge of the soul, (taught) in this whole ordinance of the Self-existent (Svayambhû), which is unknowable and unfathomable.'

I. 1. Kull. thinks that pratipûgya, 'having worshipped,' may also mean 'after mutual salutations,' and he connects, against the opinion of the other commentators, 'duly' with 'spoke.' Gov., Nâr., Râgh., and K., as well as various MSS. (Loiseleur I, p. 313; Bikaner Cat. p. 419), begin the Sa*m*hitâ with the following verse, omitted by Medh., Kull., and Nand.: 'Having adored the self-existent Brahman, possessing immeasurable power, I will declare the various eternal laws which Manu promulgated.'

2. After this verse Nand. inserts four lines, the first and last of which are also found in K.: (a) 'The origin of the whole multitude of created beings, of those born from the womb, of those born from eggs, of those produced from exudations and from germinating seeds, and their destruction;' (b) 'The settled rule of all customs and rites deign to describe at large, according to their times and fitness.'

3. 'The ordinance of the Self-existent,' i.e. 'the Veda' (Kull., Nâr., and Râgh.), or 'the Veda or the prescriptive rules (vidhi)

4. He, whose power is measureless, being thus asked by the high-minded great sages, duly honoured them, and answered, 'Listen!'

5. This (universe) existed in the shape of Darkness, unperceived, destitute of distinctive marks, unattainable by reasoning, unknowable, wholly immersed, as it were, in deep sleep.

---

contained in it' (Medh.), or 'the institutes' (Gov.). A*k*intya, 'unknowable,' i.e. 'the extent of which is unknowable' (Kull. and Râgh.), or 'unknowable on account of its depth' (Gov.), or 'the meaning of which cannot be known by reasoning' (Nâr.), or 'not perceptible by the senses' (Medh.), or 'difficult to understand' (Nand.). Aprameya, 'unfathomable,' i.e. 'not to be understood without the help of the Mîmâ*m*sâ and other methods of reasoning' (Kull.), or 'unfathomable on account of its extent' (Gov., Nand.), or 'unfathomable on account of its extent, or not directly knowable but to be inferred as the foundation of the Sm*ri*ti' (Medh.), or 'difficult to understand' (Râgh.). Kull. and Râgh. explain kâryatattvârtha by 'the purport, i.e. the rites, and the nature of the soul;' Medh., Gov., and Nand. by 'the true purport, i.e. the rites.' Nand. takes sarvasya, 'whole,' as depending on 'ordinance,' and in the sense of 'prescribed for all created beings.'

In the commentary on verse 11 Medh. gives still another explanation of this verse, according to which it has to be translated as follows: 'For thou, O Lord, alone knowest the nature and the object of the products employed in the creation of this universe, which is unthinkable on account of its greatness, and unknowable.' This version belongs to 'other' commentators, who explain Manu's whole account of the creation purely on Sâ*m*khya principles.

5. The account of the creation given in verses 5–13 bears, as Dr. Muir remarks (Sanskrit Texts, IV, p. 26), some resemblance to that contained in some passages of the *S*atapatha-brâhma*n*a, especially XI, 1, 6, 1 seqq., and is probably founded on some Vedic work, 'with an intermixture of more modern doctrines.' In explanation of the wording of verse 5, Medh. and Kull. point to passages like Rv. X, 129, 3, and Taittirîya-brâhma*n*a II, 8, 9, 4. Sâya*n*a, too, quotes the verse in his commentary on the latter passage.

The commentators Medh. and Gov. explain the fact that Manu, being asked to expound the law, gives an account of the creation,

6. Then the divine Self-existent (Svayambhû, himself) indiscernible, (but) making (all) this, the great elements and the rest, discernible, appeared with irresistible (creative) power, dispelling the darkness.

---

by the supposition that it is intended to show what a great scope the work has, and how necessary its study is, as the production of the various created beings depends on merit and demerit. Kull., on the other hand, tries to prove that the account of the creation, which belongs to the knowledge of the supreme soul, is part of the sacred law, and hence properly finds its place here. All the commentators, with the exception of Râgh., explain tama*h*, 'darkness,' by mûlaprak*ri*ti*h*, 'the root-evolvent' of the Sâ*m*khya philosophy, and tamobhûtam, 'in the shape of darkness,' by 'absorbed in the root-evolvent.' Râgh., who throughout explains Manu's sayings in the sense of the Vedânta school, takes it for an equivalent of avidyâ, 'ignorance.' The explanation of the four adjectives, which express in different terms the impossibility of knowing the mûlaprak*ri*ti, differs very much in the six commentaries. The most reasonable appears to be Kullûka's view, who assumes that the four words refer to the impossibility of attaining a knowledge of the prak*ri*ti by the three means mentioned below, XII, 105, and 'by reasoning' (tarka). He paraphrases apra*gñ*âta, 'unperceived,' by 'imperceptible by the senses;' alaksha*n*a, 'destitute of marks,' by 'uninferrible;' avi*gñ*eya, 'unknowable,' by 'undefinable by words or authoritative statement.'

6. The above translation follows Gov., Nâr., and Kull. The other three commentators take mahâbhûtâdiv*ri*ttau*g*â*h* as a relative compound. On this supposition the translation would run as follows: 'Then the divine Self-existent, (himself) undiscernible, (but) making this (universe) discernible, appeared,—he whose (creative) power works in the great elements and the rest, and who dispels the darkness.'

'Then,' i. e. at the end of the period of destruction. Avyakta*h*, '(himself) undiscernible,' i. e. 'not to be known except by Yogins' (Medh.), or 'not perceptible by the external senses' (Gov., Kull., Nâr.), or 'not to be known except through the texts of the Upanishads' (Râgh.), or 'difficult to know' (Nand.). Medh. would prefer to read avyaktam, 'this indiscernible (universe).' 'The great elements and the rest,' i.e. 'the other principles, the great one and so forth'

7. He who can be perceived by the internal organ (alone), who is subtile, indiscernible, and eternal, who contains all created beings and is inconceivable, shone forth of his own (will).

(Medh., Gov., Nâr., Kull., Nand.), or 'egoism' (Râgh.). 'Appeared,' i.e. 'assumed a body of his own free will, not in consequence of his karman, his acts in a former existence' (Medh., Gov., Kull., Nand.), or 'became discernible' (vyakta), (Nâr.), or 'became ready to create' (kâryonmukha), (Râgh.). Gov. explains v*ri*ttaugâ*h*, 'with irresistible power,' by 'who obtained power' (prâpta*m* bala*m* yena). Kull. explains tamonuda*h*, 'dispelling the darkness (i. e. of destruction),' by 'giving an impulse to the root-evolvent,' and Râgh. takes it in a similar way.

The commentators whose opinion Medh. adduces under verse 11, explained this verse also as a description of the self-evolution which the prak*ri*ti performs according to the Sâ*m*khyas. They took svayambhû*h*, 'the self-existent,' in the sense of 'which modifies itself of its own accord;' bhagavân, 'divine,' in the sense of 'which is powerful enough to perform its business' (svavyâpâra îsvara*h*). The other words presented, of course, no great difficulties.

7. 'By the two pronouns yo 'sau, "he who," he indicates the supreme soul, known in the whole world, in the Vedas, Purâ*n*as, Itihâsas, and so forth' (Kull. in accordance with Medh.). The latter proposes, besides the explanation of atîndriyagrâhya*h*, 'who can be perceived by the internal organ (or the mind alone),' which Gov., Kull., and Nand. adopt, another one, 'who, being beyond the cognisance of the senses, can be perceived by Yoga-knowledge alone.' Nâr. and Râgh., too, differ from the interpretation given above. 'Subtile,' i.e. 'who is beyond all distinctions, such as small and great' (Medh.), or 'who is unperceivable by the external senses' (Kull.), or 'who is perceivable by subtile understanding only' (Gov.), or 'who is without limbs or parts' (Râgh.). Nand. points to the common epithet of the supreme soul, 'smaller than small' (Kâ*th*. Up. II, 20; Bhagavadgîtâ VIII, 9). Avyakta*h*, 'indiscernible,' is taken by Kull. to mean 'destitute of limbs or parts.' Sarvabhûtamaya*h*, 'who contains all created beings,' means, according to Medh., either 'that he conceives the idea of creating all beings,' or 'that, in accordance with the Advaita Vedânta, all beings are illusory modifications of him.' The latter view seems to be the one adopted by all the other commentators. 'Shone forth,' i.e. either 'assumed

8. He, desiring to produce beings of many kinds from his own body, first with a thought created the waters, and placed his seed in them.

9. That (seed) became a golden egg, in brilliancy equal to the sun; in that (egg) he himself was born as Brahman, the progenitor of the whole world.

10. The waters are called nârâh, (for) the waters are, indeed, the offspring of Nara; as they were his first residence (ayana), he thence is named Nârâyana.

---

a visible body' or 'was self-luminous' (Medh.), 'assumed a body' (Gov.), 'appeared in the form of the evolutes, the great one, and so forth' (Kull.), 'became discernible' (Nand.).

8. Besides the passages quoted under verse 5, compare also the Paurânik story of the mundane egg, Wilson, Vishnu-purâna I, pp. 39–40 (ed. Hall). 'He' is according to Medh. and Râgh. 'Hiranyagarbha,' according to the other commentators, 'the supreme soul.' Medh. refers to Rig-veda X, 121, 1. According to Medh. (verse 11) those who understood the whole passage to refer to the unintelligent prakriti, explained abhidhyâya, 'with a thought,' to mean 'independently of all external action, just as a man performs an act merely by a thought.' They also asserted that the waters were produced as the first element only, but not before the great one and the other principles. Kull., on the other hand, sees in the expressions, used in this verse, the proof that Manu was an adherent of the non-dualistic Vedânta.

9. Medh., Kull., and Râghava take the epithet 'golden' figuratively, and consider it to be intended to convey the idea of purity or, as Râgh. also proposes, of brilliancy. Instead of 'he himself was born as Brahman (masc.),' the translation may also be 'Brahmâ himself was born.' Medh. gives both explanations. The other commentators adopt that given in the text. The being produced is, according to all except Râgh., Hiranyagarbha. Râgh., as a strict Vedântin, thinks that it is Virât. All the commentators point out that pitâmaha, 'the progenitor,' lit. the grandfather, is a common name of Brahman (masc.).

10. This punning explanation of Brahman's name Nârâyana occurs in most of the Purânas, see Wilson, Vishnu-purâna I, p. 56 (ed. Hall). Both Medh. and Gov. seem to have read âpo narâh,

11. From that (first) cause, which is indiscernible, eternal, and both real and unreal, was produced that male (Purusha), who is famed in this world (under the appellation of) Brahman.

12. The divine one resided in that egg during a whole year, then he himself by his thought (alone) divided it into two halves;

13. And out of those two halves he formed heaven and earth, between them the middle sphere, the eight points of the horizon, and the eternal abode of the waters.

14. From himself (âtmana*h*) he also drew forth the mind, which is both real and unreal, likewise from the mind egoism, which possesses the function of self-consciousness (and is) lordly;

15. Moreover, the great one, the soul, and all

'the waters are called narâ*h*.' Nara is another name of the supreme soul.

11. All our commentators except Râgh., whose explanation is wide off the mark, understand by the '(First) cause' the supreme soul. Sadasadâtmaka, 'who is both real and unreal,' means according to Medh., Gov., and Kull. 'who is existent or real, because he can be known through the Veda and Vedânta, but non-existent or unreal, as it were, because he cannot be perceived by the senses.' Nand.'s explanation, 'who is both the real, the efficient cause and the unreal the products, matter and the rest,' seems, however, preferable. He says, sad iti kâra*n*am asad iti prak*ri*tyâdi kâryam. Regarding the ancient Vedic term Purusha, 'the male' or 'spirit,' see Muir, Sanskrit Texts, V, pp. 367–377.

12. Kull. explains the term 'a year' by 'a year of Brahman.' But Medh. and Gov., who say that a human year is meant, are in accordance with *S*atapatha-brâhma*n*a XI, 1, 6, 2.

13. The number 'eight' is obtained by adding to the four cardinal points, 'the intermediate ones,' north-east, south-east, &c.

14–15. The commentators offer two entirely different explanations of these two difficult verses. According to Medh., Gov., Kull., and Râgh. they describe the production of the Tattvas, the (products) affected by the three qualities, and, in their order, the five organs which perceive the objects of sensation.

principles of the Sâmkhya system, the first three of which, Mahat, Ahamkâra, and Manas, have been placed in an inverted order. Though Manu clearly states (verse 14) that the creator drew the Manas (which they take to mean the internal organ) from the âtman (i. e. according to Medh. and Gov. 'from the Pradhâna,' which is his own shape [tatpradhânâd âtmanah svasvarûpât, Medh.], or according to Gov., Kull., and Râgh. 'from the Paramâtman,' the supreme soul, or according to another explanation of Râgh. 'from himself' [svasmât | gîvasya bhogârtham vâ]), that he drew the Ahamkâra, egoism, from the Manas, and that he afterwards created the mahântam âtmânam, 'the great one, the soul;' (i. e. according to Medh. the Mahat which is called the soul because like the soul it is found in all bodies, or according to Kull. the Mahat which is called the soul because it is produced from the soul or is useful to the soul), yet they think that it must be understood that the Mahat was produced first, from it the Ahamkâra, and from the latter the Manas. The next term sarvâni trigunâni, 'all the products modified by the three qualities,' they refer to all products or evolutes named and to be named hereafter. They are thus obliged to disregard the ka, 'and,' at the end of verse 15 *a*, and Râgh. states distinctly that ka indicates there a stress to be laid on the preceding word (kakâro 'vadhâranârthah). Finally, Gov., Kull., and Râgh. are of opinion that the third ka, 'and,' at the end of verse 15 *b* indicates that the organs of action and the subtile elements have to be added in accordance with the doctrine of the Sâmkhya, while Medh. holds that the subtile elements alone have to be understood.

Nand. and, to judge from the fragments of his commentary, Nâr. also give a far different explanation. According to them the first created Manas is another name for the principle usually called Mahat. In proof of this assertion Nand. adduces a passage from a Purâna, which Medh. quotes on verse 74, where Manas is given as a synonym of Mahat (see also Cowell, Sarvadarsana-samgraha, p. 222, note 1). They farther take mahântam âtmânam, 'the great one, the soul,' to denote the Manas or internal organ ([mahântam] ka mano nâma tattvam âtmânam âtmano gîvasyâvakkhedakatvâd vyapadesah, Râgh.). By the expression sarvâni trigunâni Nand. seems to understand the subtile elements (tanmâtra),

16. But, joining minute particles even of those six, which possess measureless power, with particles of himself, he created all beings.

---

and he too believes that the particle *k*a at the end of verse 15 *b* shows that the organs of action have to be understood. The object of the two verses is, according to Nand., not to give an account of the actual order of creation, but to show that the material cause of all created beings consists of portions of the creator's body, of the Mahat, Aha*m*kâra, the Manas, the Tanmâtras, and the organs of sensation and action which belong to him; (anena *s*lokadvayenaitad ukta*m* bhavati । âtmîyânâm mahadaha*m*kâramanastanmâtra*g*ñânakarmendriyâ*n*âm a*ms*â*h* sarvabhûtopâdânam iti ॥) It would seem that Nand. and Nâr.'s view, as regards the explanation of Manas (verse 14), is correct, but it may be doubted whether, with respect to the terms in verse 15, mahân âtmâ and sarvâ*n*i trigu*n*âni, they have been equally lucky. The explanation of the first four commentators seems altogether inadmissible. In conclusion, it may be stated that Nand. gives also the most acceptable explanation of the epithet of the Manas, sadasadâtmakam, which, he says, means 'partaking of the nature of an evolvent and of an evolute' (prak*ri*tivik*ri*tyâtmakam), and of î*s*varam, 'lordly,' 'which causes all actions to be done' (sarvakarmapravartakam).

16. The translation follows Nand., Râgh., and Vi*g*ñânabhikshu (Sâ*m*khyasâra, p. 19, ed. Hall), who agree that the verse derives the subtile or rudimentary bodies of individual beings from the subtile body of the creator, and the individual souls from his soul. They explain âtmamâtrâsu by apari*kkh*innasyaikasyâtmana upâdhiva*s*âd avayavavatpratîyamâneshu âtmasu (Râgh.), sva*g*îvâ*ms*eshu (Nand.), and svâ*ms*a*k*etaneshu (Vi*g*ñ.). But they differ with respect to the meaning of 'the particles of those six.' 'Those six' are, according to Râgh. and Vi*g*ñ., 'the six senses,' i.e. the five organs of sensation and the mind (which by implication indicate the whole subtile body, Vi*g*ñ.); according to Nand., the six classes of tattvas, which he believes to be mentioned in the preceding two verses, viz. (1) the great one, (2) egoism, (3) mind, (4) the subtile or rudimentary elements, (5, 6) the organs of sensation and action.

Medh., Gov., and Kull., on the other hand, take the verse as follows: 'Joining minute particles of those six (i.e. of egoism and of the five subtile elements) which possess immeasurable power to particles of the same (i.e. of evolutes from the same six [Gov., Kull.], i.e. of the gross elements produced from the Tanmâtras and the organs

17. Because those six (kinds of) minute particles, which form the (creator's) frame, enter (â-*s*ri) these (creatures), therefore the wise call his frame *s*arîra, (the body.)

produced from egoism [Medh.]), he framed all beings.' It would seem that Nand.'s explanation comes nearest to the truth, though, as stated above, his manner of showing that six principles or classes of principles are mentioned in the preceding verses is not altogether satisfactory. But, at all events, he has seen that the expression 'those six' must refer to the enumeration in the preceding two verses.

17. The translation again follows Nand., with whom Nâr. seems to have agreed. He says, 'Because six (kinds of) particles of his frame, i.e. the six before-mentioned portions of the body of Brahman, the Mahat, and the rest, enter, i.e. pervade these—all the creatures mentioned in the preceding verse are referred to—on account of that entering (*s*raya*n*ât), they call the body of that, i.e. of Brahman, *s*arîra. The meaning is as follows: The body of Hira*n*yagarbha is called *s*arîra, because it enters (*s*rayati) all beings by means of its portions, being (their) material cause; but it is not destroyed (*s*îryate) like a common body.' Nand. thinks, therefore, that the punning explanation of the word *s*arîra from sha*d* â*s*ri, or *s*ri, is given in order to show that the other etymology, which derives it from *srî*, 'to destroy,' is not applicable to the body of Brahman.

Medh., Gov., and Kull. take the verse very differently. They agree in supposing that the body is called *s*arîra, because the six elements mentioned enter into or produce the gross elements and the organs. Medh. reads tânîmani for tasyemâni, and according to his interpretation the translation would be, 'Because the six (kinds of) minute particles producing the body enter into (being their cause) or produce these (i.e. because egoism, the before-mentioned organs and the subtile elements enter the gross elements which will be mentioned hereafter), therefore the wise call the body, which is the visible shape of that (Pradhâna), *s*arîra.' Kull., who reads tasya, differs from this version only therein that he refers tasya to Brahman. Râgh. finally gives, in accordance with his explanation of 'those six,' the following version, 'Because the six (kinds of) fine particles constituting the subtile frame of that (Hira*n*yagarbha, i.e. the mind and the rest) enter these (gross bodies as their place of enjoyment), therefore the wise call the visible frame of that (i.e. of the individual soul) the *s*arîra.' He agrees, therefore, with Medh., Gov., and Kull. so far that he, too, refers the verse to the gross bodies.

18. That the great elements enter, together with their functions and the mind, through its minute parts the framer of all beings, the imperishable one.

18. The commentators give five different versions of this verse: (1) Medh., 'That (i.e. the Pradhâna is) the producer of all beings and imperishable, because these, (viz.) the gross elements with their functions (and before them) the mind with its minute particles (i.e. the subtile elements, intelligence, egoism, and the organs), enter it.' (2) Gov. and Kull., 'From that (i.e. the Brahman, which has the form of the subtile elements and of egoism) are produced the gross elements, together with their functions and the mind, which is the producer of all beings through its minute (i.e. imperceptible) portions (i.e. its products, good and bad thoughts, pleasure and pain, and so forth, the world being produced by the good and evil actions originating in the mind) and imperishable.' (3) Râgh., 'That (i.e. the gross body) the gross elements enter (as producers [or produce]) and the mind, which is the producer of all beings and imperishable, together with the actions (i.e. merit and so forth) and with the (organs which are chiefly) limbs.' (4) Nand., '(As) that (body of Hira*n*yagarbha), though through its small portions it produces all beings, yet is imperishable, (even thus) the great beings (egoism, mind, the trigu*n*as, the organs of sensation and action) and the mind (i.e. the principle, called the great one), with the actions (i.e. the individual souls) enter it.' (5) Nâr.'s explanation is mutilated, but seems to have been as follows, 'That (i.e. the subtile body) the gross elements (which produce the gross body) enter, together with the karman (i.e merit and demerit) and the mind, (which is) the producer of all beings and imperishable, together with (its functions, knowledge, desire, hatred, &c., which are, as it were, its) minute portions.'

It seems to me that not one of the above explanations can be accepted in its entirety. I agree with Nâr. in thinking that the word 'that' refers to the subtile body and that the verse describes the origin of the gross body as the result of the union of the great, i.e. the gross elements and of the manas with the subtile body. If the mahânti bhûtâni are the gross elements, it will, however, be necessary to understand by karmabhi*h*, 'their functions,' which, as Medh. and Kull. mention, are 'the function of supporting for the earth, of ripening or cooking for fire and so forth.' By manas I understand here the internal organ which forms the con-

19. But from minute body(-framing) particles of these seven very powerful Purushas springs this (world), the perishable from the imperishable.

20. Among them each succeeding (element) acquires the quality of the preceding one, and whatever place (in the sequence) each of them occupies, even so many qualities it is declared to possess.

---

necting link between the gross senses or the gross body and the individual soul, and thus may be said to frame or fashion all beings. As its nature is atomic, it is necessary to connect avayavai*h* sûkshmai*h* with sarvabhûtak*ri*t and to take avayava either in the manner proposed by Kull., or to assume that the several mind-atoms are referred to, which belong each to a different individual.

19. With respect to the explanation of the expression 'the seven Purushas,' the commentators differ as much as regarding 'the six' in ver. 16. Medh., Gov., and Kull. add 'the great one' or the Mahat to their previous enumeration, 'egoism and the five subtile elements,' while Nâr. and Nand. add the 'portions of the Âtman' (ver. 16) to those elements which they understand to be comprised by 'the six.' That is, probably, the meaning of Râgh. also, who says, purushâ*n*â*m* manaâdipurushântânâm saptânâm, 'of the Purushas, i. e. of those seven, the first of which is the mind, and the last of which is the Purusha.' All the commentators agree that the term Purusha, 'male or spirit,' is applied to the principles in a metaphorical sense, but they give various reasons for the fact, 'because they are for the sake of the soul,' purusha (Medh.), or 'because they were produced by the Purusha, the Âtman' (Kull.). Nâr. understands 'and' with avyayât and says, 'and from the imperishable, i.e. from Prak*ri*ti.' 'The perishable' designates, of course, 'the gross bodies.'

20. This verse expresses the doctrine that the first element ether (âkâ*s*a) possesses one quality, sound, alone; the next, wind two, sound and tangibility; the third, fire or light, three and so forth; see also Sâ*m*khyasâra, p. 18. Nand. places ver. 27 before this verse, and asserts that 'if some read the latter seven verses further on, that is only due to an error of the copyists.' Though vers. 20 and 27 are without any connexion with what precedes and follows, I do not think it advisable to adopt Nand.'s proposal, which I fear is based on nothing but a clever guess, against the authority of all the other commentators. If it were permissible to transpose the

21. But in the beginning he assigned their several names, actions, and conditions to all (created beings), even according to the words of the Veda.

22. He, the Lord, also created the class of the gods, who are endowed with life, and whose nature is action; and the subtile class of the Sâdhyas, and the eternal sacrifice.

23. But from fire, wind, and the sun he drew forth the threefold eternal Veda, called *Rik*, Yagus, and Sâman, for the due performance of the sacrifice.

24. Time and the divisions of time, the lunar mansions and the planets, the rivers, the oceans, the mountains, plains, and uneven ground,

25. Austerity, speech, pleasure, desire, and anger, this whole creation he likewise produced, as he desired to call these beings into existence.

---

verses, I would propose to insert here ver. 27 and to place this verse (20) after ver. 78.

22. The commentators differ very much regarding the explanation of this verse. Medh. proposes, 'And the Lord created (for the sake) of men who are intent on performing sacrificial rites (the multitude) of the gods, the subtile class of the Sâdhyas and the eternal sacrifice.' 'Others' mentioned by him, Gov. and Kull., insert another 'and' between karmâtmanâm and prâninâm, and explain, 'The Lord created the multitude of the gods whose nature is the sacrifice and of those endowed with life.' By the 'gods whose nature is the sacrifice' they understand the inanimate implements, used at sacrifices, but frequently addressed in the Veda as divine beings, while the gods endowed with life are said to be Indra, and so forth. Râgh., with whom Nâr. seems to have agreed, says, 'And the Lord created among beings endowed with life the to us invisible multitude of the gods, who by the results of their actions have obtained their divine station, or who subsist on offerings.' None of these speculations is of much use. But it may be that karman means 'sacrificial rites,' and karmâtmanâm may be translated by 'whose nature is the sacrifice,' or 'whose divinity depends on the performance of sacrifices.' Regarding the Sâdhyas, see Wilson, Vishnu-purâna II, p. 22 (ed. Hall).

26. Moreover, in order to distinguish actions, he separated merit from demerit, and he caused the creatures to be affected by the pairs (of opposites), such as pain and pleasure.

27. But with the minute perishable particles of the five (elements) which have been mentioned, this whole (world) is framed in due order.

28. But to whatever course of action the Lord at first appointed each (kind of beings), that alone it has spontaneously adopted in each succeeding creation.

29. Whatever he assigned to each at the (first) creation, noxiousness or harmlessness, gentleness or ferocity, virtue or sin, truth or falsehood, that clung (afterwards) spontaneously to it.

30. As at the change of the seasons each season of its own accord assumes its distinctive marks, even so corporeal beings (resume in new births) their (appointed) course of action.

31. But for the sake of the prosperity of the

---

26. Other pairs of opposites are desire and anger, passionate attachment and hatred, hunger and thirst, sorrow and delusion, and so forth (Kull.).

27. 'The minute perishable particles of the five (elements)' are according to Medh., Gov., and Kull. the subtile or rudimentary elements which may be called 'perishable,' because they are changed to gross elements. Râgh. explains the epithet 'perishable' by adding 'because they have been produced.' The commentators offer various explanations in order to account for the insertion of this verse which interrupts the continuity of the text. Medh. thinks that it is a résumé. Gov. and Kull. state that it is meant to remove the doubt, whether Brahman's mental creation was effected without the help of the 'principles,' and Nâr. asserts that it is meant to teach that atoms are not eternal. Nand., as stated above, note on ver. 20, places the verse immediately after ver. 19.

31. Nâr. explains lokaviv*ri*ddhyartham, 'for the sake of the

worlds, he caused the Brâhma*n*a, the Kshatriya, the Vai*s*ya, and the *S*ûdra to proceed from his mouth, his arms, his thighs, and his feet.

32. Dividing his own body, the Lord became half male and half female; with that (female) he produced Virâ*g*.

33. But know me, O most holy among the twice-born, to be the creator of this whole (world), whom that male, Virâ*g*, himself produced, having performed austerities.

34. Then I, desiring to produce created beings, performed very difficult austerities, and (thereby) called into existence ten great sages, lords of created beings,

35. Marî*k*i, Atri, Aṅgiras, Pulastya, Pulaha, Kratu, Pra*k*etas, Vasish*th*a, Bh*ri*gu, and Nârada.

36. They created seven other Manus possessing great brilliancy, gods and classes of gods and great sages of measureless power,

---

prosperity of the worlds,' by var*n*air lokaraksha*n*asa*m*vardhanârtham, 'in order to protect the world by means of the castes and to make it prosperous.' Medh., Gov., and Kull., who interpret the compound by 'in order that (the inhabitants of) the worlds might multiply,' point to the benefits conferred by sacrifices of householders, III, 76. Nand. says with reference to the bearing of the verse, 'Now he speaks of the creation of the deities representing the four castes.' Regarding the origin of the castes, see Rig-veda X, 90, 12.

32–33. 'Produced,' i. e. 'begat' (Medh., Kull.), Wilson, Vish*n*u-purâ*n*a I, p. 104, note 2 (ed. Hall).

34–35. Wilson, Vish*n*u-purâ*n*a I, p. 100, note 2 (ed. Hall).

36. 'Manus,' i.e. 'creators in the several Manvantaras' (Medh., Gov., Kull., Râgh.). 'Gods,' i.e. 'such gods as had not been created by Brahman' (verse 22, Medh., Kull.); devanikâyân, 'classes of gods' (Nand., Nâr.), means according to Medh., Kull., and Râgh. 'the abodes of the gods' (devasthânâni). Râgh. gives also the meaning 'the servants of the gods.'

37. Yakshas (the servants of Kubera, the demons called) Râkshasas and Pisâkas, Gandharvas (or musicians of the gods), Apsarases (the dancers of the gods), Asuras, (the snake-deities called) Nâgas and Sarpas, (the bird-deities called) Suparnas and the several classes of the manes,

38. Lightnings, thunderbolts and clouds, imperfect (rohita) and perfect rainbows, falling meteors, supernatural noises, comets, and heavenly lights of many kinds,

39. (Horse-faced) Kinnaras, monkeys, fishes, birds of many kinds, cattle, deer, men, and carnivorous beasts with two rows of teeth,

40. Small and large worms and beetles, moths, lice, flies, bugs, all stinging and biting insects and the several kinds of immovable things.

41. Thus was this whole (creation), both the immovable and the movable, produced by those high-minded ones by means of austerities and at my command, (each being) according to (the results of) its actions.

42. But whatever act is stated (to belong) to (each of) those creatures here below, that I will truly declare to you, as well as their order in respect to birth.

43. Cattle, deer, carnivorous beasts with two rows of teeth, Râkshasas, Pisâkas, and men are born from the womb.

44. From eggs are born birds, snakes, crocodiles,

---

37. The several classes of manes are enumerated below, III, 194–199.

38. Rohita is said to be an imperfect rainbow which appears to be straight, known according to Gov. by the name sastrotpâta.

fishes, tortoises, as well as similar terrestrial and aquatic (animals).

45. From hot moisture spring stinging and biting insects, lice, flies, bugs, and all other (creatures) of that kind which are produced by heat.

46. All plants, propagated by seed or by slips, grow from shoots; annual plants (are those) which, bearing many flowers and fruits, perish after the ripening of their fruit;

47. (Those trees) which bear fruit without flowers are called vanaspati (lords of the forest); but those which bear both flowers and fruit are called v*ri*ksha.

48. But the various plants with many stalks, growing from one or several roots, the different kinds of grasses, the climbing plants and the creepers spring all from seed or from slips.

49. These (plants) which are surrounded by multiform Darkness, the result of their acts (in former existences), possess internal consciousness and experience pleasure and pain.

50. The (various) conditions in this always terrible and constantly changing circle of births and deaths to which created beings are subject, are stated to

46. I read, with Medh., Gov., Nand., and Kull., tarava*h* instead of the sthâvarâ*h* of the editions, and translate it, as required by the context, by 'plants.'

47. My translation of ubhayata*h*, 'both,' is based on Gov.'s comment 'v*ri*kshâ*h* puna*h* pushpaphalenobhayenâpi yuktâ bhavanti,' with which Nâr. and Nand. agree. The latter, however, proposes to read 'ubhayathâ.'

49. 'Multiform Darkness,' see below, XII, 42.

50. Bhûta, 'created beings,' means according to Gov. and Kull. kshetra*g*ña, 'embodied souls.' According to Gov. and Nâr. nityam, 'always,' must be construed with ghore, 'terrible.' Nâr., however, considers nitye, 'in this eternal,' to be a better reading, which Nand. also gives.

begin with (that of) Brahman, and to end with (that of) these (just mentioned immovable creatures).

51. When he whose power is incomprehensible, had thus produced the universe and me, he disappeared in himself, repeatedly suppressing one period by means of the other.

52. When that divine one wakes, then this world stirs; when he slumbers tranquilly, then the universe sinks to sleep.

53. But when he reposes in calm sleep, the corporeal beings whose nature is action, desist from their actions and mind becomes inert.

54. When they are absorbed all at once in that great soul, then he who is the soul of all beings sweetly slumbers, free from all care and occupation.

55. When this (soul) has entered darkness, it remains for a long time united with the organs (of

51. 'Disappeared in himself,' i.e. 'he divested himself of the body which he had assumed at his own will' (Medh., Gov., Kull.). 'One period by means of the other,' i.e. 'the period of creation by means of the period of destruction' (Medh., Gov., Kull.).

52. Instead of the figurative nimîlati, 'closes the eyes, sinks to sleep,' Gov. and K., read praliyate, 'is absorbed.'

53. *S*arîri*n*ah, 'corporeal beings,' means according to Medh., Gov., and Kull. 'embodied souls.' Karmâtmâna*h*, 'whose nature is action,' i.e. who are endowed with actions (Nand., Nâr.), means according to Medh., Gov., and Kull. 'who in consequence of their actions became incorporate.'

54. According to Gov. and Kull., this verse describes the mahâpralaya, the great or total destruction at the end of a kalpa, while the preceding referred to the antarâlapralaya, the intermediate or incomplete destruction. Medh. explains 'he who is the soul of all beings' by the Sâ*m*khya term Pradhâna, 'the chief cause or Nature,' while Gov. and Kull. refer this expression as well as mahâtman 'to the supreme soul or supreme lord' of the Vedânta.

55–56. The commentators offer three different explanations of these two verses. Medh., Gov., and Kull., whom the translation

sensation), but performs not its functions; it then leaves the corporeal frame.

56. When, being clothed with minute particles (only), it enters into vegetable or animal seed, it then assumes, united (with the fine body), a (new) corporeal frame.

57. Thus he, the imperishable one, by (alternately) waking and slumbering, incessantly revivifies and destroys this whole movable and immovable (creation).

---

given above follows, think that ayam, 'this (soul),' refers to the individual soul, and that the two verses incidentally mention what happens to it on the death of the individual in which it resides. First, they say, it enters darkness, i.e. knowledge (*gñâna*) ceases, and, though for some time the soul's connection with the organs continues, it does not perform its functions of breathing, and so forth. Next it leaves the old body. It then is enveloped by the elementary body, consisting of the puryash*t*aka, the eight constituents, i.e. the rudimentary elements (bhûta) and organs (indriya), mind (manas), intelligence (buddhi), memory of past actions (vâsanâ), merit or demerit (karman), the vital airs (vâyu), and avidyâ. In this condition it enters the seed of some plant or the embryo of some animal and then assumes a new gross body. Nâr., on the other hand, considers that the first verse gives a description of the fate of the individual soul during a swoon (mûr*kh*â), and the second alone refers to its migration after death. Under this supposition verse 56 must be translated as follows: 'Being of atomic size (the soul) enters vegetable or animal seed and, united (with the rudimental body), leaves its (former) corporeal frame.' Nand. finally understands by ayam, 'this (soul),' the creator (bhagavân), and thinks that the first verse describes his behaviour during the time of destruction, while the second refers to a new creation. He says, 'When he has entered darkness,' i.e. the root-evolvent or nature, 'and has remained there for a long time,' i.e. as long as the period of destruction lasts, 'then, endowed with organs, he assumes a visible shape,' i.e. he appears in the shape of the creation. His note on verse 56, where he reads sa*m*s*ri*sh*t*au for sa*m*s*ri*sh*t*a*h*, is too short to make it intelligible how he gets over the difficulties opposed to his interpretation.

58. But he having composed these Institutes (of the sacred law), himself taught them, according to the rule, to me alone in the beginning; next I (taught them) to Marîki and the other sages.

59. Bhrigu, here, will fully recite to you these Institutes; for that sage learned the whole in its entirety from me.

60. Then that great sage Bhrigu, being thus addressed by Manu, spoke, pleased in his heart, to all the sages, 'Listen!'

61. Six other high-minded, very powerful Manus, who belong to the race of this Manu, the descendant of the Self-existent (Svayambhû), and who have severally produced created beings,

62. (Are) Svârokisha, Auttami, Tâmasa, Raivata, Kâkshusha, possessing great lustre, and the son of Vivasvat.

63. These seven very glorious Manus, the first among whom is Svâyambhuva, produced and protected this whole movable and immovable (creation), each during the period (allotted to him).

64. Eighteen nimeshas (twinklings of the eye, are one kâshthâ), thirty kâshthâs one kalâ, thirty kalâs one muhûrta, and as many (muhûrtas) one day and night.

---

58. 'According to the rule,' i.e. 'with the subsidiary ceremonies enjoined in the Sâstra' (Kull.), or 'with due attention, carefully' (Medh., Gov.).

61. 'Who belong to the race of this Manu Svâyambhuva,' i.e. 'who were born in the same race or family, for they were all immediately created by Brahman and thus belong to one race' (Medh.).

64. As tâvatah, 'as many,' stands in the accusative, Medh., Gov., and Kull. understand vidyât 'one should know to be.' But Nâr. is probably right in assuming a vibhaktivyatyaya, i.e. that the author used the accusative because the nominative did not suit the metre.

65. The sun divides days and nights, both human and divine, the night (being intended) for the repose of created beings and the day for exertion.

66. A month is a day and a night of the manes, but the division is according to fortnights. The dark (fortnight) is their day for active exertion, the bright (fortnight) their night for sleep.

67. A year is a day and a night of the gods; their division is (as follows): the half year during which the sûn progresses to the north will be the day, that during which it goes southwards the night.

68. But hear now the brief (description of) the duration of a night and a day of Brahman and of the several ages (of the world, yuga) according to their order.

69. They declare that the K*ri*ta age (consists of) four thousand years (of the gods); the twilight preceding it consists of as many hundreds, and the twilight following it of the same number.

70. In the other three ages with their twilights preceding and following, the thousands and hundreds are diminished by one (in each).

71. These twelve thousand (years) which thus have been just mentioned as the total of four (human) ages, are called one age of the gods.

72. But know that the sum of one thousand ages of the gods (makes) one day of Brahman, and that his night has the same length.

73. Those (only, who) know that the holy day of

Nand., who merely substitutes 'tâvanta*h*' for 'tavata*h*,' seems to have held the same opinion.

66. Thus the moon regulates time for the manes.

69–71. Wilson, Vish*n*u-purâ*n*a I, pp. 49–50 (ed. Hall).

73. According to the commentators the word pu*n*ya, 'holy,' is

Brahman, indeed, ends after (the completion of) one thousand ages (of the gods) and that his night lasts as long, (are really) men acquainted with (the length of) days and nights.

74. At the end of that day and night he who was asleep, awakes and, after awaking, creates mind, which is both real and unreal.

75. Mind, impelled by (Brahman's) desire to create, performs the work of creation by modifying itself, thence ether is produced; they declare that sound is the quality of the latter.

76. But from ether, modifying itself, springs the pure, powerful wind, the vehicle of all perfumes; that is held to possess the quality of touch.

77. Next from wind, modifying itself, proceeds the brilliant light, which illuminates and dispels

---

used in order to indicate that the knowledge of the duration of Brahman's day is 'meritorious.'

74. Two explanations of the second half of the verse are offered by the commentators. It may mean either that Brahman on awaking from his sleep first creates the great principle (mahat), which here, as elsewhere, is called manas, 'mind,' or that he appoints (s*ri*g*a*ti) his own internal organ or mind (manas), which at an intermediate destruction (avântara or antarâlapralaya) remains in existence, to create the world. Medh. and Kull. give both explanations, and prefer the former. Gov. gives the second alone, while Nâr. and Nand. adhere to the first. The latter takes manas as denoting the three principles, the great one, egoism, and mind, and explains sadasadâtmakam, 'which is both real and unreal,' as in verse 14, by prak*ri*tivik*ri*tyâtmakam, 'being both an evolvent and an evolute.'

75. 'Thence,' i.e. 'from mind changed to egoism,' Nâr. (similarly Kull.), or 'from Brahman.'

76. As the Sâ*m*khya doctrine (Sâ*m*khyakârikâ, ver. 25) makes all the rudimentary elements proceed from egoism, Medh. takes the first words of the verse to mean, 'But from egoism which modifies itself, wind springs next after ether.' He, of course, adopts the same trick of interpretation in the following three verses.

darkness; that is declared to possess the quality of colour;

78. And from light, modifying itself, (is produced) water, possessing the quality of taste, from water earth which has the quality of smell; such is the creation in the beginning.

79. The before-mentioned age of the gods, (or) twelve thousand (of their years), being multiplied by seventy-one, (constitutes what) is here named the period of a Manu (Manvantara).

80. The Manvantaras, the creations and destructions (of the world, are) numberless; sporting, as it were, Brahman repeats this again and again.

81. In the K*ri*ta age Dharma is four-footed and entire, and (so is) Truth; nor does any gain accrue to men by unrighteousness.

82. In the other (three ages), by reason of (unjust) gains (âgama), Dharma is deprived successively of

---

78. 'In the beginning,' i.e. 'after a total destruction' (mahâpralaya), (Kull.); 'after an intermediate destruction' (Gov., Nâr.); 'before the creation of the mundane egg' (Nand.).

81. The reason why Dharma, 'justice or law,' is said to be *k*atushpât is explained, as Kull. points out, by Manu VIII, 16. Regarding the ulterior signification of the myth which represents Dharma as a four-footed animal, the following opinions are advanced: 1. The four feet represent the four principal priests at the sacrifice (Medh.); 2. or the four chief castes (Medh., Nand.); 3. or the four chief means of gaining merit, austerities, knowledge, sacrifices, and liberality, see below, verse 86 (Medh., Kull., Nâr., K.); 4. or finally the four kinds of speech, mentioned Rig-veda I, 164, 45 (Medh.). All the commentators agree in stating that Truth, though comprised in the Dharma, is mentioned specially in order to show its paramount importance. Nand. reads the last words nâdharmo nâgama*h* kas*k*in, &c., and explains, 'Neither any demerit nor any sacred lore, *S*âstra, approached men, i. e. no Institutes of the law were necessary.'

82. Medh. explains the first half-verse differently, 'In the other three ages, Dharma, the sacred law, (which is derived) from the

one foot, and through (the prevalence of) theft, falsehood, and fraud the merit (gained by men) is diminished by one fourth (in each).

83. (Men are) free from disease, accomplish all their aims, and live four hundred years in the K*ri*ta age, but in the Tretâ and (in each of) the succeeding (ages) their life is lessened by one quarter.

84. The life of mortals, mentioned in the Veda, the desired results of sacrificial rites and the (supernatural) power of embodied (spirits) are fruits proportioned among men according to (the character of) the age.

85. One set of duties (is prescribed) for men in the K*ri*ta age, different ones in the Tretâ and in the

---

sacred lore (âgama), i.e. the Veda, is made to withdraw one foot after the other, one foot in each age, i.e. disappears (gradually) because the power of men to learn and to remember the sacred texts diminishes.' Gov. says, 'But in the Tretâ and the other ages, Dharma, the sacred law, (derived) from the sacred lore (âgama), the *S*âstra, i.e. the performance of sacrifices and so forth, is made to withdraw, i.e. is diminished successively by one quarter in each age, through (the prevalence of) theft, falsehood, and fraud.' Nand. finally differs still more, 'In the other three ages, i.e. the Tretâ and the rest, Dharma, (virtue or justice is determined) by means of the sacred lore (âgama),' the *S*âstra, but this Dharma is lessened by one quarter in each; 'lessening the Dharma' is intended to convey the meaning of 'lessening the determination of the Dharma.' The translation follows Kull., Nâr., and Râgh.

83. In order to reconcile this statement regarding the age of men in the K*ri*ta age with various passages of the Mahâbhârata and the Purâ*n*as, which attribute to certain heroes and sages lives of many thousand years, the commentators explain our passage as meaning that four hundred years were the natural term of life, which, however, might be lengthened through the performance of austerities. They further assert that in the passage Kâ*th*aka 34, 5, which names one hundred years as the term of human existence, the numeral is used in the sense of 'many.'

Dvâpara, and (again) another (set) in the Kali, in proportion as (those) ages decrease in length.

86. In the Krita age the chief (virtue) is declared to be (the performance of) austerities, in the Tretâ (divine) knowledge, in the Dvâpara (the performance of) sacrifices, in the Kali liberality alone.

87. But in order to protect this universe He, the most resplendent one, assigned separate (duties and) occupations to those who sprang from his mouth, arms, thighs, and feet.

88. To Brâhmanas he assigned teaching and studying (the Veda), sacrificing for their own benefit and for others, giving and accepting (of alms).

89. The Kshatriya he commanded to protect the people, to bestow gifts, to offer sacrifices, to study (the Veda), and to abstain from attaching himself to sensual pleasures;

90. The Vaisya to tend cattle, to bestow gifts, to offer sacrifices, to study (the Veda), to trade, to lend money, and to cultivate land.

91. One occupation only the lord prescribed to the Sûdra, to serve meekly even these (other) three castes.

92. Man is stated to be purer above the navel (than below); hence the Self-existent (Svayambhû) has declared the purest (part) of him (to be) his mouth.

93. As the Brâhmana sprang from (Brahman's)

87. See above, verse 31.

88–91. See below, X, 75–79, 99.

89. I read with Medh., Râgh., and K. samâdisat, 'he commanded,' for samâsatah, 'briefly.' Nand. reads akalpayat.

92. See below, V, 132.

93. Dharmatah prabhuh, 'by right the lord,' agrees with Nâr.'s and Nand.'s glosses. Medh., Gov., Kull., and Râgh. say, 'he is with

mouth, as he was the first-born, and as he possesses the Veda, he is by right the lord of this whole creation.

94. For the Self-existent (Svayambhû), having performed austerities, produced him first from his own mouth, in order that the offerings might be conveyed to the gods and manes and that this universe might be preserved.

95. What created being can surpass him, through whose mouth the gods continually consume the sacrificial viands and the manes the offerings to the dead?

96. Of created beings the most excellent are said to be those which are animated; of the animated, those which subsist by intelligence; of the intelligent, mankind; and of men, the Brâhma*n*as;

97. Of Brâhma*n*as, those learned (in the Veda); of the learned, those who recognise (the necessity and the manner of performing the prescribed duties); of those who possess this knowledge, those who perform them; of the performers, those who know the Brahman.

98. The very birth of a Brâhma*n*a is an eternal incarnation of the sacred law; for he is born to (fulfil) the sacred law, and becomes one with Brahman.

---

respect to the law the lord, i.e. entitled to prescribe their duties to this whole creation.'

94. Tapas taptvâ, 'having performed austerities,' is added, as Nand. says, in order to show 'particularly great consideration' (tapas taptvety âdarâti*s*aya*h*). See above, verses 33, 34, 41.

95. Medh., Nâr., and Nand. explain k*ri*tabuddhaya*h*, 'who recognise (the necessity and the manner of performing the prescribed duties),' by 'who know the meaning of the Veda.' 'Those who know the Brahman,' i.e. 'the sacred lore which leads to final emancipation.'

99. A Brâhma*n*a, coming into existence, is born as the highest on earth, the lord of all created beings, for the protection of the treasury of the law.

100. Whatever exists in the world is the property of the Brâhma*n*a; on account of the excellence of his origin the Brâhma*n*a is, indeed, entitled to it all.

101. The Brâhma*n*a eats but his own food, wears but his own apparel, bestows but his own in alms; other mortals subsist through the benevolence of the Brâhma*n*a.

102. In order to clearly settle his duties and those of the other (castes) according to their order, wise Manu sprung from the Self-existent, composed these Institutes (of the sacred law).

103. A learned Brâhma*n*a must carefully study them, and he must duly instruct his pupils in them, but nobody else (shall do it).

104. A Brâhma*n*a who studies these Institutes (and) faithfully fulfils the duties (prescribed therein), is never tainted by sins, arising from thoughts, words, or deeds.

105. He sanctifies any company (which he may enter), seven ancestors and seven descendants, and he alone deserves (to possess) this whole earth.

106. (To study) this (work) is the best means of securing welfare, it increases understanding, it procures fame and long life, it (leads to) supreme bliss.

---

100. 'On account of the excellence of his origin,' i.e. because he sprang from Brahman's mouth.

103. The verse is not intended to exclude Kshatriyas and Vai*s*yas from the right of studying the Manusa*m*hitâ, but merely from teaching it.

104. Sa*ms*itavrata*h*, 'who faithfully fulfils the duties,' is based on Gov.'s full explanation etadarthâvabodhena sa*ms*itavrato vi*s*ish*t*ayamaniyama*h* san, with which Medh. closely agrees.

107. In this (work) the sacred law has been fully stated as well as the good and bad qualities of (human) actions and the immemorial rule of conduct, (to be followed) by all the four castes (var*n*a).

108. The rule of conduct is transcendent law, whether it be taught in the revealed texts or in the sacred tradition; hence a twice-born man who possesses regard for himself, should be always careful to (follow) it.

109. A Brâhma*n*a who departs from the rule of conduct, does not reap the fruit of the Veda, but he who duly follows it, will obtain the full reward.

110. The sages who saw that the sacred law is thus grounded on the rule of conduct, have taken good conduct to be the most excellent root of all austerity.

111. The creation of the universe, the rule of the sacraments, the ordinances of studentship, and the respectful behaviour (towards Gurus), the most excellent rule of bathing (on return from the teacher's house),

---

107. 'The good and bad qualities of (human) actions,' i.e. according to Medh., Gov., Kull., and Nand. 'the good and the bad results of actions,' or according to Râgh. and Nâr. 'the prescribed actions which are good and the forbidden ones which are bad.'

108. My translation of âtmavân, 'who possesses regard for himself,' follows Medh. and Kull. Gov. explains it by 'of excellent disposition,' Nâr. by 'endowed with firmness,' and Râgh. by 'who believes in a life after death.'

109. Vedaphalam, 'the fruit of the Veda,' i.e. 'the rewards for the acts prescribed by the Veda' (Medh., Gov., Kull., and Nâr.).

110. Vas. VI, 1–8. 'The rule of conduct or good conduct' (â*k*âra), mentioned here and in the preceding verses, comprises the numerous usages prescribed partly in the Veda and partly in the Dharma*s*âstras, such as anointing oneself with butter on the occasion of particular sacrifices or sipping water on certain occasions.

112. (The law of) marriage and the description of the (various) marriage-rites, the regulations for the great sacrifices and the eternal rule of the funeral sacrifices,

113. The description of the modes of (gaining) subsistence and the duties of a Snâtaka, (the rules regarding) lawful and forbidden food, the purification of men and of things,

114. The laws concerning women, (the law) of hermits, (the manner of gaining) final emancipation and (of) renouncing the world, the whole duty of a king and the manner of deciding lawsuits,

115. The rules for the examination of witnesses, the laws concerning husband and wife, the law of (inheritance and) division, (the law concerning) gambling and the removal of (men nocuous like) thorns,

116. (The law concerning) the behaviour of Vai*s*yas and *S*ûdras, the origin of the mixed castes, the law for all castes in times of distress and the law of penances,

117. The threefold course of transmigrations, the result of (good or bad) actions, (the manner of attaining) supreme bliss and the examination of the good and bad qualities of actions,

118. The primeval laws of countries, of castes (*g*âti), of families, and the rules concerning heretics and companies (of traders and the like)—(all that) Manu has declared in these Institutes.

119. As Manu, in reply to my questions, formerly promulgated these Institutes, even so learn ye also the (whole work) from me.

CHAPTER II.

1. Learn that sacred law which is followed by men learned (in the Veda) and assented to in their hearts by the virtuous, who are ever exempt from hatred and inordinate affection.

2. To act solely from a desire for rewards is not laudable, yet an exemption from that desire is not (to be found) in this (world): for on (that) desire is grounded the study of the Veda and the performance of the actions, prescribed by the Veda.

3. The desire (for rewards), indeed, has its root in the conception that an act can yield them, and in consequence of (that) conception sacrifices are performed; vows and the laws prescribing restraints are all stated to be kept through the idea that they will bear fruit.

4. Not a single act here (below) appears ever to be done by a man free from desire; for whatever (man) does, it is (the result of) the impulse of desire.

5. He who persists in discharging these (prescribed duties) in the right manner, reaches the deathless

---

II. 2. Âp. I, 6, 20, 1–4. 'Is not laudable,' because such a disposition leads not to final liberation, but to new births' (Gov., Kull.).

3. Nand. takes the beginning of the verse differently, 'The desire for rewards is the root of the resolve to perform an act' (sa*m*kalpa). 'Vows,' i.e. 'acts to be performed during one's whole lifetime, like those of the Snâtaka' (chap. IV), Medh., Gov., Nâr.; 'the vows of a student,' Nand.; 'the laws prescribing restraints,' i.e. 'the prohibitive rules, e. g. those forbidding to injure living beings,' Medh., Gov., Nâr.; 'the rules affecting hermits and Sa*m*nyâsins,' Nand. Kull. refers both terms to the rules in chap. IV.

5. 'In the right manner,' i.e. 'as they are prescribed in the Vedas and without expecting rewards.' 'The deathless state,' i.e. 'final liberation.'

state and even in this (life) obtains (the fulfilment of) all the desires that he may have conceived.

6. The whole Veda is the (first) source of the sacred law, next the tradition and the virtuous conduct of those who know the (Veda further), also the customs of holy men, and (finally) self-satisfaction.

7. Whatever law has been ordained for any (person) by Manu, that has been fully declared in the Veda: for that (sage was) omniscient.

8. But a learned man after fully scrutinising all this with the eye of knowledge, should, in accordance with the authority of the revealed texts, be intent on (the performance of) his duties.

---

6. Âp. I, 1, 1, 1–3; Gaut. I, 1–4; XXVIII, 48; Vas. I, 4–6; Baudh. I, 1, 1, 1–6; Yâ*gñ*. I, 7.

*S*îla, 'virtuous conduct,' i.e. 'the suppression of inordinate affection and hatred,' Medh., Gov.; 'the thirteenfold *s*îla, behaving as becomes a Brâhma*n*a, devotedness to gods and parents, kindliness,' &c., Kull.; 'that towards which many men who know the Veda naturally incline,' Nâr.; 'that which makes one honoured by good men,' Nand. 'Customs,' e.g. such as tying at marriages a thread round the wrist of the bride (Medh., Gov.), wearing a blanket or a garment of bark (Kull.). Though the commentators try to find a difference between *s*îla and â*k*âra, it may be that both terms are used here, because in some Dharma-sûtras, e.g. Gaut. I, 2, the former and in some the latter (e.g. Vas. I, 5) is mentioned. The 'self-satisfaction,' i.e. of the virtuous (Medh., Gov., Nand.), is the rule for cases not to be settled by any of the other authorities (Nâr., Nand.), or for cases where an option is permitted (Medh., Gov., Kull.).

7. The last clause is taken differently by Gov., who explains it, 'for that (Veda) is made up, as it were, of all knowledge.' Medh. gives substantially the same explanation.

8. 'All this,' i.e. 'the *S*âstras' (Medh., Gov., Kull.); 'these Institutes of Manu' (Nâr.); 'these different authorities' (Nand.). 'With the eye of knowledge,' i.e. 'with the help of grammar, of the Mîmâ*m*sâ, &c.' (Medh., Kull.).

9. For that man who obeys the law prescribed in the revealed texts and in the sacred tradition, gains fame in this (world) and after death unsurpassable bliss.

10. But by *S*ruti (revelation) is meant the Veda, and by Sm*ri*ti (tradition) the Institutes of the sacred law: those two must not be called into question in any matter, since from those two the sacred law shone forth.

11. Every twice-born man, who, relying on the Institutes of dialectics, treats with contempt those two sources (of the law), must be cast out by the virtuous, as an atheist and a scorner of the Veda.

12. The Veda, the sacred tradition, the customs of virtuous men, and one's own pleasure, they declare to be visibly the fourfold means of defining the sacred law.

13. The knowledge of the sacred law is prescribed for those who are not given to the acquisition of wealth and to the gratification of their desires; to those who seek the knowledge of the sacred law the supreme authority is the revelation (*S*ruti).

14. But when two sacred texts (*S*ruti) are con-

11. 'Relying on the Institutes of dialectics,' i.e. 'relying on the atheistic institutes of reasoning, such as those of the Bauddhas and *K*ârvâkas' (Medh.); 'relying on methods of reasoning, directed against the Veda' (Kull., Nâr.).

12. The first half of this verse agrees literally with Yâ*gñ*. I, 7.

13. According to 'another' commentator, quoted by Medh., and according to Gov., Kull., and Nâr., the meaning of the first half is, 'the exhortation to learn the sacred law applies to those only who do not pursue worldly objects, because those who obey (or learn, Nâr.) the sacred law merely in order to gain worldly advantages, such as wealth, fame, &c., derive no spiritual advantage from it (because they will not really obey it,' Nâr.). Medh., on the other hand, thinks that vidhîyate, 'is prescribed,' means 'is found with.'

flicting, both are held to be law; for both are pronounced by the wise (to be) valid law.

15. (Thus) the (Agnihotra) sacrifice may be (optionally) performed, at any time after the sun has risen, before he has risen, or when neither sun nor stars are visible; that (is declared) by Vedic texts.

16. Know that he for whom (the performance of) the ceremonies beginning with the rite of impregnation (Garbhâdhâna) and ending with the funeral rite (Antyesh*t*i) is prescribed, while sacred formulas are being recited, is entitled (to study) these Institutes, but no other man whatsoever.

17. That land, created by the gods, which lies between the two divine rivers Sarasvatî and D*ri*shadvatî, the (sages) call Brahmâvarta.

18. The custom handed down in regular succession (since time immemorial) among the (four chief) castes (var*n*a) and the mixed (races) of that country, is called the conduct of virtuous men.

19. The plain of the Kurus, the (country of the) Matsyas, Pa*ñk*âlas, and *S*ûrasenakas, these (form), indeed, the country of the Brahmarshis (Brâhmanical sages, which ranks) immediately after Brahmâvarta.

---

15. The Agnihotra, here referred to, consists of two sets of oblations, one of which is offered in the morning and the other in the evening. The expression samayâdhyushite, rendered in accordance with Kull.'s gloss, 'when neither sun nor stars are visible,' is explained by Medh. as 'the time of dawn' (ushasa*h* kâla*h*), or 'as the time when the night disappears,' with which latter interpretation Gov. agrees.

16. The persons meant are the males of the three Âryan var*n*as. The sacraments may be performed for women and *S*ûdras also, but without the recitation of mantras (II, 66; X, 127).

19. This tract comprises the Doab from the neighbourhood of Delhi as far as Mathurâ, the capital of the ancient *S*ûrasenakas.

20. From a Brâhma*n*a, born in that country, let all men on earth learn their several usages.

21. That (country) which (lies) between the Himavat and the Vindhya (mountains) to the east of Prayâga and to the west of Vina*s*ana (the place where the river Sarasvatî disappears) is called Madhyade*s*a (the central region).

22. But (the tract) between those two mountains (just mentioned), which (extends) as far as the eastern and the western oceans, the wise call Âryâvarta (the country of the Âryans).

23. That land where the black antelope naturally roams, one must know to be fit for the performance of sacrifices; (the tract) different from that (is) the country of the Mle*kkh*as (barbarians).

24. Let twice-born men seek to dwell in those (above-mentioned countries); but a *S*ûdra, distressed for subsistence, may reside anywhere.

25. Thus has the origin of the sacred law been succinctly described to you and the origin of this universe; learn (now) the duties of the castes (var*n*a).

26. With holy rites, prescribed by the Veda, must the ceremony on conception and other sacraments be performed for twice-born men, which sanctify the body and purify (from sin) in this (life) and after death.

---

21. The place where the river Sarasvatî disappears lies in the Hissâr districts. Prayâga, i.e. Allahâbâd.

22. Vas. I, 9; Baudh. I, 2, 10.

23. Vas. I, 13–15; Baudh. I, 2, 12–15; Yâ*gñ*. I, 2.

25. Gov. explains dharma, 'the sacred law,' by 'spiritual merit.'

26–35. Gaut. VIII, 14–20; Vi. XXVII, 1–12; Yâ*gñ*. I, 10–13.

26. Medh. mentions another explanation for the first words, 'With holy rites, accompanied by the recitation of Vedic texts,' and Gov. thinks that 'vaidika' is to be taken in both meanings.

27. By burnt oblations during (the mother's) pregnancy, by the *G*âtakarman (the ceremony after birth), the *K*au*d*a (tonsure), and the Mau*ñg*îbandhana (the tying of the sacred girdle of Mu*ñg*a grass) is the taint, derived from both parents, removed from twice-born men.

28. By the study of the Veda, by vows, by burnt oblations, by (the recitation of) sacred texts, by the (acquisition of the) threefold sacred science, by offering (to the gods, *Ri*shis, and manes), by (the procreation of) sons, by the great sacrifices, and by (*S*rauta) rites this (human) body is made fit for (union with) Brahman.

29. Before the navel-string is cut, the *G*âtakarman (birth-rite) must be performed for a male (child); and while sacred formulas are being recited, he must be fed with gold, honey, and butter.

---

27. 'The burnt oblations during the mother's pregnancy' are the Pu*m*savana, Sîmantonnayana, and so forth; see Â*s*v. G*ri*hya-sûtra I, 13–14.

28. 'By vows,' i.e. 'the vows undertaken by the student when he learns particular portions of the Vedas, such as the Sâvitrîvrata' (Medh., Gov., Nâr.); 'voluntary restraints, such as the abstention from honey, meat, &c.' (Kull., Râgh.); 'vows such as the Prâ*g*âpatya penance' (Nand.). 'By burnt oblations,' i.e. 'the daily offerings of fuel' (II, 108). Traividyena, 'by the acquisition of the threefold sacred science,' i.e. 'by learning the meaning of the three Vedas' (Medh., Nand.); 'by undertaking the vow to study the three Vedas during thirty-six years' (III, 1; Gov., Kull., Nâr., Râgh.). I*g*yayâ, 'by offering to the gods, *Ri*shis, and manes,' i.e. by performing the so-called Tarpa*n*a (Medh., Gov., Kull., Râgh.), or 'by offering the Pâkaya*gñ*as' (Nâr., Nand.). Medh. takes brâhmî, 'fit for union with Brahman,' to mean 'connected with Brahman,' but gives our version, which all the other commentators adopt, as the opinion of 'others.'

29. Â*s*v. G*ri*hya-sûtra I, 15, 1; Mânava G*ri*hya-sûtra I, 17, 1; Pâraskara G*ri*hya-sûtra I, 16, 4. Though the text clearly says that the child is to be fed with gold, honey, and butter, it appears from the G*ri*hya-sûtras, as also some of the commentators point out,

30. But let (the father perform or) cause to be performed the Nâmadheya (the rite of naming the child), on the tenth or twelfth (day after birth), or on a lucky lunar day, in a lucky muhûrta, under an auspicious constellation.

31. Let (the first part of) a Brâhma*n*a's name (denote something) auspicious, a Kshatriya's be connected with power, and a Vai*s*ya's with wealth, but a *S*ûdra's (express something) contemptible.

32. (The second part of) a Brâhma*n*a's (name) shall be (a word) implying happiness, of a Kshatriya's (a word) implying protection, of a Vai*s*ya's (a term) expressive of thriving, and of a *S*ûdra's (an expression) denoting service.

33. The names of women should be easy to pronounce, not imply anything dreadful, possess a plain meaning, be pleasing and auspicious, end in long vowels, and contain a word of benediction.

---

that the last two substances only are to be given to the child, after they have been touched with a piece of gold, or a golden ring.

30. Â*s*v. G*ri*hya-sûtra I, 15, 4-10; Pâraskara I, 17, 1-6. Nâr. and Nand. are in doubt whether the numerals 'the tenth or twelfth' refer to lunar or solar days, because they stand in the feminine gender and either tithi or râtri may be supplied. Kull. gives an alternative version of the date, 'after the tenth (the last day of impurity, i. e.) on the eleventh or twelfth,' which Medh. also mentions, but rejects. Kull. considers that the third and fourth vâ, 'or,' which stand after muhûrta and nakshatra, have the sense of 'just,' and do not introduce a third alternative.

31-32. K. omits 31 b and 32 a. Nâr. and Râgh. think that the second part of a Brâhma*n*a's name must contain the word *s*arman and no other, while the general opinion of the others is that it may be *s*arman or some synonym, implying 'happiness or refuge.' Medh. expressly rejects the former view, and gives as examples of correct formations, Svâmidatta, Bhavabhûti, Indrasvâmin, Indrâ*s*rama, Indradatta.

33. Medh. irreverently, but pertinently, remarks that there is no

34. In the fourth month the Nishkrama*n*a (the first leaving of the house) of the child should be performed, in the sixth month the Annaprâ*s*ana (first feeding with rice), and optionally (any other) auspicious ceremony required by (the custom of) the family.

35. According to the teaching of the revealed texts, the *K*û*d*âkarman (tonsure) must be performed, for the sake of spiritual merit, by all twice-born men in the first or third year.

36. In the eighth year after conception, one should perform the initiation (upanâyana) of a Brâhma*n*a, in the eleventh after conception (that) of a Kshatriya, but in the twelfth that of a Vai*s*ya.

37. (The initiation) of a Brâhma*n*a who desires proficiency in sacred learning should take place in the fifth (year after conception), (that) of a Kshatriya who wishes to become powerful in the sixth, (and that) of a Vai*s*ya who longs for (success in his) business in the eighth.

38. The (time for the) Sâvitrî (initiation) of a

difference between 'auspiciousness' (mangala) and 'benediction' (â*s*îrvâda), and that the latter word has been added merely in order to complete the verse.

34. Â*s*v. G*ri*hya-sûtra I, 16; Pâraskara I, 17, 5; 19, 1–6. The last clause, which permits the adoption of particular family-customs, refers, according to Medh., Gov., and Kull., to all sacraments.

35. Â*s*v. G*ri*hya-sûtra I, 17, 1; Pâraskara II, 1. Nâr. and Nand. explain dharmata*h*, 'for the sake of spiritual merit,' by 'according to the law of the family' (see Â*s*v. G*ri*hya-sûtra, loc. cit.).

36–37. Âp. I, 1, 5, 8–21; Gaut. I, 5–14; Vas. II, 3; XI, 49–73; Baudh. I, 3, 7–12; Vi. XXVII, 15–28; Yâg*ñ*. I, 14.

37. As the commentators point out, the person who has the particular wish is not the boy, but his father.

38–40. Âp. I, 1, 22–2, 10; Gaut. XXI, 11; Vas. XI, 74–79;

Brâhma*n*a does not pass until the completion of the sixteenth year (after conception), of a Kshatriya until the completion of the twenty-second, and of a Vai*s*ya until the completion of the twenty-fourth.

39. After those (periods men of) these three (castes) who have not received the sacrament at the proper time, become Vrâtyas (outcasts), excluded from the Sâvitrî (initiation) and despised by the Âryans.

40. With such men, if they have not been purified according to the rule, let no Brâhma*n*a ever, even in times of distress, form a connexion either through the Veda or by marriage.

41. Let students, according to the order (of their castes), wear (as upper dresses) the skins of black antelopes, spotted deer, and he-goats, and (lower garments) made of hemp, flax or wool.

42. The girdle of a Brâhma*n*a shall consist of a triple cord of Mu*ñg*a grass, smooth and soft; (that) of a Kshatriya, of a bowstring, made of Mûrvâ fibres; (that) of a Vai*s*ya, of hempen threads.

Baudh. I, 16, 16; Vi., loc. cit., and LIV, 26; Yâ*gñ*. I, 37–38. 'Some' take the preposition â, 'until,' in the sense of 'until the beginning of,' Kull.

40. 'Connexion through the Veda,' i. e. teaching them or studying under them, sacrificing for them, or electing them to be priests, accepting religious gifts from them or giving them. Râgh. omits verse 40.

41. Âp. I, 2, 39–3, 9; Gaut. I, 16, 21; Vas. XI, 61–67; Baudh. I, 3, 14; Vi. XXVII, 19–20. Râgh. explains ruru, 'a spotted deer,' by 'a tiger.'

42. Âp. I, 2, 33–37; Gaut. I, 15; Vas. XI, 58–60; Baudh. I, 3, 13; Vi. XXVII, 18; Yâ*gñ*. I, 29. Medh. and Gov. think that the girdle of a Kshatriya is not to consist of three separate strings twisted together, and Kull. apparently holds the same opinion. Râgh. and Nâr. say that every bowstring naturally consists of three strings.

43. If Muñga grass (and so forth) be not procurable, (the girdles) may be made of Kusa, Asmantaka, and Balbaga (fibres), with a single threefold knot, or with three or five (knots according to the custom of the family).

44. The sacrificial string of a Brâhmana shall be made of cotton, (shall be) twisted to the right, (and consist) of three threads, that of a Kshatriya of hempen threads, (and) that of a Vaisya of woollen threads.

45. A Brâhmana shall (carry), according to the sacred law, a staff of Bilva or Palâsa; a Kshatriya, of Vata or Khadira; (and) a Vaisya, of Pîlu or Udumbara.

46. The staff of a Brâhmana shall be made of such length as to reach the end of his hair; that of a Kshatriya, to reach his forehead; (and) that of a Vaisya, to reach (the tip of his) nose.

47. Let all the staves be straight, without a blemish, handsome to look at, not likely to terrify men, with their bark perfect, unhurt by fire.

48. Having taken a staff according to his choice, having worshipped the sun and walked round the

43. 'With a single threefold knot' seems to mean that each of the strings of the girdle shall first be knotted, and the three knots be afterwards tied together in one. Nâr. and Râgh., however, take trivritâ, 'threefold,' separately, and refer it to the string. They thus support Sir W. Jones' translation, 'in triple strings, with one, &c.'

44. Âp. II, 4, 22; Gaut. I, 36; Vas. XII, 14; Baudh. I, 5, 5; Vi. XXVII, 19.

45–47. Âp. I, 2, 38; Gaut. I, 22; Vas. XI, 52–57; Baudh. I, 3, 15; Vi. XXVII, 22–24; Yâgñ. I, 29.

47. Anudvegakarâh, 'not likely to terrify anybody' (Medh., Gov., Kull.), means according to Nâr. 'not causing displeasure (to the wearer) by faults such as roughness.'

48–57. Âp. I, 3, 25–4, 4; Gaut. II, 35–41; Vas. XI, 68–70; Baudh. I, 3, 16–18; Vi. XXVII, 25; Yâgñ. I, 30; 51–57. Âp. II, fire, turning his right hand towards it, (the student) should beg alms according to the prescribed rule.

49. An initiated Brâhma*n*a should beg, beginning (his request with the word) lady (bhavati); a Kshatriya, placing (the word) lady in the middle, but a Vai*s*ya, placing it at the end (of the formula).

50. Let him first beg food of his mother, or of his sister, or of his own maternal aunt, or of (some other) female who will not disgrace him (by a refusal).

51. Having collected as much food as is required (from several persons), and having announced it without guile to his teacher, let him eat, turning his face towards the east, and having purified himself by sipping water.

52. (His meal will procure) long life, if he eats facing the east; fame, if he turns to the south; prosperity, if he turns to the west; truthfulness, if he faces the east.

53. Let a twice-born man always eat his food with concentrated mind, after performing an ablution; and after he has eaten, let him duly cleanse himself with water and sprinkle the cavities (of his head).

54. Let him always worship his food, and eat it without contempt; when he sees it, let him rejoice,

---

1, 2–3; 3, 11; Gaut. IX, 59; Vas. III, 69; XII, 18–20; Baudh. II, 5, 18, 21–6, 2; 13, 12; Vi. LVIII, 34–35, 40–44; Yâg*ñ*. I, 27, 31, 112.

52. Medh. and Nâr. propose for *ri*tam, 'truthfulness,' an alternative explanation, 'the sacrifice.'

53. The word nityam, 'always,' indicates that this rule refers to householders also (Gov., Kull., Nâr., Nand.).

54. 'Worship,' i.e. 'consider as a deity' (Medh., Gov., Nand.), or 'meditate on its being required to sustain life' (Medh., Gov., Kull.), or 'praise it with the verse,' Rig-veda I, 187, 1 (Nâr.).

show a pleased face, and pray that he may always obtain it.

55. Food, that is always worshipped, gives strength and manly vigour; but eaten irreverently, it destroys them both.

56. Let him not give to any man what he leaves, and beware of eating between (the two meal-times); let him not over-eat himself, nor go anywhere without having purified himself (after his meal).

57. Excessive eating is prejudicial to health, to fame, and to (bliss in) heaven; it prevents (the acquisition of) spiritual merit, and is odious among men; one ought, for these reasons, to avoid it carefully.

58. Let a Brâhma*n*a always sip water out of the part of the hand (tîrtha) sacred to Brahman, or out of that sacred to Ka (Pra*g*âpati), or out of (that) sacred to the gods, never out of that sacred to the manes.

59. They call (the part) at the root of the thumb the tîrtha sacred to Brahman, that at the root of the

55. Û*rg*am, 'manly vigour' (Gov., Kull.), or 'energy' (Nâr., Nand.), or 'bulk' (Medh.).

56. Medh. reads nâdyâd etat tathântarâ, and gives, besides the explanation adopted in the translation, two alternative interpretations: (1) 'let him not eat after interrupting his meal;' (2) 'let him not eat taking away his left hand from the dish.' Nand. reads nâdyâ*k* *k*aitat tathântarâ, 'and let him not eat such a (remnant) given to him during (a meal by one of the company).'

58–62. Âp. I, 15, 1–16; Vas. III, 26–34; Baudh. I, 8, 12–23; Vi. LXII, 1–9; Yâ*gñ*. I, 18–21.

58. Though the text speaks of the Brâhma*n*a only, the rule refers, as the commentators remark, to other Âryans too.

59. Aṅgulimûle, 'at the root of the little finger' (Kull., Nâr., Râgh.), means according to Medh. and Nand. 'at the root of the fingers.'

(little) finger (the tîrtha) sacred to Ka (Pragâpati), (that) at the tips (of the fingers, the tîrtha) sacred to the gods, and that below (between the index and the thumb, the tîrtha) sacred to the manes.

60. Let him first sip water thrice; next twice wipe his mouth; and, lastly, touch with water the cavities (of the head), (the seat of) the soul and the head.

61. He who knows the sacred law and seeks purity shall always perform the rite of sipping with water neither hot nor frothy, with the (prescribed) tîrtha, in a lonely place, and turning to the east or to the north.

62. A Brâhma*n*a is purified by water that reaches his heart, a Kshatriya by water reaching his throat, a Vai*s*ya by water taken into his mouth, (and) a *S*ûdra by water touched with the extremity (of his lips).

63. A twice-born man is called upavîtin when his right arm is raised (and the sacrificial string or the dress, passed under it, rests on the left shoulder); (when his) left (arm) is raised (and the string, or the dress, passed under it, rests on the right shoulder, he is called) prâ*k*înâvîtin; and nivîtin when it hangs down (straight) from the neck.

64. His girdle, the skin (which serves as his upper garment), his staff, his sacrificial thread, (and) his water-pot he must throw into water, when they have been damaged, and take others, reciting sacred formulas.

---

60. '(The seat of) the soul,' i. e. 'the heart' (all except Medh., who adds, or 'the navel').

61. 'Neither hot,' i. e. 'not boiled or heated on the fire' (Medh., Gov., Kull., Nâr., Nand.).

63. Baudh. I, 8, 5–10.

64. Baudh. I, 6, 7; Vi. XXVII, 29.

65. (The ceremony called) Kesânta (clipping the hair) is ordained for a Brâhmana in the sixteenth year (from conception); for a Kshatriya, in the twenty-second; and for a Vaisya, two (years) later than that.

66. This whole series (of ceremonies) must be performed for females (also), in order to sanctify the body, at the proper time and in the proper order, but without (the recitation of) sacred texts.

67. The nuptial ceremony is stated to be the Vedic sacrament for women (and to be equal to the initiation), serving the husband (equivalent to) the residence in (the house of the) teacher, and the household duties (the same) as the (daily) worship of the sacred fire.

68. Thus has been described the rule for the initiation of the twice-born, which indicates a (new) birth, and sanctifies; learn (now) to what duties they must afterwards apply themselves.

69. Having performed the (rite of) initiation, the teacher must first instruct the (pupil) in (the rules of) personal purification, of conduct, of the fire-worship, and of the twilight devotions.

---

65. Yâgñ. I, 36. This is the ceremony also called Godâna; Âsv. Grihya-sûtra I, 18; Pâraskara II, 1, 3-7.

66-67. Âsv. Grihya-sûtra I, 16, 16; Vi. XXVII, 13-14; Yâgñ. I, 13. 'The Vedic sacrament,' i.e. 'the sacrament performed with sacred texts' (Nand., Râgh.), or 'having for its object the study of Vedic texts' (Medh., Nâr.). Hence women must not be initiated. As the parallel passage of Âsv. shows, the sacraments preceding the tonsure alone are to be given to them.

68. 'Which indicates their (real) birth, because an uninitiated man is equal to one unborn' (Medh., Gov.).

69-73. Gaut. I, 46-56; Vi. XXX, 32; Yâgñ. I, 15, 27.

70. But (a student) who is about to begin the study (of the Veda), shall receive instruction, after he has sipped water in accordance with the Institutes (of the sacred law), has made the Brahmâñgali, (has put on) a clean dress, and has brought his organs under due control.

71. At the beginning and at the end of (a lesson in the) Veda he must always clasp both the feet of his teacher, (and) he must study, joining his hands; that is called the Brahmâñgali (joining the palms for the sake of the Veda).

72. With crossed hands he must clasp (the feet) of the teacher, and touch the left (foot) with his left (hand), the right (foot) with his right (hand).

73. But to him who is about to begin studying, the teacher, always unwearied, must say: Ho, recite! He shall leave off (when the teacher says): Let a stoppage take place!

74. Let him always pronounce the syllable Om at the beginning and at the end of (a lesson in) the Veda; (for) unless the syllable Om precede (the lesson) will slip away (from him), and unless it follow it will fade away.

---

70. Laghuvâsâh, '(has put on) a clean dress' (Medh., Kull.), or 'a dress which is not gorgeous' (Gov., Nâr., Nand.), i.e. less valuable than the teacher's (Râgh.).

71–72. Âp. I, 5, 19–23; Baudh. I, 3, 28; Vi. XXVIII, 14–16.

73. Nâr. and Nand. read adhyeshyamânas tu gurum, &c. 'But the pupil, desiring to study, shall say to his teacher, Venerable Sir, recite! &c.,' and this agrees with Gaut. I, 46. Nâr. mentions also the reading translated above, which the other commentators give.

74. Âp. I, 13, 6–7; Gaut. I, 57; Vi. XXX, 33. Visîryate, translated according to Kull. by 'will fade away,' means according to Medh. 'will become useless for practical purposes;' according to Gov. and Nâr. 'will not be properly understood during the lesson.' Medh. adds that the two terms contain similes, taken from boiling milk,

75. Seated on (blades of Kusa grass) with their points to the east, purified by Pavitras (blades of Kusa grass), and sanctified by three suppressions of the breath (Prânâyâma), he is worthy (to pronounce) the syllable Om.

76. Pragâpati (the lord of creatures) milked out (as it were) from the three Vedas the sounds A, U, and M, and (the Vyâhritis) Bhûh, Bhuvah, Svah.

77. Moreover from the three Vedas Pragâpati, who dwells in the highest heaven (Parameshthin), milked out (as it were) that *Ri*k-verse, sacred to Savitri (Sâvitrî), which begins with the word tad, one foot from each.

78. A Brâhmana, learned in the Veda, who recites during both twilights that syllable and that (verse), preceded by the Vyâhritis, gains the (whole) merit which (the recitation of) the Vedas confers.

79. A twice-born man who (daily) repeats those three one thousand times outside (the village), will be freed after a month even from great guilt, as a snake from its slough.

80. The Brâhmana, the Kshatriya, and the Vaisya who neglect (the recitation of) that *Ri*k-verse and the

---

and that one speaks also of the visarana, i.e. the spoiling of boiled milk.

75. Gaut. I, 48–50; Yâgñ. I, 23. 'Purified by Pavitras,' i.e. 'having touched the seat of the vital airs with blades of Kusa grass' (Medh., Gov., Nâr.); see Gaut. I, 48. Medh. mentions another explanation of Pavitra, adopted by Nand. also, according to which it means 'purificatory texts.' Regarding the term 'suppression of the breath,' see Vas. XXV, 13; Vi. LV, 9.

76. Vi. LV, 10.

77. Vi. LV, 11. The Sâvitrî, i.e. the verse tat savitur varenyam, , Rig-veda III, 62, 10.

78. Vi. LV, 12; Baudh. II, 11, 6.

79. Vi. LV, 13; Baudh. IV, 1, 29; Vas. XXVI, 4.

80. Vi. LV, 14.

timely (performance of the) rites (prescribed for) them, will be blamed among virtuous men.

81. Know that the three imperishable Mahâvyâhritis, preceded by the syllable Om, and (followed) by the three-footed Sâvitrî are the portal of the Veda and the gate leading (to union with) Brahman.

82. He who daily recites that (verse), untired, during three years, will enter (after death) the highest Brahman, move as free as air, and assume an ethereal form.

83. The monosyllable (Om) is the highest Brahman, (three) suppressions of the breath are the best (form of) austerity, but nothing surpasses the Sâvitrî; truthfulness is better than silence.

84. All rites ordained in the Veda, burnt oblations and (other) sacrifices, pass away; but know that the syllable (Om) is imperishable, and (it is) Brahman, (and) the Lord of creatures (Pragâpati).

85. An offering, consisting of muttered prayers, is ten times more efficacious than a sacrifice performed

---

81. Vi. LV, 15. Brahmano mukham, literally, 'the mouth of Brahman,' is probably meant to convey the double sense given in the translation. Both interpretations are given by Medh., Kull., and Râgh., while Gov., Nâr., and Nand. explain it merely by 'the beginning or portal of the Veda;' see also Âp. I, 13, 6.

82. Vi. LV, 16.

83. Vi. LV, 17.

84. Vi. LVI, 18. 'Pass away,' i.e. 'as far as their results are concerned' (Medh., Gov., Kull., Nâr.), 'as far as their form and their results are concerned' (Nand.). Sacrifices procure only the perishable bliss of heaven, while the constant recitation of the syllable Om secures union with Brahman. According to Medh., Gov., Kull., and Râgh., Brahman is here a neuter; according to Nâr. and Nand., a masculine. The words 'and (it is) Brahman (and) Pragâpati' (Medh., Gov., Nâr., Râgh.) are taken by Kull. as 'since it is Brahman (and) Pragâpati,' by Nand. as 'just like Brahman, the Lord of creatures.'

85. Vi. LVI, 19; Vas. XXVI, 9. The sacred texts meant are, of course, Om, the Vyâhritis, and the Gâyatrî.

according to the rules (of the Veda); a (prayer) which is inaudible (to others) surpasses it a hundred times, and the mental (recitation of sacred texts) a thousand times.

86. The four Pâkayagñas and those sacrifices which are enjoined by the rules (of the Veda) are all together not equal in value to a sixteenth part of the sacrifice consisting of muttered prayers.

87. But, undoubtedly, a Brâhmana reaches the highest goal by muttering prayers only; (whether) he perform other (rites) or neglect them, he who befriends (all creatures) is declared (to be) a (true) Brâhmana.

88. A wise man should strive to restrain his organs which run wild among alluring sensual objects, like a charioteer his horses.

89. Those eleven organs which former sages have named, I will properly (and) precisely enumerate in due order,

90. (Viz.) the ear, the skin, the eyes, the tongue, and the nose as the fifth, the anus, the organ of generation, hands and feet, and the (organ of) speech, named as the tenth.

---

86. Vi. LVI, 20; Vas. XXVI, 10. 'The Pâkayagñas,' i.e. 'the so-called great sacrifices to gods, manes, goblins, and men (III, 70) excluding the Brahmayagña' (Medh., Kull., Nâr., Nand.). Gov. and Râgh. understand the term as indicating 'all Smârta and Srauta rites;' see also Jolly on Vishnu, loc. cit.

87. Vi. LVI, 21; Vas. XXVI, 11. Maitrah, 'one who befriends (all creatures),' i.e. 'does not offer animal sacrifices.' Râgh. proposes also the interpretation 'he who worships Mitra, the Sun.' Brâhmanah, 'a (true) Brâhmana,' i.e. 'one connected with Brahman,' 'one who will be absorbed in Brahman' (Kull.), 'the best of Brâhmanas' (brahmishthah, Râgh.). Medh. and Gov. take the last clause differently, 'it is declared (in the Veda that) a Brâhmana (shall be) a friend (of all creatures).'

91. Five of them, the ear and the rest according to their order, they call organs of sense, and five of them, the anus and the rest, organs of action.

92. Know that the internal organ (manas) is the eleventh, which by its quality belongs to both (sets); when that has been subdued, both those sets of five have been conquered.

93. Through the attachment of his organs (to sensual pleasure) a man doubtlessly will incur guilt; but if he keep them under complete control, he will obtain success (in gaining all his aims).

94. Desire is never extinguished by the enjoyment of desired objects; it only grows stronger like a fire (fed) with clarified butter.

95. If one man should obtain all those (sensual enjoyments) and another should renounce them all, the renunciation of all pleasure is far better than the attainment of them.

96. Those (organs) which are strongly attached to sensual pleasures, cannot so effectually be restrained by abstinence (from enjoyments) as by a constant (pursuit of true) knowledge.

97. Neither (the study of) the Vedas, nor libera-

---

92. 'By its quality,' i.e. by the quality called sa*m*kalpa, the power of determining or shaping the impressions of the senses.

93. Dosham, 'guilt' (Nâr.), is taken by Medh., Gov., and Kull. in the sense of d*r*ish*t*âd*r*ish*t*a*m* dosham, 'misery and guilt;' by Râgh. as sa*m*sârâkhyam, 'the misery of repeated births.' 'Success (in gaining all his aims),' i.e. 'the rewards of all good works and rites' (Medh.), or 'final liberation' (Nâr., Râgh.), or 'all the aims of men, final liberation and the rest' (Gov., Kull.).

96. Asevayâ, 'by abstinence from enjoyments' (Gov., Nâr., Nand.), means according to Medh. and Kull. 'by avoiding places where enjoyments are to be obtained,' i.e. 'by dwelling in the forest' (Medh.).

lity, nor sacrifices, nor any (self-imposed) restraint, nor austerities, ever procure the attainment (of rewards) to a man whose heart is contaminated (by sensuality).

98. That man may be considered to have (really) subdued his organs, who on hearing and touching and seeing, on tasting and smelling (anything) neither rejoices nor repines.

99. But when one among all the organs slips away (from control), thereby (man's) wisdom slips away from him, even as the water (flows) through the one (open) foot of a (water-carrier's) skin.

100. If he keeps all the (ten) organs as well as the mind in subjection, he may gain all his aims, without reducing his body by (the practice) of Yoga.

101. Let him stand during the morning twilight, muttering the Sâvitrî until the sun appears, but (let him recite it), seated, in the evening until the constellations can be seen distinctly.

102. He who stands during the morning twilight muttering (the Sâvitrî), removes the guilt contracted during the (previous) night; but he who (recites it),

---

99. 'Wisdom,' i.e. 'power of control over the senses' (Medh., Gov., Râgh.), or 'knowledge of the truth' (Kull.). I read with Medh., Gov., Nâr., Nand., Râgh., K., and the Bombay edition pâdât, instead of pâtrât. The explanation of the simile has been given correctly by Haughton in his note on Sir W. Jones' translation.

100. Nâr. and Nand. take yogata*h*, 'by the practice of Yoga,' with the chief clause, and Medh. mentions this construction too.

101. Âp. I, 30, 8; Gaut. II, 10–11; Vas. VII, 16; Baudh. II, 7, Vi. XXVIII, 2–3; Yâg*ñ*. I, 24–25.

102. Vas. XXVI, 2–3; Baudh. II, 7, 18, 20. Medh. and Gov. point out that only trifling faults can be expiated in this manner, otherwise the chapter on penances would be useless.

seated, in the evening, destroys the sin he committed during the day.

103. But he who does not (worship) standing in the morning, nor sitting in the evening, shall be excluded, just like a *S*ûdra, from all the duties and rights of an Âryan.

104. He who (desires to) perform the ceremony (of the) daily (recitation), may even recite the Sâvitrî near water, retiring into the forest, controlling his organs and concentrating his mind.

105. Both when (one studies) the supplementary treatises of the Veda, and when (one recites) the daily portion of the Veda, no regard need be paid to forbidden days, likewise when (one repeats) the sacred texts required for a burnt oblation.

106. There are no forbidden days for the daily recitation, since that is declared to be a Brahmasattra (an everlasting sacrifice offered to Brahman); at that the Veda takes the place of the burnt oblations, and it is meritorious (even), when (natural phenomena, requiring) a cessation of the Veda-study, take the place of the exclamation Vasha*t*.

107. For him who, being pure and controlling his organs, during a year daily recites the Veda according to the rule, that (daily recitation) will ever cause sweet and sour milk, clarified butter and honey to flow.

---

103. Baudh. II, 17, 15.

104. Baudh. II, 11, 6. 'Even,' i.e. 'if he is unable to recite other Vedic texts.'

105–106. Âp. I, 12, 1–9; Vas. XIII, 7. The last clause of verse 106 finds its explanation by the passage from the *S*atapatha-brâhma*n*a, quoted by Âp. I, 12, 3. Anadhyâya*h* ('not studying') means 'a cause for the interruption of the study, such as thunder or a violent wind, which takes the place of the exclamation Vasha*t*.'

107. Vi. XXX, 34–38; Yâg*ñ*. I, 41–46. Nâr. and Nand. explain the four terms 'sweet and sour milk, clarified butter and

108. Let an Âryan who has been initiated, (daily) offer fuel in the sacred fire, beg food, sleep on the ground and do what is beneficial to his teacher, until (he performs the ceremony of) Samâvartana (on returning home).

109. According to the sacred law the (following) ten (persons, viz.) the teacher's son, one who desires to do service, one who imparts knowledge, one who is intent on fulfilling the law, one who is pure, a person connected by marriage or friendship, one who possesses (mental) ability, one who makes presents of money, one who is honest, and a relative, may be instructed (in the Veda).

110. Unless one be asked, one must not explain (anything) to anybody, nor (must one answer) a person who asks improperly; let a wise man, though he knows (the answer), behave among men as (if he were) an idiot.

111. Of the two persons, him who illegally explains (anything), and him who illegally asks (a question), one (or both) will die or incur (the other's) enmity.

---

honey,' as symbolical of the four objects of human existence, merit, wealth, pleasure, and liberation. Medh. quotes this interpretation as the opinion of 'others.'

108. Âp. I, 4, 16, 23, 25, 28, 32; Gaut. II, 8, 30, 35; Vas. VII, 9, 15; Vi. XXVIII, 4, 7, 9, 12; Baudh. I, 3, 16, 4, 4-8; Yâgñ. I, 25. Regarding the Samâvartana, see below, III, 3-4.

109. Yâgñ. I, 28. Dharmata*h*, 'according to the sacred law' (Kull., Nand.), means according to Medh., Gov., and Nâr. 'for the sake of spiritual merit.'

110. Âp. I, 32, 22-24; Vas. II, 12; Baudh. I, 4, 2; Vi. XXIX, 7. *Gadah*, 'an idiot,' means according to Medh. and Kull. 'dumb.'

111. Vi. XXIX, 7. The person who will die is in either case the offender. If both offend, both will die. Vidvesha*m* vâdhiga*kkh*ati, 'will incur (the other's) enmity,' means according to Medh. and Gov. 'will incur odium among men;' according to Râgh. 'will lose the reward.'

112. Where merit and wealth are not (obtained by teaching) nor (at least) due obedience, in such (soil) sacred knowledge must not be sown, just as good seed (must) not (be thrown) on barren land.

113. Even in times of dire distress a teacher of the Veda should rather die with his knowledge than sow it in barren soil.

114. Sacred Learning approached a Brâhma*n*a and said to him: 'I am thy treasure, preserve me, deliver me not to a scorner; so (preserved) I shall become supremely strong.'

115. 'But deliver me, as to the keeper of thy treasure, to a Brâhma*n*a whom thou shalt know to be pure, of subdued senses, chaste and attentive.'

116. But he who acquires without permission the Veda from one who recites it, incurs the guilt of stealing the Veda, and shall sink into hell.

117. (A student) shall first reverentially salute that (teacher) from whom he receives (knowledge), referring to worldly affairs, to the Veda, or to the Brahman.

118. A Brâhma*n*a who completely governs himself, though he know the Sâvitrî only, is better than he who knows the three Vedas, (but) does not control himself, eats all (sorts of) food, and sells all (sorts of goods).

119. One must not sit down on a couch or seat

---

112. Baudh. I, 4, 1; Vi. XXIX, 8.

113. This verse shows, as Medh. and Gov. point out, that under ordinary circumstances a learned man must teach what he knows.

114-115. Vas. II, 8-10; Vi. XXIX, 9-10; Nirukta II, 4.

116. Vi. XXX, 41-42.

117. Âp. I, 14, 7-9; Gaut. VI, 1-3, 5; Vas. XIII, 41-43; Baudh. I, 3, 25-28; Vi. XXXII, 1-4. This rule refers to any casual meeting.

119. Âp. I, 8, 11, 14, 17; Gaut. II, 21, 25.

which a superior occupies; and he who occupies a couch or seat shall rise to meet a (superior), and (afterwards) salute him.

120. For the vital airs of a young man mount upwards to leave his body when an elder approaches; but by rising to meet him and saluting he recovers them.

121. He who habitually salutes and constantly pays reverence to the aged obtains an increase of four (things), (viz.) length of life, knowledge, fame, (and) strength.

122. After the (word of) salutation, a Brâhma*n*a who greets an elder must pronounce his name, saying, 'I am N. N.'

123. To those (persons) who, when a name is pronounced, do not understand (the meaning of) the salutation, a wise man should say, 'It is I;' and (he should address) in the same manner all women.

124. In saluting he should pronounce after his name the word bho*h*; for the sages have declared that the nature of bho*h* is the same as that of (all proper) names.

125. A Brâhma*n*a should thus be saluted in return, 'May'st thou be long-lived, O gentle one!'

---

121. Âp. I, 5, 15; Baudh. I, 3, 26. Instead of vidyâ or pra*gñ*â, 'knowledge,' Medh. reads dharma*h*, 'spiritual merit,' and the same reading is given sec. man. in the text of Gov.

122. Âp. I, 5, 12; Gaut. VI, 5; Vas. XIII, 45; Baudh. I, 3, 27; Vi. XXVIII, 17; Yâ*gñ*. I, 26. 'After the word of salutation,' i. e. after the word abhivâdaye, 'I salute' (Gov., Kull., Nâr., Nand.).

123. Vas. XIII, 46. I.e. to those who either are unacquainted with grammar or with the Dharma*s*âstra (Medh.). Nand. places this verse after verse 126.

124. Vi. XXVIII, 17.

125. Âp. I, 5, 18; Vas. XIII, 46. The translation of the second half of the verse is based on the reading 'pûrvâksharapluta*h*,' which

and the vowel 'a' must be added at the end of the name (of the person addressed), the syllable preceding it being drawn out to the length of three moras.

126. A Brâhmana who does not know the form of returning a salutation, must not be saluted by a learned man; as a Sûdra, even so is he.

127. Let him ask a Brâhmana, on meeting him, after (his health, with the word) kusala, a Kshatriya (with the word) anâmaya, a Vaisya (with the word) kshema, and a Sûdra (with the word) anârogya.

128. He who has been initiated (to perform a Srauta sacrifice) must not be addressed by his name, even though he be a younger man; he who knows

---

Nand. gives, and Nâr. mentions as adopted by 'some.' It follows the interpretation of these two commentators which agrees in substance with the rule of Vasishtha. The meaning is that Devadatta is to be pronounced 'Devadattâ3a,' Harabhûte, 'Harabhûtâ3ya,' &c.

Medh. and Kull. take the passage as follows: 'and the vowel (i.e.) "a" (and so forth) at the end of the name, (or in case the word ends in a consonant) that of the preceding syllable, must be drawn out the length of the three moras.' According to this interpretation, which requires the reading 'pûrvâksharah plutah,' Manu's rule agrees with Âp. and Pânini VIII, 2, 83. The obvious objection is that Medh. and Kull. are forced to take akâra, 'the vowel a,' in the sense of 'a vowel such as a,' and to understand with pûrvâksharah the word svarah, which does not occur in the verse. Gov. and Râgh. go far off the mark. Most commentators think that the word viprah, 'a Brâhmana,' is meant to include other Âryans also; but see Âp. I, 14, 23.

126. It follows from this verse that Sûdras must never be greeted in the manner prescribed in the preceding rule.

127. Âp. I, 24, 26-29. The rule refers to friends or relatives meeting, not to every one who returns a salute (Gov.).

128. Gaut. VI, 19. The rule refers to the time between the performance of the Dîkshanîyeshti or initiatory ceremony and the final bath on completion of the sacrifice (Medh., Kull.). Besides bhoh and bhavat, the titles dikshita or yagamâna are to be used.

the sacred law must use in speaking to such (a man the particle) bho*h* and (the pronoun) bhavat (your worship).

129. But to a female who is the wife of another man, and not a blood-relation, he must say, 'Lady' (bhavati) or 'Beloved sister!'

130. To his maternal and paternal uncles, fathers-in-law, officiating priests, (and other) venerable persons, he must say, 'I am N. N.,' and rise (to meet them), even though they be younger (than himself).

131. A maternal aunt, the wife of a maternal uncle, a mother-in-law, and a paternal aunt must be honoured like the wife of one's teacher; they are equal to the wife of one's teacher.

132. (The feet of the) wife of one's brother, if she be of the same caste (var*n*a), must be clasped every day; but (the feet of) wives of (other) paternal and maternal relatives need only be embraced on one's return from a journey.

133. Towards a sister of one's father and of one's mother, and towards one's own elder sister, one must behave as towards one's mother; (but) the mother is more venerable than they.

134. Fellow-citizens are called friends (and equals though one be) ten years (older than the other), men

129. Vi. XXXII, 7.

130. Âp. I, 14, 11; Gaut. VI, 9; Vas. XIII, 41; Baudh. I, 4, 45; Vi. XXXII, 4. Gurûn, '(other) venerable persons, i.e. those venerable on account of their learning and austerities' (Kull., Râgh.), or 'his betters, because they are richer and so forth, e.g. the son of a sister' (Medh.), or 'the husband of a maternal aunt and so forth, but not those more learned than himself' (Gov.), or 'the teacher and the rest' (Nand.), or the 'sub-teachers' (upâdhyâya, Nâr.).

131–132. Gaut. VI, 9; Âp. I, 14; Vi. XXXII, 2–3.

134. Âp. I, 14, 13; Gaut. VI, 14–17. Those who are 'friends'

practising (the same) fine art (though one be) five years (older than the other), *S*rotriyas (though) three years (intervene between their ages), but blood-relations only (if the) difference of age be very small.

135. Know that a Brâhma*n*a of ten years and Kshatriya of a hundred years stand to each other in the relation of father and son; but between those two the Brâhma*n*a is the father.

136. Wealth, kindred, age, (the due performance of) rites, and, fifthly, sacred learning are titles to respect; but each later-named (cause) is more weighty (than the preceding ones).

137. Whatever man of the three (highest) castes possesses most of those five, both in number and degree, that man is worthy of honour among them; and (so is) also a *S*ûdra who has entered the tenth (decade of his life).

138. Way must be made for a man in a carriage, for one who is above ninety years old, for one diseased, for the carrier of a burden, for a woman, for a Snâtaka, for the king, and for a bridegroom.

139. Among all those, if they meet (at one time), a Snâtaka and the king must be (most) honoured;

---

and equals may address each other with the words bho*h*, bhavat, or vayasya, 'friend.' The explanation of the verse, which is substantially the same in all the commentaries, is based on Gaut.'s passage, while Haradatta's interpretation of Âp. somewhat differs.

135. Âp. I, 14, 25; Vi. XXXII, 17.

136. Gaut. VI, 20; Vas. XIII, 56–57; Vi. XXXII, 16; Yâ*gñ*. I, 116.

137. Gaut. VI, 10; Yâ*gñ*. I, 116.

138–139. Âp. II, 11, 5–7; Gaut. VI, 24–25; Vas. XIII, 58–60; Baudh. II, 6, 30; Vi. LXIII, 51; Yâ*gñ*. I, 117. For the explanation of the term Snâtaka, see below, IV, 31.

and if the king and a Snâtaka (meet), the latter receives respect from the king.

140. They call that Brâhma*n*a who initiates a pupil and teaches him the Veda together with the Kalpa and the Rahasyas, the teacher (â*k*ârya, of the latter).

141. But he who for his livelihood teaches a portion only of the Veda, or also the Aṅgas of the Veda, is called the sub-teacher (upâdhyâya).

142. That Brâhma*n*a, who performs in accordance with the rules (of the Veda) the rites, the Garbhâdhâna (conception-rite), and so forth, and gives food (to the child), is called the Guru (the venerable one).

143. He who, being (duly) chosen (for the purpose), performs the Agnyâdheya, the Pâkaya*gñ*as, (and) the (*S*rauta) sacrifices, such as the Agnish*t*oma (for another man), is called (his) officiating priest.

144. That (man) who truthfully fills both his ears with the Veda, (the pupil) shall consider as his father and mother; he must never offend him.

145. The teacher (â*k*ârya) is ten times more

140–141. Âp. I, 1, 13; Gaut. I, 9–10; Vas. III, 21–23; Vi. XXIX, 1–2; Yâ*gñ*. I, 34–35. Kalpa, i. e. the Sûtras referring to sacrifices. Rahasyas, lit. 'the secret portions,' i.e. the Upanishads and their explanation (Medh., Gov., Kull., Nand., Râgh.), or 'the extremely secret explanation of the Veda and Aṅgas, not the Upanishads, because they are included in the term Veda' (Nâr).

142. Yâ*gñ*. I, 34. The person meant is the natural father.

143. Vi. XXIX, 3; Yâ*gñ*. I, 35.

144. Âp. I, 1, 14; Vas. II, 10; Vi. XXX, 47. 'Truthfully,' i.e. in such a manner that there is no mistake in the pronunciation or in the text of the Veda.

145. Vas. XIII, 48; Yâ*gñ*. I, 35. The commentators try to reconcile the meaning of this verse and the next following one by

venerable than a sub-teacher (upâdhyâya), the father a hundred times more than the teacher, but the mother a thousand times more than the father.

146. Of him who gives natural birth and him who gives (the knowledge of) the Veda, the giver of the Veda is the more venerable father; for the birth for the sake of the Veda (ensures) eternal (rewards) both in this (life) and after death.

147. Let him consider that (he received) a (mere animal) existence, when his parents begat him through mutual affection, and when he was born from the womb (of his mother).

148. But that birth which a teacher acquainted with the whole Veda, in accordance with the law, procures for him through the Sâvitrî, is real, exempt from age and death.

149. (The pupil) must know that that man also who benefits him by (instruction in) the Veda, be it little or much, is called in these (Institutes) his Guru, in consequence of that benefit (conferred by instruction in) the Veda.

150. That Brâhma*n*a who is the giver of the birth

---

assuming, either that the term â*k*ârya refers in this case to one who merely performs the rite of initiation and teaches the Gâyatrî only (Medh., Kull.), or that the word 'father' denotes a father who initiates his own child and teaches it the Veda (Gov., Nâr.). But it is more probable that two conflicting opinions are here placed side by side, because both are based on an ancient tradition; see Gaut. II, 50–51.

146–148. Âp. I, 1, 15–17; Gaut. I, 8; Vas. II, 3–5; Vi. XXX, 44–45. Nâr. and Nand. read utpâdakabrahmapitro*h*, 'of the two fathers, i.e. him who procreates the body and him who (gives the birth) for the Veda.'

149. Iha, lit. 'here,' i.e. in these Institutes (Kull.), or 'in the chapter on saluting' (Gov.). But it may also mean 'in this world.'

for the sake of the Veda and the teacher of the prescribed duties becomes by law the father of an aged man, even though he himself be a child.

151. Young Kavi, the son of Aṅgiras, taught his (relatives who were old enough to be) fathers, and, as he excelled them in (sacred) knowledge, he called them 'Little sons.'

152. They, moved with resentment, asked the gods concerning that matter, and the gods, having assembled, answered, 'The child has addressed you properly.'

153. 'For (a man) destitute of (sacred) knowledge is indeed a child, and he who teaches him the Veda is his father; for (the sages) have always said "child" to an ignorant man, and "father" to a teacher of the Veda.'

154. Neither through years, nor through white (hairs), nor through wealth, nor through (powerful) kinsmen (comes greatness). The sages have made this law, 'He who has learnt the Veda together with the Aṅgas (Anû*k*âna) is (considered) great by us.'

155. The seniority of Brâhma*n*as is from (sacred) knowledge, that of Kshatriyas from valour, that of Vai*s*yas from wealth in grain (and other goods), but that of *S*ûdras alone from age.

---

151. Baudh. I, 3, 42. *S*i*s*u, 'young,' seems to be a name or nickname in Baudh.'s passage. Parig*ri*hya, 'as he excelled them' (Nand.), means according to Medh., Gov., Kull., Nâr., and Râgh. 'as on account of his learning he had received them (as his) pupils.' Pit*rî*n, lit. 'fathers,' means according to Nâr. 'the manes, i.e. the Agnishvâttas and the rest.'

154. Anû*k*âna*h*, 'who has learnt the Veda and the Aṅgas' (Kull., Nâr., Nand., Râgh.), means according to Medh. and Gov. 'who teaches the Veda and the Aṅgas.'

155. Vi. XXXII, 18.

156. A man is not therefore (considered) venerable because his head is gray; him who, though young, has learned the Veda, the gods consider to be venerable.

157. As an elephant made of wood, as an antelope made of leather, such is an unlearned Brâhma*n*a; those three have nothing but the names (of their kind).

158. As a eunuch is unproductive with women, as a cow with a cow is unprolific, and as a gift made to an ignorant man yields no reward, even so is a Brâhma*n*a useless, who (does) not (know) the *Rik*as.

159. Created beings must be instructed in (what concerns) their welfare without giving them pain, and sweet and gentle speech must be used by (a teacher) who desires (to abide by) the sacred law.

160. He, forsooth, whose speech and thoughts are pure and ever perfectly guarded, gains the whole reward which is conferred by the Vedânta.

161. Let him not, even though in pain, (speak words) cutting (others) to the quick; let him not injure others in thought or deed; let him not utter speeches which make (others) afraid of him, since that will prevent him from gaining heaven.

---

156. Nâr. and Nand. read sthaviro bhavati, K. sthaviro *gñ*eyo for v*ri*ddho, 'venerable.'

157. Vas. III, 11; Baudh. I, 1, 10.

158. *Rik*as, i.e. the Veda (Gov., Nâr.).

159. Âp. I, 8, 25-30; Gaut. II, 42. This and the following verses refer in the first instance to the behaviour of the teacher towards his pupils; see also below, VIII, 299-300.

160. The Vedânta are the Upanishads, and the reward meant is 'final liberation' (Gov., Kull., Nâr., Nand., Râgh.). Medh., however, prefers to take Vedânta in the sense of 'the maxims or teaching of the Veda,' and thinks that the reward includes all rewards for Vedic rites.

162. A Brâhmana should always fear homage as if it were poison; and constantly desire (to suffer) scorn as (he would long for) nectar.

163. For he who is scorned (nevertheless may) sleep with an easy mind, awake with an easy mind, and with an easy mind walk here among men; but the scorner utterly perishes.

164. A twice-born man who has been sanctified by the (employment of) the means, (described above) in due order, shall gradually and cumulatively perform the various austerities prescribed for (those who) study the Veda.

165. An Âryan must study the whole Veda together with the Rahasyas, performing at the same time various kinds of austerities and the vows prescribed by the rules (of the Veda).

166. Let a Brâhmana who desires to perform austerities, constantly repeat the Veda; for the study

---

162. This verse contains an advice to the pupil who must go begging (Medh.).

164. 'The means (described above),' i.e. 'the various sacraments.' Vedâdhigamikam tapah, 'the (various) austerities (prescribed) for (those who study) the Veda,' means according to Nâr. and Nand. 'the austerities, consisting in the study of the Veda;' see also Âp. I, 12, 1-2.

165. 'The whole Veda,' i.e. 'the Veda with the Angas' (Medh., 'others,' Nâr.), or 'one entire Sâkhâ consisting of the Mantras and the Brâhmana' (Medh., Gov., Kull.). 'Rahasyas,' i.e. 'the Upanishads' (Medh., Gov., Kull., Nand.), or 'the secret explanation of the Veda' (Nâr.). 'Various kinds of austerities,' i.e. 'fasting, Krikkhras, &c.' (Medh., Nâr., Nand.), or 'the restrictive rules applicable to students' (Medh., 'others,' Gov., Kull.), or 'particular observances, such as feeding a horse while one reads the Asvamedha texts' (Râgh.). 'The vows,' i.e. the Mahânâmnîvrata, &c.; see Sânkhâyana Grihya-sûtra II, 11-13.

166. Âp. I, 12, 1-2; Yâgñ. I, 40.

of the Veda is declared (to be) in this world the highest austerity for a Brâhma*n*a.

167. Verily, that twice-born man performs the highest austerity up to the extremities of his nails, who, though wearing a garland, daily recites the Veda in private to the utmost of his ability.

168. A twice-born man who, not having studied the Veda, applies himself to other (and worldly study), soon falls, even while living, to the condition of a *S*ûdra and his descendants (after him).

169. According to the injunction of the revealed texts the first birth of an Âryan is from (his natural) mother, the second (happens) on the tying of the girdle of Mu*ñg*a grass, and the third on the initiation to (the performance of) a (*S*rauta) sacrifice.

170. Among those (three) the birth which is symbolised by the investiture with the girdle of Mu*ñg*a grass, is his birth for the sake of the Veda; they declare that in that (birth) the Sâvitrî (verse) is his mother and the teacher his father.

171. They call the teacher (the pupil's) father because he gives the Veda; for nobody can perform a (sacred) rite before the investiture with the girdle of Mu*ñg*a grass.

172. (He who has not been initiated) should not pronounce (any) Vedic text excepting (those required for) the performance of funeral rites, since he is on a level with a *S*ûdra before his birth from the Veda.

---

167. *S*atapatha-brâhma*n*a XI, 5, 7, 4.

168. Vas. III, 2; Vi. XXVIII, 36.

169–170. Vi. XXVIII, 37–38; Vas. II, 3; Yâ*gñ*. I, 39; Aitareya-brâhma*n*a I, 1; Max Müller, Hist. Anc. Sansk. Lit., p. 390 seq.

171–172. Âp. II, 15, 19; Gaut. I, 10; II, 4–5; Vas. II, 4, 6–7; Baudh. I, 3, 6; Vi. XXVIII, 40.

173. The (student) who has been initiated must be instructed in the performance of the vows, and gradually learn the Veda, observing the prescribed rules.

174. Whatever dress of skin, sacred thread, girdle, staff, and lower garment are prescribed for a (student at the initiation), the like (must again be used) at the (performance of the) vows.

175. But a student who resides with his teacher must observe the following restrictive rules, duly controlling all his organs, in order to increase his spiritual merit.

176. Every day, having bathed, and being purified, he must offer libations of water to the gods, sages and manes, worship (the images of) the gods, and place fuel on (the sacred fire).

177. Let him abstain from honey, meat, perfumes, garlands, substances (used for) flavouring (food), women, all substances turned acid, and from doing injury to living creatures,

178. From anointing (his body), applying colly-

173–174. Vi. XXVII, 28. 'The vows,' i.e. 'the observances and the restrictive rules, such as offering fuel, the prohibition of sleeping in the day-time' (Kull., Nâr.), or 'the Veda-vows, the Godâna, &c.' (Medh., Gov., Râgh.), or 'penances, such as the Prâgâpatya' (Nand. and Nâr.). In the second verse Kull. also adopts the explanation of Medh. and Gov.

176–182. Âp. I, 2, 17, 23–30; 3, 11–25; 4, 13–23; Gaut. II, 8–9, 12–17; Vas. VII, 15, 17; Baudh. I, 3, 19–20, 23–24; Vi. XXVIII, 4–5, 11, 48–51; Yâgñ. I, 25, 33.

177. Rasân, 'substances (used for) flavouring,' i.e. 'molasses and the like' (Gov., Kull., Nâr.), 'clarified butter, oil, and the like' (Nand.). Nâr. adds that others interpret rasân to mean the poetical rasas or sentiments. Medh. mentions the same explanation and two more: (1) spices; (2) juicy fruits and canes like sugar-cane.

rium to his eyes, from the use of shoes and of an umbrella (or parasol), from (sensual) desire, anger, covetousness, dancing, singing, and playing (musical instruments),

179. From gambling, idle disputes, backbiting, and lying, from looking at and touching women, and from hurting others.

180. Let him always sleep alone, let him never waste his manhood; for he who voluntarily wastes his manhood, breaks his vow.

181. A twice-born student, who has involuntarily wasted his manly strength during sleep, must bathe, worship the sun, and afterwards thrice mutter the *Ri*k-verse (which begins), 'Again let my strength return to me.'

182. Let him fetch a pot full of water, flowers, cowdung, earth, and Ku*s*a grass, as much as may be required (by his teacher), and daily go to beg food.

183. A student, being pure, shall daily bring food from the houses of men who are not deficient in (the knowledge of) the Veda and in (performing) sacrifices, and who are famous for (following their lawful) occupations.

184. Let him not beg from the relatives of his teacher, nor from his own or his mother's blood-relations; but if there are no houses belonging to

---

179. *G*anavâda, 'idle disputes' (Medh., Gov., Kull., Râgh.), or 'gossiping' (Medh., Nâr.).

180. Vi. XXVIII, 48. Regarding the consequences of committing such an offence, see below, XI, 119–124.

181. Vi. XXVIII, 51. The verse occurs Taitt. Âr. I, 30.

182. Nand. reads udakumbhân, 'pots filled with water.'

183. Baudh. I, 3, 18; Vi. XXVIII, 9; Âp. I, 3, 25; Gaut. II, 35.

184. Gaut. II, 37–38.

strangers, let him go to one of those named above, taking the last-named first;

185. Or, if there are no (virtuous men of the kind) mentioned above, he may go to each (house in the) village, being pure and remaining silent; but let him avoid Abhisastas (those accused of mortal sin).

186. Having brought sacred fuel from a distance, let him place it anywhere but on the ground, and let him, unwearied, make with it burnt oblations to the sacred fire, both evening and morning.

187. He who, without being sick, neglects during seven (successive) days to go out begging, and to offer fuel in the sacred fire, shall perform the penance of an Avakîrnin (one who has broken his vow).

188. He who performs the vow (of studentship) shall constantly subsist on alms, (but) not eat the food of one (person only); the subsistence of a student on begged food is declared to be equal (in merit) to fasting.

189. At his pleasure he may eat, when invited, the food of one man at (a rite) in honour of the

---

186. 'From a distance,' i. e. 'from a lonely place in the forest not defiled by any impurities.' Vihâyasi, 'anywhere but on the ground,' means lit. 'in the air,' and is explained variously by 'on the roof of the house' (Medh., Gov., Kull.), 'on a platform and the like' (Nâr.), 'in the open air' (Nand.), 'in any pure place except on the ground' (Râgh.). The purpose is, as most commentators think, to preserve the wood from defilement. But, according to 'others,' quoted by Medh., with whom Nand. seems to agree, the object is to let it become dry in the open air.

187. Vi. XXVIII, 52; Yâgñ. III, 281. The penance for an Avakîrnin is mentioned below, XI, 119–120.

188. Yâgñ. I, 32.

189. Yâgñ. I, 32. 'Observing the conditions of his vow,' i.e. 'avoiding honey, meat, and the like.' *Ri*shivat, 'like a hermit' (Medh., Gov., Nâr., Nand.), or 'like an ascetic' (yati, Kull.).

gods, observing (however the conditions of) his vow, or at a (funeral meal) in honour of the manes, behaving (however) like a hermit.

190. This duty is prescribed by the wise for a Brâhma*n*a only; but no such duty is ordained for a Kshatriya and a Vai*s*ya.

191. Both when ordered by his teacher, and without a (special) command, (a student) shall always exert himself in studying (the Veda), and in doing what is serviceable to his teacher.

192. Controlling his body, his speech, his organs (of sense), and his mind, let him stand with joined hands, looking at the face of his teacher.

193. Let him always keep his right arm uncovered, behave decently and keep his body well covered, and when he is addressed (with the words), 'Be seated,' he shall sit down, facing his teacher.

194. In the presence of his teacher let him always eat less, wear a less valuable dress and ornaments

---

According to Gov., Nâr., and Nand., the last phrase means that the student is to eat at a funeral dinner a little wild-growing rice and other food fit for a hermit (munyanna), while Medh. and Kull. think that the two phrases prohibit the eating of forbidden food only.

190. 'This duty' refers to the permission given in verse 189. According to Nâr. 'others,' however, thought that this verse annulled the rule given in verse 188.

191. Âp. I, 5, 27, 4, 23; Gaut. I, 54; II, 29–30; Vi. XXVIII, 6–7; Yâ*gñ*. I, 27.

193. Âp. I, 6, 18–20. I read, with Medh., Kull., and Râgh., susa*m*vr*i*ta*h*, and translate it according to the latter two, 'keep his body well covered.' Medh. explains it, 'well guarding himself (in his speech).' Nâr. and K. read like the editions, susa*m*yata*h*, and Nand. samâhita*h*, 'concentrating his mind.' Gov. seems to have had the same reading as Nâr.

194. Âp. I, 4, 22, 28; Gaut. II, 21; Baudh. I, 3, 21; Vi. XXVIII, 13.

(than the former), and let him rise earlier (from his bed), and go to rest later.

195. Let him not answer or converse with (his teacher), reclining on a bed, nor sitting, nor eating, nor standing, nor with an averted face.

196. Let him do (that), standing up, if (his teacher) is seated, advancing towards him when he stands, going to meet him if he advances, and running after him when he runs;

197. Going (round) to face (the teacher), if his face is averted, approaching him if he stands at a distance, but bending towards him if he lies on a bed, and if he stands in a lower place.

198. When his teacher is nigh, let his bed or seat be low; but within sight of his teacher he shall not sit carelessly at ease.

199. Let him not pronounce the mere name of his teacher (without adding an honorific title) behind his back even, and let him not mimic his gait, speech, and deportment.

200. Wherever (people) justly censure or falsely defame his teacher, there he must cover his ears or depart thence to another place.

201. By censuring (his teacher), though justly, he

195–197. Âp. I, 6, 5–9; Gaut. II, 25–28; Vas. VII, 12; Baudh. I, 3, 38; Vi. XXVIII, 18–22.

197. Nidese tishthatah, 'if he stands in a lower place' (Nâr., Nand.), means according to Medh., Gov., Kull., and Râgh. 'if he stands close.'

198. Âp. I, 2, 21, 6, 13–17; Gaut. II, 14–15, 21; Vi. XXVIII, 12, 23.

199. Gaut. II, 23; Vi. XXVIII, 24–25. The epithets to be added to the teacher's name are upâdhyâya, bhatta (Medh.), âkârya (Kull.), or karana and the like (Nâr.).

200. Vi. XXVIII, 26.

201. Paribhoktâ, 'he who lives on his teacher's substance,' means

will become (in his next birth) an ass, by falsely defaming him, a dog; he who lives on his teacher's substance, will become a worm, and he who is envious (of his merit), a (larger) insect.

202. He must not serve the (teacher by the intervention of another) while he himself stands aloof, nor when he (himself) is angry, nor when a woman is near; if he is seated in a carriage or on a (raised) seat, he must descend and afterwards salute his (teacher).

203. Let him not sit with his teacher, to the leeward or to the windward (of him); nor let him say anything which his teacher cannot hear.

204. He may sit with his teacher in a carriage drawn by oxen, horses, or camels, on a terrace, on a bed of grass or leaves, on a mat, on a rock, on a wooden bench, or in a boat.

205. If his teacher's teacher is near, let him behave (towards him) as towards his own teacher; but let him, unless he has received permission from his teacher, not salute venerable persons of his own (family).

206. This is likewise (ordained as) his constant behaviour towards (other) instructors in science, towards his relatives (to whom honour is due),

according to Nâr. and Nand. 'he who eats without the teacher's permission the best food, obtained by begging.' The latter explanation is supported by the meaning of the preposition 'pari' in parivettâ and paryâdhâtâ.

202. 'Nor when a woman is near,' i.e. 'if the teacher is in the company of his wife.'

203. Âp. I, 6, 15.

204. Âp. I, 7, 7, 12–13; Vi. XXVIII, 27–28.

205. Âp. I, 7, 29–30, 8, 19–20; Vi. XXVIII, 29–30.

206. Âp. I, 8, 28.

towards all who may restrain him from sin, or may give him salutary advice.

207. Towards his betters let him always behave as towards his teacher, likewise towards sons of his teacher, born by wives of equal caste, and towards the teacher's relatives both on the side of the father and of the mother.

208. The son of the teacher who imparts instruction (in his father's stead), whether younger or of equal age, or a student of (the science of) sacrifices (or of other Aṅgas), deserves the same honour as the teacher.

209. (A student) must not shampoo the limbs of his teacher's son, nor assist him in bathing, nor eat the fragments of his food, nor wash his feet.

210. The wives of the teacher, who belong to the same caste, must be treated as respectfully as

207. Âp. I, 7, 29–30; Baudh. I, 3, 44. Âryeshu, 'born by wives of the same class,' i.e. of the Brâhma*n*a caste (Medh., Kull., Gov.), means according to Nâr. and Nand. 'who are virtuous.' It is, however, probable that it has its literal meaning, 'who are Âryans, i.e. born by wives of the first three castes.' Medh. prefers another reading, guruputre tathâ*k*ârye, 'towards the teacher's son who (takes the place of his father as) teacher.' Râgh. gives the same reading.

208. Âp. I, 7, 30; Vi. XXVIII, 31. The translation, given above, follows Medh., Gov., and Nâr. Nand. differs only slightly, 'The son of the teacher who imparts instruction (while his father is engaged) in a sacrifice (or the like), whether younger or of the same age, or a student, deserves, &c.' Kull. and Râgh. construe quite differently, 'The son of the teacher, whether younger or of equal age, or a student, if he (be able to) teach the Veda, deserves the same honour as the teacher, when (he is present) at the performance of a sacrifice.'

209–212. Âp. I, 7, 27; Gaut. II, 31–34; Baudh. I, 3, 33–37; Vi. XXVIII, 32–33; XXXII, 2, 5–7.

the teacher; but those who belong to a different caste, must be honoured by rising and salutation.

211. Let him not perform for a wife of his teacher (the offices of) anointing her, assisting her in the bath, shampooing her limbs, or arranging her hair.

212. (A pupil) who is full twenty years old, and knows what is becoming and unbecoming, shall not salute a young wife of his teacher (by clasping) her feet.

213. It is the nature of women to seduce men in this (world); for that reason the wise are never unguarded in (the company of) females.

214. For women are able to lead astray in (this) world not only a fool, but even a learned man, and (to make) him a slave of desire and anger.

215. One should not sit in a lonely place with one's mother, sister, or daughter; for the senses are powerful, and master even a learned man.

216. But at his pleasure a young student may prostrate himself on the ground before the young wife of a teacher, in accordance with the rule, and say, 'I, N. N., (worship thee, O lady).'

217. On returning from a journey he must clasp the feet of his teacher's wife and daily salute her (in the manner just mentioned), remembering the duty of the virtuous.

218. As the man who digs with a spade (into the ground) obtains water, even so an obedient (pupil) obtains the knowledge which lies (hidden) in his teacher.

219. A (student) may either shave his head, or

216–217. Vi. XXXII, 13–15.

219. Gaut. I, 27; Vas. VII, 11; Vi. XXVIII, 41; Âp. I, 30, 8; Gaut. II, 10. Instead of 'while (he sleeps) in the village' (Medh.

wear his hair in braids, or braid one lock on the crown of his head; the sun must never set or rise while he (lies asleep) in the village.

220. If the sun should rise or set while he is sleeping, be it (that he offended) intentionally or unintentionally, he shall fast during the (next) day, muttering (the Sâvitrî).

221. For he who lies (sleeping), while the sun sets or rises, and does not perform (that) penance, is tainted by great guilt.

222. Purified by sipping water, he shall daily worship during both twilights with a concentrated mind in a pure place, muttering the prescribed text according to the rule.

223. If a woman or a man of low caste perform anything (leading to) happiness, let him diligently practise it, as well as (any other permitted act) in which his heart finds pleasure.

224. (Some declare that) the chief good consists in (the acquisition of) spiritual merit and wealth, (others place it) in (the gratification of) desire and (the acquisition of) wealth, (others) in (the acqui-

---

'others,' Kull., Râgh.). Medh., Gov., Nâr., and Nand. give 'while (he stays) in the village.' The former explanation is, however, more probable on account of the following verse.

220. Âp. II, 12, 13–14; Gaut. XXIII, 21; Vas. XX, 4; Baudh. II, 7, 16; Vi. XXVIII, 53. The translation of the last words follows Gov. and Kull., while Medh., Nâr., and Râgh. state that the penance shall be performed during 'the (next) day (or night),' and that he who neglects the evening prayer, shall fast in the evening and repeat the Gâyatri during the night. The parallel passages show that a difference of opinion existed with respect to the performance of this penance.

221. Vas. I, 18; Âp. II, 12, 22.

222. Âp. I, 30, 8; Gaut. II, 11; Baudh. II, 7; Vi. XXVIII, 2.

223. Âp. II, 29, 11.

sition of) spiritual merit alone, and (others say that the acquisition of) wealth alone is the chief good here (below); but the (correct) decision is that it consists of the aggregate of (those) three.

225. The teacher, the father, the mother, and an elder brother must not be treated with disrespect, especially by a Brâhma*n*a, though one be grievously offended (by them).

226. The teacher is the image of Brahman, the father the image of Pra*g*âpati (the lord of created beings), the mother the image of the earth, and an (elder) full brother the image of oneself.

227. That trouble (and pain) which the parents undergo on the birth of (their) children, cannot be compensated even in a hundred years.

228. Let him always do what is agreeable to those (two) and always (what may please) his teacher; when those three are pleased, he obtains all (those rewards which) austerities (yield).

229. Obedience towards those three is declared to be the best (form of) austerity; let him not perform other meritorious acts without their permission.

230. For they are declared to be the three worlds, they the three (principal) orders, they the three Vedas, and they the three sacred fires.

231. The father, forsooth, is stated to be the Gârhapatya fire, the mother the Dakshi*n*âgni, but

---

225. Âp. I, 14, 6; Vi. XXXI, 1–3. This verse is placed by Kull. alone after the following one, while all the other commentators as well as K. observe the order followed above.

229. Vi. XXXI, 6.

230. Vi. XXXI, 7. 'The three worlds,' i.e. 'the earth, the middle sphere, and the sky;' 'the three orders,' i.e. 'the first three orders' (Kull., Nâr., Nand.), 'the last three orders' (Medh., Gov.).

231. Âp. I, 3, 44; Vi. XXXI, 8.

the teacher the Âhavanîya fire; this triad of fires is most venerable.

232. He who neglects not those three, (even after he has become) a householder, will conquer the three worlds and, radiant in body like a god, he will enjoy bliss in heaven.

233. By honouring his mother he gains this (nether) world, by honouring his father the middle sphere, but by obedience to his teacher the world of Brahman.

234. All duties have been fulfilled by him who honours those three; but to him who honours them not, all rites remain fruitless.

235. As long as those three live, so long let him not (independently) perform any other (meritorious acts); let him always serve them, rejoicing (to do what is) agreeable and beneficial (to them).

236. He shall inform them of everything that with their consent he may perform in thought, word, or deed for the sake of the next world.

237. By (honouring) these three all that ought to be done by man, is accomplished; that is clearly the highest duty, every other (act) is a subordinate duty.

238. He who possesses faith may receive pure learning even from a man of lower caste, the highest

---

232. Vi. XXXI, 9. 233. Vi. XXXI, 10.

238. Âp. II, 29, 11. 'The highest law,' i.e. 'the means of obtaining final liberation' (Kull.); but Medh., Gov., and Râgh. refer the expression to advice in worldly matters. 'From a base family,' i.e. 'from a family where the sacred rites are neglected' (Medh.), 'from one that is lower than oneself' (Kull.), 'from the family of a potter or a similar (low caste),' (Gov.) But probably the rule refers to the practice to take particularly desirable brides even from the families of outcasts; see Vas. XIII, 51-53.

law even from the lowest, and an excellent wife even from a base family.

239. Even from poison nectar may be taken, even from a child good advice, even from a foe (a lesson in) good conduct, and even from an impure (substance) gold.

240. Excellent wives, learning, (the knowledge of) the law, (the rules of) purity, good advice, and various arts may be acquired from anybody.

241. It is prescribed that in times of distress (a student) may learn (the Veda) from one who is not a Brâhma*n*a; and that he shall walk behind and serve (such a) teacher, as long as the instruction lasts.

242. He who desires incomparable bliss (in heaven) shall not dwell during his whole life in (the house of) a non-Brâhma*n*ical teacher, nor with a Brâhma*n*a who does not know the whole Veda and the Aṅgas.

243. But if (a student) desires to pass his whole life in the teacher's house, he must diligently serve him, until he is freed from this body.

244. A Brâhma*n*a who serves his teacher till the dissolution of his body, reaches forthwith the eternal mansion of Brahman.

245. He who knows the sacred law must not present any gift to his teacher before (the Samâvartana); but when, with the permission of his teacher, he is about to take the (final) bath, let him procure

240. Striyo ratnâni, 'excellent wives' (Kull., Râgh.), means according to Medh. and Gov. 'wives and gems.'

241. Âp. II, 4, 25; Gaut. VII, 1–3; Baudh. I, 3, 41–43.

243. Âp. II, 21, 6; Gaut. III. 5–6; Vas. VII, 4; Baudh. II, 11, 13; Vi. XXVIII, 43; Yâ*gñ*. I, 49.

245. Âp. I, 7, 19; Gaut. II, 48–49; Vi. XXVIII, 42; Yâ*gñ*. I, 51.

(a present) for the venerable man according to his ability,

246. (Viz.) a field, gold, a cow, a horse, a parasol and shoes, a seat, grain, (even) vegetables, (and thus) give pleasure to his teacher.

247. (A perpetual student) must, if his teacher dies, serve his son (provided he be) endowed with good qualities, or his widow, or his Sapi*nd*a, in the same manner as the teacher.

248. Should none of these be alive, he must serve the sacred fire, standing (by day) and sitting (during the night), and thus finish his life.

249. A Brâhma*n*a who thus passes his life as a student without breaking his vow, reaches (after death) the highest abode and will not be born again in this world.

Chapter III.

1. The vow (of studying) the three Vedas under a teacher must be kept for thirty-six years, or for

---

246. Most commentators read prîtimâharet for âvahet, and with this reading the translation must be, 'A field, gold . . . . he should give to the teacher in order to please him.'

247. Gaut. III, 7; Vi. XXVIII, 44–45; Yâ*gñ*. I, 49. Regarding the term Sapi*nd*a, see below, V, 60.

248. Gaut. III, 8; Vas. VII, 5–6; Vi. XXVIII, 46; Yâ*gñ*. I, 49. *S*arîra*m* sâdhayet, 'shall finish his life' (Medh., Gov.), means according to Kull. 'shall make the soul connected with his body perfect, i.e. fit for the union with Brahman.' Nâr. and Râgh. take the word similarly.

249. Vi. XXVIII, 49; Yâ*gñ*. I, 50.

III. 1. Âp. I, 2, 12–16; Gaut. II, 45–47; Vas. VIII, 1; Baudh. I, 3, 1–4; Vi. XXVIII, 42; Yâ*gñ*. I, 36.

The three Vedas meant are the *Ri*g-veda, Yagur-veda, and Sâma-veda. The Atharva-veda is here, as in most of the ancient Dharma-sûtras, left out altogether. Baudhâyana, alone, states that

half that time, or for a quarter, or until the (student) has perfectly learnt them.

2. (A student) who has studied in due order the three Vedas, or two, or even one only, without breaking the (rules of) studentship, shall enter the order of householders.

3. He who is famous for (the strict performance of) his duties and has received his heritage, the Veda, from his father, shall be honoured, sitting on a couch and adorned with a garland, with (the present of) a cow (and the honey-mixture).

4. Having bathed, with the permission of his teacher, and performed according to the rule the Samâvartana (the rite on returning home), a twice-born man shall marry a wife of equal caste who is endowed with auspicious (bodily) marks.

5. A (damsel) who is neither a Sapi*nd*â on the mother's side, nor belongs to the same family on

---

the term of studentship extends over forty-eight years, and that rule includes the Atharva-veda.

2. Yâg*ñ*. I, 52.

3. The meaning is, that the student who, after completing his term, has become a Snâtaka, shall receive first, i.e. before his marriage, the honour of the Madhuparka (Âp. II, 8, 5–9) from the person who instructed him. The phrase 'who has received his heritage, the Veda, from his father,' indicates, according to the commentators, that, as a rule, the father is to teach his son. As, however, the teacher is considered the spiritual father of his pupil, pitu*h* might also be translated 'from his (spiritual) father.'

4. Gaut. IV, 1; Vas. VIII, 1; Yâg*ñ*. I, 52. Regarding the 'auspicious bodily marks,' see *S*âṅkhâyana, G*ri*hya-sûtra I, 5, 10. See also below, vers. 7–10.

5. Âp. II, 11, 15–16; Gaut. IV, 2–5; Vas. VIII, 1–2; Baudh. II, 1, 32–38; Vi. XXIV, 9–10; Yâg*ñ*. I, 53.

Asagotrâ *k*a yâ pitu*h*, 'who does not belong to the same family on the father's side,' means according to Medh. and Kull. 'between whose father's and the bridegroom's family no blood-relationship is

the father's side, is recommended to twice-born men for wedlock and conjugal union.

6. In connecting himself with a wife, let him carefully avoid the ten following families, be they ever so great, or rich in kine, horses, sheep, grain, or (other) property,

7. (Viz.) one which neglects the sacred rites, one in which no male children (are born), one in which the Veda is not studied, one (the members of) which have thick hair on the body, those which are subject to hemorrhoids, phthisis, weakness of digestion, epilepsy, or white and black leprosy.

8. Let him not marry a maiden (with) reddish (hair), nor one who has a redundant member, nor one who is sickly, nor one either with no hair (on the body) or too much, nor one who is garrulous or has red (eyes),

9. Nor one named after a constellation, a tree, or a river, nor one bearing the name of a low caste, or of a mountain, nor one named after a bird, a

---

traceable.' It is, however, very probable that gotra has a double meaning, vaidika and laukika gotra, and that, in the case of Brâhma*n*as, intermarriages between families descended from the same *R*ishi, and, in the case of other Âryans, between families bearing the same name or known to be connected, are forbidden. Kull., Nâr., and Râgh. hold that the first *k*a, 'and,' indicates that asagotrâ refers to the mother's side also, and Medh., Gov., Kull., Nâr., and Râgh. think that on account of the second *k*a, the word asapi*nd*â must be taken to refer to the father's side also, and that thus intermarriages with the daughter of a paternal aunt or with the paternal grandfather's sister's descendants are forbidden. Maithune, 'for conjugal union' (Medh., Gov., Nâr.), means according to Kull. and Râgh. 'for the holy rites to be performed by the husband and wife together.' Nand. reads amaithunî, 'one who is a virgin.' Regarding the term Sapi*nd*a, see below, V, 60.

7. Vi. XXIV, 11; Yâ*gñ*. I, 54.

8. Yâ*gñ*. I, 53; Vi. XXIV, 12-16.

snake, or a slave, nor one whose name inspires terror:

10. Let him wed a female free from bodily defects, who has an agreeable name, the (graceful) gait of a Ha*m*sa or of an elephant, a moderate (quantity of) hair on the body and on the head, small teeth, and soft limbs.

11. But a prudent man should not marry (a maiden) who has no brother, nor one whose father is not known, through fear lest (in the former case she be made) an appointed daughter (and in the latter) lest (he should commit) sin.

12. For the first marriage of twice-born men (wives) of equal caste are recommended; but for those who through desire proceed (to marry again) the following females, (chosen) according to the (direct) order (of the castes), are most approved.

13. It is declared that a *S*ûdra woman alone (can be) the wife of a *S*ûdra, she and one of his own caste (the wives) of a Vai*s*ya, those two and one of his own caste (the wives) of a Kshatriya, those three and one of his own caste (the wives) of a Brâhma*n*a.

---

11. Yâg*ñ*. I, 53. 'Lest he should commit sin,' i.e. marry a Sagotrâ or one sprung from an illicit union. The translation follows Kull., Nâr., Râgh., and 'others' mentioned by Medh. But Medh. himself takes the verse differently, 'A prudent man should not marry a (maiden) who has no brother, if her father is not known (i.e. is dead or absent), through fear lest she be made an appointed daughter;' while Gov. explains it as follows, 'A prudent man should not marry a (maiden) who has no brother or whose father is not known, through fear lest she be made an appointed daughter.' According to the latter it would be possible, in case the father is not known, that she might be only the half-sister of her brother, and her real father, having no children, might make her an appointed daughter.

12. Vi. XXIV, 1–4; Baudh. I, 16, 2–5.

13. Yâg*ñ*. I, 56; Vas. I, 25–26.

14. A *S*ûdra woman is not mentioned even in any (ancient) story as the (first) wife of a Brâhma*n*a or of a Kshatriya, though they lived in the (greatest) distress.

15. Twice-born men who, in their folly, wed wives of the low (*S*ûdra) caste, soon degrade their families and their children to the state of *S*ûdras.

16. According to Atri and to (Gautama) the son of Utathya, he who weds a *S*ûdra woman becomes an outcast, according to *S*aunaka on the birth of a son, and according to Bh*ri*gu he who has (male) offspring from a (*S*ûdra female, alone).

17. A Brâhma*n*a who takes a Sûdra wife to his bed, will (after death) sink into hell; if he begets a child by her, he will lose the rank of a Brâhma*n*a.

18. The manes and the gods will not eat the (offerings) of that man who performs the rites in

14. Vas. I, 27; Gaut. XV, 18; Âp. I, 18, 33.

15. Vi. XXV, 6.

16. Baudh. II, 2–7. The above translation follows Medh., Gov., Nand., and Râgh. But Kull. takes the last clause differently, 'according to Bh*ri*gu on the birth of a son's son.' This version is supported, as a quotation given by Nâr. shows, by the Bhavishya-purâ*n*a, which, as usual, paraphrases Manu's text, putrasya putram âsâdya *S*aunaka*h* *s*ûdratâ*m* gata*h* I bh*ri*gvâdayo 'py evam eva patitatvam avâpnuyu*h* II There was, moreover, as this passage shows, an ancient explanation of our verse, according to which the various names of *Ri*shis do not refer to authors of law-books, but to founders of Gotras. This view is adopted by Nâr., and, according to him, the translation should run as follows: '(A man of the family) of Atri who weds a *S*ûdra female, becomes an outcast, (one of the race) of Utathya's son, on the birth of a son, and (one of) *S*aunaka's or Bh*ri*gu's (Gotras) by having no other but *S*ûdra offspring.' It ought to be noted that, according to Kull. alone, the three clauses refer to Brâhma*n*as, Kshatriyas, and Vai*s*yas respectively. Râgh. particularly objects to this opinion, which, according to him, 'some' hold.

18. Vas. XIV, 11; Vi. XXV, 7.

honour of the gods, of the manes, and of guests chiefly with a (*S*ûdra wife's) assistance, and such (a man) will not go to heaven.

19. For him who drinks the moisture of a *S*ûdrâ's lips, who is tainted by her breath, and who begets a son on her, no expiation is prescribed.

20. Now listen to (the) brief (description of) the following eight marriage-rites used by the four castes (var*n*a) which partly secure benefits and partly produce evil both in this life and after death.

21. (They are) the rite of Brahman (Brâhma), that of the gods (Daiva), that of the *Ri*shis (Ârsha), that of Pra*g*âpati (Prâ*g*âpatya), that of the Asuras (Âsura), that of the Gandharvas (Gândharva), that of the Râkshasas (Râkshasa), and that of the Pi*s*â*k*as (Pai*s*â*k*a).

22. Which is lawful for each caste (var*n*a) and which are the virtues or faults of each (rite), all this I will declare to you, as well as their good and evil results with respect to the offspring.

23. One may know that the first six according to the order (followed above) are lawful for a Brâhma*n*a, the four last for a Kshatriya, and the same four, excepting the Râkshasa rite, for a Vai*s*ya and a *S*ûdra.

24. The sages state that the first four are approved (in the case) of a Brâhma*n*a, one, the Râkshasa (rite

---

21–34. Âp. II, 11, 17–21; Gaut. IV, 6–15; Vas. I, 17–35; Baudh. I, 20, 1–21, 23; Vi. XXIV, 18–28; Yâ*gñ*. I, 58–61.

23. It seems extremely probable that this and the next three verses contain, as Sir W. Jones thinks, several conflicting opinions on the permissibility of the different marriage rites. The commentators, however, try to reconcile them by various tricks of interpretation.

in the case) of a Kshatriya, and the Âsura (marriage in that) of a Vaisya and of a Sûdra.

25. But in these (Institutes of the sacred law) three of the five (last) are declared to be lawful and two unlawful; the Paisâka and the Âsura (rites) must never be used.

26. For Kshatriyas those before-mentioned two rites, the Gândharva and the Râkshasa, whether separate or mixed, are permitted by the sacred tradition.

27. The gift of a daughter, after decking her (with costly garments) and honouring (her by presents of jewels), to a man learned in the Veda and of good conduct, whom (the father) himself invites, is called the Brâhma rite.

28. The gift of a daughter who has been decked with ornaments, to a priest who duly officiates at a sacrifice, during the course of its performance, they call the Daiva rite.

29. When (the father) gives away his daughter according to the rule, after receiving from the bridegroom, for (the fulfilment of) the sacred law, a cow and a bull or two pairs, that is named the Ârsha rite.

30. The gift of a daughter (by her father) after

---

26. 'Mixed,' i.e. when a girl is forcibly abducted from her father's house after a previous understanding with her lover.

27. Nâr. and Râgh. refer arkayitvâ, 'after honouring,' to the bridegroom, and take it in the sense of 'after honouring (the bridegroom with the honey-mixture).'

29. 'For the (fulfilment of) the sacred law,' i.e. 'not with the intention of selling his child' (Medh.); see also below, vers. 51–54. 'According to the rule,' i.e. 'pronouncing the words prescribed for making a gift' (Nâr.).

30. 'Has shown honour,' i.e. 'to the bridegroom by the honey-mixture' (Nâr., Nand.).

he has addressed (the couple) with the text, 'May both of you perform together your duties,' and has shown honour (to the bridegroom), is called in the Smriti the Prâgâpatya rite.

31. When (the bridegroom) receives a maiden, after having given as much wealth as he can afford, to the kinsmen and to the bride herself, according to his own will, that is called the Âsura rite.

32. The voluntary union of a maiden and her lover one must know (to be) the Gândharva rite, which springs from desire and has sexual intercourse for its purpose.

33. The forcible abduction of a maiden from her home, while she cries out and weeps, after (her kinsmen) have been slain or wounded and (their houses) broken open, is called the Râkshasa rite.

34. When (a man) by stealth seduces a girl who is sleeping, intoxicated, or disordered in intellect, that is the eighth, the most base and sinful rite of the Pisâkas.

---

31. 'According to his own will,' i. e. 'not in accordance with the injunction of the sacred law, as in the case of the Ârsha rite' (Medh., Gov., Kull., Nâr., Nand.).

32. Gov. and Nâr. here enter on a discussion of the question whether the prescribed offerings and wedding ceremonies are to be performed in the case of the Gândharva, Râkshasa, and Paisâka rites. Relying on a passage of Devala and of the Bahvrika Grihya-parisishta (Saunaka) they are of opinion that the homas must be performed, at least in the case of Âryan couples. But they hold on the strength of Manu's dictum, VIII, 226, which restricts the use of the Mantras to women, married as virgins, that the Vedic nuptial texts must not be recited. From the comment of Medh. on verse 34 it would appear that the opinions on the subject were divided, and that some held weddings with the recitation of Mantras to be permissible, while others denied the necessity of any wedding.

35. The gift of daughters among Brâhma*n*as is most approved, (if it is preceded) by (a libation of) water; but in the case of other castes (it may be performed) by (the expression of) mutual consent.

36. Listen now to me, ye Brâhma*n*as, while I fully declare what quality has been ascribed by Manu to each of these marriage-rites.

37. The son of a wife wedded according to the Brâhma rite, if he performs meritorious acts, liberates from sin ten ancestors, ten descendants and himself as the twenty-first.

38. The son born of a wife, wedded according to the Daiva rite, likewise (saves) seven ancestors and seven descendants, the son of a wife married by the Ârsha rite three (in the ascending and descending lines), and the son of a wife married by the rite of Ka (Pra*g*âpati) six (in either line).

39. From the four marriages, (enumerated) successively, which begin with the Brâhma rite spring sons, radiant with knowledge of the Veda and honoured by the *S*ish*t*as (good men).

40. Endowed with the qualities of beauty and goodness, possessing wealth and fame, obtaining as

35. Itaretarakâmyayâ, 'by (the expression of) mutual consent,' i.e. by the parents, means according to Medh. 'in consequence of the mutual desire of the bride and the bridegroom.' He mentions, however, the other explanation too. The text refers probably to customs like the sending of a cocoa-nut, which is usually adopted by Kshatriyas.

37-42. Vi. XXIV, 29-32; Gaut. IV, 29-33; Baudh. I, 21, 1; Âp. II, 12, 4; Yâ*gñ*. I, 58-60, 90.

39. Regarding the explanation of the term *S*ish*t*as, see below, XII, 109.

40. Gov. and Kull. take the first adjective differently, 'endowed with beauty, goodness, and other excellent qualities.' Regarding the term 'goodness' (sattva), see below, XII, 31.

many enjoyments as they desire and being most righteous, they will live a hundred years.

41. But from the remaining (four) blamable marriages spring sons who are cruel and speakers of untruth, who hate the Veda and the sacred law.

42. In the blameless marriages blameless children are born to men, in blamable (marriages) blamable (offspring); one should therefore avoid the blamable (forms of marriage).

43. The ceremony of joining the hands is prescribed for (marriages with) women of equal caste (var*n*a); know that the following rule (applies) to weddings with females of a different caste (var*n*a).

44. On marrying a man of a higher caste a Kshatriya bride must take hold of an arrow, a Vaisya bride of a goad, and a *S*ûdra female of the hem of the (bridegroom's) garment.

45. Let (the husband) approach his wife in due season, being constantly satisfied with her (alone); he may also, being intent on pleasing her, approach her with a desire for conjugal union (on any day) excepting the Parvans.

46. Sixteen (days and) nights (in each month),

---

43. Vi. XXIV, 5-8; Yâg*ñ*. I, 62.

44. The bridegroom takes hold of the other end of the arrow or of the goad, pronouncing the same texts which are recited on taking the hand of a bride of equal caste (Nâr.).

45. Yâg*ñ*. I, 80-81; Âp. II, 1, 17-18; Gaut. V, 1-2; Vas. XII, 21-24; Vi. LXIX, 1; Baudh. IV, 17-19. Tadvrata*h*, 'being intent on pleasing her' (Medh., Kull.), means according to Nâr. 'being careful to keep that rule (regarding the Parvans).' With respect to the Parvans, see below, IV, 128.

46. Yâg*ñ*. I, 79. The days which the virtuous declared to be unfit for conjugal intercourse are the first four after the appearance of the menses.

including four days which differ from the rest and are censured by the virtuous, (are called) the natural season of women.

47. But among these the first four, the eleventh and the thirteenth are (declared to be) forbidden; the remaining nights are recommended.

48. On the even nights sons are conceived and daughters on the uneven ones; hence a man who desires to have sons should approach his wife in due season on the even (nights).

49. A male child is produced by a greater quantity of male seed, a female child by the prevalence of the female; if (both are) equal, a hermaphrodite or a boy and a girl; if (both are) weak or deficient in quantity, a failure of conception (results).

50. He who avoids women on the six forbidden nights and on eight others, is (equal in chastity to) a student, in whichever order he may live.

51. No father who knows (the law) must take even the smallest gratuity for his daughter; for a man who, through avarice, takes a gratuity, is a seller of his offspring.

52. But those (male) relations who, in their folly, live on the separate property of women, (e. g. appropriate) the beasts of burden, carriages, and clothes of women, commit sin and will sink into hell.

---

48. Yâgñ. I, 79.

50. 'In whichever order he may live,' i. e. 'whether he be a householder or a hermit in the woods' (Kull., Nâr.). Medh. thinks that it is merely an arthavâda, and refers to no other order but that of householders, while Govinda thinks that the verse permits even to an ascetic who has lost all his children, to approach his wife during two nights in each month. Kull. justly ridicules the last opinion.

51. Âp. II, 13, 11; Vas. I, 37-38; Baudh. I, 21, 2-3.

52. Medh. gives in the first place another explanation of this

53. Some call the cow and the bull (given) at an Ârsha wedding 'a gratuity;' (but) that is wrong, since (the acceptance of) a fee, be it small or great, is a sale (of the daughter).

54. When the relatives do not appropriate (for their use) the gratuity (given), it is not a sale; (in that case) the (gift) is only a token of respect and of kindness towards the maidens.

55. Women must be honoured and adorned by their fathers, brothers, husbands, and brothers-in-law, who desire (their own) welfare.

56. Where women are honoured, there the gods are pleased; but where they are not honoured, no sacred rite yields rewards.

57. Where the female relations live in grief, the family soon wholly perishes; but that family where they are not unhappy ever prospers.

58. The houses on which female relations, not being duly honoured, pronounce a curse, perish completely, as if destroyed by magic.

59. Hence men who seek (their own) welfare, should always honour women on holidays and festivals with (gifts of) ornaments, clothes, and (dainty) food.

---

verse, which Nâr. and Nand. consider the only admissible one: 'But those (male) relations who, in their folly, live on property obtained by (the sale of) women, (e.g.) carriages or beasts of burden and clothes (received for) females, commit sin, &c.' Nand. and K. read nârîr yânâni, 'female slaves, carriages, &c.' The objection to Nâr.'s explanation is that nârîyânâni can hardly mean 'carriages received for females.' The reading 'nârî*h*' is obviously a conjectural emendation.

53. Âp. II, 13, 12; Vas. I, 36.

55–60. Yâ*gñ*. I, 82.

58. Some copies of Medh. omit verses 58–66.

59. Instead of satkâreshu (sa*m*kareshu, Gov.), 'on holidays,' like the Kaumudî, the Mahânâmnî, and so forth (Gov., Kull., Râgh.),

60. In that family, where the husband is pleased with his wife and the wife with her husband, happiness will assuredly be lasting.

61. For if the wife is not radiant with beauty, she will not attract her husband; but if she has no attractions for him, no children will be born.

62. If the wife is radiant with beauty, the whole house is bright; but if she is destitute of beauty, all will appear dismal.

63. By low marriages, by omitting (the performance of) sacred rites, by neglecting the study of the Veda, and by irreverence towards Brâhma*n*as, (great) families sink low.

64. By (practising) handicrafts, by pecuniary transactions, by (begetting) children on *S*ûdra females only, by (trading in) cows, horses, and carriages, by (the pursuit of) agriculture and by taking service under a king,

65. By sacrificing for men unworthy to offer sacrifices and by denying (the future rewards for good) works, families, deficient in the (knowledge of the) Veda, quickly perish.

66. But families that are rich in the knowledge of the Veda, though possessing little wealth, are numbered among the great, and acquire great fame.

Nâr. and Nand. read satkâre*n*a, which, according to the former, means 'by kind speech.'

64. Baudh. I, 10, 28. Nâr. says, 'by (keeping) beasts of burden, such as bullocks and horses.'

65. Baudh. I, 10, 26. Instead of kulâny â*s*u vi*n*a*s*yanti, 'families . . . perish quickly' (Gov., Kull.), Nâr., Nand., and Râgh. read kulâny akulatâ*m* yânti, '(great) families lose their rank.'

66. Baudh. I 10, 29.

67. With the sacred fire, kindled at the wedding, a householder shall perform according to the law the domestic ceremonies and the five (great) sacrifices, and (with that) he shall daily cook his food.

68. A householder has five slaughter-houses (as it were, viz.) the hearth, the grinding-stone, the broom, the pestle and mortar, the water-vessel, by using which he is bound (with the fetters of sin).

69. In order to successively expiate (the offences committed by means) of all these (five) the great sages have prescribed for householders the daily (performance of the five) great sacrifices.

70. Teaching (and studying) is the sacrifice (offered) to Brahman, the (offerings of water and food called) Tarpa*n*a the sacrifice to the manes, the burnt oblation the sacrifice offered to the gods, the

---

67. Yâg*ñ*. I, 97; Gaut. V, 7; Vi. LIX, 1; Baudh. II, 4, 22. 'The domestic ceremonies,' i. e. 'all the rites prescribed in the G*ri*hya-sûtras.'

68. Vi. LIX, 19. The translation of upaskara*h*, 'the broom,' rests on the authority of Nâr., who says, pesha*n*ena upakiraty a*s*uddhânîty upaskaro 'vaskarahetu*h* ı sa*m*mârga*n*î bhûyish*th*apipîlikâdihi*m*sâhetu*h* ıı The other commentators seem to take upaskara*h* in its usual sense, 'a household implement,' as they explain it by ku*nd*aka*t*âhâdi, 'a pot, a kettle, and the like' (Medh.), ku*nd*asa*m*mârga*n*yâdi, 'a pot, a broom, and the like' (Kull.), sa*m*mârga*n*yâdi, 'a broom and the like' (Râgh.), ulûkhalamusalâdi, 'a mortar and pestle and the like' (K.). But it is clear from the context that one implement only is meant.

69. Vi. LIX, 20.

70. Âp. I, 12, 15–13, 1; Gaut. V, 3, 9; Baudh. II, 5, 11; II, 11, 1–6; Vi. LIX, 21–25; Yâg*ñ*. I, 102. By Bhûtas either 'the goblins' or 'the living creatures' may be understood. Medh. takes it in the former sense. Nand. reads adhyâyanam for adhyâpanam, and adds adhyâyanam evâ 'dhyayanam, 'adhyâyana is the same as adhyayana, studying.'

Bali offering that offered to the Bhûtas, and the hospitable reception of guests the offering to men.

71. He who neglects not these five great sacrifices, while he is able (to perform them), is not tainted by the sins (committed) in the five places of slaughter, though he constantly lives in the (order of) house(-holders).

72. But he who does not feed these five, the gods, his guests, those whom he is bound to maintain, the manes, and himself, lives not, though he breathes.

73. They call (these) five sacrifices also, Ahuta, Huta, Prahuta, Brâhmya-huta, and Prâsita.

74. Ahuta (not offered in the fire) is the muttering (of Vedic texts), Huta the burnt oblation (offered to the gods), Prahuta (offered by scattering it on the ground) the Bali offering given to the Bhûtas, Brâhmya-huta (offered in the digestive fire of Brâhmanas), the respectful reception of Brâhmana (guests), and Prâsita (eaten) the (daily oblation to the manes, called) Tarpana.

75. Let (every man) in this (second order, at least) daily apply himself to the private recitation of the Veda, and also to the performance of the offering to the gods; for he who is diligent in the performance

72. 'Those whom he is bound to maintain,' i. e. 'aged parents and so forth' (Medh., Gov., Kull.), or 'animals unfit for work' (Medh.), or 'the Bhûtas, goblins or living beings' (Nâr., Râgh.). Nand. reads bhûtânâm for bhrityânâm, as Nâr. and Râgh. seem to have done.

73. Medh. remarks that these technical terms must belong to some particular Sâkhâ of the Veda. Two of them occur in the beginning of Baudhâyana's Grihya-sûtra, Sacred Books of the East, vol. xiv, p. xxxi, and four in Pâraskara's Grihya-sûtra I, 4, 1, as well as in Sânkhâyana's, I, 5, 1. Nâr., Nand., and K. read Brâhmahuta in this and the next verses.

of sacrifices, supports both the movable and the immovable creation.

76. An oblation duly thrown into the fire, reaches the sun; from the sun comes rain, from rain food, therefrom the living creatures (derive their subsistence).

77. As all living creatures subsist by receiving support from air, even so (the members of) all orders subsist by receiving support from the householder.

78. Because men of the three (other) orders are daily supported by the householder with (gifts of) sacred knowledge and food, therefore (the order of) householders is the most excellent order.

79. (The duties of) this order, which cannot be practised by men with weak organs, must be carefully observed by him who desires imperishable (bliss in) heaven, and constant happiness in this (life).

80. The sages, the manes, the gods, the Bhûtas, and guests ask the householders (for offerings and gifts); hence he who knows (the law), must give to them (what is due to each).

81. Let him worship, according to the rule, the sages by the private recitation of the Veda, the gods by burnt oblations, the manes by funeral offerings

---

76. Vas. XI, 13.

77–78. Vas. VIII, 14–16; Vi. LIX, 27–28.

78. Medh. points out that this verse indicates that householders alone are, as a rule, to be the teachers of the Veda, not hermits or ascetics. He adds, however, that the Institutes of the Bhikshus prescribe that men of the latter two orders, too, shall teach. Similarly Nâr. and Nand. point out that householders alone shall be teachers, 'except in times of distress' (Nand.).

79. 'Of weak organs,' i.e. 'of uncontrolled organs' (Medh., Gov., Kull.). Some MSS. of Medh. and Nand. read atyantam, 'excessive,' for nityam, 'constant.'

80. Vi. LIX, 29. 81. Yâgñ. I, 104.

(*S*râddha), men by (gifts of) food, and the Bhûtas by the Bali offering.

82. Let him daily perform a funeral sacrifice with food, or with water, or also with milk, roots, and fruits, and (thus) please the manes.

83. Let him feed even one Brâhma*n*a in honour of the manes at (the *S*râddha), which belongs to the five great sacrifices; but let him not feed on that (occasion) any Brâhma*n*a on account of the Vai*s*vadeva offering.

84. A Brâhma*n*a shall offer according to the rule (of his G*ri*hya-sûtra a portion) of the cooked food destined for the Vai*s*vadeva in the sacred domestic fire to the following deities:

85. First to Agni, and (next) to Soma, then to both these gods conjointly, further to all the gods (Vi*s*ve Devâ*h*), and (then) to Dhanvantari,

86. Further to Kuhû (the goddess of the new-moon day), to Anumati (the goddess of the full-moon day), to Pra*g*âpati (the lord of creatures), to heaven and earth conjointly, and finally to Agni Svish*t*ak*ri*t (the fire which performs the sacrifice well).

---

82. Vi. LXVII, 23-25.

83. The object of the second part of the verse is to forbid that two sets of Brâhma*n*as are to be fed at the daily *S*râddha, as is done at the Pârva*n*a *S*râddha, see below, verse 125 seq. Nâr. adds, vi*s*veshâ*m* devânâ*m* nitya*s*râddhe prî*n*ana*m* nâstîti dar*s*itam ǁ 'It is indicated (hereby) that the Vi*s*vedevas are not gladdened at the daily *S*râddha.' Medh., Nand., and Râgh. read ki*mk*it, 'any (food),' for ka*mk*it, 'any (Brâhma*n*a).'

84. Âp. II, 3, 16; Gaut. V, 10; Vi. LXVII, 3 (see also the G*ri*hya-sûtras, quoted by Professor Jolly on the last passage). The term 'a Brâhma*n*a' is not intended to exclude other Âryans (Medh., Nand., Kull., Râgh.).

85. Each offering must be presented with a mantra, consisting of the name of the deity in the dative case and the word 'svâhâ.'

87. After having thus duly offered the sacrificial food, let him throw Bali offerings in all directions of the compass, proceeding (from the east) to the south, to Indra, Yama, Varuna, and Soma, as well as to the servants (of these deities).

88. Saying, '(Adoration) to the Maruts,' he shall scatter (some food) near the door, and (some) in water, saying, '(Adoration to the waters;' he shall throw (some) on the pestle and the mortar, speaking thus, '(Adoration) to the trees.'

89. Near the head (of the bed) he shall make an offering to *S*rî (fortune), and near the foot (of his bed) to Bhadrakâlî; in the centre of the house let him place a Bali for Brahman and for Vâstoshpati (the lord of the dwelling) conjointly.

90. Let him throw up into the air a Bali for all the gods, and (in the day-time one) for the goblins roaming about by day, (and in the evening one) for the goblins that walk at night.

91. In the upper story let him offer a Bali to Sarvâtmabhûti; but let him throw what remains (from these offerings) in a southerly direction for the manes.

87–92. Âp. II, 3, 12–15, 18–4, 9; Gaut. V, 11–17; Vi. LXVII, 4–22, 26.

89. U*kk*îrshake, 'near the head of the bed' (Medh., 'others,' Nâr., Nand.), means according to Gov., Kull., and Râgh. 'in the north-eastern portion of the house, where the head of the Vâstupurusha, "the Lar," is situated.' Medh. says that the spot is known as the deva*s*ara*n*a. The same authorities refer pâdata*h*, 'at the foot,' to a spot in the south-west part of the building where the Lar keeps his feet.

91. P*ri*sh*th*avâstuni, 'in the upper story,' or (if the house has only one) 'on the top of the house' (Medh.), may also mean according to Gov. and Nâr. 'behind the house,' or according to Nand. 'outside the house.' Instead of 'Sarvâtmabhûti' (Kull.,

92. Let him gently place on the ground (some food) for dogs, outcasts, *Kandâlas* (*Svapak*), those afflicted with diseases that are punishments of former sins, crows, and insects.

93. That Brâhma*n*a who thus daily honours all beings, goes, endowed with a resplendent body, by a straight road to the highest dwelling-place (i. e. Brahman).

94. Having performed this Bali offering, he shall first feed his guest and, according to the rule, give alms to an ascetic (and) to a student.

95. A twice-born householder gains, by giving alms, the same reward for his meritorious act which (a student) obtains for presenting, in accordance with the rule, a cow to his teacher.

Râgh.), Nâr. and Nand. have 'Sarvânubhûti,' Gov. 'Sarvânnabhûti.' Nâr. mentions a various reading 'Sarvânnabhûta,' which seems to have been also Medh.'s version. The same deity occurs *S*âṅkhâyana G*ri*hya-sûtra II, 14, where Professor Oldenberg has Sarvânnabhûti, while the Petersburg Dict. gives Sarvânubhûti. Probably one of the last two readings is the original one, but without further parallel passages it is difficult to say which has to be chosen.

93. Instead of te*g*omûrti*h*, 'endowed with a resplendent body,' Kull. and Râgh. read te*g*omûrti, '(to the highest) resplendent (dwelling-place, i.e. Brahman).'

94. Vi. LIX, 14; LXVII, 27; Vas. XI, 5; Baudh. II, 5, 15; Yâ*gñ*. I, 107. Bhikshave brahma*k*âri*n*e, 'to an ascetic and to a student' (Kull., Râgh.), may mean according to Medh. (who gives Kull.'s view also), either 'to a begging student' or 'to an ascetic who is chaste.' Gov. adopts the former explanation. 'According to the rule,' i. e. 'making him wish welfare' (Medh., Nand.); see also Gaut. V, 18.

95. For vidhivad gurau or guro*h*, 'according to the rule, to his teacher,' Nand. reads agor yathâvidhi, 'according to the rule to one who has no cow.' The var. lect. is mentioned by Medh. also. The 'rule' referred to is, according to Gov. and Kull., that given Yâ*gñ*. I, 204.

96. Let him give, in accordance with the rule, to a Brâhmana who knows the true meaning of the Veda, even (a small portion of food as) alms, or a pot full of water, having garnished (the food with seasoning, or the pot with flowers and fruit).

97. The oblations to gods and manes, made by men ignorant (of the law of gifts), are lost, if the givers in their folly present (shares of them) to Brâhmanas who are mere ashes.

98. An offering made in the mouth-fire of Brâhmanas rich in sacred learning and austerities, saves from misfortune and from great guilt.

99. But let him offer, in accordance with the rule, to a guest who has come (of his own accord) a seat and water, as well as food, garnished (with seasoning), according to his ability.

100. A Brâhmana who stays unhonoured (in the house), takes away (with him) all the spiritual merit even of a man who subsists by gleaning ears of corn, or offers oblations in five fires.

101. Grass, room (for resting), water, and fourthly a kind word; these (things) never fail in the houses of good men.

102. But a Brâhmana who stays one night only is declared to be a guest (atithi); for because he stays (sthita) not long (anityam), he is called atithi (a guest).

---

96. Satkritya, 'having garnished, &c.' (Kull., Râgh.), means according to Medh. and Gov. 'having honoured the recipient' (with fruits and flowers, Gov.).

97. Vas. III, 8.

99–118. Âp. II, 4, 11, 13–20; 6, 5–9; Gaut. V, 25–45; Vas. VIII, 4–5, 11–15; Baudh. II, 5, 11–18; 6, 36–37; Vi. LXVII, 28–46; Yâgñ. I, 104–109, 112–113.

103. One must not consider as a guest a Brâhmana who dwells in the same village, nor one who seeks his livelihood by social intercourse, even though he has come to a house where (there is) a wife, and where sacred fires (are kept).

104. Those foolish householders who constantly seek (to live on) the food of others, become, in consequence of that (baseness), after death the cattle of those who give them food.

105. A guest who is sent by the (setting) sun in the evening, must not be driven away by a householder; whether he have come at (supper-)time or at an inopportune moment, he must not stay in the house without entertainment.

106. Let him not eat any (dainty) food which he does not offer to his guest; the hospitable reception of guests procures wealth, fame, long life, and heavenly bliss.

107. Let him offer (to his guests) seats, rooms,

103. Sâmgatikah, 'one who seeks his livelihood by social intercourse,' is, according to Gov., Kull., and Râgh., 'one who makes his living by telling wonderful or laughable stories and the like.' Medh. explains the word first by 'he who stays being a fellow-student (sahâdhyâyî),' and afterwards by 'a Vaisya, or Sûdra, or a friend who makes friends with everybody, possessing wonderful or laughable stories and the like, which are indicated by the word samgati.' Nâr. says that samgati means sambandha, 'connexion,' that sâmgatika is 'one who comes for such a reason.' Perhaps the term might be rendered 'a visitor on business or pleasure.' According to Kull. and Râgh., the last clause, 'where (there is) a wife and sacred fires (are kept),' indicates, that a householder who has neither, need not entertain guests. But the words are taken differently by Gov. and Nâr., 'nor him who travels with his wife or his fires' (tathâ yatra yasya pravâsino 'pi bhâryâgnayo vâ saha gakkhanti I etadanyatamam svagriha upasthitam âgatam apyathi atithim na vidyât I nâtithidharmenârkayet II Nâr.).

107. Gaut. V, 38. 'The rule refers to the case when many guests

beds, attendance on departure and honour (while they stay), to the most distinguished in the best form, to the lower ones in a lower form, to equals in an equal manner.

108. But if another guest comes after the Vaisvadeva offering has been finished, (the householder) must give him food according to his ability, (but) not repeat the Bali offering.

109. A Brâhmana shall not name his family and (Vedic) gotra in order to obtain a meal; for he who boasts of them for the sake of a meal, is called by the wise a foul feeder (vântâsin).

110. But a Kshatriya (who comes) to the house of a Brâhmana is not called a guest (atithi), nor a Vaisya, nor a Sûdra, nor a personal friend, nor a relative, nor the teacher.

111. But if a Kshatriya comes to the house of a Brâhmana in the manner of a guest, (the householder) may feed him according to his desire, after the above-mentioned Brâhmanas have eaten.

112. Even a Vaisya and a Sûdra who have approached his house in the manner of guests, he may allow to eat with his servants, showing (thereby) his compassionate disposition.

113. Even to others, personal friends and so forth, who have come to his house out of affection, he may

---

come at the same time.' Upâsanam, 'honour (while they stay),' i.e. 'sitting with them and talking to them' (Medh.).

108. 'When the Vaisvadeva offering has been finished,' i.e. 'when the dinner of the guests is over.'

111. 'In the manner of a guest,' i.e. 'having consumed his provisions while on a journey, being an inhabitant of another village or arriving at meal-time' (Medh., Gov., Kull.).

112. Nâr. says, 'he may cause them to be fed by his servants in the same manner.'

give food, garnished (with seasoning) according to his ability, (at the same time) with his wife.

114. Without hesitation he may give food, even before his guests, to the following persons, (viz.) to newly-married women, to infants, to the sick, and to pregnant women.

115. But the foolish man who eats first without having given food to these (persons) does, while he crams, not know that (after death) he himself will be devoured by dogs and vultures.

116. After the Brâhma*n*as, the kinsmen, and the servants have dined, the householder and his wife may afterwards eat what remains.

117. Having honoured the gods, the sages, men, the manes, and the guardian deities of the house, the householder shall eat afterwards what remains.

118. He who prepares food for himself (alone), eats nothing but sin; for it is ordained that the food which remains after (the performance of) the sacrifices shall be the meal of virtuous men.

119. Let him honour with the honey-mixture a king, an officiating priest, a Snâtaka, the teacher, a son-in-law, a father-in-law, and a maternal uncle, (if they come) again after a full year (has elapsed since their last visit).

---

114. Suvâsinî*h*, 'to newly-married women,' i. e. 'daughters-in-law and daughters,' may also mean according to 'others,' quoted by Medh. and Gov., 'females whose fathers or fathers-in-law live.' Nand. reads svavâsinî*h* and explains it by 'sisters.'

119-120. Âp. II, 8, 5-9; Gaut. V, 27-30; Vas. XI, 1-2; Baudh. II, 6, 36-37; Yâ*gñ*. I, 110.

119. Guru*h*, 'the teacher,' means according to Nâr. 'the teacher or the sub-teacher.' Priya*h*, which according to Gov., Kull., and Râgh. means 'a son-in-law,' is taken by Nâr. and Nand. in its etymological sense, 'a friend.'

120. A king and a *S*rotriya, who come on the performance of a sacrifice, must be honoured with the honey-mixture, but not if no sacrifice is being performed; that is a settled rule.

121. But the wife shall offer in the evening (a portion) of the dressed food as a Bali-oblation, without (the recitation of) sacred formulas; for that (rite which is called the) Vais*v*adeva is prescribed both for the morning and the evening.

122. After performing the Pit*ri*yag*ñ*a, a Brâhma*n*a who keeps a sacred fire shall offer, month by month, on the new-moon day, the funeral sacrifice (*S*râddha, called) Pi*nd*ânvâhâryaka.

123. The wise call the monthly funeral offering to the manes Anvâhârya (to be offered after the

---

120. According to one opinion, given by Medh., and according to Gov., Kull., Nâr., this rule is a limitation of verse 119, and means that the two persons mentioned shall not receive the honey-mixture, except when they come during the performance of a sacrifice, however long a period may have elapsed since their last visit. According to another explanation, mentioned by Medh., and according to Nand. and Râgh., the verse means that a king and a *S*rotriya, who come before a year since their last visit elapsed, on the occasion of a sacrifice, shall receive the madhuparka. The term *S*rotriya refers according to Medh. to a Snâtaka or to an officiating priest, according to others quoted by him to all the persons mentioned in the preceding verse, according to Gov., Kull., Nâr., and Râgh. to a Snâtaka. The latter is probably the correct opinion, as a *S*rotriya, i. e. one who knows a whole recension of the Veda, must be a Snâtaka. Medh. approves of the reading *yagñ*akarma*n*y upasthite.

121. Nand. omits this verse.

122. Yâg*ñ*. I, 217; Gaut. XV, 2. The sacrifice intended by the term Pit*ri*yag*ñ*a, 'sacrifice offered to the fathers,' is the so-called Pi*nd*apit*ri*yag*ñ*a, a *S*rauta rite (Â*s*valâyana, *S*rauta-sûtra II, 6–7), and Pi*nd*ânvâhâryaka is another name for the monthly *S*râddha.

cakes), and that must be carefully performed with the approved (sorts of) flesh (mentioned below).

124. I will fully declare what and how many Brâhma*n*as must be fed on that (occasion), who must be avoided, and on what kinds of food (they shall dine).

125. One must feed two (Brâhma*n*as) at the offering to the gods, and three at the offering to the manes, or one only on either occasion; even a very wealthy man shall not be anxious (to entertain) a large company.

126. A large company destroys these five (advantages), the respectful treatment (of the invited, the propriety of) place and time, purity and (the selection of) virtuous Brâhma*n*a (guests); he therefore shall not seek (to entertain) a large company.

127. Famed is this rite for the dead, called (the sacrifice sacred to the manes (and performed) on the new-moon day; if a man is diligent in (performing) that, (the reward of) the rite for the dead, which is performed according to Smârta rules, reaches him constantly.

---

125. Vas. XI, 27; Baudh. II, 15, 10; Vi. LXXIII, 3-4; Gaut. XV, 8, 21; Yâ*gñ*. I, 228. The offering to the gods, mentioned in this verse, is an Aṅga or subsidiary rite preceding the offering to the manes. Medh. takes the first part of this verse in a peculiar manner, 'One must feed two (Brâhma*n*as) at the offering to the gods, and three (for each ancestor, or nine in all) at the offering to the manes, or one on either occasion (i.e. one at the offering to the gods and at the offering to the manes, one for each ancestor, or three in all).'

126. Vas. XI, 28; Baudh. II, 15, 11.

127. Gov. reads vidhi*h* kshaye for vidhukshaye, 'on the new-moon day,' and explains the first half of the verse as follows: 'The ceremony called the (sacrifice) to the manes (is) a rite for the benefit of the dead, (and) prescribed on the new-moon day

128. Oblations to the gods and manes must be presented by the givers to a *S*rotriya alone; what is given to such a most worthy Brâhma*n*a yields great reward.

129. Let him feed even one learned man at (the sacrifice) to the gods, and one at (the sacrifice) to the manes; (thus) he will gain a rich reward, not (if he entertains) many who are unacquainted with the Veda.

130. Let him make inquiries even regarding the remote (ancestors of) a Brâhma*n*a who has studied an entire (recension of the) Veda; (if descended from a virtuous race) such a man is a worthy recipient of gifts (consisting) of food offered to the gods or to the manes, he is declared (to procure as great rewards as) a guest (atithi).

131. Though a million of men, unacquainted with the *Rik*as, were to dine at a (funeral sacrifice), yet a single man, learned in the Veda, who is satisfied (with his entertainment), is worth them all as far as the (production of) spiritual merit (is concerned).

132. Food sacred to the manes or to the gods must be given to a man distinguished by sacred

---

or in the house, i.e. to be performed by householders, not by men of other orders.' Medh., too, mentions another reading, which he explains much in the same way as Gov., and which therefore may have been vidhi*h* kshaye, though the MSS. read tithikshaye.

128. Vas. III, 8; Gaut. XV, 9.

130. Vi. LXXXII, 2. The examination must extend, as in the case of officiating priests, to ten ancestors on the mother's and the father's side (Medh., Gov.).

131. 'The *Rik*as,' i.e. 'the Veda.' Nâr. reads instead of prîta*h*, 'who is satisfied,' yukta*h*, and combines it with dharmata*h*, 'who is properly invited.' Nand. has vipra*h*, 'a Brâhma*n*a,' for prîta*h*. K. has prima manu vipra*h*, sec. manu yukta*h*.

knowledge; for hands, smeared with blood, cannot be cleansed with blood.

133. As many mouthfuls as an ignorant man swallows at a sacrifice to the gods or to the manes, so many red-hot spikes, spears, and iron balls must (the giver of the repast) swallow after death.

134. Some Brâhma*n*as are devoted to (the pursuit of) knowledge, and others to (the performance of) austerities; some to austerities and to the recitation of the Veda, and others to (the performance of) sacred rites.

135. Oblations to the manes ought to be carefully presented to those devoted to knowledge, but offerings to the gods, in accordance with the reason (of the sacred law), to (men of) all the four (abovementioned classes).

136. If there is a father ignorant of the sacred texts whose son has learned one whole recension of the Veda and the Aṅgas, and a son ignorant of the sacred texts whose father knows an entire recension of the Veda and the Aṅgas,

133. Nâr. thinks that the eater, not the giver of the feast will bear the punishment. Medh. gives both this explanation and that adopted in the translation. Nâr. explains *ri*sh*t*i, 'spear,' by kha*d*ga, 'sword.' Nand. reads hulân for gu*d*ân, 'balls,' and says that hula means 'a double-edged sword.'

134. 'Knowledge,' i. e. 'the knowledge of the supreme soul' (Medh., Gov., Kull., Nâr., Râgh.). Medh. and Nâr. say that ascetics, hermits, students, and householders are intended by the four divisions mentioned in the text.

135. Vas. XI, 17; Baudh. II, 14, 3. The verse indicates that ascetics are particularly desirable guests.

136–137. Kull. remarks that the object of the verse is to teach that at a *S*râddha the learned son of a learned father is to be entertained, but not to permit the admission of a fool whose father is learned.

137. Know that he whose father knows the Veda, is the more venerable one (of the two); yet the other one is worthy of honour, because respect is due to the Veda (which he has learned).

138. Let him not entertain a personal friend at a funeral sacrifice; he may gain his affection by (other) valuable gifts; let him feed at a *S*râddha a Brâhma*n*a whom he considers neither as a foe nor as a friend.

139. He who performs funeral sacrifices and offerings to the gods chiefly for the sake of (gaining) friends, reaps after death no reward for *S*râddhas and sacrifices.

140. That meanest among twice-born men who in his folly contracts friendships through a funeral sacrifice, loses heaven, because he performed a *S*râddha for the sake of friendship.

141. A gift (of food) by twice-born men, consumed with (friends and relatives), is said to be offered to the Pi*s*â*k*as; it remains in this (world) alone like a blind cow in one stable.

142. As a husbandman reaps no harvest when he has sown the seed in barren soil, even so the giver of sacrificial food gains no reward if he presented it to a man unacquainted with the *Rik*as.

143. But a present made in accordance with the rules to a learned man, makes the giver and the

138–148. Âp. II, 17, 4–6; Gaut. XV, 12–14; Baudh. II, 14, 6; Yâ*gñ*. I, 220.

141. Âp. II, 17, 8–9. According to Medh., Gov., Kull., and Râgh. pai*s*a*k*î means 'offered after the manner of the Pi*s*â*k*as.' But the version given above, which follows Nâr. and Nand., is supported by the ancient verse, quoted by Âpastamba, from which Manu's *S*loka is probably derived.

recipient partakers of rewards both in this (life) and after death.

144. (If no learned Brâhma*n*a be at hand), he may rather honour a (virtuous) friend than an enemy, though the latter may be qualified (by learning and so forth); for sacrificial food, eaten by a foe, bears no reward after death.

145. Let him (take) pains (to) feed at a *S*râddha an adherent of the *Ri*g-veda who has studied one entire (recension of that) Veda, or a follower of the Ya*g*ur-veda who has finished one *S*âkhâ, or a singer of Sâmans who (likewise) has completed (the study of an entire recension).

146. If one of these three dines, duly honoured, at a funeral sacrifice, the ancestors of him (who gives the feast), as far as the seventh person, will be satisfied for a very long time.

147. This is the chief rule (to be followed) in offering sacrifices to the gods and manes; know that the virtuous always observe the following subsidiary rule.

148. One may also entertain (on such occasions) one's maternal grandfather, a maternal uncle, a sister's son, a father-in-law, one's teacher, a daughter's son, a daughter's husband, a cognate kinsman, one's own officiating priest or a man for whom one offers sacrifices.

149. For a rite sacred to the gods, he who knows the law will not make (too close) inquiries regarding an (invited) Brâhma*n*a; but when one performs a

148. Bandhum, 'a cognate kinsman' (Kull., Râgh.), is taken by Medh. and Gov. in its widest sense, 'any remoter kinsman' (sagotrâdi*h*).

149. Vi. LXXXII, 1–2.

ceremony in honour of the manes, one must carefully examine (the qualities and parentage of the guest).

150. Manu has declared that those Brâhma*n*as who are thieves, outcasts, eunuchs, or atheists are unworthy (to partake) of oblations to the gods and manes.

151. Let him not entertain at a *S*râddha one who wears his hair in braids (a student), one who has not studied (the Veda), one afflicted with a skin-disease, a gambler, nor those who sacrifice for a multitude (of sacrificers).

152. Physicians, temple-priests, sellers of meat, and those who subsist by shop-keeping must be avoided at sacrifices offered to the gods and to the manes.

153. A paid servant of a village or of a king, a man with deformed nails or black teeth, one who opposes his teacher, one who has forsaken the sacred fire, and a usurer;

154. One suffering from consumption, one who subsists by tending cattle, a younger brother who

---

150–182. Âp. II, 17, 21; Gaut. XV, 16–19, 30–31; Vas. XI, 19; Vi. LXXXII, 3–30; Yâ*gñ*. I, 222–224.

150. For the term nâstikav*ri*tti, 'atheist,' Medh. proposes, besides the explanation given above, the other equally possible one, 'he who derives his livelihood from atheists.'

151. Anadhîyâna*m*, 'one who has not studied the Veda,' i. e. 'one who has been initiated only, but has not studied' (Kull.), or 'one who has not mastered the Veda' (Medh.), or 'one who has left off studying' (Nâr.). Medh. and Nand. read durvâlam for durbalam, 'afflicted with a skin-disease,' and the former explains his var. lect. by 'a bald or a red-haired man.' 'Those who sacrifice for a multitude,' i. e. 'who offer the (forbidden) Ahîna sacrifices, for on that occasion there are many sacrificers' (Nâr.).

154. Nirâk*ri*ti*h*, 'one who neglects the five great sacrifices' (Medh.,

marries or kindles the sacred fire before the elder, one who neglects the five great sacrifices, an enemy of the Brâhma*n*a race, an elder brother who marries or kindles the sacred fire after the younger, and one who belongs to a company or corporation,

155. An actor or singer, one who has broken the vow of studentship, one whose (only or first) wife is a *S*ûdra female, the son of a remarried woman, a one-eyed man, and he in whose house a paramour of his wife (resides);

156. He who teaches for a stipulated fee and he who is taught on that condition, he who instructs *S*ûdra pupils and he whose teacher is a *S*ûdra, he who speaks rudely, the son of an adulteress, and the son of a widow,

157. He who forsakes his mother, his father, or a teacher without a (sufficient) reason, he who has

---

Kull., Râgh.), means according to Gov. 'one who forsakes the Vedas (and the rest),' according to Nâr. and Nand. 'one who does not recite the Veda privately,' or 'who has forgotten it.' Ga*n*âbhyantara*h*, 'one who belongs to a company or corporation,' i.e. 'of men who live by one trade' (Medh., Gov., Nâr.), is further explained by Nâr. by 'the headman of a village,' or 'the leader of a caravan.' According to Kull. and Râgh. it means 'one who misappropriates the money of a corporation.'

155. Ku*s*îlava, 'an actor or singer,' is, as Medh. states, a very wide term, including all 'bards, actors, jugglers, dancers, singers, and the like.' Kull. wrongly understands by avakîr*n*în, 'one who has broken the vow of studentship,' an ascetic also who has become unchaste. Such an ascetic is called ârû*dh*apatita.

156. Vâgdush*t*a*h*, 'one who speaks rudely,' means according to 'others,' quoted by Medh. and Kull., 'one who is accused of a great crime' (abhi*s*asta).

157. According to Nâr. guro*h*, 'a teacher,' denotes the â*k*ârya alone. Medh. blames this explanation, and refers it to the subteacher. The same explains ku*nd*â*s*î, 'he who eats the food of the son of an adulteress,' by 'a glutton who eats sixty Palas of rice.'

contracted an alliance with outcasts either through the Veda or through a marriage,

158. An incendiary, a prisoner, he who eats the food given by the son of an adulteress, a seller of Soma, he who undertakes voyages by sea, a bard, an oil-man, a suborner to perjury,

159. He who wrangles or goes to law with his father, the keeper of a gambling-house, a drunkard, he who is afflicted with a disease (in punishment of former) crimes, he who is accused of a mortal sin, a hypocrite, a seller of substances used for flavouring food,

160. A maker of bows and of arrows, he who lasciviously dallies with a brother's widow, the betrayer of a friend, one who subsists by gambling, he who learns (the Veda) from his son,

---

158. Agâradâhî, 'an incendiary,' includes according to a verse, quoted by Nand. also, 'one who burns corpses for money.' Kû*t*akârakah, 'a suborner to perjury' (Gov., Kull.), means according to Medh. and Râgh. 'a false witness,' according to Nâr. and Nand. 'any one who commits fraud,' e.g. a forger, a falsifier of weights and measures. 'Others' quoted by Medh. explain somavikrayin as 'one who sells (the merit gained by) Soma (sacrifices).'

159. 'He who wrangles or goes to law with his father,' e.g. who forces him to divide the family estate (Medh.), see Gaut. XV, 19. Kitava*h*, 'the keeper of a gambling-house' (Medh.), means according to Gov. and Nand. 'one who makes others play for himself,' according to Nâr. 'a gambler for pleasure,' and according to Nand. 'a rogue.' 'Others,' however, read kekara*h*, 'a squinting man,' and construe it with madyapa*h*, 'a drunkard' (Medh., Gov., Kull., Nâr., Nand., Râgh.). Rasa, 'substances used for flavouring food,' e.g. 'sugar-cane juice' (Gov., Kull., Râgh.), 'molasses' (Nâr.). Medh. explains rasada*h* by vishada*h*, 'a poisoner.'

160. I accept Gov.'s and Râgh.'s explanation of agredidhishûpati, who believe it to be equivalent to didhishûpati explained below, verse 173. Kull. and Nand. take it as 'the husband of a younger sister married before the elder,' and Medh. as an

161. An epileptic man, one who suffers from scrofulous swellings of the glands, one afflicted with white leprosy, an informer, a madman, a blind man, and he who cavils at the Veda must (all) be avoided.

162. A trainer of elephants, oxen, horses, or camels, he who subsists by astrology, a bird-fancier, and he who teaches the use of arms,

163. He who diverts water-courses, and he who delights in obstructing them, an architect, a messenger, and he who plants trees (for money),

164. A breeder of sporting-dogs, a falconer, one who defiles maidens, he who delights in injuring living creatures, he who gains his subsistence from *S*ûdras, and he who offers sacrifices to the Ga*n*as,

165. He who does not follow the rule of conduct, a (man destitute of energy like a) eunuch, one who constantly asks (for favours), he who lives by agri-

---

irregular compound consisting of agredidhishûpati and didhishûpati, see Gaut. XV, 16. Though in some Sm*ri*tis agredidhishûpati has the meaning given by Kull., it seems here inadmissible, on account of verse 173, which is meaningless, if it is not meant to explain this term. Dyûtav*ri*tti*h*, 'one who subsists by gambling,' means according to Medh. 'one who makes others play for his profit,' according to Gov., Kull., and Râgh. 'the keeper of a gambling-house.' Nâr. and Nand. take it in its literal meaning.

162. Pakshi*n*â*m* poshaka*h*, 'a bird-fancier,' means according to Medh. 'a trainer of hunting-falcons and hawks.'

164. The commentators mention a var. lect. v*ri*shalaputra*h*, 'one who has only sons by a *S*ûdra wife,' for 'one who gains his subsistence from *S*ûdras.' Nâr. and Nand. explain ga*n*ânâ*m* yâ*g*aka*h* by 'one who sacrifices for ga*n*as,' i.e. many people or guilds. According to the explanation of Medh., Gov., Kull., and Râgh., which has been translated above, the performance of the Vinâyaka or Ga*n*e*s*ahoma (Yâ*gñ*. I, 270–294) may be meant. But it is also possible to think of the Ga*n*ahomas, which according to Baudh. IV, 8, 1 must not be performed for others.

culture, a club-footed man, and he who is censured by virtuous men,

166. A shepherd, a keeper of buffaloes, the husband of a remarried woman, and a carrier of dead bodies, (all these) must be carefully avoided.

167. A Brâhma*n*a who knows (the sacred law) should shun at (sacrifices) both (to the gods and to the manes) these lowest of twice-born men, whose conduct is reprehensible, and who are unworthy (to sit) in the company (at a repast).

168. As a fire of dry grass is (unable to consume the offerings and is quickly) extinguished, even so (is it with) an unlearned Brâhma*n*a; sacrificial food must not be given to him, since it (would be) offered in ashes.

169. I will fully declare what result the giver obtains after death, if he gives food, destined for the gods or manes, to a man who is unworthy to sit in the company.

170. The Râkshasas, indeed, consume (the food) eaten by Brâhma*n*as who have not fulfilled the vow of studentship, by a Parivett*ri* and so forth, and by other men not admissible into the company.

171. He must be considered as a Parivett*ri* who

---

168. According to Medh. and Gov. the object of this verse is to admit virtuous and learned men, afflicted with bodily defects, as guests at rites in honour of the gods; see Vas. XI, 20. Kull. thinks that the injunction to avoid ignorant men is repeated here in order to show that they are as unfit as real 'defilers of the company.'

170. Avratai*h*, 'who have not fulfilled the vow of studentship' (Gov., Kull., Râgh.), means according to Medh. 'of bad conduct,' and according to Nâr. 'who do not observe the rules prescribed for a Snâtaka and so forth.'

171. Usually a person who kindles the sacred fire before his elder brother is called a Paryâdhât*ri*, and the elder brother a Paryâhita.

marries or begins the performance of the Agnihotra before his elder brother, but the latter as a Parivitti.

172. The elder brother who marries after the younger, the younger brother who marries before the elder, the female with whom such a marriage is contracted, he who gives her away, and the sacrificing priest, as the fifth, all fall into hell.

173. He who lasciviously dallies with the widow of a deceased brother, though she be appointed (to bear a child by him) in accordance with the sacred law, must be known to be a Didhishûpati.

174. Two (kinds of) sons, a Ku*nd*a and a Golaka, are born by wives of other men; (he who is born) while the husband lives, will be a Ku*nd*a, and (he who is begotten) after the husband's death, a Golaka.

175. But those two creatures, who are born of wives of other men, cause to the giver the loss (of the rewards), both in this life and after death, for the food sacred to gods or manes which has been given (to them).

176. The foolish giver (of a funeral repast) does not reap the reward for as many worthy guests as a man, inadmissible into company, can look on while they are feeding.

177. A blind man by his presence causes to the giver (of the feast) the loss of the reward for ninety (guests), a one-eyed man for sixty, one who suffers from white leprosy for a hundred, and one punished by a (terrible) disease for a thousand.

178. The giver (of a *S*râddha) loses the reward,

172. Baudh. II, 1, 39.

177. Regarding the diseases which are punishments for sins committed in a former life, see below, XI, 49 seq.

178. Paurtikam, 'due for such a non-sacrificial gift,' i.e. 'for one

due for such a non-sacrificial gift, for as many Brâhma*n*as as a (guest) who sacrifices for *S*ûdras may touch (during the meal) with his limbs.

179. And if a Brâhma*n*a, though learned in the Veda, accepts through covetousness a gift from such (a man), he will quickly perish, like a vessel of unburnt clay in water.

180. (Food) given to a seller of Soma becomes ordure, (that given) to a physician pus and blood, but (that presented) to a temple-priest is lost, and (that given) to a usurer finds no place (in the world of the gods).

181. What has been given to a Brâhma*n*a who lives by trade that is not (useful) in this world and the next, and (a present) to a Brâhma*n*a born of a remarried woman (resembles) an oblation thrown into ashes.

182. But the wise declare that the food which (is offered) to other unholy, inadmissible men, enumerated above, (is turned into) adipose secretions, blood, flesh, marrow, and bone.

183. Now hear by what chief of twice-born men

---

which is given outside the sacrificial enclosure' (Medh., Gov.), or 'for the gift of food at a *S*râddha' (Kull., Râgh.).

179. 'From such a man,' i. e. 'from one who sacrifices for *S*ûdras.'

180. The meaning is that the giver will be born in his next life among the animals, feeding on the unclean substances enumerated (Medh., Gov., Kull., Râgh.), or that the food will be rejected by the manes and the gods as impure (Nâr.). Apratish*th*am, 'finds no place' (Medh., Gov., Kull., Râgh.), means according to Nâr. and Nand. 'secures no fame (to the giver).'

182. According to Medh., Gov., Kull., and Râgh., it must be understood that the giver will be born in his next existence as a worm, feeding on the substances mentioned.

183-186. Âp. II, 17, 22; Gaut. XV, 28, 31; Vas. III, 19; Baudh. II, 14, 2-3; Vi. LXXXIII; Yâg*ñ*. I, 219-221.

a company defiled by (the presence of) unworthy (guests) is purified, and the full (description of) the Brâhma*n*as who sanctify a company.

184. Those men must be considered as the sanctifiers of a company who are most learned in all the Vedas and in all the Aṅgas, and who are the descendants of *S*rotriyas.

185. A Tri*n*â*k*iketa, one who keeps five sacred fires, a Trisupar*n*a, one who is versed in the six Aṅgas, the son of a woman married according to the Brâhma rite, one who sings the *G*yesh*th*asâman,

186. One who knows the meaning of the Veda, and he who expounds it, a student, one who has given a thousand (cows), and a centenarian must be considered as Brâhma*n*as who sanctify a company.

187. On the day before the *S*râddha-rite is performed, or on the day when it takes place, let him invite with due respect at least three Brâhma*n*as, such as have been mentioned above.

188. A Brâhma*n*a who has been invited to a (rite) in honour of the manes shall always control himself and not recite the Veda, and he who performs the *S*râddha (must act in the same manner).

---

185. Regarding the term Tri*n*â*k*iketa, see Âp. II, 17, 22, note. Pa*ñk*âgni*h*, 'one who keeps five sacred fires' (Medh., 'others,' Gov., Kull., Nand., Râgh.), means according to Medh. and Nâr. 'one who knows the pa*ñk*âgnividyâ, taught in the *Kh*ândogyopanishad IV, 10 seq. Trisupar*n*a means according to Medh., Nâr., and Nand. 'one who knows the texts Taitt. Âr. X, 38–40; but according to Gov., Kull., and Râgh. 'one who knows the portion of the Rig-veda called Trisupar*n*a, Rig-veda X, 114, 3–5.

186. Nand. explains brahma*k*ârî, 'a student,' by 'a chaste man' (see above, verse 50).

187. Âp. II, 17, 11–15; Vas. XI, 17; Yâ*gñ*. I, 225.

188. Gaut. XV. 23; Yâ*gñ*. I, 225. 'Control himself,' i.e. 'remain chaste.'

189. For the manes attend the invited Brâhma*n*as, follow them (when they walk) like the wind, and sit near them when they are seated.

190. But a Brâhma*n*a who, being duly invited to a rite in honour of the gods or of the manes, in any way breaks (the appointment), becomes guilty (of a crime), and (in his next birth) a hog.

191. But he who, being invited to a *S*râddha, dallies with a *S*ûdra woman, takes upon himself all the sins which the giver (of the feast) committed.

192. The manes are primeval deities, free from anger, careful of purity, ever chaste, averse from strife, and endowed with great virtues.

193. Now learn fully from whom all these (manes derive) their origin, and with what ceremonies they ought to be worshipped.

194. The (various) classes of the manes are declared to be the sons of all those sages, Marî*k*i and the rest, who are children of Manu, the son of Hira*n*yagarbha.

195. The Somasads, the sons of Virâ*g*, are stated to be the manes of the Sâdhyas, and the Agnish-

189. 'Like the wind,' i.e. 'like the vital air, the breath' (Medh., Gov., Kull.). Medh. thinks that the manes enter the body of the invited guests.

190. Medh. explains atikrâman, 'breaks the appointment' (Gov., Kull., Nâr., Râgh.), by 'breaks the rules of chastity and the like.' Medh. mentions a second 'improper' explanation given by 'others,' 'does not accept the invitation.'

191. Medh., Gov., Nand., and Râgh. take v*ri*shalî, 'a *S*ûdra woman,' in the sense of 'his lascivious wife.' Probably the word is used in its proper sense and indicates, as Nâr. states, that intercourse with a *S*ûdra wife is the worst offence in such a case.

194. 'Marî*k*i and the rest,' see above, I, 35.

195. Nâr., Nand., and K. prima manu read Somasuta*h* for Somasada*h*.

vâttas, the children of Marîki, are famous in the world (as the manes) of the gods.

196. The Barhishads, born of Atri, are recorded to be (the manes) of the Daityas, Dânavas, Yakshas, Gandharvas, Snake-deities, Râkshasas, Suparnas, and Kimnaras,

197. The Somapas those of the Brâhmanas, the Havirbhugs those of the Kshatriyas, the Âgyapas those of the Vaisyas, but the Sukâlins those of the Sûdras.

198. The Somapas are the sons of Kavi (Bhrigu), the Havishmats the children of Aṅgiras, the Âgyapas the offspring of Pulastya, but the Sukâlins (the issue) of Vasishtha.

199. One should know that (other classes), the Agnidagdhas, the Anagnidagdhas, the Kâvyas, the Barhishads, the Agnishvâttas, and the Saumyas, are (the manes) of the Brâhmanas alone.

200. But know also that there exist in this (world) countless sons and grandsons of those chief classes of manes which have been enumerated.

201. From the sages sprang the manes, from the manes the gods and the Dânavas, but from the gods the whole world, both the movable and the immovable in due order.

202. Even water offered with faith (to the manes)

199. Medh. and Gov. place the Anagnidagdhas first. Nâr. reads at the end of the first half-verse bahûn, 'many,' instead of tathâ, and Nand. has vahân. The translation follows the explanation given by Gov., Kull., and Râgh. The other three commentators say that this verse gives partly different names for the several classes of manes, enumerated in the preceding verses. But their explanations are not very clear, and they are forced to ignore or transpose the particle eva which stands after viprânâm. The verse probably contains a second classification of the manes, which differs from the preceding, because it is based on a different tradition.

202. Akshayâyapakalpate, 'produces endless (bliss),' (Gov., Kull.),

in vessels made of silver or adorned with silver, produces endless (bliss).

203. For twice-born men the rite in honour of the manes is more important than the rite in honour of the gods; for the offering to the gods which precedes (the *S*râddhas), has been declared to be a means of fortifying (the latter).

204. Let him first invite a (Brâhma*n*a) in honour of the gods as a protection for the (offering to the manes); for the Râkshasas destroy a funeral sacrifice which is left without such a protection.

205. Let him make (the *S*râddha) begin and end with (a rite) in honour of the gods; it shall not begin and end with a (rite) to the manes; for he who makes it begin and end with a (rite) in honour of the manes, soon perishes together with his progeny.

206. Let him smear a pure and secluded place with cowdung, and carefully make it sloping towards the south.

207. The manes are always pleased with offerings made in open, naturally pure places, on the banks of rivers, and in secluded spots.

---

means according to Medh. 'affords to them imperishable satisfaction.'

203. The rite in honour of the gods meant is the Vai*s*vadeva which precedes each *S*râddha.

204. The above translation of the first half-verse follows Medh., Gov., and Kull. It is, however, not impossible to take, with Sir W. Jones, daiva*m* as a neuter, and to translate, 'Let him first perform the rite in honour of the gods as a protection for the (*S*râddha).'

205. The meaning of the verse is that the Brâhma*n*as, fed at the Vai*s*vadeva which precedes the *S*râddha, must be invited and served before and dismissed after the Brâhma*n*as entertained in honour of the manes (Medh., Kull., Nâr.). See also below, verse 209.

206. Âp. II, 18, 14; Gaut. XV, 25; Yâg*ñ*. I, 227.

207. Vi. LXXXV, 54–63. *K*oksheshu, 'naturally pure' (Medh.,

208. The (sacrificer) shall make the (invited) Brâhma*n*as, who have duly performed their ablutions, sit down on separate, prepared seats, on which blades of Ku*s*a grass have been placed.

209. Having placed those blameless Brâhma*n*as on their seats, he shall honour them with fragrant garlands and perfumes, beginning with (those who are invited in honour of) the gods.

210. Having presented to them water, sesamum grains, and blades of Ku*s*a grass, the Brâhma*n*a (sacrificer) shall offer (oblations) in the sacred fire, after having received permission (to do so) from (all) the Brâhma*n*a (guests) conjointly.

211. Having first, according to the rule, performed, as a means of protecting (the *S*râddha), oblations to Agni, to Soma, and to Yama, let him afterwards satisfy the manes by a gift of sacrificial food.

212. But if no (sacred) fire (is available), he shall place (the offerings) into the hand of a Brâhma*n*a; for Brâhma*n*as who know the sacred texts declare, 'What fire is, even such is a Brâhma*n*a.'

213. They (also) call those first of twice-born men the ancient deities of the funeral sacrifice, free from anger, easily pleased, employed in making men prosper.

Gov., Kull., Nâr.) or 'lovely' (Nand., Râgh.), 'such as forest glades' (Kull.).

208. Yâ*gñ*. I, 226. 209. Vi. LXXIII, 2; Yâ*gñ*. I, 231.

210. Vi. LXXXIII, 5; Âp. II, 17, 17-19; Baudh. II, 14, 7; Yâ*gñ*. I, 229.

211. Vi. LXXIII, 12; Baudh. II, 14, 7.

212. Â*s*valâyana G*ri*hya-sûtra IV, 8, 5-6. Cases, where a sacred fire is wanting, are those in which a child, an unmarried man, or a widower perform a *S*râddha (Medh., Kull., Nâr.).

213. The object of the verse is to show why the offerings may

214. After he has performed (the oblations) in the fire, (and) the whole series of ceremonies in such a manner that they end in the south, let him sprinkle water with his right hand on the spot (where the cakes are to be placed).

215. But having made three cakes out of the remainder of that sacrificial food, he must, concentrating his mind and turning towards the south, place them on (Kusa grass) exactly in the same manner in which (he poured out the libations of) water.

216. Having offered those cakes according to the (prescribed) rule, being pure, let him wipe the same hand with (the roots of) those blades of Kusa grass for the sake of the (three ancestors) who partake of the wipings (lepa).

217. Having (next) sipped water, turned round (towards the north), and thrice slowly suppressed

---

be placed into the hands of the guests. The epithet 'ancient' is explained to mean 'produced in the kalpa when the Sâdhyas were created' (Medh.), or 'those whose succession has been uninterrupted since immemorial times' (Gov., Kull., Râgh.), or 'those who were produced before all other castes' (Nâr.), or 'those who receive gifts before others' (Râgh.). Medh. prefers, however, to read purâtanâh, 'the ancients call,' &c., and this seems to have stood in Nand.'s text too.

214. 'The whole series of ceremonies,' i.e. 'the acts of sprinkling water and strewing Kusa grass round the fire and so forth, which are subsidiary to the oblations in the fire.' Apasavyam, 'in such a manner that they end in the south' (dakshinâsamstham), means according to Nâr., prâkînâvîtena, 'passing the sacrificial string over the right shoulder and under the left arm.' Apasavyena hastena, 'with his right hand' (Medh. 'others,' Kull., Râgh.), means according to Medh., Gov., Nâr., and Nand., 'out of the Tîrtha of the right hand which is sacred to the manes' (see above, II, 59).

216. The three ancestors meant are the great-grandfather, his father and grandfather; see Vi. LXXIII, 22.

217. The texts to be pronounced are, 'Adoration to Spring!' &c.,

I 2

his breath, (the sacrificer) who knows the sacred texts shall worship (the guardian deities of) the six seasons and the manes.

218. Let him gently pour out the remainder of the water near the cakes, and, with fixed attention, smell those cakes, in the order in which they were placed (on the ground).

219. But taking successively very small portions from the cakes, he shall make those seated Brâhma*n*as eat them, in accordance with the rule, before (their dinner).

220. But if the (sacrificer's) father is living, he must offer (the cakes) to three remoter (ancestors); or he may also feed his father at the funeral sacrifice as (one of the) Brâhma*n*a (guests).

221. But he whose father is dead, while his grandfather lives, shall, after pronouncing his father's name, mention (that of) his great-grandfather.

222. Manu has declared that either the grandfather may eat at that *S*râddha (as a guest), or (the

and afterwards, 'Adoration to you, oh manes!' &c. Before he recites the latter texts, the worshipper must turn round towards the south.

218. Vi. LXXIII, 23. 'The remainder of the water,' i. e. 'which is contained in the vessel from which he took the water for sprinkling the ground' (verse 214).

219. 'Those seated Brâhma*n*as,' i. e. 'those invited for the funeral rite, not those invited for the preceding rite in honour of the gods.' 'According to the rule,' i. e. 'giving to the representative of the father a piece from the cake offered to the manes of the father and so forth' (Kull.), or 'after they have sipped water and so forth' (Nâr.). Nand. inserts here verse 223, and states that it is explanatory of the term 'according to the rule.'

220. Vi. LXXV, 1, 4. Nâr. adds that this case happens when a son has kindled the sacred fire during his father's lifetime, because then the Pi*nd*apit*ri*yag*ñ*a and afterwards the Pârva*n*a *S*râddha must be performed.

221-222. Vi. LXXV, 6.

grandson) having received permission, may perform it, as he desires.

223. Having poured water mixed with sesamum, in which a blade of Kusa grass has been placed, into the hands of the (guests), he shall give (to each) that (above-mentioned) portion of the cake, saying, 'To those, Svadhâ!'

224. But carrying (the vessel) filled with food with both hands, the (sacrificer) himself shall gently place it before the Brâhmanas, meditating on the manes.

225. The malevolent Asuras forcibly snatch away that food which is brought without being held with both hands.

226. Let him, being pure and attentive, carefully place on the ground the seasoning (for the rice), such as broths and pot herbs, sweet and sour milk, and honey,

227. (As well as) various (kinds of) hard food which require mastication, and of soft food, roots, fruits, savoury meat, and fragrant drinks.

228. All this he shall present (to his guests), and, being pure and attentive, successively invite them to partake of each (dish), proclaiming its qualities.

229. Let him on no account drop a tear, become angry or utter an untruth, nor let him touch the food with his foot nor violently shake it.

---

223. Vi. LXXIII, 23. This rule is a supplement to verse 220. Instead of the pronoun the names are to be used (Medh., Gov.).

225. Vas. XI, 25; Baudh. II, 15, 3.

229. Vi. LXXIX, 19-21; LXXXI, 1; Yâgñ. I, 239. Avadhûnayet, 'nor violently shake it,' is explained according to Medh. by 'others,' 'nor remove the dust with his dress.' Nand. places verse 230 immediately after verse 228.

230. A tear sends the (food) to the Pretas, anger to his enemies, a falsehood to the dogs, contact with his foot to the Râkshasas, a shaking to the sinners.

231. Whatever may please the Brâhma*n*as, let him give without grudging it; let him give riddles from the Veda, for that is agreeable to the manes.

232. At a (sacrifice in honour) of the manes, he must let (his guests) hear the Veda, the Institutes of the sacred law, legends, tales, Purâ*n*as, and Khilas.

233. Himself being delighted, let him give delight to the Brâhma*n*as, cause them to partake gradually and slowly (of each dish), and repeatedly invite (them to eat) by (offering) the food and (praising) its qualities.

234. Let him eagerly entertain at a funeral sacrifice a daughter's son, though he be a student, and let him place a Nepâl blanket on the seat (of each guest), scattering sesamum grains on the ground.

---

231. Yâ*gñ*. I, 239. Brahmodyâ*h* kathâ*h*, 'let him give riddles from the Veda,' such as those collected in the Â*s*valâyana *S*rauta-sûtra X, 9, 2 (Medh., Nand.). Medh. thinks that the term brahmodya may also refer to Vedic stories, such as that of the fights of the Devas and Asuras, or of Saramâ and the Pa*n*is, and he mentions a var. lect. brahmâdyâ*h*, 'conversations regarding the Brahman, the supreme soul.' This latter explanation is adopted by Gov., Kull., Nâr., and Râgh., though the text everywhere has brahmodyâ*h*. As the Brahmodya-riddles were a favourite recreation of the priests during the tedious performance of their sacrifices, it is not doubtful that the explanation given in the translation is the only admissible one.

232. Baudh. II, 14, 5; Vi. LXXIII, 16; Yâ*gñ*. I, 239. 'Khilas,' i. e. 'the apocrypha of the Veda, such as the *S*rîsûkta.' 'Âkhyânâni legends, such as the Saupar*n*a, the Maitrâvâru*n*a' (Medh., Gov., Kull., Râgh.), or 'such as occur in the Brâhma*n*as' (Nâr.), or 'the death of Ka*m*sa and so forth' (Nand.).

235. There are three means of sanctification, (to be used) at a *S*râddha, a daughter's son, a Nepâl blanket, and sesamum grains; and they recommend three (other things) for it, cleanliness, suppression of anger, and absence of haste.

236. All the food must be very hot, and the (guests) shall eat in silence; (even though) asked by the giver (of the feast), the Brâhma*n*as shall not proclaim the qualities of the sacrificial food.

237. As long as the food remains warm, as long as they eat in silence, as long as the qualities of the food are not proclaimed, so long the manes partake (of it).

238. What (a guest) eats, covering his head, what he eats with his face turned towards the south, what he eats with sandals on (his feet), that the Râkshasas consume.

239. A *K*â*nd*âla, a village pig, a cock, a dog, a menstruating woman, and a eunuch must not look at the Brâhma*n*as while they eat.

240. What (any of) these sees at a burnt-oblation, at a (solemn) gift, at a dinner (given to Brâhma*n*as), or at any rite in honour of the gods and manes, that produces not the intended result.

241. A boar makes (the rite) useless by inhaling the smell (of the offerings), a cock by the air of his wings, a dog by throwing his eye (on them), a low-caste man by touching (them).

242. If a lame man, a one-eyed man, one deficient

235. Vas. XI, 35–36. 236. Vi. LXXXI, 11, 20.

237. Vi. LXXXI, 20; Vas. XI, 32.

238. Vi. LXXXI, 12–14.

239. Âp. II, 17, 20; Gaut. XV, 24.

241. 'A low-caste man,' i.e. 'a *S*ûdra.'

242. Vi. LXXXI, 15–16. According to Medh., Gov., and Kull.,

in a limb, or one with a redundant limb, be even the servant of the performer (of the *S*râddha), he also must be removed from that place (where the *S*râddha is held).

243. To a Brâhma*n*a (householder), or to an ascetic who comes for food, he may, with the permission of (his) Brâhma*n*a (guests), show honour according to his ability.

244. Let him mix all the kinds of food together, sprinkle them with water and put them, scattering them (on Ku*s*a grass), down on the ground in front of (his guests), when they have finished their meal.

245. The remnant (in the dishes), and the portion scattered on Ku*s*a grass, shall be the share of deceased (children) who received not the sacrament (of cremation) and of those who (unjustly) forsook noble wives.

246. They declare the fragments which have fallen on the ground at a (*S*râddha) to the manes, to be the share of honest, dutiful servants.

---

the word api, 'even,' indicates that others, e.g. *S*ûdras, must also be sent away.

243. Vi. LXXXI, 18. Medh., Gov., and Kull. take the first words differently, 'To a Brâhma*n*a who comes as a guest (atithi) or any other mendicant.' Nâr. and Râgh. give the explanation adopted above.

244. Vi. LXXXI, 21.

245. Vas. XI, 23–24; Vi. LXXXI, 22. Regarding the burial of children, see below, V, 69. Tyâginâ*m* kulayoshitâ*m*, 'of those who unjustly forsook noble wives' (Medh., Kull.), may also mean, according to Râgh. and to 'others,' quoted by Medh. and Kull., 'of those who forsook their Gurus and of unmarried maidens;' according to Gov., 'of women who forsook their families;' according to Nâr., 'of suicides and childless women.' Nand. explains the first word by 'of ascetics.'

246. Vi. LXXXI, 23.

247. But before the performance of the Sapi*nd*î-kara*n*a, one must feed at the funeral sacrifice in honour of a (recently-)deceased Âryan (one Brâhma*n*a) without (making an offering) to the gods, and give one cake only.

248. But after the Sapi*nd*îkara*n*a of the (deceased father) has been performed according to the sacred law, the sons must offer the cakes with those ceremonies, (described above.)

249. The foolish man who, after having eaten a *S*râddha(-dinner), gives the leavings to a *S*ûdra, falls headlong into the Kâlasûtra hell.

250. If the partaker of a *S*râddha(-dinner) enters on the same day the bed of a *S*ûdra female, the manes of his (ancestors) will lie during that month in her ordure.

251. Having addressed the question, 'Have you dined well?' (to his guests), let him give water for sipping to them who are satisfied, and dismiss them, after they have sipped water, (with the words) 'Rest either (here or at home)!'

---

247. Vi. XXI, 2-12, 19; Yâg*ñ*. I, 250. The Sapi*nd*îkara*n*a, 'the solemn reception of a dead person among the partakers of the funeral oblations,' is performed either on the thirteenth day or a year after the death. Up to the time of its performance the *S*râddhas are so-called Ekoddish*t*as, 'performed for one person only.' Medh., Gov., Nâr., Nand., and K. read the first word of the verse asapi*nd*akriyâkarma, and according to this var. lect. the translation must be, 'The rite for persons not made Sapi*nd*as (i.e. the Ekoddish*t*a *S*râddha, must be performed) for an Âryan (recently) deceased; (on that occasion) one must,' &c.

250. Medh., Gov., Kull., and Râgh. take v*ri*shalî, 'a *S*ûdra female' (Nâr.), in the sense of 'a seducing woman' (v*ri*shasyantî).

251. Yâg*ñ*. I, 242; Vi. LXXIII, 26-27. Kull. reads abhi bho ramyatâm, 'Ho, take rest!' and Râgh., abhito gamyatâm, 'Go where you please!'

252. The Brâhma*n*a (guests) shall then answer him, 'Let there be Svadhâ;' for at all rites in honour of the manes the word Svadhâ is the highest benison.

253. Next let him inform (his guests) who have finished their meal, of the food which remains; with the permission of the Brâhma*n*as let him dispose (of that), as they may direct.

254. At a (*S*râddha) in honour of the manes one must use (in asking the guests if they are satisfied, the word) svaditam; at a Gosh*th*î-*s*râddha, (the word) su*s*rutam; at a V*ri*ddhi-*s*râddha, (the word) sampannam; and at (a rite) in honour of the gods, (the word) ru*k*itam.

255. The afternoon, Ku*s*a grass, the due preparation of the dwelling, sesamum grains, liberality, the careful preparation of the food, and (the company of) distinguished Brâhma*n*as are true riches at all funeral sacrifices.

256. Know that Ku*s*a grass, purificatory (texts), the morning, sacrificial viands of all kinds, and those means of purification, mentioned above, are blessings at a sacrifice to the gods.

---

252. Yâ*gñ*. I, 243. Medh., Gov., Nand., and Râgh. read svadhetyeva, (shall then answer him) 'Svadhâ!'

254. 'One must ask,' i. e. 'the giver of the feast or any other person who comes' (Medh., Gov.), the former only (Kull.). Medh. and Gov. explain gosh*th*e, 'at a Gosh*th*î-*s*râddha' (Kull., Râgh.), by 'in a cow-pen' (goshu tish*th*antîshu, goga*n*amadhye), and Nâr. by gosh*th*e goma*nd*alârtha*m* gosh*th*e brâhma*n*abhogane. Abhyudaya or V*ri*ddhi-*s*râddhas are those performed on joyful occasions, such as marriages.

256. Pavitram, 'purificatory texts,' means according to Nâr. 'other means of purification, such as barley and water.' Nand. reads darbhapavitra*m*, 'blades of Ku*s*a grass.' 'Those means of purification mentioned above,' i. e. 'the preparation of the house

257. The food eaten by hermits in the forest, milk, Soma-juice, meat which is not prepared (with spices), and salt unprepared by art, are called, on account of their nature, sacrificial food.

258. Having dismissed the (invited) Brâhma*n*as, let him, with a concentrated mind, silent and pure, look towards the south and ask these blessings of the manes:

259. 'May liberal men abound with us! May (our knowledge of) the Vedas and (our) progeny increase! May faith not forsake us! May we have much to give (to the needy)!'

260. Having thus offered (the cakes), let him, after (the prayer), cause a cow, a Brâhma*n*a, a goat, or the sacred fire to consume those cakes, or let him throw them into water.

261. Some make the offering of the cakes after (the dinner); some cause (them) to be eaten by birds or throw them into fire or into water.

---

and so forth.' Nand. reads havishyâ*n*i *k*a *s*aktita*h*, 'sacrificial viands (prepared) according to one's ability.'

257. Anupaskr*i*tam, 'which is not prepared (with spices),' (Gov., Nâr.), means according to Nand. 'not dressed as people usually do,' according to Kull. and Râgh. 'not tainted by a bad smell,' and according to Medh. 'not forbidden, such as meat from a slaughter-house.' 'Salt unprepared by art,' i.e. 'rock salt or salt from the sea' (but not Bi*d*a, Nâr.).

259. Yâg*ñ*. I, 245; Vi. LXXIII, 28.

260. Yâg*ñ*. I, 256. 'Thus,' i. e. as described in verse 215.

261. Baudh. II, 14, 9. According to the MSS. and editions the word translated in accordance with the clear explanations of Medh., Kull., and K., and with the requirements of the context, by 'after (the dinner),' is purastât. As purastât always means 'before,' it would seem that the real reading of the three commentators was like that of Râgh.'s commentary 'parastât,' the sense of which perfectly agrees with their explanation.

262. The (sacrificer's) first wife, who is faithful and intent on the worship of the manes, may eat the middle-most cake, (if she be) desirous of bearing a son.

263. (Thus) she will bring forth a son who will be long-lived, famous, intelligent, rich, the father of numerous offspring, endowed with (the quality of) goodness, and righteous.

264. Having washed his hands and sipped water, let him prepare (food) for his paternal relations and, after giving it to them with due respect, let him feed his maternal relatives also.

265. But the remnants shall be left (where they lie) until the Brâhma*n*as have been dismissed; afterwards he shall perform the (daily) domestic Bali-offering; that is a settled (rule of the) sacred law.

266. I will now fully declare what kind of sacrificial food, given to the manes according to the rule, will serve for a long time or for eternity.

267. The ancestors of men are satisfied for one month with sesamum grains, rice, barley, mâsha beans, water, roots, and fruits, which have been given according to the prescribed rule,

268. Two months with fish, three months with the meat of gazelles, four with mutton, and five indeed with the flesh of birds,

---

Nâr. and Nand. clearly read purastât, and explain it by prâk, 'before.' But the meaning, thus obtained, is not good, because it stands to reason that the custom mentioned here should differ from that described above, verse 218 seq.

264. This is to be done after the cakes have been made and placed (Medh., Nand.). Medh., Gov., Nand. read pû*g*ayet, 'let him honour,' instead of 'let him feed.'

267–272. Âp. II, 16, 23–17, 3; Gaut. XV, 15; Vi. LXXX; Yâ*gñ*. I, 257–259.

269. Six months with the flesh of kids, seven with that of spotted deer, eight with that of the black antelope, but nine with that of the (deer called) Ruru,

270. Ten months they are satisfied with the meat of boars and buffaloes, but eleven months indeed with that of hares and tortoises,

271. One year with cow-milk and milk-rice; from the flesh of a long-eared white he-goat their satisfaction endures twelve years.

272. The (vegetable called) Kâlasâka, (the fish called) Mahâsalka, the flesh of a rhinoceros and that of a red goat, and all kinds of food eaten by hermits in the forest serve for an endless time.

273. Whatever (food), mixed with honey, one gives on the thirteenth lunar day in the rainy season under the asterism of Maghâh, that also procures endless (satisfaction).

274. 'May such a man (the manes say) be born in our family who will give us milk-rice, with honey and clarified butter, on the thirteenth lunar day (of the month of Bhâdrapada) and (in the afternoon) when the shadow of an elephant falls towards the east.'

---

269. Gov. states the Ruru is the Sambara, or Sâmbar stag.

271. Nâr. explains vârdhrînasa, which Medh., Gov., Kull., and Râgh. declare, on the strength of a verse, to be a white goat, by 'a black-necked, white-winged bird with a red head,' and quotes another nigama in favour of his view; see also Âp. II, 17, 3, where the crane called Vârdhrânasa (var. lect. Vârdhrînasa) is mentioned.

272. Another name of the pot-herb Kâlasâka is according to Medh. Krishnavâsudeva, according to Nand. Krishnanimba. The Mahâsalka is the prawn. Others mentioned by Medh. read sasalkân.

273. Vi. LXXVI, 1; Yâgñ. I, 260. The day meant is Bhâdrapada Badi 13.

274. Vi. LXXVIII, 51–52; Vas. XI, 40. Gov. omits this verse.

275. Whatever (a man), full of faith, duly gives according to the prescribed rule, that becomes in the other world a perpetual and imperishable (gratification) for the manes.

276. The days of the dark half of the month, beginning with the tenth, but excepting the fourteenth, are recommended for a funeral sacrifice; (it is) not thus (with) the others.

277. He who performs it on the even (lunar) days and under the even constellations, gains (the fulfilment of) all his wishes; he who honours the manes on odd (lunar days) and under odd (constellations), obtains distinguished offspring.

278. As the second half of the month is preferable to the first half, even so the afternoon is better for (the performance of) a funeral sacrifice than the forenoon.

Medh. says that 'others' improperly explain prâk*kh*âye ku*ñg*arasya, '(in the afternoon) when the shadow of an elephant falls towards the east' (Kull., Nâr., Râgh.), by 'during an eclipse.' He also mentions a var. lect. prâk*kh*âyâm. It seems, however, by no means certain that the explanation, adopted by him and most commentators, is the correct one. It is much more probable that a particular day (see Vi*gñ*âne*s*vara on Yâ*gñ*. I, 217) is meant. The thirteenth lunar day is, of course, the thirteenth of the dark half of Bhâdrapada, the day of the Mahâlaya *S*râddha.

276. Âp. II, 17, 6; Gaut. XV, 3; Yâ*gñ*. I, 263; Vas. XI, 16. The reason why the fourteenth is excepted, is given Vi. LXXVIII, 50, and Yâ*gñ*. loc. cit.

277. Âp. II, 17, 8–22; Gaut. XV, 4; Vi. LXXVIII, 8–49; Yâ*gñ*. I, 267. I read with Medh., Gov., Nand., Râgh., and K. pit*rî*n ar*k*an, which, to judge from the commentary, must have been Kull.'s reading also, instead of the senseless pit*rî*n sarvân of the editions. Nand. adds five verses and a half which give the details with respect to the rewards obtained by performing the *S*râddhas on particular lunar days. They are clearly an interpolation.

278. Âp. II, 17, 5.

279. Let him, untired, duly perform the (rites) in honour of the manes in accordance with the prescribed rule, passing the sacred thread over the right shoulder, proceeding from the left to the right (and) holding Ku*s*a grass in his hands, up to the end (of the ceremony).

280. Let him not perform a funeral sacrifice at night, because the (night) is declared to belong to the Râkshasas, nor in the twilight, nor when the sun has just risen.

281. Let him offer here below a funeral sacrifice, according to the rule given above, (at least) thrice a year, in winter, in summer, and in the rainy season, but that which is included among the five great sacrifices, every day.

282. The burnt-oblation, offered at a sacrifice to the manes, must not be made in a common fire; a Brâhma*n*a who keeps a sacred fire (shall) not (perform) a funeral sacrifice except on the new-moon day.

283. Even when a Brâhma*n*a, after bathing, satisfies the manes with water, he obtains thereby the whole reward for the performance of the (daily) *S*râddha.

284. They call (the manes of) fathers Vasus, (those of) grandfathers Rudras, and (those of) great-grandfathers Âdityas; thus (speaks) the eternal Veda.

---

279. Gov., Kull., and Râgh. explain apasavyam, 'proceeding from left to right' (Nâr.), by 'with the Tîrtha of the hand, that is sacred to the manes.' Medh. and Gov. think that â nidhanât, 'up to the end (of the ceremony),' (Kull., Nâr., Nand., Râgh.), means 'until death.'

280. Âp. II, 17, 23.

284. Yâg*ñ*. I, 268.

285. Let him daily partake of the vighasa and daily eat am*ri*ta (ambrosia); but vighasa is what remains from the meal (of Brâhma*n*a guests) and the remainder of a sacrifice (is called) am*ri*ta.

286. Thus all the ordinances relating to the five (daily great) sacrifices have been declared to you; hear now the law for the manner of living fit for Brâhma*n*as.

CHAPTER IV.

1. Having dwelt with a teacher during the fourth part of (a man's) life, a Brâhma*n*a shall live during the second quarter (of his existence) in his house, after he has wedded a wife.

2. A Brâhma*n*a must seek a means of subsistence which either causes no, or at least little pain (to others), and live (by that) except in times of distress.

3. For the purpose of gaining bare subsistence, let him accumulate property by (following those) irreproachable occupations (which are prescribed for) his (caste), without (unduly) fatiguing his body.

4. He may subsist by *Ri*ta (truth), and Am*ri*ta

285. Medh. and Nâr. seem to have read bh*ri*tyasesha*m*, 'what remains after those who must be supported (have been fed).' The former mentions the other reading too.

IV. 2. Medh., Gov., Kull., Nâr., and Râgh. particularly state that droha and adroha are not equivalent to hi*m*sâ and ahi*m*sâ, because 'injury to living beings' is forbidden under any circumstances. What is meant by droha is the pain caused to others by importunate begging. Hence the meaning of Manu is that householders shall, if possible, not subsist by begging, but rather by gleaning corn. Nand., however, explains droha by hi*m*sâ, and the following verses favour his opinion.

3. 'For the purpose of gaining bare subsistence, but not in order to procure many enjoyments for himself.'

(ambrosia), or by M*ri*ta (death) and by Pram*ri*ta (what causes many deaths); or even by (the mode) called Satyân*ri*ta (a mixture of truth and falsehood), but never by *S*vav*ri*tti (a dog's mode of life).

5. By *Ri*ta shall be understood the gleaning of corn; by Am*ri*ta, what is given unasked; by M*ri*ta, food obtained by begging; and agriculture is declared to be Pram*ri*ta.

6. But trade and (money-lending) are Satyân*ri*ta, even by that one may subsist. Service is called *S*vav*ri*tti; therefore one should avoid it.

7. He may either possess enough to fill a granary, or a store filling a grain-jar; or he may collect what suffices for three days, or make no provision for the morrow.

8. Moreover, among these four Brâhma*n*a householders, each later-(named) must be considered more distinguished, and through his virtue to have conquered the world more completely.

9. One of these follows six occupations, another subsists by three, one by two, but the fourth lives by the Brahmasattra.

---

7. Yâg*ñ*. I, 128. The first two clauses are variously interpreted. The first means according to Medh., 'he may keep a store of grain or other property, sufficient to maintain a large family, many servants and animals during three years;' according to Gov., 'a store of grain sufficient for twelve days;' according to Kull. and Râgh., 'a store sufficient to fill a granary which holds a supply for three years or more;' and according to Nâr., 'a store sufficient for a year, six months, or three months.' The second clause is interpreted by Medh. as 'a store sufficient for six months;' by Gov. and Nâr. as 'a store sufficient for six days;' and by Kull. and Râgh. as 'a sufficiency for one year.' For other explanations of the term Kumbhîdhânya, see Baudh. I, 1, 5 note. Nand. reads dvyahaihika*h*, 'or he may collect what suffices for two days.'

9. 'Six occupations,' i.e. 'gleaning corn, acceptance of gifts

10. He who maintains himself by picking up grains and ears of corn, must be always intent on (the performance of) the Agnihotra, and constantly offer those Ish*t*is only, which are prescribed for the days of the conjunction and opposition (of the moon), and for the solstices.

11. Let him never, for the sake of subsistence, follow the ways of the world; let him live the pure, straightforward, honest life of a Brâhma*n*a.

12. He who desires happiness must strive after a perfectly contented disposition and control himself; for happiness has contentment for its root, the root of unhappiness is the contrary (disposition).

13. A Brâhma*n*a, who is a Snâtaka and subsists by one of the (above-mentioned) modes of life, must

given unasked, begging, agriculture, trade, and teaching' (Medh.), or 'those mentioned in verses 5–6' (Gov.), or 'those mentioned in verses 5–6, excepting service and with the addition of money-lending' (Kull., Râgh.), or 'those enumerated in verses 5–6, and those six, mentioned above, I, 88' (Nâr.), or 'those mentioned above, I, 88' (Nand.). 'Subsists by three,' i.e. 'by the first three, mentioned in verses 5–6' (Medh.), or 'by teaching, sacrificing, and accepting gifts' (Gov., Kull., Râgh., Nand.), or 'by teaching, sacrificing and accepting gifts, and by the first three, mentioned in verses 5–6' (Nâr.). 'One by two,' i.e. 'by gleaning and accepting voluntary gifts' (Medh.), or 'by sacrificing and teaching' (Gov., Kull., Râgh., Nand.), or 'by gleaning ears and single grains' (Nâr.). 'The Brahmasattra,' i.e. 'gleaning either ears or single grains' (Nâr.), or 'teaching' (Gov., Kull., Râgh., Nand.). Elsewhere the term Brahmasattra is applied to the daily recitation of the Veda, and it probably means here 'teaching.'

10. The Agnihotra, i.e. the daily morning and evening oblations in the sacred fire or fires. The sacrifices intended are the Dar*s*a-paur*n*amâsas and the Âgraya*n*as.

11. Yâ*gñ*. I, 123.

12–17. Yâ*gñ*. I, 129.

13. Nand. places verse 15 immediately after verse 12. Regarding the term Snâtaka, see below, verse 31, Âp. I, 30, 1–3.

discharge the (following) duties which secure heavenly bliss, long life, and fame.

14. Let him, untired, perform daily the rites prescribed for him in the Veda; for he who performs those according to his ability, attains to the highest state.

15. Whether he be rich or even in distress, let him not seek wealth through pursuits to which men cleave, nor by forbidden occupations, nor (let him accept presents) from any (giver whosoever he may be).

16. Let him not, out of desire (for enjoyments), attach himself to any sensual pleasures, and let him carefully obviate an excessive attachment to them, by (reflecting on their worthlessness in) his heart.

17. Let him avoid all (means of acquiring) wealth which impede the study of the Veda; (let him maintain himself) anyhow, but study, because that (devotion to the Veda-study secures) the realisation of his aims.

18. Let him walk here (on earth), bringing his dress, speech, and thoughts to a conformity with his age, his occupation, his wealth, his sacred learning, and his race.

19. Let him daily pore over those Institutes of science which soon give increase of wisdom, those

---

15. Prasaṅgena, 'through pursuits to which men cleave,' e.g. 'music and singing' (Medh., Gov., Kull., Râgh., Nand.). Nâr. interprets the word by 'with too great eagerness.'

17. Vi. LXXI, 4.

18. Yâgñ. I, 123; Vi. LXXI, 5–6. 'His race,' e.g. let him wear his hair in the manner prescribed by the usage of his family (Vas. II, 21).

19. Yâgñ. I, 99; Vi. LXXI, 8. The various sciences meant are the Itihâsas, Purâṇas, and Nyâya, the Arthaṣâstra, medicine, and

which teach the acquisition of wealth, those which are beneficial (for other worldly concerns), and likewise over the Nigamas which explain the Veda.

20. For the more a man completely studies the Institutes of science, the more he fully understands (them), and his great learning shines brightly.

21. Let him never, if he is able (to perform them), neglect the sacrifices to the sages, to the gods, to the Bhûtas, to men, and to the manes.

22. Some men who know the ordinances for sacrificial rites, always offer these great sacrifices in their organs (of sensation), without any (external) effort.

23. Knowing that the (performance of the) sacrifice in their speech and their breath yields imperishable (rewards), some always offer their breath in their speech, and their speech in their breath.

24. Other Brâhma*n*as, seeing with the eye of knowledge that the performance of those rites has knowledge for its root, always perform them through knowledge alone.

25. A Brâhma*n*a shall always offer the Agnihotra at the beginning or at the end of the day and of the night, and the Dar*s*a and Paur*n*amâsa (Ish*t*is) at the end of each half-month,

26. When the old grain has been consumed the

astrology. The Nigamas are the Aṅgas (Medh.). Gov., Kull., and Nâr. consider the Nigamas to be a separate class of works, teaching the meaning of the Veda, i. e. the naigamakâ*nd*a of the Nirukta.

22. This and the next two verses refer to various symbolical ways of performing the great sacrifices, which are mentioned in the Upanishads.

23. Kaushîtaki-Up. II, 5. 24. Nand. omits this verse.

25–27. Gaut. VIII, 19–20; Vas. XI, 46; Vi. LIX, 2–9; Baudh. II, 4, 23; Yâ*g*ñ. I, 97, 124–125.

(Âgrayana) Ishti with new grain, at the end of the (three) seasons the (Kâturmâsya-)sacrifices, at the solstices an animal (sacrifice), at the end of the year Soma-offerings.

27. A Brâhmana, who keeps sacred fires, shall, if he desires to live long, not eat new grain or meat, without having offered the (Âgrayana) Ishti with new grain and an animal-(sacrifice).

28. For his fires, not being worshipped by offerings of new grain and of an animal, seek to devour his vital spirits, (because they are) greedy for new grain and flesh.

29. No guest must stay in his house without being honoured, according to his ability, with a seat, food, a couch, water, or roots and fruits.

30. Let him not honour, even by a greeting, heretics, men who follow forbidden occupations, men who live like cats, rogues, logicians, (arguing against the Veda,) and those who live like herons.

31. Those who have become Snâtakas after studying the Veda, or after completing their vows, (and) householders, who are Srotriyas, one must worship by (gifts of food) sacred to gods and manes, but one must avoid those who are different.

---

30. Yâgñ. I, 130. Pâshandinah, 'heretics,' i.e. 'non-Brâhmanical ascetics' (vâhyalinginah, Medh.), or 'ascetics wearing red dresses and the like' (Gov.), or 'non-Brâhmanical ascetics, such as Bauddhas' (Kull., Nâr.), or 'those who do not believe in the Vedas' (Râgh.). The term does not necessarily refer to the Buddhists and Gainas, though the latter may be designated by it. The correct explanation of the word pâshanda or pâshandin, 'a sectarian,' has been given by Kern, Jaartelling der zuidelijke Buddhisten, p. 67. Regarding the men who act like cats or herons, see below, verses 195–196.

31. Nand. reads griham âgatân, 'who have come to his house,' instead of grihamedhinah, 'who are householders.'

32. A householder must give (as much food) as he is able (to spare) to those who do not cook for themselves, and to all beings one must distribute (food) without detriment (to one's own interest).

33. A Snâtaka who pines with hunger, may beg wealth of a king, of one for whom he sacrifices, and of a pupil, but not of others; that is a settled rule.

34. A Snâtaka who is able (to procure food) shall never waste himself with hunger, nor shall he wear old or dirty clothes, if he possesses property.

35. Keeping his hair, nails, and beard clipped, subduing his passions by austerities, wearing white garments and (keeping himself) pure, he shall be always engaged in studying the Veda and (such acts as are) conducive to his welfare.

36. He shall carry a staff of bamboo, a pot full of water, a sacred string, a bundle of Ku*s*a grass, and (wear) two bright golden ear-rings.

---

32. Âp. II, 4, 14; Gaut. V, 22; Baudh. II, 5, 20. 'Those who do not cook for themselves,' i.e. students and ascetics. According to Gov. Pâsha*nd*as are included by this term.

33. Gaut. IX, 63–64; Vas. XII, 2; Yâ*gñ*. I, 130. 'A king,' i.e. 'a Kshatriya king who rules in accordance with the *S*âstras;' see below, verse 84.

34. Vas. XII, 4; Vi. LXXI, 9; Gaut. IX, 3; Âp. I, 30, 13. *S*akta*h*, 'who is able (to procure food),' (Nâr.), means according to Nand. 'he who is able to dine, shall not stint himself through avarice.' Gov., Kull., and K. explain the phrase, 'A Ṣnâtaka, who is a fit (recipient of gifts), must not pine with hunger (as long as the king has anything to give),' i.e. he must be relieved. Râgh. reads yukta*h* instead of *s*akta*h*, 'A Snâtaka who is suffering hunger shall not despair.' If taken in the second sense the rule is identical with that given Âp. II, 25, 11; Gaut. X, 9–10; Vi. III, 79.

35. Âp. I, 30, 10–12; Gaut. IX, 4, 7; Yâ*gñ*. I, 131; Baudh. I, 5, 7.

36. Vas. XII, 14–17; Baudh. I, 5, 3–5; 6, 1–5; II, 6, 7; Vi. LXXI, 13–16; Yâ*gñ*. I, 133.

37. Let him never look at the sun, when he sets or rises, is eclipsed or reflected in water, or stands in the middle of the sky.

38. Let him not step over a rope to which a calf is tied, let him not run when it rains, and let him not look at his own image in water; that is a settled rule.

39. Let him pass by (a mound of) earth, a cow, an idol, a Brâhma*n*a, clarified butter, honey, a cross-way, and well-known trees, turning his right hand towards them.

40. Let him, though mad with desire, not approach his wife when her courses appear; nor let him sleep with her in the same bed.

41. For the wisdom, the energy, the strength, the sight, and the vitality of a man who approaches a woman covered with menstrual excretions, utterly perish.

42. If he avoids her, while she is in that condition, his wisdom, energy, strength, sight, and vitality will increase.

43. Let him not eat in the company of his wife, nor look at her, while she eats, sneezes, yawns, or sits at her ease.

44. A Brâhma*n*a who desires energy must not

37. Âp. I, 31, 20; Vas. XII, 10; Baudh. II, 6, 10; Vi. LXXI, 17–21; Yâ*g*ñ. I, 135.

38. Âp. I, 31, 15; Vas. XII, 9; Baudh. II, 6, 15; Vi. LXXI, 23; LXIII, 41–43.

39. Gaut. IX, 66; Vi. LXIII, 26–28; Yâ*g*ñ. I, 133.

40–42. Gaut. IX, 29–30; Vas. XII, 7; Vi. LXIX, 11.

42. Medh. and Nand. read lakshmî, 'luck,' instead of te*g*a*h*, 'energy.'

43. Vas. XII, 31; Vi. LXVIII, 46; Yâ*g*ñ. I, 131; Gaut. IX, 32.

44. Gaut. IX, 32.

look at (a woman) who applies collyrium to her eyes, has anointed or uncovered herself or brings forth (a child).

45. Let him not eat, dressed with one garment only; let him not bathe naked; let him not void urine on a road, on ashes, or in a cow-pen,

46. Nor on ploughed land, in water, on an altar of bricks, on a mountain, on the ruins of a temple, nor ever on an ant-hill,

47. Nor in holes inhabited by living creatures, nor while he walks or stands, nor on reaching the bank of a river, nor on the top of a mountain.

48. Let him never void faeces or urine, facing the wind, or a fire, or looking towards a Brâhma*n*a, the sun, water, or cows.

49. He may ease himself, having covered (the ground) with sticks, clods, leaves, grass, and the like, restraining his speech, (keeping himself) pure, wrapping up his body, and covering his head.

50. Let him void faeces and urine, in the daytime turning to the north, at night turning towards the south, during the two twilights in the same (position) as by day.

---

45. Âp. I, 30, 18; Gaut. IX, 40, 45; Vas. XII, 11; Baudh. II, 6, 24, 39; Vi. LXVIII, 14; LXIV, 5; LX, 11, 16, 19; Yâ*gñ*. I, 131, 134. Govra*g*e, 'in a cow-pen' (Gov., Kull.), means according to Medh. 'a place where cows graze.'

46. Âp. I, 30, 18; Gaut. IX, 40; Vi. LX, 4, 21, 10. 'Some omit verses 46–47' (Nâr.), and they are not found in Nand.

47. Vi. LX, 9.

48. Âp. I, 30, 20; Gaut. II, 12; Vi. LX, 22; Yâ*gñ*. I, 134. 'Looking at (things moved by) the wind' (Medh., Kull.). Medh. places verse 52 immediately after this.

49. Âp. I, 30, 14–15; Gaut. IX, 37–38, 41–43; Vas. XII, 13; Vi. LX, 2–3, 23.

50. Âp. I, 31, 1; Vi. LX, 2–3.

51. In the shade or in darkness a Brâhma*n*a may, both by day and at night, do it, assuming any position he pleases; likewise when his life is in danger.

52. The intellect of (a man) who voids urine against a fire, the sun, the moon, in water, against a Brâhma*n*a, a cow, or the wind, perishes.

53. Let him not blow a fire with his mouth; let him not look at a naked woman; let him not throw any impure substance into the fire, and let him not warm his feet at it.

54. Let him not place (fire) under (a bed or the like); nor step over it, nor place it (when he sleeps) at the foot-(end of his bed); let him not torment living creatures.

55. Let him not eat, nor travel, nor sleep during the twilight; let him not scratch the ground; let him not take off his garland.

56. Let him not throw urine or faeces into the water, nor saliva, nor (clothes) defiled by impure substances, nor any other (impurity), nor blood, nor poisonous things.

57. Let him not sleep alone in a deserted dwelling; let him not wake (a superior) who is sleeping; let him not converse with a menstruating woman;

---

52. Medh. and Nâr. mention a var. lect. for prativâtam, 'against the wind,' pratisa*m*dhya*m*, 'in the twilights,' which Nand. adopts.

53. Âp. I, 15, 20–21; Gaut. IX, 32; Vas. XII, 27; Vi. LXXI, 32–34, 37; Yâ*gñ*. I, 137.

54. Vi. LXXI, 36; Yâ*gñ*. I, 135, 137; Gaut. IX, 73.

55. Vi. LXIII, 8; LXVIII, 12; LXXI, 41, 55.

56. Âp. I, 30, 19; Vi. LXXI, 35; Yâ*gñ*. I, 137.

57. Gaut. IX, 54–55; Vas. XII, 42; Vi. LXIII, 21; LXX, 13; LXXI, 58; Yâ*gñ*. I, 138.

nor let him go to a sacrifice, if he is not chosen (to be officiating priest).

58. Let him keep his right arm uncovered in a place where a sacred fire is kept, in a cow-pen, in the presence of Brâhma*n*as, during the private recitation of the Veda, and at meals.

59. Let him not interrupt a cow who is suckling (her calf), nor tell anybody of it. A wise man, if he sees a rainbow in the sky, must not point it out to anybody.

60. Let him not dwell in a village where the sacred law is not obeyed, nor (stay) long where diseases are endemic; let him not go alone on a journey, nor reside long on a mountain.

61. Let him not dwell in a country where the rulers are *S*ûdras, nor in one which is surrounded by unrighteous men, nor in one which has become subject to heretics, nor in one swarming with men of the lowest castes.

62. Let him not eat anything from which the oil has been extracted; let him not be a glutton; let him not eat very early (in the morning), nor very late (in the evening), nor (take any food) in the evening, if he has eaten (his fill) in the morning.

63. Let him not exert himself without a purpose; let him not drink water out of his joined palms; let

---

58. Baudh. II, 6, 38; Vi. LXXI, 60.

59. Âp. I, 31, 10, 18; Gaut. IX, 23; Vas. XII, 33; Baudh. II, 6, 11, 17; Vi. LXIII, 2; LXXI, 62. All the commentators except Râgh. explain dhayantîm, 'who is suckling (her calf),' by pibantîm, 'who is drinking' (milk or water, see Yâg*ñ*. I, 140).

60–61. Âp. I, 15, 22, 32, 18; Gaut. IX, 65; Baudh. II, 6, 21, 31; Vi. LXXI, 64–68.

62. Vi. LXVIII, 27, 48; see above, II, 56–57.

63. Gaut. IX, 9, 50, 56; Baudh. II, 6, 5; Vi. LXXI, 69.

him not eat food (placed) in his lap; let him not show (idle) curiosity.

64. Let him not dance, nor sing, nor play musical instruments, nor slap (his limbs), nor grind his teeth, nor let him make uncouth noises, though he be in a passion.

65. Let him never wash his feet in a vessel of white brass; let him not eat out of a broken (earthen) dish, nor out of one that (to judge) from its appearance (is) defiled.

66. Let him not use shoes, garments, a sacred string, ornaments, a garland, or a water-vessel which have been used by others.

67. Let him not travel with untrained beasts of burden, nor with (animals) that are tormented by hunger or disease, or whose horns, eyes, and hoofs have been injured, or whose tails have been disfigured.

68. Let him always travel with (beasts) which are well broken in, swift, endowed with lucky marks, and perfect in colour and form, without urging them much with the goad.

69. The morning sun, the smoke rising from a (burning) corpse, and a broken seat must be avoided. Let him not clip his nails or hair, and not tear his nails with his teeth.

---

64. Âp. II, 20, 13; Vi. LXXI, 70–71. Na kshve*d*et, 'let him not grind his teeth,' means according to Nâr., 'let him not roar like a lion;' according to Nand., 'let him not snap his fingers.' Na spho*t*aye*t*, 'he shall not slap (his limbs),' means according to Nand., 'he shall not make his fingers crack.'

65. Vi. LXVIII, 20; LXXI, 39.

66. Vi. LXXI, 47. 67–68. Vi. LXIII, 13–18.

69. Vi. LXXI, 44, 46; Yâ*gñ*. I, 139. Bâlâtapa*h*, 'the morning sun,' is according to 'some,' mentioned by Nâr., and according to

70. Let him not crush earth or clods, nor tear off grass with his nails; let him not do anything that is useless or will have disagreeable results in the future.

71. A man who crushes clods, tears off grass, or bites his nails, goes soon to perdition, likewise an informer and he who neglects (the rules of) purification.

72. Let him not wrangle; let him not wear a garland over (his hair). To ride on the back of cows (or of oxen) is anyhow a blamable act.

73. Let him not enter a walled village or house except by the gate, and by night let him keep at a long distance from the roots of trees.

74. Let him never play with dice, nor himself take off his shoes; let him not eat, lying on a bed, nor what has been placed in his hand or on a seat.

Râgh. 'the sun in the sign of Kanyâ, or Virgo,' i.e. 'the sun in autumn.' The same explanation is mentioned by Nandapa*nd*ita in his comment on the parallel passage of Vish*n*u. It is, however, probably wrong: see the Introduction. 'Let him not clip his nails or hair,' i.e. 'not himself, but let him employ a barber' (Medh., Gov.), or 'before they have grown long' (Kull.), or 'except at the proper time for clipping' (Nand.).

70. Âp. I, 32, 18; Gaut. IX, 51; Vi. LXXI, 42–43.

72. Âp. I, 32, 5; Gaut. IX, 32; Baudh. II, 69. I read with all the commentators 'vig*ri*hya' instead of the 'vigarhya' of the editions. 'Let him not wear a garland over (his dress),' (Medh.), or 'let him not wear a garland outside (the house),' or 'one that is not fragrant' (others, Medh.).

73. Âp. I, 31, 23; Gaut. IX, 32; Baudh. II, 6, 13; Yâ*g*ñ. I, 140.

74. Gaut. IX, 32; Vas. XII, 36; Baudh. II, 6, 6; Vi. LXVIII, 23; Vi. LXXI, 45; Yâ*g*ñ. I, 138. 'Nor what has been placed in his hand,' i.e. 'in his left hand or in a vessel held in that hand' (Nâr.). This is no doubt the best explanation, as Hindus always eat with the fingers of the right hand, and the left hand is considered unclean for very good reasons.

75. Let him not eat after sunset any (food) containing sesamum grains; let him never sleep naked, nor go anywhere unpurified (after meals).

76. Let him eat while his feet are (yet) wet (from the ablution), but let him not go to bed with wet feet. He who eats while his feet are (still) wet, will attain long life.

77. Let him never enter a place, difficult of access, which is impervious to his eye; let him not look at urine or ordure, nor cross a river (swimming) with his arms.

78. Let him not step on hair, ashes, bones, potsherds, cotton-seed or chaff, if he desires long life.

79. Let him not stay together with outcasts, nor with *K*â*nd*âlas, nor with Pukkasas, nor with fools, nor with overbearing men, nor with low-caste men, nor with Antyâvasâyins.

80. Let him not give to a *S*ûdra advice, nor the remnants (of his meal), nor food offered to the gods; nor let him explain the sacred law (to such a man), nor impose (upon him) a penance.

81. For he who explains the sacred law (to a *S*ûdra) or dictates to him a penance, will sink together with that (man) into the hell (called) Asa*m*v*ri*ta.

82. Let him not scratch his head with both hands

75. Gaut. IX, 60; Vi. LXVIII, 29; LXXI, 3; see above, II, 56.
76. Vi. LXVIII, 34; LXX, 1.
77. Âp. I, 32, 26; Gaut. IX, 32; Vas. XII, 45; Baudh. II, 6, 26; Vi. LXIII, 46.
78. Âp. II, 20, 11; Gaut. IX, 15; Baudh. II, 6, 16; Yâ*gñ*. I, 139.
79. Regarding the Pukkasas and Antyâvasâyins, see below, X, 18, 39.
80. Âp. I, 31, 24; Vi. LXXI, 48–52; Vas. XVIII, 14.
81. Vas. XVIII, 15.
82. Vi. LXXI, 53.

joined; let him not touch it while he is impure, nor bathe without (submerging) it.

83. Let him avoid (in anger) to lay hold of (his own or other men's) hair, or to strike (himself or others) on the head. When he has bathed (submerging) his head, he shall not touch any of his limbs with oil.

84. Let him not accept presents from a king who is not descended from the Kshatriya race, nor from butchers, oil-manufacturers, and publicans, nor from those who subsist by the gain of prostitutes.

85. One oil-press is as (bad) as ten slaughter-houses, one tavern as (bad as) ten oil-presses, one brothel as (bad as) ten taverns, one king as (bad as) ten brothels.

86. A king is declared to be equal (in wickedness) to a butcher who keeps a hundred thousand slaughter-houses; to accept presents from him is a terrible (crime).

87. He who accepts presents from an avaricious king who acts contrary to the Institutes (of the sacred law), will go in succession to the following twenty-one hells:

88. Tâmisra, Andhatâmisra, Mahâraurava, Raurava, the Kâlasûtra hell, Mahânaraka,

89. Sa*m*gîvana, Mahâvî*k*i, Tapana, Sampratâpana, Sa*m*ghâta, Sakâkola, Ku*d*mala, Pûtim*ri*ttika,

83. Vi. LXIV, 12. 'When he has bathed (submerging) his head' should be according to others (mentioned by Kull. and Râgh.) 'when he has anointed his head with oil.'

84. Yâ*gñ*. I, 140.

85. Yâ*gñ*. I, 141. Medh., Gov., Nâr., and Nand. say, 'one king as bad as ten prostitutes' (vesyâ).

88–90. Vi. XLIII, 2–22. Nâr. and Gov. say expressly that naraka*m* kâlasûtra*m* *k*a means 'the Kâlasûtra hell,' and Nâr. that 'Vaita-

90. Lohasanku, *Rig*îsha, Pathin, the (flaming) river, *S*âlmala, Asipatravana, and Loha*k*âraka.

91. Learned Brâhma*n*as, who know that, who study the Veda and desire bliss after death, do not accept presents from a king.

92. Let him wake in the muhûrta, sacred to Brahman, and think of (the acquisition of) spiritual merit and wealth, of the bodily fatigue arising therefrom, and of the true meaning of the Veda.

93. When he has risen, has relieved the necessities of nature and carefully purified himself, let him stand during the morning twilight, muttering for a long time (the Gâyatrî), and at the proper time (he must similarly perform) the evening (devotion).

94. By prolonging the twilight devotions, the sages obtained long life, wisdom, honour, fame, and excellence in Vedic knowledge.

95. Having performed the Upâkarman according to the prescribed rule on (the full moon of the month) *S*râva*n*a, or on that of Praush*th*apada (Bhâdrapada),

---

ra*n*î' must be understood with nadî, 'the river,' while Gov. speaks of a hell called Nadî, 'the river.' The corresponding passage of Vish*n*u shows that the Dîpanadî is meant. The editions read Sa*m*hâta instead of Sa*m*ghâta, *S*âlmalî instead of *S*âlmala, and Lohadâraka, which Râgh. has also, instead of Loha*k*âraka.

92. Vas. XII, 47; Vi. LX, 1. Kull. and Râgh. say, 'in the muhûrta, sacred to Brâhmî,' or Bhâratî, the goddess of speech. But this explanation is wrong, as the expression prâ*g*âpatya muhûrta, used in other Sm*ri*tis, shows.

93. Vi. LXXI, 77.

94. I read with Gov., Nand., and K., avâpnuvan, 'obtained,' instead of avâpnuyu*h* (Medh., Kull., Nâr., Râgh.).

95-97. Âp. I, 9, 1-3, 10, 2; Gaut. XVI, 1-2, 40; Vas. XIII, 1-5; Baudh. I, 12-16; Vi. XXX, 1-2, 24-25; Yâ*gñ*. I, 142-144. The Upâkarman is the solemn opening of the Brâhma*n*ical school-term, and the Utsar*g*ana or Utsarga its closing. Their

a Brâhma*n*a shall diligently study the Vedas during four months and a half.

96. When the Pushya-day (of the month Pausha), or the first day of the bright half of Mâgha has come, a Brâhma*n*a shall perform in the forenoon the Utsar*g*ana of the Vedas.

97. Having performed the Utsarga outside (the village), as the Institutes (of the sacred law) prescribe, he shall stop reading during two days and the intervening night, or during that day (of the Utsarga) and (the following) night.

98. Afterwards he shall diligently recite the Vedas during the bright (halves of the months), and duly study all the Aṅgas of the Vedas during the dark fortnights.

99. Let him not recite (the texts) indistinctly, nor in the presence of *S*ûdras; nor let him, if in the latter part of the night he is tired with reciting the Veda, go again to sleep.

100. According to the rule declared above, let him recite the daily (portion of the) Mantras, and a zealous Brâhma*n*a, (who is) not in distress, (shall study) the Brâhma*n*a and the Mantrasa*m*hitâ.

101. Let him who studies always avoid (reading) on the following occasions when the Veda-study is

---

description is found in the G*ri*hya-sûtras, e.g. *S*âṅkhâyana IV, 5–6. The Pushya-day is the sixth lunar day of each month: *S*râva*n*a, July–August; Bhâdrapada, August–September; Pausha, December–January; Mâgha, January–February.

97. But see below, verse 119.

98–129. Âp. I, 9, 4–11, 38; 32, 12–15; Gaut. I, 58–60; XVI, 5–49; Vas. XIII, 6–40; XVIII, 13; Baudh. I, 21, 4–22; Vi. XXX, 3–30; Yâ*gñ*. I, 144–151.

100. 'The daily (portion of the) Mantras,' i.e. 'the Gâyatrî and other portions of the *Rik*as, Ya*g*us, and Sâmans.'

forbidden, and (let) him who teaches pupils according to the prescribed rule (do it likewise).

102. Those who know the (rules of) recitation declare that in the rainy season the Veda-study must be stopped on these two (occasions), when the wind is audible at night, and when it whirls up the dust in the day-time.

103. Manu has stated, that when lightning, thunder, and rain (are observed together), or when large fiery meteors fall on all sides, the recitation must be interrupted until the same hour (on the next day, counting from the occurrence of the event).

104. When one perceives these (phenomena) all together (in the twilight), after the sacred fires have been made to blaze (for the performance of the Agnihotra), then one must know the recitation of the Veda to be forbidden, and also when clouds appear out of season.

105. On (the occasion of) a preternatural sound from the sky, (of) an earthquake, and when the lights of heaven are surrounded by a halo, let him know that (the Veda-study must be) stopped until the same hour (on the next day), even if (these phenomena happen) in the (rainy) season.

106. But when lightning and the roar of thunder (are observed) after the sacred fires have been made to blaze, the stoppage shall last as long as the light (of the sun or of the stars is visible); if the remaining (above-named phenomenon, rain, occurs, the reading shall cease), both in the day-time and at night.

---

105. Medh. proposes as another explanation of *g*yotishâ*m k*opasar*g*ane, 'when the heavenly lights trouble each other,' i. e. obscure each other, and Nâr., Kull., and Râgh. refer the phrase to eclipses.

107. For those who wish to acquire exceedingly great merit, a continual interruption of the Veda-study (is prescribed) in villages and in towns, and (the Veda-study must) always (cease) when any kind of foul smell (is perceptible).

108. In a village where a corpse lies, in the presence of a (man who lives as unrighteously as a) *S*ûdra, while (the sound of) weeping (is heard), and in a crowd of men the (recitation of the Veda must be) stopped.

109. In water, during the middle part of the night, while he voids excrements, or is impure, and after he has partaken of a funeral dinner, a man must not even think in his heart (of the sacred texts).

110. A learned Brâhma*n*a shall not recite the Veda during three days, when he has accepted an invitation to a (funeral rite) in honour of one ancestor (ekoddish*t*a), or when the king has become impure through a birth or death in his family (sûtaka), or when Râhu by an eclipse makes the moon impure.

111. As long as the smell and the stains of the (food given) in honour of one ancestor remain on the body of a learned Brâhma*n*a, so long he must not recite the Veda.

112. While lying on a bed, while his feet are raised (on a bench), while he sits on his hams with a cloth tied round his knees, let him not study, nor when he has eaten meat or food given by a person impure on account of a birth or a death,

107. With respect to this verse, see especially Baudh. II, 6, 33–34.

109. Medh. mentions a var. lect. udaye, 'at sunrise,' for udake, 'in water.'

110. Eclipses of the sun are of course included.

113. Nor during a fog, nor while the sound of arrows is audible, nor during both the twilights, nor on the new-moon day, nor on the fourteenth and the eighth (days of each half-month), nor on the full-moon day.

114. The new-moon day destroys the teacher, the fourteenth (day) the pupil, the eighth and the full-moon days (destroy all remembrance of) the Veda; let him therefore avoid (reading on) those (days).

115. A Brâhma*n*a shall not recite (the Veda) during a dust-storm, nor while the sky is preternaturally red, nor while jackals howl, nor while the barking of dogs, the braying of donkeys, or the grunting of camels (is heard), nor while (he is seated) in a company.

116. Let him not study near a burial-ground, nor near a village, nor in a cow-pen, nor dressed in a garment which he wore during conjugal intercourse, nor after receiving a present at a funeral sacrifice.

117. Be it an animal or a thing inanimate, whatever be the (gift) at a *S*râddha, let him not, having just accepted it, recite the Veda; for the hand of a Brâhma*n*a is his mouth.

118. When the village has been beset by robbers, and when an alarm has been raised by fire, let him know that (the Veda-study must be) interrupted until the same hour (on the next day), and on (the occurrence of) all portents.

---

113. Vâ*n*a, 'arrows,' may also mean 'a large lute.'

115. Paṅktau, 'in a company' (Gov., Kull., Nâr., 'others'), means according to Medh., Nâr., and Râgh. 'in the midst of dogs, donkeys, or camels.' Nâr. mentions a third explanation, 'in the company of unworthy persons' (apâṅktya).

117. I.e. it is as sinful to recite the Veda after accepting a present at a *S*râddha, as to study after partaking of a funeral dinner.

119. On (the occasion of) the Upâkarman and (of) the Vedotsarga an omission (of the Veda-study) for three days has been prescribed, but on the Ash*t*akâs and on the last nights of the seasons for a day and a night.

120. Let him not recite the Veda on horseback, nor on a tree, nor on an elephant, nor in a boat (or ship), nor on a donkey, nor on a camel, nor standing on barren ground, nor riding in a carriage,

121. Nor during a verbal altercation, nor during a mutual assault, nor in a camp, nor during a battle, nor when he has just eaten, nor during an indigestion, nor after vomiting, nor with sour eructations,

122. Nor without receiving permission from a guest (who stays in his house), nor while the wind blows vehemently, nor while blood flows from his body, nor when he is wounded by a weapon.

123. Let him never recite the *Ri*g-veda or the Ya*g*ur-veda while the Sâman (melodies) are heard; (let him stop all Veda-study for a day and a night) after finishing a Veda or after reciting an Âra*n*yaka.

124. The *Ri*g-veda is declared to be sacred to the gods, the Ya*g*ur-veda sacred to men, and the Sâma-veda sacred to the manes; hence the sound of the latter is impure (as it were).

---

119. The Ash*t*akâs are the three or four days for the Ash*t*akâ *S*râddhas, which are placed differently by different writers; see Weber, Die Nakshatras II, 337.

121. Nâr. interprets na vivâde na kalahe by 'neither during a dispute on legal matters nor during an altercation.'

124. 'Is impure (as it were),' i.e. 'it is not really impure, but when it is heard, one must not study, just as in the presence of some impure thing or person' (Medh.).

125. Knowing this, the learned daily repeat first in due order the essence of the three (Vedas) and afterwards the (text of the) Veda.

126. Know that (the Veda-study must be) interrupted for a day and a night, when cattle, a frog, a cat, a dog, a snake, an ichneumon, or a rat pass between (the teacher and his pupil).

127. Let a twice-born man always carefully interrupt the Veda-study on two (occasions, viz.) when the place where he recites is impure, and when he himself is unpurified.

128. A twice-born man who is a Snâtaka shall remain chaste on the new-moon day, on the eighth (lunar day of each half-month), on the full-moon day, and on the fourteenth, even (if they fall) in the period (proper for conjugal intercourse).

129. Let him not bathe (immediately) after a meal, nor when he is sick, nor in the middle of the night, nor frequently dressed in all his garments, nor in a pool which he does not perfectly know.

130. Let him not intentionally step on the shadow of (images of) the gods, of a Guru, of a king, of a Snâtaka, of his teacher, of a reddish-brown animal, or of one who has been initiated to the performance of a *S*rauta sacrifice (Dîkshita).

---

125. 'The essence of three (Vedas),' i.e. the syllable Om and the Gâyatrî; see above, II, 76–77.

128. Vi. LXIX, 1; Vas. XII, 21. According to others, quoted by Medh., the word brahma*k*ârî translated by 'chaste' indicates that a Snâtaka must also in other respects behave like a student. Medh. thinks it possible that the abstention from honey and meat may also be indicated.

129. Âp. I, 32, 8; Baudh. II, 6, 25; Vi. LXIV, 3–4, 6. 'Not frequently,' i.e. 'only for particular reasons, such as being touched by a *K*â*nd*âla.'

130. Yâ*gñ*. I, 152; Vi. LXIII, 40. Babhru, 'a reddish-brown

131. At midday and at midnight, after partaking of meat at a funeral dinner, and in the two twilights let him not stay long on a cross-road.

132. Let him not step intentionally on things used for cleansing the body, on water used for a bath, on urine or ordure, on blood, on mucus, and on anything spat out or vomited.

133. Let him not show particular attention to an enemy, to the friend of an enemy, to a wicked man, to a thief, or to the wife of another man.

134. For in this world there is nothing so detrimental to long life as criminal conversation with another man's wife.

135. Let him who desires prosperity, indeed, never despise a Kshatriya, a snake, and a learned Brâhma*n*a, be they ever so feeble.

136. Because these three, when treated with disrespect, may utterly destroy him; hence a wise man must never despise them.

137. Let him not despise himself on account of former failures; until death let him seek fortune, nor despair of gaining it.

138. Let him say what is true, let him say what is pleasing, let him utter no disagreeable truth, and let him utter no agreeable falsehood; that is the eternal law.

---

animal,' is not clearly explained by Gov., Kull., and Râgh. Medh. thinks that 'a brown cow' or 'the Soma creeper' may be meant. Nand. adopts the former view, and Nâr. explains it by 'a brown creature.'

132. Vi. LXIII, 41; Yâ*gñ*. I, 152. Apasnânam, 'water used for a bath,' means according to Nâr. and Nand. 'water used for washing a corpse.'

135–136. Yâ*gñ*. I, 153. 137. Vi. LXXI, 76; Yâ*gñ*. I, 153.

138. Gaut. IX, 68; Vi. LXXI, 73–74; Yâ*gñ*. I, 132.

139. (What is) well, let him call well, or let him say 'well' only; let him not engage in a useless enmity or dispute with anybody.

140. Let him not journey too early in the morning, nor too late in the evening, nor just during the midday (heat), nor with an unknown (companion), nor alone, nor with *S*ûdras.

141. Let him not insult those who have redundant limbs or are deficient in limbs, nor those destitute of knowledge, nor very aged men, nor those who have no beauty or wealth, nor those who are of low birth.

142. A Brâhma*n*a who is impure must not touch with his hand a cow, a Brâhma*n*a, or fire; nor, being in good health, let him look at the luminaries in the sky, while he is impure.

143. If he has touched these, while impure, let him always sprinkle with his hand water on the organs of sensation, all his limbs, and the navel.

144. Except when sick he must not touch the cavities (of the body) without a reason, and he must avoid (to touch) the hair on the secret (parts).

145. Let him eagerly follow the (customs which are) auspicious and the rule of good conduct, be careful of purity, and control all his organs, let him mutter (prayers) and, untired, daily offer oblations in the fire.

139. Âp. I, 32, 11–14; Gaut. IX, 19–20; Vi. LXXI, 57; Yâg*ñ*. I, 132; Gaut. IX, 32. 'Only,' i.e. even if things go wrong. I follow Nâr.'s explanation, which is the only correct one: bhadra*m* vastuto ya*kkh*obhana*m* I bhadram ity eva vâ 'bhadram api, '(let him call) well what is really well; or (let him call) well even that which is not well.'

140. Baudh. II, 6, 22–23; Vi. LXIII, 4, 6–7, 9.

141. Vi. LXXI, 2. 142. Yâg*ñ*. I, 155. 144. Vi. LXXI, 79.

146. No calamity happens to those who eagerly follow auspicious customs and the rule of good conduct, to those who are always careful of purity, and to those who mutter (sacred texts) and offer burnt-oblations.

147. Let him, without tiring, daily mutter the Veda at the proper time; for they declare that to be one's highest duty; (all) other (observances) are called secondary duties.

148. By daily reciting the Veda, by (the observance of the rules of) purification, by (practising) austerities, and by doing no injury to created beings, one (obtains the faculty of) remembering former births.

149. He who, recollecting his former existences, again recites the Veda, gains endless bliss by the continual study of the Veda.

150. Let him always offer on the Parva-days oblations to Savitri and such as avert evil omens, and on the Ashtakâs and Anvashtakâs let him constantly worship the manes.

151. Far from his dwelling let him remove urine (and ordure), far (let him remove) the water used for washing his feet, and far the remnants of food and the water from his bath.

152. Early in the morning only let him void

---

146. Vas. XXVI, 14. 147. Gaut. IX, 72.

150. Vi. LXXI, 86. Nand. reads sâvitryâ, 'with the Sâvitrî,' for sâvitrân, 'to Savitri,' and Nâr. has the same explanation.

151. Âp. I, 31, 2–3; Gaut. IX, 39; Yâgñ. I, 153. Âvasatha, 'his dwelling,' means according to Kull. 'the room where the fires are kept.' Kull. explains nishekam, 'the water from his bath,' by 'seminal impurity.' Gov. and Nâr. read ukkhishtânnanishekam ka, and explain nisheka by tyâga, 'throwing away.'

152. According to Medh., 'others' explained maitram, 'defecation,' by 'friendly service,' or by 'the worship of Mitra.'

fæces, decorate (his body), bathe, clean his teeth, apply collyrium to his eyes, and worship the gods.

153. But on the Parva-days let him go to visit the (images of the) gods, and virtuous Brâhma*n*as, and the ruler (of the country), for the sake of protection, as well as his Gurus.

154. Let him reverentially salute venerable men (who visit him), give them his own seat, let him sit near them with joined hands and, when they leave, (accompany them), walking behind them.

155. Let him, untired, follow the conduct of virtuous men, connected with his occupations, which has been fully declared in the revealed texts and in the sacred tradition (Sm*ri*ti) and is the root of the sacred law.

156. Through virtuous conduct he obtains long life, through virtuous conduct desirable offspring, through virtuous conduct imperishable wealth; virtuous conduct destroys (the effect of) inauspicious marks.

157. For a man of bad conduct is blamed among people, constantly suffers misfortunes, is afflicted with diseases, and short-lived.

158. A man who follows the conduct of the virtuous, has faith and is free from envy, lives a hundred years, though he be entirely destitute of auspicious marks.

159. Let him carefully avoid all undertakings (the success of) which depends on others; but let

153. Âp. I, 31, 21-22. Medh. omits verses 153-158.
154. Baudh. II, 6, 35. 155. Vas. LXXI, 90; Yâ*gñ*. I, 154.
156. Vas. VI, 7; Vi. LXXI, 91. 157. Vas. VI, 6.
158. Vas. VI, 8; Vi. LXXI, 92.

him eagerly pursue that (the accomplishment of) which depends on himself.

160. Everything that depends on others (gives) pain, everything that depends on oneself (gives) pleasure; know that this is the short definition of pleasure and pain.

161. When the performance of an act gladdens his heart, let him perform it with diligence; but let him avoid the opposite.

162. Let him never offend the teacher who initiated him, nor him who explained the Veda, nor his father and mother, nor (any other) Guru, nor cows, nor Brâhma*n*as, nor any men performing austerities.

163. Let him avoid atheism, cavilling at the Vedas, contempt of the gods, hatred, want of modesty, pride, anger, and harshness.

164. Let him, when angry, not raise a stick against another man, nor strike (anybody) except a son or a pupil; those two he may beat in order to correct them.

---

161. This rule refers to indifferent acts or cases where there is an option; see above, II, 12.

162. Yâg*ñ*. I, 157–158. Na hi*m*syât, 'let him never offend' (Medh., Kull., Nâr., Nand.), means according to Gov. 'let him never injure them, though they attempt his life, when self-defence is permitted' (see VIII, 350). Tapasvina*h* means according to Medh. and Gov. 'all those engaged in the performance of austerities,' e.g. even sinners who perform penances (Medh.), while the other commentators understand it to denote 'ascetics.'

163. Âp. I, 30, 25; Vas. XIII, 41; Vi. LXXI, 83. I read with all the commentators instead of dambham, 'hypocrisy,' stambham, which according to Medh., Gov., and Nâr. means 'want of modesty,' and according to Kull. 'want of energy in the fulfilment of duties.'

164. Vi. LXXI, 81–82. See also below, VIII, 299–300.

165. A twice-born man who has merely threatened a Brâhma*n*a with the intention of (doing him) a corporal injury, will wander about for a hundred years in the Tâmisra hell.

166. Having intentionally struck him in anger, even with a blade of grass, he will be born during twenty-one existences in the wombs (of such beings where men are born in punishment of their) sins.

167. A man who in his folly caused blood to flow from the body of a Brâhma*n*a who does not attack him, will suffer after death exceedingly great pain.

168. As many particles of dust as the blood takes up from the ground, during so many years the spiller of the blood will be devoured by other (animals) in the next world.

169. A wise man should therefore never threaten a Brâhma*n*a, nor strike him even with a blade of grass, nor cause his blood to flow.

170. Neither a man who (lives) unrighteously, nor he who (acquires) wealth (by telling) falsehoods, nor he who always delights in doing injury, ever attain happiness in this world.

171. Let him, though suffering in consequence of his righteousness, never turn his heart to unrighteousness; for he will see the speedy overthrow of unrighteous, wicked men.

172. Unrighteousness, practised in this world, does not at once produce its fruit, like a cow; but, advancing slowly, it cuts off the roots of him who committed it.

165–167. Gaut. XXI, 20-22; Yâ*gñ*. I, 155.

172. 'Like a cow,' i.e. 'which at once yields benefits by its milk, &c.' (Gov., Nâr., Nand.). Medh., Kull., and Râgh. take gau*h*

173. If (the punishment falls) not on (the offender) himself, (it falls) on his sons, if not on the sons, (at least) on his grandsons; but an iniquity (once) committed, never fails to produce fruit to him who wrought it.

174. He prospers for a while through unrighteousness, then he gains great good fortune, next he conquers his enemies, but (at last) he perishes (branch and) root.

175. Let him always delight in truthfulness, (obedience to) the sacred law, conduct worthy of an Âryan, and purity; let him chastise his pupils according to the sacred law; let him keep his speech, his arms, and his belly under control.

176. Let him avoid (the acquisition of) wealth and (the gratification of his) desires, if they are opposed to the sacred law, and even lawful acts which may cause pain in the future or are offensive to men.

177. Let him not be uselessly active with his hands and feet, or with his eyes, nor crooked (in his ways), nor talk idly, nor injure others by deeds or even think of it.

178. Let him walk in that path of holy men

---

in its other sense, 'the earth,' i.e. 'which does not at once yield a harvest,' but mention the first explanation too. It is not impossible that the word has to be taken both ways, and that the author wishes to give with it both a sâdharmya and a vaidharmyad*r*ish*t*ânta.

175. Gaut. IX, 50, 68–69.

176. Gaut. IX, 47, 73; Vi. LXXI, 84–85; Yâ*gñ*. I, 156. As an example of 'a lawful act causing pain in the future,' Medh. adduces 'the gift of one's whole property.'

177. The last portion of the verse, 'nor injure others, &c.,' may also be translated, 'let him not be intent on deeds (calculated) to injure others.'

which his fathers and his grandfathers followed; while he walks in that, he will not suffer harm.

179. With an officiating or a domestic priest, with a teacher, with a maternal uncle, a guest and a dependant, with infants, aged and sick men, with learned men, with his paternal relatives, connexions by marriage and maternal relatives,

180. With his father and his mother, with female relatives, with a brother, with his son and his wife, with his daughter and with his slaves, let him not have quarrels.

181. If he avoids quarrels with these persons, he will be freed from all sins, and by suppressing (all) such (quarrels) a householder conquers all the following worlds.

182. The teacher is the lord of the world of Brahman, the father has power over the world of the Lord of created beings (Pra*g*âpati), a guest rules over the world of Indra, and the priests over the world of the gods.

183. The female relatives (have power) over the world of the Apsarases, the maternal relatives over that of the Vi*s*ve Devâs, the connexions by marriage over that of the waters, the mother and the maternal uncle over the earth.

184. Infants, aged, poor and sick men must be considered as rulers of the middle sphere, the eldest

179–184. Yâ*gñ*. I, 157–158.

179. Vaidyai*h*, 'with learned men,' may also mean 'with physicians.'

181. Instead of etair *g*itai*s k*a, 'by suppressing (all) such (quarrels),' (Medh., Gov., Kull., Râgh.), Nâr. and Nand. read etair *g*ita*s k*a, 'allowing himself to be conquered by these,' i.e. 'by bearing with these persons.' This reading, though less well attested than the vulgata, is perhaps preferable.

brother as equal to one's father, one's wife and one's son as one's own body,

185. One's slaves as one's shadow, one's daughter as the highest object of tenderness; hence if one is offended by (any one of) these, one must bear it without resentment.

186. Though (by his learning and sanctity) he may be entitled to accept presents, let him not attach himself (too much) to that (habit); for through his accepting (many) presents the divine light in him is soon extinguished.

187. Without a full knowledge of the rules, prescribed by the sacred law for the acceptance of presents, a wise man should not take anything, even though he may pine with hunger.

188. But an ignorant (man) who accepts gold, land, a horse, a cow, food, a dress, sesamum-grains, (or) clarified butter, is reduced to ashes like (a piece of) wood.

189. Gold and food destroy his longevity, land and a cow his body, a horse his eye(sight), a garment his skin, clarified butter his energy, sesamum-grains his offspring.

190. A Brâhma*n*a who neither performs austerities nor studies the Veda, yet delights in accepting gifts, sinks with the (donor into hell), just as (he who attempts to cross over in) a boat made of stone (is submerged) in the water.

191. Hence an ignorant (man) should be afraid of accepting any presents; for by reason of a very small (gift) even a fool sinks (into hell) as a cow into a morass.

---

186. Vi. LVII, 6-7. 187. Vi. LVII, 8.
188. Yâg*ñ*. I, 201. 191. Yâg*ñ*. I, 202.

192. (A man) who knows the law should not offer even water to a Brâhma*n*a who acts like a cat, nor to a Brâhma*n*a who acts like a heron, nor to one who is unacquainted with the Veda.

193. For property, though earned in accordance with prescribed rules, which is given to these three (persons), causes in the next world misery both to the giver and to the recipient.

194. As he who (attempts to) cross water in a boat of stone sinks (to the bottom), even so an ignorant donor and an ignorant donee sink low.

195. (A man) who, ever covetous, displays the flag of virtue, (who is) a hypocrite, a deceiver of the people, intent on doing injury, (and) a detractor (from the merits) of all men, one must know to be one who acts like a cat.

196. That Brâhma*n*a, who with downcast look, of a cruel disposition, is solely intent on attaining his own ends, dishonest and falsely gentle, is one who acts like a heron.

197. Those Brâhma*n*as who act like herons, and those who display the characteristics of cats, fall in consequence of that wicked mode of acting into (the hell called) Andhatâmisra.

198. When he has committed a sin, let him not

192. Vi. XCIII, 7. 195. Vi. XCIII, 8.

196–200. Vi. XCIII, 9–13.

196. I have everywhere translated the word baka or vaka by 'heron,' though, like its modern representative baglâ, it is used also as a name of the white ibis and of the bittern. But from other verses, which speak of the baka cautiously wading in the water as if it were afraid of hurting the aquatic animals, it would seem that the proceedings of the heron, which one can watch in India at every village tank, gave rise to the proverbial expressions bakavrata and bakavratin.

198. Several penances, e.g. the *K*ândrâya*n*a or the lunar penance,

perform a penance under the pretence (that the act is intended to gain) spiritual merit, (thus) hiding his sin under (the pretext of) a vow and deceiving women and *S*ûdras.

199. Such Brâhma*n*as are reprehended after death and in this (life) by those who expound the Veda, and a vow, performed under a false pretence, goes to the Râkshasas.

200. He who, without being a student, gains his livelihood by (wearing) the dress of a student, takes upon himself the guilt of (all) students and is born again in the womb of an animal.

201. Let him never bathe in tanks belonging to other men; if he bathes (in such a one), he is tainted by a portion of the guilt of him who made the tank.

202. He who uses without permission a carriage, a bed, a seat, a well, a garden or a house belonging to an(other man), takes upon himself one fourth of (the owner's) guilt.

203. Let him always bathe in rivers, in ponds, dug by the gods (themselves), in lakes, and in water-holes or springs.

204. A wise man should constantly discharge the paramount duties (called yama), but not always the minor ones (called niyama); for he who does not

---

may be performed either by a sinner in order to atone for a crime or by a guiltless man in order to gain spiritual merit; see Baudh. III, 8, 27-31.

201. Vi. LXIV, 1; Yâg*ñ*. I, 159; Baudh. II, 5, 6.

202. Yâg*ñ*. I, 160; Baudh. II, 6, 29.

203. Vi. LXIV, 16; Yâg*ñ*. I, 159. Garta, 'water-holes' (Gov., Nâr.), means according to Kull., who quotes a verse of the *Kh*ândogya-pari*s*ish*t*a, Nand., and Râgh., 'a brook.'

204. Regarding the two classes of duties, see Yâg*ñ*. III, 313-314. Though the commentators give various explanations of yama

discharge the former, while he obeys the latter alone, becomes an outcast.

205. A Brâhma*n*a must never eat (a dinner given) at a sacrifice that is offered by one who is not a *S*rotriya, by one who sacrifices for a multitude of men, by a woman, or by a eunuch.

206. When those persons offer sacrificial viands in the fire, it is unlucky for holy (men) and it displeases the gods; let him therefore avoid it.

207. Let him never eat (food given) by intoxicated, angry, or sick (men), nor that in which hair or insects are found, nor what has been touched intentionally with the foot,

208. Nor that at which the slayer of a learned Brâhma*n*a has looked, nor that which has been touched by a menstruating woman, nor that which has been pecked at by birds or touched by a dog,

209. Nor food at which a cow has smelt, nor particularly that which has been offered by an invitation to all comers, nor that (given) by a multitude or by harlots, nor that which is declared to be bad by a learned (man),

210. Nor the food (given) by a thief, a musician, a carpenter, a usurer, one who has been initiated (for the performance of a *S*rauta sacrifice), a miser, one bound with fetters,

---

and niyama, it is highly probable that Kull. is right in supposing Manu to have held the same opinion as Yâg*ñ*.

205. Nâr. mentions a var. lect. *s*ûdre*n*a, 'by a *S*ûdra,' for 'by a eunuch.'

209. Gov. and Kull. give as an instance of 'a multitude,' 'a fraternity of Brâhma*n*as inhabiting a monastery.'

210. I translate baddhasya niga*d*asya *k*a according to Kull. by 'one bound with fetters,' because in the older Sanskrit the genitive is occasionally used for the instrumental with passive perfect parti-

211. By one accused of a mortal sin (Abhi*s*asta), a hermaphrodite, an unchaste woman, or a hypocrite, nor (any sweet thing) that has turned sour, nor what has been kept a whole night, nor (the food) of a *S*ûdra, nor the leavings (of another man),

212. Nor (the food given) by a physician, a hunter, a cruel man, one who eats the fragments (of another's meal), nor the food of an Ugra, nor that prepared for a woman in childbed, nor that (given at a dinner) where (a guest rises) prematurely (and) sips water, nor that (given by a woman) whose ten days of impurity have not elapsed,

213. Nor (food) given without due respect, nor (that which contains) meat eaten for no sacred purpose, nor (that given) by a female who has no male (relatives), nor the food of an enemy, nor that (given) by the lord of a town, nor that (given) by outcasts, nor that on which anybody has sneezed;

---

ciples, and because niga*d*a does not mean 'bound with fetters,' as the other commentators assume. Nand. adds that the correct reading is nigalena, which is found in some southern MSS.

211. *S*ûdrasyo*kk*ish*t*am eva *k*a, 'nor (the food) of a *S*ûdra, nor the leavings (of any other man),' (Kull., Nâr.); or, 'the leavings of a *S*ûdra,' which are mentioned in order to show that a very heavy penance has to be performed (Medh., Râgh.); or, 'that food of which a *S*ûdra has eaten, and has left a remnant in the dish' (Gov., Nand., Medh., 'others'). Medh. mentions also a var. lect. u*kk*ish*t*am aguros tathâ, 'nor the leavings of any man excepting a Guru.'

212. Ugra is explained variously as 'a man of the Ugra caste' (Medh., Gov., Nâr., Nand., Râgh.); or, 'a king' (Medh., Gov. in the Ma*ñg*arî); or, 'a man who perpetrates dreadful deeds' (Kull., Râgh.).

213. Kull. and Gov. seem to take nagaryannam, 'food given by the lord of a town,' i.e. a king (Medh., Nâr., Râgh.), in the sense of nagarânnam, 'food given by a whole town.'

214. Nor the food (given) by an informer, by one who habitually tells falsehoods, or by one who sells (the rewards for) sacrifices, nor the food (given) by an actor, a tailor, or an ungrateful (man),

215. By a blacksmith, a Nishâda, a stage-player, a goldsmith, a basket-maker, or a dealer in weapons,

216. By trainers of hunting dogs, publicans, a washerman, a dyer, a pitiless (man), and a man in whose house (lives) a paramour (of his wife),

217. Nor (the food given) by those who knowingly bear with paramours (of their wives), and by those who in all matters are ruled by women, nor food (given by men) whose ten days of impurity on account of a death have not passed, nor that which is unpalatable.

218. The food of a king impairs his vigour, the food of a *S*ûdra his excellence in sacred learning, the food of a goldsmith his longevity, that of a leather-cutter his fame;

219. The food of an artisan destroys his offspring, that of a washerman his (bodily) strength; the food of a multitude and of harlots excludes him from (the higher) worlds.

220. The food of a physician (is as vile as) pus, that of an unchaste woman (equal to) semen, that of a usurer (as vile as) ordure, and that of a dealer in weapons (as bad as) dirt.

221. The food of those other persons who have

215. According to 'others,' quoted by Medh., Nand., and Râgh., *s*ailûsha, 'an actor,' may also mean 'one who prostitutes his wife.'

216. N*ri*s*am*sa, 'a pitiless man' (Medh., Gov., Kull., Nand., Râgh.), may also mean 'a bard' (Medh., Nâr., Râgh.).

220. I.e. it causes him to be reborn as an animal feeding on pus or other impure substances (Gov.).

M 2

been successively enumerated as such whose food must not be eaten, the wise declare (to be as impure as) skin, bones, and hair.

222. If he has unwittingly eaten the food of one of those, (he must) fast for three days; if he has eaten it intentionally, or (has swallowed) semen, ordure, or urine, he must perform a K*rikkh*ra penance.

223. A Brâhma*n*a who knows (the law) must not eat cooked food (given) by a *S*ûdra who performs no *S*râddhas; but, on failure of (other) means of subsistence, he may accept raw (grain), sufficient for one night (and day).

224. The gods, having considered (the respective merits) of a niggardly *S*rotriya and of a liberal usurer, declared the food of both to be equal (in quality).

225. The Lord of created beings (Pra*g*âpati) came and spake to them, 'Do not make that equal, which is unequal. The food of that liberal (usurer) is purified by faith; (that of the) other (man) is defiled by a want of faith.'

226. Let him, without tiring, always offer sacrifices and perform works of charity with faith; for offerings and charitable works made with faith and with lawfully-earned money, (procure) endless rewards.

227. Let him always practise, according to his

---

222. Gaut. XXIII, 23–24. Regarding the K*rikkh*ra penance, see below, XI, 211.

224. Nâr. explains a*s*râddhina*h*, 'who performs no *S*râddhas,' by 'destitute of faith,' and Nand. writes asraddhina*h*.

224–225. Baudh. I, 10, 5; Vas. XIV, 17.

226–227. Gov. gives and explains 226a and 227b only.

ability, with a cheerful heart, the duty of liberality, both by sacrifices and by charitable works, if he finds a worthy recipient (for his gifts).

228. If he is asked, let him always give something, be it ever so little, without grudging; for a worthy recipient will (perhaps) be found who saves him from all (guilt).

229. A giver of water obtains the satisfaction (of his hunger and thirst), a giver of food imperishable happiness, a giver of sesamum desirable offspring, a giver of a lamp a most excellent eyesight.

230. A giver of land obtains land, a giver of gold long life, a giver of a house most excellent mansions, a giver of silver (rûpya) exquisite beauty (rûpa),

231. A giver of a garment a place in the world of the moon, a giver of a horse (a*s*va) a place in the world of the A*s*vins, a giver of a draught-ox great good fortune, a giver of a cow the world of the sun;

232. A giver of a carriage or of a bed a wife, a giver of protection supreme dominion, a giver of grain eternal bliss, a giver of the Veda (brahman) union with Brahman;

233. The gift of the Veda surpasses all other gifts, water, food, cows, land, clothes, sesamum, gold, and clarified butter.

234. For whatever purpose (a man) bestows any gift, for that same purpose he receives (in his next birth) with due honour its (reward).

226–235. Vas. XXX; Vi. XCI–XCII; Yâ*gñ*. I, 201, 203–212.

234. Medh., Gov., Nâr., and Râgh. take the verse differently. 'With whatever disposition (a man) bestows any gift, with that same disposition he receives (in his next birth its reward), being duly honoured.' Nand. omits it. K. follows Kull.'s explanation, which is mentioned by Medh. also.

235. Both he who respectfully receives (a gift), and he who respectfully bestows it, go to heaven; in the contrary case (they both fall) into hell.

236. Let him not be proud of his austerities; let him not utter a falsehood after he has offered a sacrifice; let him not speak ill of Brâhma*n*as, though he be tormented (by them); when he has bestowed (a gift), let him not boast of it.

237. By falsehood a sacrifice becomes vain, by self-complacency (the reward for) austerities is lost, longevity by speaking evil of Brâhma*n*as, and (the reward of) a gift by boasting.

238. Giving no pain to any creature, let him slowly accumulate spiritual merit, for the sake (of acquiring) a companion to the next world, just as the white ant (gradually raises its) hill.

239. For in the next world neither father, nor mother, nor wife, nor sons, nor relations stay to be his companions; spiritual merit alone remains (with him).

240. Single is each being born; single it dies; single it enjoys (the reward of its) virtue; single (it suffers the punishment of its) sin.

241. Leaving the dead body on the ground like a log of wood, or a clod of earth, the relatives depart with averted faces; but spiritual merit follows the (soul).

242. Let him therefore always slowly accumulate spiritual merit, in order (that it may be his) companion (after death); for with merit as his companion he will traverse a gloom difficult to traverse.

243. (That companion) speedily conducts the man who is devoted to duty and effaces his sins by

austerities, to the next world, radiant and clothed with an ethereal body.

244. Let him, who desires to raise his race, ever form connexions with the most excellent (men), and shun all low ones.

245. A Brâhma*n*a who always connects himself with the most excellent (ones), and shuns all inferior ones, (himself) becomes most distinguished; by an opposite conduct he becomes a *S*ûdra.

246. He who is persevering, gentle, (and) patient, shuns the company of men of cruel conduct, and does no injury (to living creatures), gains, if he constantly lives in that manner, by controlling his organs and by liberality, heavenly bliss.

247. He may accept from any (man), fuel, water, roots, fruit, food offered without asking, and honey, likewise a gift (which consists in) a promise of protection.

248. The Lord of created beings (Pra*g*âpati) has declared that alms freely offered and brought (by the giver himself) may be accepted even from a sinful man, provided (the gift) had not been (asked for or) promised beforehand.

249. During fifteen years the manes do not eat (the food) of that man who disdains a (freely-offered gift), nor does the fire carry his offerings (to the gods).

250. A couch, a house, Ku*s*a grass, perfumes,

---

247. Âp. I, 18, 1; Gaut. XVII, 5; Vas. XIV, 12; Vi. LVII, 11.

248. Âp. I, 10, 12–14; Vas. XIV, 16; Vi. LVII, 11; Yâ*gñ*. I, 215. Medh., Gov., and Nâr. take apra*k*oditâm, 'not asked for or promised,' in the sense of 'not promised' only, and so does Nand., who reads apraveditâm.

249. Âp. I, 19, 14; Vas. XIV, 18; Vi. LVII, 12.

250. Gaut. XVII, 5; Vas. XIV, 12; Vi. LVII, 11; Yâ*gñ*. I, 214.

water, flowers, jewels, sour milk, grain, fish, sweet milk, meat, and vegetables let him not reject, (if they are voluntarily offered.)

251. He who desires to relieve his Gurus and those whom he is bound to maintain, or wishes to honour the gods and guests, may accept (gifts) from anybody; but he must not satisfy his (own hunger) with such (presents).

252. But if his Gurus are dead, or if he lives separate from them in (another) house, let him, when he seeks a subsistence, accept (presents) from good men alone.

253. His labourer in tillage, a friend of his family, his cow-herd, his slave, and his barber are, among *S*ûdras, those whose food he may eat, likewise (a poor man) who offers himself (to be his slave).

254. As his character is, as the work is which he desires to perform, and as the manner is in which he means to serve, even so (a voluntary slave) must offer himself.

255. He who describes himself to virtuous (men), in a manner contrary to truth, is the most sinful (wretch) in this world; he is a thief who makes away with his own self.

256. All things (have their nature) determined by speech; speech is their root, and from speech they proceed; but he who is dishonest with respect to speech, is dishonest in everything.

---

251. Âp. I, 7, 20; Gaut. XVII, 4; Vas. XIV, 13; Vi. LVII, 13; Yâ*gñ*. I, 216.

252. Vi. LVII, 15.

253. Âp. I, 18, 14; Gaut. XVII, 5-6; Vi. LVII, 16.

255. I.e. by denying who he really is, he destroys his own identity.

257. When he has paid, according to the law, his debts to the great sages, to the manes, and to the gods, let him make over everything to his son and dwell (in his house), not caring for any worldly concerns.

258. Alone let him constantly meditate in solitude on that which is salutary for his soul; for he who meditates in solitude attains supreme bliss.

259. Thus have been declared the means by which a Brâhma*n*a householder must always subsist, and the summary of the ordinances for a Snâtaka, which cause an increase of holiness and are praiseworthy.

260. A Brâhma*n*a who, being learned in the lore of the Vedas, conducts himself in this manner and daily destroys his sins, will be exalted in Brahman's world.

Chapter V.

1. The sages, having heard the duties of a Snâtaka thus declared, spoke to great-souled Bh*ri*gu, who sprang from fire:

2. 'How can Death have power over Brâhma*n*as

---

257. Regarding the three debts, see Vas. XI, 48. This verse and the next describe, as Medh. points out, a kind of informal sa*m*nyâsa.

260. Vas. VIII, 17; Baudh. II, 3, 1; Gaut. IX, 74.

V. 1. Medh., Gov., and Râgh. state correctly that Bh*ri*gu, though above, I, 35, he is said to have been created by Manu, and has therefore been named Mânava below, V, 3, is here called the offspring of Fire, in accordance with other passages of the Veda and of the Mahâbhârata.

2. I.e. 'how can they be deprived of the length of life, one hundred years, allotted to men in the Veda?' (Gov., Kull.)

who know the sacred science, the Veda, (and) who fulfil their duties as they have been explained (by thee), O Lord?'

3. Righteous Bh*ri*gu, the son of Manu, (thus) answered the great sages: 'Hear, (in punishment) of what faults Death seeks to shorten the lives of Brâhma*n*as!'

4. 'Through neglect of the Veda-study, through deviation from the rule of conduct, through remissness (in the fulfilment of duties), and through faults (committed by eating forbidden) food, Death becomes eager to shorten the lives of Brâhma*n*as.'

5. Garlic, leeks and onions, mushrooms and (all plants), springing from impure (substances), are unfit to be eaten by twice-born men.

6. One should carefully avoid red exudations from trees and (juices) flowing from incisions, the *S*elu (fruit), and the thickened milk of a cow (which she gives after calving).

7. Rice boiled with sesamum, wheat mixed with butter, milk and sugar, milk-rice and flour-cakes which are not prepared for a sacrifice, meat which has not been sprinkled with water while sacred texts were recited, food offered to the gods and sacrificial viands,

8. The milk of a cow (or other female animal) within ten days after her calving, that of camels,

---

5-25. Âp. I, 17, 18-39; Gaut. XVII, 22-36; Vas. XIV, 33-48; Baudh. I, 12, 1-15; Vi. LI, 3-6, 21-42; Yâgñ. I, 169-178. *S*elu, i.e. Cordia Myxa.

7. 'Food offered to the gods,' i.e. the so-called Naivedya. This and sacrificial viands, i.e. those destined for burnt-oblations, must not be eaten before the offering has been made, afterwards the remnants may be eaten (Medh., Gov., Kull.).

8. Sandhinî, 'a cow in heat' (Kull., Nâr., Râgh.), means according

of one-hoofed animals, of sheep, of a cow in heat, or of one that has no calf with her,

9. (The milk) of all wild animals excepting buffalo-cows, that of women, and all (substances turned) sour must be avoided.

10. Among (things turned) sour, sour milk, and all (food) prepared of it may be eaten, likewise what is extracted from pure flowers, roots, and fruit.

11. Let him avoid all carnivorous birds and those living in villages, and one-hoofed animals which are not specially permitted (to be eaten), and the *Titt*ibha (Parra Jacana),

12. The sparrow, the Plava, the Ha*m*sa, the Brâhma*n*î duck, the village-cock, the Sârasa crane, the Ra*gg*udâla, the woodpecker, the parrot, and the starling,

13. Those which feed striking with their beaks, web-footed birds, the Koyash*t*i, those which scratch with their toes, those which dive and live on fish, meat from a slaughter-house and dried meat,

14. The Baka and the Balâkâ crane, the raven, the Kha*ñg*arî*t*aka, (animals) that eat fish, village-pigs, and all kinds of fishes.

15. He who eats the flesh of any (animal) is

---

to Medh. and Gov. 'one who gives milk once a day only,' and according to Nand. and K. 'one big with a calf.'

11. The permission to eat one-hoofed animals is, as the commentators observe, not given in the Sm*ri*ti. The expression refers to the cases where the Veda prescribes horses, &c., to be slain and eaten at sacrifices.

12. I read with all the commentators Ra*gg*udâla instead of Ra*gg*uvâla, which the printed editions give. The Ra*gg*udâla is according to Vi*gñ*âne*s*vara the jungle-fowl, according to Nâr. an aquatic bird.

14. Regarding the Vaka or Baka, see above, IV, 196.

called the eater of the flesh of that (particular creature), he who eats fish is an eater of every (kind of) flesh; let him therefore avoid fish.

16. (But the fish called) Pâ*th*îna and (that called) Rohita may be eaten if used for offerings to the gods or to the manes; one may eat) likewise Râ*g*îvas, Si*m*hatu*nd*as, and Sa*s*alkas on all (occasions).

17. Let him not eat solitary or unknown beasts and birds, though they may fall under (the categories of) eatable (creatures), nor any five-toed (animals).

18 The porcupine, the hedgehog, the iguana, the rhinoceros, the tortoise, and the hare they declare to be eatable likewise those (domestic animals) that have teeth in one jaw only, excepting camels.

19. A twice-born man who knowingly eats mushrooms, a village-pig, garlic, a village-cock, onions, or leeks, will become an outcast.

20. He who unwittingly partakes of (any of) these six, shall perform a Sâ*m*tapana (K*rikkh*ra) or the lunar penance (*K*ândrâya*n*a) of ascetics; in case (he has eaten) any other (kind of forbidden food) he shall fast for one day (and a night).

21. Once a year a Brâhma*n*a must perform a K*rikkh*ra penance, in order to atone for unintentionally eating (forbidden food); but for intentionally (eating forbidden food he must perform the penances prescribed) specially.

22. Beasts and birds recommended (for con-

16. Nâr. explains eka*k*arân, 'solitary animals,' by 'those who go in herds' (sa*m*gha*k*âri*n*a*h*).

20. Regarding the Sâ*m*tapana K*rikkh*ra and the lunar penance of ascetics, see below, XI, 213 and 219.

21. Regarding the K*rikkh*ra penance, see below, XI, 212.

22. Vas. XIV, 15.

sumption) may be slain by Brâhma*n*as for sacrifices, and in order to feed those whom they are bound to maintain; for Agastya did this of old.

23. For in ancient (times) the sacrificial cakes were (made of the flesh) of eatable beasts and birds at the sacrifices offered by Brâhma*n*as and Kshatriyas.

24. All lawful hard or soft food may be eaten, though stale, (after having been) mixed with fatty (substances), and so may the remains of sacrificial viands.

25. But all preparations of barley and wheat, as well as preparations of milk, may be eaten by twice-born men without being mixed with fatty (substances), though they may have stood for a long time.

26. Thus has the food, allowed and forbidden to twice-born men, been fully described; I will now propound the rules for eating and avoiding meat.

27. One may eat meat when it has been sprinkled with water, while Mantras were recited, when Brâhma*n*as desire (one's doing it), when one is engaged (in the performance of a rite) according to the law, and when one's life is in danger.

28. The Lord of creatures (Pra*g*âpati) created this whole (world to be) the sustenance of the vital spirit; both the immovable and the movable (creation is) the food of the vital spirit.

29. What is destitute of motion is the food of those endowed with locomotion; (animals) without fangs (are the food) of those with fangs, those without hands of those who possess hands, and the timid of the bold.

30. The eater who daily even devours those

27–56. Vas. IV, 5–8; Vi. LI, 59–78; Yâ*gñ*. I, 178–181.

27. Meat is sprinkled with water at the *S*rauta sacrifices.

destined to be his food, commits no sin; for the creator himself created both the eaters and those who are to be eaten (for those special purposes).

31. 'The consumption of meat (is befitting) for sacrifices,' that is declared to be a rule made by the gods; but to persist (in using it) on other (occasions) is said to be a proceeding worthy of Râkshasas.

32. He who eats meat, when he honours the gods and manes, commits no sin, whether he has bought it, or himself has killed (the animal), or has received it as a present from others.

33. A twice-born man who knows the law, must not eat meat except in conformity with the law; for if he has eaten it unlawfully, he will, unable to save himself, be eaten after death by his (victims).

34. After death the guilt of one who slays deer for gain is not as (great) as that of him who eats meat for no (sacred) purpose.

35. But a man who, being duly engaged (to officiate or to dine at a sacred rite), refuses to eat meat, becomes after death an animal during twenty-one existences.

36. A Brâhma*n*a must never eat (the flesh of) animals unhallowed by Mantras; but, obedient to the primeval law, he may eat it, consecrated with Vedic texts.

37. If he has a strong desire (for meat) he may make an animal of clarified butter or one of flour, (and eat that); but let him never seek to destroy an animal without a (lawful) reason.

---

34. 'Of one who slays deer for gain,' i. e. of a professional hunter of the *S*abara or other low castes.

35. Vas. XI, 34.

37. Saṅge, 'if (he has) a strong desire (for meat),' (Kull., Râgh.),

38. As many hairs as the slain beast has, so often indeed will he who killed it without a (lawful) reason suffer a violent death in future births.

39. Svayambhû (the Self-existent) himself created animals for the sake of sacrifices; sacrifices (have been instituted) for the good of this whole (world); hence the slaughtering (of beasts) for sacrifices is not slaughtering (in the ordinary sense of the word).

40. Herbs, trees, cattle, birds, and (other) animals that have been destroyed for sacrifices, receive (being reborn) higher existences.

41. On offering the honey-mixture (to a guest), at a sacrifice and at the rites in honour of the manes, but on these occasions only, may an animal be slain; that (rule) Manu proclaimed.

42. A twice-born man who, knowing the true meaning of the Veda, slays an animal for these purposes, causes both himself and the animal to enter a most blessed state.

43. A twice-born man of virtuous disposition, whether he dwells in (his own) house, with a teacher, or in the forest, must never, even in times of distress, cause an injury (to any creature) which is not sanctioned by the Veda.

44. Know that the injury to moving creatures and to those destitute of motion, which the Veda has

means according to Medh. and K. 'if an occasion (arises to slay an animal at a non-Vedic rite),' according to Gov. 'in case (one suffers from) an attack by evil spirits (Bhûtas and the like),' and according to Nand. 'on the occasion of social meetings.' Râgh. mentions Medh.'s view as an optional explanation, and Nâr. objects to Gov.'s interpretation. His own explanation saṅgetyantekâyâm is corrupt, but is probably intended for atyante*kkh*â-yâm, and thus agrees with Kull.'s.

prescribed for certain occasions, is no injury at all; for the sacred law shone forth from the Veda.

45. He who injures innoxious beings from a wish to (give) himself pleasure, never finds happiness, neither living nor dead.

46. He who does not seek to cause the sufferings of bonds and death to living creatures, (but) desires the good of all (beings), obtains endless bliss.

47. He who does not injure any (creature), attains without an effort what he thinks of, what he undertakes, and what he fixes his mind on.

48. Meat can never be obtained without injury to living creatures, and injury to sentient beings is detrimental to (the attainment of) heavenly bliss; let him therefore shun (the use of) meat.

49. Having well considered the (disgusting) origin of flesh and the (cruelty of) fettering and slaying corporeal beings, let him entirely abstain from eating flesh.

50. He who, disregarding the rule (given above), does not eat meat like a Pisâka, becomes dear to men, and will not be tormented by diseases.

51. He who permits (the slaughter of an animal), he who cuts it up, he who kills it, he who buys or sells (meat), he who cooks it, he who serves it up, and he who eats it, (must all be considered as) the slayers (of the animal).

52. There is no greater sinner than that (man) who, though not worshipping the gods or the manes, seeks to increase (the bulk of) his own flesh by the flesh of other (beings).

46. The latter part of the verse may also be translated 'will obtain endless bliss, because he is a man who desires the good of all creatures' (Gov.).

53. He who during a hundred years annually offers a horse-sacrifice, and he who entirely abstains from meat, obtain the same reward for their meritorious (conduct).

54. By subsisting on pure fruit and roots, and by eating food fit for ascetics (in the forest), one does not gain (so great) a reward as by entirely avoiding (the use of) flesh.

55. 'Me he (mâ*m* sa*h*)' will devour in the next (world), whose flesh I eat in this (life); the wise declare this (to be) the real meaning of the word 'flesh' (mâ*m*sa*h*).

56. There is no sin in eating meat, in (drinking) spirituous liquor, and in carnal intercourse, for that is the natural way of created beings, but abstention brings great rewards.

57. I will now in due order explain the purification for the dead and the purification of things as they are prescribed for the four castes (var*n*a).

58. When (a child) dies that has teethed, or that before teething has received (the sacrament of) the tonsure (*K*û*d*âkara*n*a) or (of the initiation), all relatives (become) impure, and on the birth (of a child) the same (rule) is prescribed.

---

54. Munyannâni, 'food fit for ascetics (in the forest),' i.e. 'wild rice and other produce of the forest.'

56. 'There is no sin,' i.e. in doing these things when they are permitted by law.

58–104. Âp. I, 15, 18; II, 15, 2–11; Gaut. XIV; Vas. IV, 16–37; Baudh. I, 11, 1–8, 17–23, 27–32; Vi. XXII; Yâ*gñ*. III, 1–30.

58. Medh. and Gov. explain anu*g*âte, translated freely by 'before teething,' as the conventional designation of 'a child that is younger than one that has teethed' (*g*âtadantâd bâlatara iti smaranti), and Nâr. and Râgh. agree to this interpretation. Kull., however, seems to take it in the sense of 'after teething,' and Nand. explains it as 'one who has been born again, i.e. has been initiated.' Gov.,

59. It is ordained (that) among Sapi*nd*as the impurity on account of a death (shall last) ten days, (or) until the bones have been collected, (or) three days or one day only.

60. But the Sapi*nd*a-relationship ceases with the seventh person (in the ascending and descending lines), the Samânodaka-relationship when the (common) origin and the (existence of a common family)-name are no (longer) known.

61. As this impurity on account of a death is prescribed for (all) Sapi*nd*as, even so it shall be (held) on a birth by those who desire to be absolutely pure.

62. (Or while) the impurity on account of a death is common to all (Sapi*nd*as), that caused by a birth (falls) on the parents alone; (or) it shall fall on the mother alone, and the father shall become pure by bathing;

Nâr., Kull., and Râgh. think that on account of the second *k*a, 'or,' the words 'of the initiation' must be understood.

59. The bones of a Brâhma*n*a are collected on the fourth day; see Vi. XIX, 10. The commentators are of opinion that the length of the period of impurity depends, in accordance with the express teaching of other Sm*ri*tis, on the status of the mourner, and that a man who knows the Mantras only of one *S*âkhâ shall be impure during four days, one who knows a whole *S*âkhâ (or two Vedas) during three days, one who knows the Veda (or three Vedas) and keeps three or five sacred fires, during one day. Medh., however, mentions another interpretation, according to which the four periods correspond to the four ages of the deceased, which have been mentioned in the preceding verse. According to this view the Sapi*nd*as shall mourn for an initiated person ten days, for one who had received the tonsure four days, &c. But see verse 67.

61-62. Medh. and Gov. have only one verse instead of the two: *g*anane 'py eva*m* syân mâtâpitros tu sûtakam ı sûtaka*m* mâtur eva syâd upasp*ri*sya pitâ *s*u*k*i*h* ıı 'Even thus it shall be (held) on a birth, or the impurity shall fall on the parents alone,

63. But a man, having spent his strength, is purified merely by bathing; after begetting a child (on a remarried female), he shall retain the impurity during three days.

64. Those who have touched a corpse are purified after one day and night (added to) three periods of three days; those who give libations of water, after three days.

65. A pupil who performs the Pit*ri*medha for his deceased teacher, becomes also pure after ten days, just like those who carry the corpse out (to the burial-ground).

66. (A woman) is purified on a miscarriage in as many (days and) nights as months (elapsed after conception), and a menstruating female becomes pure by bathing after the menstrual secretion has ceased (to flow).

---

or it shall fall on the mother alone, and the father (shall become) pure by bathing.' Nand. leaves out the first half of verse 61, and combines the second half of 61 with the first half of 62. He continues in this manner down to 65, the second half of which he takes by itself. Hence his interpretation of the following verses is perfectly useless.

63. The translation given above follows Gov., Kull., Nâr., and Râgh. Medh. differs.

64. According to Gov. and Nâr. the rule refers to such Brâhma*n*as who for money carry a dead body to the cemetery; according to Kull. and Râgh. to Sapi*nd*as who in any way touch a corpse out of affection. Medh. thinks that it applies to all who touch or carry out a dead body, be it for love or for money. Râgh. thinks that the text mentions three alternative periods of impurity, one day, three days, and ten days.

65. The Pit*ri*medha, i.e. the Antyesh*t*i (Medh., Gov., Kull., Râgh.), or 'the whole of the obsequies' ('others,' Medh.).

66. Thus according to Kull.; Nâr. and Râgh. think that this rule refers to miscarriages which happen during the first six months of pregnancy; and that from the seventh month, whether the child

N 2

67. (On the death) of children whose tonsure (*K*û*d*âkarman) has not been performed, the (Sapi*nd*as) are declared to become pure in one (day and) night; (on the death) of those who have received the tonsure (but not the initiation, the law) ordains (that) the purification (takes place) after three days.

68. A child that has died before the completion of its second year, the relatives shall carry out (of the village), decked (with flowers, and bury it) in pure ground, without collecting the bones (afterwards).

69. Such (a child) shall not be burnt with fire, and no libations of water shall be offered to it; leaving it like a (log of) wood in the forest, (the relatives) shall remain impure during three days only.

70. The relatives shall not offer libations to (a child) that has not reached the third year; but if it had teeth, or the ceremony of naming it (Nâmakarman) had been performed, (the offering of water is) optional.

71. If a fellow-student has died, the Sm*ri*ti prescribes an impurity of one day; on a birth the purification of the Samânodakas is declared (to take place) after three (days and) nights.

72. (On the death) of females (betrothed but) not married (the bridegroom and his) relatives are purified after three days, and the paternal relatives become pure according to the same rule.

---

lives or not, the full period of impurity must be kept. Nâr., moreover, asserts that in the first and second months the impurity shall last three days. Sâdhvî, 'becomes pure,' i.e. 'fit to perform sacred rites' (Gov.). Nâr. takes the word in the sense of 'chaste.'

67. Nand. inserts verse 78 immediately after verse 66.

72. 'According to the same rule,' i.e. 'according to that given in verse 67' (Medh., Gov., Nand.), or 'just as the husband's relatives, i.e. after three days' (Kull., Nâr., Râgh.).

73. Let (mourners) eat food without factitious salt, bathe during three days, abstain from meat, and sleep separate on the ground.

74. The above rule regarding impurity on account of a death has been prescribed (for cases where the kinsmen live) near (the deceased); (Sapi*nd*a) kinsmen and (Samânodaka) relatives must know the following rule (to refer to cases where deceased lived) at a distance (from them).

75. He who may hear that (a relative) residing in a distant country has died, before ten (days after his death have elapsed), shall be impure for the remainder of the period of ten (days and) nights only.

76. If the ten days have passed, he shall be impure during three (days and) nights; but if a year has elapsed (since the occurrence of the death), he becomes pure merely by bathing.

77. A man who hears of a (Sapi*nd*a) relative's death, or of the birth of a son after the ten days (of impurity have passed), becomes pure by bathing, dressed in his garments.

78. If an infant (that has not teethed), or a (grown-up relative who is) not a Sapi*nd*a, die in a distant country, one becomes at once pure after bathing in one's clothes.

79. If within the ten days (of impurity) another birth or death happens, a Brâhma*n*a shall remain impure only until the (first) period of ten days has expired.

80. They declare that, when the teacher (â*k*ârya) has died, the impurity (lasts) three days; if the

73. Nand. reads anvaham, (bathe) 'daily' instead of 'during three days.'

(teacher's) son or wife (is dead, it lasts) a day and a night; that is a settled (rule).

81. For a *S*rotriya who resides with (him out of affection), a man shall be impure for three days; for a maternal uncle, a pupil, an officiating priest, or a maternal relative, for one night together with the preceding and following days.

82. If the king in whose realm he resides is dead, (he shall be impure) as long as the light (of the sun or stars shines), but for (an intimate friend) who is not a *S*rotriya (the impurity lasts) for a whole day, likewise for a Guru who knows the Veda and the Aṅgas.

83. A Brâhma*n*a shall be pure after ten days, a Kshatriya after twelve, a Vai*s*ya after fifteen, and a *S*ûdra is purified after a month.

84. Let him not (unnecessarily) lengthen the period of impurity, nor interrupt the rites to be performed with the sacred fires; for he who performs that (Agnihotra) rite will not be impure, though (he be) a (Sapi*nd*a) relative.

---

81. Upasampanne, 'who resides with (him out of affection),' may according to Medh. also mean 'who is virtuous.' According to Nâr. it means 'who is a neighbour.'

82. Anû*k*âne tathâ gurau, 'likewise for a Guru who knows the Veda and Aṅgas,' i.e. 'such a one who is mentioned above, II, 149' (Gov., Kull., Râgh.). Nâr. takes the two words separately. Medh. connects anû*k*âne with a*s*rotriye, and thinks that a man is meant who does not know the Veda, but the Aṅgas. He also mentions the explanation adopted above. Nand. finally reads anû*k*âne tathâ 'gurau, 'likewise for one who knows the Veda and the Aṅgas, but is not a Guru.'

84. According to Medh. the meaning of the first clause is that, if there is an option between shorter or longer periods of impurity, the mourner is not to choose the longer one in order to escape the performance of his sacred duties. He adds, that others think

85. When he has touched a *Kandâla*, a menstruating woman, an outcast, a woman in childbed, a corpse, or one who has touched a (corpse), he becomes pure by bathing.

86. He who has purified himself by sipping water shall, on seeing any impure (thing or person), always mutter the sacred texts, addressed to Sûrya, and the Pâvamânî (verses).

87. A Brâhmana who has touched a human bone to which fat adheres, becomes pure by bathing; if it be free from fat, by sipping water and by touching (afterwards) a cow or looking at the sun.

88. He who has undertaken the performance of a vow shall not pour out libations (to the dead) until the vow has been completed; but when he has

---

it to be an exhortation not to delay the bath which must be taken at the expiration of the period of impurity. The other commentators mention the first explanation only. The second clause, which refers to the continued offering of the *S*rauta Agnihotra, means according to Medh., Gov., and Nand., that an Agnihotrin who is in mourning shall not perform the offerings in person, but make others, who may even be his near relatives, do it for him. Kull., Nâr., and Râgh. think that the performer himself may also offer them. Nand. explains sanâbhya*h*, 'a Sapi*nd*a' (Gov., Kull., Nâr., Râgh.), by sahodara*h*, 'a full brother.'

85. Tatsprish*t*inam, 'one who has touched a (corpse),' (Medh., 'others;' Gov., Kull., Râgh.), means according to Medh., Nâr., and Nand. 'one who has touched any of those enumerated before, a *Kandâ*la and so forth.'

86. 'He who has purified himself,' i. e. 'before he begins to worship the gods or manes' (Medh., 'others;' Kull., Nâr., Râgh.). 'An impure (thing or person),' i.e. 'those mentioned above.' Medh. and Gov. take the verse differently, 'On seeing one of those impure persons mentioned above, let him sip water and, thus purified, recite, &c.' The texts addressed to Sûrya are found Rig-veda I, 50, 1 seq.; the Pâvamânîs in Ma*nd*ala IX.

88. The rule refers to a student, who must not during his studentship perform the last rites for any deceased relative except

offered water after its completion, he becomes pure in three days only.

89. Libations of water shall not be offered to those who (neglect the prescribed rites and may be said to) have been born in vain, to those born in consequence of an illegal mixture of the castes, to those who are ascetics (of heretical sects), and to those who have committed suicide,

90. To women who have joined a heretical sect, who through lust live (with many men), who have caused an abortion, have killed their husbands, or drink spirituous liquor.

91. A student does not break his vow by carrying out (to the place of cremation) his own dead teacher (â*k*ârya), sub-teacher (upâdhyâya), father, mother, or Guru.

92. Let him carry out a dead *S*ûdra by the southern gate of the town, but (the corpses of)

---

his mother (Medh.), or except his mother and father (Gov.), or except his parents and his teacher; see below, verse 91 (Kull., Râgh.). According to K. 'others' think that the rule refers to those performing a lunar penance or other vows.

89. 'To those who (neglect the prescribed rites and may be said to) have been born in vain' (Gov., Kull., Nand., Râgh.), i.e. 'to those who for a year belonged to no order' (Medh.), or 'to eunuchs' (Nâr.). The term sa*m*kara*g*â*h*, 'born in consequence of an illegal mixture of the castes,' includes besides those sprung from mothers of a higher and fathers of a lower caste, sons of widows not appointed and of adulteresses (Medh., Gov., Nand.). 'Ascetics (of heretical sects),' i.e. Kâpâlikas, those wearing red garments, &c. (Medh.). Nâr. and Râgh. refer the term to orthodox ascetics.

90. Pâsha*nd*am, 'a heretical sect,' i.e. the Kâpâlikas, those wearing red garments' (Medh.), or 'Bauddhas and so forth' (Nâr.).

91. 'Guru,' i. e. 'one who explains the Veda' (Nâr., Kull.), or 'him who is mentioned above, II, 149' (Medh., Gov.).

92. I.e. a Vais*y*a by the western gate, a Kshatriya by the

twice-born men, as is proper, by the western, northern, or eastern (gates).

93. The taint of impurity does not fall on kings, and those engaged in the performance of a vow, or of a Sattra; for the (first are) seated on the throne of Indra, and the (last two are) ever pure like Brahman.

94. For a king, on the throne of magnanimity, immediate purification is prescribed, and the reason for that is that he is seated (there) for the protection of (his) subjects.

95. (The same rule applies to the kinsmen) of those who have fallen in a riot or a battle, (of those who have been killed) by lightning or by the king, and (of those who perished fighting) for cows and Brâhma*n*as, and to those whom the king wishes (to be pure).

96. A king is an incarnation of the eight guardian deities of the world, the Moon, the Fire, the Sun, the Wind, Indra, the Lords of wealth and water (Kubera and Varu*n*a), and Yama.

97. Because the king is pervaded by (those)

---

northern, and a Brâhma*n*a by the eastern (Medh., Gov., Kull., Nand., Râgh.).

93. 'A vow,' i.e. 'the studentship (Nâr.), also a lunar penance and the like' (Medh., Gov., Kull.); 'a Sattra,' i.e. 'a long sacrifice such as the Gavâmayana.' Brahmabhûtâ*h*, 'pure like Brahman' (Kull., Nâr., Râgh.), means according to Medh. 'they have reached Brahmahood.'

95. Nand. and K. explain *d*imbha, 'in a riot,' to mean 'by infants.' 'Whom the king wishes (to be pure),' i.e. 'his servants and ministers whom he wants for his affairs.' Nâr. inserts another class, '(the kinsmen of those who have been killed) by Brâhma*n*as, i.e. by incantations.' But I do not understand how the word could be made to suit the verse.

96. See below, VII, 4.

97. Medh. reads loke*s*aprabhavâpyayau, and the second half

lords of the world, no impurity is ordained for him; for purity and impurity of mortals is caused and removed by (those) lords of the world.

98. By him who is slain in battle with brandished weapons according to the law of the Kshatriyas, a (*S*rauta) sacrifice is instantly completed, and so is the period of impurity (caused by his death); that is a settled rule.

99. (At the end of the period of impurity) a Brâhma*n*a who has performed the necessary rites, becomes pure by touching water, a Kshatriya by touching the animal on which he rides, and his weapons, a Vai*s*ya by touching his goad or the nose-string (of his oxen), a *S*ûdra by touching his staff.

100. Thus the purification (required) on (the death of) Sapi*nd*as has been explained to you, O best of twice-born men; hear now the manner in which men are purified on the death of any (relative who is) not a Sapi*nd*a.

101. A Brâhma*n*a, having carried out a dead

---

verse must then be translated 'purity and impurity affect mortals, they are caused and removed by the guardians of the world.' Nâr., Nand., and K. read loke*s*aprabhavo hy ayam, 'but he (the) king springs from the guardians of the world.' Nâr. mentions also a reading loke*s*aprabhave 'pyaya*h*, 'for him who springs from the guardians of the world, (purity and impurity) do not exist.'

98. According to Medh. some contend that this rule refers only to those who die on the battle-field, not to those who die later of their wounds. Yag*ñ*a*h*, 'a (*S*rauta) sacrifice' (Medh., Kull., Râgh.), means according to Nâr. 'the funeral sacrifice.'

99. 'Touching water,' i.e. 'bathing' (Medh., Kull., Nâr.), 'washing his hands' (Gov.).

101. 'The relatives of his mother and (the Sagotras of his father), or connexions by marriage, are meant' (Nâr.).

Brâhma*n*a who is not a Sapi*nd*a, as (if he were) a (near) relative, or a near relative of his mother, becomes pure after three days;

102. But if he eats the food of the (Sapi*nd*as of the deceased), he is purified in ten days, (but) in one day, if he does not eat their food nor dwells in their house.

103. Having voluntarily followed a corpse, whether (that of) a paternal kinsman or (of) a stranger, he becomes pure by bathing, dressed in his clothes, by touching fire and eating clarified butter.

104. Let him not allow a dead Brâhma*n*a to be carried out by a *S*ûdra, while men of the same caste are at hand; for that burnt-offering which is defiled by a *S*ûdra's touch is detrimental to (the deceased's passage to) heaven.

105. The knowledge (of Brahman) austerities, fire, (holy) food, earth, (restraint of) the internal organ, water, smearing (with cowdung), the wind, sacred rites, the sun, and time are the purifiers of corporeal (beings).

106. Among all modes of purification, purity in (the acquisition of) wealth is declared to be the best; for he is pure who gains wealth with clean hands, not he who purifies himself with earth and water.

---

102. In case he stays in the house of the mourners, he becomes impure for three days (Gov., Kull., Râgh., K.).

104. According to Nâr. the rule refers exclusively to Brâhma*n*as, according to Medh. and Kull. to all Âryans. The burning of the body is euphemistically called a burnt-offering.

105. Vi. XXII, 88; Yâ*gñ*. III, 31; Baudh. I, 8, 52. Mana*h* kshamâkhya*h* (?) niyamayukta*m* mano *g*îvasya (Nâr.). The other commentators take mana*h*, 'the mind or internal organ,' in the sense of 'a sanctified heart.'

106. Vi. XXII, 89; Yâ*gñ*. III, 32.

107. The learned are purified by a forgiving disposition, those who have committed forbidden actions by liberality, secret sinners by muttering (sacred texts), and those who best know the Veda by austerities.

108. By earth and water is purified what ought to be made pure, a river by its current, a woman whose thoughts have been impure by the menstrual secretion, a Brâhma*n*a by abandoning the world (sa*m*nyâsa).

109. The body is cleansed by water, the internal organ is purified by truthfulness, the individual soul by sacred learning and austerities, the intellect by (true) knowledge.

110. Thus the precise rules for the purification of the body have been declared to you; hear now the decision (of the law) regarding the purification of the various (inanimate) things.

111. The wise ordain that all (objects) made of metal, gems, and anything made of stone are to be cleansed with ashes, earth, and water.

112. A golden vessel which shows no stains, becomes pure with water alone, likewise what is produced in water (as shells and coral), what is made of stone, and a silver (vessel) not enchased.

---

107. Vi. XXII, 90; Yâ*gñ*. III, 33.

108. Vi. XXII, 91; Vas. III, 58; Yâ*gñ*. III, 32.

109. Vi. XXII, 92; Vas. III, 60; Yâ*gñ*. III, 33–34.

110. Vi. XXII, 93.

111–126. Âp. I, 17, 8–13; II, 3, 9; Gaut. I, 29–34; Vas. III, 44–57, 59, 61–63; Baudh. I, 8, 32–53, 9, 1–4, 7–12, 10, 1–9; 13, 11–14, 19; Vi. XXIII, 2–46, 56; Yâ*gñ*. I, 182–190.

112. Anupask*ri*tam, 'not enchased,' may also mean according to Medh. and Nand. 'not defiled very much.' Medh. and Nâr. add

113. From the union of water and fire arose the glittering gold and silver; those two, therefore, are best purified by (the elements) from which they sprang.

114. Copper, iron, brass, pewter, tin, and lead must be cleansed, as may be suitable (for each particular case), by alkaline (substances), acids or water.

115. The purification prescribed for all (sorts of) liquids is by passing two blades of Ku*s*a grass through them, for solid things by sprinkling (them with water), for (objects) made of wood by planing them.

116. At sacrifices the purification of (the Soma cups called) *K*amasas and Grahas, and of (other) sacrificial vessels (takes place) by rubbing (them) with the hand, and (afterwards) rinsing (them with water).

117. The *K*aru and (the spoons called) Sru*k* and Sruva must be cleaned with hot water, likewise (the wooden sword, called) Sphya, the winnowing-basket (*S*ûrpa), the cart (for bringing the grain), the pestle and the mortar.

118. The manner of purifying large quantities of grain and of cloth is to sprinkle them with water;

---

that this last term applies to all the various objects mentioned in the verse.

113. Medh., Gov., and Kull. quote a Vedic passage which derives the origin of gold from Agni and the goddess Varu*n*ânî.

115. Utpavanam or utplavanam (Gov., Kull., Râgh.), 'passing two blades of Ku*s*a grass through them,' means according to Medh., 'others,' and K. 'purifying by pouring them into another vessel, filled with pure liquids of the same kind,' according to Nâr. by 'straining through a cloth.' 'Solid things,' i.e. 'a couch, a seat, and the like.'

but the purification of small quantities is prescribed (to take place) by washing them.

119. Skins and (objects) made of split cane must be cleaned like clothes; vegetables, roots, and fruit like grain;

120. Silk and woollen stuffs with alkaline earth; blankets with pounded Arish*t*a (fruit); A*ms*upa*tt*as with Bel fruit; linen cloth with (a paste of) yellow mustard.

121. A man who knows (the law) must purify conch-shells, horn, bone and ivory, like linen cloth, or with a mixture of cow's urine and water.

122. Grass, wood, and straw become pure by being sprinkled (with water), a house by sweeping and smearing (it with cowdung or whitewash), an earthen (vessel) by a second burning.

123. An earthen vessel which has been defiled by spirituous liquor, urine, ordure, saliva, pus or blood cannot be purified by another burning.

124. Land is purified by (the following) five (modes, viz.) by sweeping, by smearing (it with cow-dung), by sprinkling (it with cows' urine or milk), by scraping, and by cows staying (on it during a day and night).

125. (Food) which has been pecked at by birds,

---

119. Vaidalânâm, 'objects made of split cane' (Kull., K., Râgh., Nâr., Nand.), means according to Medh. and Gov. 'made of the bark of trees and the like.' Medh. remarks that this and other rules, where skins and so forth are mentioned, apply also to objects made of such things, e.g. shoes.

120. Arish*t*a, i.e. Sapindus detergens, the soap-berry tree. A*ms*upa*tt*a means according to Gov., Nand., and Nâr. 'cloth made of thinned bark,' according to Kull. and Râgh. 'upper garments for women (Sârîs) made of fine cloth' (pa*tt*a*s*â*t*aka, pa*tt*a*s*â*t*î).

125. 'By birds,' i.e. 'by parrots and the like, not by crows,

smelt at by cows, touched (with the foot), sneezed on, or defiled by hair or insects, becomes pure by scattering earth (over it).

126. As long as the (foul) smell does not leave an (object) defiled by impure substances, and the stain caused by them (does not disappear), so long must earth and water be applied in cleansing (inanimate) things.

127. The gods declared three things (to be) pure to Brâhma*n*as, that (on which) no (taint is) visible, what has been washed with water, and what has been commended (as pure) by the word (of a Brâhma*n*a).

128. Water, sufficient (in quantity) in order to slake the thirst of a cow, possessing the (proper) smell, colour, and taste, and unmixed with impure substances, is pure, if it is collected on (pure) ground.

129. The hand of an artisan is always pure, so is (every vendible commodity) exposed for sale in

---

vultures, and other impure ones' (Medh., Gov., Kull.). Avadhûtam, 'touched (with the foot),' (Kull., Râgh.), means according to Medh. 'blown upon with the mouth,' or 'dusted with a dress,' according to Gov. 'dusted with a dress,' according to Nâr. 'moved by the wind (caused by the motion) of a cloth, the foot or the like,' according to Nand. 'defiled by the dust of a broom or of the air moved by the wings (of a bird).'

127. Vas. XIV, 24; Baudh. I, 9, 9; Vi. XXIII, 47; Yâ*gñ*. I, 191. In conformity with the opinion of the commentators I translate pavitrâ*n*i by 'pure.' But the word has also the meaning of 'means of purification,' in which I have taken it in the translations of the parallel passages. The general sense remains the same.

128. Vas. III, 35–36, 47; Baudh. I, 9, 10; Vi. XXIII, 43; Yâ*gñ*. I, 192.

129. Baudh. I, 9, 1; Vi. XXIII, 48.

the market, and food obtained by begging which a student holds (in his hand) is always fit for use; that is a settled rule.

130. The mouth of a woman is always pure, likewise a bird when he causes a fruit to fall; a calf is pure on the flowing of the milk, and a dog when he catches a deer.

131. Manu has declared that the flesh (of an animal) killed by dogs is pure, likewise (that) of a (beast) slain by carnivorous (animals) or by men of low caste (Dasyu), such as *Kand*âlas.

132. All those cavities (of the body) which lie above the navel are pure, (but) those which are below the navel are impure, as well as excretions that fall from the body.

133. Flies, drops of water, a shadow, a cow, a horse, the rays of the sun, dust, earth, the wind, and fire one must know to be pure to the touch.

134. In order to cleanse (the organs) by which urine and faeces are ejected, earth and water must be used, as they may be required, likewise in removing the (remaining ones among) twelve impurities of the body.

---

130. Baudh. I, 9, 2; Vi. XXIII, 49; Yâ*gñ*. I, 193.

131. Vas. III, 45; Vi. XXIII, 50; Yâ*gñ*. I, 192.

132. Vi. XXIII, 51; Yâ*gñ*. I, 194.

133. Vi. XXIII, 51; Yâ*gñ*. I, 193. 'Drops of water,' i.e. 'such as are only perceptible by the touch' (Medh., Gov.), or 'such as come from the mouth, i.e. of saliva' (Kull., Râgh., Nâr.). Râgh. adds, 'and a continuous stream of water.'

134. Âp. I, 16, 15; Gaut. I, 43; Vas. VI, 14; Yâ*gñ*. I, 17. 'As they may be required,' i.e. 'for removing the first six kinds of impurities enumerated in the next verse, as much water and earth as may be required, and for the last six water only' (Gov., Kull., Nâr., Râgh.).

135. Oily exudations, semen, blood, (the fatty substance of the) brain, urine, faeces, the mucus of the nose, ear-wax, phlegm, tears, the rheum of the eyes, and sweat are the twelve impurities of human (bodies).

136. He who desires to be pure, must clean the organ by one (application of) earth, the anus by (applying earth) three (times), the (left) hand alone by (applying it) ten (times), and both (hands) by (applying it) seven (times).

137. Such is the purification ordained for householders; (it shall be) double for students, treble for hermits, but quadruple for ascetics.

138. When he has voided urine or faeces, let him, after sipping water, sprinkle the cavities, likewise when he is going to recite the Veda, and always before he takes food.

139. Let him who desires bodily purity first sip water three times, and then twice wipe his mouth; but a woman and a *S*ûdra (shall perform each act) once (only).

140. *S*ûdras who live according to the law, shall each month shave (their heads); their mode of purification (shall be) the same as that of Vai*s*yas, and their food the fragments of an Âryan's meal.

---

136. Vas. VI, 18; Vi. LX, 25.

137. Vas. VI, 19; Vi. LX, 26.

138. Gaut. I, 36; Baudh. I, 8, 26; Vi. LXII, 8. 'The cavities,' i.e. of the head (Gov.), and also the navel, the heart, and the crown of the head (Nâr., Kull.).

139. Âp. I, 16, 3–8; Gaut. I, 36; Vas. III, 27–28; Baudh. I, 8, 20–22; Vi. LXII, 6–8; Yâ*gñ*. I, 20.

140. Âp. II, 3, 4–6. 'Who live according to the law,' i.e. 'who serve Âryans' (Medh., Gov., Kull., Râgh.). Nand. thinks that mâsika*m* vapana*m* kârya*m*, 'shall shave each month,' means 'shall offer the monthly *S*râddha.'

141. Drops (of water) from the mouth which do not fall on a limb, do not make (a man) impure, nor the hair of the moustache entering the mouth, nor what adheres to the teeth.

142. Drops which trickle on the feet of him who offers water for sipping to others, must be considered as equal to (water) collected on the ground; they render him not impure.

143. He who, while carrying anything in any manner, is touched by an impure (person or thing), shall become pure, if he performs an ablution, without putting down that object.

144. He who has vomited or purged shall bathe, and afterwards eat clarified butter; but if (the attack comes on) after he has eaten, let him only sip water; bathing is prescribed for him who has had intercourse with a woman.

145. Though he may be (already) pure, let him sip water after sleeping, sneezing, eating, spitting, telling untruths, and drinking water, likewise when he is going to study the Veda.

146. Thus the rules of personal purification for men of all castes, and those for cleaning (inanimate) things, have been fully declared to you: hear now the duties of women.

---

141. Âp. I, 16, 13; Gaut. I, 38–41; Vas. III, 37, 40–41; Baudh. I, 8, 23–25; Vi. XXIII, 53; Yâgñ. I, 195. I read with Medh., Gov., Nâr., Nand., and K., aṅgam na yanti yâh, instead of aṅge patanti, 'which fall on a limb,' the reading of Kull. and Râgh.

142. Vas. III, 42; Vi. XXIII, 54.

143. Gaut. I, 28; Vas. III, 43; Baudh. I, 8, 27–29; Vi. XXIII, 55.

145. Âp. I, 16, 14; Gaut. I, 37; Vi. XXII, 75; Yâgñ. I, 196. According to Medh., some refer this verse to a repeated sipping of water.

147. By a girl, by a young woman, or even by an aged one, nothing must be done independently, even in her own house.

148. In childhood a female must be subject to her father, in youth to her husband, when her lord is dead to her sons; a woman must never be independent

149. She must not seek to separate herself from her father, husband, or sons; by leaving them she would make both (her own and her husband's) families contemptible.

150. She must always be cheerful, clever in (the management of her) household affairs, careful in cleaning her utensils, and economical in expenditure.

151. Him to whom her father may give her, or her brother with the father's permission, she shall obey as long as he lives, and when he is dead, she must not insult (his memory).

152. For the sake of procuring good fortune to (brides), the recitation of benedictory texts (svastyayana), and the sacrifice to the Lord of creatures (Pra*g*âpati) are used at weddings; (but) the betrothal (by the father or guardian) is the cause of (the husband's) dominion (over his wife).

147–149. See below, IX, 2–3; Vi. XXVI, 12–13; Yâ*gñ*. I, 85–86.

150. Vi. XXVI, 4–6; Yâ*gñ*. I, 83.

151. Vi. XXVI, 14; Yâ*gñ*. I, 63.

152. Svastyayanam, 'the recitation of benedictory texts,' i. e. 'of those intended for averting evil omens' (Gov., Kull.); or 'the Pu*n*yâhavâ*k*ana and the rest' (Nâr.); or 'the recitation of the texts which precede the nuptial burnt-oblation' (Râgh., Nand.). Medh. connects the word with *yagñah*, and explains it by 'that whereby welfare is obtained.' Medh. explains the expression 'the sacrifice to Pra*g*âpati' by stating that 'some' prescribe at a wedding an oblation with the verse Pra*g*âpate na tvad evânya*h* (? tvadetâny, Rig-veda X, 121, 10), and that the offerings to the other gods are

153. The husband who wedded her with sacred texts, always gives happiness to his wife, both in season and out of season, in this world and in the next.

154. Though destitute of virtue, or seeking pleasure (elsewhere), or devoid of good qualities, (yet) a husband must be constantly worshipped as a god by a faithful wife.

155. No sacrifice, no vow, no fast must be performed by women apart (from their husbands); if a wife obeys her husband, she will for that (reason alone) be exalted in heaven.

156. A faithful wife, who desires to dwell (after death) with her husband, must never do anything that might displease him who took her hand, whether he be alive or dead.

157. At her pleasure let her emaciate her body by (living on) pure flowers, roots, and fruit; but she must never even mention the name of another man after her husband has died.

158. Until death let her be patient (of hardships), self-controlled, and chaste, and strive (to fulfil) that most excellent duty which (is prescribed) for wives who have one husband only.

159. Many thousands of Brâhma*n*as who were chaste from their youth, have gone to heaven without continuing their race.

---

implied by this expression. Nâr. thinks that the Pra*g*âpati called Manu is the guardian deity of the bride, and hence the nuptial oblations are called 'the sacrifice to Pra*g*âpati.'

155. Vi. XXVI, 15; Yâ*gñ*. I, 77.

156–166. See below, IX, 64–68; Yâ*gñ*. I, 75, 87.

157. Medh. takes this opportunity to strongly object to the practice of widows burning themselves with their husbands' corpses.

159. Gov. and Kull. think that the verse refers to the Vâlakhilya *Ri*shis.

160. A virtuous wife who after the death of her husband constantly remains chaste, reaches heaven, though she have no son, just like those chaste men.

161. But a woman who from a desire to have offspring violates her duty towards her (deceased) husband, brings on herself disgrace in this world, and loses her place with her husband (in heaven).

162. Offspring begotten by another man is here not (considered lawful), nor (does offspring begotten) on another man's wife (belong to the begetter), nor is a second husband anywhere prescribed for virtuous women.

163. She who cohabits with a man of higher caste, forsaking her own husband who belongs to a lower one, will become contemptible in this world, and is called a remarried woman (parapûrvâ).

164. By violating her duty towards her husband, a wife is disgraced in this world, (after death) she enters the womb of a jackal, and is tormented by diseases (the punishment of) her sin.

165. She who, controlling her thoughts, words, and deeds, never slights her lord, resides (after death) with her husband (in heaven), and is called a virtuous (wife).

166. In reward of such conduct, a female who controls her thoughts, speech, and actions, gains in this (life) highest renown, and in the next (world) a place near her husband.

---

160. Vi. XXVI, 17.

162. Medh., Nâr., and Nand. take the first part of the verse differently: 'Offspring begotten by another man does not belong (to the mother).' The other explanation is given by Gov. and Kull.

165. Medh. omits verses 165–166.

167. A twice-born man, versed in the sacred law, shall burn a wife of equal caste who conducts herself thus and dies before him, with (the sacred fires used for) the Agnihotra, and with the sacrificial implements.

168. Having thus, at the funeral, given the sacred fires to his wife who dies before him, he may marry again, and again kindle (the fires).

169. (Living) according to the (preceding) rules, he must never neglect the five (great) sacrifices, and, having taken a wife, he must dwell in (his own) house during the second period of his life.

CHAPTER VI.

1. A twice-born Snâtaka, who has thus lived according to the law in the order of householders, may, taking a firm resolution and keeping his organs in subjection, dwell in the forest, duly (observing the rules given below).

2. When a householder sees his (skin) wrinkled, and (his hair) white, and the sons of his sons, then he may resort to the forest.

167–168. Yâgñ. I, 88.

VI. 1–32. Âp. II, 21, 18–23, 2; Gaut. III, 26–35; Vas. VI, 19–20; IX; Baudh. II, 11, 14–15; III, 18–4, 22; Vi. XCIV–XCV; Yâgñ. III, 45–55.

1. Niyata*h*, 'taking a firm resolution' (Gov., Kull.), means according to Nâr. 'devoted to the restrictive duties, austerities, reciting the Veda, and so forth.' Kull. connects yathâvad, 'duly observing,' &c. (Gov., Nâr.), with 'keeping his organs in subjection.'

2. Medh. notes particularly that the *S*ish*t*as insist on the necessity that he who takes to forest-life must have sons and sons' sons, and that hence apatya, 'offspring,' is to be taken in this restricted sense. Nâr. holds that the verse gives three separate grounds for entering the third order, each of which is sufficient by itself, while

3. Abandoning all food raised by cultivation, and all his belongings, he may depart into the forest, either committing his wife to his sons, or accompanied by her.

4. Taking with him the sacred fire and the implements required for domestic (sacrifices), he may go forth from the village into the forest and reside there, duly controlling his senses.

5. Let him offer those five great sacrifices according to the rule, with various kinds of pure food fit for ascetics, or with herbs, roots, and fruit.

6. Let him wear a skin or a tattered garment; let him bathe in the evening or in the morning; and let him always wear (his hair in) braids, the hair on his body, his beard, and his nails (being unclipped).

7. Let him perform the Bali-offering with such food as he eats, and give alms according to his ability; let him honour those who come to his hermitage with alms consisting of water, roots, and fruit.

8. Let him be always industrious in privately reciting the Veda; let him be patient of hardships, friendly (towards all), of collected mind, ever liberal

---

Medh. thinks that the three conditions must exist together. Others, however, mentioned by Medh., took the verse to give a description of the approach of old age, which entitles the householder to turn hermit.

3. 'If his wife desires to accompany him, she may do so. But others say that he is to leave his wife behind if she is young, but shall take her with him if she is aged' (Medh.).

6. *K*îram, 'a tattered garment' (vastrakha*nd*am, Medh., Gov., Kull.), may also mean 'a dress made of bark, Ku*s*a grass, or the like' (Gov., Nâr., Râgh.).

8. Dânta*h*, 'patient of hardships,' means according to Medh. and Nâr. 'free from pride.' Gov. reads in the beginning of the second

and never a receiver of gifts, and compassionate towards all living creatures.

9. Let him offer, according to the law, the Agnihotra with three sacred fires, never omitting the new-moon and full-moon sacrifices at the proper time.

10. Let him also offer the Nakshatresh*t*i, the Âgraya*n*a, and the *K*âturmâsya (sacrifices), as well as the Turâya*n*a and likewise the Dâkshâya*n*a, in due order.

11. With pure grains, fit for ascetics, which grow in spring and in autumn, and which he himself has collected, let him severally prepare the sacrificial cakes (puro*d*â*s*a) and the boiled messes (*k*aru), as the law directs.

12. Having offered those most pure sacrificial viands, consisting of the produce of the forest, he may use the remainder for himself, (mixed with) salt prepared by himself.

---

half-verse, tyaktadvandvo 'ni*s*a*m* dâtâ, 'let him not care for the pairs of opposites, let him be ever liberal and compassionate towards all creatures.'

9. Yogata*h*, 'at the proper time' (Kull., Râgh.), means according to Medh. and Gov. 'as required by law;' according to Nâr. 'diligently.'

10. Medh. reads Dar*s*esh*t*i for *Ri*ksheshi*t*i, 'the Nakshatresh*t*i.' I read with Medh., Nâr., Nand., and Râgh., Turâya*n*a (see *S*âṅkh. *S*rauta-sûtra IV, 11) instead of Uttarâya*n*a, 'the sacrifice at the winter-solstice,' which Gov., Kull., and K. give. The first reads also more consistently than Kull. and K.: Dakshi*n*âya*n*a*m*, 'the sacrifice at the summer-solstice,' for Dakshasyâya*n*am, 'the Dâkshâya*n*a.' The Nakshatresh*t*i is a *S*rauta sacrifice offered to the lunar mansions. Regarding the variety of the Dar*s*apaur*n*amâsa, called Dâkshâya*n*a, see Â*s*v. *S*rauta-sûtra II, 14.

12. According to Kull., the hermit is to collect the salt from ûsharas, i.e. salt-marshes; according to Nâr., he is to prepare it from the kshâra, 'salt or alcaline elements' of trees and the like.

13. Let him eat vegetables that grow on dry land or in water, flowers, roots, and fruits, the productions of pure trees, and oils extracted from forest-fruits.

14. Let him avoid honey, flesh, and mushrooms growing on the ground (or elsewhere, the vegetables called) Bhûstri*n*a, and *S*igruka, and the *S*leshmântaka fruit.

15. Let him throw away in the month of Â*s*vina the food of ascetics, which he formerly collected, likewise his worn-out clothes and his vegetables, roots, and fruit.

16. Let him not eat anything (grown on) ploughed (land), though it may have been thrown away by somebody, nor roots and fruit grown in a village, though (he may be) tormented (by hunger).

17. He may eat either what has been cooked with fire, or what has been ripened by time; he either may use a stone for grinding, or his teeth may be his mortar.

18. He may either at once (after his daily meal) cleanse (his vessel for collecting food), or lay up a

---

14. Bhûst*ri*na, i.e. Andropogon Schoenanthus, *S*igruka, according to Nâr., the same as the *S*obhanâ*ñg*ana, i.e. Moringa Pterygosperma, the horse-radish tree, the leaves of which are said to be used as a vegetable. According to Medh., these two vegetables are known among the Bâhîkas, in the Panjâb; according to Gov., Kull., Râgh., the former is found in Mâlvâ. *S*leshmântaka, i.e. Cordia Myxa. According to Medh., bhaumâni, 'those which grow on or come from the ground,' has to be taken as a separate word, and denotes a plant, known to the woodmen, named Go*g*ihvikâ, Phlomnis or Premna Esculenta. Gov., Nâr., and Kull. give the construction adopted above, and the latter two declare that mushrooms growing on trees are likewise forbidden.

16. 'Though he may be in distress,' i.e. 'tormented by hunger' (Gov., Kull.), or 'sick' (Nâr.).

18. 'He may either at once (after his daily meal) cleanse (his

store sufficient for a month, or gather what suffices for six months or for a year.

19. Having collected food according to his ability, he may either eat at night (only), or in the day-time (only), or at every fourth meal-time, or at every eighth.

20. Or he may live according to the rule of the lunar penance (*K*ândrâya*n*a, daily diminishing the quantity of his food) in the bright (half of the month) and (increasing it) in the dark (half); or he may eat on the last days of each fortnight, once (a day only), boiled barley-gruel.

21. Or he may constantly subsist on flowers, roots, and fruit alone, which have been ripened by time and have fallen spontaneously, following the rule of the (Institutes) of Vikhanas.

22. Let him either roll about on the ground, or stand during the day on tiptoe, (or) let him alternately stand and sit down; going at the Savanas (at sunrise, at midday, and at sunset) to water in the forest (in order to bathe).

23. In summer let him expose himself to the heat of five fires, during the rainy season live under the open sky, and in winter be dressed in wet clothes, (thus) gradually increasing (the rigour of) his austerities.

---

vessel for collecting food),' (Nâr.), means 'he may either gather only as much as suffices for one day.' This mode of subsistence is apparently the same as that called Samprakshâlanî v*ri*tti by Baudhâyana, III, 2, 11.

21. All the commentators except Nâr. expressly state that the text refers to a particular set of Sûtras, ascribed to the *Ri*shi Vikhanas, which contained rules for hermits. Medh. adds that the hermit is to learn other practices also from that work.

23. 'Five fires,' i.e. 'four fires and the sun from above.'

24. When he bathes at the three Savanas (sunrise, midday, and sunset), let him offer libations of water to the manes and the gods, and practising harsher and harsher austerities, let him dry up his bodily frame.

25. Having reposited the three sacred fires in himself, according to the prescribed rule, let him live without a fire, without a house, wholly silent, subsisting on roots and fruit,

26. Making no effort (to procure) things that give pleasure, chaste, sleeping on the bare ground, not caring for any shelter, dwelling at the roots of trees.

27. From Brâhma*n*as (who live as) ascetics, let him receive alms, (barely sufficient) to support life, or from other householders of the twice-born (castes) who reside in the forest.

28. Or (the hermit) who dwells in the forest may bring (food) from a village, receiving it either in a hollow dish (of leaves), in (his naked) hand, or in a broken earthen dish, and may eat eight mouthfuls.

29. These and other observances must a Brâhma*n*a who dwells in the forest diligently practise, and in order to attain complete (union with) the (supreme) Soul, (he must study) the various sacred texts contained in the Upanishads,

---

24. Gov. says that these harsher austerities are those prescribed in the Vaikhânasa *S*âstra. Medh. gives as instances, standing with uplifted arms, fasting for a month, and the Dvâda*s*arâtra.

25. 'According to the rule,' i.e. 'by swallowing ashes and so forth' (Medh., Gov., Kull.), which mode has to be learned from the *S*râva*n*aka [*S*râma*n*aka Sûtra] (Medh.), or by reciting the text 'Yâ te agne ya*gñ*iyâ,' Taitt. Sa*m*h. II, 5, 8, 8 (Nâr.).

29. Âtmasa*m*siddhaye, 'in order to attain complete (union with the (supreme) Soul,' may also mean 'in order to make himself or his soul perfect.' Nâr. gives the correct etymology of Upanishad, explaining upanisha*nn*â yo*k*yata ity upanishat, 'Upanishad means (a text) which is recited (while the pupils are) seated near (the teacher).'

30. (As well as those rites and texts) which have been practised and studied by the sages (*Ri*shis), and by Brâhma*n*a householders, in order to increase their knowledge (of Brahman), and their austerity, and in order to sanctify their bodies;

31. Or let him walk, fully determined and going straight on, in a north-easterly direction, subsisting on water and air, until his body sinks to rest.

32. A Brâhma*n*a, having got rid of his body by one of those modes practised by the great sages, is exalted in the world of Brahman, free from sorrow and fear.

33. But having thus passed the third part of (a

---

30. Gov. and Kull. separate the two words 'Brâhma*n*a householders.' The former explains Brâhma*n*a by 'hermit,' and the latter by 'acquainted with the Brahman, i. e. ascetic.' By 'householders' Kull. understands 'hermits in the forest.' Râgh. explains Brâhma*n*a by 'those who know Brahman.'

31. Gov. and Kull. take yukta, 'firmly resolved' (Nâr., Râgh.), in the sense of 'intent on the practice of Yoga.' Gov. and Kull. (see also Medh. on the next verse) say that a man may undertake the Mahâprasthâna, or 'Great Departure,' on a journey which ends in death, when he is incurably diseased or meets with a great misfortune, and that, because it is taught in the *S*âstras, it is not opposed to the Vedic rules which forbid suicide. From the parallel passage of Âp. II, 23, 2, it is, however, evident that a voluntary death by starvation was considered the befitting conclusion of a hermit's life. The antiquity and general prevalence of the practice may be inferred from the fact that the *G*aina ascetics, too, consider it particularly meritorious.

32. 'By one of those modes,' i.e. 'drowning oneself in a river, precipitating oneself from a mount, burning oneself or starving oneself to death' (Medh.); or 'by one of those modes of practising austerities, mentioned above, verse 23' (Gov., Kull., Nâr., Nand.). Medh. adds a long discussion, trying to prove that 'the world of Brahman,' which the ascetic thus gains, is not the real complete liberation.

33–85. Âp. II, 21, 2–17; Gaut. III, 11–25; Vas. VI, 19–20; X;

man's natural term of) life in the forest, he may live as an ascetic during the fourth part of his existence, after abandoning all attachment to worldly objects.

34. He who after passing from order to order, after offering sacrifices and subduing his senses, becomes, tired with (giving) alms and offerings of food, an ascetic, gains bliss after death.

35. When he has paid the three debts, let him apply his mind to (the attainment of) final liberation; he who seeks it without having paid (his debts) sinks downwards.

36. Having studied the Vedas in accordance with the rule, having begat sons according to the sacred law, and having offered sacrifices according to his ability, he may direct his mind to (the attainment of) final liberation.

37. A twice-born man who seeks final liberation, without having studied the Vedas, without having begotten sons, and without having offered sacrifices, sinks downwards.

38. Having performed the Ish*t*i, sacred to the Lord of creatures (Pra*g*âpati), where (he gives) all his property as the sacrificial fee, having reposited the sacred fires in himself, a Brâhma*n*a may depart from his house (as an ascetic).

39. Worlds, radiant in brilliancy, become (the portion) of him who recites (the texts regarding) Brahman and departs from his house (as an ascetic), after giving a promise of safety to all created beings.

Baudh. II, 11, 16–26; 17, 1–18, 27; Vi. XCVI–XCVII; Yâ*gñ*. III, 56–65.

33. Nâr. takes âsaṅga, 'attachment' (Gov., Kull.), in the sense of 'possessions.'

38. The description of the rites to be performed on entering the order of ascetics is given in detail in Baudh. II, 17.

40. For that twice-born man, by whom not the smallest danger even is caused to created beings, there will be no danger from any (quarter), after he is freed from his body.

41. Departing from his house fully provided with the means of purification (Pavitra), let him wander about absolutely silent, and caring nothing for enjoyments that may be offered (to him).

42. Let him always wander alone, without any companion, in order to attain (final liberation), fully understanding that the solitary (man, who) neither forsakes nor is forsaken, gains his end.

43. He shall neither possess a fire, nor a dwelling, he may go to a village for his food, (he shall be) indifferent to everything, firm of purpose, meditating (and) concentrating his mind on Brahman.

44. A potsherd (instead of an alms-bowl), the roots of trees (for a dwelling), coarse worn-out garments,

41. Pavitropa*k*ita*h*, 'provided with the means of purification,' i. e. 'his staff, his water-pot, and so forth' (Gov., Kull., Nand.), means according to Medh. either 'applying himself to the recitation of purificatory texts and provided with the means of purifications, i.e. a staff, &c.,' or 'performing penances which purify.' Nâr. takes it to mean, 'having been made most eminent during his life as a householder by acts which purify, i.e. austerities and recitals of the Veda and so forth;' and Râgh., 'possessing a rich store of sanctifying knowledge taught in the Upanishads.' Nâr. takes muni*h*, 'wholly silent' (Gov., Kull.), in the sense of 'intent on meditation.' Nand. explains samupo*dh*eshu, 'which may be offered to him' (Medh., Gov., Kull.), by 'which he collected in his house;' and Nâr. by 'which he has duly enjoyed.'

43. Medh. explains muni*h*, 'meditating' (Gov., Kull.), by 'wholly silent.' Instead of asa*m*kasuka*h* or a*s*a*m*kasuka*h*, 'firm of purpose' (Gov., Kull.), Nâr., Nand., and K. prima manu read asa*mk*ayika*h*, 'destitute of any store of provisions,' and Râgh. a*s*aṅkasûka*h*, 'free from doubts.' Medh., whose text now reads asa*m*kasuka*h*, gives this word as the var. lect. of others, and probably originally read, like Nâr. and Nand., asa*mk*ayika*h*.

life in solitude and indifference towards everything, are the marks of one who has attained liberation.

45. Let him not desire to die, let him not desire to live; let him wait for (his appointed) time, as a servant (waits) for the payment of his wages.

46. Let him put down his foot purified by his sight, let him drink water purified by (straining with) a cloth, let him utter speech purified by truth, let him keep his heart pure.

47. Let him patiently bear hard words, let him not insult anybody, and let him not become anybody's enemy for the sake of this (perishable) body.

48. Against an angry man let him not in return show anger, let him bless when he is cursed, and let him not utter speech, devoid of truth, scattered at the seven gates.

49. Delighting in what refers to the Soul, sitting (in the postures prescribed by the Yoga), independent (of external help), entirely abstaining from sensual enjoyments, with himself for his only companion, he shall live in this world, desiring the bliss (of final liberation).

---

45. The correct reading is nirvesam (Medh., Nâr., var. lect., Nand.) instead of nirdesam (Gov., K.) or nidesa*m* (Kull., Râgh.). The latter reading can, as Nâr. remarks, only mean 'command.'

46. I. e. 'let him look before he puts down his foot, lest he injure any small animal, see ver. 68' (Gov., Medh., Râgh.), or 'lest he step on something impure' (Kull.).

48. 'The seven gates' are, according to Medh. and Gov., 'Dharma, Artha, and Kâma separately, Dharma and Artha, Dharma and Kâma, Artha and Kâma, and finally Dharmârthakâma conjointly; according to Kull. and Medh., 'mind, intellect, and the five senses;' and according to Nâr., 'the five senses, mind, and Aha*m*kâra, or egoism.' Kull. mentions another explanation, 'the seven worlds,' and Medh. gives as a third meaning, 'the seven vital airs located in the head.' The general sense, 'what refers to worldly matters,' remains always the same.

50. Neither by (explaining) prodigies and omens, nor by skill in astrology and palmistry, nor by giving advice and by the exposition (of the *S*âstras), let him ever seek to obtain alms.

51. Let him not (in order to beg) go near a house filled with hermits, Brâhma*n*as, birds, dogs, or other mendicants.

52. His hair, nails, and beard being clipped, carrying an alms-bowl, a staff, and a water-pot, let him continually wander about, controlling himself and not hurting any creature.

53. His vessels shall not be made of metal, they shall be free from fractures; it is ordained that they shall be cleansed with water, like (the cups, called) *K*amasa, at a sacrifice.

54. A gourd, a wooden bowl, an earthen (dish), or one made of split cane, Manu, the son of Svayambhu, has declared (to be) vessels (suitable) for an ascetic.

55. Let him go to beg once (a day), let him not be eager to obtain a large quantity (of alms); for an ascetic who eagerly seeks alms, attaches himself also to sensual enjoyments.

---

50. According to Nâr. and Râgh., aṅgavidyâ, 'palmistry' (Medh., Kull., Nand.), means 'the science of grammar and the other five Aṅgas of the Veda.' Gov. takes nakshatrâṅgavidyâ as a determinative compound, meaning 'astrology.' Anu*s*âsana, 'giving advice' (Medh., Gov., Kull., Râgh.), means according to Nâr. and Nând. 'teaching the Veda.' Vâda, 'the exposition (of the *S*âstras),' (Gov., Kull.), means according to Medh. and Nâr. 'disputations;' according to Nand. and Râgh. 'the science of dialectics.' This verse, which occurs also in Vas. X, 21, is historically important, as it shows that in ancient as in modern times, ascetics followed worldly pursuits and were the teachers or advisers of the people.

55. 'Let him not go oftener to beg' is Gov.'s explanation, instead of 'let him not be eager to obtain a large quantity of alms.'

56. When no smoke ascends from (the kitchen), when the pestle lies motionless, when the embers have been extinguished, when the people have finished their meal, when the remnants in the dishes have been removed, let the ascetic always go to beg.

57. Let him not be sorry when he obtains nothing, nor rejoice when he obtains (something), let him (accept) so much only as will sustain life, let him not care about the (quality of his) utensils.

58. Let him disdain all (food) obtained in consequence of humble salutations, (for) even an ascetic who has attained final liberation, is bound (with the fetters of the Sa*m*sâra) by accepting (food given) in consequence of humble salutations.

59. By eating little, and by standing and sitting in solitude, let him restrain his senses, if they are attracted by sensual objects.

60. By the restraint of his senses, by the destruction of love and hatred, and by the abstention from injuring the creatures, he becomes fit for immortality.

61. Let him reflect on the transmigrations of men, caused by their sinful deeds, on their falling into hell, and on the torments in the world of Yama,

62. On the separation from their dear ones, on their union with hated men, on their being overpowered by age and being tormented with diseases,

63. On the departure of the individual soul from this body and its new birth in (another) womb, and

57. Mâtrâ, 'utensils,' i.e. his staff, water-pot, &c. (Medh., Gov., Kull., Râgh.), means according to Nâr. and Nand. 'a portion, e.g. a mouthful' (kavalâdi*h*, Nâr.), or 'a portion, i.e. enough to fill his stomach' (udarapûra*n*âvadhir mâtrâ).

on its wanderings through ten thousand millions of existences,

64. On the infliction of pain on embodied (spirits), which is caused by demerit, and the gain of eternal bliss, which is caused by the attainment of their highest aim, (gained through) spiritual merit.

65. By deep meditation let him recognise the subtile nature of the supreme Soul, and its presence in all organisms, both the highest and the lowest.

66. To whatever order he may be attached, let him, though blemished (by a want of the external marks), fulfil his duty, equal-minded towards all creatures; (for) the external mark (of the order) is not the cause of (the acquisition of) merit.

67. Though the fruit of the Kataka tree (the clearing-nut) makes water clear, yet the (latter) does not become limpid in consequence of the mention of the (fruit's) name.

68. In order to preserve living creatures, let him always by day and by night, even with pain to his body, walk, carefully scanning the ground.

69. In order to expiate (the death) of those creatures which he unintentionally injures by day or by night, an ascetic shall bathe and perform six suppressions of the breath.

---

65. Nand. omits this verse. 'The highest aim' is 'the recognition of the Brahman' (Kull.), and the good fortune of attaining that falls only to the lot of those who have accumulated a rich store of merit.

66. Instead of dûshito 'pi, 'though blemished (by a want of the external marks of the order),' (Kull., Nand., Râgh.), Medh., Gov., Nâr., and K. read bhûshito 'pi, 'though adorned (with garlands and the like).'

69. Regarding the term 'suppression of the breath,' see Vas. XXV, 13, and Wilson, Vish*n*upurâ*n*a, V, p. 231 (ed. Hall).

70. Three suppressions of the breath even, performed according to the rule, and accompanied with the (recitation of the) Vyâhr*i*tis and of the syllable Om, one must know to be the highest (form of) austerity for every Brâhma*n*a.

71. For as the impurities of metallic ores, melted in the blast (of a furnace), are consumed, even so the taints of the organs are destroyed through the suppression of the breath.

72. Let him destroy the taints through suppressions of the breath, (the production of) sin by fixed attention, all sensual attachments by restraining (his senses and organs), and all qualities that are not lordly by meditation.

73. Let him recognise by the practice of meditation the progress of the individual soul through beings of various kinds, (a progress) hard to understand for unregenerate men.

74. He who possesses the true insight (into the

71. Vas. XXV, 6; Baudh. IV, 1, 24.

72. Regarding the term dhâra*n*â, 'fixed attention,' see Wilson, Vish*n*upurâ*n*a, V, p. 237 (ed. Hall), and Jacob, Vedântasâra, p. 109.

Anî*s*varân gu*n*ân, 'all qualities that are not lordly.' Medh. explains the qualities by 'goodness, passion, and darkness,' and the epithet 'not lordly' by 'depending upon another,' and adds that 'the conceit (abhimâna) of the soul (purusha) that it possesses qualities and is affected by pleasure or pain and the like must be destroyed.' Gov. and K. assert that the qualities opposed to 'virtue, knowledge, absence of passion and power' (Davies, Sâ*m*khya, p. 81) are to be destroyed by 'meditation,' as defined in the Yoga*s*âstra. Similarly Nâr., who (as also Nand.) reads anai*s*varân, says that the qualities that are opposed to true knowledge and power, and are modifications of passion and darkness, must be destroyed by meditating on the formless. Kull. and Râgh., on the other hand, interpret the passage on Vedânta principles, and explain the qualities as 'such which do not belong to the lord, Brahman, i.e. anger, greed, envy, and so forth.'

nature of the world), is not fettered by his deeds; but he who is destitute of that insight, is drawn into the circle of births and deaths.

75. By not injuring any creatures, by detaching the senses (from objects of enjoyment), by the rites prescribed in the Veda, and by rigorouslypra ctising austerities, (men) gain that state (even) in this (world).

76–77. Let him quit this dwelling, composed of the five elements, where the bones are the beams, which is held together by tendons (instead of cords), where the flesh and the blood are the mortar, which is thatched with the skin, which is foul-smelling, filled with urine and ordure, infested by old age and sorrow, the seat of disease, harassed by pain, gloomy with passion, and perishable.

78. He who leaves this body, (be it by necessity) as a tree (that is torn from) the river-bank, or (freely) like a bird (that) quits a tree, is freed from the misery (of this world, dreadful like) a shark.

79. Making over (the merit of his own) good actions to his friends and (the guilt of) his evil deeds to his enemies, he attains the eternal Brahman by the practice of meditation.

80. When by the disposition (of his heart) he

---

75. 'By the rites prescribed in the Veda,' i. e. the daily rites (Medh., Gov., Kull.), or 'the daily rites and those prescribed for certain occasions' (Nâr., Nand.). 'That state,' i. e. 'the union with Brahman' (Gov., Kull., Râgh.), means according to Medh. 'that place, i.e. the world of Brahman.' Nâr. and Nand. read tatparam, 'that highest (Brahman).'

76–77. Maitr. Up. III, 4.

79. 'Making over (the merit of his own) good actions' means according to Gov. and Medh. '(the merit of anybody's) good actions.'

80. 'In this world,' i.e. he becomes a *G*îvanmukta, one liberated during this life (Nâr.).

becomes indifferent to all objects, he obtains eternal happiness both in this world and after death.

81. He who has in this manner gradually given up all attachments and is freed from all the pairs (of opposites), reposes in Brahman alone.

82. All that has been declared (above) depends on meditation; for he who is not proficient in the knowledge of that which refers to the Soul reaps not the full reward of the performance of rites.

83. Let him constantly recite (those texts of) the Veda which refer to the sacrifice, (those) referring to the deities, and (those) which treat of the Soul and are contained in the concluding portions of the Veda (Vedânta).

84. That is the refuge of the ignorant, and even

---

81. 'The pairs of opposites,' i.e. hunger and satiety and so forth (Gov.), or honour and dishonour (Kull.).

82. I follow Gov., Nâr., and Nand., who explain the verse to mean that all the teaching of the preceding chapters with respect to the four orders depends, as far as its ultimate result is concerned, on meditation, because, however well a man may fulfil the prescribed rites, he cannot reap the full reward without knowing and meditating on the Brahman. Kull. refers the phrase 'All that has been declared' to the contents of the last verse, and says that 'the complete freedom from all attachments and the repose in Brahman' depend on the recognition of the unity of the individual soul and of Brahman. He understands by kriyâphalam, 'the reward for the act of meditating.' Medh. begins with an explanation similar to that of Kull., but he takes finally kriyâphalam in the same sense as Gov., Nâr., and Nand. Râgh. explains yad etad abhi*s*abditam by 'what can be expressed by words.'

83. 'Which refer to the sacrifice,' i.e. 'the Brâhma*n*as' (Medh., Gov., Nand.), or 'the Brahmaveda' (Kull., Nâr.), or 'the Karmakâ*nd*a,' e.g. ishe tvâ ûrge tvâ (Vâ*g*. Sa*m*h. I, 1), Râgh. 'Those referring to the deities,' i.e. 'Mantras describing the various deities' (Medh., Gov.), e.g. Rig-veda VIII, 44, 16 (Gov.). The third class of texts mentioned is that of the Upanishads; but see also Goldstücker, Sansk. Dict., s. v. adhyâtma.

that (the refuge) of those who know (the meaning of the Veda); that is (the protection) of those who seek (bliss in) heaven and of those who seek endless (beatitude).

85. A twice-born man who becomes an ascetic, after the successive performance of the above-mentioned acts, shakes off sin here below and reaches the highest Brahman.

86. Thus the law (valid) for self-restrained ascetics has been explained to you; now listen to the (particular) duties of those who give up (the rites prescribed by) the Veda.

87. The student, the householder, the hermit, and the ascetic, these (constitute) four separate orders, which all spring from (the order of) householders.

88. But all (or) even (any of) these orders, assumed successively in accordance with the Institutes (of the sacred law), lead the Brâhma*n*a who acts by the preceding (rules) to the highest state.

89. And in accordance with the precepts of the Veda and of the Sm*ri*ti, the housekeeper is declared

86. Gov. is of opinion that the persons named above, IV, 22, are here intended. But from what follows, verses 94, 95, it appears that those Brâhma*n*as are meant who, though solely intent on the acquisition of supreme knowledge, and retired from all worldly affairs, continue to reside in their houses; see also IV, 257. Gov. and Nâr. assume that they remain householders, while Kull. counts them among the ascetics.

87–93. Âp. II, 23–24; Gaut. III, 36; Vas. VIII, 14–16; X, 30; Baudh. II, 11, 9–34; Vi. LIX, 27–29.

According to the commentators, the following discussion is introduced in order to show, (1) that there are four orders only, and that the Vedasa*m*nyâsika belongs to these, and does not form a fifth order, or stand outside the orders; (2) that as the order of the householders is the most distinguished, it is proper that a man may continue to live in his house under the protection of his son.

to be superior to all of them; for he supports the other three.

90. As all rivers, both great and small, find a resting-place in the ocean, even so men of all orders find protection with householders.

91. By twice-born men belonging to (any of) these four orders, the tenfold law must be ever carefully obeyed.

92. Contentment, forgiveness, self-control, abstention from unrighteously appropriating anything, (obedience to the rules of) purification, coercion of the organs, wisdom, knowledge (of the supreme Soul), truthfulness, and abstention from anger, (form) the tenfold law.

93. Those Brâhma*n*as who thoroughly study the tenfold law, and after studying obey it, enter the highest state.

94. A twice-born man who, with collected mind, follows the tenfold law and has paid his (three) debts, may, after learning the Vedânta according to the prescribed rule, become an ascetic.

95. Having given up (the performance of) all rites, throwing off the guilt of his (sinful) acts, subduing his organs and having studied the Veda, he may live at his ease under the protection of his son.

---

92. Dh*ri*ti*h*, 'contentment,' means according to Nâr., Nand., and Râgh. 'firmness of purpose or in the discharge of duties.' Dama*h*, 'self-control,' means according to Medh. and Nand. 'humility;' according to Gov. and Nâr. 'patience under sufferings;' according to Kull. and Râgh. 'the subjugation of the internal organ.' Dhî*h*, 'wisdom,' means according to Medh. and Gov. 'freedom from doubts and errors;' according to Kull. and Râgh. 'knowledge of the true meaning of the *S*âstras.' Nâr. and Nand. read hrî*h*, 'modesty or shame.'

94. Vas. X, 26.

95. 'Having studied the Veda,' i. e. 'the Upanishads' (Kull.).

96. He who has thus given up (the performance of) all rites, who is solely intent on his own (particular) object, (and) free from desires, destroys his guilt by his renunciation and obtains the highest state.

97. Thus the fourfold holy law of Brâhma*n*as, which after death (yields) imperishable rewards, has been declared to you; now learn the duty of kings.

Chapter VII.

1. I will declare the duties of kings, (and) show how a king should conduct himself, how he was created, and how (he can obtain) highest success.

2. A Kshatriya, who has received according to the rule the sacrament prescribed by the Veda, must duly protect this whole (world).

3. For, when these creatures, being without a king, through fear dispersed in all directions, the Lord created a king for the protection of this whole (creation),

4. Taking (for that purpose) eternal particles of Indra, of the Wind, of Yama, of the Sun, of Fire, of Varu*n*a, of the Moon, and of the Lord of wealth (Kubera).

Gov., Nâr., Nand., Râgh., and K. read abhyasyan, 'studying the Veda,' and the same reading is mentioned by Medh. as a var. lect.

96. 'His own object,' i. e. 'final liberation.'

97. According to Medh. the word 'Brâhma*n*a' is not intended to exclude other Âryans; but according to Gov., Kull., and Nâr. it is meant to prescribe that asceticism is permissible for Brâhma*n*as alone.

VII. 2. 'The sacrament,' i. e. 'the initiation' (Medh., Gov., Nâr., Kull.), or 'the initiation and the rest' (Râgh.), or 'the sacrament of the coronation' (Nand.). The last opinion seems the correct one.

5. Because a king has been formed of particles of those lords of the gods, he therefore surpasses all created beings in lustre;

6. And, like the sun, he burns eyes and hearts; nor can anybody on earth even gaze on him.

7. Through his (supernatural) power he is Fire and Wind, he Sun and Moon, he the Lord of justice (Yama), he Kubera, he Varu*n*a, he great Indra.

8. Even an infant king must not be despised, (from an idea) that he is a (mere) mortal; for he is a great deity in human form.

9. Fire burns one man only, if he carelessly approaches it, the fire of a king's (anger) consumes the (whole) family, together with its cattle and its hoard of property.

10. Having fully considered the purpose, (his) power, and the place and the time, he assumes by turns many (different) shapes for the complete attainment of justice.

11. He, in whose favour resides Padmâ, the goddess of fortune, in whose valour dwells victory, in whose anger abides death, is formed of the lustre of all (gods).

12. The (man), who in his exceeding folly hates him, will doubtlessly perish; for the king quickly makes up his mind to destroy such (a man).

---

5. The commentators explain tegas, 'lustre,' by 'prowess or valour' (vîrya). The next verse, however, shows that at least a play on the word is intended.

10. According to the commentators, the verse is meant as a warning to those who are too confident of possessing a king's favour.

11. 'Padmâ, the goddess of fortune,' must be taken according to Nâr. and Nand. as 'who carries a lotus in her hand,' and according to Râgh. 'whose dwelling is the lotus.' According to Medh., Gov., and Kull., the epithet is added in order to give the idea of greatness.

13. Let no (man), therefore, transgress that law which the king decrees with respect to his favourites, nor (his orders) which inflict pain on those in disfavour.

14. For the (king's) sake the Lord formerly created his own son, Punishment, the protector of all creatures, (an incarnation of) the law, formed of Brahman's glory.

15. Through fear of him all created beings, both the immovable and the movable, allow themselves to be enjoyed and swerve not from their duties.

16. Having fully considered the time and the place (of the offence), the strength and the knowledge (of the offender), let him justly inflict that (punishment) on men who act unjustly.

---

13. Medh. gives the following instances. If a king orders that during the celebration of a wedding in the house of a minister or other favourite, a public festival is to be held in the town, that everybody is to appear on the occasion, or that during so and so many days no animals are to be killed, no birds to be snared, and no debtors to be imprisoned by their creditors, everybody must obey. The same shall be the case if the king orders with respect to persons in disfavour that they are to be shunned by everybody, that nobody is to enter their houses. Gov., Kull., and Râgh. give the same explanation, and they as well as Medh. add, that this rule refers to lawful orders in worldly matters only. Nâr. seems to have taken the verse differently, in a sense similar to that contained in Sir W. Jones' translation.

14. Yâg*ñ*. I, 353.

15. Bhogâya kalpante, 'allow themselves to be enjoyed' (Medh., Gov., Nâr., Nand., Râgh.), means according to Kull. 'are able to enjoy their own.' Gov. says, *kh*edanâdibhayena v*ri*kshâdisthâvarâ*n*y api phalapushpâdidvâre*n*opabhogârtha*m* sa*m*padyante niyatakâlam pushpâdidânavyavasthâ*m* nâtikrâmanti, 'through fear of being cut down and the like immovable things such as trees become fit to be enjoyed by means of their fruit, flowers, and so forth, (i. e.) they transgress not the law according to which they must give flowers, &c. at the appointed time;' see also below, verse 23.

16. Gaut. XII, 51; Vas. XIX, 9; Vi. III, 91; Yâg*ñ*. I, 367.

17. Punishment is (in reality) the king (and) the male, that the manager of affairs, that the ruler, and that is called the surety for the four orders' obedience to the law.

18. Punishment alone governs all created beings, punishment alone protects them, punishment watches over them while they sleep; the wise declare punishment (to be identical with) the law.

19. If (punishment) is properly inflicted after (due) consideration, it makes all people happy; but inflicted without consideration, it destroys everything.

20. If the king did not, without tiring, inflict punishment on those worthy to be punished, the stronger would roast the weaker, like fish on a spit;

21. The crow would eat the sacrificial cake and the dog would lick the sacrificial viands, and ownership would not remain with any one, the lower ones would (usurp the place of) the higher ones.

22. The whole world is kept in order by punishment, for a guiltless man is hard to find; through fear of punishment the whole world yields the enjoyments (which it owes).

23. The gods, the Dânavas, the Gandharvas, the Râkshasas, the bird and snake deities even give the enjoyments (due from them) only, if they are tormented by (the fear of) punishment.

24. All castes (var*n*a) would be corrupted (by intermixture), all barriers would be broken through,

---

17. 'That is the male,' i. e. 'compared with him all others are (weak) women' (Kull.).

19. Yâ*gñ*. I, 355.

23. The commentators quote in explanation of this verse a passage from the Ya*g*ur-veda, 'Through fear the fire warms, through fear the sun shines, through fear move Indra, the Wind, and Death, as the fifth.'

and all men would rage (against each other) in consequence of mistakes with respect to punishment.

25. But where Punishment with a black hue and red eyes stalks about, destroying sinners, there the subjects are not disturbed, provided that he who inflicts it discerns well.

26. They declare that king to be a just inflicter of punishment, who is truthful, who acts after due consideration, who is wise, and who knows (the respective value of) virtue, pleasure, and wealth.

27. A king who properly inflicts (punishment), prospers with respect to (those) three (means of happiness); but he who is voluptuous, partial, and deceitful will be destroyed, even through the (unjust) punishment (which he inflicts).

28. Punishment (possesses) a very bright lustre, and is hard to be administered by men with unimproved minds; it strikes down the king who swerves from his duty, together with his relatives.

29. Next it will afflict his castles, his territories, the whole world together with the movable and immovable (creation), likewise the sages and the gods, who (on the failure of offerings) ascend to the sky.

30. (Punishment) cannot be inflicted justly by one who has no assistant, (nor) by a fool, (nor) by a covetous man, (nor) by one whose mind is unimproved, (nor) by one addicted to sensual pleasures.

25. Vi. III, 96. 26. Gaut. XI, 2.

27. Vishama*h*, 'partial' (Nâr.), means according to Gov., Kull., and Râgh. 'wrathful.'

28 'By men with unimproved minds,' i. e. 'who have not learnt the *S*âstras' (Gov., Kull.).

30–31. Gaut. XI, 4; Yâg*ñ*. I, 308–309, 354.

31. By him who is pure (and) faithful to his promise, who acts according to the Institutes (of the sacred law), who has good assistants and is wise, punishment can be (justly) inflicted.

32. Let him act with justice in his own domain, with rigour chastise his enemies, behave without duplicity towards his friends, and be lenient towards Brâhma*n*as.

33. The fame of a king who behaves thus, even though he subsist by gleaning, is spread in the world, like a drop of oil on water.

34. But the fame of a king who acts in a contrary manner and who does not subdue himself, diminishes in extent among men like a drop of clarified butter in water.

35. The king has been created (to be) the protector of the castes (var*n*a) and orders, who, all according to their rank, discharge their several duties.

36. Whatever must be done by him and by his servants for the protection of his people, that I will fully declare to you in due order.

37. Let the king, after rising early in the morning, worship Brâhma*n*as who are well versed in the threefold sacred science and learned (in polity), and follow their advice.

38. Let him daily worship aged Brâhma*n*as who know the Veda and are pure; for he who always worships aged men, is honoured even by Râkshasas.

---

31. Pure, i. e. 'with respect to the acquisition of wealth,' or 'not covetous' (Medh., Gov., Kull., Nâr., Râgh.). Satyasa*m*dha, 'faithful to his promise' (Gov., Kull., Râgh.), means according to Medh. 'who cares for truth alone.'

32. Vi. III, 96; Yâg*ñ*. I, 333. 33. Vi. III, 97.

37-38. Vi. III, 76-77.

39. Let him, though he may already be modest, constantly learn modesty from them; for a king who is modest never perishes.

40. Through a want of modesty many kings have perished, together with their belongings; through modesty even hermits in the forest have gained kingdoms.

41. Through a want of humility Vena perished, likewise king Nahusha, Sudâs, the son of Pi*g*avana, Sumukha, and Nemi.

42. But by humility P*ri*thu and Manu gained sovereignty, Kubera the position of the Lord of wealth, and the son of Gâdhi the rank of a Brâhma*n*a.

43. From those versed in the three Vedas let him learn the threefold (sacred science), the primeval science of government, the science of dialectics, and the knowledge of the (supreme) Soul; from the people (the theory of) the (various) trades and professions.

44. Day and night he must strenuously exert himself to conquer his senses; for he (alone) who has conquered his own senses, can keep his subjects in obedience.

45. Let him carefully shun the ten vices, springing

41. I read with Medh., Gov., Nâr., Râgh., and K., Sudâ*h* pai*g*avana*s* *k*aiva, instead of Sudâso yavana*s* *k*aiva (Kull.). Nand. has Vai*g*avana, a mere clerical mistake. As Medh. remarks, the legends regarding the worthies mentioned here occur in the Mahâbhârata.

42. The son of Gâdhi, i.e. Vi*s*vâmitra; see Muir, Original Sanskrit Texts, I, p. 83 seqq.

43. Gaut. XI, 3; Yâ*gñ*. I, 310. Nâr. takes ânvîkshikî*m* *k*âtmavidyâm to mean 'and the science of dialectics, i.e. the Nyâya, Sâ*m*khya, and so forth, which is useful for obtaining final liberation.' Medh. too is not certain if ânvîkshikî is to be taken by itself, but proposes 'the science of dialectics which will be useful to him.'

45–48. Vi. III, 50–51.

from love of pleasure, and the eight, proceeding from wrath, which (all) end in misery.

46. For a king who is attached to the vices springing from love of pleasure, loses his wealth and his virtue, but (he who is given) to those arising from anger, (loses) even his life.

47. Hunting, gambling, sleeping by day, censoriousness, (excess with) women, drunkenness, (an inordinate love for) dancing, singing, and music, and useless travel are the tenfold set (of vices) springing from love of pleasure.

48. Tale-bearing, violence, treachery, envy, slandering, (unjust) seizure of property, reviling, and assault are the eightfold set (of vices) produced by wrath.

49. That greediness which all wise men declare to be the root even of both these (sets), let him carefully conquer; both sets (of vices) are produced by that.

50. Drinking, dice, women, and hunting, these four (which have been enumerated) in succession, he must know to be the most pernicious in the set that springs from love of pleasure.

51. Doing bodily injury, reviling, and the seizure of property, these three he must know to be the most pernicious in the set produced by wrath.

52. A self-controlled (king) should know that in this set of seven, which prevails everywhere, each

49. 'Greediness (lobha) is the root of all (these vices), because (the king) acts in some (of these cases) from a desire for money, and in others from a greediness of sensual pleasures' (Gov.).

52. Medh., Nand., and K. read âtmana*h* instead of âtmavân, and in that case the translation must be, 'Let him know that in this set . . . each earlier-named vice is more pernicious for him (than . . .).'

earlier-named vice is more abominable (than those named later).

53. (On a comparison) between vice and death, vice is declared to be more pernicious; a vicious man sinks to the nethermost (hell), he who dies, free from vice, ascends to heaven.

54. Let him appoint seven or eight ministers whose ancestors have been royal servants, who are versed in the sciences, heroes skilled in the use of weapons and descended from (noble) families and who have been tried.

55. Even an undertaking easy (in itself) is (sometimes) hard to be accomplished by a single man; how much (harder is it for a king), especially (if he has) no assistant, (to govern) a kingdom which yields great revenues.

56. Let him daily consider with them the ordinary (business, referring to) peace and war, (the four subjects called) sthâna, the revenue, the (manner of) protecting (himself and his kingdom), and the sanctification of his gains (by pious gifts).

---

54. Vi. III, 71; Yâgñ. I, 311. Labdhalakshân, 'skilled in the use of weapons' (Kull., Nâr.), means according to Medh., Gov., Nand., and Râgh. 'who fail not in their undertakings.' Parîkshitân (Gov., Kull., and K.), or suparîkshitân (Medh., Nâr.), 'who have been tried,' i. e. by tempting them in various ways (Medh.), or 'if they are incorruptible' (Nâr.), or 'who have been examined by spies' (Gov.), or 'who have been bound to fidelity by touching images of the gods, &c.' (Kull., Râgh.). Nand. reads parîkshakân, 'who examine (the state-affairs).'

55. The correct reading is kimu, 'how much harder' (Medh., Gov., sec. manu, Nâr., Nand., Râgh., K.), instead of the ki*m* tu, 'but,' of the editions.

56. Yâgñ. I, 311. Sthâna means according to Gov., Kull., Nâr., Râgh. 'the army, the treasury, the town, and the kingdom;' according to Medh. either that or 'the loss of his kingdom;' according to Nand. 'halting' (âsana).

57. Having (first) ascertained the opinion of each (minister) separately and (then the views) of all together, let him do what is (most) beneficial for him in his affairs.

58. But with the most distinguished among them all, a learned Brâhma*n*a, let the king deliberate on the most important affairs which relate to the six measures of royal policy.

59. Let him, full of confidence, always entrust to that (official) all business; having taken his final resolution with him, let him afterwards begin to act.

60. He must also appoint other officials, (men) of integrity, (who are) wise, firm, well able to collect money, and well tried.

61. As many persons as the due performance of his business requires, so many skilful and clever (men), free from sloth, let him appoint.

62. Among them let him employ the brave, the skilful, the high-born, and the honest in (offices for the collection of) revenue, (e.g.) in mines, manufactures, and storehouses, (but) the timid in the interior of his palace.

63. Let him also appoint an ambassador who is versed in all sciences, who understands hints, expressions of the face and gestures, who is honest, skilful, and of (noble) family.

---

58. Yâg*ñ*. I, 311.

60. Nâr. mentions kulodgatân, 'of noble families,' as a var. lect. for avasthitân, 'firm.'

62. Vi. III, 18, 21. Medh. refers karmânta, literally 'management,' to 'sugar-mills, distilleries, and so forth;' Gov. and Kull. add 'storehouses of grain;' Nâr. explains it by 'manufactories of ornaments and weapons and so forth.' It is, however, not impossible that the compound âkarakarmânte may mean 'for superintending mines and manufactories.' Âkara has very frequently that double meaning.

64. (Such) an ambassador is commended to a king (who is) loyal, honest, skilful, possessing a good memory, who knows the (proper) place and time (for action, who is) handsome, fearless, and eloquent.

65. The army depends on the official (placed in charge of it), the due control (of the subjects) on the army, the treasury and the (government of) the realm on the king, peace and its opposite (war) on the ambassador.

66. For the ambassador alone makes (kings') allies and separates allies; the ambassador transacts that business by which (kings) are disunited or not.

67. With respect to the affairs let the (ambassador) explore the expression of the countenance, the gestures and actions of the (foreign king) through the gestures and actions of his confidential (advisers), and (discover) his designs among his servants.

68. Having learnt exactly (from his ambassador) the designs of the foreign king, let (the king) take such measures that he does not bring evil on himself.

---

64. Anurakta*h*, 'loyal' (Medh., Gov., Râgh.), means according to Kull. 'who is beloved among the people.'

66. Instead of bhidyante yena vâ na vâ, 'by which (kings) are disunited or not' (Kull., Râgh.), Medh., Nand., and K. read bhidyante yena mânavâ*h*, and Gov. bhidyante yena bândhavâ*h*, 'by which men or relatives are disunited.'

67. Nigû*dh*eṅgita*k*esh*t*itai*h*, 'through the gestures and actions of his confidential (advisers),' (Kull., Râgh.), means according to Medh. and Gov. 'by his own hidden gestures and actions,' or perhaps 'while suppressing all significant gestures and actions on his own part;' according to Nand. 'through men who hide their own gestures and actions.'

68. Medh., Gov., Nand., and Râgh. take the verse differently. 'Having learnt exactly the designs of the foreign king, (the ambassador) shall take such measures that he does not bring evil on himself (and his master).'

69. Let him settle in a country which is open and has a dry climate, where grain is abundant, which is chiefly (inhabited) by Âryans, not subject to epidemic diseases (or similar troubles), and pleasant, where the vassals are obedient and his own (people easily) find their livelihood.

70. Let him build (there) a town, making for his safety a fortress, protected by a desert, or a fortress built of (stone and) earth, or one protected by water or trees, or one (formed by an encampment of armed) men or a hill-fort.

71. Let him make every effort to secure a hill-fort, for amongst all those (fortresses mentioned) a hill-fort is distinguished by many superior qualities.

72. The first three of those (various kinds of fortresses) are inhabited by wild beasts, animals living in holes and aquatic animals, the last three by monkeys, men, and gods respectively.

73. As enemies do not hurt these (beings, when they are) sheltered by (their) fortresses, even so foes (can)not injure a king who has taken refuge in his fort.

74. One bowman, placed on a rampart, is a match in battle for one hundred (foes), one hundred for ten

---

69. Vi. III, 4–5; Yâgñ. I, 320. The full definition of *gâṅgalah*, 'which is open and has a dry climate,' is, according to a verse quoted by Gov., Râgh., and Kull., 'That country is called *gâṅgala*, which has little water and grass, where strong breezes prevail, the heat is great, where grain and the like are abundant.' Anâvila, 'not subject to epidemic diseases (or similar troubles),' (Kull. and Râgh.), means according to Medh. 'where the people are not quarrelsome;' according to Nâr. and Nand. 'free from defilement such as a mixture of the castes.'

70. Vi. III, 6.

thousand; hence it is prescribed (in the *S*âstras that a king shall possess) a fortress.

75. Let that (fort) be well supplied with weapons, money, grain and beasts of burden, with Brâhma*n*as, with artisans, with engines, with fodder, and with water.

76. Let him cause to be built for himself, in the centre of it, a spacious palace, (well) protected, habitable in every season, resplendent (with white-wash), supplied with water and trees.

77. Inhabiting that, let him wed a consort of equal caste (var*n*a), who possesses auspicious marks (on her body), and is born in a great family, who is charming and possesses beauty and excellent qualities.

78. Let him appoint a domestic priest (purohita) and choose officiating priests (*ri*tvi*g*); they shall perform his domestic rites and the (sacrifices) for which three fires are required.

79. A king shall offer various (*S*rauta) sacrifices at which liberal fees (are distributed), and in order

75. Yantrai*h*, 'with engines,' i.e. 'with catapults and so forth' (kshepyâdibhi*h*, Nâr.), or 'made of iron and so forth' (Râgh.).

76. Âp. II, 25, 2–3. Sarvartukam, 'habitable in every season' (Nâr., Nand.), means according to Medh., Gov., Kull., and Râgh. 'supplied with the produce of every season.'

78. Gaut. XI, 12–18; Vas. XIX, 3–6; Baudh. I, 18, 7–8; Vi. III, 70; Yâ*gñ*. I, 312–313. Medh., Gov., Râgh., and K. read, as the sense requires, *ri*tvi*g*a*h*, 'officiating priests,' while Kull. alone gives the singular.

79. Âp. II, 26, 1; Vi. III, 81, 84; Yâ*gñ*. I, 314. 'Enjoyments,' i.e. 'garlands, perfumes, unguents, and so forth' (Medh.), or 'houses, couches, and so forth' (Gov., Râgh.), or 'gold, clothes, &c.' (Kull.), or 'wives, houses, clothes, and so forth' (Nâr.), or 'cows and buffalos' (Nand.).

to acquire merit, he shall give to Brâhma*n*as enjoyments and wealth.

80. Let him cause the annual revenue in his kingdom to be collected by trusty (officials), let him obey the sacred law in (his transactions with) the people, and behave like a father towards all men.

81. For the various (branches of business) let him appoint intelligent supervisors; they shall inspect all (the acts) of those men who transact his business.

82. Let him honour those Brâhma*n*as who have returned from their teacher's house (after studying the Veda); for that (money which is given) to Brâhma*n*as is declared to be an imperishable treasure for kings.

83. Neither thieves nor foes can take it, nor can it be lost; hence an imperishable store must be deposited by kings with Brâhma*n*as.

84. The offering made through the mouth of a Brâhma*n*a, which is neither spilt, nor falls (on the ground), nor ever perishes, is far more excellent than Agnihotras.

85. A gift to one who is not a Brâhma*n*a (yields) the ordinary (reward; a gift) to one who calls himself a Brâhma*n*a, a double (reward); a gift to a well-

80. Yâg*ñ*. I, 321. 'Let him obey the sacred law in (his transactions with his) people,' i. e. 'let him not take higher taxes and duties than the law permits.'

83. Yâg*ñ*. I, 314.

84. Vas. XXX, 7; Yâg*ñ*. I, 315. Na vyathate, 'nor falls (on the ground),' (Gov., Nâr.), means according to Kull. 'nor is dried up.' Medh. reads *k*yavate, 'falls (on the ground),' and Nâr. prefers that reading. Nand. explains na vyadhate (sic) by 'is not spoilt by hairs or insects falling into it.' Râgh. takes it, like K*ri*sh*n*apa*nd*ita in his comm. on Vas. XXX, 7, in the sense of 'nor causes pain.'

85. Gaut. V, 20; Vi. XCIII, 1–4. Samam phalam, 'the ordinary

read Brâhma*n*a, a hundred-thousandfold (reward); (a gift) to one who knows the Veda and the Aṅgas (Vedapâraga, a reward) without end.

86. For according to the particular qualities of the recipient and according to the faith (of the giver) a small or a great reward will be obtained for a gift in the next world.

87. A king who, while he protects his people, is defied by (foes), be they equal in strength, or stronger, or weaker, must not shrink from battle, remembering the duty of Kshatriyas.

88. Not to turn back in battle, to protect the people, to honour the Brâhma*n*as, is the best means for a king to secure happiness.

89. Those kings who, seeking to slay each other in battle, fight with the utmost exertion and do not turn back, go to heaven.

90. When he fights with his foes in battle, let him not strike with weapons concealed (in wood), nor with (such as are) barbed, poisoned, or the points of which are blazing with fire.

91. Let him not strike one who (in flight) has

---

reward,' i.e. 'just as much as the Veda promises for the object given' (Gov., Kull., Râgh.). Medh. takes samam in the sense of 'middling,' and Nâr. explains it by 'a reward equal to the kindness shown.' Instead of prâdhîte, 'to a well-read Brâhma*n*a,' Medh., Gov., Nâr., and K. read â*k*ârye, 'to the teacher,' and Nand. *s*rotriye, 'to a *S*rotriya.' Moreover, Gov., K., and Nand. have sahasragunam or sahasra*m* .. dânam, 'a thousandfold reward.'

87–89. Âp. II, 26, 2; Gaut. X, 16; Baudh. I, 18, 9; Vi. III, 43–45; Yâ*gñ*. I, 322–323.

90. Baudh. I, 18, 10. Kû*t*ai*h*, 'concealed (in wood),' (Medh., Gov., Kull., Nâr., Râgh.), means according to Nand. 'treacherous.'

91–93. Âp. II, 10, 11; Gaut. X, 18; Baudh. I, 18, 11; Yâ*gñ*. I, 325.

91. Sthalârû*dh*am, 'one who (in flight) has climbed on an eminence' (Nâr.), means according to Medh., Kull., and Râgh. 'one

climbed on an eminence, nor a eunuch, nor one who joins the palms of his hands (in supplication), nor one who (flees) with flying hair, nor one who sits down, nor one who says 'I am thine;'

92. Nor one who sleeps, nor one who has lost his coat of mail, nor one who is naked, nor one who is disarmed, nor one who looks on without taking part in the fight, nor one who is fighting with another (foe);

93. Nor one whose weapons are broken, nor one afflicted (with sorrow), nor one who has been grievously wounded, nor one who is in fear, nor one who has turned to flight; (but in all these cases let him) remember the duty (of honourable warriors).

94. But the (Kshatriya) who is slain in battle, while he turns back in fear, takes upon himself all the sin of his master, whatever (it may be);

95. And whatever merit (a man) who is slain in flight may have gained for the next (world), all that his master takes.

96. Chariots and horses, elephants, parasols, money, grain, cattle, women, all sorts of (marketable) goods and valueless metals belong to him who takes them (singly) conquering (the possessor).

97. A text of the Veda (declares) that (the soldiers) shall present a choice portion (of the booty) to the king; what has not been taken singly, must be distributed by the king among all the soldiers.

---

who has alighted on the ground,' i. e. 'while the assailant stands on his chariot.'

92. Medh. mentions a var. lect. bhagnam, 'who is broken' (?), for nagnam, 'who is naked.'

94–95. Yâgñ. I, 324. 96–97. Gaut. X, 20–23.

97. According to the commentators the Vedic text alluded to is Aitareya-brâhma*n*a III, 21.

98. Thus has been declared the blameless, primeval law for warriors; from this law a Kshatriya must not depart, when he strikes his foes in battle.

99. Let him strive to gain what he has not yet gained; what he has gained let him carefully preserve; let him augment what he preserves, and what he has augmented let him bestow on worthy men.

100. Let him know that these are the four means for securing the aims of human (existence); let him, without ever tiring, properly employ them.

101. What he has not (yet) gained, let him seek (to gain) by (his) army; what he has gained, let him protect by careful attention; what he has protected, let him augment by (various modes of) increasing it; and what he has augmented, let him liberally bestow (on worthy men).

102. Let him be ever ready to strike, his prowess constantly displayed, and his secrets constantly concealed, and let him constantly explore the weaknesses of his foe.

103. Of him who is always ready to strike, the whole world stands in awe; let him therefore make all creatures subject to himself even by the employment of force.

104. Let him ever act without guile, and on no

99. Yâg*ñ*. I, 316; Vas. XVI, 6.

101. Medh., Gov., Râgh., Nand., and K. read at the end of the verse pâtreshu nikshipet, 'let him bestow on worthy recipients,' and this may have been Kull.'s reading too.

102. Nityam udyatada*nd*a*h* syât, 'let him be always ready to strike' (Nâr., Nand.), means according to Medh., Gov., and Kull. 'let him keep his army always ready or exercised.'

104. I read with Gov., Nâr., Nand., Râgh., and K., susa*m*v*ri*ta*h*, 'carefully guarding himself.' Medh. reads atandrita*h*, 'untired.'

account treacherously; carefully guarding himself, let him always fathom the treachery which his foes employ.

105. His enemy must not know his weaknesses, but he must know the weaknesses of his enemy; as the tortoise (hides its limbs), even so let him secure the members (of his government against treachery), let him protect his own weak points.

106. Let him plan his undertakings (patiently meditating) like a heron; like a lion, let him put forth his strength; like a wolf, let him snatch (his prey); like a hare, let him double in retreat.

107. When he is thus engaged in conquest, let him subdue all the opponents whom he may find, by the (four) expedients, conciliation and the rest.

108. If they cannot be stopped by the three first expedients, then let him, overcoming them by force alone, gradually bring them to subjection.

109. Among the four expedients, conciliation and the rest, the learned always recommend conciliation and (the employment of) force for the prosperity of kingdoms.

110. As the weeder plucks up the weeds and preserves the corn, even so let the king protect his kingdom and destroy his opponents.

111. That king who through folly rashly oppresses his kingdom, (will), together with his relatives, ere long be deprived of his life and of his kingdom.

112. As the lives of living creatures are destroyed by tormenting their bodies, even so the lives of kings are destroyed by their oppressing their kingdoms.

---

106. The position of the second and fourth clauses is interchanged according to Medh., Gov., Nand.

113. In governing his kingdom let him always observe the (following) rules; for a king who governs his kingdom well, easily prospers.

114. Let him place a company of soldiers, commanded (by a trusty officer), in the midst of two, three, five or hundreds of villages, (to be) a protection of the kingdom.

115. Let him appoint a lord over (each) village, as well as lords of ten villages, lords of twenty, lords of a hundred, and lords of a thousand.

116. The lord of one village himself shall inform the lord of ten villages of the crimes committed in his village, and the ruler of ten (shall make his report) to the ruler of twenty.

117. But the ruler of twenty shall report all such (matters) to the lord of a hundred, and the lord of a hundred shall himself give information to the lord of a thousand.

118. Those (articles) which the villagers ought to furnish daily to the king, such as food, drink, and fuel, the lord of one village shall obtain.

---

114. Kull. says, 'in the midst of two, three, or five hundred villages.' Nâr. remarks that the plural 'hundreds' is used in order to leave the number doubtful. It is, however, not impossible that here, as elsewhere in ancient Sanskrit, *s*atânâm means 'a hundred.' Medh. explains sa*m*graha, 'protection,' by 'an official,' or 'a royal granary.' Gov. states correctly that the pickets mentioned are the so-called Sthânakas, the *Th*â*n*âs of modern India.

115-124. Âp. II, 26, 4-5; Vi. III, 7-15; Yâ*gñ*. I, 337.

116. The rule refers, as Medh., Gov., Kull., and Râgh. remark, to offences with which the persons who report them, are unable to deal. Nâr. thinks that chiefly refusals to pay the revenue or disputes on such matters are meant.

118. The lord of one village is apparently the modern Pâ*t*îl, the Pa*tt*akîla or Grâmakû*t*a of the inscriptions, and the articles to be furnished to him the so-called 'haks.' The other officials correspond

119. The ruler of ten (villages) shall enjoy one kula (as much land as suffices for one family), the ruler of twenty five kulas, the superintendent of a hundred villages (the revenues of) one village, the lord of a thousand (the revenues of) a town.

120. The affairs of these (officials), which are connected with (their) villages and their separate business, another minister of the king shall inspect, (who must be) loyal and never remiss;

121. And in each town let him appoint one superintendent of all affairs, elevated in rank, formidable, (resembling) a planet among the stars.

122. Let that (man) always personally visit by turns all those (other officials); let him properly explore their behaviour in their districts through spies (appointed to) each.

123. For the servants of the king, who are appointed to protect (the people), generally become knaves who seize the property of others; let him protect his subjects against such (men).

124. Let the king confiscate the whole property of

to the modern Naib-sûbâs, Sûbâs, or Mahâlkarîs, Mâmlatdârs, and so forth, and to the Vishayapatis, Râsh*t*rapatis, Râ*g*asthânîyas, &c. of the inscriptions.

119. Kulam, '(as much land as suffices for one) family,' is really a technical term which Medh. explains by gha*nt*a, a term known 'in some districts.' Gov., Kull., Nâr., and Râgh. state that it is the double of a 'middling plough,' i. e. as much as can be cultivated with twelve oxen, while Nand. interprets it by 'the share of one cultivator.'

120. Nâr. explains p*ri*thakkâryâ*n*i, 'separate affairs,' by 'quarrels among each other;' Nand. by 'the separate affairs of the villagers.' Snigdha*h*, 'loyal' (Kull., Râgh.), means according to Medh. 'impartial.'

121. Graham, 'a planet' (Kull., Râgh.), or 'the planet Mars' (Medh.), or 'the sun' (Gov.), or 'the moon' (Nâr.).

those (officials) who, evil-minded, may take money from suitors, and banish them.

125. For women employed in the royal service and for menial servants, let him fix a daily maintenance, in proportion to their position and to their work.

126. One pa*n*a must be given (daily) as wages to the lowest, six to the highest, likewise clothing every six months and one dro*n*a of grain every month.

127. Having well considered (the rates of) purchase and (of) sale, (the length of) the road, (the expense for) food and condiments, the charges of securing the goods, let the king make the traders pay duty.

128. After (due) consideration the king shall always fix in his realm the duties and taxes in such a manner that both he himself and the man who does the work receive (their due) reward.

129. As the leech, the calf, and the bee take their food little by little, even so must the king draw from his realm moderate annual taxes.

130. A fiftieth part of (the increments on) cattle

126. 'One pa*n*a;' see below, VIII, 136. 'A dro*n*a,' i.e. 'four â*dh*akas' (Medh., Kull., Râgh.), or '512 palas' (Gov.); see below, VIII, 135. Gov., Kull., Nâr., and Râgh. state that the highest servants shall receive six times as much grain and clothes as the lowest, and they add that the middle-class servants, of course, receive three times as much as the lowest.

127. 'The food and condiments,' i.e. 'what is consumed by the people employed by the merchants.' According to Kull. and Nâr., yoga means 'the net profits,' and kshema 'the charges for securing the goods against robbers and so forth.' According to Medh., Gov., and Râgh., the whole compound denotes the latter charges alone.

130–132. Âp. II, 26, 9; Gaut. X, 24–27; Vas. XIX, 26–27; Baudh. I, 18, 1, 13, 15; Vi. III, 22–25, 29–30.

and gold may be taken by the king, and the eighth, sixth, or twelfth part of the crops.

131. He may also take the sixth part of trees, meat, honey, clarified butter, perfumes, (medical) herbs, substances used for flavouring food, flowers, roots, and fruit;

132. Of leaves, pot-herbs, grass, (objects) made of cane, skins, of earthen vessels, and all (articles) made of stone.

133. Though dying (with want), a king must not levy a tax on *S*rotriyas, and no *S*rotriya, residing in his kingdom, must perish from hunger.

134. The kingdom of that king, in whose dominions a *S*rotriya pines with hunger, will even, ere long, be afflicted by famine.

135. Having ascertained his learning in the Veda and (the purity of) his conduct, the king shall provide for him means of subsistence in accordance with the sacred law, and shall protect him in every way, as a father (protects) the lawful son of his body.

136. Whatever meritorious acts (such a Brâhma*n*a) performs under the full protection of the king, thereby the king's length of life, wealth, and kingdom increase.

137. Let the king make the common inhabitants of his realm who live by traffic, pay annually some trifle, which is called a tax.

---

132. Medh. and Kull. add 'from the profits (made on the seventeen articles enumerated).'

133. Âp. II, 26, 10; 25, 11; Gaut. X, 9; Vas. XIX. 23; Vi. III, 26, 79.

135–136. Yâ*gñ*. III, 44.

137. P*ri*thagganam, 'the common inhabitants,' i. e. small dealers in vegetables, leaves, and so forth (Kull., Râgh.), or in cakes (Gov.).

138. Mechanics and artisans, as well as *S*ûdras who subsist by manual labour, he may cause to work (for himself) one (day) in each month.

139. Let him not cut up his own root (by levying no taxes), nor the root of other (men) by excessive greed; for by cutting up his own root (or theirs), he makes himself or them wretched.

140. Let the king, having carefully considered (each) affair, be both sharp and gentle; for a king who is both sharp and gentle is highly respected.

141. When he is tired with the inspection of the business of men, let him place on that seat (of justice) his chief minister, (who must be) acquainted with the law, wise, self-controlled, and descended from a (noble) family.

142. Having thus arranged all the affairs (of) his (government), he shall zealously and carefully protect his subjects.

143. That (monarch) whose subjects are carried off by robbers (Dasyu) from his kingdom, while they loudly call (for help), and he and his servants are (quietly) looking on, is a dead and not a living (king).

144. The highest duty of a Kshatriya is to protect his subjects, for the king who enjoys the rewards, just mentioned, is bound to (discharge that) duty.

145. Having risen in the last watch of the night, having performed (the rite of) personal purification,

---

138. Gaut. X, 31; Vas. XIX, 28; Vi. III, 32.

141. Vi. III, 73–74; Yâg*ñ*. II, 1–3. Medh. reads *s*ântam, 'of a tranquil disposition,' for prâg*ñ*am, 'wise.'

142–144. Âp. II, 10, 6; Gaut. X, 7–8; Vas. XIX, 1; Baudh. I, 18, 1; Vi. III, 1; Yâg*ñ*. I, 334–335.

having, with a collected mind, offered oblations in the fire, and having worshipped Brâhma*n*as, he shall enter the hall of audience which must possess the marks (considered) auspicious (for a dwelling).

146. Tarrying there, he shall gratify all subjects (who come to see him by a kind reception) and afterwards dismiss them; having dismissed his subjects, he shall take counsel with his ministers.

147. Ascending the back of a hill or a terrace, (and) retiring (there) in a lonely place, or in a solitary forest, let him consult with them unobserved.

148. That king whose secret plans other people, (though) assembled (for the purpose), do not discover, (will) enjoy the whole earth, though he be poor in treasure.

149. At the time of consultation let him cause to be removed idiots, the dumb, the blind, and the deaf, animals, very aged men, women, barbarians, the sick, and those deficient in limbs.

150. (Such) despicable (persons), likewise animals, and particularly women betray secret council; for that reason he must be careful with respect to them.

151. At midday or at midnight, when his mental and bodily fatigues are over, let him deliberate, either with himself alone or with his (ministers), on virtue, pleasure, and wealth,

152. On (reconciling) the attainment of these

147–148. Yâ*g*ñ. I, 343.

147. Ni*h*salâke, 'solitary' (Nâr., Kull., Râgh.), means according to Medh., Gov., and Nand. 'free from grass and so forth.'

149. 'Animals,' i. e. 'parrots, starlings, and other talking birds' (Kull., Gov., Râgh., Nand.), 'for such creatures divulge secret plans' (Medh.).

(aims) which are opposed to each other, on bestowing his daughters in marriage, and on keeping his sons (from harm),

153. On sending ambassadors, on the completion of undertakings (already begun), on the behaviour of (the women in) his harem, and on the doings of his spies.

154. On the whole eightfold business and the five classes (of spies), on the goodwill or enmity and the conduct of the circle (of neighbours he must) carefully (reflect).

155. On the conduct of the middlemost (prince), on the doings of him who seeks conquest, on the behaviour of the neutral (king), and (on that) of the foe (let him) sedulously (meditate).

---

154. 'The eightfold business' consists according to Medh. either of 'conciliation, division, employment of force, gifts,' or 'of agriculture, trade, building bridges and embankments, building fortresses or repairing them, catching elephants, digging mines, settling desert districts, cutting down forests,' or 'of collecting revenue, expenditure, dismissing bad servants, prohibiting bad conduct on the part of the castes and orders, deciding difficult points in one's own affairs, deciding legal cases, punishing, and imposing penances.' The second explanation, which is said to belong to Antaka (Yama), is adopted by Nand.; the third, which is taken from the Nîtisâstra of Usanas, by Gov., Kull., Nâr., and Râgh. 'The five classes (of spies),' i. e. 'kârpa*t*ika, a pilgrim or a rogue, an ascetic who has violated his vows, a distressed agriculturist, a decayed merchant, and a fictitious devotee' (Medh., Gov., Kull., Râgh.). Nâr. and Nand. explain pa*ñk*avarga by 'the collection of the five (requisites for an undertaking).' Regarding 'the circle,' see the following verses.

155–159. Vi. III, 38; Yâ*gñ*. I, 344.

155. 'The middlemost prince' is he whose territory lies between that of the king seeking conquest and that of his foe, and who, though unable to resist both, may become dangerous to them when they are at war with each other; see Kâmandaki, Nîtisâra VIII, 18, which passage the commentators quote. 'The foe' may be of three

156. These (four) constituents (prakriti, form), briefly (speaking), the foundation of the circle (of neighbours); besides, eight others are enumerated (in the Institutes of Polity) and (thus) the (total) is declared to be twelve.

157. The minister, the kingdom, the fortress, the treasury, and the army are five other (constituent elements of the circle); for, these are mentioned in connexion with each (of the first twelve; thus the whole circle consists), briefly (speaking, of) seventy-two (constituent parts).

158. Let (the king) consider as hostile his immediate neighbour and the partisan of (such a) foe, as friendly the immediate neighbour of his foe, and as neutral (the king) beyond those two.

159. Let him overcome all of them by means of the (four) expedients, conciliation and the rest, (employed) either singly or conjointly, (or) by bravery and policy (alone).

160. Let him constantly think of the six measures of royal policy (guna, viz.) alliance, war, marching, halting, dividing the army, and seeking protection.

161. Having carefully considered the business (in hand), let him resort to sitting quiet or marching,

---

kinds, 'natural,' 'artificial' (i. e. one who has a particular reason for his enmity), and 'an immediate neighbour' (see below, verse 158).

156. 'The eight other constituents' are according to Kâmandaki VIII, 16–17, (a) in front beyond the foe's territory, 1. a friend, 2. the foe's friend, 3. the friend's friend, 4. the foe's friend's friend; (b) in the rear, 1. he who attacks in the rear (pârshnigrâha), 2. he who restrains the latter (âkranda), 3, 4. the supporters of these two. All the commentators except Medh. quote Kâmandaki more or less correctly. Kâmandaki VIII, 24 states that this doctrine, with respect to the constituent parts of the system of states which requires the attention of each king, is peculiar to the Mânavas.

160–161. Vi. III, 39; Yâgñ. I, 345–346.

alliance or war, dividing his forces or seeking protection (as the case may require).

162. But the king must know that there are two kinds of alliances and of wars, (likewise two) of both marching and sitting quiet, and two (occasions for) seeking protection.

163. An alliance which yields present and future advantages, one must know to be of two descriptions, (viz.) that when one marches together (with an ally) and the contrary (when the allies act separately).

164. War is declared to be of two kinds, (viz.) that which is undertaken in season or out of season, by oneself and for one's own purposes, and (that waged to avenge) an injury done to a friend.

165. Marching (to attack) is said to be twofold, (viz. that undertaken) by one alone when an urgent matter has suddenly arisen, and (that undertaken) by one allied with a friend.

---

163. Medh. proposes besides the explanation given above another, 'An alliance one must know to be of two kinds, (viz.) that where (the allies) share the danger and the fruits of the expedition and the contrary' (yânaphalasahitau ga*kkh*âva*h* samânaphalabhâgitayâ na *k*a tvayâham uttambhanîyo yatnato lipsite tatas tava bhâgo bhavishyati). Nâr. thinks that the adjective tadâtvâyatisa*m*yukta*h*, too, refers to two different cases, and means 'which yields either immediate or future advantages.' Nand. adopts the latter view as well as Medh.'s second explanation of the first part of the verse.

164. Regarding the expression 'in season,' see below, verse 182. Medh. takes 'out of season' with the second clause, 'and (that waged) out of season (in order to avenge) an injury done to a friend.' He also mentions a var. lect. mitre*n*âpak*ri*te (which Gov. has adopted), with the following explanation, 'and that waged out of season when the enemy has been weakened by an ally.' Gov. agrees with this latter view except that he takes akâle with the first clause. The other commentators give the explanation adopted in the translation.

166. Sitting quiet is stated to be of two kinds, (viz. that incumbent) on one who has gradually been weakened by fate or in consequence of former acts, and (that) in favour of a friend.

167. If the army stops (in one place) and its master (in another) in order to effect some purpose, that is called by those acquainted with the virtues of the measures of royal policy, the twofold division of the forces.

168. Seeking refuge is declared to be of two kinds, (first) for the purpose of attaining an advantage when one is harassed by enemies, (secondly) in order to become known among the virtuous (as the protégé of a powerful king).

169. When (the king) knows (that) at some future time his superiority (is) certain, and (that) at the time present (he will suffer) little injury, then let him have recourse to peaceful measures.

170. But when he thinks all his subjects to be

166. Pûrvakr*i*tena, 'in consequence of former acts,' i. e. 'in consequence of acts committed in a former existence, or in consequence of former imprudence' (Medh., Gov., Kull.). Nand. and Râgh. give only the second explanation; Nâr. says 'by an enemy whom he formerly made.'

167. The text really mentions only one method of 'division.' Hence Medh. thinks that, in order to obtain the two kinds required, it must be understood that the measure may be resorted to either for one's own sake or for the sake of somebody else. Nâr. makes the two methods out by supposing that in the one case the army stops in front of the enemy under the command of a general, while the king marches with a portion of his forces, and that in the other case the contrary takes place. Gov., after giving the explanation adopted in the translation, quotes Kâmandaki, Nîtisâra XI, 24, where a different meaning, 'duplicity,' is attributed to the term dvaidhîbhâva. Nand.'s whole explanation consists of this quotation.

170. I read with all the commentators and K., prahr*i*sh*t*â instead of prakr*i*sh*t*â (editions).

R 2

exceedingly contented, and (that he) himself (is) most exalted (in power), then let him make war.

171. When he knows his own army to be cheerful in disposition and strong, and (that) of his enemy the reverse, then let him march against his foe.

172. But if he is very weak in chariots and beasts of burden and in troops, then let him carefully sit quiet, gradually conciliating his foes.

173. When the king knows the enemy to be stronger in every respect, then let him divide his army and thus achieve his purpose.

174. But when he is very easily assailable by the forces of the enemy, then let him quickly seek refuge with a righteous, powerful king.

175. That (prince) who will coerce both his (disloyal) subjects and the army of the foe, let him ever serve with every effort like a Guru.

176. When, even in that (condition), he sees (that) evil is caused by (such) protection, let him without hesitation have recourse to war.

177. By all (the four) expedients a politic prince must arrange (matters so) that neither friends, nor neutrals, nor foes are superior to himself.

178. Let him fully consider the future and the immediate results of all undertakings, and the good and bad sides of all past (actions).

179. He who knows the good and the evil (which will result from his acts) in the future, is quick in forming resolutions for the present, and understands the consequences of past (actions), will not be conquered.

176. I read with Gov. and K. sa yuddham instead of suyuddham (Medh., Kull., Râgh., Nand.), 'let him fight bravely.'

180. Let him arrange everything in such a manner that no ally, no neutral or foe may injure him; that is the sum of political wisdom.

181. But if the king undertakes an expedition against a hostile kingdom, then let him gradually advance, in the following manner, against his foe's capital.

182. Let the king undertake his march in the fine month Mârgasîrsha, or towards the months of Phâlguna and *K*aitra, according to the (condition of his) army.

183. Even at other times, when he has a certain prospect of victory, or when a disaster has befallen his foe, he may advance to attack him.

184. But having duly arranged (all affairs) in his original (kingdom) and what relates to the expedition, having secured a basis (for his operations) and having duly dispatched his spies;

185. Having cleared the three kinds of roads, and (having made) his sixfold army (efficient), let him leisurely proceed in the manner prescribed for warfare against the enemy's capital.

---

182. Vi. III, 40; Yâg*ñ*. I, 347. 'Fine,' i. e. 'when fodder and grain are abundant and the roads dry' (Gov., Kull., Râgh.). Mârgasîrsha, i. e. November–December; Phâlguna, i. e. February–March; *K*aitra, i. e. March–April.

184. 'Having secured a basis (for his operations),' i. e. 'having won over the servants of his foe who may be at enmity with their master' (Medh., Gov., Kull., Râgh.), or 'having established a camp in the country which he intends to attack' (Nâr.).

185. 'The three kinds of roads,' i. e. 'through the open country, through marshy ground or such as is cut by watercourses, and through forests' (*g*âṅgalânûpâ*t*avika), (Medh., Gov., Kull., Râgh., Nand.). Nâr. gives the same explanation, but adds that the proper interpretation is 'through villages, forests, and hills.' 'The sixfold army,' i. e. consisting of 'elephants, horses, chariots, infantry, the

186. Let him be very much on his guard against a friend who secretly serves the enemy and against (deserters) who return (from the enemy's camp); for such (men are) the most dangerous foes.

187. Let him march on his road, arraying (his troops) like a staff (i.e. in an oblong), or like a waggon (i.e. in a wedge), or like a boar (i.e. in a rhombus), or like a Makara (i.e. in two triangles, with the apices joined), or like a pin (i.e. in a long line), or like a Garu*d*a (i.e. in a rhomboid with far-extended wings).

188. From whatever (side) he apprehends danger, in that (direction) let him extend his troops, and let him always himself encamp in an array, shaped like a lotus.

189. Let him allot to the commander-in-chief, to the (subordinate) general, (and to the superior officers) places in all directions, and let him turn his front in that direction whence he fears danger.

---

general, and workmen' (Medh., Gov., Kull., Râgh.). Medh. adds that some name as the fifth component 'the treasury,' and that others explain the term by 'the sixfold division, mentioned by Kâmandi,' Nîtisâra XVI, 6. The latter view is adopted by Nand. Nâr. enumerates besides elephants, horses, chariots, and infantry, the riders on elephants and sâstropanâyakas (?).

187. The details regarding the various ways of arranging the troops are found in the Kâmandaki, Nîtisâra XIX.

188. My translation of the last clause follows Gov., Nâr., and Râgh. Medh. says that the king shall leave the town with his army in the lotus-array, and Kull. speaks of a 'feigned encampment' (kapa*t*anive*s*ana*m* kuryât). The lotus-array is stated to be 'equally extended on all sides and perfectly circular, the centre being occupied by the king.'

189. Medh. remarks that, as the subordinate general and the commander-in-chief are only two persons, they cannot possibly be stationed 'in all directions,' as the text prescribes, and that hence their servants (i. e. the superior officers) must also be intended.

190. On all sides let him place troops of soldiers, on whom he can rely, with whom signals have been arranged, who are expert both in sustaining a charge and in charging, fearless and loyal.

191. Let him make a small number of soldiers fight in close order, at his pleasure let him extend a large number in loose ranks; or let him make them fight, arranging (a small number) in the needle-array, (and a large number) in the thunderbolt-array.

192. On even ground let him fight with chariots and horses, in water-bound places with boats and elephants, on (ground) covered with trees and shrubs with bows, on hilly ground with swords, targets, (and other) weapons.

193. (Men born in) Kurukshetra, Matsyas, Pa*ñk*âlas, and those born in *S*ûrasena, let him cause to fight in the van of the battle, as well as (others who are) tall and light.

194. After arranging his troops, he should encourage them (by an address) and carefully inspect them; he should also mark the behaviour (of the soldiers) when they engage the enemy.

195. When he has shut up his foe (in a town), let him sit encamped, harass his kingdom, and continually spoil his grass, food, fuel, and water.

---

190. Nâr. explains gulmân, 'troops of soldiers,' by gulmade*s*asthân, '(soldiers) standing in thickets' (?).

192. Sthale, 'on hilly ground' (nimnonnate, Râgh.), means according to Medh., Gov., and Kull. 'on ground free from stones, trees, creepers, thorns, pits, and the like.'

193. Kurukshetra, i.e. the neighbourhood of Delhi; Matsyas, i.e. the inhabitants of Bairâ*t*a or Vairâ*t*a, north of Jepur (Bhogapure, Medh.); Pa*ñk*âlas, i.e. the inhabitants of Kânyakub*g*a (Kanog); *S*ûrasenas, i.e. the inhabitants of the country near Mathurâ (Ahi*kk*hatra, Gov.).

196. Likewise let him destroy the tanks, ramparts, and ditches, and let him assail the (foe unawares) and alarm him at night.

197. Let him instigate to rebellion those who are open to such instigations, let him be informed of his (foe's) doings, and, when fate is propitious, let him fight without fear, trying to conquer.

198. He should (however) try to conquer his foes by conciliation, by (well-applied) gifts, and by creating dissension, used either separately or conjointly, never by fighting, (if it can be avoided.)

199. For when two (princes) fight, victory and defeat in the battle are, as experience teaches, uncertain; let him therefore avoid an engagement.

200. (But) if even those three before-mentioned expedients fail, then let him, duly exerting himself, fight in such a manner that he may completely conquer his enemies.

201. When he has gained victory, let him duly worship the gods and honour righteous Brâhma*n*as, let him grant exemptions, and let him cause promises of safety to be proclaimed.

201–205. Vi. III, 47–49; Yâg*ñ*. I, 342, 348–351.

201. 'The gods,' i.e. of the conquered country. Parihârân, 'exemptions,' i.e. 'from taxes and dues for a year or two' (Medh., Nand.), means according to Gov. 'gifts to *S*rotriyas and others' (*s*rotriyâdigatâva*s*yadâneshu mayaitad anug*ñ*âtam ity evam); according to Kull. 'gifts to gods and Brâhma*n*as;' according to Nâr. 'Agrahâras or villages presented to Brâhma*n*as;' according to Râgh. 'gifts of clothes and ornaments to the inhabitants.' The term parihâra occurs very frequently in the inscriptions (see e.g. Arch. Reports of Western India, vol. iv, p. 104 seq.), and means, as the details adduced there show, 'exemption from taxes and payments as well as other immunities.' These parihâras were regularly attached to all grants to Brâhma*n*as or temples. In our passage a general temporary remission of the taxes is probably intended.

202. But having fully ascertained the wishes of all the (conquered), let him place there a relative of the (vanquished ruler on the throne), and let him impose his conditions.

203. Let him make authoritative the lawful (customs) of the (inhabitants), just as they are stated (to be), and let him honour the (new king) and his chief servants with precious gifts.

204. The seizure of desirable property which causes displeasure, and its distribution which causes pleasure, are both recommendable, (if they are) resorted to at the proper time.

205. All undertakings (in) this (world) depend both on the ordering of fate and on human exertion; but among these two (the ways of) fate are unfathomable; in the case of man's work action is possible.

206. Or (the king, bent on conquest), considering a friend, gold, and land (to be) the triple result (of an expedition), may, using diligent care, make peace with (his foe) and return (to his realm).

207. Having paid due attention to any king in the circle (of neighbouring states) who might attack him in the rear, and to his supporter who opposes

205. Yâgñ. I, 348. 'Action,' i. e. 'careful investigation,' hence one should strive to attain one's ends by exertion (Gov., Kull.), or 'remedial action' (pratikriyâ, Nâr.), or 'an effort' (purushakâra, Râgh.). Nand. takes the last clause differently, 'if there is a human effort, the action of fate takes place' (mânushe purushakâre sati daivasya kriyâ vidyate).

206. According to Gov., Kull., and Nâr. the meaning is that, if the foe is willing to make an alliance, to pay tribute, and to cede some territory, the king, bent on conquest, may also make peace with him without actually fighting and return home. In the MSS. of Medh. this and the next verses down to verse 211 are wanting, and the commentary on verse 211 is partly given.

207. The meaning of the verse is according to Gov., Kull., and

the latter, let (the conqueror) secure the fruit of the expedition from (the prince whom he attacks), whether (he may have become) friendly or (remained) hostile.

208. By gaining gold and land a king grows not so much in strength as by obtaining a firm friend, (who), though weak, (may become) powerful in the future.

209. A weak friend (even) is greatly commended, who is righteous (and) grateful, whose people are contented, who is attached and persevering in his undertakings.

210. The wise declare him (to be) a most dangerous foe, who is wise, of noble race, brave, clever, liberal, grateful, and firm.

211. Behaviour worthy of an Âryan, knowledge of men, bravery, a compassionate disposition, and great liberality are the virtues of a neutral (who may be courted).

212. Let the king, without hesitation, quit for his own sake even a country (which is) salubrious, fertile, and causing an increase of cattle.

Râgh. that the king, bent on conquest, shall secure his back before he undertakes an expedition. The prince immediately in his rear, who in the terms of the Nîti is called the pârsh*n*igrâha, 'the heel-catcher,' may be supposed to be hostile to him and may be expected to invade his territory during his absence. It is, therefore, essential for the conqueror either to settle matters with him beforehand, or to secure the support of the next neighbour of the pârsh*n*igrâha, who is technically called the âkranda and may be supposed to be inclined to check the pârsh*n*igrâha.

208. Yâ*gñ*. I, 351.

211. Sthaulalakshyam, 'great liberality' (Kull., Nâr., Râgh., Nand.), is explained, as Kull. asserts, by Medh. and Gov. 'being not sharp-sighted.' The Government copy of Gov. has, however, just the contrary, sûkshmadar*s*itvam. Medh.'s explanation is not decipherable.

213. For times of need let him preserve his wealth; at the expense of his wealth let him preserve his wife; let him at all events preserve himself even by (giving up) his wife and his wealth.

214. A wise (king), seeing that all kinds of misfortunes violently assail him at the same time, should try all (the four) expedients, be it together or separately, (in order to save himself.)

215. On the person who employs the expedients, on the business to be accomplished, and on all the expedients collectively, on these three let him ponder and strive to accomplish his ends.

216. Having thus consulted with his ministers on all these (matters), having taken exercise, and having bathed afterwards, the king may enter the harem at midday in order to dine.

217. There he may eat food, (which has been prepared) by faithful, incorruptible (servants) who know the (proper) time (for dining), which has been well examined (and hallowed) by sacred texts that destroy poison.

218. Let him mix all his food with medicines (that are) antidotes against poison, and let him always be careful to wear gems which destroy poison.

---

215. 'The person who employs the expedients,' i. e. 'himself' (Gov., Kull., Nâr., Râgh.); 'his minister or the like' (Nand.). Âsritya, 'let him ponder on' (manasâ balâbalâdidvârâ niskitya, Nâr., Râgh.), means according to Medh., Gov., Kull. 'let him depend on.'

217-220. Vi. III, 85, 87-88; Yâgñ. I, 326.

218. Medh., Gov., Nâr., and Nand. read negayet, and Râgh. sodhayet, 'let him purify,' instead of yogayet (Kull., K.), 'let him mix.' Nâr. explains niyatah (Medh., Nâr., Râgh.) or prayatah, 'careful' (yatnavân, Gov., Kull., Râgh.), by 'being pure.'

219. Well-tried females whose toilet and ornaments have been examined, shall attentively serve him with fans, water, and perfumes.

220. In like manner let him be careful about his carriages, bed, seat, bath, toilet, and all his ornaments.

221. When he has dined, he may divert himself with his wives in the harem; but when he has diverted himself, he must, in due time, again think of the affairs of state.

222. Adorned (with his robes of state), let him again inspect his fighting men, all his chariots and beasts of burden, the weapons and accoutrements.

223. Having performed his twilight-devotions, let him, well armed, hear in an inner apartment the doings of those who make secret reports and of his spies.

224. But going to another secret apartment and dismissing those people, he may enter the harem, surrounded by female (servants), in order to dine again.

225. Having eaten there something for the second time, and having been recreated by the sound of music, let him go to rest and rise at the proper time free from fatigue.

226. A king who is in good health must observe these rules; but, if he is indisposed, he may entrust all this (business) to his servants.

223. Yâgñ. I, 329. 'Of those who make secret reports,' i. e. 'of the ministers and the rest' (Nâr.), or 'of citizens who may have come' (Medh.).

225. Yâgñ. I, 330. 'Something,' i. e. 'not too much.'

Chapter VIII.

1. A king, desirous of investigating law cases, must enter his court of justice, preserving a dignified demeanour, together with Brâhma*n*as and with experienced councillors.

2. There, either seated or standing, raising his right arm, without ostentation in his dress and ornaments, let him examine the business of suitors,

3. Daily (deciding) one after another (all cases) which fall under the eighteen titles (of the law) according to principles drawn from local usages and from the Institutes of the sacred law.

4. Of those (titles) the first is the non-payment of debts, (then follow), (2) deposit and pledge, (3) sale without ownership, (4) concerns among partners, and (5) resumption of gifts,

5. (6) Non-payment of wages, (7) non-performance of agreements, (8) rescission of sale and purchase, (9) disputes between the owner (of cattle) and his servants,

6. (10) Disputes regarding boundaries, (11) assault and (12) defamation, (13) theft, (14) robbery and violence, (15) adultery,

---

VIII. 1. Vi. III, 72; Yâg*ñ*. I, 359; II, 1; Gaut. XIII, 26; Vas. XVI, 2.

2. 'Standing,' i. e. 'in important cases' (Medh., Gov., Kull., Râgh.). 'Raising his right arm,' i. e. 'keeping it uncovered' (Nâr., Nand., Râgh., Gov.). Regarding the meaning of the action, see above, IV, 58.

3. Gaut. XI, 19–24; Vas. XVI, 4–5. 'Local usages,' i. e. 'the law of custom which is not opposed to the *S*âstras' (Medh., Gov., Kull., Nâr.).

4. 'Non-payment of debts' (*ri*n*a*sya adânam, Nâr., Nand.) may also be translated 'recovery of debts' (*rin*asya âdânam).

7. (16) Duties of man and wife, (17) partition (of inheritance), (18) gambling and betting; these are in this world the eighteen topics which give rise to lawsuits.

8. Depending on the eternal law, let him decide the suits of men who mostly contend on the titles just mentioned.

9. But if the king does not personally investigate the suits, then let him appoint a learned Brâhma*n*a to try them.

10. That (man) shall enter that most excellent court, accompanied by three assessors, and fully consider (all) causes (brought) before the (king), either sitting down or standing.

11. Where three Brâhma*n*as versed in the Vedas and the learned (judge) appointed by the king sit down, they call that the court of (four-faced) Brahman.

12. But where justice, wounded by injustice, approaches and the judges do not extract the dart, there (they also) are wounded (by that dart of injustice).

13. Either the court must not be entered, or the truth must be spoken; a man who either says nothing or speaks falsely, becomes sinful.

---

7. Vyavahârasthitau, 'which give rise to lawsuits' (Gov.), means according to Nâr. 'in deciding lawsuits.'

8. The word 'mostly' is intended to show that there are other titles besides, as Nârada declared (Medh., Gov., Kull., Nâr., Râgh.). Nand. omits this verse.

9. Vi. III, 73; Yâg*ñ*. II, 3; Gaut. XIII, 26; Vas. XVI, 2.

10. Medh. says 'by (at least) three assessors.'

13. 'Must not be entered,' i. e. 'for the purpose of deciding causes' (Gov., Kull., Râgh.). But the further details show that the verse is intended as a general maxim, applicable to witnesses also.

14. Where justice is destroyed by injustice, or truth by falsehood, while the judges look on, there they shall also be destroyed.

15. 'Justice, being violated, destroys; justice, being preserved, preserves: therefore justice must not be violated, lest violated justice destroy us.'

16. For divine justice (is said to be) a bull (v*ri*sha); that (man) who violates it (kurute 'lam) the gods consider to be (a man despicable like) a *S*ûdra (v*ri*shala); let him, therefore, beware of violating justice.

17. The only friend who follows men even after death is justice; for everything else is lost at the same time when the body (perishes).

18. One quarter of (the guilt of) an unjust (decision) falls on him who committed (the crime), one quarter on the (false) witness, one quarter on all the judges, one quarter on the king.

19. But where he who is worthy of condemnation is condemned, the king is free from guilt, and the judges are saved (from sin); the guilt falls on the perpetrator (of the crime alone).

20. A Brâhma*n*a who subsists only by the name of his caste (*g*âti), or one who merely calls himself a Brâhma*n*a (though his origin be uncertain), may, at the king's pleasure, interpret the law to him, but never a *S*ûdra.

---

15. This admonition must be addressed by the assessors to a judge who acts against the law (Gov., Kull., Râgh.). Nand. reads va*h*, 'you,' instead of na*h*, 'us.'

18. Gaut. XIII, 11; Baudh. I, 19, 8. Sabhâsada*h*, 'the judges,' means according to Gov. 'all those in court who look on.' The judge and his assessors are, however, the persons really intended.

20. 'One who subsists only by the name of his caste,' i.e. 'a man of Brâhma*n*a descent, who neither studies nor performs any other

21. The kingdom of that monarch, who looks on while a *S*ûdra settles the law, will sink (low), like a cow in a morass.

22. That kingdom where *S*ûdras are very numerous, which is infested by atheists and destitute of twice-born (inhabitants), soon entirely perishes, afflicted by famine and disease.

23. Having occupied the seat of justice, having covered his body, and having worshipped the guardian deities of the world, let him, with a collected mind, begin the trial of causes.

24. Knowing what is expedient or inexpedient, what is pure justice or injustice, let him examine the causes of suitors according to the order of the castes (var*n*a).

---

act required by the sacred law' (Kull., Râgh.), or 'one who has not been initiated' (Nâr.). Brâhma*n*abruva*h*, 'one who merely calls himself a Brâhma*n*a (though his origin be doubtful,' Kull., Râgh.), means according to Nâr. 'an initiated Brâhma*n*a who does not study the Veda.' Medh. and Gov. take the two terms as referring to one person only, 'Even a despicable Brâhma*n*a, who subsists merely by the name of his race,' i. e. neither studies the Veda, nor performs the rites, &c. The commentators point out that, as the employment of a *S*ûdra is emphatically forbidden, Kshatriyas and Vai*s*yas may be employed in cases of necessity.

22. *S*ûdrabhûyish*th*am, 'where *S*ûdras are very numerous' (Gov., Kull., Râgh.), means according to Medh. 'where *S*ûdras mostly decide the law-cases,' according to Nand. 'where *S*ûdras are mostly employed in high offices.' Nâr. adds that each of the blemishes enumerated is sufficient to cause destruction.

24. Medh. and Râgh. give another optional explanation of the participial clause, 'Understanding that pure justice secures advantages and mere injustice disadvantages.' According to Kull. it means 'Knowing what is expedient and what inexpedient, but paying attention to justice and injustice alone.' Nâr. and Nand. give still more unacceptable interpretations. Gov., who considers the explanation adopted above the only correct one, explains 'what is expedient' by 'what will please the people,' and 'what is inex-

25. By external signs let him discover the internal disposition of men, by their voice, their colour, their motions, their aspect, their eyes, and their gestures.

26. The internal (working of the) mind is perceived through the aspect, the motions, the gait, the gestures, the speech, and the changes in the eye and of the face.

27. The king shall protect the inherited (and other) property of a minor, until he has returned (from his teacher's house) or until he has passed his minority.

28. In like manner care must be taken of barren women, of those who have no sons, of those whose family is extinct, of wives and widows faithful to their lords, and of women afflicted with diseases.

---

pedient' by 'what will make them angry;' Kull. and Râgh. by 'what will protect the people' and 'what will destroy them.'

25–26. Yâ*gñ*. II, 15.

25. Gov. omits svara, 'voice,' and writes mukha, 'by the colour of the face.' Iṅgita, 'motions,' i.e. 'trembling, horripilation, &c.' (Medh., Gov., Râgh.), or 'looking down, &c.' (Kull.), or 'unintentionally moving the arms, &c.' (Nâr.). Âkâra, 'aspect,' i.e. 'pallor, &c.' (Gov.), or 'sweating, horripilation, &c.' (Kull., Nâr.). Medh. and Râgh. take âkâra to mean 'the manner' of the voice, &c., not as a separate class of signs. *K*esh*t*ita, 'gestures,' i.e. 'moving, wringing the hands, &c.' (Gov., Kull., Râgh.), or 'intentional movements' (Nâr.).

27–29. Gaut. X, 48; Vas. XVI, 8; Vi. III, 65.

27. 'The minority ends with the sixteenth year' (Kull., Nâr.); see Nârada III, 37. The second term is intended to provide for the case of those who finish their Veda-study before the sixteenth year (Medh., Kull.), or of *S*ûdras (Medh.).

28. 'Those whose family is extinct,' i.e. 'maidens in that condition' (Gov.), or 'those who have quitted their families and become harlots' (Medh. 'others'). 'Wives faithful to their lords,' i.e. 'those whose husbands are absent' (Gov., Râgh.). The conditions

29. A righteous king must punish like thieves those relatives who appropriate the property of such females during their lifetime.

30. Property, the owner of which has disappeared, the king shall cause to be kept as a deposit during three years; within the period of three years the owner may claim it, after (that term) the king may take it.

31. He who says, 'This belongs to me,' must be examined according to the rule; if he accurately describes the shape, and the number (of the articles found) and so forth, (he is) the owner, (and) ought (to receive) that property.

32. But if he does not really know the time and the place (where it was) lost, its colour, shape, and size, he is worthy of a fine equal (in value) to the (object claimed).

33. Now the king, remembering the duty of good men, may take one-sixth part of property lost and afterwards found, or one-tenth, or at least one-twelfth.

---

of the king's protection are in every case that the relatives are either dead or unable to provide for the females or try to oppress them.

30–34. Âp. II, 28, 7–9; Gaut. X, 36–38; Vas. XVI, 20; Yâgñ. II, 33.

30. 'Property the owner of which has disappeared' means according to the commentators, 'property, found by the royal servants (in a forest or elsewhere, Medh.), the owner of which is not known.' Such property shall be proclaimed by beat of drum (Gov., Kull.). 'Others,' quoted by Medh., think that after three years the king may use it as his own, but has still to restore it, if the owner appears. Nand. points out that the rule does not refer to Brâhma*n*ical property (see Gaut. loc. cit.).

33. The amount to be taken by the king depends according to Medh. on the length of time for which it has been kept (so also

34. Property lost and afterwards found (by the king's servants) shall remain in the keeping of (special) officials; those whom the king may convict of stealing it, he shall cause to be slain by an elephant.

35. From that man who shall truly say with respect to treasure-trove, 'This belongs to me,' the king may take one-sixth or one-twelfth part.

36. But he who falsely says (so), shall be fined in one-eighth of his property, or, a calculation of (the value of) the treasure having been made, in some smaller portion (of that).

37. When a learned Brâhma*n*a has found treasure, deposited in former (times), he may take even the whole (of it); for he is master of everything.

38. When the king finds treasure of old concealed in the ground, let him give one half to Brâhma*n*as and place the (other) half in his treasury.

39. The king obtains one half of ancient hoards and metals (found) in the ground, by reason of

Râgh.), or on the trouble which it gave (so also Gov.) and the king's compassion; according to Kull. and Nâr., on the virtues of the owner. Medh. places this verse after verse 34.

35-39. Gaut. X, 43-45; Vas. III, 13-14; Vi. III, 56-64; Yâg*ñ*. II, 34-35.

35. 'Treasure-trove,' i.e. 'valuables secretly buried in the ground' (Medh.). The amount to be taken depends on the 'virtues' of the finder (Medh., Gov., Kull., Râgh.), or on his caste (Nâr.), or on the place and time, the caste, &c. (Gov.).

36. The amount of the fine depends on the circumstances of the case or the 'virtues' of the offender (Medh.), or on the 'virtues' of the offender alone (Gov., Kull., Râgh.).

37. Medh., Gov., Nâr. take, as Kull. points out, most improperly pûrvopanihitam, 'deposited in former times,' to mean 'deposited by his ancestors.' The parallel passages of Vish*n*u and others are perfectly clear on the point.

39. I take the last clause, which might also be translated '(and)

S 2

(his giving) protection, (and) because he is the lord of the soil.

40. Property stolen by thieves must be restored by the king to (men of) all castes (var*n*a); a king who uses such (property) for himself incurs the guilt of a thief.

41. (A king) who knows the sacred law, must inquire into the laws of castes (*g*âti), of districts, of guilds, and of families, and (thus) settle the peculiar law of each.

42. For men who follow their particular occupations and abide by their particular duty, become dear to people, though they may live at a distance.

43. Neither the king nor any servant of his shall

---

because he is the lord of the earth,' as a distinct recognition of the principle that the ownership of all land is vested in the king. Medh. says, 'he is the lord of the soil (bhûmi); it is just that a share should be given to him of that which is found in the soil belonging to him (tadiyâyâ bhuvo yallabdham).'

40. Âp. II, 26, 8; Gaut. X, 46–47; Vi. III, 66–67; Yâg*ñ*. II, 36. I. e. 'if he recovers it' (Medh., Gov., Kull., Nâr., Râgh., Nand.). Medh. reads *k*aurîhr*i*tam, and mentions another reading, *k*aurahr*i*tam, which Râgh. has, and thinks that it may mean that the king must make good stolen property which is not recovered.

41. Âp. II, 15, 1; Gaut. XI, 20; Vas. XIX, 7; Baudh. I, 2, 1–8; Vi. III, 3; Yâg*ñ*. I, 360. *G*âti, 'castes,' i. e. 'Brâhma*n*as and so forth' (Kull., Nâr., Râgh., Nand.). *G*ânapada, 'the laws of districts, e. g. of the Kuru, Kâ*s*i or Kâ*s*mîra countries' (Medh.), or 'of certain districts' (de*s*a, Gov., Kull., Râgh.), or 'of the inhabitants of one and the same village' (Nâr.). Medh. gives also other explanations of the compound *g*âti*g*ânapadân, 'of local castes' or 'natives of different countries.' *S*re*n*î, 'guilds,' i. e. 'of merchants, &c.' (Medh. Kull., Nâr., Râgh.), or 'of merchants and husbandmen, &c.' (Gov.), or 'of merchants and actors, &c.' (Nand.). Râgh. reads paripâlayet, 'and protect the peculiar law of each.' It must, of course, be understood that the customs are not opposed to the sacred law (Medh., Gov., Kull., Râgh.).

43. Gaut. XIII, 27. '(Some) other (man),' i. e. 'the plaintiff'

themselves cause a lawsuit to be begun, or hush up one that has been brought (before them) by (some) other (man).

44. As a hunter traces the lair of a (wounded) deer by the drops of blood, even so the king shall discover on which side the right lies, by inferences (from the facts).

45. When engaged in judicial proceedings he must pay full attention to the truth, to the object (of the dispute), (and) to himself, next to the witnesses, to the place, to the time, and to the aspect.

46. What may have been practised by the virtuous, by such twice-born men as are devoted to the law, that he shall establish as law, if it be not

(Medh.), or 'the plaintiff or the defendant' (Kull.), or 'any suitor.' 'Others' explain the second half of the verse according to Medh., as follows, 'and let him not appropriate money brought to him in any other manner than for the suit.'

44. Thus Kull. and Râgh. But Medh. and Gov. take the verse a little differently, 'As the hunter tracks the steps of (a wounded) deer,' &c.

45. 'The truth,' i. e. 'removing all fraud' (Kull., Râgh.), or 'what portion (of this suit) is based on truth' (Nâr., Nand.). Artham, 'the object of the dispute,' i. e. 'if it be not too insignificant, in which case the plaint must not be accepted' (Medh., Gov., Kull., Râgh.). Nâr. explains artha by 'the money realised by a fine and the like,' Nand. by 'the aim.' 'Himself,' i. e. 'that he will obtain heaven by a just decision' (Kull., Râgh.). 'The place and the time,' i. e. 'what is befitting the place and the time' (Kull.), or 'the place, e. g. Banâras, and the time (e. g. of a famine) where and when the offence has been committed, and which may make the case lighter or heavier' (Medh., Râgh.), or 'the customs of the country and what is befitting the time' (Nâr.), or 'the place where the offence was committed and the age of the offender' (Gov.). Rûpam, 'the aspect,' i. e. 'the nature of the object' (Medh., Nand.), or 'the nature of the case' (Kull.), or 'the looks of the parties' (Medh. 'others,' Gov., Nâr., Râgh.).

46. Thus Kull., Nâr., Râgh., and Nand. But Medh. takes the verse differently, 'What has been practised by the virtuous and by

opposed to the (customs of) countries, families, and castes (*g*âti).

47. When a creditor sues (before the king) for the recovery of money from a debtor, let him make the debtor pay the sum which the creditor proves (to be due).

48. By whatever means a creditor may be able to obtain possession of his property, even by those means may he force the debtor and make him pay.

49. By moral suasion, by suit of law, by artful management, or by the customary proceeding, a creditor may recover property lent; and fifthly, by force.

50. A creditor who himself recovers his property from his debtor, must not be blamed by the king for retaking what is his own.

51. But him who denies a debt which is proved by good evidence, he shall order to pay that debt

twice-born men . . . . that he shall establish as law for countries, families, and castes, if it is not opposed (to texts of the *S*ruti and Smr*i*ti).' Gov. reads anurûpam, 'conform with,' instead of aviruddham, 'not opposed,' and seems to agree with Medh. He says, 'And thus let him punish in lawsuits the litigant who acts in a contrary manner; and as here the phrase "what is practised by the virtuous" is used, this (rule) must refer to good conduct.' But the rule, given in verse 41, must refer to laws other than '(those relating to) good conduct.'

49. Vyavahâre*n*a, 'by suit of law' (Gov., Kull., Nâr.), or 'by threatening a lawsuit' (Nand.), or 'by forced labour' (Medh.), or 'by a forcible sale of property' (Râgh.). Â*k*arita, 'the customary proceeding,' i. e. 'by killing one's wife, children, and cattle, and sitting at the debtor's door.' B*ri*haspati, quoted by Kull. and Râgh., or 'by fasting' (Gov.), or 'by the creditor's starving himself to death' (Nâr.). This custom corresponds to the so-called prâyopave*s*ana, or Dhar*n*a, and to the Traga of the bards.

50. Vi. VI, 19; Yâ*gñ*. II, 40.

51. 'In this case self-help must not be used' (Medh.). Regarding the amount of the fine, see below, verse 139.

to the creditor and a small fine according to his circumstances.

52. On the denial (of a debt) by a debtor who has been required in court to pay it, the complainant must call (a witness) who was present (when the loan was made), or adduce other evidence.

53. (The plaintiff) who calls a witness not present at the transaction, who retracts his statements, or does not perceive that his statements (are) confused or contradictory;

54. Or who having stated what he means to prove afterwards varies (his case), or who being questioned on a fact duly stated by himself does not abide by it;

55. Or who converses with the witnesses in a place improper for such conversation; or who declines to answer a question, properly put, or leaves (the court);

56. Or who, being ordered to speak, does not answer, or does not prove what he has alleged; or who does not know what is the first (point), and what the second, fails in his suit.

57. Him also who says 'I have witnesses,' and,

---

52. Instead of de*s*yam, '(a witness) who was present (when the loan was made,' K., Râgh., Kull.), Medh., Gov., Nâr., and Nand. read de*s*am, '(must point out) the place.'

53–56. Yâg*ñ*. II, 16.

53. Medh., Gov., Nâr., and Nand. read apade*s*am, 'a wrong or impossible place,' instead of ade*s*yam, 'a witness not present.' Kull. reads according to the editions, 'ade*s*yam,' but his explanation agrees with the other reading.

54. Pra*n*ihitam, 'duly stated (by himself),' (Kull., Nand.), i. e. 'in the plaint' (Gov.), means according to Râgh. and Nâr. 'duly ascertained.'

56. 'Who does not know what is the first (point) and what is the second,' i. e. 'what is the proof and what the matter to be proved' (Kull., Râgh.), or 'what ought to be said first and what later' (Nâr., Nand.).

being ordered to produce them, produces them not, the judge must on these (same) grounds declare to be non-suited.

58. If a plaintiff does not speak, he may be punished corporally or fined according to the law; if (a defendant) does not plead within three fortnights, he has lost his cause.

59. In the double of that sum which (a defendant) falsely denies or on which (the plaintiff) falsely declares, shall those two (men) offending against justice be fined by the king.

60. (A defendant) who, being brought (into court) by the creditor, (and) being questioned, denies (the debt), shall be convicted (of his falsehood) by at least three witnesses (who must depose) in the presence of the Brâhma*n*a (appointed by) the king.

61. I will fully declare what kind of men may be made witnesses in suits by creditors, and in what manner those (witnesses) must give true (evidence).

62. Householders, men with male issue, and indigenous (inhabitants of the country, be they) Kshatriyas, Vai*s*yas, or *S*ûdras, are competent, when called by a suitor, to give evidence, not any persons whatever (their condition may be) except in cases of urgency.

58. 'If a plaintiff does not speak,' i.e. 'after bringing a suit' (Kull.). Corporal punishment is for heavy cases (Kull.).

59. Yâ*gñ*. II, 59.

60. Thus Gov., Kull., Râgh., but the last words may also mean 'in the presence of the king and of the Brâhma*n*as.'

61-72. Âp. II, 29, 7; Gaut. XIII, 1-4; Vas. XVI, 28-30; Baudh. I, 19, 13; Vi. VIII, 7-9; Yâ*gñ*. II, 68-72.

62. Medh. and Nâr. refer the expression 'not any person whatever (their condition may be),' to such as volunteer to give evidence without being summoned. The 'cases of urgency' are those mentioned below, verse 69.

63. Trustworthy men of all the (four) castes (var*n*a) may be made witnesses in lawsuits, (men) who know (their) whole duty, and are free from covetousness; but let him reject those (of an) opposite (character).

64. Those must not be made (witnesses) who have an interest in the suit, nor familiar (friends), companions, and enemies (of the parties), nor (men) formerly convicted (of perjury), nor (persons) suffering under (severe) illness, nor (those) tainted (by mortal sin).

65. The king cannot be made a witness, nor mechanics and actors, nor a *S*rotriya, nor a student of the Veda, nor (an ascetic) who has given up (all) connexion (with the world),

66. Nor one wholly dependent, nor one of bad fame, nor a Dasyu, nor one who follows forbidden

64. 'Who have an interest in the suit' (Nâr.) means according to Medh., Gov., Kull., and Râgh. 'connected by money, i. e. creditors or debtors of the parties,' or according to Nand. 'men who have received benefits from one of the parties.' Sahâya, 'companions,' i.e. 'sureties and the like' (Medh.), or 'servants' (Kull., Nâr.). D*ri*sh*t*adosha, 'men formerly convicted (of perjury),' (Medh., Gov., Kull., Nâr., Râgh., Nand.), may according to Medh. also mean 'men who have been convicted (of any serious offence).' Men afflicted with serious illnesses must not be made witnesses, because such men are liable to become angry or to forget and thus to give false evidence (Medh.). Dûshita, 'tainted,' i. e. by mortal crimes or numerous smaller offences (Medh., Kull., Râgh.), means according to Nâr. and Nand. Abhi*s*astas, 'those accused of such crimes.'

65. Ku*s*îlava, 'actors' (Nâr.), or 'dancers, musicians, and singers' (Medh.), or 'actors and so forth' (Gov., Kull.), or 'singers' (Nand.). A *S*rotriya, or Brâhma*n*a learned in the Vedas, cannot be made a witness, because he has to attend to his studies and to the Agnihotra (Medh., Kull., Nâr., Râgh., Gov., Nand.). The same remark applies to the last two classes. Liṅgastha, 'a student,' includes according to Nâr., Gov., Nand., Medh. also 'ascetics.'

66. 'One wholly dependent,' i. e. 'a slave by birth' (Medh., Gov.,

occupations, nor an aged (man), nor an infant, nor one (man alone), nor a man of the lowest castes, nor one deficient in organs of sense,

67. Nor one extremely grieved, nor one intoxicated, nor a madman, nor one tormented by hunger or thirst, nor one oppressed by fatigue, nor one tormented by desire, nor a wrathful man, nor a thief.

68. Women should give evidence for women, and for twice-born men twice-born men (of the) same (kind), virtuous *S*ûdras for *S*ûdras, and men of the lowest castes for the lowest.

69. But any person whatsoever, who has personal knowledge (of an act committed) in the interior apartments (of a house), or in a forest, or of (a crime causing) loss of life, may give evidence between the parties.

70. On failure (of qualified witnesses, evidence)

Kull., Nâr., Râgh.). Vaktavya, 'one of bad fame,' may according to Medh. also mean 'one afflicted with leprosy or some other bad disease.' Dasyu, i. e. 'a servant for wages' (Medh., Gov., Râgh.), or 'a hard-hearted man' (Medh.), or 'an angry man' (Kull.), or 'a murderer' (Râgh.), or 'a low-caste man' (Nand.). The term denotes, however, properly the aboriginal robber-tribes, and probably includes all those resembling them. 'One who follows forbidden occupations,' i. e. 'a Brâhma*n*a who has become a warrior or a trader and the like' (Medh.), or 'a butcher and the like' (Nâr.).

68. Vas. XVI, 30. 'Women should give evidence for women only in cases between women or in matters concerning the female sex, which they alone may be supposed to know' (Medh., Gov., Kull.). 'Twice-born men of the same kind,' i. e. 'of the same caste' (Kull., Nâr., Nand.), or 'of the same caste and equally virtuous' (Gov.), or 'of the same place,' or 'of the same caste, occupations, &c.' (Medh.).

69. 'Of (a crime causing) loss of life,' i.e. 'of robberies, murders, and the like' (Medh., Gov., Kull.).

70. The rule refers to the cases mentioned in verse 69 (Gov., Kull.), or to the last only (Nâr.).

may be given (in such cases) by a woman, by an infant, by an aged man, by a pupil, by a relative, by a slave, or by a hired servant.

71. But the (judge) should consider the evidence of infants, aged and diseased men, who (are apt to) speak untruly, as untrustworthy, likewise that of men with disordered minds.

72. In all cases of violence, of theft and adultery, of defamation and assault, he must not examine the (competence of) witnesses (too strictly).

73. On a conflict of the witnesses the king shall accept (as true) the (evidence of the) majority; if (the conflicting parties are) equal in number, (that of) those distinguished by good qualities; on a difference between (equally) distinguished (witnesses, that of) the best among the twice-born.

74. Evidence in accordance with what has actually been seen or heard, is admissible; a witness who speaks truth in those (cases), neither loses spiritual merit nor wealth.

75. A witness who deposes in an assembly of honourable men (Ârya) anything else but what he has seen or heard, falls after death headlong into hell and loses heaven.

---

73. Vi. VIII, 39; Yâ*gñ*. II, 78, 80. 'The best of the twice-born,' i.e. 'Brâhma*n*as' (Gov., Nâr.), or 'particularly distinguished Brâhma*n*as, who fulfil their sacred duties' (Kull., Râgh.).

74–75. Âp. II, 29, 9–10; Gaut. XIII, 7; Baudh. I, 19, 14–15; Vas. XVI, 36; Vi. VIII, 13–14.

74. 'Nor wealth,' i.e. 'he will not be fined.'

75. 'In an assembly of honourable men,' i.e. in court (Medh.), or 'in an assembly of Brâhma*n*as' (Gov.). 'And loses heaven,' i.e. which he may have earned by good works (Medh., Gov., Kull., Nand.), or 'even after passing through hell, he cannot get into heaven, because his merit is extinct' (Nâr.).

76. When a man (originally) not appointed to be a witness sees or hears anything and is (afterwards) examined regarding it, he must declare it (exactly) as he saw or heard it.

77. One man who is free from covetousness may be (accepted as) witness; but not even many pure women, because the understanding of females is apt to waver, nor even many other men, who are tainted with sin.

78. What witnesses declare quite naturally, that must be received on trials; (depositions) differing from that, which they make improperly, are worthless for (the purposes of) justice.

79. The witnesses being assembled in the court in the presence of the plaintiff and of the defendant, let the judge examine them, kindly exhorting them in the following manner:

80. 'What ye know to have been mutually transacted in this matter between the two men before us, declare all that in accordance with the truth; for ye are witnesses in this (cause).

81. 'A witness who speaks the truth in his evidence, gains (after death) the most excellent regions (of bliss) and here (below) unsurpassable fame; such testimony is revered by Brahman (himself).

---

76. '(Originally) not appointed (to be a witness),' i.e. 'not entered as a witness in the document' (Medh.), 'but accidentally present at the transaction' (Kull., Nâr., Nand.).

78. 'Quite naturally,' i.e. 'not out of compassion, in the belief of gaining merit, or depending on women' (Medh.), or 'not out of fear and the like' (Kull.), or 'without hesitation, quickly' (Nâr.). Gov. and Nand. explain it 'in accordance with the truth.'

79. Gaut. XIII, 5.

80–101. Âp. II, 29, 9–10; Gaut. XIII, 14–22; Vas. XVI, 32–34; Baudh. I, 19, 9–12; Vi. VIII, 19–37; Yâ*gñ*. II, 73–75.

82. 'He who gives false evidence is firmly bound by Varu*n*a's fetters, helpless during one hundred existences; let (men therefore) give true evidence.

83. 'By truthfulness a witness is purified, through truthfulness his merit grows; truth must, therefore, be spoken by witnesses of all castes (var*n*a).

84. 'The Soul itself is the witness of the Soul, and the Soul is the refuge of the Soul; despise not thy own Soul, the supreme witness of men.

85. 'The wicked, indeed, say in their hearts, "Nobody sees us;" but the gods distinctly see them and the male within their own breasts.

86. 'The sky, the earth, the waters, (the male in) the heart, the moon, the sun, the fire, Yama and the wind, the night, the two twilights, and justice know the conduct of all corporeal beings.'

87. The (judge), being purified, shall ask in the forenoon the twice-born (witnesses) who (also have been) purified, (and stand) facing the north or the east, to give true evidence in the presence of (images of) the gods and of Brâhma*n*as.

88. Let him examine a Brâhma*n*a (beginning with) 'Speak,' a Kshatriya (beginning with) 'Speak the truth,' a Vai*s*ya (admonishing him) by (mentioning) his kine, grain, and gold, a *S*ûdra (threatening

82. 'Varu*n*a's fetters,' i. e. 'terrible snake-bonds or dropsy' (Medh., Kull.). Gov. mentions the snake-bonds alone, and Râgh. says that the verse threatens the punishment of hell. Dropsy is a disease specially attributed to Varu*n*a, see Rig-veda VII, 89, 1, and the story of *S*una*h*sepha, Ait. Brâhm. VII, 15. The fetters of Varu*n*a are mentioned as the punishment of liars, Atharva-veda IV, 16, 6.

86. '(The male in) the heart,' i. e. 'the male or spirit (purusha) who resides in the human heart, clothed with a rudimentary body' (Medh.), and similarly the other commentators.

88. '(Admonishing him) by (mentioning) his kine, grain, or gold,' i. e. 'threatening him with the guilt of all offences committed against

him) with (the guilt of) every crime that causes loss of caste;

89. (Saying), 'Whatever places (of torment) are assigned (by the sages) to the slayer of a Brâhma*n*a, to the murderer of women and children, to him who betrays a friend, and to an ungrateful man, those shall be thy (portion), if thou speakest falsely.

90. '(The reward) of all meritorious deeds which thou, good man, hast done since thy birth, shall become the share of the dogs, if in thy speech thou departest from the truth.

91. 'If thou thinkest, O friend of virtue, with respect to thyself, "I am alone," (know that) that sage who witnesses all virtuous acts and all crimes, ever resides in thy heart.

92. 'If thou art not at variance with that divine Yama, the son of Vivasvat, who dwells in thy heart, thou needest neither visit the Ganges nor the (land of the) Kurus.

93. 'Naked and shorn, tormented with hunger and thirst, and deprived of sight, shall the man who gives false evidence, go with a potsherd to beg food at the door of his enemy.

94. 'Headlong, in utter darkness shall the sinful man tumble into hell, who being interrogated in a judicial inquiry answers one question falsely.

95. 'That man who in a court (of justice) gives an untrue account of a transaction (or asserts a fact) of which he was not an eye-witness, resembles a blind man who swallows fish with the bones.

96. 'The gods are acquainted with no better man

---

kine, &c.' (Medh.), or 'with the guilt of the theft of kine, &c.' (Gov., Kull., Râgh.), or 'with the loss of his kine, &c.' (Nâr.), or 'by making him touch a cow, &c.' (Nand.).

in this world than him, of whom his conscious Soul has no distrust, when he gives evidence.

97. 'Learn now, O friend, from an enumeration in due order, how many relatives he destroys who gives false evidence in several particular cases.

98. 'He kills five by false testimony regarding (small) cattle, he kills ten by false testimony regarding kine, he kills a hundred by false evidence concerning horses, and a thousand by false evidence concerning men.

99. 'By speaking falsely in a cause regarding gold, he kills the born and the unborn; by false evidence concerning land, he kills everything; beware, therefore, of false evidence concerning land.

100. 'They declare (false evidence) concerning water, concerning the carnal enjoyment of women, and concerning all gems, produced in water, or consisting of stones (to be) equally (wicked) as a lie concerning land.

101. 'Marking well all the evils (which are pro-

---

97. Hanti, 'destroys or kills,' i. e. 'causes to fall into hell' (Medh., Gov., Kull., Nâr.), or 'causes to fall from heaven and to be reborn in the wombs of animals' (Râgh.). Medh. and Kull. (verse 99) give another explanation of this expression, viz. 'incurs a guilt as great as if he had killed them.'

98. 'Men,' i. e. 'slaves.'

99. 'Everything,' i. e. 'everything animated' (Gov., Kull), or 'even more than a thousand' (Nâr., Râgh.).

100. 'Water,' i. e. 'wells, tanks, &c.' 'Gems produced in water,' i. e. 'pearls, coral, &c.'

Verse 99 is placed by Nand. before verse 100, and some others are inserted between and after them, but the confusion is probably owing merely to clerical errors, as no commentary is given.

101. *Añg*asâ, 'openly,' means according to Gov. and Kull. 'truly,' according to Nâr. 'quickly.'

duced) by perjury, declare thou openly everything as (thou hast) heard or seen (it).'

102. Brâhma*n*as who tend cattle, who trade, who are mechanics, actors (or singers), menial servants or usurers, the (judge) shall treat like *S*ûdras.

103. In (some) cases a man who, though knowing (the facts to be) different, gives such (false evidence) from a pious motive, does not lose heaven; such (evidence) they call the speech of the gods.

104. Whenever the death of a *S*ûdra, of a Vai*s*ya, of a Kshatriya, or of a Brâhma*n*a would be (caused) by a declaration of the truth, a falsehood may be spoken; for such (falsehood) is preferable to the truth.

105. Such (witnesses) must offer to Sarasvatî oblations of boiled rice (*k*aru) which are sacred to the goddess of speech, (thus) performing the best penance in order to expiate the guilt of that falsehood.

106. Or such (a witness) may offer according to the rule clarified butter in the fire, reciting the Kûshmâ*nd*a texts, or the *Rik*, sacred to Varu*n*a, 'Untie, O Varu*n*a, the uppermost fetter,' or the three verses addressed to the Waters.

107. A man who, without being ill, does not give evidence in (cases of) loans and the like within three fortnights (after the summons), shall become respon-

102. Vas. III, 1.

103–104. Gaut. XIII, 24–25; Vas. XVI, 36; Vi. VIII, 15; Yâg*ñ*. II, 83.

103. Nand. omits this verse.

105–106. Baudh. I, 19, 16; Vi. VIII, 16; Yâg*ñ*. II, 83.

106. The Kûshmâ*nd*a texts are found Taitt. Âr. X, 3–5; the verse addressed to Varu*n*a, Rig-veda I, 24, 15; and the three verses addressed to the Waters, Rig-veda X, 9, 1–3.

107. Yâg*ñ*. II, 76.

sible for the whole debt and (pay) a tenth part of the whole (as a fine to the king).

108. The witness to whom, within seven days after he has given evidence, happens (a misfortune through) sickness, a fire, or the death of a relative, shall be made to pay the debt and a fine.

109. If two (parties) dispute about matters for which no witnesses are available, and the (judge) is unable to really ascertain the truth, he may cause it to be discovered even by an oath.

110. Both by the great sages and the gods oaths have been taken for the purpose of (deciding doubtful) matters; and Vasish*th*a even swore an oath before king (Sudâs), the son of Pi*g*avana.

111. Let no wise man swear an oath falsely, even in a trifling matter; for he who swears an oath falsely is lost in this (world) and after death.

112. No crime, causing loss of caste, is committed by swearing (falsely) to women, the objects of one's desire, at marriages, for the sake of fodder for a cow, or of fuel, and in (order to show) favour to a Brâhma*n*a.

---

108. Yâ*gñ*. II, 113.

109. Gaut. XIII, 12–13; Vi. IX, 2–9. According to Medh. *s*apatha, 'oath,' is used for the whole daiva anumâna, 'divine proof,' and thus includes the ordeals.

110. Medh. and Gov. point out that the seven sages purified themselves by oaths when they mutually accused each other of a theft of lotus-fibres (Mah. XIII, 93, 13 seqq.), and that Indra swore an oath when he was accused of an intrigue with Ahalyâ, the wife of Gautama. Vasish*th*a finally cleared himself of the accusation which Vi*s*vâmitra brought against him before king Sudâs, that he was a Râkshasa and had devoured his hundred sons (Medh., Gov., Kull., Nâr., Râgh., Nand.). See Sâya*n*a on Rig-veda VII, 104, and especially on verse 15, which is considered to contain the oath sworn.

112. Gaut. XXIII, 29; Vas. XVI, 35. 'Fuel,' i. e. 'for a burnt-

113. Let the (judge) cause a Brâhma*n*a to swear by his veracity, a Kshatriya by his chariot or the animal he rides on and by his weapons, a Vai*s*ya by his kine, grain, and gold, and a *S*ûdra by (imprecating on his own head the guilt) of all grievous offences (pâtaka).

114. Or the (judge) may cause the (party) to carry fire or to dive under water, or severally to touch the heads of his wives and children.

115. He whom the blazing fire burns not, whom the water forces not to come (quickly) up, who meets with no speedy misfortune, must be held innocent on (the strength of) his oath.

116. For formerly when Vatsa was accused by his younger brother, the fire, the spy of the world, burned not even a hair (of his) by reason of his veracity.

117. Whenever false evidence has been given in any suit, let the (judge) reverse the judgment, and whatever has been done must be (considered as) undone.

---

oblation' (Medh., Gov., Kull., Nâr.). In the last cases the sacredness of the purpose excuses the crime.

113. The Kshatriya and Vai*s*ya must touch the things mentioned, and say, 'May they become useless to me!' (Medh., Gov., Kull.)

114. This verse refers, as the commentators assert, to the two ordeals described by Vi. XI–XII, and Yâ*g*ñ. II, 103–109. Medh., Gov., and Kull. assert that ordeals are to be used in particularly important cases only; see also Vi. IX, 10–14.

116. Maitreya, the step-brother of Vatsa, accused the latter of being the offspring of a *S*ûdra woman. In order to prove the falseness of this allegation, Vatsa passed through a fire (Medh., Gov., Kull., Nâr., Râgh.). I read spa*s*a*h* instead of sp*ri**s*a*h*.

117. Vi. VIII, 40. 'Fines imposed must be remitted' (Gov., Kull., Nâr.).

118. Evidence (given) from covetousness, distraction, terror, friendship, lust, wrath, ignorance, and childishness is declared (to be) invalid.

119. I will propound in (due) order the particular punishments for him who gives false evidence from any one of these motives.

120. (He who commits perjury) through covetousness shall be fined one thousand (pa*n*as), (he who does it) through distraction, in the lowest amercement; (if a man does it) through fear, two middling amercements shall be paid as a fine, (if he does it) through friendship, four times the amount of the lowest (amercement).

121. (He who does it) through lust, (shall pay) ten times the lowest amercement, but (he who does it) through wrath, three times the next (or second amercement); (he who does it) through ignorance, two full hundreds, but (he who does it) through childishness, one hundred (pa*n*as).

122. They declare that the wise have prescribed these fines for perjury, in order to prevent a failure of justice, and in order to restrain injustice.

123. But a just king shall fine and banish (men of) the three (lower) castes (var*n*a) who have given false evidence, but a Brâhma*n*a he shall (only) banish.

124. Manu, the son of the Self-existent (Svayambhu), has named ten places on which punishment

---

119–123. Yâg*ñ*. II, 81.

120. Regarding the three amercements, see below, verse 138.

123. Vivâsayet, 'he shall (only) banish' (Kull., Nâr., Râgh., Nand.), means according to Medh. 'he shall deprive him of his clothes or of his house.' Gov. gives Medh.'s first explanation only.

124. Âp. II, 27; 8, 17–19; Gaut. XII, 46–47; Vi. V, 2–8.

may be (made to fall) in the cases of the three (lower) castes (var*n*a); but a Brâhma*n*a shall depart unhurt (from the country).

125. (These are) the organ, the belly, the tongue, the two hands, and fifthly the two feet, the eye, the nose, the two ears, likewise the (whole) body.

126. Let the (king), having fully ascertained the motive, the time and place (of the offence), and having considered the ability (of the criminal to suffer) and the (nature of the) crime, cause punishment to fall on those who deserve it.

127. Unjust punishment destroys reputation among men, and fame (after death), and causes even in the next world the loss of heaven; let him, therefore, beware of (inflicting) it.

128. A king who punishes those who do not deserve it, and punishes not those who deserve it, brings great infamy on himself and (after death) sinks into hell.

129. Let him punish first by (gentle) admonition, afterwards by (harsh) reproof, thirdly by a fine, after that by corporal chastisement.

130. But when he cannot restrain such (offenders) even by corporal punishment, then let him apply to them even all the four (modes conjointly).

131. Those technical names of (certain quantities of) copper, silver, and gold, which are generally used

---

126. Gaut. XII, 51; Yâg*ñ*. I, 367. Anubandham, 'the motive,' includes according to Gov. and Kull. also 'the frequency of the offence.' Nâr. gives the latter meaning alone. Nand. reads aparâdham, 'the offence.' Instead of sârâparâdhau Nand. reads sârâsâram, 'the strength or weakness (of the offender).'

127-128. Yâg*ñ*. I, 356; Vi. XIX, 43.

129-130. Yâg*ñ*. I, 366.

131-138. Vi. IV, 1-14; Yâg*ñ*. I, 361-365.

on earth for the purpose of business transactions among men, I will fully declare.

132. The very small mote which is seen when the sun shines through a lattice, they declare (to be) the least of (all) quantities and (to be called) a trasare*n*u (a floating particle of dust).

133. Know (that) eight trasare*n*us (are equal) in bulk (to) a likshâ (the egg of a louse), three of those to one grain of black mustard (râ*g*asarshapa), and three of the latter to a white mustard-seed.

134. Six grains of white mustard are one middle-sized barley-corn, and three barley-corns one k*ri*sh*n*ala (raktikâ, or gu*ñg*a-berry); five k*ri*sh*n*alas are one mâsha (bean), and sixteen of those one suvar*n*a.

135. Four suvar*n*as are one pala, and ten palas one dhara*n*a; two k*ri*sh*n*alas (of silver), weighed together, must be considered one mâshaka of silver.

136. Sixteen of those make a silver dhara*n*a, or purâ*n*a; but know (that) a karsha of copper is a kârshâpa*n*a, or pa*n*a.

137. Know (that) ten dhara*n*as of silver make one *s*atamâna; four suvar*n*as must be considered (equal) in weight to a nishka.

138. Two hundred and fifty pa*n*as are declared (to be) the first (or lowest) amercement, five (hundred) are considered as the mean (or middlemost), but one thousand as the highest.

139. A debt being admitted as due, (the defendant)

134. The k*ri*sh*n*ala or raktikâ (ratti) is still used by jewellers and goldsmiths. It corresponds to 0.122 grammes, or 1.875 grains.

136. A karsha = 16 mâshas = 80 k*ri*sh*n*alas.

139. Vi. VI, 20–21; Yâ*gñ*. II, 42. According to Nâr. 'some' only have this verse.

shall pay five in the hundred (as a fine), if it be denied (and proved) twice as much; that is the teaching of Manu.

140. A money-lender may stipulate as an increase of his capital, for the interest, allowed by Vasish*th*a, and take monthly the eightieth part of a hundred.

141. Or, remembering the duty of good men, he may take two in the hundred (by the month), for he who takes two in the hundred becomes not a sinner for gain.

142. Just two in the hundred, three, four, and five (and not more), he may take as monthly interest according to the order of the castes (var*n*a).

143. But if a beneficial pledge (i.e. one from which profit accrues, has been given), he shall receive no interest on the loan; nor can he, after keeping (such) a pledge for a very long time, give or sell it.

---

140. Gaut. XII, 29; Yâ*gñ*. II, 37. The rule occurs in our Vâsish*th*a Dharma*s*âstra II, 51. The amount is fifteen per cent per annum. According to Kull. (on verse 141), Nâr., Râgh., and Nand. this rule refers to a debt secured by a pledge, and the correctness of this view is proved by the parallel passage of Yâ*gñ*.

141-142. Vas. II, 48; Vi. VI, 2; Yâ*gñ*. II, 37. This rule refers, according to the same commentators, to unsecured loans. A Brâhma*n*a is to pay two per cent per month, a Kshatriya three, a Vai*s*ya four, and a *S*ûdra five. Med. and Gov. think that the rule refers to cases where the creditor is unable to live on the smaller interest.

143. Gaut. XII, 32; Vi. VI, 5. 'A beneficial pledge,' i.e. 'land, cattle, slaves, &c.' According to Medh., Gov., and Nâr., the last clause refers to pledges which are not used. But Kull. objects that this is contrary to the common practice of the *S*ish*t*as, and Râgh. refers to Yâ*gñ*. II, 58, where it is clearly stated that beneficial pledges only are never lost, while those which are merely kept are lost when the original debt is doubled by unpaid interest.

144. A pledge (to be kept only) must not be used by force, (the creditor), so using it, shall give up his (whole) interest, or, (if it has been spoilt by use) he shall satisfy the (owner) by (paying its) original price; else he commits a theft of the pledge.

145. Neither a pledge nor a deposit can be lost by lapse of time; they are both recoverable, though they have remained long (with the bailee).

146. Things used with friendly assent, a cow, a camel, a riding-horse, and (a beast) made over for breaking in, are never lost (to the owner).

147. (But in general) whatever (chattel) an owner sees enjoyed by others during ten years, while, though present, he says nothing, that (chattel) he shall not recover.

148. If (the owner is) neither an idiot nor a minor and if (his chattel) is enjoyed (by another) before his eyes, it is lost to him by law; the adverse possessor shall retain that property.

149. A pledge, a boundary, the property of infants, an (open) deposit, a sealed deposit, women, the property of the king and the wealth of a *S*rotriya are not lost in consequence of (adverse) enjoyment.

---

144. Vi. VI, 5; Yâ*gñ*. II, 59. According to Medh. clothes, &c., are meant; according to Kull. and Râgh. clothes, ornaments, &c.; according to Nâr. beds and so forth. Nâr. thinks that the expression 'the value' refers to the profit made by the use of the pledge.

145. Vi. VI, 7–8; Yâ*gñ*. II, 58. According to Medh. the pledge spoken of here is 'a pledge for keeping which is forcibly used.' Upanidhi, 'a deposit,' means according to Medh., Gov., Kull. (who however refers the term also to deposits), Râgh., and Nand. 'anything lent to another out of friendship;' according to Nâr. 'an additional pledge, given subsequently, in order to complete the security for the loan.'

147–148. Gaut. XII, 37; Vas. XVI, 16–17; Yâ*gñ*. II, 24.

149. Vas. XVI, 18; Gaut. XII, 38–39; Yâ*gñ*. II, 25. 'Women,'

150. The fool who uses a pledge without the permission of the owner, shall remit half of his interest, as a compensation for (such) use.

151. In money transactions interest paid at one time (not by instalments) shall never exceed the double (of the principal); on grain, fruit, wool or hair, (and) beasts of burden it must not be more than five times (the original amount).

152. Stipulated interest beyond the legal rate, being against (the law), cannot be recovered; they call that a usurious way (of lending); (the lender) is (in no case) entitled to (more than) five in the hundred.

153. Let him not take interest beyond the year, nor such as is unapproved, nor compound interest, periodical interest, stipulated interest, and corporal interest.

---

i. e. 'female slaves and the like.' Râgh. adds that their offspring is not lost to the owner. Upanidhi*h*, 'a sealed deposit' (Gov., Kull., Nâr., and Râgh.).

150. According to the commentators this is the consequence, resulting from the secret unpermitted use of a pledge in ordinary cases, while the loss of the whole interest ensues in the case of a forcible use in contravention of a special prohibition.

151. Gaut. XII, 31, 36; Vi. VI, 11–15; Yâ*gñ*. II, 39. The interest here intended is such which is not paid by instalments, but becomes due together with the principal. According to the commentators, the whole sum payable, i. e. the interest together with the principal, shall not exceed the double of the sum lent, or, in the special cases mentioned, five times that amount.

152. According to Gov. and Nâr. this verse entitles the money-lender to take five per cent from Âryans, not from *S*ûdras only.

153. Gaut. XII, 30, 34–35. 'A creditor may take for the term of a year interest which has been settled by the following agreement, "When one, two, or three months have passed, the interest on the (capital) shall be calculated and be paid to me at one time;" but he shall not take the interest according to the agreement after

154. He who, unable to pay a debt (at the fixed time), wishes to make a new contract, may renew the agreement, after paying the interest which is due.

155. If he cannot pay the money (due as interest), he may insert it in the renewed (agreement); he must pay as much interest as may be due.

156. He who has made a contract to carry goods by a wheeled carriage for money and has agreed to a certain place or time, shall not reap that reward, if he does not keep to the place and the time (stipulated).

---

a year has passed' (Kull., Râgh.). According to Gov. this clause means, 'If (the creditor) does not take the money (due) for two or three years and (the debtor) pays then, (the creditor) shall not take more interest than for one year.' Nâr. says, 'atisâ*m*vatsarîm ("beyond the year") means that (interest) which after the lapse of one year only is redundant,' i. e. 'exceeds that which has been doubled' (see verse 151). Ad*ri*sh*t*âm, 'unapproved,' i. e. 'in the law-books' (Kull., Râgh), or 'in the law-books and in daily life' (Nand.), means according to Medh. and Gov. anupa*k*itâm, 'which has not accumulated,' i. e. 'which is taken for one, two, or three days.' Nâr. agrees with the latter view. Kâlav*ri*ddhi*h*, 'periodical interest,' i. e. 'monthly interest' (Gov., Nâr.), or 'interest in contravention of verse 151' (Kull., Râgh.). Kâritâ, 'stipulated interest,' i. e. 'an illegal rate of interest, or interest which runs on after the principal has been doubled, agreed to by the debtor on account of distress' (Medh., Gov., Nâr., Kull., Râgh.). Kâyikâ, 'corporal interest,' i. e. 'to be paid by bodily labour or by the use of the body of a pledged animal or slave' (Medh.). Kull., Râgh., and Nand. give the second explanation. According to 'some,' quoted by Medh. and Nâr., the last four kinds of interest are not forbidden. Medh. and Gov. think all or some of them are permissible for merchants. See also for the explanation of the terms, Gaut. XII, 34–35, notes; and Colebrooke I, Digest 35–45.

154. Kara*n*a, 'the agreement,' i. e. 'the written bond' (Kull., Râgh.), or 'the written bond and so forth' (Gov., Nâr.). According to the latter two, with whom Medh. seems to agree, kara*n*a may also refer to a verbal agreement before witnesses.

155. 'Pay,' i. e. promise to pay in the new agreement.

156. Thus Medh., Gov., Kull., and Râgh. But Nâr. and Nand.

157. Whatever rate men fix, who are expert in sea-voyages and able to calculate (the profit) according to the place, the time, and the objects (carried), that (has legal force) in such cases with respect to the payment (to be made).

158. The man who becomes a surety in this (world) for the appearance of a (debtor), and produces him not, shall pay the debt out of his own property.

159. But money due by a surety, or idly promised, or lost at play, or due for spirituous liquor, or what remains unpaid of a fine and a tax or duty, the son (of the party owing it) shall not be obliged to pay.

160. This just mentioned rule shall apply to the case of a surety for appearance (only); if a surety for payment should die, the (judge) may compel even his heirs to discharge the debt.

161. On what account then is it that after the death of a surety other than for payment, whose

---

explain *k*akravr*i*ddhi, 'a contract to carry goods by a wheeled carriage,' by 'compound interest;' and Medh. on verse 157 mentions this opinion too.

157. The expression 'in sea-voyages' includes voyages by land (Medh., Gov., Kull., Râgh.), or all voyages (Nâr.). The commentators, who explain the preceding verse as referring to compound interest, explain this to mean that merchants trading by sea must pay any rate of interest for money borrowed which experts may fix (see Yâ*gñ*. II, 38). The others, of course, understand by 'the rate' (vr*i*ddhi) the carrier's or shipowner's wages.

158–160. Gaut. XII, 42; Vi. VI, 41; Yâ*gñ*. II, 47, 53–54.

159. 'Idly promised,' i.e. 'to clowns and so forth' (Kull.), or 'to bards and the like' (Nâr.), or 'not for a religious purpose, but to singers and the like' (Nand.), or 'in jest, to bards and the like' (Râgh.), or 'a pour-boire and the like' (Gov.).

161. 'Whose affairs are fully known,' i.e. 'the cause for which

affairs are fully known, the creditor may (in some cases) afterwards demand the debt (of the heirs)?

162. If the surety had received money (from him for whom he stood bail) and had money enough (to pay), then (the heir of him) who received it, shall pay (the debt) out of his property; that is the settled rule.

163. A contract made by a person intoxicated, or insane, or grievously disordered (by disease and so forth), or wholly dependent, by an infant or very aged man, or by an unauthorised (party) is invalid.

164. That agreement which has been made contrary to the law or to the settled usage (of the virtuous), can have no legal force, though it be established (by proofs).

165. A fraudulent mortgage or sale, a fraudulent gift or acceptance, and (any transaction) where he detects fraud, the (judge) shall declare null and void.

166. If the debtor be dead and (the money borrowed) was expended for the family, it must be paid by the relatives out of their own estate even if they are divided.

---

he became a surety (e. g. for appearance or good behaviour) being fully known' (Nâr., Râgh.).

162. Ala*m*dhana*h*, 'had money enough (to pay),' i.e. 'had received a sum equal to the loan contracted by him for whose appearance he stood surety' (Medh., Gov., Kull., Nâr.). According to Râgh. the adjective refers to the heir, and means 'if he has money enough to pay.' Nand. reads alakshita*h*, 'if a surety who received money be not found' (i. e. has died or disappeared, &c.).

163. Yâ*gñ*. II, 32.

164. 'The sale of wife and children, giving away one's whole property, though one may have issue' (Medh.).

166. Vi. VI, 39; Yâ*gñ*. II, 45. The meaning is, as Nand. points out, that if a debt was contracted for the benefit of a united family,

167. Should even a person wholly dependent make a contract for the behoof of the family, the master (of the house), whether (living) in his own country or abroad, shall not rescind it.

168. What is given by force, what is enjoyed by force, also what has been caused to be written by force, and all other transactions done by force, Manu has declared void.

169. Three suffer for the sake of others, witnesses, a surety, and judges; but four enrich themselves (through others), a Brâhma*n*a, a money-lender, a merchant, and a king.

170. No king, however indigent, shall take anything that ought not to be taken, nor shall he,

---

it must be repaid by the members of the family, though they may have separated afterwards.

167. Adhyadhîna*h*, 'a person wholly dependent,' i. e. 'a servant (Nâr.), or 'a slave' (Kull.), or 'the youngest (brother) or one in a similar position' (Râgh.). Gov. reads vâ instead of api, and for vi*k*âlayet (Medh., Kull., Râgh.) or vi*k*ârayet (Nand.), vilambayet; and with this reading the translation must be, 'or one wholly dependent, who makes a contract for the sake of the family, must wait for (the arrival of) the master of the house, whether he be at home or abroad.'

168. Vi. VII, 6; Yâg*ñ*. II, 89.

169. Kulam, 'the judges' (Medh., Gov., Kull.), has, according to Nâr., Nand., and Râgh., its usual meaning, 'the family.' Nâr. and Nand. say that the undivided relatives have to suffer by paying the debts of a deceased coparcener; and Râgh. explains the sufferings of a family by the ruin caused through a bad son. Medh., Gov., and Kull. state that the object of the verse is to inculcate that men must not be forced to become witnesses and so forth against their will, and that Brâhma*n*as, &c., must not force others to those transactions from which they gain advantages, e. g. to lawsuits. (Râgh. similarly.) Nâr. takes the first half as a warning not to become a witness or surety or to remain undivided.

170. Vas. XIX, 14–15.

however wealthy, decline taking that which he ought to take, be it ever so small.

171. In consequence of his taking what ought not to be taken, or of his refusing what ought to be received, a king will be accused of weakness and perish in this (world) and after death.

172. By taking his due, by preventing the confusion of the castes (var*n*a), and by protecting the weak, the power of the king grows, and he prospers in this (world) and after death.

173. Let the prince, therefore, like Yama, not heeding his own likings and dislikings, behave exactly like Yama, suppressing his anger and controlling himself.

174. But that evil-minded king who in his folly decides causes unjustly, his enemies soon subjugate.

175. If, subduing love and hatred, he decides the causes according to the law, (the hearts of) his subjects turn towards him as the rivers (run) towards the ocean.

176. (The debtor) who complains to the king that his creditor recovers (the debt) independently (of the court), shall be compelled by the king to pay (as a fine) one quarter (of the sum) and to his (creditor) the money (due).

177. Even by (personal) labour shall the debtor make good (what he owes) to his creditor, if he be of the same caste or of a lower one; but

---

171. 'For if a king takes from his subjects what he ought not to take, they will say, "He fines us, because he is unable to overcome the vassals, neighbours, and the forest tribes (and to obtain money from them),"' Medh.

176. Vi. VI, 19. See above, verses 49–50.

177. The last clause refers to Brâhma*n*as (Medh., Kull., Râgh.).

a (debtor) of a higher caste shall pay it gradually (when he earns something).

178. According to these rules let the king equitably decide between men, who dispute with each other the matters, which are proved by witnesses and (other) evidence.

179. A sensible man should make a deposit (only) with a person of (good) family, of good conduct, well acquainted with the law, veracious, having many relatives, wealthy, and honourable (ârya).

180. In whatever manner a person shall deposit anything in the hands of another, in the same manner ought the same thing to be received back (by the owner); as the delivery (was, so must be) the re-delivery.

181. He who restores not his deposit to the depositor at his request, may be tried by the judge in the depositor's absence.

182. On failure of witnesses let the (judge) actually deposit gold with that (defendant) under some pretext or other through spies of suitable age and appearance (and afterwards demand it back).

183. If the (defendant) restores it in the manner and shape in which it was bailed, there is nothing

---

178. Pratyaya, '(other) evidence,' i. e. 'by inference and divine proof' (Medh.), or 'by inference, oaths, and so forth' (Gov.), or 'by oaths' (Nâr., Nand.).

180. Yâgñ. II, 65. See also below, verse 195. Nand. omits 184, and places the other verses as follows: 180, 195, 188 b, 185, 186, 189, 194, 187, 188 a, 181, 182, 183, 196, 190, 191, 192, 193.

181. The order of the verses referring to the trial of the bailee, is according to Gov. 181, 183, 184, 182, and according to Nâr. 181, 183, 182, 184.

(of that description) in his hands, for which others accuse him.

184. But if he restores not that gold, as he ought, to those (spies), then he shall be compelled by force to restore both (deposits); that is a settled rule of law.

185. An open or a sealed deposit must never be returned to a near relative (of the depositor during the latter's lifetime); for if (the recipient) dies (without delivering them), they are lost, but if he does not die, they are not lost.

186. But (a depositary) who of his own accord returns them to a near relative of a deceased (depositor), must not be harassed (about them) by the king or by the depositor's relatives.

187. And (in doubtful cases) he should try to obtain that object by friendly means, without (having recourse to) artifice, or having inquired into the (depositary's) conduct, he should settle (the matter) with gentle means.

188. Such is the rule for obtaining back all those open deposits; in the case of a sealed deposit (the depositary) shall incur no (censure), unless he has taken out something.

189. (A deposit) which has been stolen by thieves

---

185. Pratyanantare, 'to a near relative,' i. e. 'to his son, brother, or wife' (Medh.).

187. According to Nâr., this verse refers to cases when one believes a deposit to be with another, but has not made it over oneself; according to Gov. and Kull., to cases where there may be an error. Gov. and Kull. think that the person who should act in the manner described is the king, and they explain anvi*kkh*et, 'one should try to obtain,' by 'he should decide.' Nâr. and Râgh., on the other hand, think that the depositor should act thus. The former explanation is perhaps preferable.

189. Yâ*gñ*. II, 66.

or washed away by water or burned by fire, (the bailee) shall not make it good, unless he took part of it (for himself).

190. Him who appropriates a deposit and him (who asks for it) without having made it, (the judge) shall try by all (sorts of) means, and by the oaths prescribed in the Veda.

191. He who does not return a deposit and he who demands what he never bailed shall both be punished like thieves, or be compelled to pay a fine equal (to the value of the object retained or claimed).

192. The king should compel him who does not restore an open deposit, and in like manner him who retains a sealed deposit, to pay a fine equal (to its value).

193. That man who by false pretences may possess himself of another's property, shall be publicly punished by various (modes of) corporal (or capital) chastisement, together with his accomplices.

---

190. 'By all (sorts of) means,' i. e. 'by the four expedients, kindness and so forth' (Gov., Kull., Râgh.), or 'by spies and so forth' (Nâr.), or 'by blows, imprisonment, and so forth' (Medh.). 'By the oaths prescribed in the Veda,' i. e. 'by the ordeals, such as carrying fire' (Gov., Kull., Nâr.). Nâr. quotes a passage of the Veda, in which it is prescribed that the accused shall take hold of a hot axe.

191. Vi. V, 169–171. The former punishment, which consists of mutilation and other corporal punishments (Medh., Nâr., Râgh.), or the highest amercement and the like (Gov.), shall be inflicted on others than Brâhma*n*as in particularly bad cases and for a repetition of the offence (Medh., Gov., Kull., Nâr., Râgh.).

192. Medh., Gov., and Kull. refer this rule to first offences. Nâr. takes avi*s*eshe*n*a, 'in like manner,' to mean 'without making a distinction on account of the caste of the offender.' Medh. explains upanidhi, 'a sealed deposit,' by 'an object lent in a friendly manner.'

193. 'By false pretences,' i. e. 'by frightening others with the

194. If a deposit of a particular description or quantity is bailed by anybody in the presence of a number (of witnesses), it must be known to be of that particular (description and quantity; the depositary) who makes a false statement (regarding it) is liable to a fine.

195. But if anything is delivered or received privately, it must be privately returned; as the bailment (was, so should be) the re-delivery.

196. Thus let the king decide (causes) concerning a deposit and a friendly loan (for use) without showing (undue) rigour to the depositary.

197. If anybody sells the property of another man, without being the owner and without the assent of the owner, the (judge) shall not admit him who is a thief, though he may not consider himself as a thief, as a witness (in any case).

198. If the (offender) is a kinsman (of the owner), he shall be fined six hundred paṇas; if he is not a kinsman, nor has any excuse, he shall be guilty of theft.

---

king's anger, by promising to obtain for them favours from the king, or the love of a maiden, and so forth' (Medh.). 'By (various) modes of corporal chastisement,' i. e. 'by cutting off his hands, feet, or his head, &c.' (Gov., Kull., Râgh.), or 'by decapitating or impaling the offender, or having him trampled to death by elephants, and so forth' (Medh.).

194. I. e. the witnesses must be examined regarding it, and their evidence is conclusive.

196. This conclusion makes it somewhat doubtful if the term upanidhi, which occurs verses 185 and 191, and has been translated by 'a sealed deposit' in accordance with the opinion of most commentators, has really that meaning.

198. 'Any excuse,' e. g. 'that he received it as a present, or bought it from the son or other relative of the owner, and so forth' (Gov., Kull.). Nâr. reads anavasare, 'and buys at an improper (time or place).'

199. A gift or sale, made by anybody else but the owner, must be considered as null and void, according to the rule in judicial proceedings.

200. Where possession is evident, but no title is perceived, there the title (shall be) a proof (of ownership), not possession; such is the settled rule.

201. He who obtains a chattel in the market before a number (of witnesses), acquires that chattel with a clear legal title by purchase.

202. If the original (seller) be not producible, (the buyer) being exculpated by a public sale, must be dismissed by the king without punishment, but (the former owner) who lost the chattel shall receive it (back from the buyer).

203. One commodity mixed with another must not be sold (as pure), nor a bad one (as good), nor less (than the proper quantity or weight), nor anything that is not at hand or that is concealed.

---

199. Nand. omits this verse, and inserts instead, 'He who ignorantly makes a sale without ownership shall be punished according to the above rule (i. e. be fined); but he who does it knowingly shall be punished like a thief.' Nâr. has no trace of verse 199, but quotes the beginning of the verse just translated (anena vidhineti).

200. Nand. places this verse after 202.

201–202. Vi. V, 164–166; Yâg*n*. II, 168–170.

202. Thus Medh., Kull., Nâr., and Râgh. (Kull., however, taking *s*odhita, 'exculpated,' in the sense of nis*k*ita, 'determined.') But Gov. takes the first part differently. 'If the price cannot be produced by him (the seller)—because he has gone to another country—then the buyer must not be punished by the king, being held to be guiltless on account of the open sale, in accordance with the rule of the preceding verse;' similarly Nand. The difference is caused thereby that Gov. apparently objects to the explanation of mûlam (mûlyam, Nand.) by 'the original (seller).' According to Kull. the buyer receives half the value from the original owner.

203. Yâg*n*. II, 245. 'Concealed,' i.e. 'in a cloth' (Medh., Nâr.), or 'in the earth' (Nand.), or 'covered with paint' (Gov., Kull., Râgh.).

204. If, after one damsel has been shown, another be given to the bridegroom, he may marry them both for the same price; that Manu ordained.

205. He who gives (a damsel in marriage), having first openly declared her blemishes, whether she be insane, or afflicted with leprosy, or have lost her virginity, is not liable to punishment.

206. If an officiating priest, chosen to perform a sacrifice, abandons his work, a share only (of the fee) in proportion to the work (done) shall be given to him by those who work with him.

207. But he who abandons his work after the sacrificial fees have been given, shall obtain his full share and cause to be performed (what remains) by another (priest).

208. But if (specific) fees are ordained for the several parts of a rite, shall he (who performs the part) receive them, or shall they all share them?

209. The Adhvaryu priest shall take the chariot, and the Brahman at the kindling of the fires (Agnyâdhâna) a horse, the Hot*ri* priest shall also take a horse, and the Udgât*ri* the cart, (used) when (the Soma) is purchased.

---

204. This rule is rather astonishing after what has been said, III, 51–54, regarding the sale of daughters, and it proves that, in spite of all directions to the contrary, wives were purchased in ancient India as frequently as in our days.

207. Yâ*gñ*. II, 265. 'After the sacrificial fees have been given,' i.e. 'at the midday oblation and so forth' (Medh., Kull., Gov.). According to Medh. the sacrificer is to pay the substitute, according to the other commentators the priest who receives the fee.

208. Medh. mentions that specific fees are prescribed at the Râ*g*asûya and similar sacrifices; see Âsv. *S*rauta-sûtra IX, 3, 14–15; 4, 7–20.

209. According to Medh. and Kull. all the three first-mentioned gifts are given according to the precepts of some *S*âkhâs at the Agnyâdhâna, the kindling of the fires. But Gov. says that the

210. The (four) chief priests among all (the sixteen), who are entitled to one half, shall receive a moiety (of the fee), the next (four) one half of that, the set entitled to a third share, one third, and those entitled to a fourth a quarter.

211. By the application of these principles the allotment of shares must be made among those men who here (below) perform their work conjointly.

212. Should money be given (or promised) for a pious purpose by one man to another who asks for it, the gift shall be void, if the (money is) afterwards not (used) in the manner (stated).

213. But if the (recipient) through pride or greed tries to enforce (the fulfilment of the promise), he shall be compelled by the king to pay one suvar*n*a as an expiation for his theft.

214. Thus the lawful subtraction of a gift has

Brahman priest receives a swift horse at the Agnyâdhâna, and Nâr. adds that the Hot*ri* receives a horse at the *G*yotish*t*oma.

210. The four classes of priests, regarding whose functions see Max Müller, History Anc. Sansk. Lit., p. 468 seqq., are: 1. Hot*ri*, Adhvaryu, Brahman, Udgât*ri*; 2. Maitrâvaru*n*a, Pratiprasthât*ri*, Brâhma*n*â*kkh*a*m*sin, Prastot*ri*; 3. A*kkh*âvâka, Nesh*t*ri, Agnîdhra, Pratihart*ri*; 4. Pot*ri*, Subrahma*n*yâ, Grâvash*t*ut, Net*ri*. Medh. gives the total as 112, and the shares as 56, 28, 16, 12; Gov., Kull., Nâr., and Râgh. the total as 100, and the shares as 48, 24, 16, 8. But Nand. says that the total of the fee, whatever it may be, shall be divided into 25 shares, and the several classes shall receive 12, 6, 4, and 3 such shares respectively. See also Âsv. *S*rauta-sûtra IX, 4, 3–5. The rule, given in this verse, applies to all ordinary cases.

211. Yâ*gñ*. II, 259, 265. I. e. each is to be paid according to the amount of work which he performs.

212. 'For a pious purpose,' i. e. 'for a sacrifice or a wedding' (Medh.).

213. Sa*m*sâdhayet, 'tries to enforce (the fulfilment of the promise),' i. e. 'by a complaint before the king' (Medh.), or 'tries to obtain the money forcibly or refuses to return it' (Kull., Râgh., Gov.).

been fully explained; I will next propound (the law for) the non-payment of wages.

215. A hired (servant or workman) who, without being ill, out of pride fails to perform his work according to the agreement, shall be fined eight k*ri*sh*n*alas and no wages shall be paid to him.

216. But (if he is really) ill, (and) after recovery performs (his work) according to the original agreement, he shall receive his wages even after (the lapse of) a very long time.

217. But if he, whether sick or well, does not (perform or) cause to be performed (by others) his work according to his agreement, the wages for that work shall not be given to him, even (if it be only) slightly incomplete.

218. Thus the law for the non-payment of wages has been completely stated; I will next explain the law concerning men who break an agreement.

219. If a man belonging to a corporation inhabiting a village or a district, after swearing to an agreement, breaks it through avarice, (the king) shall banish him from his realm,

220. And having imprisoned such a breaker of an agreement, he shall compel him to pay six

---

215. Âp. II, 28, 2–3; Vi. V, 153–154; Yâ*gñ*. II, 193. 'Eight k*ri*sh*n*alas,' i. e. 'of gold, silver or copper, according to the case' (Medh., Gov.), or 'of gold' (Kull.).

216. I read with Medh., Gov., Nâr., Râgh., and K. sudîrghasya for sa dîrghasya (Kull., Nand.).

219. Vi. V, 168; Yâ*gñ*. II, 192. By 'corporations inhabiting a village or district' are meant according to Medh., village communities and corporations of merchants, mendicants or monks, *K*aturvedîs and so forth, and he mentions regulations regarding the grazing of the cattle on a common as one of the agreements which all must observe.

220. According to others mentioned by Medh. the translation

nishkas, (each of) four suvar*n*as, and one *s*atamâna of silver.

221. A righteous king shall apply this law of fines in villages and castes (*g*âti) to those who break an agreement.

222. If anybody in this (world), after buying or selling anything, repent (of his bargain), he may return or take (back) that chattel within ten days.

223. But after (the lapse of) ten days he may neither give nor cause it to be given (back); both he who takes it (back) and he who gives it (back, except by consent) shall be fined by the king six hundred (pa*n*as).

224. But the king himself shall impose a fine of ninety-six pa*n*as on him who gives a blemished damsel (to a suitor) without informing (him of the blemish).

225. But that man who, out of malice, says of a maiden, 'She is not a maiden,' shall be fined one hundred (pa*n*as), if he cannot prove her blemish.

226. The nuptial texts are applied solely to virgins, (and) nowhere among men to females who have lost their virginity, for such (females) are excluded from religious ceremonies.

---

should be 'four suvar*n*as or six nishkas or one *s*atamâna.' Kull. and Râgh. also think it possible that three separate fines may be inflicted according to the circumstances of the case.

222. Yâ*g*ñ. II, 177. According to Medh., Gov., Kull., the rule refers to things which are not easily spoilt, such as land, copper, &c., not to flowers, fruit, and the like; according to Nâr., to grain and seeds, 'because in other Sm*ri*tis different periods are mentioned for other objects' (see Yâ*g*ñ. loc. cit.).

224–225. Yâ*g*ñ. I, 66.

224. Regarding the blemishes, see above, verse 205.

226. K. omits this verse.

227. The nuptial texts are a certain proof (that a maiden has been made a lawful) wife; but the learned should know that they (and the marriage-ceremony) are complete with the seventh step (of the bride around the sacred fire).

228. If anybody in this (world) repent of any completed transaction, (the king) shall keep him on the road of rectitude in accordance with the rules given above.

229. I will fully declare in accordance with the true law (the rules concerning) the disputes, (arising) from the transgressions of owners of cattle and of herdsmen.

230. During the day the responsibility for the safety (of the cattle rests) on the herdsman, during the night on the owner, (provided they are) in his house; (if it be) otherwise, the herdsman will be responsible (for them also during the night).

231. A hired herdsman who is paid with milk, may milk with the consent of the owner the best (cow) out of ten; such shall be his hire if no (other) wages (are paid).

232. The herdsman alone shall make good (the loss of a beast) strayed, destroyed by worms, killed by dogs or (by falling) into a pit, if he did not duly exert himself (to prevent it).

---

227. Nand. omits this verse and the next. After the seventh step has been made the marriage cannot be rescinded (Medh., Gov., Kull., Nâr.).

228. I.e. he may be allowed to rescind a contract for wages and the like within ten days, but not later (Gov., Kull.).

231. Nand. omits this verse.

232. Vi. V, 137–138; Yâgñ. I, 164–165. 'By worms,' i.e. according to Medh. by a kind called Ârohakas, who enter the sexual parts of the cows and destroy them; Râgh. says, 'by snakes and the like.' 'By dogs,' the word is according to Medh. merely intended as an instance for any wild animal.

233. But for (an animal) stolen by thieves, though he raised an alarm, the herdsman shall not pay, provided he gives notice to his master at the proper place and time.

234. If cattle die, let him carry to his master their ears, skin, tails, bladders, tendons, and the yellow concrete bile, and let him point out their particular marks.

235. But if goats or sheep are surrounded by wolves and the herdsman does not hasten (to their assistance), he shall be responsible for any (animal) which a wolf may attack and kill.

236. But if they, kept in (proper) order, graze together in the forest, and a wolf, suddenly jumping on one of them, kills it, the herdsman shall bear in that case no responsibility.

237. On all sides of a village a space, one hundred dhanus or three *s*amyâ-throws (in breadth), shall be reserved (for pasture), and thrice (that space) round a town.

238. If the cattle do damage to unfenced crops on that (common), the king shall in that case not punish the herdsmen.

239. (The owner of the field) shall make there a hedge over which a camel cannot look, and stop

---

234. I read with Medh. and Gov. aṅkâ*ms k*a, 'their particular marks,' instead of aṅgâni, 'their (other) limbs' (Râgh., Nand., K., and the editions). To judge from the commentary, Kull. must have had the same reading as Medh. and Gov.

235. Vi. V, 137.

237. Yâ*gñ*. II, 167. Dhanus, literally 'a bow's length'=4 hastas or about 6 feet. The *s*amyâ is a short, thick piece of wood, used at sacrifices. A *s*amyâ-throw is mentioned as a measure also by Âp. I, 9, 6.

every gap through which a dog or a boar can thrust his head.

240. (If cattle do mischief) in an enclosed field near a highway or near a village, the herdsman shall be fined one hundred (pa*n*as); (but cattle), unattended by a herdsman, (the watchman in the field) shall drive away.

241. (For damage) in other fields (each head of) cattle shall (pay a fine of) one (pa*n*a) and a quarter, and in all (cases the value of) the crop (destroyed) shall be made good to the owner of the field; that is the settled rule.

242. But Manu has declared that no fine shall be paid for (damage done by) a cow within ten days after her calving, by bulls and by cattle sacred to the gods, whether they are attended by a herdsman or not.

243. If (the crops are destroyed by) the husbandman's (own) fault, the fine shall amount to ten times as much as (the king's) share; but the fine (shall be) only half that amount if (the fault lay) with the servants and the farmer had no knowledge of it.

240–242. Âp. II, 28, 5; Gaut. XII, 19–26; Vi. V, 140–150; Yâ*gñ*. II, 161–163.

241. 'The cattle,' i.e. 'the herdsman shall pay for the cattle.' 'In all cases,' i.e. 'whether the cattle were attended by a herdsman or not' (Medh., Gov., Kull., Râgh.).

242. A cow is, according to Nâr., during the first days after calving utterly unmanageable. 'Bulls,' i.e. 'those set at liberty (see Vi. LXXXVI) are meant' (Nâr., Kull.), which may be met with near many Indian villages and in many towns. 'Cattle sacred to the gods,' i.e. either 'such as are set apart for sacrifices,' or 'such as are dedicated to temples' (Medh.). The other commentators prefer the second explanation.

243. Âp. II, 28, 1. 'The husbandman's (own) fault,' i.e. 'if he

244. To these rules a righteous king shall keep in (all cases of) transgressions by masters, their cattle, and herdsmen.

245. If a dispute has arisen between two villages concerning a boundary, the king shall settle the limits in the month of *G*yaish*th*a, when the landmarks are most distinctly visible.

246. Let him mark the boundaries (by) trees, (e.g.) Nyagrodhas, A*s*vatthas, Ki*ms*ukas, cotton-trees, *S*âlas, Palmyra palms, and trees with milky juice,

247. By clustering shrubs, bamboos of different kinds, *S*amîs, creepers and raised mounds, reeds, thickets of Kub*g*aka; thus the boundary will not be forgotten.

248. Tanks, wells, cisterns, and fountains should be built where boundaries meet, as well as temples,

249. And as he will see that through men's ignorance of the boundaries trespasses constantly occur in the world, let him cause to be made other hidden marks for boundaries,

250. Stones, bones, cow's hair, chaff, ashes, potsherds, dry cowdung, bricks, cinders, pebbles, and sand,

---

has allowed his crops to be eaten by cattle, or has not sown the field in proper time, &c.' (Medh., Gov., Kull., Nâr., Râgh.).

245. *G*yaish*th*a, i. e. May–June, 'when the grass has been dried up by the heat' (Medh., Kull., Râgh.).

246. Yâ*gñ*. II, 151. Nyagrodha, Ficus Indica; A*s*vattha, Ficus Religiosa; Ki*ms*uka, Butea Frondosa; *S*âla, Shorea Robusta. 'Trees with milky juice,' i.e. 'Arka (Calatropis Gigantea), Udumbara (Ficus Glomerata), &c.'

247. *S*amî, Acacia Suma; 'mounds,' i. e. the heaps of earth are meant which now are used generally as landmarks in British districts. Instead of Kub*g*aka Nand. reads Kulyaka.

251. And whatever other things of a similar kind the earth does not corrode even after a long time, those he should cause to be buried where one boundary joins (the other).

252. By these signs, by long continued possession, and by constantly flowing streams of water the king shall ascertain the boundary (of the land) of two disputing parties.

253. If there be a doubt even on inspection of the marks, the settlement of a dispute regarding boundaries shall depend on witnesses.

254. The witnesses, (giving evidence) regarding a boundary, shall be examined concerning the landmarks in the presence of the crowd of the villagers and also of the two litigants.

255. As they, being questioned, unanimously decide, even so he shall record the boundary (in writing), together with their names.

256. Let them, putting earth on their heads, wearing chaplets (of red flowers) and red dresses, being sworn each by (the rewards for) his meritorious deeds, settle (the boundary) in accordance with the truth.

257. If they determine (the boundary) in the

---

251. According to Kull., who relies on a passage of B*ri*haspati, these objects are to be placed in jars.

254. According to the commentators the verse refers to a dispute between two villages, and the two litigants are persons deputed by each village to conduct the case (see also below, verse 261).

255. All the commentators explain nibadhnîyât by 'he shall record in writing,' and as it is specially mentioned that the names of the witnesses shall be given, it seems impossible to take the word in any other sense. Medh. says that, if the witnesses disagree, the opinion of the majority shall be taken.

256–260. Yâg*ñ*. II, 150–152.

manner stated, they are guiltless (being) veracious witnesses; but if they determine it unjustly, they shall be compelled to pay a fine of two hundred (pa*n*as).

258. On failure of witnesses (from the two villages, men of) the four neighbouring villages, who are pure, shall make (as witnesses) a decision concerning the boundary in the presence of the king.

259. On failure of neighbours (who are) original inhabitants (of the country and can be) witnesses with respect to the boundary, (the king) may hear the evidence even of the following inhabitants of the forest,

260. (Viz.) hunters, fowlers, herdsmen, fishermen, root-diggers, snake-catchers, gleaners, and other foresters.

261. As they, being examined, declare the marks for the meeting of the boundaries (to be), even so the king shall justly cause them to be fixed between the two villages.

262. The decision concerning the boundary-marks of fields, wells, tanks, of gardens and houses depends upon (the evidence of) the neighbours.

263. Should the neighbours give false evidence,

258. Men from the four surrounding villages are meant, as Kull. suggests. The correctness of this opinion is proved by the fact that the land-grants usually mention 'the four boundaries' (*k*aturâghâ*t*anâni) of the villages given away. Medh. and Nand. read gramasâmântavâsina*h*, 'four men living in, &c.'

259. Maulânâm, 'original inhabitants,' i.e. 'whose ancestors have lived there since the settlement of the village' (Medh., Gov., Kull., Râgh.).

260. 'Other foresters,' i.e. 'those who collect flowers, fruit, and fuel' (Medh., Gov., Kull.), or '*S*abaras and the rest' (Nâr.).

262. Vas. XVI, 13–15; Yâ*gñ*. II, 154.

263. Yâ*gñ*. I, 153.

when men dispute about a boundary-mark, the king shall make each of them pay the middlemost amercement as a fine.

264. He who by intimidation possesses himself of a house, a tank, a garden, or a field, shall be fined five hundred (pa*n*as); (if he trespassed) through ignorance, the fine (shall be) two hundred (pa*n*as).

265. If the boundary cannot be ascertained (by any evidence), let a righteous king with (the intention of) benefiting them (all), himself assign (his) land (to each); that is the settled rule.

266. Thus the law for deciding boundary (disputes) has been fully declared, I will next propound the (manner of) deciding (cases of) defamation.

267. A Kshatriya, having defamed a Brâhma*n*a, shall be fined one hundred (pa*n*as); a Vai*s*ya one hundred and fifty or two hundred; a *S*ûdra shall suffer corporal punishment.

268. A Brâhma*n*a shall be fined fifty (pa*n*as) for defaming a Kshatriya; in (the case of) a Vai*s*ya the fine shall be twenty-five (pa*n*as); in (the case of) a *S*ûdra twelve.

269. For offences of twice-born men against those of equal caste (var*n*a, the fine shall be) also twelve (pa*n*as); for speeches which ought not to be uttered, that (and every fine shall be) double.

270. A once-born man (a *S*ûdra), who insults a

---

265. Yâ*gñ*. II, 153.

267–277. Âp. II, 27, 14; Gaut. XII, 1, 8–14; Vas. IX, 9; Vi. V, 23–39; Yâ*gñ*. II, 204–211.

269. 'Speeches that ought not to be uttered,' i. e. 'insinuations against the honour of another's female relatives, especially mothers and sisters' (Medh., Gov., Kull., Râgh.), with which the Hindus, like other Orientals, are very ready.

270. The last clause refers, according to the commentators, to the

twice-born man with gross invective, shall have his tongue cut out; for he is of low origin.

271. If he mentions the names and castes (*g*âti) of the (twice-born) with contumely, an iron nail, ten fingers long, shall be thrust red-hot into his mouth.

272. If he arrogantly teaches Brâhma*n*as their duty, the king shall cause hot oil to be poured into his mouth and into his ears.

273. He who through arrogance makes false statements regarding the learning (of a caste-fellow), his country, his caste (*g*âti), or the rites by which his body was sanctified, shall be compelled to pay a fine of two hundred (pa*n*as).

274. He who even in accordance with the true facts (contemptuously) calls another man one-eyed, lame, or the like (names), shall be fined at least one kârshâpa*n*a.

275. He who defames his mother, his father, his wife, his brother, his son, or his teacher, and he who gives not the way to his preceptor, shall be compelled to pay one hundred (pa*n*as).

276. (For mutual abuse) by a Brâhma*n*a and a

origin of the *S*ûdra from Brahman's feet; see above, I, 31. According to Medh. the expression 'once-born' includes men born from high-caste fathers and low-caste mothers.

271. I.e. if he says 're Ya*gñ*adatta,' or 'thou scum of the Brâhma*n*as.'

273. '(Of a caste-fellow),' (Kull., Râgh.), Gov. too states that the rule cannot refer to *S*ûdras, because the punishment is too light. Medh. explains karma by 'occupation,' and *s*ârîram by 'bodily (deficiencies),' while the others refer karma *s*ârîram to a denial of the initiation.

275. Âkshârayati, 'defames,' i.e. 'accuses them of a mortal sin' (Gov., Kull., Râgh.), or 'of incest' (Nâr.), or 'causes dissensions between them and others' (Medh.), or 'makes them angry' (Nand.).

Kshatriya a fine must be imposed by a discerning (king), on the Brâhma*n*a the lowest amercement, but on the Kshatriya the middlemost.

277. A Vai*s*ya and a *S*ûdra must be punished exactly in the same manner according to their respective castes, but the tongue (of the *S*ûdra) shall not be cut out; that is the decision.

278. Thus the rules for punishments (applicable to cases) of defamation have been truly declared; I will next propound the decision (of cases) of assault.

279. With whatever limb a man of a low caste does hurt to (a man of the three) highest (castes), even that limb shall be cut off; that is the teaching of Manu.

280. He who raises his hand or a stick, shall have his hand cut off; he who in anger kicks with his foot, shall have his foot cut off.

281. A low-caste man who tries to place himself on the same seat with a man of a high caste, shall be branded on his hip and be banished, or (the king) shall cause his buttock to be gashed.

282. If out of arrogance he spits (on a superior), the king shall cause both his lips to be cut off; if he urines (on him), the penis; if he breaks wind (against him), the anus.

---

277. I.e. if a *S*ûdra defames a Vai*s*ya his tongue is not cut out, but he pays the middlemost amercement.

279–280. Vi. V, 19; Yâg*ñ*. II, 215.

280. Praharet, 'kicks,' i.e. 'lifts his foot in order to kick' (Medh., Nâr., Nand.).

281. Âp. II, 27, 15; Gaut. XII, 7; Vi. V, 20. According to Medh., Gov., Kull., the rule refers to a Brâhma*n*a and a *S*ûdra; according to Râgh., to the latter and an Âryan; according to Nâr., to a Kshatriya, Vai*s*ya, or *S*ûdra offending against a Brâhma*n*a.

282. Vi. V, 21–22.

283. If he lays hold of the hair (of a superior), let the (king) unhesitatingly cut off his hands, likewise (if he takes him) by the feet, the beard, the neck, or the scrotum.

284. He who breaks the skin (of an equal) or fetches blood (from him) shall be fined one hundred (pa*n*as), he who cuts a muscle six nishkas, he who breaks a bone shall be banished.

285. According to the usefulness of the several (kinds of) trees a fine must be inflicted for injuring them; that is the settled rule.

286. If a blow is struck against men or animals in order to (give them) pain, (the judge) shall inflict a fine in proportion to the amount of pain (caused).

287. If a limb is injured, a wound (is caused), or blood (flows, the assailant) shall be made to pay (to the sufferer) the expenses of the cure, or the whole (both the usual amercement and the expenses of the cure as a) fine (to the king).

---

284. Vi. V, 66–70; Yâg*ñ*. II, 218. '(Of an equal),' (Medh., Kull., Nand.) According to Râgh., the rule refers to *S*ûdras assaulting *S*ûdras. According to Nâr., the last offender's property shall be confiscated.

285. Vi. V, 55–59; Yâg*ñ*. II, 227–228. The expression 'trees' includes all plants (Medh., Kull.). According to Gov., the fine for injuring trees which give shade only is to be very small; in the case of flower-bearing trees, middling; in the case of fruit-trees, high (see Vi. loc. cit.). Medh. remarks that the position of the trees, e.g. whether they are boundary-marks, or stand on a cross-road, in a hermitage, &c., has to be taken into account (see Yâg*ñ*. loc. cit.).

286–287. Vi. V, 75–76; Yâg*ñ*. II, 219, 222.

287. Instead of vra*n*a, 'a wound' (Kull., Nâr.), Medh., Gov., Râgh., Nand., and K. read prâ*n*a. Medh. explains the latter reading by 'if the vital strength is injured,' and Gov. and Râgh. by 'if the breathing power is injured by gagging.' 'Or the whole (as a) fine,' i. e. if the person injured refuses the compensation. Nâr. says, 'and shall pay the whole fine, mentioned above.'

288. He who damages the goods of another, be it intentionally or unintentionally, shall give satisfaction to the (owner) and pay to the king a fine equal to the (damage).

289. In the case of (damage done to) leather, or to utensils of leather, of wood, or of clay, the fine (shall be) five times their value; likewise in the case of (damage to) flowers, roots, and fruit.

290. They declare with respect to a carriage, its driver and its owner, (that there are) ten cases in which no punishment (for damage done) can be inflicted; in other cases a fine is prescribed.

291. When the nose-string is snapped, when the yoke is broken, when the carriage turns sideways or back, when the axle or a wheel is broken,

292. When the leather-thongs, the rope around the neck or the bridle are broken, and when (the driver) has loudly called out, 'Make way,' Manu has declared (that in all these cases) no punishment (shall be inflicted).

293. But if the cart turns off (the road) through the driver's want of skill, the owner shall be fined, if damage (is done), two hundred (pa*n*as).

294. If the driver is skilful (but negligent), he alone shall be fined; if the driver is unskilful, the occupants of the carriage (also) shall be each fined one hundred (pa*n*as).

295. But if he is stopped on his way by cattle or

---

288. 'The goods,' i.e. 'such objects as are not mentioned specially' (Medh., Gov., Kull., Râgh.).

291–295. Yâg*ñ*. II, 298–299.

291. 'When the carriage turns sideways or backwards,' i.e. 'off the road owing to its badness, to the animals taking fright, &c.' (Medh., Gov., Kull., Râgh.).

295. There are two readings, avi*k*ârita*h*, 'without doubt' (lit. 'not

by (another) carriage, and he causes the death of any living being, a fine shall without doubt be imposed.

296. If a man is killed, his guilt will be at once the same as (that of) a thief; for large animals such as cows, elephants, camels or horses, half of that.

297. For injuring small cattle the fine (shall be) two hundred (pa*n*as); the fine for beautiful wild quadrupeds and birds shall amount to fifty (pa*n*as).

298. For donkeys, sheep, and goats the fine shall be five mâshas; but the punishment for killing a dog or a pig shall be one mâsha.

299. A wife, a son, a slave, a pupil, and a (younger) brother of the full blood, who have committed faults, may be beaten with a rope or a split bamboo,

300. But on the back part of the body (only), never on a noble part; he who strikes them otherwise will incur the same guilt as a thief.

301. Thus the whole law of assault (and hurt) has been declared completely; I will now explain the rules for the decision (in cases) of theft.

302. Let the king exert himself to the utmost to

---

considered'), and vi*k*ârita*h*, 'is considered (to be just).' Medh. gives besides the explanation, adopted in the translation according to Kull., another one, 'is not considered (just).' He mentions also the second reading, which Gov., Râgh., Nâr., and Nand. have, and explains it with them by 'is considered (to be just).'

296. 'The same as that of a thief,' i. e. 'he must pay the highest amercement, or 1000 pa*n*as' (Medh., Gov., Nâr., Kull., Râgh., Nand.).

297–298. Vi. V, 50–54.

299–300. Âp. I, 8, 31; Gaut. II, 43–44.

300. 'Not on a noble part,' i. e. 'not on the chest or the head, &c.' (Medh., Kull.).

punish thieves; for, if he punishes thieves, his fame grows and his kingdom prospers.

303. That king, indeed, is ever worthy of honour who ensures the safety (of his subjects); for the sacrificial session (sattra, which he, as it were, performs thereby) ever grows in length, the safety (of his subjects representing) the sacrificial fee.

304. A king who (duly) protects (his subjects) receives from each and all the sixth part of their spiritual merit; if he does not protect them, the sixth part of their demerit also (will fall on him).

305. Whatever (merit a man gains by) reading the Veda, by sacrificing, by charitable gifts, (or by) worshipping (Gurus and gods), the king obtains a sixth part of that in consequence of his duly protecting (his kingdom).

306. A king who protects the created beings in accordance with the sacred law and smites those worthy of corporal punishment, daily offers (as it were) sacrifices at which hundred thousands (are given as) fees.

307. A king who does not afford protection, (yet) takes his share in kind, his taxes, tolls and duties, daily presents and fines, will (after death) soon sink into hell.

303–311. Âp. II, 25, 15; Vas. I, 42–44; Vi. V, 196; Yâgñ. I, 335–336, 358; see also below, IX, 252 seqq.

307. 'The share in kind,' i.e. 'the sixth part of the harvest' (Medh., Gov., Kull., Nâr., Râgh.), or 'the choice portions of fruit, grain, &c. to be given to the king.' 'Taxes,' i.e. gaṅghâdâna (Medh.), or the land-tax paid in money (Nâr.), 'monthly taxes, or taxes payable in certain months by the villagers' (Gov., Kull., Râgh.). Sulka, i.e. 'the tolls and duties payable by merchants and traders' (Medh., Gov., Kull., Nâr., Râgh.). For pratibhâgam, i.e. 'the daily presents of fruit, vegetables, &c.,' the so-called Dâlîs (Medh., Kull.),

308. They declare that a king who affords no protection, (yet) receives the sixth part of the produce, takes upon himself all the foulness of his whole people.

309. Know that a king who heeds not the rules (of the law), who is an atheist, and rapacious, who does not protect (his subjects, but) devours them, will sink low (after death).

310. Let him carefully restrain the wicked by three methods,—by imprisonment, by putting them in fetters, and by various (kinds of) corporal punishments.

311. For by punishing the wicked and by favouring the virtuous, kings are constantly sanctified, just as twice-born men by sacrifices.

312. A king who desires his own welfare must always forgive litigants, infants, aged and sick men, who inveigh against him.

313. He who, being abused by men in pain, pardons (them), will in reward of that (act) be exalted in heaven; but he who, (proud) of his kingly state,

---

Nâr. and Râgh. read pratibhogam, Gov. bhûtibhogam, and Nand. prîtibhogam, but the explanation of the first two var. lect. is the same. Prîtibhoga would however denote all 'benevolences,' which usually are called prîtidâna and are levied on particular occasions.

308. Medh. and Nâr. read arakshitâram attâram, '(a king) who affords no protection, (yet) devours (his subjects and) takes, &c.'

309. Nand. reads at the end of the verse asatya*m* *k*a n*r*ipa*m* tya*g*et, 'Let him forsake a king who heeds not the rules . . . . and is untruthful.' This var. lect. is mentioned by Medh. Vipralumpakam (or °lopakam), 'rapacious,' means according to Nâr., Nand., and Râgh. 'who takes the goods of Brâhma*n*as or injures them.'

310. 'The wicked,' i.e. 'thieves, because the topic (is theft),' (Medh.).

311. 'Twice-born men,' i.e. 'Brâhma*n*as' (Medh., Nâr.).

forgives them not, will for that (reason) sink into hell.

314. A thief shall, running, approach the king, with flying hair, confessing that theft (and saying), 'Thus have I done, punish me;'

315. (And he must) carry on his shoulder a pestle, or a club of Khadira wood, or a spear sharp at both ends, or an iron staff.

316. Whether he be punished or pardoned, the thief is freed from the (guilt of) theft; but the king, if he punishes not, takes upon himself the guilt of the thief.

317. The killer of a learned Brâhma*n*a throws his guilt on him who eats his food, an adulterous wife on her (negligent) husband, a (sinning) pupil or sacrificer on (their negligent) teacher (or priest), a thief on the king (who pardons him).

318. But men who have committed crimes and have been punished by the king, go to heaven, being pure like those who performed meritorious deeds.

319. He who steals the rope or the water-pot from a well, or damages a hut where water is distri-

---

314–316. Âp. I, 25, 4–5; Gaut. XII, 43–45; Vas. XX, 41; Baudh. II, 1, 16–17; Vi. LII, 1–2; Yâg*ñ*. III, 257.

314. Medh. and Nand. read instead of dhâvatâ, 'running,' dhîmatâ, (shall approach the king) 'with firm determination.' But Medh. mentions the other reading too, the correctness of which is attested by Vas. loc. cit. According to the commentators and the parallel passages, a repentant thief is meant who has stolen gold belonging to a Brâhma*n*a; see also below, XI, 199–201.

317. Vas. XIX, 44. Medh. gives verse 317 after 318, but remarks that the order ought to be inverted. He says that a priest must leave a disobedient sacrificer; else the guilt of irregularities committed by the latter will fall upon the priest.

319. 'Damages,' i.e. 'takes away the wood belonging to it' (Nâr.).

buted, shall pay one mâsha as a fine and restore the (article abstracted or damaged) in its (proper place).

320. On him who steals more than ten kumbhas of grain corporal punishment (shall be inflicted); in other cases he shall be fined eleven times as much, and shall pay to the (owner the value of his) property.

321. So shall corporal punishment be inflicted for stealing more than a hundred (palas) of articles sold by the weight, (i. e.) of gold, silver, and so forth, and of most excellent clothes.

322. For (stealing) more than fifty (palas) it is enacted that the hands (of the offender) shall be cut off; but in other cases, let him inflict a fine of eleven times the value.

323. For stealing men of noble family and especially women and the most precious gems, (the offender) deserves corporal (or capital) punishment.

324. For stealing large animals, weapons, or medicines, let the king fix a punishment, after considering the time and the purpose (for which they were destined).

'One mâsha,' i. e. 'of copper' (Medh.), 'of gold' (Gov., Kull., Nâr., Râgh.).

320. Vi. V, 12. 'A kumbha is equal to 20 or 22 prasthas of 32 palas each' (Medh.), or 'to 20 dro*n*as of 200 palas each' (Gov., Kull., Râgh.), or 'to 200 palas' (Nâr.). Vadha*h*, 'corporal punishment,' i. e. 'flogging, mutilation, or even capital punishment, according to the quality of the person robbed' (Gov., Kull., Râgh.).

321. Vi. V, 13. According to Nâr. and Râgh., other things than gold and silver are to be understood by dharima, 'sold by the weight.' But Medh., Gov., and Kull. explain as above.

322. Vi. V, 81–82. Nâr. thinks that this rule refers to copper and the like metals of small value. But it is also possible to remove the seeming inconsistency, by explaining the term vadha*h* in the preceding verse by 'capital punishment.'

324–325. Vi. V, 77–78.

324. 'The purpose for which the object was destined,' i. e. 'whether

325. For (stealing) cows belonging to Brâhma*n*as, for piercing (the nostrils of) a barren cow, and for stealing (other) cattle (belonging to Brâhma*n*as, the offender) shall forthwith lose half his feet.

326. (For stealing) thread, cotton, drugs causing fermentation, cowdung, molasses, sour milk, sweet milk, butter-milk, water, or grass,

327. Vessels made of bamboo or other cane, salt of various kinds, earthen (vessels), earth and ashes,

328. Fish, birds, oil, clarified butter, meat, honey, and other things that come from beasts,

329. Or other things of a similar kind, spirituous liquor, boiled rice, and every kind of cooked food, the fine (shall be) twice the value (of the stolen article).

330. For flowers, green corn, shrubs, creepers, trees, and other unhusked (grain) the fine (shall be) five k*ri*sh*n*alas.

---

weapons were stolen during a combat, or medicines from a very sick man' (Medh., Gov., Râgh.).

325. Instead of the reading of the editions, '*kh*ûrikâyâ*s* *k*a bhedane,' Medh., Nâr., Râgh., Nand., and K. have 'sthûrikâyâ*s* *k*a bhedane,' which is no doubt the correct version, the vulgata being caused by a mislecture of the old form of the letter 'tha.' Kull. and Râgh. explain the phrase in the manner given above, and Gov., who reads 'nâsa[si]kâyâ*s* *k*a bhedane,' agrees with them. Medh., on the other hand, says that sthûrikâ means 'an ox' (balîvarda*h*), and the phrase must be taken 'for pricking with a goad (and using for one's purpose) the ox (of another man).' Nâr. finally asserts that sthûrikâ means 'a load placed on an ox,' and interprets the words by 'for cutting open a sack carried by an ox and abstracting its contents.'

326–331. Vi. V, 83–86.

328. 'Other things that come from beasts,' i. e. 'skins, horns, goro*k*anâ, &c.' (Gov., Nâr., Kull., Râgh.).

329. 'Other things of a similar kind,' i. e. 'red arsenic, red lead, &c.' (Gov., Kull.), or 'other eatables' (Nand.).

330. Gaut. XII, 18. Gov. reads alpeshu, 'for a little unhusked

331. For husked grain, vegetables, roots, and fruit the fine (shall be) one hundred (pa*n*as) if there is no connexion (between the owner and the thief), fifty (pa*n*as) if such a connexion exists.

332. An offence (of this description), which is committed in the presence (of the owner) and with violence, will be robbery; if (it is committed) in his absence, it will be theft; likewise if (the possession of) anything is denied after it has been taken.

333. On that man who may steal (any of) the above-mentioned articles, when they are prepared for (use), let the king inflict the first (or lowest) amercement; likewise on him who may steal (a sacred) fire out of the room (in which it is kept).

334. With whatever limb a thief in any way commits (an offence) against men, even of that (the king) shall deprive him in order to prevent (a repetition of the crime).

(grain),' instead of anyeshu, 'other.' 'Five k*ri*sh*n*alas,' i. e. 'of gold' (Medh.), 'of gold or silver' (Gov., Kull., Râgh.).

331. Niranvaye, 'if there be no connexion (between the owner and the thief),' means according to Medh. either 'if there be no connexion by friendly mutual leading,' or 'if there be no connexion such as residence in the same village,' or 'if there was no watchman in the field.' Gov. and Nâr. agree with the first explanation, Kull. and Râgh. with the second; but see above, verse 198.

332. Yâg*ñ*. II, 230. Medh. and Nâr. place this verse after the next.

333. 'Prepared for use,' i.e. 'for eating' (Medh., Nâr.), or 'thread worked into cloth' (Medh., Gov., Kull., Râgh.). 'Fire,' i. e. either the sacred fire (Medh., Kull., Nâr., Râgh.), or also the common fire (Gov.). Medh. and Nand. read *s*atam, 'one hundred pa*n*as,' instead of âdyam, 'the lowest amercement,' which latter reading Medh. mentions too.

334. Pratyâde*s*âya, 'in order to prevent (a repetition of the offence),' (Gov., Kull., Râgh.. Nand.), means according to Medh. and Nâr. 'in order to deter (others).'

335. Neither a father, nor a teacher, nor a friend, nor a mother, nor a wife, nor a son, nor a domestic priest must be left unpunished by a king, if they do not keep within their duty.

336. Where another common man would be fined one kârshâpa*n*a, the king shall be fined one thousand; that is the settled rule.

337. In (a case of) theft the guilt of a *S*ûdra shall be eightfold, that of a Vai*s*ya sixteenfold, that of a Kshatriya two-and-thirtyfold,

338. That of a Brâhma*n*a sixty-fourfold, or quite a hundredfold, or (even) twice four-and-sixtyfold; (each of them) knowing the nature of the offence.

339. (The taking of) roots and of fruit from trees, of wood for a (sacrificial) fire, and of grass for feeding cows, Manu has declared (to be) no theft.

340. A Brâhma*n*a, seeking to obtain property from a man who took what was not given to him, either by sacrificing for him or by teaching him, is even like a thief.

341. A twice-born man, who is travelling and whose provisions are exhausted, shall not be fined, if he takes two stalks of sugar-cane or two (esculent) roots from the field of another man.

---

335. Yâ*gñ*. I, 357.

336. The king shall throw the money, due as a fine for an offence he may have committed, into the water or give it to Brâhma*n*as (Medh., Gov., Kull.), in accordance with IX, 245.

337–338. Gaut. XII, 15–17.

337. 'The guilt' means of course that the offender has to pay a fine in proportion.

339. Âp. I, 28, 3; Gaut. XII, 28; Yâ*gñ*. II, 166. According to Medh., Gov., Kull., Nâr., and Râgh., the condition is that the things taken were unenclosed.

341. Gaut. XII, 49–50; see also below, IX, 239, 241.

342. He who ties up unbound or sets free tied up (cattle of other men), he who takes a slave, a horse, or a carriage will have incurred the guilt of a thief.

343. A king who punishes thieves according to these rules, will gain fame in this world and after death unsurpassable bliss.

344. A king who desires to gain the throne of Indra and imperishable eternal fame, shall not, even for a moment, neglect (to punish) the man who commits violence.

345. He who commits violence must be considered as the worst offender, (more wicked) than a defamer, than a thief, and than he who injures (another) with a staff.

346. But that king who pardons the perpetrator of violence quickly perishes and incurs hatred.

347. Neither for friendship's sake, nor for the sake of great lucre, must a king let go perpetrators of violence, who cause terror to all creatures.

348. Twice-born men may take up arms when (they are) hindered (in the fulfilment of) their duties, when destruction (threatens) the twice-born castes (var*n*a) in (evil) times,

---

342. 'Takes a slave, &c.,' i. e. 'makes them do his work' (Nâr.). The other commentators think of actual theft.

344. Sâhasa, 'violence,' comprises according to Medh. robbery (see also above, verse 332), rape, arson, cutting clothes, or forcibly destroying property.

348–351. Gaut. VII, 25; Vas. III, 15–18, 24; Baudh. I, 18–23; Vi. V, 189–192.

348. I. e. when robbers and so forth do not allow the twice-born to offer sacrifices or to fulfil other sacred duties (Medh.), or when in times of a foreign invasion (Gov., Kull., Nâr., Râgh.), or of a famine (Nâr.), the twice-born castes are threatened by an improper intermixture (sa*m*kara).

349. In their own defence, in a strife for the fees of officiating priests, and in order to protect women and Brâhma*n*as; he who (under such circumstances) kills in the cause of right, commits no sin.

350. One may slay without hesitation an assassin who approaches (with murderous intent), whether (he be one's) teacher, a child or an aged man, or a Brâhma*n*a deeply versed in the Vedas.

351. By killing an assassin the slayer incurs no guilt, whether (he does it) publicly or secretly; in that case fury recoils upon fury.

352. Men who commit adultery with the wives of others, the king shall cause to be marked by punishments which cause terror, and afterwards banish.

353. For by (adultery) is caused a mixture of the castes (var*n*a) among men; thence (follows) sin, which cuts up even the roots and causes the destruction of everything.

354. A man formerly accused of (such) offences, who secretly converses with another man's wife, shall pay the first (or lowest) amercement.

355. But a man, not before accused, who (thus) speaks with (a woman) for some (reasonable) cause, shall not incur any guilt, since in him there is no transgression.

---

350. According to Kull. the condition is that one must be unable to save oneself by flight, according to Nâr. one must not wound such a man 'excessively.'

351. 'Secretly,' i. e. 'by incantations or spells' (Gov., Nâr., Nand.).

353. I. e. if a mixture of the castes takes place, the sacrifices cannot be offered properly, because duly qualified sacrificers are wanting. If sacrifices are not duly offered, no rain will fall (see above, III, 76), and everything will perish (Medh., Gov., Kull., Râgh.).

354–358. Âp. II, 26, 18–19; Yâg*ñ*. II, 284.

356. He who addresses the wife of another man at a Tîrtha, outside the village, in a forest, or at the confluence of rivers, shall suffer (the punishment for) adulterous acts (sa*m*graha*n*a).

357. Offering presents (to a woman), romping (with her), touching her ornaments and dress, sitting with her on a bed, all (these acts) are considered adulterous acts (sa*m*graha*n*a).

358. If one touches a woman in a place (which ought) not (to be touched) or allows (oneself to be touched in such a spot), all (such acts done) with mutual consent are declared (to be) adulterous (sa*m*graha*n*a).

359. A man who is not a Brâhma*n*a ought to suffer death for adultery (sa*m*graha*n*a); for the wives of all the four castes even must always be carefully guarded.

360. Mendicants, bards, men who have performed the initiatory ceremony of a Vedic sacrifice, and artisans are not prohibited from speaking to married women.

---

356. 'A Tîrtha,' i. e. 'a place on the river-bank where the women fetch water' (Medh., Nâr., Râgh.). The punishment is the highest amercement (Kull.). Nand. places this verse after 357.

358. Nand. says, 'If one touches a woman in a lonely place.' Gov. also mentions this explanation.

359. According to Gov., Kull., Râgh. this rule refers to adultery committed by a *S*ûdra with a Brâhma*n*î (Râgh.) or to the violation of a Brâhma*n*î by a *S*ûdra (Gov., Kull.). Medh., too, thinks that a *S*ûdra alone is to suffer capital punishment for adultery with an Âryan woman. Nand., finally, says that Kshatriyas, Vai*s*yas, and *S*ûdras are meant, who offend with a female of a higher caste. Possibly the correct explanation of prâ*n*ânta*m* da*n*d*a*m, 'death,' may, however, be 'a punishment, even death.' This rendering at least removes all the difficulties created by the parallel passages and the following verses.

361. Let no man converse with the wives of others after he has been forbidden (to do so); but he who converses (with them), in spite of a prohibition, shall be fined one suvar*n*a.

362. This rule does not apply to the wives of actors and singers, nor (of) those who live on (the intrigues of) their own (wives); for such men send their wives (to others) or, concealing themselves, allow them to hold criminal intercourse.

363. Yet he who secretly converses with such women, or with female slaves kept by one (master), and with female ascetics, shall be compelled to pay a small fine.

364. He who violates an unwilling maiden shall instantly suffer corporal punishment; but a man who enjoys a willing maiden shall not suffer corporal punishment, if (his caste be) the same (as hers).

365. From a maiden who makes advances to a (man of) high (caste), he shall not take any fine; but her, who courts a (man of) low (caste), let him force to live confined in her house.

---

361. Yâ*gñ*. II, 285.

362. Baudh. II, 4, 3. I translate *k*âra*n*a according to the commentators by 'actors and singers,' but it may also be the name of a caste which is well known in Western India.

363. 'Female ascetics,' i. e. 'Rakshakâs (?), *S*îlamitrâs (?), and so forth' (Medh.), or 'Buddhist nuns' (Gov., Kull., Râgh.). Nâr. says 'female mendicants.' It deserves to be noted that according to a passage attributed by Gov. and Nâr. to Baudhâyana, but not found in our text, 'some' permitted even orthodox females to become ascetics. Female ascetics were probably in ancient India as common as they are now, and were considered equally disreputable.

364–368. Yâ*gñ*. II, 288.

365. 'From a maiden,' i. e. 'from her relatives or guardians' (Medh.). According to Kull. and Nâr. the girl is to be fettered, according to Medh. to be guarded by her relatives. The confinement is to last until she is cured of her attachment.

366. A (man of) low (caste) who makes love to a maiden (of) the highest (caste) shall suffer corporal punishment; he who addresses a maiden (of) equal (caste) shall pay the nuptial fee, if her father desires it.

367. But if any man through insolence forcibly contaminates a maiden, two of his fingers shall be instantly cut off, and he shall pay a fine of six hundred (pa*n*as).

368. A man (of) equal (caste) who defiles a willing maiden shall not suffer the amputation of his fingers, but shall pay a fine of two hundred (pa*n*as) in order to deter him from a repetition (of the offence).

369. A damsel who pollutes (another) damsel must be fined two hundred (pa*n*as), pay the double of her (nuptial) fee, and receive ten (lashes with a) rod.

370. But a woman who pollutes a damsel shall instantly have (her head) shaved or two fingers cut off, and be made to ride (through the town) on a donkey.

371. If a wife, proud of the greatness of her relatives or (her own) excellence, violates the duty which she owes to her lord, the king shall cause

366. The meaning of the second clause is that if the father wishes it, the offender is to marry the girl, after paying the nuptial fee (Kull., Nâr.). If the father does not wish to receive the fee, the offender is to pay an equal sum as a fine to the king (Medh., Gov., Râgh.).

370. According to Medh. and Nâr. the verse prescribes three different punishments, and a Brâhma*n*î offender is to be shaved, a Kshatriyâ to be led through the streets on a donkey, while women of other castes are to lose two fingers. According to Gov., Kull., and Râgh. the punishment is to be regulated by the circumstances.

371–372. Gaut. XXIII, 14–15; Vi. V, 18.

her to be devoured by dogs in a place frequented by many.

372. Let him cause the male offender to be burnt on a red-hot iron bed; they shall put logs under it, (until) the sinner is burned (to death).

373. On a man (once) convicted, who is (again) accused within a year, a double fine (must be inflicted); even thus (must the fine be doubled) for (repeated) intercourse with a Vrâtyâ and a *Kand*âlî.

374. A *S*ûdra who has intercourse with a woman of a twice-born caste (var*n*a), guarded or unguarded, (shall be punished in the following manner): if she was unguarded, he loses the part (offending) and all his property; if she was guarded, everything (even his life).

375. (For intercourse with a guarded Brâhma*n*î) a Vai*s*ya shall forfeit all his property after imprisonment for a year; a Kshatriya shall be fined one thousand (pa*n*as) and be shaved with the urine (of an ass).

376. If a Vai*s*ya or a Kshatriya has connexion with an unguarded Brâhma*n*î, let him fine the Vai*s*ya five hundred (pa*n*as) and the Kshatriya one thousand.

377. But even these two, if they offend with a

373. 'A Vrâtyâ,' i.e. 'the wife of an Âryan who has not been initiated' (Gov., Kull., Râgh.); see above, II, 39; or 'one not married in proper time' (Nâr. and Medh.), which latter attempts also another explanation, 'a public woman' or 'one common to several men.' The fine intended is two thousand pa*n*as (Gov., Kull., Râgh.).

374. Âp. II, 26, 20; 27, 9; Gaut. XII, 2–3; Vas. XXI, 5, 5; Baudh. II, 3, 52; Yâ*gñ*. II, 286, 294. 'Guarded,' i.e. 'by her husband or relatives' (Medh., Kull., Râgh.).

377. Âp. II, 26, 20; Vas. XXI, 2–3; Yâ*gñ*. II, 286. 'Like a *S*ûdra,' see verse 374.

Brâhmanî (not only) guarded (but the wife of an eminent man), shall be punished like a *S*ûdra or be burnt in a fire of dry grass.

378. A Brâhmana who carnally knows a guarded Brâhmanî against her will, shall be fined one thousand (panas); but he shall be made to pay five hundred, if he had connexion with a willing one.

379. Tonsure (of the head) is ordained for a Brâhmana (instead of) capital punishment; but (men of) other castes shall suffer capital punishment.

380. Let him never slay a Brâhmana, though he have committed all (possible) crimes; let him banish such an (offender), leaving all his property (to him) and (his body) unhurt.

381. No greater crime is known on earth than slaying a Brâhmana; a king, therefore, must not even conceive in his mind the thought of killing a Brâhmana.

382. If a Vaisya approaches a guarded female of the Kshatriya caste, or a Kshatriya a (guarded) Vaisya woman, they both deserve the same punishment as in the case of an unguarded Brâhmana female.

383. A Brâhmana shall be compelled to pay a fine of one thousand (panas) if he has intercourse with guarded (females of) those two (castes); for (offending with) a (guarded) *S*ûdra female a fine of one thousand (panas shall be inflicted) on a Kshatriya or a Vaisya.

384. For (intercourse with) an unguarded Kshatriyâ a fine of five hundred (panas shall fall) on a

382. According to the commentators the rule of verse 376 applies.

Vais*ya; but (for the same offence) a Kshatriya shall be shaved with the urine (of a donkey) or (pay) the same fine.

385. A Brâhma*n*a who approaches unguarded females (of the) Kshatriya or Vais*ya (castes), or a *S*ûdra female, shall be fined five hundred (pa*n*as); but (for intercourse with) a female (of the) lowest (castes), one thousand.

386. That king in whose town lives no thief, no adulterer, no defamer, no man guilty of violence, and no committer of assaults, attains the world of *S*akra (Indra).

387. The suppression of those five in his dominions secures to a king paramount sovereignty among his peers and fame in the world.

388. A sacrificer who forsakes an officiating priest, and an officiating priest who forsakes a sacrificer, (each being) able to perform his work and not contaminated (by grievous crimes), must each be fined one hundred (pa*n*as).

389. Neither a mother, nor a father, nor a wife, nor a son shall be cast off; he who casts them off, unless guilty of a crime causing loss of caste, shall be fined by the king six hundred (pa*n*as).

390. If twice-born men dispute among each other

---

385. 'A female of the lowest castes,' i.e. 'a *Kand*âlî' (Gov., Kull., Râgh.), or 'belonging to the castes of washermen, leather-workers, actors, basket-makers, fishermen, Medas, or Bhillas' (Nâr.).

386. Vi. V, 196.

388. 'An officiating priest,' i.e. 'one who has sacrificed for his family since many generations' (Gov., Nâr.).

389. Vi. V, 163; Yâ*gñ*. II, 237. 'Shall not be cast off,' i.e. 'shall not be refused maintenance or the due respect' (Medh., Gov., Kull.).

390. 'Of the orders,' i.e. 'of the four orders' (Nâr., Râgh.), or 'of the householders' (Gov., Kull.). Medh. and Nand. take âs*rama

concerning the duty of the orders, a king who desires his own welfare should not (hastily) decide (what is) the law.

391. Having shown them due honour, he should, with (the assistance of) Brâhma*n*as, first soothe them by gentle (speech) and afterwards teach them their duty.

392. A Brâhma*n*a who does not invite his next neighbour and his neighbour next but one, (though) both (be) worthy (of the honour), to a festival at which twenty Brâhma*n*as are entertained, is liable to a fine of one mâsha.

393. A *S*rotriya who does not entertain a virtuous *S*rotriya at auspicious festive rites, shall be made to pay him twice (the value of) the meal and a mâsha of gold (as a fine to the king).

394. A blind man, an idiot, (a cripple) who moves with the help of a board, a man full seventy years old, and he who confers benefits on *S*rotriyas, shall not be compelled by any (king) to pay a tax.

---

not in the sense of 'order,' but of 'hermitage,' and 'twice-born men' in the sense of 'hermits.' Nâr. explains na vibrûyât, 'shall not (hastily) decide,' by 'shall not wrongly decide by himself.'

392. Vi. V, 94; Yâ*gñ*. II, 263. 'A festival,' i.e. 'a wedding and so forth' (Medh.), or 'at which a dinner is given' (Nand.). Anuve*s*ya, 'his next neighbour but one' (Kull., Nâr., Râgh.), means according to Medh., Gov., and Nand. 'he who lives at the back of his house,' while the neighbour living opposite is the prâtive*s*ya. 'Twenty,' i.e. 'twenty or more other Brâhma*n*as' (Gov.). 'A mâsha,' i.e. 'of silver' (Gov., Kull., Râgh.), or 'of gold' (Medh., Nâr.).

393. 'A virtuous *S*rotriya,' i.e. 'a neighbour' (Gov., Kull., Râgh.), or 'living in the same village' (Nâr.). Medh. says, 'one who is not a neighbour.'

394. Âp. II, 26, 10–15; Vas. XIX, 23–24. '(A cripple) who moves with the help of a board' is not an uncommon sight in the streets of Indian towns. 'By any (king),' i.e. 'even by one whose treasury is empty.'

395. Let the king always treat kindly a *S*rotriya, a sick or distressed man, an infant and an aged or an indigent man, a man of high birth, and an honourable man (Ârya).

396. A washerman shall wash (the clothes of his employers) gently on a smooth board of *S*âlmalî-wood; he shall not return the clothes (of one person) for those (of another), nor allow anybody (but the owner) to wear them.

397. A weaver (who has received) ten palas (of thread), shall return (cloth weighing) one pala more; he who acts differently shall be compelled to pay a fine of twelve (pa*n*as).

398. Let the king take one-twentieth of that (amount) which men, well acquainted with the settlement of tolls and duties (and) skilful in (estimating the value of) all kinds of merchandise, may fix as the value for each saleable commodity.

399. Let the king confiscate the whole property of (a trader) who out of greed exports goods of which the king has a monopoly or (the export of which is) forbidden.

---

396. Yâ*gñ*. II, 238. *S*âlmalî, or cotton-tree wood, is naturally soft (Medh.).

397. Yâ*gñ*. II, 179. Instead of 'twelve (pa*n*as),' (Kull., Râgh.), Medh. proposes 'twelve (palas),' Gov. 'twelve (times the value of the thread),' and Nâr. 'one-twelfth (of the value of the thread).' Nand. reads da*s*aphalam and ekaphalâdhikam, and says that the weaver is to pay to the king the profit of each eleventh piece of work which he performs.

398. Yâ*gñ*. II, 261. Instead of 'of that (amount),' (Medh., Nâr.), Gov., Kull., and Râgh. say 'of the profit on that.'

399. Yâ*gñ*. II, 261. Medh. gives as instances of monopolies, elephants; in Ka*s*mîr, saffron; in the east, fine cloth and wool; in the west, horses; in the south, precious stones and pearls. Saffron is still a royal monopoly in Ka*s*mîr.

400. He who avoids a custom-house (or a toll), he who buys or sells at an improper time, or he who makes a false statement in enumerating (his goods), shall be fined eight times (the amount of duty) which he tried to evade.

401. Let (the king) fix (the rates for) the purchase and sale of all marketable goods, having (duly) considered whence they come, whither they go, how long they have been kept, the (probable) profit and the (probable) outlay.

402. Once in five nights, or at the close of each fortnight, let the king publicly settle the prices for the (merchants).

403. All weights and measures must be duly marked, and once in six months let him re-examine them.

404. At a ferry an (empty) cart shall be made to pay one pa*n*a, a man's (load) half a pa*n*a, an animal and a woman one quarter of a (pa*n*a), an unloaded man one-half of a quarter.

405. Carts (laden) with vessels full (of merchandise) shall be made to pay toll at a ferry according to the value (of the goods), empty vessels and men without luggage some trifle.

---

400. Yâ*gñ*. II, 262. 'At an improper time,' i.e. 'at night and so forth' (Medh., Gov., Nâr., Kull., Râgh.).

402. Yâ*gñ*. II, 251. Gov. and Kull. say, 'let the king settle the price in the presence of those (experts,' see verse 398). The translation follows Râgh. The length of the periods depends thereon, whether the goods vary much in price. Medh. omits this and the next four verses.

403. Vas. XIX, 13.

405. 'Empty vessels,' i.e. such as serve for the transport of merchandise, jars, leather-bags, baskets, &c. Apari*kkh*adâ*h*, 'men without luggage,' may also be translated 'men without attendants.' Kull. and Râgh. say, 'poor men.'

406. For a long passage the boat-hire must be proportioned to the places and times; know that this (rule refers) to (passages along) the banks of rivers; at sea there is no settled (freight).

407. But a woman who has been pregnant two months or more, an ascetic, a hermit in the forest, and Brâhma*n*as who are students of the Veda, shall not be made to pay toll at a ferry.

408. Whatever may be damaged in a boat by the fault of the boatmen, that shall be made good by the boatmen collectively, (each paying) his share.

409. This decision in suits (brought) by passengers (holds good only) in case the boatmen are culpably negligent on the water; in the case of (an accident) caused by (the will of) the gods, no fine can be (inflicted on them).

410. (The king) should order a Vai*s*ya to trade, to lend money, to cultivate the land, or to tend cattle, and a *S*ûdra to serve the twice-born castes.

411. (Some wealthy) Brâhma*n*a shall compassionately support both a Kshatriya and a Vai*s*ya, if they are distressed for a livelihood, employing them on work (which is suitable for) their (castes).

412. But a Brâhma*n*a who, because he is powerful, out of greed makes initiated (men of the) twice-born (castes) against their will do the work of slaves, shall be fined by the king six hundred (pa*n*as).

---

407. Vi. V, 132. According to Medh., heterodox monks must pay, because the word Brâhma*n*a (taken above with students) refers to all the persons mentioned.

408. 'Whatever,' i.e. 'merchandise' (Medh., Nâr.), or 'luggage' (Gov., Kull., Râgh.).

411. I.e. he shall employ a poor Kshatriya as watchman, and a Vai*s*ya as herdsman (Medh.). If he employs them in this way, he is not punishable (Gov., Kull.).

413. But a *S*ûdra, whether bought or unbought, he may compel to do servile work; for he was created by the Self-existent (Svayambhû) to be the slave of a Brâhma*n*a.

414. A *S*ûdra, though emancipated by his master, is not released from servitude; since that is innate in him, who can set him free from it?

415. There are slaves of seven kinds, (viz.) he who is made a captive under a standard, he who serves for his daily food, he who is born in the house, he who is bought and he who is given, he who is inherited from ancestors, and he who is enslaved by way of punishment.

416. A wife, a son, and a slave, these three are declared to have no property; the wealth which they earn is (acquired) for him to whom they belong.

---

413. 'Whether bought or unbought,' i. e. 'whether maintained in consideration of service or not' (Gov., Kull., Ragh.), or 'whether bought or hired' (Nâr.).

414. Medh. says that the last clause is 'an arthavâda, because further on it will be shown that a slave can be emancipated.' Kull. thinks that an emancipated *S*ûdra must still serve Brâhma*n*as or other Âryans in order to gain spiritual merit.

415. Medh. rejects the notion that a captive Kshatriya can be made a slave, and thinks that a captured *S*ûdra must be meant; but see Yâ*gñ*. II, 183, where it is laid down that Kshatriyas may become the slaves of Brâhma*n*as and Vai*s*yas of Brâhma*n*as and Kshatriyas. Nâr. explains dhva*g*âh*ri*ta*h*, 'one made a captive under a standard,' by 'one who has become a slave by marrying a female slave.' 'Enslaved by way of punishment,' i. e. 'because he cannot pay a debt or a fine' (Medh., Gov., Kull., Râgh.), or 'also because he left a religious order' (see Vi. V, 152), (Nâr., Nand.)

416. According to Medh., Gov., Kull., Râgh., the verse means only that these persons are unable to dispose of their property independently. Nâr.'s short note (adhiga*kkh*a*m*ti parakarmakara*n*âdinâ) seems to indicate that he took it to refer to their incapacity to earn money by working for others.

417. A Brâhma*n*a may confidently seize the goods of (his) *S*ûdra (slave); for, as that (slave) can have no property, his master may take his possessions.

418. (The king) should carefully compel Vai*s*yas and *S*ûdras to perform the work (prescribed) for them; for if these two (castes) swerved from their duties, they would throw this (whole) world into confusion.

419. Let him daily look after the completion of his undertakings, his beasts of burden, and carriages, (the collection of) his revenues and the disbursements, his mines and his treasury.

420. A king who thus brings to a conclusion all the legal business enumerated above, and removes all sin, reaches the highest state (of bliss).

CHAPTER IX.

1. I will now propound the eternal laws for a husband and his wife who keep to the path of duty, whether they be united or separated.

2. Day and night women must be kept in depend-

417. 'Confidently' means according to Medh., Nâr., and Nand. 'without fearing that he commits the sin of accepting a present from a *S*ûdra.'

419. Karmântân, 'the completion of his undertakings' (Kull., Râgh.), means according to Medh., Gov., and Nand. 'the works,' i. e. 'agriculture, offices for collecting tolls and duties, and so forth' (Medh., Gov.), according to Nâr. 'the workshops, e. g. for making arms.' The last explanation is perhaps the best.

IX. 1. According to Medh., Gov., and Kull. the duties of husband and wife are placed in the section on civil and criminal law, because the king can and even is bound to enforce their observance by punishments, if either of the two raises a complaint. 'Separated,' i. e. 'when the husband is absent or dead' (Nâr., Râgh.).

2-3. Gaut. XVIII, 1; Vas. V, 1-2; Baudh. II, 3, 44-45; Vi. V, 1-2; Yâg*ñ*. I, 85.

ence by the males (of) their (families), and, if they attach themselves to sensual enjoyments, they must be kept under one's control.

3. Her father protects (her) in childhood, her husband protects (her) in youth, and her sons protect (her) in old age; a woman is never fit for independence.

4. Reprehensible is the father who gives not (his daughter in marriage) at the proper time; reprehensible is the husband who approaches not (his wife in due season), and reprehensible is the son who does not protect his mother after her husband has died.

5. Women must particularly be guarded against evil inclinations, however trifling (they may appear); for, if they are not guarded, they will bring sorrow on two families.

6. Considering that the highest duty of all castes, even weak husbands (must) strive to guard their wives.

7. He who carefully guards his wife, preserves (the purity of) his offspring, virtuous conduct, his family, himself, and his (means of acquiring) merit.

---

2. 'Must be kept under one's control,' i. e. 'they must be restrained from their vicious attachment' (âtmano va*s*e sthâpyâ yathâ na sa*g*yante), (Nâr.)

4. Yâ*gñ*. I, 64. 'At the proper time,' i. e. before she is marriageable; see Gaut. XVIII, 21; Vas. XVII, 67–71. 'The husband,' see Baudh. IV, 1, 17–19, and above, III, 45. After this verse K. inserts another, not mentioned by the commentators, 'If the wife is guarded, the (purity of the) offspring is secured thereby; if the (purity of the) offspring is secured, oneself is secure.'

6. Yâ*gñ*. I, 81. 'Weak husbands,' i. e. 'blind, lame, or poor ones, &c.' (Kull., Râgh.).

7. 'His family,' i. e. 'his ancestors,' because legitimate sons alone can offer the *S*râddhas (Medh., Gov., Kull.), or 'his relatives,' because adultery brings dishonour (Medh., Râgh.), or 'the position of the

8. The husband, after conception by his wife, becomes an embryo and is born again of her; for that is the wifehood of a wife (*g*âyâ), that he is born (*g*âyate) again by her.

9. As the male is to whom a wife cleaves, even so is the son whom she brings forth; let him therefore carefully guard his wife, in order to keep his offspring pure.

10. No man can completely guard women by force; but they can be guarded by the employment of the (following) expedients:

11. Let the (husband) employ his (wife) in the collection and expenditure of his wealth, in keeping (everything) clean, in (the fulfilment of) religious duties, in the preparation of his food, and in looking after the household utensils.

12. Women, confined in the house under trustworthy and obedient servants, are not (well) guarded; but those who of their own accord keep guard over themselves, are well guarded.

13. Drinking (spirituous liquor), associating with wicked people, separation from the husband, rambling abroad, sleeping (at unseasonable hours), and dwelling in other men's houses, are the six causes of the ruin of women.

---

family' (Nâr.), or 'his property' (Râgh.). 'Himself,' i. e. 'because legitimate children alone can offer the *S*râddhas' (Gov., Kull., Râgh.), or 'because an adulteress and her paramour are likely to attempt his life' (Medh.). 'His (means of acquiring) merit,' i. e. 'because the husband of an adulteress is not entitled to kindle the sacred fire' (Gov., Kull., Râgh.). Nâr. says, 'his duty (as a householder).'

8. Yâ*gñ*. I, 56. The idea is taken from the Veda; see e.g. Aitareya-brâhma*n*a VII, 13, to which Kull. refers.

13. 'Associating with wicked people,' i. e. 'with other unfaithful wives' (Nâr.), or 'with adulterers' (Râgh.).

14. Women do not care for beauty, nor is their attention fixed on age; (thinking), '(It is enough that) he is a man,' they give themselves to the handsome and to the ugly.

15. Through their passion for men, through their mutable temper, through their natural heartlessness, they become disloyal towards their husbands, however carefully they may be guarded in this (world).

16. Knowing their disposition, which the Lord of creatures laid in them at the creation, to be such, (every) man should most strenuously exert himself to guard them.

17. (When creating them) Manu allotted to women (a love of their) bed, (of their) seat and (of) ornament, impure desires, wrath, dishonesty, malice, and bad conduct.

18. For women no (sacramental) rite (is performed) with sacred texts, thus the law is settled; women (who are) destitute of strength and destitute of (the knowledge of) Vedic texts, (are as impure as) falsehood (itself), that is a fixed rule.

19. And to this effect many sacred texts are sung also in the Vedas, in order to (make) fully known the true disposition (of women); hear (now those texts which refer to) the expiation of their (sins).

20. 'If my mother, going astray and unfaithful, conceived illicit desires, may my father keep that seed from me,' that is the scriptural text.

18. The sacramental rites meant are the birth-ceremony and so forth; see also above, II, 66. 'Destitute of strength' (Gov.), i. e. 'of firmness, intelligence, bodily strength, &c.' (Medh., Nand.). The second half verse is closely allied to that quoted Baudh. II, 3, 46, and, like the latter, probably a modification of a Vedic passage.

20. The verse is a slightly altered Mantra which occurs in the

21. If a woman thinks in her heart of anything that would pain her husband, the (above-mentioned text) is declared (to be a means for) completely removing such infidelity.

22. Whatever be the qualities of the man with whom a woman is united according to the law, such qualities even she assumes, like a river (united) with the ocean.

23. Akshamâlâ, a woman of the lowest birth, being united to Vasish*th*a and Sârangî, (being united) to Mandapâla, became worthy of honour.

24. These and other females of low birth have

---

*S*âṅkhâyana G*ri*hya-sûtra III, 13, and in the *K*âturmâsya portion of the Kâ*th*aka recension of the Black Ya*g*ur-veda. According to the former work it is to be recited by an Anyatrakara*n*a, 'the son of a paramour.' But the Ka*th*as prescribe its use by every sacrificer who offers a *K*âturmâsya sacrifice. Medh., Gov., and Kull. probably allude to the custom of the latter school when they say that the Mantra must be recited by every sacrificer, and that its viniyoga or destination is to be repeated at the *K*âturmâsya and at the Anvash*t*akâ-*s*râddha. Gov., Kull., Râgh., Nâr., and Nand. explain reta*h*, 'seed,' by mât*ri*ra*g*orûpa*m* skannam, and v*ri*ṅktâm, 'may he keep away,' either by bha*g*atâm (svîkarotu, Nâr., Nand.), 'may he take for himself,' or by *s*odhayatu, 'may he purify' (Gov., Kull., Râgh.). Medh. likewise knows the last explanation. But he gives also another, reta*h* pitu*h* sambandhi yad reta*h* *s*ukram, and v*ri*ṅktâm, apanudatu, which comes nearer to that given above. Nidar*s*anam, 'a scriptural text,' means according to Medh., d*ri*sh*t*ânta*h*, 'an example,' and the other commentators explain it similarly.

22. I.e. as a river becomes salt after uniting with the ocean. It must be borne in mind that, according to the Indian poets, the rivers are the wives of the ocean.

23. Akshamâlâ or Arundhatî was a *K*â*nd*âlî (Gov., Râgh.), and became, as the *S*ruti states (Râgh.), with the permission of the *Ri*shis, the wife of the sage Vasish*th*a. The story of Mandapâla is told in the Mahâbhârata I, 8335 seq. (Adhy. 229). Medh., Gov., and K. read *S*ârṅgî instead of *S*ârangî or Sârangî.

attained eminence in this world by the respective good qualities of their husbands.

25. Thus has been declared the ever pure popular usage (which regulates the relations) between husband and wife; hear (next) the laws concerning children which are the cause of happiness in this world and after death.

26. Between wives (striya*h*) who (are destined) to bear children, who secure many blessings, who are worthy of worship and irradiate (their) dwellings, and between the goddesses of fortune (*s*riya*h*, who reside) in the houses (of men), there is no difference whatsoever.

27. The production of children, the nurture of those born, and the daily life of men, (of these matters) woman is visibly the cause.

28. Offspring, (the due performance of) religious rites, faithful service, highest conjugal happiness and heavenly bliss for the ancestors and oneself, depend on one's wife alone.

29. She who, controlling her thoughts, speech, and acts, violates not her duty towards her lord, dwells with him (after death) in heaven, and in this world is called by the virtuous a faithful (wife, sâdhvî).

30. But for disloyalty to her husband a wife is censured among men, and (in her next life) she is born in the womb of a jackal and tormented by diseases, the punishment of her sin.

27. Instead of pratyaham, 'the daily (life of men),' Medh. and Nâr. read pratyartham, '(the life of men) in all its details,' and Gov. prîtyartham, 'the friendly intercourse of men,' because he who has no wife cannot entertain others (Gov., Kull., Râgh.). Medh. mentions also another reading, pratyardham.

29. Identical with V, 165.

30. Vas. XXI, 14; see also above, V, 164.

31. Listen (now) to the following holy discussion, salutary to all men, which the virtuous (of the present day) and the ancient great sages have held concerning male offspring.

32. They (all) say that the male issue (of a woman) belongs to the lord, but with respect to the (meaning of the term) lord the revealed texts differ; some call the begetter (of the child the lord), others declare (that it is) the owner of the soil.

33. By the sacred tradition the woman is declared to be the soil, the man is declared to be the seed; the production of all corporeal beings (takes place) through the union of the soil with the seed.

34. In some cases the seed is more distinguished, and in some the womb of the female; but when both are equal, the offspring is most highly esteemed.

35. On comparing the seed and the receptacle (of the seed), the seed is declared to be more important; for the offspring of all created beings is marked by the characteristics of the seed.

36. Whatever (kind of) seed is sown in a field, prepared in due season, (a plant) of that same kind,

32. Âp. II, 13, 6–7; Gaut. XVIII, 9–14; Vas. XVII, 6–9, 63–64. Thus Gov., Kull., Râgh., and Nand. But Medh., Nâr., and K. (prima manu) read kartari instead of bhartari, and with this reading the verse has to be translated as follows: 'They (all) declare that a (lawfully begotten) son belongs to the husband, but with respect to the begetter (of a child on another's wife) there is a conflict between the revealed texts; some declare the begetter (to be the owner of the son), others that (he belongs to the) owner of the soil.'

34. The commentators point out the cases of Vyâsa and *Ri*shya*s*riṅga as instances of the truth of the first proposition, and of Dh*ri*tarâsh*t*ra and other Kshetra*g*as as instances of the second. 'Equal,' i. e. 'belonging to the same owner and to the same class' (Medh.).

marked with the peculiar qualities of the seed, springs up in it.

37. This earth, indeed, is called the primeval womb of created beings; but the seed develops not in its development any properties of the womb.

38. In this world seeds of different kinds, sown at the proper time in the land, even in one field, come forth (each) according to its kind.

39. The rice (called) vrîhi and (that called) *s*âli, mudga-beans, sesamum, mâsha-beans, barley, leeks, and sugar-cane, (all) spring up according to their seed.

40. That one (plant) should be sown and another be produced cannot happen; whatever seed is sown, (a plant of) that kind even comes forth.

41. Never therefore must a prudent well-trained man, who knows the Veda and its Aṅgas and desires long life, cohabit with another's wife.

42. With respect to this (matter), those acquainted with the past recite some stanzas, sung by Vâyu (the Wind, to show) that seed must not be sown by (any) man on that which belongs to another.

43. As the arrow, shot by (a hunter) who afterwards hits a wounded (deer) in the wound (made by

37. 'Develops not any properties of the womb,' i. e. 'shows no properties such as being composed of earth' (Medh., Gov., Kull.).

39. Vrîhi, i.e. such rice as ripens in sixty days (shash*t*ikâ); *s*âli, i.e. 'red rice, which ripens in the cold season' (Gov., Nâr.). Mudga, i.e. Phaseolus Mungo (mûg); mâsha, i.e. Phaseolus Radiatus.

41. Vig*ñ*âna, 'the knowledge of the Aṅgas' (Kull.), means according to Medh. and Nâr., 'profane knowledge;' according to Râgh., 'the tradition.' Nand. inverts the order, and says, 'profane and sacred learning.'

43. Or, according to a second explanation offered by Medh., 'As the arrow of the hunter who hits a wounded deer is shot into the air (as it were) and becomes useless.'

another), is shot in vain, even so the seed, sown on what belongs to another, is quickly lost (to the sower).

44. (Sages) who know the past call this earth (p*ri*thivî) even the wife of P*ri*thu; they declare a field to belong to him who cleared away the timber, and a deer to him who (first) wounded it.

45. He only is a perfect man who consists (of three persons united), his wife, himself, and his offspring; thus (says the Veda), and (learned) Brâhma*n*as propound this (maxim) likewise, 'The husband is declared to be one with the wife.'

46. Neither by sale nor by repudiation is a wife released from her husband; such we know the law to be, which the Lord of creatures (Pra*g*âpati) made of old.

47. Once is the partition (of the inheritance) made, (once is) a maiden given in marriage, (and) once does (a man) say, 'I will give;' each of those three (acts is done) once only.

---

44. 'Though the earth, after she belonged to P*ri*thu, was possessed by many kings, yet she is called P*ri*thivî, or P*ri*thvî, after her first owner P*ri*thu' (Medh., Nâr.).

45. In confirmation of the first maxim the commentators adduce a passage of the Vâ*g*asaneyi-brâhma*n*a; see also Âp. II, 14, 16.

46. The meaning is that a wife, sold or repudiated by her husband, can never become the legitimate wife of another who may have bought or received her after she was repudiated (Medh.).

47. Yâ*gñ*. I, 65. 'A partition (of the inheritance),' i. e. 'one which has been made in accordance with the law, not one made unjustly' (Gov., Kull., Râgh.). Medh. mentions two other explanations: 1. 'if one of the coparceners complains afterwards that he has received too little, he is entitled only to have the particular point readjusted, not to annul the whole division;' 2. 'if after the division it appears that one of the coparceners was disqualified by bodily defects and ought not to have received a share, the portion

48. As with cows, mares, female camels, slave-girls, buffalo-cows, she-goats, and ewes, it is not the begetter (or his owner) who obtains the offspring, even thus (it is) with the wives of others.

49. Those who, having no property in a field, but possessing seed-corn, sow it in another's soil, do indeed not receive the grain of the crop which may spring up.

50. If (one man's) bull were to beget a hundred calves on another man's cows, they would belong to the owner of the cows; in vain would the bull have spent his strength.

51. Thus men who have no marital property in women, but sow their seed in the soil of others, benefit the owner of the woman; but the giver of the seed reaps no advantage.

52. If no agreement with respect to the crop has been made between the owner of the field and the owner of the seed, the benefit clearly belongs to the owner of the field; the receptacle is more important than the seed.

53. But if by a special contract (a field) is made over (to another) for sowing, then the owner of the seed and the owner of the soil are both considered in this world as sharers of the (crop).

54. If seed be carried by water or wind into

made over to him cannot be resumed by the others.' Nâr. refers the phrase 'I will give' to a verbal promise to give a girl, made without a libation of water. I read with Medh., Gov., Râgh., Nand., and K. sak*ri*t sak*ri*t, instead of satâ*m* sak*ri*t, 'those three (acts are done) once among good men.' The object of the verse is to show that a marriage is indissoluble, because a girl can be given once only (Kull., Nand.).

50. Vas. XVII, 8.

54. I read with Gov., Râgh., and K. bî*g*î, 'the owner of the

somebody's field and germinates (there), the (plant sprung from that) seed belongs even to the owner of the field, the owner of the seed does not receive the crop.

55. Know that such is the law concerning the offspring of cows, mares, slave-girls, female camels, she-goats, and ewes, as well as of females of birds and buffalo-cows.

56. Thus the comparative importance of the seed and of the womb has been declared to you; I will next propound the law (applicable) to women in times of misfortune.

57. The wife of an elder brother is for his younger (brother) the wife of a Guru; but the wife of the younger is declared (to be) the daughter-in-law of the elder.

58. An elder (brother) who approaches the wife of the younger, and a younger (brother who approaches) the wife of the elder, except in times of misfortune, both become outcasts, even though (they were duly) authorised.

59. On failure of issue (by her husband) a woman who has been authorised, may obtain, (in the) proper (manner prescribed), the desired offspring by (cohabitation with) a brother-in-law or (with some other) Sapi*nd*a (of the husband).

---

seed,' instead of vaptâ, 'the sower of the seed' (Medh., Kull., Nand.).

55. 'Such is the law,' i.e. what has been stated in verses 48–54.

56. 'In times of misfortune,' i.e. 'when there is no male offspring.'

57. Guru means here, according to Râgh., 'the father.' As the younger brother's wife is called 'the daughter-in-law' of the elder, the explanation is probably correct.

58–63. Gaut. XVIII, 4–8; Vas. XVII, 56–61; Baudh. II, 4, 9–10; Yâg*ñ*. I, 68–69.

59. A woman can be authorised by her husband, or after his

60. He (who is) appointed to (cohabit with) the widow shall (approach her) at night anointed with clarified butter and silent, (and) beget one son, by no means a second.

61. Some (sages), versed in the law, considering the purpose of the appointment not to have been attained by those two (on the birth of the first), think that a second (son) may be lawfully procreated on (such) women.

62. But when the purpose of the appointment to (cohabit with) the widow has been attained in accordance with the law, those two shall behave towards each other like a father and a daughter-in-law.

63. If those two (being thus) appointed deviate from the rule and act from carnal desire, they will both become outcasts, (as men) who defile the bed of a daughter-in-law or of a Guru.

64. By twice-born men a widow must not be appointed to (cohabit with) any other (than her husband); for they who appoint (her) to another (man), will violate the eternal law.

---

death by his relatives. 'On failure of issue,' i. e. 'of sons' (Gov., Râgh., Nand.), or 'of sons and of an appointed daughter' (Medh.). If the son born is not fit to offer the *S*râddhas, a second may be begot (Medh., Kull., Nâr.).

60. According to the commentators, the expression 'the widow' is not intended to prohibit an appointment by a diseased or impotent husband.

61. 'Because the *S*ish*t*as say, "He who has one son only, has no son"' (Medh., Gov., Kull., Râgh.).

62. 'Those two,' i.e. 'the elder brother and the female appointed.'

63. 'Those two,' i. e. 'an elder or younger brother.' 'The rule,' see verse 60. For the last clause, compare verse 57.

64–68. These verses flatly contradict the rules given in the preceding ones. But it by no means follows that they are a modern

65. In the sacred texts which refer to marriage the appointment (of widows) is nowhere mentioned, nor is the re-marriage of widows prescribed in the rules concerning marriage.

66. This practice which is reprehended by the learned of the twice-born castes as fit for cattle is said (to have occurred) even among men, while Vena ruled.

67. That chief of royal sages who formerly possessed the whole world, caused a confusion of the castes (var*n*a), his intellect being destroyed by lust.

68. Since that (time) the virtuous censure that (man) who in his folly appoints a woman, whose husband died, to (bear) children (to another man).

69. If the (future) husband of a maiden dies after troth verbally plighted, her brother-in-law shall wed her according to the following rule.

70. Having, according to the rule, espoused her (who must be) clad in white garments and be intent

addition. For the same view is expressed by Âp. II, 27, 2–6, and was held, according to Baudh. II, 3, 34, by Aupa*g*andhani. Moreover the B*ri*haspati Sm*ri*ti states expressly (Colebrooke IV, Dig. CLVII) that the contradictory statement occurred in the Mânava Dharma*s*âstra, known to its author.

65. In his commentary on verse 66 Medh. points out that in other sacred texts, Rig-veda X, 40, 2, the Niyoga is mentioned.

66. According to the epic and Paurâ*n*ic tradition Vena was the father of P*ri*thu, and a godless king, who demanded that the sacrifices should be offered to himself, not to the gods. He was, therefore, cut to pieces by the Brâhma*n*as with blades of Ku*s*a grass. But hitherto no other passage has been found where it is stated that he introduced the practice of Niyoga. Possibly the assertion of the Mânava may have grown out of the etymological import of the word vena, 'full of desire or lust.'

70. The child born by a female thus married belongs, as the commentators point out, to her deceased betrothed.

on purity, he shall approach her once in each proper season until issue (be had).

71. Let no prudent man, after giving his daughter to one (man), give her again to another; for he who gives (his daughter) whom he had before given, incurs (the guilt of) speaking falsely regarding a human being.

72. Though (a man) may have accepted a damsel in due form, he may abandon (her if she be) blemished, diseased, or deflowered, and (if she have been) given with fraud.

73. If anybody gives away a maiden possessing blemishes without declaring them, (the bridegroom) may annul that (contract) with the evil-minded giver.

74. A man who has business (abroad) may depart after securing a maintenance for his wife; for a wife, even though virtuous, may be corrupted if she be distressed by want of subsistence.

75. If (the husband) went on a journey after providing (for her), the wife shall subject herself to restraints in her daily life; but if he departed without providing (for her), she may subsist by blameless manual work.

---

71. Yâ*gñ*. I, 65; Vi. XXV, 9–10. Regarding the guilt incurred, see above, VIII, 98. Medh. and Nand. say that the verse is meant to forbid the marriage of a girl whose betrothed died. But Kull. thinks that it refers to all cases where a betrothal has taken place, and that it removes a doubt which might arise through a too strict interpretation of VIII, 227.

72. 'In due form,' i. e. 'with a libation of water and in the presence of Brâhma*n*as' (Medh., Kull., Râgh.). 'Blemished,' i. e. 'by evil bodily marks' (Medh., Kull., Râgh., Nand.), or 'by being of a base family' (Nâr.).

73. See above, VIII, 205, 224.

74. Nand. inserts verses 95–96 after this.

75. Yâ*gñ*. I, 84. 'Shall subject herself to restraints in her daily

76. If the husband went abroad for some sacred duty, (she) must wait for him eight years, if (he went) to (acquire) learning or fame six (years), if (he went) for pleasure three years.

77. For one year let a husband bear with a wife who hates him; but after (the lapse of) a year let him deprive her of her property and cease to cohabit with her.

78. She who shows disrespect to (a husband) who is addicted to (some evil) passion, is a drunkard, or diseased, shall be deserted for three months (and be) deprived of her ornaments and furniture.

79. But she who shows aversion towards a mad or outcast (husband), a eunuch, one destitute of manly strength, or one afflicted with such diseases as punish crimes, shall neither be cast off nor be deprived of her property.

80. She who drinks spirituous liquor, is of bad

---

life,' i.e. 'shall not adorn herself, nor visit the houses of strangers, or go to festivals' (Medh., Kull., Râgh.).

76. Gaut. XVIII, 15, 17; Vas. XVII, 75–80. Kull., Nâr., and Râgh. declare that after the expiration of the terms mentioned the wife shall go to seek her husband. Nand. says, 'the meaning is that no sin is committed if she afterwards takes another husband.' Medh. holds that she shall support herself, as before, by blameless occupations and remain chaste. He mentions the opinion of others, according to which she may take another husband in accordance with Nârada's and Parâsara's precepts, but rejects it. 'For pleasure,' i. e. 'in order to gain the favours of another woman whom he prefers' (Medh., Kull., Râgh.).

77. 'Her property,' i.e. 'the ornaments and other wealth given to her by himself' (Kull., Râgh., Nand.), or 'her separate property, which he may have given to her' (strîdhana, Nâr.). The commentators add that she must, however, be maintained.

78. 'Addicted to (some evil) passion,' i.e. 'to gambling and so forth' (Kull., Nâr.), or 'to avarice' (Râgh.).

80–81. Baudh. II, 4, 6; Yâgñ. I, 73.

80. 'Diseased,' i. e. 'afflicted with leprosy or the like' (Kull.);

conduct, rebellious, diseased, mischievous, or wasteful, may at any time be superseded (by another wife).

81. A barren wife may be superseded in the eighth year, she whose children (all) die in the tenth, she who bears only daughters in the eleventh, but she who is quarrelsome without delay.

82. But a sick wife who is kind (to her husband) and virtuous in her conduct, may be superseded (only) with her own consent and must never be disgraced.

83. A wife who, being superseded, in anger departs from (her husband's) house, must either be instantly confined or cast off in the presence of the family.

84. But she who, though having been forbidden, drinks spirituous liquor even at festivals, or goes to public spectacles or assemblies, shall be fined six k*ri*sh*n*alas.

85. If twice-born men wed women of their own and of other (lower castes), the seniority, honour, and habitation of those (wives) must be (settled) according to the order of the castes (var*n*a).

86. Among all (twice-born men) the wife of equal caste alone, not a wife of a different caste by any means, shall personally attend her husband and assist him in his daily sacred rites.

87. But he who foolishly causes that (duty) to be

'mischievous,' i.e. 'who beats or ill-treats her children, servants, &c.' (Medh., Nâr., Kull.).

83. 'Of the family,' i.e. 'of her own and the husband's family' (Medh.), or 'of her own family' (Kull., Nâr.).

86. Vi. XXVI, 1; Yâg*ñ*. I, 88. 'Personally attend,' i. e. 'prepare and bring his food, &c.' (Medh., Kull., Râgh.).

87. Vi. XXVI, 2. Instead of 'by the ancients' (Kull., Râgh.,

performed by another, while his wife of equal caste is alive, is declared by the ancients (to be) as (despicable) as a *Kândâla* (sprung from the) Brâhma*n*a (caste).

88. To a distinguished, handsome suitor (of) equal (caste) should (a father) give his daughter in accordance with the prescribed rule, though she have not attained (the proper age).

89. (But) the maiden, though marriageable, should rather stop in (the father's) house until death, than that he should ever give her to a man destitute of good qualities.

90. Three years let a damsel wait, though she be marriageable; but after that time let her choose for herself a bridegroom (of) equal (caste and rank).

91. If, being not given in marriage, she herself seeks a husband, she incurs no guilt, nor (does) he whom she weds.

92. A maiden who choses for herself, shall not take with her any ornaments, given by her father or her mother, or her brothers; if she carries them away, it will be theft.

93. But he who takes (to wife) a marriageable

Nand.), Medh. says, 'since olden times,' Nâr. 'in the Purâ*n*a.' Regarding the origin of the *Kând*âlas, see below, X, 12.

88–92. Gaut. XVIII, 20–23; Vas. XVII, 69–71; Baudh. IV, 1, 11–14; Vi. XXIV, 40–41; Yâ*gñ*. I, 64.

88. 'Though she have not attained (the proper age),' i.e. 'the age of eight years' (Kull., Nâr., Râgh.), or 'before she is bodily fit for marriage' (Medh., Nand.). Medh. specially objects to the first opinion, 'because men greedy of money give even an infant in marriage.'

92. I read with Medh. and Nand., steya*m* syât, instead of stenâ syât, 'she will be a thief' (Kull., Râgh., K.). Medh. mentions another reading, stena*h* syât, 'he, i.e. the bridegroom, will be a thief.'

93. Medh. says that this verse, according to 'some,' does not belong to Manu (ke*k*id âhu*h* amânavo 'ya*m* *s*loka*h*).

damsel, shall not pay any nuptial fee to her father; for the (latter) will lose his dominion over her in consequence of his preventing (the legitimate result of the appearance of) her menses.

94. A man, aged thirty years, shall marry a maiden of twelve who pleases him, or a man of twenty-four a girl eight years of age; if (the performance of) his duties would (otherwise) be impeded, (he must marry) sooner.

95. The husband receives his wife from the gods, (he does not wed her) according to his own will; doing what is agreeable to the gods, he must always support her (while she is) faithful.

96. To be mothers were women created, and to be fathers men; religious rites, therefore, are ordained in the Veda to be performed (by the husband) together with the wife.

97. If, after the nuptial fee has been paid for a maiden, the giver of the fee dies, she shall be given in marriage to his brother, in case she consents.

---

94. Medh. and Kull. point out that this verse is not intended to lay down a hard and fast rule, but merely to give instances of suitable ages. 'If (the performance of) his duties would be impeded, &c.,' i. e. 'if he has finished his studentship earlier, he must marry at once in order to be able to fulfil his duties as a householder' (Kull., Nâr., Râgh.).

95. 'From the gods,' i. e. 'from those mentioned in the Mantras recited at the wedding, e. g. from Bhaga, Aryaman, Savit*ri*, &c.' (Kull., Râgh.), or 'from Agni' (Nâr.), or 'from Soma, the Gandharva, and Agni' (Medh., Nand.). Medh. reads vindetâni*kkh*ayâ, 'shall wed without a wish on his part,' but mentions the other reading, vindate ne*kkh*ayâ, too. According to Medh., Kull., and Râgh., a faithful wife must be supported, even if she does not love her husband.

97. 'His brother,' i. e. 'his full brother, who is even (as) the deceased himself' (Nâr.). Regarding the nuptial fee, and the

98. Even a *S*ûdra ought not to take a nuptial fee, when he gives away his daughter; for he who takes a fee sells his daughter, covering (the transaction by another name).

99. Neither ancients nor moderns who were good men have done such (a deed) that, after promising (a daughter) to one man, they gave her to another;

100. Nor, indeed, have we heard, even in former creations, of such (a thing as) the covert sale of a daughter for a fixed price, called a nuptial fee.

101. 'Let mutual fidelity continue until death,' this may be considered as the summary of the highest law for husband and wife.

102. Let man and woman, united in marriage, constantly exert themselves, that (they may not be) disunited (and) may not violate their mutual fidelity.

103. Thus has been declared to you the law for a husband and his wife, which is intimately connected with conjugal happiness, and the manner of raising offspring in times of calamity; learn (now the law concerning) the division of the inheritance.

104. After the death of the father and of the mother, the brothers, being assembled, may divide among themselves in equal shares the paternal (and the maternal) estate; for, they have no power (over it) while the parents live.

---

contradiction between this and the next verses, see note on VIII, 204.

99. Nand. places this verse after the next.

104. Gaut. XXVIII, 1; Baudh. II, 3, 8; Yâ*gñ*. II, 117. The father's estate is to be divided after the father's death, and the mother's estate after the mother's death (Kull., Nâr., Râgh., Nand.). The mother's estate devolves on the sons only on failure of daughters (Nâr.). The word ûrdhvam, 'after,' indicates by implication that the rule holds good in the case of the (father's)

105. (Or) the eldest alone may take the whole paternal estate, the others shall live under him just as (they lived) under their father.

106. Immediately on the birth of his first-born a man is (called) the father of a son and is freed from the debt to the manes; that (son), therefore, is worthy (to receive) the whole estate.

107. That son alone on whom he throws his debt and through whom he obtains immortality, is begotten for (the fulfilment of) the law; all the rest they consider the offspring of desire.

108. As a father (supports) his sons, so let the eldest support his younger brothers, and let them also in accordance with the law behave towards their eldest brother as sons (behave towards their father).

109. The eldest (son) makes the family prosperous or, on the contrary, brings it to ruin; the eldest (is considered) among men most worthy of honour, the eldest is not treated with disrespect by the virtuous.

110. If the eldest brother behaves as an eldest brother (ought to do), he (must be treated) like a

---

turning ascetic (Râgh.). The equal division takes place if the eldest does not desire to receive an additional share (Kull.). The last clause shows that a division of the property may take place with the parents' permission during their lifetime (Kull., Nâr., Râgh.).

105. Gaut. XXVIII, 3; Baudh. II, 3, 13. I. e. if the eldest son is virtuous (Kull., Râgh.), or possesses particularly eminent qualities, while the others are less distinguished (Nâr.).

106. Regarding the debt, see Vas. XI, 48.

107. This verse alludes to the Vedic text quoted, Vas. XVII, 1; Vi. XV, 45.

108. I. e. if they make no division and the eldest takes the whole estate (Kull.). Nand. places this verse after the next.

110. 'Behaves as an eldest brother (ought to do),' i. e. 'duly protects and educates the younger ones' (Medh., Kull., Nâr., Râgh.).

mother and like a father; but if he behaves in a manner unworthy of an eldest brother, he should yet be honoured like a kinsman.

111. Either let them thus live together, or apart, if (each) desires (to gain) spiritual merit; for (by their living) separate (their) merit increases, hence separation is meritorious.

112. The additional share (deducted) for the eldest shall be one-twentieth (of the estate) and the best of all chattels, for the middlemost half of that, but for the youngest one-fourth.

113. Both the eldest and the youngest shall take (their shares) according to (the rule just) stated; (each of) those who are between the eldest and the youngest, shall have the share (prescribed for the) middlemost.

114. Among the goods of every kind the eldest shall take the best (article), and (even a single chattel) which is particularly good, as well as the best of ten (animals).

'Like a kinsman,' i.e. 'like a maternal or paternal uncle' (Medh., Kull., Râgh.); see also below, verse 213.

111. Gaut. XXVIII, 4. '(Their) merit increases,' i.e. 'each of them has to kindle the sacred fire, to offer separately the Agnihotra, the five great sacrifices and so forth, and hence each gains separately merit' (Medh., Kull.).

112. Gaut. XXVIII, 5–7; Baudh. II, 3, 9; Vi. XVIII, 37; Yâgñ. II, 114. 'The remainder shall be divided equally,' see verse 116 (Medh., Kull., Nâr., Râgh.). Medh. says that 'some' declare that the rules on the unequal partition refer to past times, and have no authority for the Kaliyuga. But he rejects this view.

113. The object of the verse is to show that no difference shall be made between sons intervening between the eldest and the youngest, however great their number may be (Kull., Râgh.).

114. Gaut. XXVIII, 11–13; Baudh. II, 3, 6. '(Even a single chattel) which is particularly good,' i.e. 'a dress or an ornament' (Medh.), or 'something impartible like an idol' (Nand.).

115. But among (brothers) equally skilled in their occupations, there is no additional share, (consisting of the best animal) among ten; some trifle only shall be given to the eldest as a token of respect.

116. If additional shares are thus deducted, one must allot equal shares (out of the residue to each); but if no deduction is made, the allotment of the shares among them shall be (made) in the following manner.

117. Let the eldest son take one share in excess, the (brother) born next after him one (share) and a half, the younger ones one share each; thus the law is settled.

118. But to the maiden (sisters) the brothers shall severally give (portions) out of their shares, each out of his share one-fourth part; those who refuse to give (it), will become outcasts.

'The best of ten animals,' thus Kull., Nâr., Râgh., according to Gaut. XXVIII, 12, where they read da*s*ata*h* pa*s*ûnâm, instead of da*s*atam. Medh. gives the same explanation, but applies the rule also to clothes and ornaments. He adds, that 'others' explain the text in accordance with Vas. XVII, 43, 'And a tithe (of the cattle and horses).' Nand. nearly agrees with Medh.'s opinion, as he says that everything shall be divided into ten shares, and the eldest shall take one in excess. All the commentators agree that this additional share belongs to an eldest brother only, if he is endowed with particularly good qualities and the rest are inferior to him.

115. Âp. II, 13, 13. 'Their occupations,' i. e. 'reciting the Veda and so forth' (Kull., Râgh.). According to Nâr., the phrase 'no additional share (consisting of the best animals) among ten' indicates that none of the other additions, mentioned in verse 114, shall be given. Nand. omits this verse.

116. Gaut. XXVIII, 8.

117. Gaut. XXVIII, 9–10; Vas. XVII, 42. 'One share in excess,' i. e. 'two shares' (Medh., Kull., Nâr., Râgh., Nand.). The latter four point out that this division is to be made when the eldest and the second brothers are more eminent than the rest.

118. Vi. XVIII, 35; Yâg*ñ*. II, 124. According to all the com-

119. Let him never divide (the value of) a single goat or sheep, or a (single beast) with uncloven hoofs; it is prescribed (that) a single goat or sheep (remaining after an equal division, belongs) to the eldest alone.

120. If a younger brother begets a son on the wife of the elder, the division must then be made equally; thus the law is settled.

---

mentators the meaning is that, if a man leaves children by wives of different castes, the brothers are to provide for the dowry of the unmarried sisters of the same caste, i.e. a Brâhma*n*a's sons by a Brâhma*n*a wife for the daughters of the latter, the sons by a Kshatriya wife for the daughters of the latter, &c. This meaning is more clearly expressed by Medh.'s reading, svâbhya*h* svâbhyas tu kanyâbha*h*, 'But the brothers shall give (portions) to the maiden (sisters), each to those of his own (caste).' Kull. adds, that the duty of providing for sisters devolves in the first instance on brothers of the full blood, and in default of such on half-brothers.

As regards the expression 'a fourth share,' Medh. says that a brother shall receive three-fourths and the sister one-fourth, and that, if there are many sisters, they shall receive one-fourth of the share of a brother of equal caste. Kull. agrees with the first part of the explanation, but adds, 'Hence it must be understood that even if there are many brothers and sisters of the same caste, but born of different mothers, one-fourth part must be given to the sisters of the full blood' (i. e. by their full brothers). Nâr. says, 'They shall give each one-fourth part of their share, and take three parts; and the same division must be made if there are many daughters. But if there are many sons and one daughter, they must deduct from their several shares as much money as will be equal to a fourth part of one brother's share and give that.' Medh. censures those commentators who think that one-fourth share need not be actually given, but only as much as will suffice to defray the marriage expenses.

119. I. e. such an animal is not to be sold and the proceeds to be divided; nor shall its value be made good to the other brothers by giving them other objects (Medh.. Kull., Nâr., Râgh.).

120. I. e. the Kshetra*g*a receives no preferential share, as his father would have done. Kull. infers from this verse that, though

121. The representative (the son begotten on the wife) is not invested with the right of the principal (the eldest brother to an additional share); the principal (became) a father on the procreation (of a son by his younger brother); hence one should give a share to the (son begotten on the wife of the elder brother) according to the rule (stated above).

122. If there be a doubt, how the division shall be made, in case the younger son is born of the elder wife and the elder son of the younger wife,

123. (Then the son) born of the first wife shall

---

above, verse 104, brothers (i.e. sons of the deceased) only are named, grandsons inherit, also according to Manu, just like sons and with sons; see also below, verse 186.

121. Thus Kull.; Nand. agrees with respect to the first half-verse, but explains the second as follows, 'The father is the principal in the procreation of children; hence one must give a share to the (son begotten on the wife of the eldest) according to the law (declared above).' Nâr. also differs, 'The subsidiary (son) does not by law take the place of the principal, (and cannot for that reason receive an additional share); his father (the eldest was) the principal for continuing the line; hence one should give a share (to his subsidiary son) in accordance with the law.' Râgh. goes off still further, 'The principal (the eldest) must according to the law not be treated like the substitute (i.e. not be deprived of an additional share, yet as) the father is the chief person in the procreation (of children), one should give a share to the (son of the wife) in accordance with the law (applicable to his real father).' Medh. has a similar explanation, '(To say) that the substitute (i.e. the Kshetraga) is equal to the principal is not proper according to the sacred law; the father (i.e. the begetter) is the principal in the procreation of children, hence one must give a share (to the Kshetraga) in accordance (with the law declared above).'

122. The point to be decided is, if the seniority is to be according to the mothers or according to actual birth. The eldest wife is, of course, the one married first.

123. Gaut. XXVIII, 14.

take as his additional share one (most excellent) bull; the next best bulls (shall belong) to those (who are) inferior on account of their mothers.

124. But the eldest (son, being) born of the eldest wife, shall receive fifteen cows and a bull, the other sons may then take shares according to (the seniority of) their mothers; that is a settled rule.

125. Between sons born of wives equal (in caste) (and) without (any other) distinction no seniority in right of the mother exists; seniority is declared (to be) according to birth.

126. And with respect to the Subrahma*n*yâ (texts) also it is recorded that the invocation (of Indra shall be made) by the first-born, of twins likewise, (conceived at one time) in the wombs (of their mothers) the seniority is declared (to depend) on (actual) birth.

---

124. Gaut. XXVIII, 15. 'May take shares,' i. e. 'may divide the (other) cows' (Medh., Kull.), or 'shall each receive one bull, a very good one, a less excellent one, in due order, according to the seniority of their mothers' (Nâr.).

125. As this verse and the following one contradict the rules given in verses 123–124, the commentators try to reconcile them in various ways. Medh. thinks that verses 123–124 are an arthavâda and have no legal force, and Râgh. inclines to the same opinion. Nâr. and Nand. hold that the seniority according to the mother's marriage is of importance for the law of inheritance (verses 123–124), but that it has no value with respect to salutations and the like or to prerogatives at sacrifices (verses 125–126). Kull., finally relying on Gov.'s opinion, thinks that the rules leave an option, and that their application depends on the existence of good qualities and the want of such. It is, however, probable that, according to the custom of Hindu writers, the two conflicting opinions are placed side by side, and that it is intended that the learned should find their way out of the difficulty as they can.

126. The Subrahma*n*yâ texts contain an invitation, addressed to Indra, to partake of the Soma; see Aitareya-brâhma*n*a VI, 3. Nand. reads yamayo*s* *k*aikagarbhe 'pi.

127. He who has no son may make his daughter in the following manner an appointed daughter (putrikâ, saying to her husband), 'The (male) child, born of her, shall perform my funeral rites.'

128. According to this rule Daksha, himself, lord of created beings, formerly made (all his female offspring) appointed daughters in order to multiply his race.

129. He gave ten to Dharma, thirteen to Kasyapa, twenty-seven to King Soma, honouring (them) with an affectionate heart.

130. A son is even (as) oneself, (such) a daughter is equal to a son; how can another (heir) take the estate, while such (an appointed daughter who is even) oneself, lives?

131. But whatever may be the separate property of the mother, that is the share of the unmarried daughter alone; and the son of an (appointed) daughter shall take the whole estate of (his maternal grandfather) who leaves no son.

---

127. Gaut. XXVIII, 18; Vas. XVII, 17; Baudh. II, 3, 15; Vi. XV, 5.

128. The story of Daksha's fifty, sixty, or twenty-four daughters occurs in the Mahâbhârata and the Purâ*n*as. The twenty-seven given to King Soma, the moon, are the lunar mansions or Nakshatras.

130. 'A son is even (as) oneself;' see the verse quoted, Baudh. II, 3, 14. The commentators state that the word duhitâ, 'daughter,' means here putrikâ, 'an appointed daughter.' Medh. adds that in accordance with this verse, an appointed daughter who has no son, when her father dies, does not inherit his property (?).

131. Gaut. XXVIII, 24; Vi. XVII, 21. The correctness of the translation of the term yautakam by 'separate property' (Medh.), follows from its being used below, verse 214, to denote the separate hoard made by an elder brother. According to Medh., Kull., and Nâr. all strîdhana is meant; according to 'others' mentioned by Medh., Nand., and Râgh., the so-called saudâyikam or property derived from the

132. The son of an (appointed) daughter, indeed, shall (also) take the estate of his (own) father, who leaves no (other) son; he shall (then) present two funeral cakes to his own father and to his maternal grandfather.

133. Between a son's son and the son of an (appointed) daughter there is no difference, neither with respect to worldly matters nor to sacred duties; for their father and mother both sprang from the body of the same (man).

134. But if, after a daughter has been appointed, a son be born (to her father), the division (of the inheritance) must in that (case) be equal; for there is no right of primogeniture for a woman.

135. But if an appointed daughter by accident dies without (leaving) a son, the husband of the appointed daughter may, without hesitation, take that estate.

---

father's family. Kumârî, 'an unmarried daughter' (Medh., Kull.), means according to Nâr. 'a daughter who has no sons.' Dauhitra*h*, literally 'the son of a daughter,' means according to the commentators 'the son of an appointed daughter,' putrikâputra*h*. The first rule is, according to Kull., Nâr., and Nand., a general maxim, which refers not merely to the case of a putrikâ. The second rule shows, according to Nand., that the appointed daughter herself does not inherit her father's estate, if she has a son.

132. Medh. mentions a var. lect., aputrasya hared yadi, 'If the son of an (appointed) daughter takes the entire estate of (his maternal grandfather), &c.,' which is also found in Gov.'s text, but considers it to be wrong.

133. Yâ*gñ*. II, 128. Loke dharmata*h*, 'neither with respect to worldly affairs nor to sacred duties' (Kull.), means according to Râgh. and Nand. 'with respect to sacred duties, according to the law.'

135. 'That estate,' i.e. 'what the appointed daughter received from her father either during his lifetime or after his death' (Nâr.). Kull. adds that the verse is intended to forbid the father's inheriting his pre-deceased daughter's property, on the plea that she was like a son (see verse 185). Nand. says that the paternal uncles &c. shall not take the putrikâ's estate.

136. Through that son whom (a daughter), either not appointed or appointed, may bear to (a husband) of equal (caste), his maternal grandfather (has) a son's son; he shall present the funeral cake and take the estate.

137. Through a son he conquers the worlds, through a son's son he obtains immortality, but through his son's grandson he gains the world of the sun.

138. Because a son delivers (trâyate) his father from the hell called Put, he was therefore called put-tra (a deliverer from Put) by the Self-existent (Svayambhû) himself.

139. Between a son's son and the son of a daughter there exists in this world no difference; for even the son of a daughter saves him (who has no sons) in the next world, like the son's son.

---

136. Kull. explains akritâ vâ kritâ vâpi by '(a daughter) either appointed not (explicitly but by a mental reservation), or appointed (explicitly, at the betrothal, according to verse 127).' He adds that Gov. takes the word akritâ in its usual sense, and asserts that the verse allows the son of a daughter not appointed to inherit his maternal grandfather's estate. The latter opinion is held also by Nâr., who remarks that the son of a daughter not appointed inherits on failure of a wife or of daughters of his grandfather; and by Nand. Râgh. and Medh. side with Kull., whose explanation is supported by Gaut. XXVIII, 20, and still more by Vi. XV, 6. The latter passage clearly prescribes that the daughter of a man who has no sons is in every case 'an appointed daughter.'

137. Vas. XVII, 5; Vi. XV, 46; Yâgñ. I, 78. 'The worlds,' i. e. 'the ten, called visoka (free from sorrow), the first of which is svarga' (Medh.). 'Immortality, i. e. a very long residence in those same (worlds),' (Medh., Kull.) 'The sun,' i. e. 'Hiranyagarbha' (Nâr.). The verse shows that sons and grandsons inherit, though a wife and the rest may be living (Kull.).

138. Vi. XV, 44.

139. Vi. XV, 47. According to Medh. and Kull., dauhitrah, 'the

140. Let the son of an appointed daughter first present a funeral cake to his mother, the second to her father, the third to his father's father.

141. Of the man who has an adopted (Datrima) son possessing all good qualities, that same (son) shall take the inheritance, though brought from another family.

142. An adopted son shall never take the family (name) and the estate of his natural father; the funeral cake follows the family (name) and the estate, the funeral offerings of him who gives (his son in adoption) cease (as far as that son is concerned).

---

son of a daughter,' means here also 'the son of an appointed daughter.' Nand. reads putravat, 'like a son;' Gov. pûrva*g*ân, '(and) the ancestors.'

140. Baudh. II, 3, 16. Medh. mentions a var. lect., pitus tasya, 'the second to his father,' which he, however, justly considers to be bad.

141. Vas. XV, 9–10; Baudh. Pari*s*ish*t*a 16. Medh., Kull., and Râgh. refer this rule to the case where a man has a legitimate son and an adopted son, and think that in such a case the latter, being eminently virtuous, shall receive, like a Kshetra*g*a (see verse 146), a fifth or sixth part of the estate. Medh. remarks that some think he is to have half, but that their opinion is improper, and finally that Upâdhyâya, i.e. his teacher, allots to the adopted son less than to the Kshetra*g*a. Kull. and Râgh. state that Gov. took the verse to mean that an eminently virtuous adopted son shall inherit on failure of a legitimate son and of the son of the wife, but that this explanation is inadmissible on account of verse 165. Nevertheless Râgh. reproduces Gov.'s opinion. Nâr. says, 'It has been declared that an adopted son receives a share like the chief son, when he is eminently virtuous.' Nand. reads at the end of the second line, samprâpto 'sya na putraka*h*, 'shall take the inheritance, (provided) the (adoptive father) has no son.'

142. Medh. mentions another 'improper' explanation, according to which haret, 'shall take,' is to mean hârayet, 'shall allow to be taken,' and the purport of the verse is that 'he is to benefit both (fathers) like a Dvyâmushyâya*n*a.'

143. The son of a wife, not appointed (to have issue by another), and he whom (an appointed female, already) the mother of a son, bears to her brother-in-law, are both unworthy of a share, (one being) the son of an adulterer and (the other) produced through (mere) lust.

144. Even the male (child) of a female (duly) appointed, not begotten according to the rule (given above), is unworthy of the paternal estate; for he was procreated by an outcast.

145. A son (legally) begotten on such an appointed female shall inherit like a legitimate son of the body; for that seed and the produce belong, according to the law, to the owner of the soil.

146. He who takes care of his deceased brother's estate and of his widow, shall, after raising up a son for his brother, give that property even to that (son).

147. If a woman (duly) appointed bears a son to her brother-in-law or to another (Sapi*nd*a), that (son, if he is) begotten through desire, they declare (to be) incapable of inheriting and to be produced in vain.

148. The rules (given above) must be understood (to apply) to a distribution among sons of women of the same (caste); hear (now the law) concerning

144. 'The rule (given above),' i. e. that given above, verse 60. Nand. omits this verse.

145. Medh. and Kull. state that the object of this verse is to teach that a Kshetra*g*a, if endowed with good qualities, may even receive (against verse 120) the additional share of an eldest son, because it is said that he inherits 'like a legitimate son.' Nâr. says, '(the expression) like a legitimate son (is used) in order to establish (the title to) an equal share.' Nand. omits this verse.

146. 'This rule refers to the case where the two brothers are divided, while verse 120 refers to those who live in union' (Medh., Kull., Râgh.). Nand. places this verse after 147.

those begotten by one man on many wives of different (castes).

149. If there be four wives of a Brâhma*n*a in the direct order of the castes, the rule for the division (of the estate) among the sons born of them is as follows:

150. The (slave) who tills (the field), the bull kept for impregnating cows, the vehicle, the ornaments, and the house shall be given as an additional portion to the Brâhma*n*a (son), and one most excellent share.

151. Let the son of the Brâhma*n*î (wife) take three shares of the (remainder of the) estate, the son of the Kshatriyâ two, the son of the Vai*s*yâ a share and a half, and the son of the *S*ûdrâ may take one share.

152. Or let him who knows the law make ten shares of the whole estate, and justly distribute them according to the following rule:

149–156. Gaut. XXVIII, 35–39; Vas. XVII, 48–50; Baudh. II, 3, 10; Vi. XVIII, 1–33, 38–40; Yâ*gñ*. II, 125.

150. 'The ornaments,' i. e. 'the ring which the father used to wear, and the like' (Medh., Kull.). 'The house,' i. e. 'the principal mansion' (Medh., Kull., Râgh.). Ekâ*ms*a*s* *k*a pradhânata*h*, 'one most excellent share' (Medh., Kull.), means according to Nâr., with whom Nand. agrees, 'and one share consisting of the chief, i. e. best property' (pradhânato mukhyadhanâd utk*ri*sh*t*âd ity artha*h*), and according to Râgh. 'and one share, because he is the chief person.' According to Nâr. this 'one share' must be equal in value to one of the three shares mentioned in the next verse.

151. Medh. and Kull. remark that the rule holds good also if there are more sons than one in each class.

152. According to Nâr. this rule refers to the case when each of the wives has several sons, while the preceding one is applicable when each wife has one son only. Râgh. thinks that the first rule shall be followed when the son of the Brâhma*n*î possesses good qualities, the second when he is destitute of them.

153. The Brâhma*n*a (son) shall take four shares, the son of the Kshatriyâ (wife) three, the son of the Vai*s*yâ shall have two parts, the son of the *S*ûdrâ may take one share.

154. Whether (a Brâhma*n*a) have sons or have no sons (by wives of the twice-born castes), the (heir) must, according to the law, give to the son of a *S*ûdra (wife) no more than a tenth (part of his estate).

155. The son of a Brâhma*n*a, a Kshatriya, and a Vai*s*ya by a *S*ûdra (wife) receives no share of the inheritance; whatever his father may give to him, that shall be his property.

156. All the sons of twice-born men, born of wives of the same caste, shall equally divide the estate, after the others have given to the eldest an additional share.

157. For a *S*ûdra is ordained a wife of his own caste only (and) no other; those born of her shall have equal shares, even if there be a hundred sons.

153. Medh. points out that according to other Sm*r*itis the Brâhma*n*a son alone receives land, given to his father, and that the *S*ûdra son receives no share in land, if there is other property.

154. Hence on failure of other sons the other heirs, the Sapi*nd*as (Medh.), or the widow and the rest (Nâr.), shall take the rest of the estate. Nâr. adds that he may obtain more than a tenth, if his father give it to him.

155. The son of a *S*ûdra wife receives no share of his father's estate in case the mother was not legally married (Medh. 'others,' Kull.), or in case he is destitute of good qualities (Kull., Râgh.). According to Medh. and Nâr., na rikthabhâk, 'receives no share of the inheritance,' means 'receives no (larger) share (than one-tenth, except if the father himself has given more to him).' But it seems more probable, that the verse is intended to inculcate the maxim that a son by a *S*ûdra wife cannot claim any fixed portion of the inheritance from his father who divides his estate.

156. Medh., Gov., and K. read vâ, 'or,' instead of ye (*g*âtâ*h*), but this gives no good sense, as Medh. remarks.

158. Among the twelve sons of men whom Manu, sprung from the Self-existent (Svayambhû), enumerates, six are kinsmen and heirs, and six not heirs, (but) kinsmen.

159. The legitimate son of the body, the son begotten on a wife, the son adopted, the son made, the son secretly born, and the son cast off, (are) the six heirs and kinsmen.

160. The son of an unmarried damsel, the son received with the wife, the son bought, the son begotten on a re-married woman, the son self-given, and the son of a *S*ûdra female, (are) the six (who are) not heirs, (but) kinsmen.

161. Whatever result a man obtains who (tries to) cross a (sheet of) water in an unsafe boat, even that result obtains he who (tries to) pass the gloom (of the next world) with (the help of) bad (substitutes for a real) son.

162. If the two heirs of one man be a legitimate

158–159. Gaut. XXVIII, 31–33; Vas. XVII, 25, 38; Baudh. II, 3, 31–32.

158. I.e. the first six inherit the family estate and offer the funeral oblations, the last six do not inherit, but offer libations of water and so forth as remoter kinsmen (Kull., Nâr., Râgh., Nand. 'some'). Medh., Nâr., and Nand. take adâyâdabândhavâ*h* to mean 'not heirs nor kinsmen.' But Kull. rightly objects that the parallel passage of Baudh. proves this explanation to be wrong. Nâr. finally interprets bandhudâyâdâ*h*, 'heirs and kinsmen,' as 'heirs to the kinsmen,' i.e. 'inheritors of the estate of kinsmen, such as paternal uncles, on failure of sons, wives, and so forth.' Nâr. and Nand., as well as Medh. in his commentary on verse 166, add that the son of an appointed daughter is not mentioned, because he has been declared above to be equal to a legitimate son.

161. Medh. mentions another explanation of the expression kuputrai*h*, 'by bad (substitutes for a real) son,' according to which 'sons of a wife or widow not duly appointed' are meant.

162. According to Medh. and Gov. (quoted by Kull. and Râgh.),

son of his body and a son begotten on his wife, each (of the two sons), to the exclusion of the other, shall take the estate of his (natural) father.

163. The legitimate son of the body alone (shall be) the owner of the paternal estate; but, in order to avoid harshness, let him allow a maintenance to the rest.

164. But when the legitimate son of the body divides the paternal estate, he shall give one-sixth or one-fifth part of his father's property to the son begotten on the wife.

---

the rule refers to the case where a legitimate son and the son of a wife not appointed both claim the inheritance. But 'others,' quoted by Medh., Kull., and Râgh., think that it applies to the case where a wife first was appointed by her husband to procreate a son with his brother, and afterwards a legitimate son was born. The difficulty which under this explanation arises with respect to verse 164, is removed by assuming that the latter applies to the case where the natural father of the Kshetra*g*a has likewise sons, while verse 162 presupposes that he has none. Nâr. and Nand. say that the case which the rule contemplates, is that two brothers were undivided, and when the one died, the other, who himself had sons, begat with the widow a Kshetra*g*a son. On the death of the second brother, the Kshetra*g*a is entitled to receive only the share of the husband of his mother, not to claim a portion of the estate of his natural father. Under this supposition the translation would be, 'If a legitimate son (of one brother) and the son of the wife (of another) have a claim to one (undivided) estate, each shall receive the share of his father.'

163–165. Vi. XV, 28–30; Yâ*gñ*. II, 132.

163. This rule refers to the case where one man leaves several substitutes for sons and a legitimate son (Medh., Kull., Nâr., Râgh.). 'To the rest,' i.e. 'to all except the son begotten on the wife' (which latter is exempted by verses 164–165; Medh., Kull., Râgh., Nand.). 'He who does not maintain them, commits sin' (Medh., Kull.); but not, if they have other means of subsistence (Nand.).

164. This rule refers to the case where a Kshetra*g*a was begotten before the legitimate son, and received no property from his natural father (Râgh.); see also Kull.'s notes on verses 162–163. According

165. The legitimate son and the son of the wife (thus) share the father's estate; but the other ten become members of the family, and inherit according to their order (each later named on failure of those named earlier).

166. Him whom a man begets on his own wedded wife, let him know to be a legitimate son of the body (Aurasa), the first in rank.

167. He who was begotten according to the peculiar law (of the Niyoga) on the appointed wife of a dead man, of a eunuch, or of one diseased, is called a son begotten on a wife (Kshetra*g*a).

168. That (boy) equal (by caste) whom his mother or his father affectionately give, (confirming the gift)

---

to Nâr. it refers, however, to the case where a man died, leaving several widows, and one was appointed to bear a son by her brother-in-law, while another afterwards proved to be pregnant and bore a legitimate son. 'The Kshetra*g*a receives one-fifth, if he is endowed with good qualities, else one-sixth' (Medh., Kull., Nâr., Râgh., Nand.).

165. Vas. XVII, 39. Gotrarikthâ*ms*abhâgina*h*, 'become members of the family (i. e. succeed to the family rights and duties) and inherit' (Medh., Kull., Nand.), may also be translated, 'share the family estate,' as Nâr. proposes. But his suggestion that the family estate is here mentioned in order to exclude them from their father's self-acquired property is doubtlessly wrong. Equally inadmissible seems another explanation, mentioned by Nâr. and Nand., according to which a*ms*abhâgina*h*, 'they share,' is to mean 'they obtain (such) a share (as will suffice for their maintenance).'

166. Âp. II, 18, 1; Vas. XVII, 13; Baudh. II, 3, 14; Vi. XV, 2; Yâ*gñ*. II, 128. I read prâthamakalpikam with Medh., Gov., Nâr., and K. Râgh. gives prathamakalpikam. Kull. and Nâr. think that the wife must be of equal caste, while Medh. says that sva means 'his own,' not 'of his own caste.' Medh. mentions Kull.'s opinion as that of 'others.'

167. Vas. XVII, 14; Baudh. II, 3, 18; Vi. XV, 3; Yâ*gñ*. I, 69, II, 127–128.

168. Vas. XVII, 29; Baudh. II, 3, 20; Vi. XV, 18–19; Yâ*gñ*.

with (a libation of) water, in times of distress (to a man) as his son, must be considered as an adopted son (Datrima).

169. But he is considered a son made (K*ri*trima) whom (a man) makes his son, (he being) equal (by caste), acquainted with (the distinctions between) right and wrong, (and) endowed with filial virtues.

170. If (a child) be born in a man's house and his father be not known, he is a son born secretly in the house (Gûdhotpanna), and shall belong to him of whose wife he was born.

171. He whom (a man) receives as his son, (after he has been) deserted by his parents or by either of them, is called a son cast off (Apaviddha).

II, 130. Sad*ri*sam, 'equal (by caste),' (Kull., Nâr., Râgh., Nand.), means according to Medh. 'equal by virtues, not by caste.' 'His mother or his father,' i. e. 'after mutually agreeing' (Kull.), 'the mother, if there is no father' (Râgh.). Medh. and Nand. read mâtâ pitâ *k*a, 'his mother and his father,' but Medh. adds that vâ is the proper reading. 'Affectionately,' i. e. 'not out of avarice' (Medh.), or 'not out of fear and so forth' (Kull., Nand.), or 'not by force or fraud' (Râgh.). 'In times of distress,' i. e. 'if the adopter has no son' (Kull., Râgh.), or 'if the adoptee's parents are in distress' (Nâr.).

169. Baudh. II, 3, 21; Yâ*gñ*. II, 131. Medh. again says, 'equal by qualities.' 'Acquainted with (the distinctions between) right and wrong,' i. e. 'by performing or not performing *S*râddhas and other sacred rites merit or sin will follow' (Kull.), or 'I am now the son of so and so, and if I do not serve him I shall become an outcast' (Râgh.), or 'not an infant' (Medh. 'some,' Nâr.). Nâr. adds that some read gu*n*adoshavi*k*aksha*n*a*h*, and refer the adjective to the adopter, who is thereby warned not to take an outcast or the like.

170. Vas. XVII, 24; Baudh. II, 3, 22; Vi. XV, 13–14; Yâ*gñ*. II, 129. According to the commentators the condition is that there is no suspicion that the wife had intercourse with a man of lower caste. Nâr. says that the case contemplated is, that a wife had intercourse with several men of equal caste.

171. Vas. XVII, 37; Baudh. II, 3, 23; Vi. XV, 24–25; Yâ*gñ*.

172. A son whom a damsel secretly bears in the house of her father, one shall name the son of an unmarried damsel (Kânîna, and declare) such offspring of an unmarried girl (to belong) to him who weds her (afterwards).

173. If one marries, either knowingly or unknowingly, a pregnant (bride), the child in her womb belongs to him who weds her, and is called (a son) received with the bride (Saho*dh*a).

174. If a man buys a (boy), whether equal or unequal (in good qualities), from his father and mother for the sake of having a son, that (child) is called a (son) bought (Krîtaka).

175. If a woman abandoned by her husband, or a widow, of her own accord contracts a second marriage and bears (a son), he is called the son of a re-married woman (Paunarbhava).

176. If she be (still) a virgin, or one who returned (to her first husband) after leaving him, she is worthy to again perform with her second (or first deserted) husband the (nuptial) ceremony.

II, 132. The reason of the desertion may be either extreme distress of the parents, or the commission of some fault on the part of the boy (Medh.). 'Provided the father of the child was of equal caste' (Nâr., Nand.).

172. Vas. XVII, 22–23; Baudh. II, 3, 24; Vi. XV, 10–11; Yâg*ñ*. II, 129. 'Provided the lover was of equal or higher caste' (Nâr.).

173. Vas. XVII, 26–27; Baudh. II, 3, 25; Vi. XV, 15–16; Yâg*ñ*. II, 131. Medh.'s commentary on verses 173–178 is missing in the I. O. copies.

174. Vas. XVII, 30–32; Baudh. II, 3, 26; Vi. XV, 20–21; Yâg*ñ*. II, 131. 'Equal or unequal,' i. e. 'by good qualities, not by caste' (Kull., Râgh.), means according to Nâr. 'whether of equal or of lower caste.'

175. Vas. XVII, 18; Baudh. II, 3, 27; Vi. XV, 7–9; Yâg*ñ*. II, 130.

176. Vas. XVII, 74. 'Hence a re-married woman, who is not a

177. He who, having lost his parents or being abandoned (by them) without (just) cause, gives himself to a (man), is called a son self-given (Svayamdatta).

178. The son whom a Brâhmana begets through lust on a *S*ûdra female is, (though) alive (pârayan), a corpse (*s*ava), and hence called a Pâra*s*ava (a living corpse).

179. A son who is (begotten) by a *S*ûdra on a female slave, or on the female slave of his slave, may, if permitted (by his father), take a share (of the inheritance); thus the law is settled.

180. These eleven, the son begotten on the wife and the rest as enumerated (above), the wise call substitutes for a son, (taken) in order (to prevent) a failure of the (funeral) ceremonies.

181. Those sons, who have been mentioned in connection with (the legitimate son of the body),

---

virgin, is unworthy of the sacrament' (Nâr.). Râgh., relying on Yâgñ. II, 130, expresses the contrary view, and thinks that the word vâ, 'or,' at the end of the first half-verse, permits the insertion of 'or not a virgin.'

177. Vas. XVII, 33–35; Baudh. II, 3, 28; Vi. XV, 22–23; Yâgñ. II, 131.

178. Vas. XVII, 38; Baudh. II, 3, 30; Vi. XV, 27. 'On a *S*ûdra-female' i. e. 'one married to him' (Kull.). The designation 'a corpse' indicates that his father derives imperfect benefits from his offerings (Kull., Nâr., Râgh.), or that he is blameable (Râgh.). The term Brâhmana includes Kshatriyas by implication (Nâr.).

179. Yâgñ. II, 133. 'A share,' i. e. 'a share equal to that of a legitimate son' (Kull.), in case the division is made in the father's lifetime, else half a share according to Yâgñ. (Medh.).

180. Kriyâlopât, 'in (order to prevent) a failure of the (funeral) ceremonies,' means according to Medh. 'in (order to prevent) a failure of the duty (to beget offspring).' Kull. mentions this explanation also. Nand. says, 'when there is no legitimateness in consequence of the absence of the action of begetting one.'

181. Âp. II, 13, 7; Baudh. II, 3, 34–35. Hence they should not

being begotten by strangers, belong (in reality) to him from whose seed they sprang, but not to the other (man who took them).

182. If among brothers, sprung from one (father), one have a son, Manu has declared them all to have male offspring through that son.

183. If among all the wives of one husband one have a son, Manu declares them all (to be) mothers of male children through that son.

184. On failure of each better (son), each next inferior (one) is worthy of the inheritance; but if there be many (of) equal (rank), they shall all share the estate.

185. Not brothers, nor fathers, (but) sons take the paternal estate; but the father shall take the inheritance of (a son) who leaves no male issue, and his brothers.

---

be taken, if there is a legitimate son (Medh.), or an appointed daughter (Kull.).

182. Vas. XVII, 10; Vi. XV, 42. Hence no subsidiary sons (Kull., Râgh.), or no Kshetra*g*as (Nâr.), are necessary in such a case. Kull. and Râgh. add that the brother will take estate and give the funeral offerings on failure of a wife, daughters, and so forth (Yâ*gñ*. II, 135).

183. Vas. XVII, 11; Vi. XV, 41. Hence no adoption or other substitution (Kull., Râgh.), or no appointment (Nâr.), shall be made in such a case.

184. 'Each better (son),' i. e. 'each earlier named among the twelve' (Kull., Nâr., Râgh., Nand.). Kull. and Râgh. add that, as the son of a *S*ûdra wife is enumerated among the twelve, and not considered like the son of Kshatriya and Vai*s*ya wives a legitimate son, he inherits only on failure of all other subsidiary sons. 'Many (of) equal rank,' i.e. 'many Paunarbhavas and so forth' (Kull., Râgh.).

185. Kull. and Râgh. insert after 'who leaves no son,' 'nor widow and daughters,' and before 'brothers,' 'who leaves no parents.' Nâr., who (as also Gov., Nand., and K.) reads eva vâ, 'or brothers,' says that the father inherits the estate of an undivided

186. To three (ancestors) water must be offered, to three the funeral cake is given, the fourth (descendant is) the giver of these (oblations), the fifth has no connection (with them).

187. Always to that (relative within three degrees) who is nearest to the (deceased) Sapi*nd*a the

son, leaving no male issue, or the brothers with his permission, and that the estate of a divided son descends to his wife, and other heirs mentioned by Yâg*ñ*. II, 135–136. All these interpolations are most probably improper, as Manu nowhere mentions the right of a wife or a daughter, not appointed, to the estate. The verse can only refer to a divided coparcener or to the separate property of an undivided one, and Manu's opinion seems to be that on failure of sons, grandsons, and great-grandsons, whose rights are indicated by verse 137, the father shall inherit, and after him the brothers.

186. 'To three,' i. e. 'to the father, the grandfather, and the great-grandfather' (Kull., Nâr., Râgh., Nand.). To these same three the cakes are offered (Kull., Râgh.). Kull. and Râgh. state that the object of the verse is to indicate the right of Kshetra*g*as and other subsidiary sons to inherit the estate of a grandfather and so forth deceased without leaving issue. Kull. adds that the right of sons and grandsons of a legitimate son is indicated by verse 137. Nand., however, thinks that the verse serves to prove the right of grandsons and great-grandsons to inherit before 'brothers and the rest.'

187. Vas. XVII, 81–82; Gaut. XXVIII, 33; Âp. II, 14, 2–3. The above translation does not fully agree with any of the explanations given by the four commentators. On philological grounds it seems to me improbable that anantara*h* sapi*nd*ât can mean anything else than 'nearest to the Sapi*nd*a,' and that this Sapi*nd*a can be anybody else than the deceased. Further, as verse 186 apparently contains a definition of the term, limiting Sapi*nd*a-relationship to three degrees, and as in the second half of verse 187 the Sakulyas, 'those belonging to the same family,' are mentioned as the next heirs, it seems certain that 'the nearest' here meant is 'the nearest Sapi*nd*a or relative within three degrees.' Practically the proposed translation is not much different from that extracted by Kull. and others by the grammatically inadmissible expedient of taking sapi*nd*ât for sapi*nd*amadhyât, 'among the Sapi*nd*as.' The correctness of the above explanation is also attested by the closely allied parallel passage of Baudhâyana I, 11, 9–13, the first Sûtra of

estate shall belong; afterwards a Sakulya shall be (the heir, then) the spiritual teacher or the pupil.

---

which corresponds to verse 186, while the other four express the same sense as verse 187. There too the term Sakulya occurs, which *G*îmûtavâhana takes to denote the three descendants beyond the great-grandson and the three ascendants beyond the great-grandfather, while others explain it as a general term, 'members of one family.' What Manu's precise acceptation of the word was cannot be said with certainty. But, as no technical definition is given by him, it will be safest to take it in its etymological and widest sense, 'the (remoter) members of the family,' and to assume that the principle of nearness to the deceased regulated the succession.

As regards the explanations of the commentators, Kull. says, 'As this general rule would be meaningless, if it were referred to the legitimate son and those other Sapi*nd*as alone, who have already been mentioned, its object must therefore be (to teach) that the wife and the rest, who have not been mentioned, shall inherit. To that Sapi*nd*a who is the nearest among the Sapi*nd*as, be he a male or a female, the estate of the deceased shall belong.' He then goes on to enumerate the heirs in the following order: 1. the legitimate son, sharing with a Kshetra*g*a (verse 164), and a virtuous adoptive son (verse 141); 2. the appointed daughter and her son; 3. the Kshetra*g*a and the other ten subsidiary sons, each on failure of the earlier named, with the proviso that the son of a *S*ûdra wife receives one-tenth of the estate only (verse 154); 4. the widow (on this point a great many passages are quoted, and Medh. is censured, because in his commentary, which is missing in the I. O. MSS., like the whole passage 182–201, he denied her right to inherit); 5. the daughter, not appointed; 6. the father and the mother; 7. full brothers; 8. sons of full brothers; 9. the paternal grandmother (verse 227); 10. any other near Sapi*nd*a, (a) of the grandfather's line, (b) of the great-grandfather's line, and so forth; 11. the Samânodakas, or relatives allied by libations of water (Kull. considering Sakulya as equivalent to Samânodaka); 12. the teacher; 13. the pupil. According to Kull. the translation should be, 'To the nearest among the Sapi*nd*as (male or female) the estate shall belong; afterwards (on failure of Sapi*nd*as) a Samânodaka shall be (the heir), next the teacher, and (then) the pupil.' Râgh. in substance agrees with this explanation, but in order to make the rule still more fully agree with Yâ*gñ*. II, 135–136, he asserts that the

188. But on failure of all (heirs) Brâhma*n*as (shall) share the estate, (who are) versed in the three Vedas, pure and self-controlled; thus the law is not violated.

Bandhus or cognates are also implied by the term Sakulya. His explanation of the first words also differs from Kull.'s, and is more in accordance with the rules of grammar, 'He who is the nearest to the Sapi*nd*a, i.e. to the legitimate son and the son of the daughter —(viz.) the five, the wife and the rest (mentioned by Yâ*gñ*. II, 135–136).' Râgh. and Kull. are clearly under the spell of Yâ*gñ*., and most improperly transfer into Manu's text the ideas of the latter. Nâr.'s short disjointed remarks are not very clear. He explains the first words by eshâ*m* madhye sapi*nd*ânâm ato tho[yo]nantaro yathâ putrasya pitâ tasya tatpitetyâdi tasya tasya taddhanam, 'Among those Sapi*nd*as the nearest to him, i.e. the father to his son, his father to him, and so forth; always to him that estate (shall belong).' He then enumerates, on failure of the father, the brother and his son, the grandfather, the Samânodaka, the Sagotra, and the 'Bandhu, i.e. the maternal uncle and the rest,' as successive heirs, and explains Sakulya by Bandhu.

Nand., whose text has a faulty reading sapi*nd*ârha*h*, asserts that pi*nd*a (sapi*nd*a?) means 'the deceased,' and explains the first line by saying, 'Always to him who is the Sapi*nd*a nearest to the deceased the wealth, the estate, shall belong—the repetition (of the word tasya) shows the successive order.' The Sakulyas are, according to him, the Samânodakas. He reads sakulyâ*h* syu*h*, 'Sakulyas shall be the heirs.'

188. Gaut. XXVIII, 41; Vas. XVII, 84–86; Baudh. I, 13, 14; Vi. XVII, 13–14. The phrase 'on failure of all (heirs),' i.e. 'of those mentioned' (Râgh.), or 'of all males and females, related in any way (to the deceased),' (Nand.), indicates according to Kull. that other unnamed persons, such as fellow-students, are also entitled to inherit. 'Brâhma*n*as,' i.e. 'such as live in the same village' (Nâr.). 'Pure,' i.e. 'careful of external and internal purity' (Kull.), or better 'who are of good conduct' (Nâr.). According to Kull. and Râgh., the meaning of the last clause is that the Brâhma*n*as who inherit the estate will offer the funeral sacrifices, and thus no violation of the law regarding the *S*râddhas will occur. Nâr. points out that this rule, as the following verse shows, refers solely to the property of a Brâhma*n*a.

189. The property of a Brâhma*n*a must never be taken by the king, that is a settled rule; but (the property of men) of other castes the king may take on failure of all (heirs).

190. (If the widow) of (a man) who died without leaving issue, raises up to him a son by a member of the family (Sagotra), she shall deliver to that (son) the whole property which belonged to the (deceased).

191. But if two (sons), begotten by two (different men), contend for the property (in the hands) of their mother, each shall take, to the exclusion of the other, what belonged to his father.

---

189. Âp. II, 14, 5; Gaut. XXVIII, 42; Vas. XVII, 83; Baudh. I, 13, 15–16. According to Kull. and Râgh., the repetition of the prohibition to take the property of a Brâhma*n*a shows that, if no learned and virtuous Brâhma*n*as are to be found, the king shall give the estate of a Brâhma*n*a deceased without heirs, even to men who have nothing but the name of the Brâhma*n*a caste.

190. According to Kull. and Râgh., this verse refers to the case in which a duly authorised widow bears a son to a relative of her husband, and repeats the rule given above, verse 146, which here however is made imperative on the widow. Kull. adds that the object of the repetition is to show that not only a brother-in-law or a Sapi*nd*a, as stated above, verse 59, but also a remoter relative, a Sagotra, may beget a son for a man deceased without issue. Nâr., on the other hand, thinks that in accordance with this verse a child which a widow bears, even without authorisation, to a Sagotra shall inherit the estate of the widow's deceased husband (sagotrâd yadi tantu*m* sa*m*tânam âhared aniyuktâpi strî tadâ golakatve 'pi tasya *gñ*âtyantarâbhâve kshetrapatidhanahâritvam ity artha*h*). He adds that some apply this rule to *S*ûdra females only, and that in the opinion of these persons Gû*dh*a*g*as, Kânînas, and Saho*dh*as also are considered as sons in the case of *S*ûdras only, not in the case of Âryans.

191. Kull. and Nand. think that the verse refers to the case in which a woman married successively two husbands and bore a son to either. If the two husbands died and their property remained in

192. But when the mother has died, all the uterine brothers and the uterine sisters shall equally divide the mother's estate.

193. Even to the daughters of those (daughters) something should be given, as is seemly, out of the estate of their maternal grandmother, on the score of affection.

194. What (was given) before the (nuptial) fire, what (was given) on the bridal procession, what was

---

the hands of the wife, she is to make over the entire property of her first husband to his son, and the property of the second husband to the son of the latter. Râgh. gives the same explanation, but proposes as an alternative, 'If two (sons), begotten by two (different men), contend for the separate property of their mother, &c.' For a twice-married woman will have received nuptial and other presents from both husbands. After her death her sons shall each receive what came to her from his father. Nâr. finally holds that the verse refers to a contention between a legitimate son and a Golaka or a Paunarbhava for the estates of their respective fathers which their mother holds. He construes striyâ*h* with *g*âtau, 'begotten by two (different men) on one woman.'

192. Kull. and Râgh. restrict this rule, in accordance with a passage of B*ri*haspati, to unmarried daughters, and hold that married daughters receive merely 'a token of respect.' The latter amounts according to Kull. to 'one-fourth of a share;' see above, verse 118. Nâr. says that the term 'the mother's estate' refers to 'other property than strîdhana or separate property,' and adds to the expression 'the sisters' aputrâ*h*, 'those who have no sons.' He, however, gives the opinion, held by Kull. and Râgh. also, stating that it belongs to 'some.'

193. Kull. holds that the granddaughters should be unmarried. Nâr. says, 'When the married daughters are dead, their daughters shall be presented at will by their maternal uncles with the share which their mothers would have received as a token of respect.' Râgh., too, thinks that 'on the score of affection' means 'at the pleasure (of the heirs).' But Nand. deduces from the same term the absolute necessity of the gift.

194. Vi. XVII, 17; Yâ*gñ*. II, 143. 'What was given in token of love,' i.e. 'by the husband' (ratikâle, Nâr.).

given in token of love, and what was received from her brother, mother, or father, that is called the sixfold property of a woman.

195. (Such property), as well as a gift subsequent and what was given (to her) by her affectionate husband, shall go to her offspring, (even) if she dies in the lifetime of her husband.

196. It is ordained that the property (of a woman married) according to the Brâhma, the Daiva, the Ârsha, the Gândharva, or the Prâ*g*âpatya rite (shall belong) to her husband alone, if she dies without issue.

197. But it is prescribed that the property which may have been given to a (wife) on an Âsura marriage or (one of the) other (blamable marriages, shall go) to her mother and to her father, if she dies without issue.

198. Whatever property may have been given by her father to a wife (who has co-wives of different castes), that the daughter (of the) Brâhma*n*î (wife) shall take, or that (daughter's) issue.

---

195. Yâ*gñ*. II, 144. Kull. and Nâr. state that both the separate property of a woman, enumerated in verse 194, and that named in verse 195, descend to her children, i.e. 'to her sons and the rest' (Râgh.), or 'to her sons or daughters' (Nand.). Nâr. remarks that 'a gift subsequent' and 'the husband's affectionate gift' are not strîdhana, or separate property, and that hence the wife has no right of free disposal with respect to these two.

196–197. Vi. XVII, 19–20; Yâ*gñ*. II, 145.

196. Nâr. adds to the term 'property,' strîdhanâstrîdhanarûpam, 'whether separate property or not.'

198. I. e. if a Brâhma*n*a has wives of the Brâhma*n*a and Kshatriya castes, property given in any way to the Kshatriya wife by her own family, goes to the daughter of the Brâhma*n*a wife, or if that daughter of the Brâhma*n*a wife is dead and has left issue, to the latter. 'Thus the sons of the Brâhma*n*a wife are excluded' (Kull., Nâr.). Nâr. states expressly that the term 'issue' refers to daughters alone.

199. Women should never make a hoard from (the property of) their families which is common to many, nor from their own (husbands' particular) property without permission.

200. The ornaments which may have been worn by women during their husbands' lifetime, his heirs shall not divide; those who divide them become outcasts.

201. Eunuchs and outcasts, (persons) born blind or deaf, the insane, idiots and the dumb, as well as those deficient in any organ (of action or sensation), receive no share.

---

199. Kull. and Râgh., whose explanation the translation given above follows, take the first clause to refer to the property of a united family, and the second to the separate property of the husbands. But according to Nâr. and Nand. the translation should be as follows, 'Wives should never take anything (for their private expenses) from (their husbands' property, destined for the support of) their families, on which many have a claim, nor from their own property (which is not strîdhana), without the consent of their husbands.' Nâr.'s explanation of nirhâra*m* kuryu*h*, 'should (never) take anything,' seems preferable to that given by Kull. and Râgh.

200. Vi. XVII, 22. 'His heirs,' i. e. 'the sons and the rest' (Kull., Nâr.). Nand., who differs from the above explanation, says, 'Since the ornaments are the husband's property, because they have not been mentioned as strîdhana, the object of this utterance is to forbid their going to the heirs, while the husband lives' (ala*m*kârasya strîdhane 'nudish*t*atvâd bhart*ri*dhanatvena bhart*ri*bhâve dâyâdânâm prâptyapavâdârtho 'yam ârambha*h*). Nand. appears, therefore, to construe patyau *g*îvati with bha*g*eran, just as Nandapa*nd*ita does in the parallel passage of Vish*n*u (see Professor Jolly's note).

201–203. Âp. II, 14, 1, 15; Gaut. XXVIII, 23, 40, 43; Vas. XVII, 52–53; Baudh. II, 3, 37–40; Vi. XV, 32–37; Yâ*gñ*. II, 140–141.

201. 'Eunuchs,' i. e. 'those who are incurable;' 'outcasts,' i. e. 'those guilty of a mortal sin (mahâpâtaka) before they perform a penance;' 'the insane,' i. e. 'those who are incurable' (Nâr.). 'Those deficient in any organ, i. e. of action' (Nand.), such as lame men (Kull., Nand.), such as men without hands (Râgh.), or

202. But it is just that (a man) who knows (the law) should give even to all of them food and raiment without stint, according to his ability; he who gives it not will become an outcast.

203. If the eunuch and the rest should somehow or other desire to (take) wives, the offspring of such among them as have children is worthy of a share.

204. Whatever property the eldest (son) acquires (by his own exertion) after the father's death, a share of that (shall belong) to his younger (brothers), provided they have made a due progress in learning.

---

also 'of sensation,' such as men who have lost the faculty of touch (Nâr.).

202. Medh. and Kull. take atyantam, 'without stint,' in the sense of 'for life.' Nâr. construes the word with adadat, and explains 'he who does not give it at all.' Nand. reads abhyaṅgam, 'ointments,' for atyantam, 'without stint.'

203. Medh. is of opinion that some of the persons disqualified from inheriting, the vâtaretas klîba, those born blind and the lame, may marry, while outcasts, madmen, and the rest cannot do so. Hence the conditional clause may be taken in the sense adopted above in the translation. He, however, adds that the rule may also refer to cases in which the cause of the disqualification arose after marriage. Nâr.'s explanation is substantially the same. But he considers that a eunuch and an outcast cannot contract a legal marriage, and that the expression klibâdaya*h*, literally 'those among whom the eunuch is the first,' refers to 'men born blind and the rest.' He admits also the rights of the Kshetra*g*a sons of eunuchs and outcasts who contracted a marriage before their disqualification arose. Kull. says, 'By the employment of the term "somehow or other" it is indicated that a eunuch and the rest are not worthy to marry.' In the sequel he explains the word 'offspring' by Kshetra*g*a. Râgh. and Nand. follow him with respect to the latter point.

204. The rule refers of course to a united family only (Kull.). Medh. infers from the expression vidyânupâlina*h*, 'provided they have made a due progress in learning,' that 'persons subsisting by learning, mechanics and artisans, such as physicians, actors, singers,'

205. But if all of them, being unlearned, acquire property by their labour, the division of that shall be equal, (as it is) not property acquired by the father; that is a settled rule.

206. Property (acquired) by learning belongs solely to him to whom (it was given), likewise the gift of a friend, a present received on marriage or with the honey-mixture.

---

are meant. Nâr. and Nand. hold that no part of an acquisition, made under the same circumstances by the youngest brother, can be claimed by the eldest, because this verse specifies the eldest alone, and because the next verse declares that the acquisitions only made by any member of an unlearned family, shall be partible.

205. Gaut. XXXVIII, 31. This rule refers to acquisitions by trade (Medh., Kull., Nâr.), by agriculture (Medh., Kull. Nand.), or by royal service (Medh.). 'As the division is to be equal, the eldest receives no preferential share' (Medh., Kull., Nand.). Medh. adds that, since the expression 'as it is not property acquired by the father,' gives the reason for the equal division, the same rule holds good for the division of the estate of any other person deceased without issue. Nand. takes apitrya iti for apitrya*h* iti and explains it by 'since (the division) has not been made by the father.'

206. Yâg*ñ*. II, 118–119. 'Property acquired by learning,' i. e. 'a fee for teaching or money received for proficiency in an art' (Medh., Nand.), includes according to a text of Kâtyâyana, quoted by Kull. and Râgh. (see Colebrooke V, Digest CCCXLVII), gifts from pupils, gratuities for performing a sacrifice, a fee for answering a difficult question in casuistry, or for ascertaining a doubtful point in law, rewards for displaying knowledge or for victory in a learned contest, or for reciting the Veda with transcendent ability. Instances in which land was given as vidyâdhana occur in the inscriptions, see e. g. Indian Antiquary, XII, p. 195 b, l. 6. 'A present received on marriage,' i. e. 'what (the bridegroom) receives from the relatives of his wife' (Medh., Nâr.), or 'from any other person' (Medh. 'others'), means according to Nand., 'strîdhana received at the time of marriage' (?). 'A present received with the honey-mixture' is explained by Medh. and, as Kull. asserts, by Gov. also, by 'the fee given for the performance of a sacrifice.' But the explanation given by Kull., Nâr., Râgh., and Nand., 'any

207. But if one of the brothers, being able (to maintain himself) by his own occupation, does not desire (a share of the family) property, he may be made separate (by the others) receiving a trifle out of his share to live upon.

208. What one (brother) may acquire by his labour without using the patrimony, that acquisition, (made solely) by his own effort, he shall not share unless by his own will (with his brothers).

209. But if a father recovers lost ancestral pro-

---

present received, in token of respect, with the honey-mixture,' e. g. a silver vase (Râgh.), is preferable. Regarding the persons worthy of the honey-mixture, see above, III, 119–120. Kull. points out that this rule is a restriction of that given above, verse 204. Râgh. adds that, as the parallel passage of Yâgñ. shows, such acquisitions become the private property of the donee, only if they were obtained 'without detriment to the paternal estate;' see also below, verse 208.

207. Yâgñ. II, 116. The translation given above follows the second explanation offered by Medh., and the glosses of Kull. and Nâr. According to Medh.'s first explanation, with which Nand. agrees, the translation would agree with Sir W. Jones's, 'he may debar himself from his share.' The reason why a trifle should be given is, according to all commentators, that future disputes may be prevented.

208. Yâgñ. II, 118; Vi. XVIII, 42. 'By his labour,' i. e. 'by agriculture and the like' (Medh., Kull., Nand.), or 'by any occupation entailing trouble' (*s*ramaganyakarma*n*â, Nâr.). Anupaghnan, 'without using' (Nand.), or 'without living upon' (Râgh.), is explained by Kull. 'without detriment to,' and Nand. mentions this interpretation also. Nâr. remarks that acquisitions made without labour or trouble are liable to partition. Nand. says that the rule, given in this verse, may be reconciled with that contained in verse 205, by assuming that the latter presupposes that all brothers exert themselves according to their ability (pûrva*m* sarveshu yathâsâmarthyam îhamâneshu bhrât*ri*shu labdhasya samavibhâga ukta ity avirodho 'nusa*m*dheya*h*).

209. Yâgñ. II, 119; Vi. XVIII, 43. The translation of pait*ri*kam, lit. 'paternal,' by 'ancestral,' is based on Nâr.'s gloss svapit*ri*-

perty, he shall not divide it, unless by his own will, with his sons, (for it is) self-acquired (property).

210. If brothers, (once) divided and living (again) together (as coparceners), make a second partition, the division shall in that case be equal; in such a case there is no right of primogeniture.

211. If the eldest or the youngest (brother) is deprived of his share, or if either of them dies, his share is not lost (to his immediate heirs).

212. His uterine brothers, having assembled together, shall equally divide it, and those brothers who were reunited (with him) and the uterine sisters.

---

sambandhi and on Râgh.'s pit*ri*pitâmahâdisambandhi. The latter refers also to the parallel passage of Yâ*gñ*. Anavâptam, 'lost,' means literally 'not obtained (by his father).' The translation of svayamar*g*itam by 'for it is self-acquired' agrees with Nand.'s remark, svayamar*g*itatvâd ity artha*h*. Nâr. adds, 'And thus it has been declared that property of the father which has not been acquired by him with exceedingly great trouble must be divided at the will of the sons, and to this refers the passage of Yâ*gñ*. II, 121, "Over land acquired by the grandfather, &c."' Medh., whose commentary on this verse is very corrupt, seems likewise to have inferred from it that Manu admitted the equal ownership of a father and his sons in ancestral property (see also Colebrooke V, Digest XCI). But he combats the theory that sons may without a violation of their duty force the father to divide the ancestral property.

210. Vi. XVIII, 41.

211. 'Be deprived of his share,' i. e. 'because he has become an outcast or the like' (Medh.), or 'because he has become an ascetic' (Kull., Nand.), or 'because he has emigrated' (Nand.), or 'because he has become a eunuch after the (first) partition' (Nâr.). Na lupyate, 'is not lost (to his immediate heirs),' is explained by Nâr. as follows, 'His share, being formerly determined, is not lost, i. e. must not be divided by all the reunited coparceners and thus be made to disappear' (see also the text of B*ri*haspati, Colebrooke V, Digest CCCCVII, 2). 'What is to be done with the share is shown in the next verse' (Medh., Nâr., Râgh., Nand.).

212. Vi. XVII, 17; Gaut. XXVIII, 21; Yâ*gñ*. II, 138. The

213. An eldest brother who through avarice may defraud the younger ones, shall no (longer hold the position of) the eldest, shall not receive an (eldest son's additional) share, and shall be punished by the king.

214. All brothers who habitually commit forbidden acts, are unworthy of (a share of) the property, and the eldest shall not make (anything his) separate property without giving (an equivalent) to his younger brothers.

---

meaning of the verse is: 1. according to Medh., with whose opinion the not very clear glosses of Kull. and Râgh. seem to agree, 'the share of a deceased reunited brother goes first to the reunited brothers of the full blood and to such sisters of the full blood who are not married (aputrâ*h*, MSS. for aprattâ*h*)—married sisters (pravr*i*ttâ*h*, MSS. for pradattâ*h*) being excluded, because they belong to another family—next to not reunited brothers of the full blood, finally to reunited half-brothers;' 2. according to Nâr., 'the share of a reunited brother devolves first on reunited brothers of the whole blood, next on reunited half-brothers, further on sisters of the full blood, then on the sons of brothers [of the whole blood?], and finally on sons of half-brothers [? tadabhâve tvasodarâdy api].' Nand. has the same order of heirs as Nâr., but stops with 'the sisters of the whole blood.' Nâr.'s and Nand.'s explanation, which strictly follows the order of the enumeration in the text, agrees with Br*i*haspati's rule (Colebrooke V, Digest CCCCVII, 3), which likewise seems to be a paraphrase of Manu's words. Kull., Râgh., and Nâr. hold that the heirs, named in the verse, inherit only on failure of sons, wives, daughters, and parents. Nâr. further remarks that some refer this verse and the preceding one to the division of the estate of one who died before partition, while others believe that it applies to the estate of a reunited brother only.

213. 'Shall no (longer hold the position of) the eldest,' i. e. 'shall not receive the honours, e. g. in saluting, due to the eldest brother' (Medh., Kull., Nâr., Râgh.). The insertion of the words 'an eldest son's additional' before 'share,' is made on the authority of Medh. and Kull. 'Shall be punished,' i. e. 'by reprimand (vâgda*nd*adhigda*nd*âbhyâm) or by a fine as the case may require' (Medh.).

214. Âp. II, 14, 15; Gaut. XXVIII, 40; Baudh. II, 3, 38. 'Who

215. If undivided brethren, (living with their father,) together make an exertion (for gain), the father shall on no account give to them unequal shares (on a division of the estate).

216. But a son, born after partition, shall alone take the property of his father, or if any (of the other sons) be reunited with the (father), he shall share with them.

217. A mother shall obtain the inheritance of a son (who dies) without leaving issue, and, if the mother be dead, the paternal grandmother shall take the estate.

---

habitually commit forbidden acts,' i. e. 'who are addicted to gambling, drinking, and the like vices' (Kull., Râgh.), or 'who, being Brâhma*n*as, follow despicable modes of living, such as tending cattle, serving *S*ûdras and the like' (Nâr.). Na . . . . kurvîta yautukam, 'shall not make (anything his) separate property,' means according to Nand. 'shall not give a marriage-portion to his daughter without having made a division of the estate.' The correct interpretation is, however, that given by the other commentators, according to which the eldest is not to appropriate anything out of the common stock for himself 'without giving an equivalent to the others' (kanish*th*ebhyas tâvad adattvâ, Nâr.).

215. Yâ*g*ñ. II, 120. Medh. remarks that this rule is a restriction of the general power of the father to make an unequal division (Yâ*g*ñ. II, 116), and thinks that it is not necessary that all the brothers should have been associated in the same kind of work. According to him it is sufficient that all have exerted themselves to gain money. Nâr. and Nand. clearly express the contrary view (sahotthâna*m* sambhûyavâ*n*i*g*yâdinâ vittâr*g*anam, Nâr.).

216. Gaut. XXVIII, 29; Vi. XVII, 3; Yâ*g*ñ. II, 122.

217. Vi. XVII, 7; Yâ*g*ñ. II, 135. Kull., Nâr., and Nand. all three hold that the mother inherits only on failure of sons [grandsons and great-grandsons, Nand.], widows, and daughters. But they disagree with respect to the sequence of the next following heirs. Kull. holds that the mother and the father, whose right has been mentioned above, verse 185, follow next, inheriting conjointly, then brothers, afterwards brothers' sons, and after

218. And if, after all the debts and assets have been duly distributed according to the rule, any (property) be afterwards discovered, one must divide it equally.

219. A dress, a vehicle, ornaments, cooked food, water, and female (slaves), property destined for pious uses or sacrifices, and a pasture-ground, they declare to be indivisible.

---

them the paternal grandmother. Nâr. gives the following order: 1. mother, 2. father, 3. brothers, 4. brothers' sons, 5. maternal grandmother. Medh. says that this verse has been explained formerly. The portion of his commentary where the explanation occurred, has, however, been lost; see note on verse 187.

218. Yâgñ. II, 126. Medh., Kull., and Nâr. point out that on the division of property discovered after partition, the eldest, according to this text, receives no preferential share. Nâr. adds that this rule applies also to debts, discovered after partition. Nâr. inserts this verse after verse 219.

219. Gaut. XXVIII, 46-47; Vi. XVIII, 44. Instead of pattram, 'a vehicle,' i. e. 'a horse or cart, used exclusively by one of the coparceners during union' (Medh., Kull., Nâr., Râgh.), Nand. reads pâtram, 'a drinking-vessel.' Striya*h*, 'female (slaves),' means according to Nâr. 'wives.' My translation of yogakshemam, which I take with Medh., Nâr., and Nand. as a copulative compound in the neuter gender, by 'property destined for pious uses and sacrifices,' rests on the explanation given by Vigñâne*s*vara (Colebrooke, Mit. I, 4, 23), and adopted by Haradatta and Nandapa*nd*ita on the parallel passages of Gaut. and Vi. I prefer it to all others, chiefly on account of the explicit passage of Laugâkshi which Vigñâne*s*vara quotes. In its favour speaks also that numerous royal grants allow villages or land to Brâhma*n*as and their descendants for the performance of certain sacrifices, or for charitable purposes, such as the daily distribution of food (annasattra or sadâvrata), and that the occurrence of a rule in the Sm*ri*tis, declaring property given under such conditions to be impartible, is no more than might be expected. The commentators on Manu, on the other hand, give the following explanations: 1. 'the means of securing protection, i.e. royal councillors, family priests, ministers, old women (v*ri*ddhâ?), a house, and a *k*âra, a spy (?), or a pasture-ground (?) and the like' (Medh.); 2. 'a royal councillor, a domestic priest and the like' (Kull.

220. The division (of the property) and the rules for allotting (shares) to the (several) sons, those begotten on a wife and the rest, in (due) order, have been thus declared to you; hear (now) the laws concerning gambling.

221. Gambling and betting let the king exclude from his realm; those two vices cause the destruction of the kingdoms of princes.

222. Gambling and betting amount to open theft; the king shall always exert himself in suppressing both (of them).

223. When inanimate (things) are used (for staking money on them), that is called among men gambling (dyûta), when animate beings are used (for the same purpose), one must know that to be betting (samâhvaya).

224. Let the king corporally punish all those (persons) who either gamble and bet or afford (an

---

and Râgh., which latter reads, however, yogakshemapra*k*âram); 3. 'means of gain, i. e. a grant and the like, received from a king and the like, and gained by oneself, and means of protection' (prâkâre *k*a ish*t*akâdi*h*? Nâr.); 4. 'sources of gain, i. e. persons for whom one sacrifices and the like, sources of protection, i. e. doorkeepers and the like, and sources of gain and protection, i. e. lords of villages and the like' (Nand.). Pra*k*âra, 'a pasture-ground,' means according to Nâr. and Nand. 'a road leading to a field, a garden and the like.'

Medh., Kull., and Nâr. state that the first four articles shall in general be kept by the coparcener who used them or for whose use they were prepared, but that articles or quantities of exceptional value must be sold or exchanged for other property. Wells and so forth are to be used by all the coparceners (Kull., Nand.). Female slaves are to do work for all coparceners (Kull.).

221-229. Âp. II, 25, 12-15; Gaut. XXV, 18; Baudh. II, 2, 16; Yâg*ñ*. II, 199-203. In the I. O. MSS. Medh.'s commentary on verses 221-227 is missing.

224. Yâg*ñ*. II, 304. 'The distinctive marks of twice-born men,'

opportunity for it), likewise *S*ûdras who assume the distinctive marks of twice-born (men).

225. Gamblers, dancers and singers, cruel men, men belonging to an heretical sect, those following forbidden occupations, and sellers of spirituous liquor, let him instantly banish from his town.

226. If such (persons who are) secret thieves, dwell in the realm of a king, they constantly harass his good subjects by their forbidden practices.

227. In a former Kalpa this (vice of) gambling has been seen to cause great enmity; a wise man, therefore, should not practise it even for amusement.

228. On every man who addicts himself to that (vice) either secretly or openly, the king may inflict punishment according to his discretion.

---

i. e. 'the sacrificial thread and the like' (Kull., Nâr.). 'Shall punish corporally,' i. e. 'shall cause them to be flogged, &c.' (Nâr.), or 'shall cause their hands and feet to be cut off and so forth according to the gravity of the offence' (Kull., Râgh.).

225. Instead of krûrân, 'cruel men,' i. e. 'those who hate men learned in the Veda' (Kull.), Nâr. and Râgh. read kerân, which the former explains by 'men of exceedingly crooked behaviour,' and the latter in accordance with Kull.'s explanation of krûrân. Nand. reads kailân, 'given to sports' (kelî*s*ilân), and K. *k*orân, 'thieves.' Sau*nd*ikân, 'distillers or sellers of spirituous liquor' (Kull., Nâr.), may also mean 'drunkards,' as Nand. explains it.

226. Instead of 'who are secret thieves' (Kull.), Nâr. says, 'and secret thieves.' Bâdhante, 'harass' (Kull.), means according to Nâr., Râgh., and Nand. 'corrupt.'

227. Nâr. explains purâkalpe, 'in a former Kalpa,' by 'in the ancient stories,' and Râgh. and Nand. point to the adventures of king Nala and Yudhish*th*ira, which, no doubt, are alluded to in the text.

228. Râgh. and Nand. point out that not only corporal punishment (according to verse 224), but also a fine may be inflicted; see also the next verse.

229. But a Kshatriya, a Vaisya, and a Sûdra who are unable to pay a fine, shall discharge the debt by labour; a Brâhmana shall pay it by instalments.

230. On women, infants, men of disordered mind, the poor and the sick, the king shall inflict punishment with a whip, a cane, or a rope and the like.

231. But those appointed (to administer public) affairs, who, baked by the fire of wealth, mar the business of suitors, the king shall deprive of their property.

232. Forgers of royal edicts, those who corrupt his ministers, those who slay women, infants, or Brâhmanas, and those who serve his enemies, the king shall put to death.

233. Whenever any (legal transaction) has been completed or (a punishment) been inflicted according to the law, he shall sanction it and not annul it.

---

229. Yâgñ. II, 43. Compare the rule given at VIII, 177.

230. Siphâ, 'a whip,' is explained by Râgh. as 'a rod measuring five fingers,' or 'the pendent root of a fig-tree.' Nâr. and Nand. give the latter meaning. Medh., Nâr., and Nand. read daridrânâtharoginâm, 'the poor, the unprotected, and the sick.'

231. See above, VII, 124; Vi. V, 180. 'Those appointed, &c.,' i.e. viceroys and so forth (Medh.), or judges and so forth (Nâr.). 'Baked by the fire of wealth' is a simile taken from the burning of earthen pots, and means that such persons by the influence of wealth undergo a change for the worse, just as a pot heated in a fire changes its colour, or, as the Vaiseshikas hold, its nature. According to Medh., 'others' read ye 'niyuktâs tu, and referred the verse to non-official persons meddling with administrative or judicial business.

232. Yâgñ. II, 240; Vi. V, 9, 11.

233. Medh. and Kull. refer this prohibition to cases which have been properly decided in the king's courts, while Nâr. thinks that it applies to orders passed by former kings. Nand. gives a different explanation of the words tîrita and anusishta. He adduces a verse of Kâtyâyana, according to which the former means 'a cause or

234. Whatever matter his ministers or the judge may settle improperly, that the king himself shall (re-)settle and fine (them) one thousand (pa*n*as).

235. The slayer of a Brâhma*n*a, (a twice-born man) who drinks (the spirituous liquor called) Surâ, he who steals (the gold of a Brâhma*n*a), and he who violates a Guru's bed, must each and all be considered as men who committed mortal sins (mahâpâtaka).

236. On those four even, if they do not perform a penance, let him inflict corporal punishment and fines in accordance with the law.

237. For violating a Guru's bed, (the mark of) a female part shall be (impressed on the forehead with a hot iron); for drinking (the spirituous liquor called) Surâ, the sign of a tavern; for stealing (the gold of a Brâhma*n*a), a dog's foot; for murdering a Brâhma*n*a, a headless corpse.

---

plaint declared to be just or unjust by the assessors,' and the latter 'a cause or plaint confirmed by witnesses.'

234. Yâ*gñ*. II, 305. Medh. and Kull. think that this rule refers to cases where the cause of the unjust decision is not a bribe, because the punishment of corrupt judges has been prescribed above, verse 231. But Nâr. and Râgh. think that it applies to cases of bribery also, and that the fine shall vary according to the nature of the case, 1000 pa*n*as being the lowest punishment.

235–242. Baudh. I, 18, 18; Vi. V, 3–7.

235. Instead of '(a twice-born man) who drinks the spirituous liquor, &c.' (Kull., Nâr.), Medh. and Râgh. say, 'a Brâhma*n*a who, &c.;' but see below, XI, 94.

236. Medh. remarks that 'others' refer this rule, on account of the word api, 'even, likewise,' to the fifth Mahâpatakin also, i. e. to him who associates with one of the other four (see below, XI, 55); and Râgh., as well as Nand., approves of this explanation.

237. 'The sign of a tavern,' i. e. 'a wine-cup.' It follows from the rule given in verse 240, that the forehead is the place where they shall be branded.

238. Excluded from all fellowship at meals, excluded from all sacrifices, excluded from instruction and from matrimonial alliances, abject and excluded from all religious duties, let them wander over (this) earth.

239. Such (persons) who have been branded with (indelible) marks must be cast off by their paternal and maternal relations, and receive neither compassion nor a salutation; that is the teaching of Manu.

240. But (men of) all castes who perform the prescribed penances, must not be branded on the forehead by the king, but shall be made to pay the highest amercement.

241. For (such) offences the middlemost amercement shall be inflicted on a Brâhma*n*a, or he may be banished from the realm, keeping his money and his chattels.

242. But (men of) other (castes), who have unintentionally committed such crimes, ought to be deprived of their whole property; if (they committed them) intentionally, they shall be banished.

---

238. Medh. reads asa*m*yogyâ*h*, 'excluded from all intercourse,' instead of asa*m*yâgyâ*h*, 'excluded from all sacrifices.'

240. 'All castes,' i. e. 'the three Âryan castes.' Nâr. and Nand. read pûrve, 'the before-mentioned castes.' 'The highest amercement,' see above, VIII, 138.

241. According to Medh., the meaning of the verse is that a Brâhma*n*a, endowed with good qualities, who unintentionally (verse 242) committed a mortal sin, shall either be fined in the middlemost amercement and be made to perform the prescribed penance, or, if he refuses to do that, be banished without the infliction of a fine. Kull. and Nand. partly agree, but think that the offender is to be banished, if he committed the crime intentionally.

242. The translation follows Nâr. and Nand., who think that persons, performing no penance, shall be deprived of their whole

243. A virtuous king must not take for himself the property of a man guilty of mortal sin; but if he takes it out of greed, he is tainted by that guilt (of the offender).

244. Having thrown such a fine into the water, let him offer it to Varuna, or let him bestow it on a learned and virtuous Brâhmana.

245. Varuna is the lord of punishment, for he holds the sceptre even over kings; a Brâhmana who has learnt the whole Veda is the lord of the whole world.

246. In that (country), where the king avoids taking the property of (mortal) sinners, men are born in (due) time (and are) long-lived,

247. And the crops of the husbandmen spring up, each as it was sown, and the children die not, and no misshaped (offspring) is born.

---

property, if the offence was committed unintentionally, and be banished after being branded, if their crime was intentional. Nâr., moreover, adds, 'this refers to light cases; it has been declared that he shall slay the offender in bad cases.' Kull. and Râgh. think that confiscation of the whole property shall be inflicted in particularly bad cases, instead of the fine of 1000 panas prescribed in verse 240; and Medh. says that this is the opinion of 'some.' Medh., Kull., and Râgh. explain pravâsanam, 'shall be banished,' by 'shall be punished corporally.' Though it is not absolutely impossible that pravâs may mean 'to hurt, or punish corporally,' it seems not advisable to take the word in the latter sense, on account of verses 238 and 241; compare also VIII, 284. Medh. remarks that a *S*ûdra who offends unintentionally, shall be branded and be deprived of his whole property, else he shall be put to death.

244. Yâ*gñ*. II, 307.

245. Varuna is the supreme ruler (adhirâ*g*a) of kings; see Taittirîya-brâhmana III, 1, 2, 7. Regarding the position of a learned Brâhmana, see above, I, 98–101.

246. Instead of kâlena, 'in (due) time,' i.e. 'after the full period of gestation' (Kull., Nâr., Râgh.), Nand. reads loke tu, 'but in that country.'

248. But the king shall inflict on a base-born (*S*ûdra), who intentionally gives pain to Brâhma*n*as, various (kinds of) corporal punishment which cause terror.

249. When a king punishes an innocent (man), his guilt is considered as great as when he sets free a guilty man; but (he acquires) merit when he punishes (justly).

250. Thus the (manner of) deciding suits (falling) under the eighteen titles, between two litigant parties, has been declared at length.

251. A king who thus duly fulfils his duties in accordance with justice, may seek to gain countries which he has not yet gained, and shall duly protect them when he has gained them.

252. Having duly settled his country, and having built forts in accordance with the Institutes, he shall use his utmost exertions to remove (those men who are nocuous like) thorns.

253. By protecting those who live as (becomes) Âryans and by removing the thorns, kings, solely intent on guarding their subjects, reach heaven.

254. The realm of that king who takes his share

---

248. See above, VIII, 279–284. Though all the commentators take avara*g*a*m* in the sense of 'a base-born *S*ûdra,' the word may have its etymological meaning, 'a man of lower caste.' Medh. explains 'who gives pain' by 'who takes their property or wives;' Nâr., 'who causes exceedingly great misery.'

249. See above, VIII, 19, 310–311, 317.

250. 'This verse is the conclusion of the section on the eighteen titles of the law' (Medh.), 'and now follows a supplement on the duties of a king' (Nâr.).

252. See above, VII, 69–70.

253–254. See above, VIII, 307, 386–387.

in kind, though he does not punish thieves, (will be) disturbed and he (will) lose heaven.

255. But if his kingdom be secure, protected by the strength of his arm, it will constantly flourish like a (well)-watered tree.

256. Let the king who sees (everything) through his spies, discover the two sorts of thieves who deprive others of their property, both those who (show themselves) openly and those who (lie) concealed.

257. Among them, the open rogues (are those) who subsist by (cheating in the sale of) various marketable commodities, but the concealed rogues are burglars, robbers in forests, and so forth.

258. Those who take bribes, cheats and rogues, gamblers, those who live by teaching (the performance of) auspicious ceremonies, sanctimonious hypocrites, and fortune-tellers,

---

258. Aupâdhikâ*h*, 'cheats,' means according to Medh. 'persons of crooked behaviour who promise kindnesses, but secretly do evil to others,' or 'such as take money under false pretences,' or 'such as extort money by threats.' The last explanation is adopted by Kull. and Râgh., while Nâr. and Nand. interpret the term to mean 'persons who cheat by using false weights and measures.' Vañ*k*akâ*h*, 'rogues,' i.e. 'men who promise to transact business for others, and do not keep their word' (Medh.), or 'alchemists who pretend to change base metals into precious metals' (rasa*m* vidya*m* [rasavidyayâ] tâmrâdi ra*g*atâdirûpe*n*a dar*s*ayitvâ suvar*n*âdika*m* g*ri*h*n*anti, Râgh., Kull.), or 'men who take money on false pretences' (Nâr.). Mañgalâde*s*av*ri*ttâ*h*, 'those who live by teaching the performance of, or by performing for others, auspicious ceremonies' (Medh., Kull., Râgh.), means according to Nâr. 'men who live by reciting auspicious hymns' (mañgalastutipâ*th*o v*ri*tta*m* *k*arita*m* yeshâm), and Medh. proposes a similar alternative explanation. Medh. reads bhadrapreksha*n*ikai*h* saha, and explains the compound by 'eulogists' (prâ*s*a*m*sikapurushalaksha*n*â*h*). Nâr. explains îksha*n*ikâ*h*, 'fortune-tellers,' by 'actors and jugglers.'

259. Officials of high rank and physicians who act improperly, men living by showing their proficiency in arts, and clever harlots,

260. These and the like who show themselves openly, as well as others who walk in disguise (such as) non-Âryans who wear the marks of Âryans, he should know to be thorns (in the side of his people).

261. Having detected them by means of trustworthy persons, who, disguising themselves, (pretend) to follow the same occupations and by means of spies, wearing various disguises, he must cause them to be instigated (to commit offences), and bring them into his power.

---

259. Mahâmâtra, 'officials of high rank,' i.e. 'courtiers such as councillors and domestic priests' (Medh.), or 'ministers' (Nâr.), is taken by Kull. and Râgh. in its other sense, 'elephant-breakers.' *S*ilpopa*k*ârayuktâ*h*, 'men living by showing their proficiency in arts,' i. e. 'such as cut figures out of chips of cane and the like' (Medh., Râgh.), or 'painters and the like' (Kull.). Nâr. and Nand. read *s*ilpopakârayuktâ*h*, i. e. 'artists such as painters and persons adorning (upakâra) people such as hairdressers' (Nâr.), or 'umbrella and fan makers' (Nand.). Medh. says that asamyakkâri*n*a*h*, 'who act improperly,' must be taken with all the four classes of persons enumerated.

260. Nâr. and Nand. read vi*g*âtîyân, 'such and the like open (rogues) of many kinds,' and connect the accusatives in this verse with viditvâ in the next. Kull. takes vi*g*ânîyât, 'let him know (to be),' in the sense of 'let him discover (through spies).'

261. The translation follows Nâr.'s explanation, who reads protsâhya (likewise found in Gov., Râgh., and K.) instead of protsâdya, found in the editions, in Kull.'s and probably also in Medh.'s version. The reading protsâdya, 'having destroyed them,' is objectionable on account of the following verse. Râgh. explains protsâhya differently; he says, 'having inspired them with energy by saying, "you must give up this livelihood and earn money by agriculture, trade, and the like," he shall induce to adopt a honest mode of line through desire for money.' Nand. seems to

262. Then having caused the crimes, which they committed by their several actions, to be proclaimed in accordance with the facts, the king shall duly punish them according to their strength and their crimes.

263. For the wickedness of evil-minded thieves, who secretly prowl over this earth, cannot be restrained except by punishment.

264. Assembly-houses, houses where water is distributed or cakes are sold, brothels, taverns and victualler's shops, cross-roads, well-known trees, festive assemblies, and play-houses and concert-rooms,

265. Old gardens, forests, the shops of artisans, empty dwellings, natural and artificial groves,

266. These and the like places the king shall cause to be guarded by companies of soldiers, both stationary and patrolling, and by spies, in order to keep away thieves.

267. By the means of clever reformed thieves, who associate with such (rogues), follow them and know their various machinations, he must detect and destroy them.

268. Under the pretext of (offering them) various dainties, of introducing them to Brâhma*n*as, and on the pretence of (showing them) feats of strength, the (spies) must make them meet (the officers of justice).

---

read protsârya (protsâryâ, MS.). Kull. explains anekasa*m*sthânai*h*, 'wearing various disguises' (Nâr., Nand.), by 'stationed in various places.' Medh.'s commentary on the end of verse 261 and on verses 262–274 is missing in the I. O. MSS.

267. Instead of utsâdayet, 'he shall destroy them' (Kull., K., editions), Gov., Nâr., Nand., and Râgh. read utsâhayet, i.e. 'he shall incite them to commit (crimes,' Nâr., Râgh.).

269. Those among them who do not come, and those who suspect the old (thieves employed by the king), the king shall attack by force and slay together with their friends, blood relations, and connexions.

270. A just king shall not cause a thief to be put to death, (unless taken) with the stolen goods (in his possession); him who (is taken) with the stolen goods and the implements (of burglary), he may, without hesitation, cause to be slain.

271. All those also who in villages give food to thieves or grant them room for (concealing their implements), he shall cause to be put to death.

272. Those who are appointed to guard provinces and his vassals who have been ordered (to help), he shall speedily punish like thieves, (if they remain) inactive in attacks (by robbers).

273. Moreover if (a man), who subsists by (the fulfilment of) the law, departs from the established rule of the law, the (king) shall severely punish him by a fine, (because he) violated his duty.

---

269. Mûlapra*n*ihitâ*h*, 'who suspect the old thieves employed by the king' (Kull., Râgh.), means according to Nâr. 'who have been sent by ministers and the like staying in his kingdom,' and according to Nand. 'who have discovered the root, i. e. the reasons (of the proceedings of the spies).' All the three explanations are, however, doubtful.

271. Bhâ*nd*âvakâ*s*adâ*h*, 'who give them room for (concealing) their implements' (Kull.), means according to Nâr. 'who give them money (for buying arms and the like) and shelter.'

272. The commentators take sâmantân, 'his vassals,' in its etymological sense of 'neighbours.' But it has here no doubt the usual technical meaning.

273. According to the commentators officiating priests and other Brâhma*n*as are meant, who subsist by obtaining alms on the strength of their piety.

274. Those who do not give assistance according to their ability when a village is being plundered, a dyke is being destroyed, or a highway robbery committed, shall be banished with their goods and chattels.

275. On those who rob the king's treasury and those who persevere in opposing (his commands), he shall inflict various kinds of capital punishment, likewise on those who conspire with his enemies.

276. But the king shall cut off the hands of those robbers who, breaking into houses, commit thefts at night, and cause them to be impaled on a pointed stake.

277. On the first conviction, let him cause two fingers of a cut-purse to be amputated; on the second, one hand and one foot; on the third, he shall suffer death.

278. Those who give (to thieves) fire, food, arms, or shelter, and receivers of stolen goods, the ruler shall punish like thieves.

---

274. Vi. V, 74. Instead of hitâbhaṅge, 'when an embankment is destroyed' (Kull., editions), Râgh. reads hi*d*âbhaṅge, and Gov. as well as Nand. i*d*âbhaṅge with the same explanation. Nâr. has ta*d*âgabhaṅge, probably a mistake for idâbhaṅge, and mentions a var. lect. hi*tt*âbhaṅge, adding that hi*tt*â is 'a dam thrown across a river.' K. finally reads setubhaṅge.

276. Yâ*gñ*. II, 273.

277. Vi. V, 136; Yâ*gñ*. II, 274. 'Two fingers,' i. e. 'the thumb and the index' (Kull., Râgh., Nâr.), or 'the index and the middle finger' (Nand.).

278. Yâ*gñ*. II, 276. 'Those who give (to thieves) fire,' i. e. 'in order that they may warm themselves, or for similar purposes' (Medh.), or 'in order that they may put fire to houses' (Nâr.). Moshasya sa*m*nidhât*ri*n, 'receivers of stolen goods' (Kull.), means according to Nâr. 'those who conduct thieves to the place where they can commit their crime, or helpers and abettors.' The best copy of Medh. has mokshasya, both in the text and in the

279. Him who breaks (the dam of) a tank he shall slay (by drowning him) in water or by (some other) simple (mode of) capital punishment; or the offender may repair the (damage), but shall be made to pay the highest amercement.

280. Those who break into a (royal) storehouse, an armoury, or a temple, and those who steal elephants, horses, or chariots, he shall slay without hesitation.

281. But he who shall take away the water of a tank, made in ancient times, or shall cut off the supply of water, must be made to pay the first (or lowest) amercement.

282. But he who, except in a case of extreme necessity, drops filth on the king's high-road, shall pay two kârshâpa*n*as and immediately remove (that) filth.

283. But a person in urgent necessity, an aged man, a pregnant woman, or a child, shall be reprimanded and clean the (place); that is a settled rule.

284. All physicians who treat (their patients) wrongly (shall pay) a fine; in the case of animals, the

commentary, and the other gives it in the text, while the explanation is rakshitâra*h*, 'protectors or abettors.' Nand., too, reads in the text mokshasya, and says, 'mokshasya moshitadravyasya mokshasâdhanasyeti vâ.' It would, therefore, seem that an ancient var. lect. mokshasya really existed.

279. Yâ*gñ*. II, 278. 'By (some other) simple (mode of) capital punishment,' i. e. 'by cutting off his head' (Nâr., Râgh.).

280. Yâ*gñ*. II, 273. This verse and the next are omitted in the I. O. MSS. of Medh.

281. Nâr. says that the offender must also make good the damage done.

282. Vi. V, 106–107. Medh. says that he shall pay the *K*a*n*d*âla, i.e. the sweeper, to remove the filth.

284. Vi. V, 175–177; Yâ*gñ*. II, 242. Nâr. adds, 'But this

first (or lowest); in the case of human beings, the middlemost (amercement).

285. He who destroys a bridge, the flag (of a temple or royal palace), a pole, or images, shall repair the whole (damage) and pay five hundred (pa*n*as).

286. For adulterating unadulterated commodities, and for breaking gems or for improperly boring (them), the fine is the first (or lowest) amercement.

287. But that man who behaves dishonestly to honest (customers) or cheats in his prices, shall be fined in the first or in the middlemost amercement.

288. Let him place all prisons near a high-road, where the suffering and disfigured offenders can be seen.

289. Him who destroys the wall (of a town), or fills up the ditch (round a town), or breaks a (town)-gate, he shall instantly banish.

290. For all incantations intended to destroy life,

---

refers to cases when death is not (the result of the wrong treatment); for if that is the case the punishment is greater.'

285. Vi. V, 174; Yâ*gñ*. II, 297. 'A pole,' i. e. the flagstaff of a village (Nâr.), or 'such as stand in tanks and the like' (Kull.). 'Images,' i.e. 'statues of men; but death as the punishment for destroying images of the gods, because (above, verse 280) capital punishment has been prescribed for breaking into temples' (Nâr.). Kull. and Râgh. say 'common images, made of clay and so forth.'

286. Vi. V, 124; Yâ*gñ*. II, 245-246. Medh. thinks that the fine must be proportionate to the value of the spoiled gem, and Kull. adds that in every case the owner of the spoilt article shall receive compensation.

287. Thus Kull. and Nâr. But Medh. takes the first clause differently: 'That man who gives unequal (quantities) for (such goods as ought to be bartered for) equal (quantities).'

288. Nand. reads kash*t*âni, 'where the treatment is severe,' instead of sarvâ*n*i, 'all.'

290. According to the commentators the abhi*k*ârâ*h* comprise

for magic rites with roots (practised by persons) not related (to him against whom they are directed), and for various kinds of sorcery, a fine of two hundred (pa*n*as) shall be inflicted.

291. He who sells (for seed-corn that which is) not seed-corn, he who takes up seed (already sown), and he who destroys a boundary(-mark), shall be punished by mutilation.

292. But the king shall cause a goldsmith who behaves dishonestly, the most nocuous of all the thorns, to be cut to pieces with razors.

293. For the theft of agricultural implements, of arms and of medicines, let the king award punishment, taking into account the time (of the offence) and the use (of the object).

---

all incantations and sacrifices, taught either in the Veda or in secular works, which are intended to destroy life. The magic rites, performed with roots, are those which are intended to bring a person into one's power. These are permitted, if practised against a husband or a relative (Nâr.). The k*ri*tyâ*h*, 'sorcery,' are such spells as produce diseases, or cause the failure of an adversary's undertakings. If the abhi*k*âras are successful, the punishment is that of murder (Medh., Kull.).

291. Instead of bî*g*otk*ri*sh*t*am (Kull.), which is explained 'who sells seed-corn placed (at the top of a bag of worthless grain),' the correct reading seems to be bî*g*otkrash*t*â, 'he who takes up seed (already sown).' Bî*g*otkrash*t*â occurs in Nâr.'s commentary only, where it is explained bî*g*akâle mahârghatâkâmotkarshakârî, 'he who at sowing time plucks (the seed) out, desiring to raise the price of grain.' All the other commentators give more or less corrupt readings, which, however, all point to the form bî*g*otkrash*t*â, viz. Medh., bî*g*etkrush*t*a*h* or bî*g*otk*ri*ptya*h*, explained by vandhyâ-nîti kshetra *gñ*âtu [kshetrâ*n*i kartu*m*] bî*g*am utkarshati *s*obhana*m* yad bî*g*a*m* kshetre [ta]devoddh*ri*tya nayati; Gov., bî*g*otk*ri*sh*t*â*h*; Nand., bî*g*otk*ri*sh*t*o*h* and bî*g*otk*ri*sh*t*â, explained by bî*g*ânâm uptânâm uddhartâ; K., bîryâtkrash*t*â, marked as corrupt.

293. Thus a theft of a plough in the season for ploughing, or of

294. The king and his minister, his capital, his realm, his treasury, his army, and his ally are the seven constituent parts (of a kingdom); (hence) a kingdom is said to have seven limbs (aṅga).

295. But let him know (that) among these seven constituent parts of a kingdom (which have been enumerated) in due order, each earlier (named) is more important and (its destruction) the greater calamity.

296. Yet in a kingdom, containing seven constituent parts, which is upheld like the triple staff (of an ascetic), there is no (single part) more important (than the others), by reason of the importance of the qualities of each for the others.

297. For each part is particularly qualified for (the accomplishment of) certain objects, (and thus) each is declared to be the most important for that particular purpose which is effected by its means.

298. By spies, by a (pretended) display of energy, and by carrying out (various) undertakings, let the king constantly ascertain his own and his enemy's strength;

299. Moreover, all calamities and vices; afterwards, when he has fully considered their relative importance, let him begin his operations.

---

arms just before or during a fight, should be punished more heavily than if it had been committed at any other time.

294. See above, VII, 257; Yâgñ. I, 352.

296. The verse is meant, as the commentators remark, to show that one must not infer from verse 295 that the Aṅgas, named later in the enumeration, may be neglected. According to Nâr., the simile is not taken from the triple staff of an ascetic, but from the three beams of a house and the like.

298. See above, VII. Medh., Gov., Nâr., Nand., and K. read at the end of the line, parâtmano*h*, instead of mahîpati*h*.

299. 'All calamities and vices,' i. e. 'those affecting his enemy

300. (Though he be) ever so much tired (by repeated failures), let him begin his operations again and again; for fortune greatly favours the man who (strenuously) exerts himself in his undertakings.

301. The various ways in which a king behaves (resemble) the Krita, Tretâ, Dvâpara, and Kali ages; hence the king is identified with the ages (of the world).

302. Sleeping he represents the Kali (or iron age), waking the Dvâpara (or brazen) age, ready to act the Tretâ (or silver age), but moving (actively) the Krita (or golden) age.

303. Let the king emulate the energetic action of Indra, of the Sun, of the Wind, of Yama, of Varuna, of the Moon, of the Fire, and of the Earth.

304. As Indra sends copious rain during the four months of the rainy season, even so let the king, taking upon himself the office of Indra, shower benefits on his kingdom.

305. As the Sun during eight months (imperceptibly) draws up the water with his rays, even so let him gradually draw his taxes from his kingdom; for that is the office in which he resembles the Sun.

306. As the Wind moves (everywhere), entering (in the shape of the vital air) all created beings, even so let him penetrate (everywhere) through his

---

and his enemy's party' (Nâr.), or 'those affecting both his own and the enemy's parties' (Kull.). Nand. reads the second line as follows, gurulâghavato gñâtvâ tatah karma samâkaret.

302. This verse closely agrees with the fourth exhortation, addressed by Indra to Rohita, Aitareya-brâhmana VII, 15.

305. Instead of nityam, 'gradually,' Nand. reads samyak, 'duly.'

spies; that is the office in which he resembles the Wind.

307. As Yama at the appointed time subjects to his rule both friends and foes, even so all subjects must be controlled by the king; that is the office in which he resembles Yama.

308. As (a sinner) is seen bound with ropes by Varu*n*a, even so let him punish the wicked; that is his office in which he resembles Varu*n*a.

309. He is a king, taking upon himself the office of the Moon, whose (appearance) his subjects (greet with as great joy) as men feel on seeing the full moon.

310. (If) he is ardent in wrath against criminals and endowed with brilliant energy, and destroys wicked vassals, then his character is said (to resemble) that of Fire.

311. As the Earth supports all created beings equally, thus (a king) who supports all his subjects, (takes upon himself) the office of the Earth.

312. Employing these and other means, the king shall, ever untired, restrain thieves both in his own dominions and in (those of) others.

313. Let him not, though fallen into the deepest distress, provoke Brâhma*n*as to anger; for they,

---

308. Nand. reads the first line differently, Varu*n*enâpi pâ*s*ai*s* *k*a badhyate vâru*n*air nara*h*, 'As men are bound by Varu*n*a with Varu*n*a's fetters.' The expression 'the fetters of Varu*n*a' is a common designation of dropsy.

310. Nâr. adds, 'As the fire at an ordeal injures wicked men, even so he should destroy wicked neighbours.'

312. 'In (those of) others,' i. e. 'those thieves who live in other kingdoms, and come to rob in his own' (Kull., Nâr.). Nand. omits this and the next two verses.

313. 'Let him not provoke Brâhma*n*as to anger,' i.e. 'by taking their

when angered, could instantly destroy him together with his army and his vehicles.

314. Who could escape destruction, when he provokes to anger those (men), by whom the fire was made to consume all things, by whom the (water of the) ocean was made undrinkable, and by whom the moon was made to wane and to increase again?

315. Who could prosper, while he injures those (men) who provoked to anger, could create other worlds and other guardians of the world, and deprive the gods of their divine station?

316. What man, desirous of life, would injure them to whose support the (three) worlds and the gods ever owe their existence, and whose wealth is the Veda?

317. A Brâhma*n*a, be he ignorant or learned, is a great divinity, just as the fire, whether carried forth (for the performance of a burnt-oblation) or not carried forth, is a great divinity.

318. The brilliant fire is not contaminated even in burial-places, and, when presented with oblations (of butter) at sacrifices, it again increases mightily.

---

property' (Medh., Nâr.), or 'treating them with contumely' (Medh.). 'They could destroy him,' i. e. 'by magic rites and curses' (Kull.).

314. This verse refers to certain stories, told, as Medh. and Nâr. point out, in the section of the Mahâbhârata, called Mokshadharmâ*h* XII, 344, 55, 57–58, 60–61. There it is said that Bh*ri*gu made the fire consume all things, that the moon became 'consumptive' in consequence of the curse of Daksha, and that Va*d*avâmukha made the ocean salt in punishment for his disobedience.

315. This verse also contains allusions to the Mahâbhârata. Vi*s*vâmitra tried to create other worlds (Medh.), the Vâlakhilyas another Indra and Vâyu, and others deprived the gods of their station. With respect to the latter point, Râgh. quotes the story of Mâ*nd*avya cursing Yama (Mahâbhârata I, 108, 16), and causing him to be born as a *S*ûdra.

316. See above, I, 93-95.

319. Thus, though Brâhma*n*as employ themselves in all (sorts of) mean occupations, they must be honoured in every way; for (each of) them is a very great deity.

320. When the Kshatriyas become in any way overbearing towards the Brâhma*n*as, the Brâhma*n*as themselves shall duly restrain them; for the Kshatriyas sprang from the Brâhma*n*as.

321. Fire sprang from water, Kshatriyas from Brâhma*n*as, iron from stone; the all-penetrating force of those (three) has no effect on that whence they were produced.

322. Kshatriyas prosper not without Brâhma*n*as, Brâhma*n*as prosper not without Kshatriyas; Brâhma*n*as and Kshatriyas, being closely united, prosper in this (world) and in the next.

323. But (a king who feels his end drawing nigh) shall bestow all his wealth, accumulated from fines, on Brâhma*n*as, make over his kingdom to his son, and then seek death in battle.

---

321. 'Fire sprang from water, thus speak the Paurâ*n*ikas' (Nand.); '(that origin is) visible in the case of lightning and in that of the (submarine) Va*d*avâgni' (Râgh.). According to Râgh., the statement that the Kshatriyas sprang from the Brâhma*n*as is based on a Vedic passage. But Nâr. thinks that it alludes to a Paurâ*n*ik story, according to which the Brâhma*n*as produced with the Kshatriyâ females a new Kshatriya race after the destruction of the second var*n*a by Para*s*urâma.

322. Gaut. XI, 14; Vas. XIX, 4.

323. Medh. says that others explain the expression 'all his wealth, accumulated from fines,' as including 'all the king's possessions, excepting horses and chariots, arms, land, and slaves,' but that this is improper. He adds that, if the king cannot die in battle, he may burn or drown himself. Kull. says that he may kill himself by starvation. In later times kings followed this rule; see e.g. Vikramâṅka*k*arita IV, 44–68.

324. Thus conducting himself (and) ever intent on (discharging) his royal duties, a king shall order all his servants (to work) for the good of his people.

325. Thus the eternal law concerning the duties of a king has been fully declared; know that the following rules apply in (due) order to the duties of Vai*s*yas and *S*ûdras.

326. After a Vai*s*ya has received the sacraments and has taken a wife, he shall be always attentive to the business whereby he may subsist and to (that of) tending cattle.

327. For when the Lord of creatures (Pra*g*âpati) created cattle, he made them over to the Vai*s*ya; to the Brâhma*n*a, and to the king he entrusted all created beings.

328. A Vai*s*ya must never (conceive this) wish, 'I will not keep cattle;' and if a Vai*s*ya is willing (to keep them), they must never be kept by (men of) other (castes).

329. (A Vai*s*ya) must know the respective value of gems, of pearls, of coral, of metals, of (cloth) made of thread, of perfumes, and of condiments.

330. He must be acquainted with the (manner of) sowing of seeds, and of the good and bad qualities of fields, and he must perfectly know all measures and weights.

331. Moreover, the excellence and defects of commodities, the advantages and disadvantages of (different) countries, the (probable) profit and loss on merchandise, and the means of properly rearing cattle.

332. He must be acquainted with the (proper)

---

326. Regarding the 'business whereby a Vai*s*ya may subsist,' see below, X, 77-78.

wages of servants, with the various languages of men, with the manner of keeping goods, and (the rules of) purchase and sale.

333. Let him exert himself to the utmost in order to increase his property in a righteous manner, and let him zealously give food to all created beings.

334. But to serve Brâhma*n*as (who are) learned in the Vedas, householders, and famous (for virtue) is the highest duty of a *S*ûdra, which leads to beatitude.

335. (A *S*ûdra who is) pure, the servant of his betters, gentle in his speech, and free from pride, and always seeks a refuge with Brâhma*n*as, attains (in his next life) a higher caste.

336. The excellent law for the conduct of the (four) castes (var*n*a), (when they are) not in distress, has been thus promulgated; now hear in order their (several duties) in times of distress.

CHAPTER X.

1. Let the three twice-born castes (var*n*a), discharging their (prescribed) duties, study (the Veda); but among them the Brâhma*n*a (alone) shall teach it, not the other two; that is an established rule.

333. 'If a rich Vai*s*ya is not liberal, he shall be punished by the king' (Medh.).

334–336. See below, X, 121–129.

335. I read with Medh., Gov., and Nâr., brâhma*n*âpâ*s*rayo nityam.

X. 1. Medh. has one line more in the beginning, 'Hereafter I will declare the rules applicable to that which must be studied.' According to Nâr., the expression svakarmasthâ*h*, 'discharging their prescribed duties,' means 'if they follow their prescribed

2. The Brâhma*n*a must know the means of subsistence (prescribed) by law for all, instruct the others, and himself live according to (the law).

3. On account of his pre-eminence, on account of the superiority of his origin, on account of his observance of (particular) restrictive rules, and on account of his particular sanctification the Brâhma*n*a is the lord of (all) castes (var*n*a).

4. The Brâhma*n*a, the Kshatriya, and the Vai*s*ya castes (var*n*a) are the twice-born ones, but the fourth, the *S*ûdra, has one birth only; there is no fifth (caste).

5. In all castes (var*n*a) those (children) only which are begotten in the direct order on wedded wives, equal (in caste and married as) virgins, are to be

---

occupations,' and indicates that those who follow forbidden occupations, i. e. live like *S*ûdras, shall not study the Veda. The commentators entirely forget to mention that, according to II, 241–242, a Brâhma*n*a may learn the Veda from a non-Brâhma*n*ical teacher, and that hence this rule is not absolute.

2. Gaut. XI, 25; Vas. I, 39–41. Medh. points out that this rule gives an exception to IV, 80, where it is said that a Brâhma*n*a shall not give spiritual advice to a *S*ûdra.

3. See above, I, 93. 'On account of his pre-eminence,' i. e. 'through his qualities' (Medh.), or 'by race' (Gov., Kull., Nâr., Râgh.). Niyamasya *k*a dhâra*n*ât, 'on account of his observance of (particular) restrictive rules,' i. e. 'of the rules prescribed for a Snâtaka' (Medh., Gov., Nâr., Râgh.), means according to Kull. 'on account of his possessing a particularly great knowledge of the Veda.' 'On account of his particular sanctification,' i. e. 'because special observances are required from him in sipping water and so forth, or because he must be initiated earlier than a Kshatriya' (Medh.). The other commentators give the second explanation only. 'The lord,' i. e. 'the adviser and instructor.'

4. Âp. I, 1, 3; Vas. II, 1–2; Baudh. I, 16, 1; Yâ*gñ*. I, 10.

5. Âp. II, 13, 1; Vi. XVI, 1; Yâ*gñ*. I, 90. 'In the direct order,' i. e. 'by a Brâhma*n*a on a Brâhma*n*î, by a Kshatriya on a Kshatriyâ, and so forth' (Medh., Gov., Kull.), means according to Nâr., that

considered as belonging to the same caste (as their fathers).

6. Sons, begotten by twice-born men on wives of the next lower castes, they declare to be similar (to their fathers, but) blamed on account of the fault (inherent) in their mothers.

7. Such is the eternal law concerning (children) born of wives one degree lower (than their husbands); know (that) the following rule (is applicable) to those born of women two or three degrees lower.

8. From a Brâhma*n*a with the daughter of a Vai*s*ya is born (a son) called an Ambash*th*a, with the daughter of a *S*ûdra a Nishâda, who is also called a Pâra*s*ava.

---

in each case the bridegroom must be older than the wife. He adds, 'Hence it has been declared that the son of a woman who is older than (her husband) is not a Brâhma*n*a, though she may have been legally married, and may be of the same caste (as her husband).' The commentators are at great pains to prove that subsidiary sons, such as Saho*dh*as, Kânînas, and so forth, and all offspring of illicit unions are outcasts. Medh. and Gov. even take the trouble to discuss the Vedic story of *G*âbâla Satyakâma (*Kh*ândogya Up. IV, 4), whose mother did not know by whom he was begotten, and who, nevertheless, was admitted to be a Brâhma*n*a. They are of opinion that *G*abâlâ had been legally married, and had forgotten her husband's family-name during her troubles.

6–56. Gaut. IV, 16–28; Vas. XVIII; Baudh. I, 16, 6–17, 15; Vi. XVI, 2–15; Yâ*gñ*. I, 91–95.

6. 'Blamed,' i. e. 'excluded from the fathers' caste' (Nâr.). With the expression 'similar,' compare Baudh.'s term 'savar*n*a.' Nand. places verse 14 immediately after this, and adds that if the latter is placed lower down, that is owing to a mistake of the copyists.

7. Regarding the term Pâra*s*ava, see above, IX, 178. Gov. and Nâr. remark that the second name Parâ*s*ava is added in order to distinguish this Nishâda from the other Nishâda, who is a Pratiloma, and subsists by catching fish.

8. Medh. does not give this verse.

9. From a Kshatriya and the daughter of a *S*ûdra springs a being, called Ugra, resembling both a Kshatriya and a *S*ûdra, ferocious in his manners, and delighting in cruelty.

10. Children of a Brâhma*n*a by (women of) the three (lower) castes, of a Kshatriya by (wives of) the two (lower) castes, and of a Vai*s*ya by (a wife of) the one caste (below him) are all six called base-born (apasada).

11. From a Kshatriya by the daughter of a Brâhma*n*a is born (a son called) according to his caste (*g*âti) a Sûta; from a Vai*s*ya by females of the royal and the Brâhma*n*a (castes) spring a Mâgadha and a Vaideha.

12. From a *S*ûdra are born an Âyogava, a Kshatt*ri*, and a *K*â*nd*âla, the lowest of men, by Vai*s*ya, Kshatriya, and Brâhma*n*a females, (sons who owe their origin to) a confusion of the castes.

13. As an Ambash*th*a and an Ugra, (begotten) in the direct order on (women) one degree lower (than their husbands) are declared (to be), even so are a Kshatt*ri* and a Vaidehaka, though they were born in the inverse order of the castes (from mothers one degree higher than the fathers).

14. Those sons of the twice-born, begotten on wives of the next lower castes, who have been enumerated in due order, they call by the name

12. Nâr. and K. read Ayogava. Medh. and Nand. read *K*a*nd*âla, instead of *K*â*nd*âla (Gov., Kull.).

13. The meaning is that the Kshatt*ri* and the Vaidehaka, though Pratilomas, hold the same position with respect to sacred rites, but not with respect to studying and so forth, and are as fit to be touched as the two Anulomas (Medh.). Gov. and Kull. mention the second point of equality only.

14. The meaning is that they are reckoned as belonging to the

Anantaras (belonging to the next lower caste), on account of the blemish (inherent) in their mothers.

15. A Brâhma*n*a begets on the daughter of an Ugra an Âv*ri*ta, on the daughter of an Ambash*th*a an Âbhîra, but on a female of the Âyogava (caste) a Dhigva*n*a.

16. From a *S*ûdra spring in the inverse order (by females of the higher castes) three base-born (sons, apasada), an Âyogava, a Kshatt*ri*, and a *K*â*nd*âla, the lowest of men;

17. From a Vai*s*ya are born in the inverse order of the castes a Mâgadha and a Vaideha, but from a Kshatriya a Sûta only; these are three other base-born ones (apasada).

18. The son of a Nishâda by a *S*ûdra female becomes a Pukkasa by caste (*g*âti), but the son of a *S*ûdra by a Nishâda female is declared to be a Kukku*t*aka.

19. Moreover, the son of a Kshatt*ri* by an Ugra female is called a *S*vapâka; but one begotten by a Vaidehaka on an Ambash*th*a female is named a Ve*n*a.

20. Those (sons) whom the twice-born beget on wives of equal caste, but who, not fulfilling their

---

mothers' caste and receive the sacraments according to the law prescribed for the mothers' caste (Medh., Gov., Kull., Nâr., Nand.); see also below, verse 41.

15. The Âbhîra is the modern Ahir.

16–17. Kull. thinks that the Pratilomas are enumerated once more, 'in order to show that they are unfit to fulfil the duties of sons.' Nand. places these two verses before verse 15.

18. Nand. reads Pulkasa instead of Pukkasa.

19. Gov., Nand., and K. read Vena instead of Ve*n*a. Râgh. adds that the modern name is Baru*d*a, the name of caste of basket-makers.

20. Gov. and Nand. read at the end of the first line sutân for

sacred duties, are excluded from the Sâvitrî, one must designate by the appellation Vrâtyas.

21. But from a Vrâtya (of the) Brâhma*n*a (caste) spring the wicked Bh*r*igg*a*ka*n*t*aka, the Âvantya, the Vâ*t*adhâna, the Pushpadha, and the *S*aikha.

22. From a Vrâtya (of the) Kshatriya (caste), the *Gh*alla, the Malla, the Li*kkh*ivi, the Na*t*a, the Kara*n*a, the Khasa, and the Dravi*d*a.

---

tu yân (Medh., Kull., K.), 'not fulfilling their sacred duties,' i. e. 'not being initiated at the proper time;' see above, II, 39. Medh. mentions a var. lect. avratâ*h*, 'Those sons whom men neglecting their sacred duties, &c.' But he rejects it.

21. I read with Medh., Gov., Nâr., and K., Bh*r*igg*a*ka*n*t*aka instead of Bhûrg*a*ka*n*t*aka (editions), or Bhûtyaka*n*t*aka (Nand.); see also Gaut. IV, 20, where the form Bh*r*igyaka*n*t*a occurs. Regarding the Âvantya (Âpa*ñk*a, Nand.), see also Baudh. I, 2, 13. Instead of Vâ*t*adhâna Nand. has Vâ*d*aghâna, and K. Vâ*dh*adhâna, marked as corrupt. Medh. reads (one MS. Pushpa*s*aikhara*h*) Pushpa*s*ekhara instead of pushpadha*h* *s*aikha eva *k*a (editions). Gov. has in the text Pushya*h* *s*aikhakastathâ, in the commentary pushyavasai*s*akha; K. pushpa . . . kharas tathâ; Nand. Pushpa*s*îbaka eva *k*a. It would seem that according to Medh. and Nand. only four tribes, sprung from a Vrâtya Brâhma*n*a, are enumerated. But the form of the last name remains doubtful. The commentators think all the races named are descended from a Vrâtya Brâhma*n*a and a female of his own caste. Gov. remarks that according to U*s*anas' Nîti*s*âstra the Bh*r*igg*a*ka*n*t*as live by sorcery, the Âvantyas and Vâ*t*adhânas serve in war, and all other Vrâtyas are spies. It is very probable that all these names originally denote nations, but the Âvantyas, the inhabitants of Western Mâlvâ, and the Vâ*t*adhânas, who are enumerated among the northern tribes, are alone traceable in other works.

22. I read with Medh. and Gov. Li*kkh*ivi instead of Ni*kkh*ivi (editions). K. has Li*kh*avi (*kh*a being marked as corrupt), and Nand. Li*kk*ikhi. As 'a' and 'i' in thesi are constantly exchanged, Li*kkh*ivi may be considered as a vicarious form for Li*kkh*avi, and it may be assumed that the Manusa*m*hitâ considered the famous Kshatriya race of Magadha and Nepâl as unorthodox. Gov. says that, according to U*s*anas, the Na*t*as and Kara*n*as are spies, and

23. From a Vrâtya (of the) Vai*s*ya (caste) are born a Sudhanvan, an Â*k*ârya, a Kârusha, a Vi*g*anman, a Maitra, and a Sâtvata.

24. By adultery (committed by persons) of (different) castes, by marriages with women who ought not to be married, and by the neglect of the duties and occupations (prescribed) to each, are produced (sons who owe their origin) to a confusion of the castes.

25. I will (now) fully enumerate those (sons) of mixed origin, who are born of Anulomas and of Pratilomas, and (thus) are mutually connected.

26. The Sûta, the Vaidehaka, the *K*a*nd*âla, that lowest of mortals, the Mâgadha, he of the Kshatt*ri* caste (*g*âti), and the Âyogava,

27. These six (Pratilomas) beget similar races (var*n*a) on women of their own (caste), they (also) produce (the like) with females of their mother's caste (*g*âti), and with females (of) higher ones.

---

the Khasas and Dravi*d*as are water-carriers and distributors of waters at drinking fountains.

23. K. reads Pârusha, and Nand. Kâru*g*a, instead of Kârusha (Medh., Gov., Kull.). Instead of Vi*g*anman Nand. has Ni*g*aṅgha. Gov. remarks that, according to U*s*anas, Â*k*âryas and Sâtvatas subsist by worshipping the gods, or serving as temple-priests (â*k*âryasâtvatai*h* devapû*g*anam).

25. 'Anulomas,' see above, verse 8.

27. Thus Nâr. and Nand., with whom Kull. agrees, except that he adds 'on higher and (on lower) castes.' Medh. reads in the second line mât*rig*âtyâ*h* prasûyante pravarâsu *k*a yonishu, and explains as follows, 'Those who belong to the mother's caste, i.e. the Anulomas, called Anantara (verse 14), beget similar sons on females of their own caste, and (more degraded children) on females of higher castes.' He mentions that others read mat*rig*âtau prasûyante, and says that the meaning then is, 'The Anulomas beget sons of their own race on females of their own and of their mothers' castes.' Gov. reads mât*rig*âtau svayonyâ*m* tu sad*ris*a*m* *g*anayanti vai, and

28. As a (Brâhma*n*a) begets on (females of) two out of the three (twice-born castes a son similar to) himself, (but inferior) on account of the lower degree (of the mother), and (one equal to himself) on a female of his own race, even so is the order in the case of the excluded (races, vâhya).

29. Those (six mentioned above) also beget, the one on the females of the other, a great many (kinds of) despicable (sons), even more sinful than their (fathers), and excluded (from the Âryan community, vâhya).

30. Just as a *S*ûdra begets on a Brâhma*n*a female a being excluded (from the Âryan community), even so (a person himself) excluded pro-

---

likewise refers the line to the Anulomas. 'But (the Anulomas) beget similar sons on females of their mothers' and of their own castes.' Râgh. likewise differs.

28. I read with all the commentators and K., krama*h* instead of kramât (editions). 'Even so is the order in the case of the excluded (races),' means according to Gov. and Kull., that there is a difference in rank between Pratilomas, similar to that existing between Anulomas, and that Pratilomas sprung from Âryan fathers are more respectable than those begotten by *S*ûdra fathers, according to Medh., whose opinion is controverted by Gov., Kull., and Râgh., that Pratilomas, sprung from Âryan fathers and mothers, are to be considered Âryans, and worthy of being initiated just as Anulomas. According to Nâr. and Nand., the translation should be as follows: 'As among the three castes a (man) produces (a son similar to) himself on two wives, (i. e.) on her who belongs to his own caste and on her who belongs to the next lower one, even so is the order with those excluded (from the four chief castes),' i. e. even so is it with Anulomas, e. g. with a Mûrdhâvasikta, who begets a Mûrdhâvasikta on a Mûrdhâvasikta female and on an Âvantya female (Nâr.), and with Pratilomas, e. g. with a Kshatt*ri* who begets a Kshatt*ri* both on a female of his own caste and on a *K*a*nd*âlî (Nand.). It must be added that Nand. reads anantaryâm instead of ânantaryât.

creates with (females of) the four castes (var*n*a, sons) more (worthy of being) excluded (than he himself).

31. But men excluded (by the Âryans, vâhya), who approach females of higher rank, beget races (var*n*a) still more worthy to be excluded, low men (hîna) still lower races, even fifteen (in number).

---

31. In order to show that fifteen lower castes are produced, the commentators propose various interpretations of the verse, among which those of Kull., Nâr., and Râgh. alone deserve to be mentioned. Kull. thinks that the terms vâhya and hîna may either refer to two sets of men or to one only. Under the former supposition, the Vâhyas must be understood to be the Pratiloma offspring of a *S*ûdra, i.e. Âyogavas, Kshatt*r*is, and *K*a*nd*âlas; and the Hînas, the Pratiloma offspring of Kshatriyas and Vai*s*yas, i.e. Sûtas, Mâgadhas, and Vaidehas. Each of these two sets produce fifteen lower races by unions with women of the four chief castes and of their own (verse 27), i.e. Âyogavas beget five, with Brâhma*n*a, Kshatriya, Vai*s*ya, *S*ûdra, and Âyogava women; Kshatt*r*is likewise five, with Brâhma*n*a, Kshatriya, Vai*s*ya, *S*ûdra, and Kshatt*r*î women, and so forth. But if the two terms vâhya and hîna are referred to one set of males only, they must be understood to denote the six Pratilomas, *K*a*nd*âlas, Kshatt*r*is, Âyogavas, Vaidehas, Mâgadhas, and Sûtas; and it must be assumed that the verse refers to unions between these six Pratiloma races alone. Then the lowest among them, the *K*a*nd*âla, may produce with females of the five higher Pratiloma tribes five more degraded races; the Kshatt*r*i, with the four above him, four; the Âyogava, the three above him, three; the Vaideha, two; and the Mâgadha, one. The total of 5+4+3+2+1 is thus 15. Râgh. agrees with this interpretation. Nâr., on the other hand, refers the terms vâhya and hîna to one set of males, the three Pratilomas sprung from the *S*ûdra, and assumes that the verse refers to unions of these three with females of the four principal castes and of their own. According to the calculation given under Kull.'s first explanation, the total of more degraded races which may be thus produced, is thirty. It seems to me that Kull.'s second explanation is the best, though I am not prepared to deny that his first explanation, and even Nâr.'s version, may be defended. The commentators point out that var*n*a is used here in a figurative sense, because it has been declared above, verse 4, that there are only four real var*n*as.

32. A Dasyu begets on an Âyogava (woman) a Sairandhra, who is skilled in adorning and attending (his master), who, (though) not a slave, lives like a slave, (or) subsists by snaring (animals).

33. A Vaideha produces (with the same) a sweet-voiced Maitreyaka, who, ringing a bell at the appearance of dawn, continually praises (great) men.

34. A Nishâda begets (on the same) a Mârgava (or) Dâ*s*a, who subsists by working as a boatman, (and) whom the inhabitants of Âryâvarta call a Kaivarta.

35. Those three base-born ones are severally begot on Âyogava women, who wear the clothes of the dead, are wicked, and eat reprehensible food.

---

32. I read with Medh., Gov., Nâr., Nand., and K., Sairandhra instead of Sairandhri (editions). 'A Dasyu,' i.e. 'one of those tribes described below, verse 45' (Medh., Gov., Kull.), or 'one of the afore-mentioned fifteen Pratiloma races' (Nâr., Nand.). Prasâdhanopa*k*âra*g*ñam, 'skilled in adorning and attending (his master),' i.e. 'in dressing hair, anointing him with oil and so forth, and in shampooing' (Gov., Nâr., Nand.), means according to Kull., who takes prasâdhanopa*k*âra, not as a copulative, but as a tatpurusha compound, 'skilled in serving (his master) at his toilet.' Medh.'s explanation is ambiguous. With respect to his second occupation, 'snaring animals,' Medh., Gov., and Kull. say that the Sairandhra resorts to it in order to support himself in times of distress, or in order to obtain meat for the worship of the gods and manes, or at the order of the king. Nand. remarks, 'As the Dasyus are many, there are also many Sairandhras, and that is indicated by the addition of a different mode of subsistence.'

34. Gov. and K. read Mâgadha instead of Mârgava. Gov. thinks that, as the section treats of Pratilomas, the Nishâda mentioned here is the Pratiloma Nishâda enumerated by Vyâsa.

35. I follow Medh., Gov., Nâr., Nand., and K., who read m*ri*tavastrabh*ri*tsvanâryâsu, 'who wear the clothes of the dead, are wicked,' instead of m*ri*tavastrabh*ri*tsu nârîshu, 'women who wear the clothes of the dead' (editions). Kull. also seems to have had the

36. From a Nishâda springs (by a woman of the Vaideha caste) a Kârâvara, who works in leather; and from a Vaidehaka (by women of the Kârâvara and Nishâda castes), an Andhra and a Meda, who dwell outside the village.

37. From a *Kand*âla by a Vaideha woman is born a Pâ*nd*usopâka, who deals in cane; from a Nishâda (by the same) an Âhi*nd*ika.

38. But from a *Kand*âla by a Pukkasa woman is born the sinful Sopâka, who lives by the occupations of his sire, and is ever despised by good men.

39. A Nishâda woman bears to a *Kand*âla a son (called) Antyâvasâyin, employed in burial-grounds, and despised even by those excluded (from the Âryan community).

40. These races, (which originate) in a confusion (of the castes and) have been described according to their fathers and mothers, may be known by their occupations, whether they conceal or openly show themselves.

---

former reading, as he copies the explanation sukrûrâsu, 'very cruel,' which Gov. gives. Medh. explains anâryâsu by 'not to be touched by Âryans.'

36. Thus according to Medh. and Kull. But Gov. and Râgh. understand in the second line with 'from a Vaidehaka,' the words 'by women of the Vaideha caste.' Nâr., who in the preceding verse takes the words ete traya*h*, 'those three,' in the sense of 'the following three other races,' assumes of course that the mothers of Kârâvaras, Medas, and Andhras are Âyogava females. The latter two 'castes' are the well-known nations inhabiting Mevâ*d* (Medapâ*t*a) in south-eastern Râgputâna, and the eastern Dekkan.

38. Râgh. and Nand. read Paulkasa instead of Pukkasa. Mûlavyasanav*ri*ttimân means according to Gov., Kull., and Râgh. 'who lives by executing criminals,' according to Nâr. and Nand. 'who lives by digging roots,' i. e. 'in order to sell them as medicine,' or 'by curing hemorrhoids' (Nand.). Medh. gives both explanations. The translation, given above, follows the Petersburg Dict., sub voce.

41. Six sons, begotten (by Âryans) on women of equal and the next lower castes (Anantara), have the duties of twice-born men; but all those born in consequence of a violation (of the law) are, as regards their duties, equal to *S*ûdras.

42. By the power of austerities and of the seed (from which they sprang), these (races) obtain here among men more exalted or lower rank in successive births.

43. But in consequence of the omission of the sacred rites, and of their not consulting Brâhma*n*as, the following tribes of Kshatriyas have gradually sunk in this world to the condition of *S*ûdras;

44. (Viz.) the Pau*nd*rakas, the *K*o*d*as, the Dravi*d*as, the Kâmbo*g*as, the Yavanas, the *S*akas, the Pâradas, the Pahlavas, the *K*înas, the Kirâtas, and the Daradas.

---

41. Medh. adds, 'The mention of the Anantaras is intended to include all Anulomas.'

42. 'These,' i. e. 'those born of wives of equal castes and Anantaras' (Gov., Kull.). Medh. and Nâr. include all Anulomas, and Râgh. even Pratilomas, sprung from Âryan fathers. Yuge yuge, 'in successive births' (Medh., Nâr., Nand.), means according to Kull. 'in each of the ages of the world.' Kull. refers to the stories regarding Vi*s*vâmitra and *R*ishya*s*ri*n*ga, while Medh. points to the discussion, given below, verse 64 seq.

43. Medh. and Gov. read brâhma*n*âtikrame*n*a, 'by disrespect towards Brâhma*n*as,' instead of brâhma*n*âdar*s*anena, 'by not consulting Brâhma*n*as' (Kull., Nâr., Nand., Râgh., K.).

44. Instead of Pau*nd*rakas (Kull.), Medh., Nâr., Nand., and K. read Pu*nd*rakas, and Gov. Pau*ndh*rakas. My reading *K*o*d*as is a correction of *K*o*md*ra, which is found in some MSS. of Medh. and in K. We have plainly *K*ola in Nand., while some MSS. of Medh. and Gov. read *K*â*m*dra or *K*â*md*ra, and the editions give *K*au*d*ra. Sir W. Jones' opinion that *k*au*d*ra stands for *k*a O*d*ra is improbable, because the particle 'and' is clearly not wanted after the first word. Instead of Pahlava, some MSS. of Medh. and some editions

45. All those tribes in this world, which are excluded from (the community of) those born from the mouth, the arms, the thighs, and the feet (of Brahman), are called Dasyus, whether they speak the language of the Mle*kkh*as (barbarians) or that of the Âryans.

46. Those who have been mentioned as the base-born (offspring, apasada) of Âryans, or as produced in consequence of a violation (of the law, apadhva*m*sa*g*a), shall subsist by occupations reprehended by the twice-born.

47. To Sûtas (belongs) the management of horses and of chariots; to Ambash*th*as, the art of healing; to Vaidehakas, the service of women; to Mâgadhas, trade;

48. Killing fish to Nishâdas; carpenters' work to the Âyogava; to Medas, Andhras, *K*uñ*k*us, and Madgus, the slaughter of wild animals;

---

read Pahnava. Gov. gives Pallava. The editions give the Khasas after the Daradas. But Medh., Gov., Nand., and K. have tathâ at the end of the verse. The commentators state that the names enumerated in the first instance denote countries, and next, particular races living in them.

45. 'Those born from the mouth, &c.,' i. e. the four Var*n*as; see above, I, 87.

46. 'Base-born offspring of Âryans;' see above, verses 17 and 41.

47. 'The service of women,' i.e. 'the office of guardians in the harem.'

48. Instead of *K*uñ*k*u (editions, Râgh.), Medh., Gov., and Nâr. seem to have read *K*û*k*u. Nand. reads Ma*m*su for Madgu. Nâr. says that these two words are synonyms of *Gh*alla and Malla; see above, verse 22. But Gov. quotes a verse of Yama, according to which the *K*û*k*uka is the son of a Vai*s*ya by a Kshatriya female, and the Madgu the offspring of a *S*ûdra and a Kshatriyâ. Kull.'s and Râgh.'s reference to Baudh. is, according to the MSS. of the Baudh. Dharmasûtra, erroneous.

49. To Kshattris, Ugras, and Pukkasas, catching and killing (animals) living in holes; to Dhigvanas, working in leather; to Venas, playing drums.

50. Near well-known trees and burial-grounds, on mountains and in groves, let these (tribes) dwell, known (by certain marks), and subsisting by their peculiar occupations.

51. But the dwellings of *Kand*âlas and *S*vapa*k*as shall be outside the village, they must be made Apapâtras, and their wealth (shall be) dogs and donkeys.

52. Their dress (shall be) the garments of the dead, (they shall eat) their food from broken dishes, black iron (shall be) their ornaments, and they must always wander from place to place.

53. A man who fulfils a religious duty, shall not seek intercourse with them; their transactions (shall be) among themselves, and their marriages with their equals.

54. Their food shall be given to them by others (than an Âryan giver) in a broken dish; at night they shall not walk about in villages and in towns.

---

49. Nand. omits this verse.

50. Nand. places verse 50 after verse 52.

51. Medh. and Nâr. read avapâtrâ*h* instead of apapâtrâ*h* (Kull., Râgh., K., and Gov.?), and Medh. gives three explanations of the term: 1. vessels used by them must be thrown away; 2. if food is given to them, it must not be placed in vessels which they hold in their hands, but in such as stand on the ground or are held by others; 3. they shall use bad, i.e. broken vessels, as is stated in the next verse. The other commentators adopt the first explanation, which is no doubt the correct one.

53. Gov. and Nand. say, 'A righteous man,' instead of 'A man who fulfils a religious duty.'

54. Gov. and Nâr. take the beginning of the verse differently,

55. By day they may go about for the purpose of their work, distinguished by marks at the king's command, and they shall carry out the corpses (of persons) who have no relatives; that is a settled rule.

56. By the king's order they shall always execute the criminals, in accordance with the law, and they shall take for themselves the clothes, the beds, and the ornaments of (such) criminals.

57. A man of impure origin, who belongs not to any caste, (varna, but whose character is) not known, who, (though) not an Âryan, has the appearance of an Âryan, one may discover by his acts.

58. Behaviour unworthy of an Âryan, harshness, cruelty, and habitual neglect of the prescribed duties betray in this world a man of impure origin.

59. A base-born man either resembles in character his father, or his mother, or both; he can never conceal his real nature.

60. Even if a man, born in a great family, sprang from criminal intercourse, he will certainly possess the faults of his (father), be they small or great.

61. But that kingdom in which such bastards, sullying (the purity of) the castes, are born, perishes quickly together with its inhabitants.

'Their food shall be given to them by others in a broken vessel,' i. e. 'they shall not cook for themselves in their houses.'

55. 'Distinguished by marks,' i. e. 'by a thunderbolt and the like, or by axes, adzes, and so forth, used for executing criminals, and carried on the shoulder' (Medh.), or 'by sticks and so forth' (Gov.), or 'by iron ornaments and peacock's feathers and the like' (Nâr.). Râgh. thinks that they are to be branded on the forehead and on other parts of the body. In olden times the depressed races of Gujarat used to wear a horn as their distinguishing mark.

57-59. Vas. XVIII, 7; Vi. XVI, 17.

62. Dying, without the expectation of a reward, for the sake of Brâhma*n*as and of cows, or in the defence of women and children, secures beatitude to those excluded (from the Âryan community, vâhya).

63. Abstention from injuring (creatures), veracity, abstention from unlawfully appropriating (the goods of others), purity, and control of the organs, Manu has declared to be the summary of the law for the four castes.

64. If (a female of the caste), sprung from a Brâhma*n*a and a *S*ûdra female, bear (children) to one of the highest caste, the inferior (tribe) attains the highest caste within the seventh generation.

---

62. Vi. XVI, 18.

63. Gaut. VIII, 23; Yâ*gñ*. I, 122; and above, IV, 246, V, 107. Nand. reads sarvavar*n*e, 'for all castes,' instead of *k*âturvar*n*ye, 'for the four castes.'

64. Âp. II, 10-11; Gaut. IV, 22; Yâ*gñ*. I, 96. According to Medh., Gov., Kull., and Râgh., the meaning is that, if the daughter of a Brâhma*n*a and of a *S*ûdra female and her descendants all marry Brâhma*n*as, the offspring of the sixth female descendant of the original couple will be a Brâhma*n*a. While this explanation agrees with Haradatta's comment on the parallel passage of Gautama, Nâr. and Nand. take the verse very differently. They say that if a Pâra*s*ava, the son of a Brâhma*n*a and of a *S*ûdra female, marries a most excellent Pâra*s*ava female, who possesses a good moral character and other virtues, and if his descendants do the same, the child born in the sixth generation will be a Brâhma*n*a. Nand. quotes in support of his view Baudhâyana I, 16, 13-14 (left out in my translation of the Sacred Books of the East, II, p. 197), nishâdena nishâdyâm â pa*ñk*amâ*g g*âter apahanti [*g*âto 'pahanti] *s*ûdratâm | tam upanayet shash*th*am yâ*g*ayet, '(Offspring), begotten by a Nishâda on a Nishâdî, removes within five generations the *S*ûdra-hood; one may initiate him (the fifth descendant), one may sacrifice for the sixth.' This passage of Baudhâyana, the reading of which is supported by a new MS. from Madras, clearly shows that Baudhâyana allowed the male offspring of Brâhma*n*as and *S*ûdra females to be raised to the level of Âryans. It is also not impossible

65. (Thus) a *S*ûdra attains the rank of a Brâhma*n*a, and (in a similar manner) a Brâhma*n*a sinks to the level of a *S*ûdra; but know that it is the same with the offspring of a Kshatriya or of a Vai*s*ya.

66. If (a doubt) should arise, with whom the preeminence (is, whether) with him whom an Âryan by chance begot on a non-Âryan female, or (with the son) of a Brâhma*n*a woman by a non-Âryan,

67. The decision is as follows: 'He who was begotten by an Âryan on a non-Âryan female, may become (like to) an Âryan by his virtues; he whom an Âryan (mother) bore to a non-Âryan father (is and remains) unlike to an Âryan.'

---

that the meaning of Manu's verse may be the same, and that the translation should be, 'If the offspring of a Brâhma*n*a and of a *S*ûdra female begets children with a most excellent (male of the Brâhma*n*a caste or female of the Pâra*s*ava tribe), the inferior (tribe) attains the highest caste in the seventh generation.' The chief objection to this version, which consists in the fact that *s*reg*a*sâ, 'with a most excellent,' stands in the masculine, may be met by Manu's peculiar use of the masculine instead of the feminine above in verse 32, where âyogave is used for âyogavyâm.

65. The manner in which a Brâhma*n*a sinks to the level of a *S*ûdra is, according to Medh., Gov., and Kull., the following. If the son of a Brâhma*n*a and of a *S*ûdra female and his descendants marry *S*ûdra wives, the seventh descendant will be a pure *S*ûdra. Medh., Gov., and Kull. hold that the offspring of a Brâhma*n*a and of a Kshatriya female obtains the higher or lower rank in the third generation, and the offspring of a Brâhma*n*a and of a Vai*s*ya female in the fifth. Medh. and Gov. expressly state that 'they,' i.e. the older commentators, give this explanation.

66. 'A non-Âryan female,' i.e. 'a *S*ûdra female' (Medh., Gov., Kull., Râgh., Nand.), or 'the daughter of a Vrâtya and the like' (Nâr.). 'By chance,' i.e. even on an unmarried one (Medh., Gov., Kull., Râgh., Nand.), or 'unknowingly' (Nâr.). 'An Âryan female,' i.e. 'a Brâhma*n*î' (Medh., Gov., Kull., Râgh., Nâr., Nand.).

67. 'May become (like to) an Âryan by his virtues,' i.e. 'may become most excellent or praiseworthy by offering the Pâkaya*gñ*as

68. The law prescribes that neither of the two shall receive the sacraments, the first (being excluded) on account of the lowness of his origin, the second (because the union of his parents was) against the order of the castes.

69. As good seed, springing up in good soil, turns out perfectly well, even so the son of an Âryan by an Âryan woman is worthy of all the sacraments.

70. Some sages declare the seed to be more important, and others the field; again others (assert that) the seed and the field (are equally important); but the legal decision on this point is as follows:

71. Seed, sown on barren ground, perishes in it; a (fertile) field also, in which no (good) seed (is sown), will remain barren.

72. As through the power of the seed (sons) born of animals became sages who are honoured and praised, hence the seed is declared to be more important.

73. Having considered (the case of) a non-Âryan who acts like an Âryan, and (that of) an Âryan who acts like a non-Âryan, the creator declared, 'Those two are neither equal nor unequal.'

---

and the like, which according to other Smritis are permitted to him' (Medh., Gov., Kull., Nâr.). 'Unlike to an Âryan,' i. e. 'unworthy of praise or respect' (Gov., Kull.).

69-72. See also the discussion which occurs above, IX, 33-41.

71. Gov., Kull., and Nand. say 'a field in which no seed (is sown) remains barren.' The translation follows Medh. The commentators refer to the stories of Mandapâla and *Ri*shyas*ri*ṅga, see above, IX, 23.

72. 'Not equal,' i. e. because they differ in caste; 'not unequal,' i. e. because both do what is forbidden to them. Hence nobody should do acts which are not permitted to him (Gov., Kull., Râgh.).

74. Brâhma*n*as who are intent on the means (of gaining union with) Brahman and firm in (discharging) their duties, shall live by duly performing the following six acts, (which are enumerated) in their (proper) order.

75. Teaching, studying, sacrificing for himself, sacrificing for others, making gifts and receiving them are the six acts (prescribed) for a Brâhma*n*a.

76. But among the six acts (ordained) for him three are his means of subsistence, (viz.) sacrificing for others, teaching, and accepting gifts from pure men.

77. (Passing) from the Brâhma*n*a to the Kshatriya, three acts (incumbent on the former) are forbidden, (viz.) teaching, sacrificing for others, and, thirdly, the acceptance of gifts.

78. The same are likewise forbidden to a Vai*s*ya, that is a settled rule; for Manu, the lord of creatures (Pra*g*âpati), has not prescribed them for (men of) those two (castes).

79. To carry arms for striking and for throwing (is prescribed) for Kshatriyas as a means of subsistence; to trade, (to rear) cattle, and agriculture

74–80. Âp. II, 10, 4–7; Gaut. X, 1–7, 49; Vas. II, 13–19; Baudh. I, 18, 1–4; Vi. II, 1–7; Yâ*g*ñ. I, 118–119; see also above, I, 88–90.

74. Brahmayonisthâ*h*, 'who are intent on the means of gaining union with Brahman' (Medh., Gov., Kull.), means according to Nâr. and Râgh. 'who are of pure Brâhma*n*ical race,' according to Nand. 'who abide by that which springs from the Veda, i. e. the sacred law,' or 'who are the dwelling-place of the Veda.'

77. Nâr. reads brâhma*n*â*h* kshatriya*m* prati, 'To a Kshatriya three acts incumbent on a Brâhma*n*a' are forbidden,' instead of brâhma*n*ât kshatriya*m* prati. Nand., whose text is corrupt, seems to have had the same reading as Nâr.

for Vaisyas; but their duties are liberality, the study of the Veda, and the performance of sacrifices.

80. Among the several occupations the most commendable are, teaching the Veda for a Brâhmana, protecting (the people) for a Kshatriya, and trade for a Vaisya.

81. But a Brâhmana, unable to subsist by his peculiar occupations just mentioned, may live according to the law applicable to Kshatriyas; for the latter is next to him in rank.

82. If it be asked, 'How shall it be, if he cannot maintain himself by either (of these occupations?' the answer is), he may adopt a Vaisya's mode of life, employing himself in agriculture and rearing cattle.

83. But a Brâhmana, or a Kshatriya, living by a Vaisya's mode of subsistence, shall carefully avoid (the pursuit of) agriculture, (which causes) injury to many beings and depends on others.

84. (Some) declare that agriculture is something excellent, (but) that means of subsistence is blamed

---

80. Vârttâ, 'trade' (Nand.), means according to Kull. 'trade and rearing cattle,' and according to Gov. 'trade, rearing cattle, and agriculture.' But the context makes it probable that one occupation only is intended.

81–98. Âp. I, 20, 10–21, 4; Gaut. VII, 1–26; Vas. II, 22–39; Baudh. II, 4, 16–21; Vi. II, 15; LIV, 18–21; Yâgñ. III, 35–40.

82. Nâr. thinks that krishi, 'agriculture,' means here asvayamkritâ, 'at which the Brâhmana does not work personally,' while Gov. and Kull. hold the contrary opinion. For according to them the asvayamkritâ krishih has been permitted even for ordinary times, above, IV, 4–5.

83. 'Depends on others,' i. e. 'on bullocks and so forth' (Gov., Kull.). It has been taught above, IV, 159–160, that a Snâtaka is to avoid all that depends upon others.

84. Medh. points out that this verse is directed against the teaching of Vas. II, 32–36.

by the virtuous; (for) the wooden (implement) with iron point injures the earth and (the beings) living in the earth

85. But he who, through a want of means of subsistence, gives up the strictness with respect to his duties, may sell, in order to increase his wealth, the commodities sold by Vaisyas, making (however) the (following) exceptions.

86. He must avoid (selling) condiments of all sorts, cooked food and sesamum, stones, salt, cattle, and human (beings),

87. All dyed cloth, as well as cloth made of hemp, or flax, or wool, even though they be not dyed, fruit, roots, and (medical) herbs;

88. Water, weapons, poison, meat, Soma, and perfumes of all kinds, fresh milk, honey, sour milk, clarified butter, oil, wax, sugar, Kusa-grass;

89. All beasts of the forest, animals with fangs or tusks, birds, spirituous liquor, indigo, lac, and all one-hoofed beasts.

90. But he who subsists by agriculture, may at pleasure sell unmixed sesamum grains for sacred

86. Medh. says, 'and cooked food, mixed with sesamum grains.' The same commentator thinks that, as salt which is also a condiment is specially forbidden, other condiments may be sold optionally. But Gov. and Kull. point out that it is specially named, because the penance is heavier. Nâr. explains rasân, 'condiments,' by 'exudations of leaves, wood, and so forth.'

88. Nâr. reads kshâram, 'alcaline substances,' instead of kshîram, 'fresh milk,' but mentions the latter reading, and Nand. kshâram for kshaudram.

89. Nâr. reads maggâ, 'marrow,' instead of madyam, 'spirituous liquor.' Medh. says that some read ekasaphân bahûn, 'many one-hoofed beasts,' and permit the sale of a single one. Nand. reads pasûn, 'animals.'

90. Suddhân, 'unmixed' (Medh., Gov., Kull., Râgh.), means

purposes, provided he himself has grown them and has not kept them long.

91. If he applies sesamum to any other purpose but food, anointing, and charitable gifts, he will be born (again) as a worm and, together with his ancestors, be plunged into the ordure of dogs.

92. By (selling) flesh, salt, and lac a Brâhma*n*a at once becomes an outcast; by selling milk he becomes (equal to) a *S*ûdra in three days.

93. But by willingly selling in this world other (forbidden) commodities, a Brâhma*n*a assumes after seven nights the character of a Vai*s*ya.

94. Condiments may be bartered for condiments, but by no means salt for (other) condiments; cooked food (may be exchanged) for (other kinds of) cooked food, and sesamum seeds for grain in equal quantities.

95. A Kshatriya who has fallen into distress, may subsist by all these (means); but he must never arrogantly adopt the mode of life (prescribed for his) betters.

---

according to Nand. 'white,' according to Nâr. 'of good quality.' 'Provided he has not kept them long,' i. e. 'if he has not kept them long after the harvest, in order to increase his profit' (Medh., Gov., Kull., Nâr.).

91. K. reads k*ri*mir bhûtvâ sa vish*th*âyâm, 'he will be plunged into ordure;' and Medh. seems likewise to have read sa, 'he,' for *s*va, 'dog.'

93. Kâmata*h*, 'willingly,' means according to Medh. and Nand. 'not in times of distress, but in ordinary times.'

94. I read with Medh. and Nand., k*ri*tânna*m* *k*a k*ri*tânnena instead of *k*âk*ri*tânnena (Gov., Kull., Nâr.), 'for undressed grain,' because all the other Sm*ri*tis have the former rule. K. reads vâ k*ri*tânnena, and thus shows how the misreading *k*â° arose. Nand. reads na tveva lava*n*a*m* tilai*h*, 'but not salt for sesamum grains,' and Medh. mentions the reading as a var. lect.

96. A man of low caste who through covetousness lives by the occupations of a higher one, the king shall deprive of his property and banish.

97. It is better (to discharge) one's own (appointed) duty incompletely than to perform completely that of another; for he who lives according to the law of another (caste) is instantly excluded from his own.

98. A Vaisya who is unable to subsist by his own duties, may even maintain himself by a *S*ûdra's mode of life, avoiding (however) acts forbidden (to him), and he should give it up, when he is able (to do so).

99. But a *S*ûdra, being unable to find service with the twice-born and threatened with the loss of his sons and wife (through hunger), may maintain himself by handicrafts.

100. (Let him follow) those mechanical occupations and those various practical arts by following which the twice-born are (best) served.

101. A Brâhma*n*a who is distressed through a want of means of subsistence and pines (with hunger), (but) unwilling to adopt a Vai*s*ya's mode of life and resolved to follow his own (prescribed) path, may act in the following manner.

---

97. Nâr. gives as an instance of an ill or incomplete performance of a Brâhma*n*a's duty, which is better than completely discharging the duties of another caste, the acceptance of alms from an impure person. Nand. omits this verse, which, indeed, is here out of place and ought to stand in the discussion beginning verse 101.

98. 'Acts forbidden to him,' i. e. 'eating the leavings of the others and so forth' (Gov., Kull., Nâr.), or 'eating forbidden food and the like' (Nand.).

99–100. Vi. III, 14; Gaut. X, 60.

101–114. Gaut. VII, 4–5, 23; Âp. I, 18, 5–8, 14–15.

102. A Brâhma*n*a who has fallen into distress may accept (gifts) from anybody; for according to the law it is not possible (to assert) that anything pure can be sullied.

103. By teaching, by sacrificing for, and by accepting gifts from despicable (men) Brâhma*n*as (in distress) commit not sin; for they (are as pure) as fire and water.

104. He who, when in danger of losing his life, accepts food from any person whatsoever, is no more tainted by sin than the sky by mud.

105. A*g*îgarta, who suffered hunger, approached in order to slay (his own) son, and was not tainted by sin, since he (only) sought a remedy against famishing.

106. Vâmadeva, who well knew right and wrong, did not sully himself when, tormented (by hunger), he desired to eat the flesh of a dog in order to save his life.

107. Bharadvâ*g*a, a performer of great austerities, accepted many cows from the carpenter B*ri*bu, when he was starving together with his sons in a lonely forest.

102. 'Anything pure,' i. e. 'the Ganges and the like' (Medh., Gov., Kull.), or 'fire and the like' (Nâr., Râgh.).

103. Vas. XXVII, 9.

105. Regarding the story of A*g*îgarta, see Aitareya-brâhma*n*a VII, 13–16.

107. I read with Gov. and Sâya*n*a on Rig-veda VI, 45, 31, B*ri*bu instead of V*ri*dhu (Kull., Râgh., K.), and B*ri*hat (Nâr., Nand.). The corrected copies of Medh. have V*ri*dhu, but the oldest reads v*ri*ddha in the text, and in the commentary d*ri*bu, i. e. b*ri*bu. It is not doubtful that B*ri*bu is the correct reading. For in the hymn quoted that personage is described as the carpenter of the Pa*n*is, and his liberality is highly praised. Moreover the *S*âṅkhâyana

108. Visvâmitra, who well knew what is right or wrong, approached, when he was tormented by hunger, (to eat) the haunch of a dog, receiving it from the hands of a *Kand*âla.

109. On (comparing) the acceptance (of gifts from low men), sacrificing (for them), and teaching (them), the acceptance of gifts is the meanest (of those acts) and (most) reprehensible for a Brâhma*n*a (on account of its results) in the next life.

110. (For) assisting in sacrifices and teaching are (two acts) always performed for men who have received the sacraments; but the acceptance of gifts takes place even in (case the giver is) a *S*ûdra of the lowest class.

111. The guilt incurred by offering sacrifices for teaching (unworthy men) is removed by muttering (sacred texts) and by burnt offerings, but that incurred by accepting gifts (from them) by throwing (the gifts) away and by austerities.

112. A Brâhma*n*a who is unable to maintain himself, should (rather) glean ears or grains from (the field of) any (man); gleaning ears is better than accepting gifts, picking up single grains is declared to be still more laudable.

113. If Brâhma*n*as, who are Snâtakas, are pining with hunger, or in want of (utensils made of) common metals, or of other property, they may ask the

---

*S*rauta-sûtra (see the Petersburg Dictionary, sub voce B*ri*bu) alludes to the legend mentioned by Manu.

108. Regarding the legend of Visvâmitra, see Mahâbh. XII, 141, 28 seqq.

110. Nâr. says, 'a *S*ûdra (or) one of the lowest class, i. e. a *Kand*âla.'

111. Âp. I, 28, 11; Vas. XX, 45; Vi. LIV, 28. 'By austerities,' i. e. 'by penances,' see below, XI, 194.

113. Kupyam, '(utensils made of) common metals,' includes

king for them; if he is not disposed to be liberal, he must be left.

114. (The acceptance of) an untilled field is less blamable than (that of) a tilled one; (with respect to) cows, goats, sheep, gold, grain, and cooked food, (the acceptance of) each earlier-named (article is less blamable than of the following ones).

115. There are seven lawful modes of acquiring property, (viz.) inheritance, finding or friendly donation, purchase, conquest, lending at interest, the performance of work, and the acceptance of gifts from virtuous men.

---

according to Medh. 'pots, kettles, wooden stools, and the like; according to Gov. 'all property of small value such as beds, seats;' according to Kull., Râgh., and Nand. 'also grain and clothes.' But Nâr. takes it in its usual sense, 'common metals such as brass and copper.' I translate the last clause according to the first explanation of Medh., Gov., Nâr., and Râgh., who think that all Brâhmanas should leave the realm of a king who does not support famishing Snâtakas. Nand., however, says that such a king is to be excluded from instruction and admission to sacrifices. Medh.'s second interpretation, according to which tyâgah means dharmahânih, 'a loss of spiritual merit,' agrees with Nand.'s view. Kull. finally takes the phrase very differently, 'but he who does not wish to give anything, being known for his avarice, must be left to himself, i. e. must not be asked.' Kull. and Gov. hold that 'the prince' meant here is a Kshatriya king who does not follow the *S*âstras, or a *S*ûdra king (see note on IV, 33), and that the verse thus rescinds the prohibition given above, IV, 84 seq.

114. Vas. XII, 3.

115. Gaut. X, 39–42. Lâbha, 'finding or friendly donation' (Medh., Gov., Kull.), refers according to Nâr. and Nand. to the acquisition of treasure-trove alone, not to the acceptance of presents from friends, from a father-in-law, &c. *G*aya, 'conquest,' means according to Nand. 'gaining lawsuits.' The same commentator takes prayoga, 'lending money at interest,' in the sense of 'teaching,' and karmayoga, 'performance of labour,' in the sense of 'sacrificing for others.' All the commentators, except Nand., point out that the first three modes of acquisition are lawful for all castes, the fourth for Ksha-

116. Learning, mechanical arts, work for wages, service, rearing cattle, traffic, agriculture, contentment (with little), alms, and receiving interest on money, are the ten modes of subsistence (permitted to all men in times of distress).

117. Neither a Brâhma*n*a, nor a Kshatriya must lend (money at) interest; but at his pleasure (either of them) may, in times of distress (when he requires money) for sacred purposes, lend to a very sinful man at a small interest.

118. A Kshatriya (king) who, in times of distress, takes even the fourth part (of the crops), is free from guilt, if he protects his subjects to the best of his ability.

119. His peculiar duty is conquest, and he must not turn back in danger; having protected the Vai*s*yas by his weapons, he may cause the legal tax to be collected;

120. (Viz.) from Vai*s*yas one-eighth as the tax on

---

triyas, the fifth and sixth for Vai*s*yas (or the fifth for Vai*s*yas, the sixth for *S*ûdras, Nâr.), and the seventh for Brâhma*n*as.

116. 'Learning,' i. e. (teaching) other than Vedic sciences, e. g. logic, exorcising evil spirits, or charms against poison (Medh., Kull., Nâr., Râgh.). Gov. thinks that 'teaching for a stipulated fee' is also permissible under this rule.

117. Vas. II, 40–43. Gov., Nâr., and K. read alpakam instead of alpikâm, and with this var. lect. the last clause might be translated with Nâr. by '. . . (either of them) . . . may lend a small (sum) to a very sinful man.'

119. I read with Gov. and K. na bhaye instead of nâhave (editions). Medh.'s text has the latter reading, but the commentary bhaye upasthite parâṅmukho yuddhe na syât, 'when danger threatens he shall not turn back in battle,' indicates that his reading was bhaye. The same inference may be drawn from Kull.'s commentary. Nand. gives na bhave, probably a mistake for na bhaye.

120. According to Medh., the first line refers to the profits of

grain, one-twentieth (on the profits on gold and cattle), which amount at least to one Kârshâpa*n*a; *S*ûdras, artisans, and mechanics (shall) benefit (the king) by (doing) work (for him).

121. If a *S*ûdra, (unable to subsist by serving Brâhma*n*as,) seeks a livelihood, he may serve Kshatriyas, or he may also seek to maintain himself by attending on a wealthy Vai*s*ya.

122. But let a (*S*ûdra) serve Brâhma*n*as, either

---

subjects dealing in corn or in gold. From the former the king may take in times of distress one-eighth, and from the latter one-twentieth. The second line indicates that artisans who, according to VII, 138, in ordinary times furnish one piece of work in each month, may be made to work more for the king. According to Gov. and Kull., husbandmen (k*ri*shig*î*vinâm, Gov.) shall give from the increments on grain (upa*k*aya) one-eighth (instead of one-twelfth, and in the direst distress one-fourth, according to verse 118, Kull.), from all increments on gold and so forth amounting to more than a Kârshâpa*n*a one-twentieth instead of one-fiftieth, as prescribed above, VII, 130. Râgh. in substance agrees with this explanation. Nâr. and Nand. read, as it would seem, vi*ms*atkârshâpa*n*âvara*m* (*n*âpara*m*, Nand.), and take the verse differently. Nâr. says that the tax on grain is to be one-fourth in the case of *S*ûdras, and one-eighth in the case of Vai*s*yas, that the tax on everything else is to be at least one Kârshâpa*n*a in twenty, and that artisans who work for wages shall pay the same rate (vi*ms*atkârshâpanam iti । dhânyâd anyeshu vi*ms*ad vi*ms*atikârshâpa*n*amûlya*m* tâd*ris*alâbhe kârshâpa*n*a eko râ*gñ*â grâhya ity avara*h* paksha*h* । sambhave tv adhikam api grâhyam ity artha*h* । dharmopakara*n*â*h* [karmo°] dharmibhir [karmabhir] vi*s*vam upakurvantas tantuvâyâdaya*h* । *s*ûdrâ*h* kâravo var*n*avâhyâ na*t*a*k*itrakârâdyâ*h* । *s*ilpina*s* *k*a rathakârâdyâs te 'pi karma k*ri*tvâ bh*ri*titve 'pi vi*ms*atikârshâpa*n*alâbhe kârshâpa*n*âvara*m* *s*ulka*m* dadyur iti *s*esha*h*). According to Nâr. the translation would be: '(Viz.) one-eighth as the tax (payable) by Vai*s*yas on grain, (and on everything else) at least one Kârshâpa*n*a out of twenty; *S*ûdra artisans and mechanics who benefit (men) by their work (shall pay the same rate).' Nâr. adds that some read tri*ms*atkârshâpa*n*âvaram, 'at least one Kârshâpa*n*a out of thirty.'

121-129. Gaut. X, 50-65; Yâ*gñ*. I, 120-121.

for the sake of heaven, or with a view to both (this life and the next); for he who is called the servant of a Brâhma*n*a thereby gains all his ends.

123. The service of Brâhma*n*as alone is declared (to be) an excellent occupation for a *S*ûdra; for whatever else besides this he may perform will bear him no fruit.

124. They must allot to him out of their own family(-property) a suitable maintenance, after considering his ability, his industry, and the number of those whom he is bound to support.

125. The remnants of their food must be given to him, as well as their old clothes, the refuse of their grain, and their old household furniture.

126. A *S*ûdra cannot commit an offence, causing loss of caste (pâtaka), and he is not worthy to receive the sacraments; he has no right to (fulfil) the sacred law (of the Âryans, yet) there is no prohibition against (his fulfilling certain portions of) the law.

127. (*S*ûdras) who are desirous to gain merit, and know (their) duty, commit no sin, but gain praise, if they imitate the practice of virtuous men, without reciting sacred texts.

128. The more a (*S*ûdra), keeping himself free from envy, imitates the behaviour of the virtuous, the more he gains, without being censured, (exaltation in) this world and the next.

---

126. 'Cannot commit an offence causing loss of caste,' i.e. 'by eating garlic and the like forbidden fruit' (Gov., Kull.), or 'by (keeping) a slaughter-house' (Râgh.).

127. In what particulars the practice of the Âryans may be imitated by *S*ûdras, may be learnt from the parallel passages quoted above.

129. No collection of wealth must be made by a *S*ûdra, even though he be able (to do it); for a *S*ûdra who has acquired wealth, gives pain to Brâhma*n*as.

130. The duties of the four castes (var*n*a) in times of distress have thus been declared, and if they perform them well, they will reach the most blessed state.

131. Thus all the legal rules for the four castes have been proclaimed; I next will promulgate the auspicious rules for penances.

CHAPTER XI.

1. Him who wishes (to marry for the sake of having) offspring, him who wishes to perform a sacrifice, a traveller, him who has given away all his property, him who begs for the sake of his teacher, his father, or his mother, a student of the Veda, and a sick man,

2. These nine Brâhma*n*as one should consider as

129. 'Gives pain to Brâhma*n*as,' i.e. 'by becoming proud and not serving them' (Gov., Kull., Râgh.).

XI. 1. Âp. II, 10, 1–2; Gaut. V, 21; Baudh. II, 5, 19. 'He who has given away all his property,' i.e. 'on performing a Vi*s*vagit sacrifice' (Medh., Gov., Kull., Râgh.), or 'other Kratus' (Nâr.). 'For the sake of his teacher, his father, or his mother,' i.e. 'in order to maintain them' (Gov., Kull., Râgh.), or 'in order to procure the fee for the teacher' (Râgh., Nâr.). The commentators try to excuse the introduction of the miscellaneous rules, contained in verses 1–43, before the discussion of the penances, which according to X, 131 ought to follow at once, either by assuming that the object is to show the necessity of performing penances in case these rules are violated, or by pointing out that, as gifts are the means for removing sin, the enumeration of the Pâtras or worthy recipients is required.

Snâtakas, begging in order to fulfil the sacred law; to such poor men gifts must be given in proportion to their learning.

3. To these most excellent among the twice-born, food and presents (of money) must be given; it is declared that food must be given to others outside the sacrificial enclosure.

4. But a king shall bestow, as is proper, jewels of all sorts, and presents for the sake of sacrifices on Brâhmanas learned in the Vedas.

5. If a man who has a wife weds a second wife, having begged money (to defray the marriage expenses, he obtains) no advantage but sensual enjoyment; but the issue (of his second marriage belongs) to the giver of the money.

6. One should give, according to one's ability, wealth to Brâhmanas learned in the Veda and living alone; (thus) one obtains after death heavenly bliss.

---

3. Gaut. V, 22; Baudh. II, 5, 20. The translation follows Medh., Gov., and Nâr. The interpretation adopted by Kull. is, 'To these most excellent Brâhmanas food together with presents must be given (inside the sacrificial enclosure).' Nand. reads etebhyo 'pi instead of etebhyo hi, and thinks that bahirvede is to be construed with api, 'To these most excellent among the twice-born food .... must be given even outside the sacrificial enclosure.' The correct explanation of the force of the word bahirvedi, 'outside the sacrificial enclosure,' is given by Nâr., who adds, vedyâm tu yâkitam sarvam eva deyam, 'but near the fire-altar everything asked for must be given to them.' The meaning of the verse, therefore, is that the nine mendicants, mentioned in verses 1–2, shall always receive what they ask for, and other mendicants ordinary food only, but that if they beg at the performance of a sacrifice, other property also must be given to them.

5. Âp. II, 10, 3. The object of the verse is to forbid that alms shall be asked or given for such a purpose (Gov., Kull.). Medh., Gov., Nâr., Râgh., and K. omit this verse. It looks very much like an interpolation, intended to explain the preceding rule.

7. He who may possess (a supply of) food sufficient to maintain those dependant on him during three years or more than that, is worthy to drink the Soma-juice.

8. But a twice-born man, who, though possessing less than that amount of property, nevertheless drinks the Soma-juice, does not derive any benefit from that (act), though he may have formerly drunk the Soma-juice.

9. (If) an opulent man (is) liberal towards strangers, while his family lives in distress, that counterfeit virtue will first make him taste the sweets (of fame, but afterwards) make him swallow the poison (of punishment in hell).

10. If (a man) does anything for the sake of his happiness in another world, to the detriment of those whom he is bound to maintain, that produces evil results for him, both while he lives and when he is dead.

11. If a sacrifice, (offered) by (any twice-born) sacrificer, (and) especially by a Brâhma*n*a, must remain incomplete through (the want of) one requisite, while a righteous king rules,

---

7. Vas. VIII, 10; Vi. LIX, 8; Yâ*gñ*. I, 124. 'Drink the Soma-juice,' i.e. 'perform a Soma-sacrifice, in order to obtain the fulfilment of some wish' (Medh., Gov., Kull., Râgh.).

8. 'Though he formerly may have drunk the Soma,' i.e. 'at the nitya (i.e. the annual, see above, IV, 26, VI, 10) Soma-sacrifice' (Gov., Kull., Râgh.). The same commentators and Medh. point out that this and the preceding verses do not forbid the performance of the nitya Soma-sacrifices, but only of those called kâmya. He who performs the latter without possessing the requisite property, loses also the rewards for the former.

11–15. Gaut. XVIII, 24–27.

11. 'While a righteous king rules,' i. e. 'because such a king will not punish a man who acts in accordance with the *S*âstras' (Medh., Gov., Kull., Nâr.).

12. That article (required) for the completion of the sacrifice, may be taken (forcibly) from the house of any Vaisya, who possesses a large number of cattle, (but) neither performs the (minor) sacrifices nor drinks the Soma-juice;

13. (Or) the (sacrificer) may take at his pleasure two or three (articles required for a sacrifice) from the house of a Sûdra; for a Sûdra has no business with sacrifices.

14. If (a man) possessing one hundred cows, kindles not the sacred fire, or one possessing a thousand cows, drinks not the Soma-juice, a (sacrificer) may unhesitatingly take (what he requires) from the houses of those two, even (though they be Brâhmanas or Kshatriyas);

15. (Or) he may take (it by force or fraud) from one who always takes and never gives, and who refuses to give it; thus the fame (of the taker) will spread and his merit increase.

16. Likewise he who has not eaten at (the time of) six meals, may take at (the time of) the seventh meal (food) from a man who neglects his sacred

12. Nâr. and Nand. think that 'the king' is the agent to be understood with the verb 'may be taken.' The latter relies on the parallel passage of the Mahâbhârata, where the last Pâda of the verse is yagñârtham pârthivo haret. 'The (minor) sacrifices,' i.e. 'the Pâkayagñas and so forth' (Kull.), or 'the five great sacrifices' (Nâr.).

14. Gov. thinks that this verse refers to a Kshatriya alone, while Medh., Kull., Râgh. refer it to Brâhmanas also.

15. Gov., Kull., and Râgh. explain âdânanitya, 'one who always takes,' by 'a Brâhmana who always accepts presents,' while Medh. and Nâr. refer the word to men of all castes who constantly amass wealth.

16–23. Gaut. XVIII, 28–32; Yâgñ. III, 43–44.

16. 'At the seventh meal-time,' i.e. 'on the fourth day of his starving.'

duties, without (however) making a provision for the morrow,

17. Either from the threshing-floor, or from a field, or out of the house, or wherever he finds it; but if (the owner) asks him, he must confess to him that (deed and its cause).

18. (On such occasions) a Kshatriya must never take the property of a (virtuous) Brâhma*n*a; but he who is starving may appropriate the possessions of a Dasyu, or of one who neglects his sacred duties.

19. He who takes property from the wicked and bestows it on the virtuous, transforms himself into a boat, and carries both (over the sea of misfortune).

20. The property of those who zealously offer sacrifices, the wise call the property of the gods; but the wealth of those who perform no sacrifices is called the property of the Âsuras.

21. On him (who, for the reasons stated, appropriates another's possessions), a righteous king shall not inflict punishment; for (in that case) a Brâhma*n*a pines with hunger through the Kshatriya's want of care.

22. Having ascertained the number of those dependent on such a man, and having fully considered his learning and his conduct, the king shall allow him, out of his own property, a maintenance whereon he may live according to the law;

23. And after allotting to him a maintenance, the

18. 'A Dasyu,' see above, X, 45. According to Nâr., this verse too refers to the king.

19. 'Both,' i. e. 'him from whom he takes it by saving him from sin (or, from the trouble of protecting his property, Gov.), and the recipient' (Kull., Gov.). Nand. omits verses 19–21.

21–22. See above, VII, 134–135.

23. See above, VIII, 304.

king must protect him in every way; for he obtains from such (a man) whom he protects, the sixth part of his spiritual merit.

24. A Brâhma*n*a shall never beg from a *S*ûdra property for a sacrifice; for a sacrificer, having begged (it from such a man), after death is born (again) as a *K*a*nd*âla.

25. A Brâhma*n*a who, having begged any property for a sacrifice, does not use the whole (for that purpose), becomes for a hundred years a (vulture of the kind called) Bhâsa, or a crow.

26. That sinful man, who, through covetousness, seizes the property of the gods, or the property of Brâhma*n*as, feeds in another world on the leavings of vultures.

27. In case the prescribed animal and Soma-sacrifices cannot be performed, let him always offer at the change of the year a Vai*s*vânarî Ish*t*i as a penance (for the omission).

28. But a twice-born, who, without being in distress, performs his duties according to the law for times of distress, obtains no reward for them in the next world; that is the opinion (of the sages).

29. By the Visve-devas, by the Sâdhyas, and by the great sages (of the) Brâhma*n*a (caste), who were afraid of perishing in times of distress, a substitute was made for the (principal) rule.

---

24. Vi. LIX, 11; Yâ*gñ*. I, 127.

25. Yâ*gñ*. I, 127. Medh., Gov., and Nâr. say, 'A Brâhma*n*a who . . . . does not give the whole of it (to Brâhma*n*as).'

26. Pare loke, 'in another world,' means according to Gov. and Kull., 'in his next birth.'

27. Vi. LIX, 10; Yâ*gñ*. I, 126. The Vai*s*vânarî Ish*t*i is according to Medh., a rite described in the G*ri*hya-sûtras. Regarding the prescribed *S*rauta sacrifices, see above, IV, 25–26.

30. That evil-minded man, who, being able (to fulfil) the original law, lives according to the secondary rule, reaps no reward for that after death.

31. A Brâhma*n*a who knows the law need not bring any (offence) to the notice of the king; by his own power alone he can punish those men who injure him.

32. His own power is greater than the power of the king; the Brâhma*n*a, therefore, may punish his foes by his own power alone.

33. Let him use without hesitation the sacred texts, revealed by Atharvan and by Aṅgiras; speech, indeed, is the weapon of the Brâhma*n*a, with that he may slay his enemies.

34. A Kshatriya shall pass through misfortunes which have befallen him by the strength of his arms, a Vai*s*ya and a *S*ûdra by their wealth, the chief of the twice-born by muttered prayers and burnt-oblations.

35. The Brâhma*n*a is declared (to be) the creator (of the world), the punisher, the teacher, (and hence) a benefactor (of all created beings); to him let no man say anything unpropitious, nor use any harsh words.

31. This and the following verses rescind the rules given above, IX, 290.

32. See above, IX, 313–321.

33. 'The sacred texts, revealed by Atharvan and Aṅgiras,' i.e. the charms and incantations contained in the Atharva-veda. Nâr. reads abhi*k*ârayan, 'using magic,' instead of avi*k*ârayan (Medh., Gov., Kull., K.). Nand. reads, *s*rutîr atharvâṅgirasî*h* kuryâd ity abhi*k*âritam.

34. Vas. XXVI, 16.

35. I read with Medh., Gov., Nâr., Râgh., Nand., and K., maitro for maitrî, and *s*uktâm for *s*ushkâm (editions). The commentators differ

36. Neither a girl, nor a (married) young woman, nor a man of little learning, nor a fool, nor a man in great suffering, nor one uninitiated, shall offer an Agnihotra.

37. For such (persons) offering a burnt-oblation sink into hell, as well as he to whom that (Agnihotra) belongs; hence the person who sacrifices (for another) must be skilled in (the performance of) Vaitâna (rites), and know the whole Veda.

---

much with respect to the explanation of the first line. Vidhâtâ, 'the creator (of the world,' Medh., Nâr.), means according to Gov. and Kull. 'the performer of the prescribed rites;' according to Râgh. 'able to do, to undo, and to change;' according to Nand. 'the performer of magic rites and so forth.' *S*âsitâ, 'the punisher' (Medh. Kull., Râgh.), i. e. 'of others, of the king' (Medh.), or 'of his sons, pupils, and so forth' (Kull.), is interpreted by Nâr. to mean 'the instructor in the sacred law,' by Nand. 'the instigator (of incantations).' Vaktâ, 'the teacher' (Gov., Nâr.), means according to Medh. 'the giver of good advice,' according to Kull. and Râgh. 'the expounder of the sacred law.' The explanations of Gov. and Kull. allow also the translation adopted by Sir W. Jones, 'He who performs his duties .... is truly called a Brâhma*n*a.' As regards the second line Medh. offers two explanations. First he interprets it 'to him, i. e. when he uses magic, let no man say anything unpropitious, i. e. he must not punish him, nor use any harsh words, i. e. admonish or sharply reprimand him.' Gov. and Kull. agree with this explanation, but omit the specification 'when he uses magic.' According to Medh.'s second rendering the line contains an advice, addressed to men of all castes, not to anger or disquiet a Brâhma*n*a; and this view is adopted by Râgh. and Nand., who explain aku*s*alam, 'unpropitious,' by anish*t*am, 'anything disagreeable.' Nâr.'s readings seem to have differed. He has kuryât instead of brûyât, and explains the first phrase, 'to him let no man do anything unpropitious,' i. e. anything unbecoming, such as a bodily injury. In the second clause he reads *s*uktam (suktam, MS.), which he explains by paryushitam, 'stale,' but he does not give the remainder of his text.

36–37. Âp. II, 15, 18–19; Gaut. II, 4; Vas. II, 6: see also above, II, 172; V, 155; IX, 18. The Vaitâna rites are those performed in the vitâna, the three sacred fires. Hence it follows that the Agnihotra meant here is the *S*rauta Agnihotra.

38. A Brâhma*n*a who, though wealthy, does not give, as fee for the performance of an Agnyâdheya, a horse sacred to Pra*g*âpati, becomes (equal to one) who has not kindled the sacred fires.

39. Let him who has faith and controls his senses perform other meritorious acts, but let him on no account offer sacrifices at which he gives smaller fees (than those prescribed).

40. The organs (of sense and action), honour, (bliss in) heaven, longevity, fame, offspring, and cattle are destroyed by a sacrifice at which (too) small sacrificial fees are given; hence a man of small means should not offer a (*S*rauta) sacrifice.

41. A Brâhma*n*a who, being an Agnihotrin, voluntarily neglects the sacred fires, shall perform a lunar penance during one month; for that (offence) is equal to the slaughter of a son.

42. Those who, obtaining wealth from *S*ûdras, (and using that) offer an Agnihotra, are priests officiating for *S*ûdras, (and hence) censured among those who recite the Veda.

---

38. The translation of prâ*g*âpatya, 'sacred to Pra*g*âpati,' follows Gov., Kull., Nâr., and Râgh. Medh. says that the epithet may be used merely by way of laudation, or may mean that the animal is to be neither very good nor very bad, or that it may be derived from a phrase current among the people. Nand. explains it by 'to be given to the Brahman priest.'

40. Gov. and Kull. explain, here and above, IV, 94, *yasah*, 'honour,' by 'a good name during one's life,' and kîrtim, 'fame,' by 'fame after death.' Nâr. takes the former as 'being known to others for one's virtues,' and the latter as 'being praised by others.'

41. Gaut. XXII, 34; Vas. I, 18; XXI, 27; Vi. LIV, 13. Nand. explains vîra, 'son' (Gov., Kull., Nâr., Râgh.), by a Kshatriya, and Râgh. says that it may also mean 'a deity.'

42. See above, XI, 24.

43. Treading with his foot on the heads of those fools who worship a fire (kindled at the expense) of a *S*ûdra, the giver (of the wealth) shall always pass over his miseries (in the next world).

44. A man who omits a prescribed act, or performs a blamable act, or cleaves to sensual enjoyments, must perform a penance.

45. (All) sages prescribe a penance for a sin unintentionally committed; some declare, on the evidence of the revealed texts, (that it may be performed) even for an intentional (offence).

46. A sin unintentionally committed is expiated by the recitation of Vedic texts, but that which (men) in their folly commit intentionally, by various (special) penances.

47. A twice-born man, having become liable to perform a penance, be it by (the decree of) fate or by (an act) committed in a former life, must not, before the penance has been performed, have intercourse with virtuous men.

48. Some wicked men suffer a change of their

---

43. Nand. reads the first line differently, pâpânâ*m* satata*m* teshâm agni*m* *s*ûdrasya *g*uhvatâm, but the general sense remains the same.

44–46. Gaut. XIX; Vas. XX, 1–3; XXII; Baudh. III, 10; Yâ*gñ*. III, 219, 226.

45. Vedic texts which prescribe penances for offences committed intentionally, are quoted Gaut. XIX, 7–10. The commentators adduce also Aitareya-brâhma*n*a VII, 28.

47. Daivât, 'by (the decree of) fate,' i.e. 'through carelessness' (Medh., Nâr., Kull., Râgh.). Medh. mentions a var. lect. mohât, 'through delusion of mind.' 'By (an act) committed in a former life,' i.e. 'if he has black teeth or some other bodily defect from which his having committed a crime in a former birth may be inferred.'

48–54. Vas. I, 18; XX, 6; XXI, 43–44; Vi. XLV; Yâ*gñ*. III, 207–215.

(natural) appearance in consequence of crimes committed in this life, and some in consequence of those committed in a former (existence).

49. He who steals the gold (of a Brâhma*n*a) has diseased nails; a drinker of (the spirituous liquor called) Surâ, black teeth; the slayer of a Brâhma*n*a, consumption; the violator of a Guru's bed, a diseased skin;

50. An informer, a foul-smelling nose; a calumniator, a stinking breath; a stealer of grain, deficiency in limbs; he who adulterates (grain), redundant limbs;

51. A stealer of (cooked) food, dyspepsia; a stealer of the words (of the Veda), dumbness; a stealer of clothes, white leprosy; a horse-stealer, lameness.

52. The stealer of a lamp will become blind; he who extinguishes it will become one-eyed; injury (to sentient beings) is punished by general sickliness; an adulterer (will have) swellings (in his limbs).

53. Thus in consequence of a remnant of (the guilt of former) crimes, are born idiots, dumb, blind, deaf, and deformed men, who are (all) despised by the virtuous.

54. Penances, therefore, must always be performed for the sake of purification, because those

51. 'A stealer of the words (of the Veda),' i.e. 'one who learns the Veda without permission, by hearing another man recite it' (Gov., Kull., Râgh.), means according to Nâr. 'a plagiator.'

52. Gov., Nâr., Nand., and K. omit this verse, and Râgh. says that it is found kvâpi, in some MSS.

53. I read with Nâr., Nand., and K., karmâva*s*eshe*n*a instead of karmavi*s*eshe*n*a (editions). The explanations of Medh., Gov., and Kull. likewise point to the former reading.

whose sins have not been expiated, are born (again) with disgraceful marks.

55. Killing a Brâhma*n*a, drinking (the spirituous liquor called) Surâ, stealing (the gold of a Brâhma*n*a), adultery with a Guru's wife, and associating with such (offenders), they declare (to be) mortal sins (mahâpâtaka).

56. Falsely attributing to oneself high birth, giving information to the king (regarding a crime), and falsely accusing one's teacher, (are offences) equal to slaying a Brâhma*n*a.

57. Forgetting the Veda, reviling the Vedas, giving false evidence, slaying a friend, eating forbidden food, or (swallowing substances) unfit for food, are six (offences) equal to drinking Surâ.

58. Stealing a deposit, or men, a horse, and silver, land, diamonds and (other) gems, is declared to be equal to stealing the gold (of a Brâhma*n*a).

59. Carnal intercourse with sisters by the same mother, with (unmarried) maidens, with females of

55–71. Âp. I, 21, 7–19; Gaut. XXI, 1–12; Vas. I, 19–23; Baudh. II, 2, 1–8; 12–13; 15–16; Vi. XXXIV, 1; XXXV–XXXVIII, 6; XXXIX–XLII; Yâ*gñ*. III, 227–242.

55. See above, IX, 235.

56. Guro*s* *k*âlîkanirbandha*h*, 'falsely accusing one's teacher' (Medh., Gov., Kull.), may also mean according to Medh. 'wrongfully going to law with the teacher.' Nâr. and Nand. explain it by 'persevering in doing what is disagreeable to the teacher.'

57. Garhitânâdya, 'forbidden food and (substances) unfit for food' (Gov., Kull., Râgh.), means according to Medh. 'forbidden food and such which one has resolved not to eat;' according to Nâr. and Nand. 'food blemished by the contact with impure men or things, and such as is by its nature unfit for eating, e. g. garlic.'

59. The commentators point out that, though the crimes enumerated in verses 56–59 are stated to be equal to mortal sins, the penances are not always the same, but frequently less heavy.

the lowest castes, with the wives of a friend, or of a son, they declare to be equal to the violation of a Guru's bed.

60. Slaying kine, sacrificing for those who are unworthy to sacrifice, adultery, selling oneself, casting off one's teacher, mother, father, or son, giving up the (daily) study of the Veda, and neglecting the (sacred domestic) fire,

61. Allowing one's younger brother to marry first, marrying before one's elder brother, giving a daughter to, or sacrificing for, (either brother),

62. Defiling a damsel, usury, breaking a vow, selling a tank, a garden, one's wife, or child,

63. Living as a Vrâtya, casting off a relative, teaching (the Veda) for wages, learning (the Veda) from a paid teacher, and selling goods which one ought not to sell,

64. Superintending mines (or factories) of any

60. 'Selling oneself,' i.e. 'for money into slavery' (Medh.), 'refers to Âryans only' (Nâr.). Medh. mentions another reading, pâradâryam avikraya*h*, 'adultery and the sale of forbidden merchandise.' Medh. and Nâr. say, 'forgetting the sacred texts required for the daily private recitation;' and Medh. adds that, as the same offence has been mentioned above, verse 57, 'forgetting the Veda,' may be either reckoned as equal to a Mahâpâtaka or as an Upapâtaka crime. Nâr. refers the term 'the fire' to the three sacred *S*rauta fires.

62. 'Breaking a vow,' i.e. 'any vow voluntarily undertaken' (Medh., Nâr.), means according to Gov., Kull., and Râgh. 'breaking the vow of studentship.'

63. 'Living as a Vrâtya,' see above, X, 20. 'Casting off a relative,' i.e. 'not supporting him in distress, though one possesses money enough to do so' (Medh.). Medh. takes bândhava in the sense of 'maternal relatives,' and understands that it includes the mother, sisters, maternal uncles, &c., while the other commentators take it in a wider sense.

64. Mahâyantrapravartana, 'executing great mechanical works,'

sort, executing great mechanical works, injuring (living) plants, subsisting on (the earnings of) one's wife, sorcery (by means of sacrifices), and working (magic by means of) roots, (and so forth),

65. Cutting down green trees for firewood doing acts for one's own advantage only, eating prohibited food,

66. Neglecting to kindle the sacred fires, theft, non-payment of (the three) debts, studying bad books, and practising (the arts of) dancing and singing,

67. Stealing grain, base metals, or cattle, inter-

---

e. g. 'constructing dams across rivers in order to stop the water' (Medh., Gov., Kull., Râgh., K.), means according to Nâr. 'making machines for killing great animals such as boars,' according to Nand. '(making) great machines such as sugar-mills.' Stryâgîva, 'subsisting on (the earnings of) one's wife, i. e. by making her go into service (Nâr., Nand.), or by forcing her to become a harlot' (Kull.), means according to Medh. 'subsisting on (the separate property of) one's wife,' according to Râgh. 'living on (the money obtained by selling one's wife.' Nand. reads him*s*raushadhistry-upâgîvah, 'subsisting on (money earned by the sale of) noxious herbs or on (the earnings of) one's wife.'

65. 'Doing acts for one's own advantage only,' i. e. 'cooking only for oneself, and so forth' (Medh., Nâr., Kull., Nand., Râgh.); see above, III, 118. By ninditânna, 'forbidden food,' Medh. understands the same kinds, mentioned above, verse 57; Kull., 'forbidden food such as garlic;' Nâr., Râgh., and Nand., 'food given by persons from whom it must not be accepted, e. g. by a king, a gambler, &c.' Medh. and Kull. state expressly that, if such food be eaten once and unintentionally, the offence is an Upapâtaka, but in worse cases equal to a Mahâpâtaka.

66. 'Theft,' i. e. 'of valuable objects' (Kull.), 'excepting gold and the other articles specially mentioned' (Medh., Râgh.), e. g. 'of clothes' (Nâr.). Regarding the three debts, see Vas. XI, 45. 'Bad books,' i. e. 'those of the *K*ârvâkas, Nirgranthas (*G*ainas,' Medh.), or 'of heretics in general' (Nâr.).

67. 'Cattle,' i. e. other than cows; see above, verse 60.

course with women who drink spirituous liquor, slaying women, *S*ûdras, Vai*s*yas, or Kshatriyas, and atheism, (are all) minor offences, causing loss of caste (Upapâtaka).

68. Giving pain to a Brâhma*n*a (by a blow), smelling at things which ought not to be smelt at, or at spirituous liquor, cheating, and an unnatural offence with a man, are declared to cause the loss of caste (*G*âtibhra*m*s*a).

69. Killing a donkey, a horse, a camel, a deer, an elephant, a goat, a sheep, a fish, a snake, or a buffalo, must be known to degrade (the offender) to a mixed caste (Sa*m*karîkara*n*a).

70. Accepting presents from blamed men, trading, serving *S*ûdras, and speaking a falsehood, make (the offender) unworthy to receive gifts (Apâtra).

71. Killing insects, small or large, or birds, eating anything kept close to spirituous liquors, stealing fruit, firewood, or flowers, (are offences) which make impure (Malâvaha).

72. Learn (now) completely those penances, by means of which all the several offences mentioned (can) be expiated.

73. For his purification the slayer of a Brâhma*n*a shall make a hut in the forest and dwell (in it)

---

68. 'Things which ought not to be smelt at,' e. g. 'garlic, onions, ordure, &c.' (Medh., Gov., Kull., Nâr.).

70. 'Blamed men,' i. e. those from whom no gifts must be accepted; see above, IV, 84 seq.

73–87. Âp. I, 24, 10–25; 25, 11–12; 28, 21–29, 1; Gaut. XXII, 2–10; Vas. XX, 25–28; Baudh. II, 1, 2–6; Vi. XXV, 6; L, 1–6, 15; Yâg*ñ*. III, 243–250.

73. According to Kull., Nâr., and Râgh. this penance is to be performed in case the homicide was committed unintentionally.

during twelve years, subsisting on alms and making the skull of a dead man his flag;

74. Or let him, of his own free will, become (in a battle) the target of archers who know (his purpose); or he may thrice throw himself headlong into a blazing fire;

75. Or he may offer a horse-sacrifice, a Svar*g*it, a Gosava, an Abhi*g*it, a Vi*s*va*g*it, a Triv*ri*t, or an Agnish*t*ut;

76. Or, in order to remove (the guilt of) slaying a Brâhma*n*a, he may walk one hundred yo*g*anas, reciting one of the Vedas, eating little, and controlling his organs;

77. Or he may present to a Brâhma*n*a, learned in

---

74. Vidushâm, 'who know (his purpose),' (Medh., Gov., Kull.), may also mean according to Medh. 'who are expert in archery,' and Nand. adopts this explanation. Nâr. thinks that this penance must be performed by one who intentionally murdered a Brâhma*n*a, and that it must end in his death. According to the Bhavishyapurâ*n*a which Kull. and Râgh. quote, these two penances and that mentioned in the next verse are to be performed by a Kshatriya who slew a Brâhma*n*a, those ending in death by an offender who himself, destitute of good qualities, killed a learned *S*rotriya, and the lighter ones by an eminent king who unintentionally caused the death of a worthless Brâhma*n*a.

75. According to the Bhavishyapurâ*n*a, Nâr. and Kull., Svar*g*it is the name of a sacrifice, but Medh. (on verse 78) and Râgh. take the word as an adjective qualifying Gosava. Regarding the Gosava, see Kâtyâyana *S*r. Sûtras XXII, 11, 3; regarding the Abhi*g*it, Â*s*v. *S*r. Sûtras VIII, 5, 13. According to Gov. and Nâr., Triv*ri*t is equivalent to Triv*ri*tstoma, and to be taken separately; but according to Medh. and Râgh., triv*ri*tâ qualifies Agnish*t*ut. Regarding the Agnish*t*ut, see Â*s*v. *S*r. Sûtras IX, 7, 22–25.

76. According to Nâr., Kull., and Râgh. (the latter two quoting the Bhavishyapurâ*n*a as their authority), this penance suffices to expiate the unintentional slaughter of one who has nothing but the name of a Brâhma*n*a.

77. I read with Medh., Gov., and K., dhana*m* hi instead of

the Vedas, his whole property, as much wealth as suffices for the maintenance (of the recipient), or a house together with the furniture;

78. Or, subsisting on sacrificial food, he may walk against the stream along (the whole course of the river) Sarasvatî; or, restricting his food (very much), he may mutter thrice the Sa*m*hitâ of a Veda.

79. Having shaved off (all his hair), he may dwell at the extremity of the village, or in a cow-pen, or in a hermitage, or at the root of a tree, taking pleasure in doing good to cows and Brâhma*n*as.

---

dhana*m* vâ (Nâr., Nand., Râgh., editions), 'or as much wealth as.' Kull.'s explanation, too, points to the former reading, the meaning of which is that 'the whole property' must be sufficient to maintain the recipient. According to the Bhavishyapurâ*n*a, quoted by Kull. and Râgh., the penance is prescribed for the case that a rich, unlearned Brâhma*n*a who keeps no sacred fire, unintentionally slew an utterly worthless Brâhma*n*a.

78. According to the Bhavishyapurâ*n*a, quoted by Kull. and Râgh., the first penance is to be performed by an unlearned Brâhma*n*a who intentionally killed an utterly worthless caste-fellow, the second by an exceedingly distinguished *S*rotriya who unintentionally caused the death of a man merely a Brâhma*n*a in name. Medh. and Gov. attach their views regarding the particular cases to their explanations of this Sûtra. Gov. does not go beyond generalities. But Medh. says that the penance mentioned in verse 73 and the first described in verse 74 may be optionally performed for intentionally slaying an ordinary Brâhma*n*a. If a *S*rotriya or one who is performing a *S*rauta sacrifice has been killed, the offender is to burn himself. The sacrifices will atone for the guilt of a homicide committed unintentionally, by a most distinguished member of the Âryan castes, provided that the person slain was a Brâhma*n*a in name only.

79. Medh., Kull., and Gov. think that the rule allows an option with respect to the residence during the penance of twelve years (verse 73). Nâr. says that the verse contains a general rule for all penances.

80. He who unhesitatingly abandons life for the sake of Brâhma*n*as or of cows, is freed from (the guilt of) the murder of a Brâhma*n*a, and (so is he) who saves (the life of) a cow, or of a Brâhma*n*a.

81. If either he fights at least three times (against robbers in defence of) a Brâhma*n*a's (property), or reconquers the whole property of a Brâhma*n*a, or if he loses his life for such a cause, he is freed (from his guilt).

82. He who thus (remains) always firm in his vow, chaste, and of concentrated mind, removes after the lapse of twelve years (the guilt of) slaying a Brâhma*n*a.

83. Or he who, after confessing his crime in an assembly of the gods of the earth (Brâhma*n*as), and the gods of men (Kshatriyas), bathes (with the priests) at the close of a horse-sacrifice, is (also) freed (from guilt).

84. The Brâhma*n*a is declared (to be) the root of the sacred law and the Kshatriya its top; hence he who has confessed his sin before an assembly of such men, becomes pure.

85. By his origin alone a Brâhma*n*a is a deity even for the gods, and (his teaching is) authoritative for men, because the Veda is the foundation for that.

---

80. This holds good also before the twelve years' penance is finished (Gov., Kull., Nâr.).

83. Gov. holds that this penance is efficacious only if the offender is engaged in the performance of the twelve years' penance. Kull. and Râgh. think that it is a separate penance, because the subject of the twelve years' penance has been finished in the preceding verse, and because the Bhavishyapurâ*n*a specially prescribes it for an eminent Brâhma*n*a who unintentionally causes the death of a worthless caste-fellow. Medh. mentions both opinions, and states that he believes the penance to be efficacious in any case.

86. (If) only three of them who are learned in the Veda proclaim the expiation for offences, that shall purify the (sinners); for the words of learned men are a means of purification.

87. A Brâhmana who, with a concentrated mind, follows any of the (above-mentioned) rules, removes the sin committed by slaying a Brâhmana through his self-control.

88. For destroying the embryo (of a Brâhmana, the sex of which was) unknown, for slaying a Kshatriya or a Vaisya who are (engaged in or) have offered a (Vedic) sacrifice, or a (Brâhmana) woman who has bathed after temporary uncleanness (Âtreyî), he must perform the same penance,

89. Likewise for giving false evidence (in an important cause), for passionately abusing the teacher, for stealing a deposit, and for killing (his) wife or his friend.

90. This expiation has been prescribed for unin-

88–89. Âp. I, 24, 6–9, 23; Gaut. XXII, 11–14; Vas. XX, 34–36; Baudh. II, 1, 12; Vi. L, 7–10; LII, 4; Yâgñ. III, 251.

88. Medh. and several other commentators propose, in explanation of the term Âtreyî, besides the interpretation given above, also the erroneous one, 'a female of the tribe of Atri.'

89. 'Giving false evidence,' i.e. 'in a case where the life of the accused is involved' (Medh., Gov., Nâr.), or 'where gold, land and the like is at stake' (Kull., Râgh.). 'Abusing the teacher,' see above, verse 56. 'Stealing a deposit,' i.e. 'gold belonging to a Kshatriya or Vaisya, or silver and other property belonging to a Brâhmana' (Kull., Nâr., Râgh.), or property belonging to a poor Brâhmana (Medh.). Strî, 'his wife' (Nâr., Nand.), means according to Gov., Kull., and Râgh. 'the virtuous wife of a distinguished Brâhmana who keeps sacred fires.' Medh. (on verse 88) seems to agree to a similar explanation. 'His friend,' i.e. 'though he may not be a Brâhmana' (Nâr.).

90. The verse is identical with Baudh. II, 1, 6. The correct

tentionally killing a Brâhma*n*a; but for intentionally slaying a Brâhma*n*a no atonement is ordained.

91. A twice-born man who has (intentionally) drunk, through delusion of mind, (the spirituous liquor called) Surâ shall drink that liquor boiling-hot; when his body has been completely scalded by that, he is freed from his guilt;

92. Or he may drink cow's urine, water, milk, clarified butter or (liquid) cowdung boiling-hot, until he dies;

93. Or, in order to remove (the guilt of) drinking Surâ, he may eat during a year once (a day) at night grains (of rice) or oilcake, wearing clothes made of cowhair and his own hair in braids and carrying (a wine cup as) a flag.

---

interpretation of this verse is that Manu, just as Âp. I, 24, 24, held the intentional murder of a true Brâhma*n*a to be inexpiable during the criminal's life, and meant to teach that the murderer had either to perform a penance which caused his death or to live according to the twelve years' rule during the term of his natural life. This is the doctrine attributed to Manu by Gaut. XXI, 7. While Gov. and Nâr. agree with this explanation, Medh., 'others' quoted by Gov., Kull., Nand., and Râgh. refer iya*m*, 'this,' to verse 73, and hold that in the case of wilful murder the penance has only to be made severer by doubling or trebling the term of twelve years.

91-98. Âp. I, 25, 3, 10; 27, 10; Gaut. XXIII, 10-12; Vas. XX, 19, 22; Baudh. II, 1, 18-22; Vi. LI, 1-4; Yâ*gñ*. III, 253-254.

91. This and the next penances are prescribed for an intentional offence; see below, verse 147. According to Medh., Gov., Kull., and Râgh. (the latter two quoting the Bhavishyapurâ*n*a), the spirituous liquor here intended is the paish*t*ikî surâ, that distilled from ground rice. According to Nâr. the penance ending in death must be performed by all Âryans who have drunk paish*t*ikî surâ, and by Brâhma*n*as who have drunk any of the three kinds of surâ mentioned in verse 95. Nand. reads amohât, and explains it by matipûrvakam, 'intentionally.'

93. According to Gov., Kull., Nand., and Râgh., this penance is prescribed for drinking unintentionally paish*t*ikî surâ; according

94. Surâ, indeed, is the dirty refuse (mala) of grain, sin also is called dirt (mala); hence a Brâhma*n*a, a Kshatriya, and a Vai*s*ya shall not drink Surâ.

95. Surâ one must know to be of three kinds, that distilled from molasses (gau*d*î), that distilled from ground rice, and that distilled from Madhûka-flowers (mâdhvî); as the one (named above) even so are all (three sorts) forbidden to the chief of the twice-born.

96. Surâ, (all other) intoxicating drinks and decoctions and flesh are the food of the Yakshas, Râkshasas, and Pi*s*â*k*as; a Brâhma*n*a who eats (the remnants of) the offerings consecrated to the gods, must not partake of such (substances).

97. A Brâhma*n*a, stupefied by drunkenness, might fall on something impure, or (improperly) pronounce Vedic (texts), or commit some other act which ought not to be committed.

98. When the Brahman (the Veda) which dwells in his body is (even) once (only) deluged with spirituous liquor, his Brahmanhood forsakes him and he becomes a *S*ûdra.

---

to 'others' quoted by Medh. and Râgh., for drinking gau*d*î or mâdhvî surâ; according to Nâr., for intentionally drinking water mixed with madhusurâ. Medh. himself says idam prâ*n*âtyaya aushadhârtham, 'this (is intended) as a medicine for death.'

94. This verse shows, as the commentators point out, the distinction between spirituous liquor distilled from ground grain, paish*t*ikî surâ, and the other two sorts mentioned in the next verse. The first alone is forbidden to all Âryans, the other two sorts to Brâhma*n*as; see also Gaut. II, 20.

95. Mâdhvî, 'distilled from Madhûka (Mauâ) flowers' (Kull.), means according to Medh. 'distilled from honey,' according to Nâr. 'distilled either from grapes or from Madhûka flowers or from honey.'

99. The various expiations for drinking (the spirituous liquors called) Surâ have thus been explained; I will next proclaim the atonement for stealing the gold (of a Brâhmana).

100. A Brâhmana who has stolen the gold (of a Brâhmana) shall go to the king and, confessing his deed, say, 'Lord, punish me!'

101. Taking (from him) the club (which he must carry), the king himself shall strike him once, by his death the thief becomes pure; or a Brâhmana (may purify himself) by austerities.

102. He who desires to remove by austerities the guilt of stealing the gold (of a Brâhmana), shall perform the penance (prescribed) for the slayer of a Brâhmana, (living) in a forest and dressed in (garments made of) bark.

103. By these penances a twice-born man may remove the guilt incurred by a theft (of gold); but he may atone for connexion with a Guru's wife by the following penances.

104. He who has violated his Guru's bed, shall,

100–101. See above, VIII, 314–316.

101. At the end of the verse Gov., Kull., Nâr., Râgh., Nand., and K. read vâ instead of tu (Medh. (?) editions), which is variously explained. According to Nâr. and Nand., it means 'but.' Kull. thinks that it indicates that, while a Brâhmana must never be slain by the king, other Âryans also may perform austerities. According to Râgh., it refers to the optional recitation of the Gâyatrî, repeated 700,000 times; according to Nâr., to other penances, even such as end in death. But Gov. is probably right in assuming that 'the austerities' meant are those prescribed in the next verse.

102. Âp. I, 25, 10; Yâgñ. III, 258; Vi. LII, 3. According to Nâr., this verse refers to an 'unintentional' offence; according to Kull. and Râgh., to the theft of a small sum.

104–107. Âp. I, 25, 1–2, 10; 28, 15–18; Gaut. XXIII, 8–12;

after confessing his crime, extend himself on a heated iron bed, or embrace the red-hot image (of a woman); by dying he becomes pure;

105. Or, having himself cut off his organ and his testicles and having taken them in his joined hands, he may walk straight towards the region of Nir*ri*ti (the south-west), until he falls down (dead);

106. Or, carrying the foot of a bedstead, dressed in (garments of) bark and allowing his beard to grow, he may, with a concentrated mind, perform during a whole year the K*rikkh*ra (or hard, penance), revealed by Pra*g*âpati, in a lonely forest;

107. Or, controlling his organs, he may during three months continuously perform the lunar penance, (subsisting) on sacrificial food or barley-gruel, in order to remove (the guilt of) violating a Guru's bed.

108. By means of these penances men who have committed mortal sins (Mahâpâtaka) may remove their guilt, but those who committed minor offences, causing loss of caste, (Upapâtaka, can do it) by the various following penances.

Vas. XX, 13–14; Baudh. II, 1, 13–15; Vi. XXXIV, 2; LIII, 1; Yâ*gñ*. III, 259–260.

104. According to Medh., the term 'Guru' denotes here 'the teacher or the father;' according to Kull., Nâr., and Râgh., 'the father;' and Nâr. particularly excludes an offence with a stepmother.

106. According to Medh., Kull., Râgh., this penance expiates incest committed by mistake; according to Nâr., the rule applies to the case when the offence was committed with a stepmother. Regarding the K*rikkh*ra penance, see below, verse 212.

107. According to Medh. and Râgh., the rule refers to an offence committed with the wife of a paternal or of a maternal uncle, or of other minor Gurus; according to Kull., to an offence with an unfaithful or low-caste wife of a Guru. Regarding the lunar penance or *K*ândrâya*n*a, see below, verse 217.

108. Nâr. takes mahâpâtakina*h*, 'those who committed mortal

109. He who has committed a minor offence by slaying a cow (or bull) shall drink during (the first) month (a decoction of) barley-grains; having shaved all his hair, and covering himself with the hide (of the slain cow), he must live in a cow-house.

110. During the two (following) months he shall eat a small (quantity of food) without any factitious salt at every fourth meal-time, and shall bathe in the urine of cows, keeping his organs under control.

111. During the day he shall follow the cows and, standing upright, inhale the dust (raised by their hoofs); at night, after serving and worshipping them, he shall remain in the (posture, called) vîrâsana.

112. Controlling himself and free from anger, he must stand when they stand, follow them when they walk, and seat himself when they lie down.

113. (When a cow is) sick, or is threatened by danger from thieves, tigers, and the like, or falls, or sticks in a morass, he must relieve her by all possible means:

114. In heat, in rain, or in cold, or when the wind blows violently, he must not seek to shelter himself, without (first) sheltering the cows according to his ability.

115. Let him not say (a word), if a cow eats (anything) in his own or another's house or field or on the threshing-floor, or if a calf drinks (milk).

116. The slayer of a cow who serves cows in this

---

sins,' in the sense of 'those equal to mortal sinners,' i.e. those offenders who have been enumerated above, verse 56 seq.

109–117. Âp. I, 26, 1; Gaut. XXII, 18; Vi. L, 16–24; Yâgñ. III, 263–264.

111. 'In the (posture, called) vîrâsana,' i.e. 'seated without leaning against a wall or the like' (Kull., Nand.).

manner, removes after three months the guilt which he incurred by killing a cow.

117. But after he has fully performed the penance, he must give to (Brâhma*n*as) learned in the Veda ten cows and a bull, (or) if he does not possess (so much property) he must offer to them all he has.

118. Twice-born men who have committed (other) minor offences (Upapâtaka), except a student who has broken his vow (Avakîr*n*in), may perform, in order to purify themselves, the same penance or also a lunar penance.

119. But a student who has broken his vow shall offer at night on a crossway to Nir*ri*ti a one-eyed ass, according to the rule of the Pâkaya*gñ*as.

120. Having offered according to the rule oblations in the fire, he shall finally offer (four) oblations of clarified butter to Vâta, to Indra, to the teacher (of the gods, B*ri*haspati) and to Agni, reciting the *Ri*k verse 'May the Maruts grant me,' &c.

121. Those who know the Veda declare that a voluntary effusion of semen by a twice-born (youth) who fulfils the vow (of studentship constitutes) a breach of that vow.

122. The divine light which the Veda imparts to

117. Yâ*gñ*. III, 265.

118–124. Âp. I, 26, 8; Gaut. XXV, 1–4; Vas. XXIII, 1–4; Baudh. II, 1, 30–35; Vi. XXVIII, 49–50; Yâ*gñ*. III, 280.

118. According to Nâr. and Nand., the lunar penance is to be performed if the offence was committed unintentionally.

119. 'According to the rule of the Pâkaya*gñ*as,' i. e. 'according to the Pa*s*ukalpa, found in Â*s*valâyana's and other G*ri*hya Sûtras,' Â*s*v. G*ri*. Sûtras I, 11 (Nâr.).

120. The verse is found Taittirîya Âra*n*yaka II, 18, 4.

122. I read with Medh., Gov., and K., maruta*h*, instead of mâruta*m* (Nand., editions).

the student, enters, if he breaks his vow, the Maruts, Puruhûta (Indra), the teacher (of the gods, B*ri*haspati) and Pâvaka (Fire).

123. When this sin has been committed, he shall go begging to seven houses, dressed in the hide of the (sacrificed) ass, proclaiming his deed.

124. Subsisting on a single (daily meal that consists) of the alms obtained there and bathing at (the time of) the three savanas (morning, noon, and evening), he becomes pure after (the lapse of) one year.

125. For committing with intent any of the deeds which cause loss of caste (*G*âtibhra*ms*akara), (the offender) shall perform a Sâ*m*tapana K*rikkh*ra; (for doing it) unintentionally, (the K*rikkh*ra) revealed by Pra*g*âpati.

126. As atonement for deeds which degrade to a mixed caste (Sa*m*kara), and for those which make a man unworthy to receive gifts (Apâtra), (he shall perform) the lunar (penance) during a month; for (acts) which render impure (Malinîkara*n*îya) he shall scald himself during three days with (hot) barley-gruel.

127. One-fourth (of the penance) for the murder of a Brâhma*n*a is prescribed (as expiation) for (intentionally) killing a Kshatriya, one-eighth for

125. Regarding the offences called *G*âtibhra*ms*akara, see above, verse 68. The Sâ*m*tapana K*rikkh*ra is described below, verse 213.

126. Regarding the three classes of offences, see above, 69–71. The penance of subsisting on barley-gruel is described Vi. XLVIII; Baudh. III, 6.

127–131. Âp. I, 24, 1–4; Gaut. XXII, 14–16; Vas. XX, 31–33; Baudh. I, 19, 1–2; II, 8–10; Vi. L, 12–14; Yâ*gñ*. III, 266–267.

127. The word 'virtuous' is, according to the commentators, to be understood with 'a Kshatriya' and 'a Vai*s*ya,' and the rule

killing a Vaisya; know that it is one-sixteenth for killing a virtuous Sûdra.

128. But if a Brâhmana unintentionally kills a Kshatriya, he shall give, in order to purify himself, one thousand cows and a bull;

129. Or he may perform the penance prescribed for the murderer of a Brâhmana during three years, controlling himself, wearing his hair in braids, staying far away from the village, and dwelling at the root of a tree.

130. A Brâhmana who has slain a virtuous Vaisya, shall perform the same penance during one year, or he may give one hundred cows and one (bull).

(verse 66), according to which the murder of a Sûdra, a Vaisya, and a Kshatriya is an Upapâtaka, to be expiated by a three months' Govrata or a lunar penance, refers to the cases of persons who do not live in accordance with the sacred law.

128. I read with Medh., Gov., Kull. (commentary), Nand., K., suddhyartham âtmanah, instead of sukaritavratah (editions), which latter reading is evidently wrong.

129. According to Medh. and Râgh., this verse is merely a repetition of the rule given in verse 127. But others, mentioned by him, Gov., Kull., and Nâr., think that the special observances prescribed during the twelve years' penance, e. g. carrying a skull instead of a flag, which this verse does not expressly mention, need not be kept. Nand. reads dvyabdam, 'two years,' instead of tryabdam.

130. I read with Gov., Kull., Nâr., Râgh., Nand., and K. dadyâd vaikasatam, instead of dadyâkkaikasatam (Medh., editions, and probably mentioned by Nâr.). According to Gov. and Kull. the two penances are to be performed optionally, in case a virtuous Vaisya has been killed unintentionally. Râgh. seems to hold the same opinion. But Medh. says that the first penance is to be performed for the murder of a Vaisya who was less distinguished than the one referred to in verse 127. Nâr. finally thinks that the verse refers to a Vaisya engaged in the performance of a sacrifice, and that the

131. He who has slain a *S*ûdra, shall perform that whole penance during six months, or he may also give ten white cows and one bull to a Brâhma*n*a.

132. Having killed a cat, an ichneumon, a blue jay, a frog, a dog, an iguana, an owl, or a crow, he shall perform the penance for the murder of a *S*ûdra;

133. Or he may drink milk during three days, or walk one hundred yo*g*anas, or bathe in a river, or mutter the hymn addressed to the Waters.

134. For killing a snake, a Brâhma*n*a shall give a spade of black iron, for a eunuch a load of straw and a mâsha of lead;

---

particle vâ, 'or,' takes the place of the copula, and thus one penance only is prescribed.

131. Gov. and Kull. hold that these penances, too, are to be performed in the case of an unintentional homicide. Medh. explains sitâ*h*, 'white,' to mean 'not white in colour, but (called so) because they resemble in purity (white substances), and give much milk and are accompanied by their calves.'

132. Âp. I, 25, 13; Gaut. XXII, 19; Vas. XXI, 24; Vi. L, 30–32; Yâ*gñ*. III, 270. Gov., Kull., Nand. expressly state that the penance for the murder of a *S*ûdra is to be performed for intentionally (thus also Nâr.) killing any single one of these animals, while Medh. thinks that the rule holds good only if one has killed all of them. The penance intended is, according to Gov., Kull., Nâr., and Râgh., not that mentioned in the preceding verse, but the lunar penance (Gov., Kull., Râgh.), or the Govrata (Gov., Kull.), or the Tapta K*rikkh*ra (Nâr.).

133. According to Gov., Kull., Nâr., Râgh., these penances are to be performed if the animal has been killed unintentionally; according to Medh. they serve to expiate the slaughter of a single animal. The choice among the four penances depends according to Kull. and Râgh. on the strength of the offender, according to Gov. and Nâr. on his caste and other circumstances. 'A yo*g*ana,' i.e. 2½–9 miles. The hymn mentioned is found Rig-veda X, 9.

134. Gaut. XXII, 23, 25; Vi. L, 34–35; Yâ*gñ*. III, 273. 'A Brâhma*n*a,' i.e. 'even a Brâhma*n*a' (Nâr.). The recipient of the gift is in every case a Brâhma*n*a.

135. For a boar a pot of clarified butter, for a partridge a drona of sesamum-grains, for a parrot a calf two years old, for a crane (a calf) three years old.

136. If he has killed a Hamsa, a Balâka, a heron, a peacock, a monkey, a falcon, or a Bhâsa, he shall give a cow to a Brâhmana.

137. For killing a horse, he shall give a garment, for (killing) an elephant, five black bulls, for (killing) a goat, or a sheep, a draught-ox, for killing a donkey, (a calf) one year old;

138. But for killing carnivorous wild beasts, he shall give a milch-cow, for (killing) wild beasts that are not carnivorous, a heifer, for killing a camel, one krishnala.

139. For killing adulterous women of the four castes, he must give, in order to purify himself, respectively a leathern bag, a bow, a goat, or a sheep.

140. A twice-born man, who is unable to atone by gifts for the slaughter of a serpent and the other (creatures mentioned), shall perform for each of them, a Krikkhra (penance) in order to remove his guilt.

141. But for destroying one thousand (small)

135. Gaut. XXII, 24; Vi. L, 36–39; Yâgñ. III, 271, 273–274. Kumbha, 'a pot,' i. e. 'of 200 palas' (Nâr.). A drona, i. e. four âdhakas (Medh.), or 128 palas (Nâr.).

136. Vi. L, 33; Yâgñ. III, 272.

137. Vi. L, 25–28; Yâgñ. III, 271, 274.

138. Vi. L, 29, 40–41; Yâgñ. III, 272–273. 'A krishnala,' i. e. 'of gold' (Medh., Gov., Kull., Nâr., Nand., Râgh.).

139. Gaut. XXII, 26; Yâgñ. III, 268. 'Respectively,' i. e. according to the order of the castes. Râgh. adds 'unintentionally.'

140. Yâgñ. III, 274; Vas. XXI, 26.

141. Gaut. XXII, 20–21; Âp. I, 26, 2; Vas. XXI, 25; Vi. L, 46;

animals that have bones, or a whole cart-load of boneless (animals), he shall perform the penance (prescribed) for the murder of a *S*ûdra.

142. But for killing (small) animals which have bones, he should give some trifle to a Brâhma*n*a; if he injures boneless (animals), he becomes pure by suppressing his breath (prâ*n*âyâma).

143. For cutting fruit-trees, shrubs, creepers, lianas, or flowering plants, one hundred *Rik*as must be muttered.

144. (For destroying) any kind of creature, bred in food, in condiments, in fruit, or in flowers, the expiation is to eat clarified butter.

145. If a man destroys for no good purpose plants produced by cultivation, or such as spontaneously spring up in the forest, he shall attend a cow during one day, subsisting on milk alone.

146. The guilt incurred intentionally or unintentionally by injuring (created beings) can be removed by means of these penances; hear (now, how) all

---

Yâg*ñ*. III, 269. '(Small) animals that have bones,' i. e. 'lizards and the like' (Gov., Kull., Nâr.).

142. Vi. L, 47; Yâg*ñ*. III, 275; Gaut. XXII, 22. The rule refers in each case to the destruction of a single animal (Medh., Gov., Kull., Râgh.), or of a number less than that mentioned in the preceding verse (Nâr.). 'Something,' i. e. one pa*n*a (Nâr.) or 'eight handfuls of grain' (Nand.).

143. Vi. L, 48; Yâg*ñ*. III, 276. According to Kull. this penance must be performed for an offence committed once and unintentionally, because 'the cutting of green trees' has been declared above, verse 65, to be an Upapâtaka for which at least a lunar penance has to be performed. 'One hundred *Rik*as,' 'the Gâyatrî and the like' (Kull.), or 'the Gâyatrî one hundred times' (Nâr.).

144. Vi. L, 49; Yâg*ñ*. III, 275. Rasa, 'condiments,' i. e. 'molasses, butter-milk and the like' (Medh., Gov., Kull.).

145. Vi. L, 50; Yâg*ñ*. III, 144.

(sins) committed by partaking of forbidden food (or drink, can be expiated).

147. He who drinks unintentionally (the spirituous liquor, called) Vâru*n*î, becomes pure by being initiated (again); (even for drinking it) intentionally (a penance) destructive to life must not be imposed; that is a settled rule.

148. He who has drunk water which has stood in a vessel used for keeping (the spirituous liquor, called) Surâ, or other intoxicating drinks, shall drink during five (days and) nights (nothing but) milk in which the *S*ankhapushpî (plant) has been boiled.

---

147. Âp. I, 25, 10; Gaut. XXIII, 2; Vas. XX, 19; Baudh. II, 1, 19; Vi. LI, 1, 4; Yâg*ñ*. III, 255. 'Vâru*n*î,' i. e. 'liquor distilled from molasses or Mauâ flowers (gau*d*î mâdhvî *k*a), not that distilled from ground grain, because another penance has been prescribed above, verse 93' (Medh., Gov.). The other commentators agree with this explanation, as well as with the additional rule that a Tapta K*r*i*kkh*ra must be performed before the second initiation. Râgh. and Kull. quote also the Bhavishyapurâ*n*a, which gives the same interpretation. The explanation of the second part of the verse is everywhere that which the translation follows except in Medh.'s and Nand.'s commentaries, where it is rendered '(for drinking even these two kinds of Surâ) intentionally (this penance) must not be prescribed, (but) one whereby death ensues.' In my opinion the commentators are totally wrong. I think that Vâru*n*î means here, as elsewhere, Surâ, and that the first half of the verse prescribes the performance of a second initiation after the penance, mentioned in verse 93, has been performed, while the second line teaches that the intentional drinking of Surâ can be expiated by death alone. I would therefore propose, 'If a man unintentionally drinks Surâ, he becomes pure only by being initiated again; but (the guilt of him who drinks it) intentionally, cannot be expiated, it remains as long as he lives, that is a settled rule.' The correctness of my interpretation of the words anirde*s*yam prâ*n*ântikam follows from Gaut. XXI, 7.

148. Vas. XX, 21; Vi. LI, 23–24; Baudh. II, 1, 22.

149. He who has touched spirituous liquor, has given it away, or received it in accordance with the rule, or has drunk water left by a *S*ûdra, shall drink during three days water in which Ku*s*a-grass has been boiled.

150. But when a Brâhma*n*a who has partaken of Soma-juice, has smelt the odour exhaled by a drinker of Surâ, he becomes pure by thrice suppressing his breath in water, and eating clarified butter.

151. (Men of) the three twice-born castes who have unintentionally swallowed ordure or urine, or anything that has touched Surâ, must be initiated again.

152. The tonsure, (wearing) the sacred girdle, (carrying) a staff, going to beg, and the vows (incumbent on a student), are omitted on the second initiation of twice-born men.

153. But he who has eaten the food of men, whose food must not be eaten, or the leavings of women and *S*ûdras, or forbidden flesh, shall drink barley(-gruel) during seven (days and) nights.

---

149. 'According to the rule,' i. e. 'pronouncing a benediction (on the giver),' (Gov., Kull., Nâr., Râgh.), or 'at a Sautrâma*n*î sacrifice' (Nand.).

150. Gaut. XXIII, 6; Vi. LI, 25.

151. Gaut. XXIII, 3; Vas. XX, 20; Vi. LI, 2; Yâ*gñ*. III, 235.

152. Vas. XX, 18; Baudh. II, 1, 20; Vi. LI, 5. 'The vows,' i. e. 'serving the fire, avoiding meat, honey and so forth' (Gov., Kull., Râgh.), and 'the Veda-vows' (Nâr.).

153. Vas. XIV, 33; Vi. LI, 50, 54, 56. See above, IV, 222, where another penance is prescribed for unknowingly eating food given by persons whose food must not be eaten. According to Kull. the two penances may be performed optionally, but according to Medh. and Nâr. this rule refers to an offence committed intentionally.

154. A twice-born man who has drunk (fluids that have turned) sour, or astringent decoctions, becomes, though (these substances may) not (be specially) forbidden, impure until they have been digested.

155. A twice-born man, who has swallowed the urine or ordure of a village pig, of a donkey, of a camel, of a jackal, of a monkey, or of a crow, shall perform a lunar penance.

156. He who has eaten dried meat, mushrooms growing on the ground, or (meat, the nature of) which is unknown, (or) such as had been kept in a slaughter-house, shall perform the same penance.

157. The atonement for partaking of (the meat of) carnivorous animals, of pigs, of camels, of cocks, of crows, of donkeys, and of human flesh, is a Tapta K*r*i*kkh*ra (penance).

158. If a twice-born man, who has not returned

154. 'Astringent decoctions,' i.e. 'those known to physicians are prepared from various herbs' (Medh.). Râgh. and Nand. think that pîtvâmedhyânyapi stands for pîtvâ amedhyâni api, and explain amedhya by 'garlic and the like.'

156. Vi. LI, 27, 34. Gov. and Râgh. take ag*ñ*âtam, 'the nature of which is unknown,' to mean 'unintentionally.' Râgh. takes bhaumâni, 'growing on the ground,' separately, and interprets kavakâni, 'mushrooms,' by 'mushrooms growing on trees.' But Medh. says 'the word bhaumâni is used in order to exclude those growing in the holes (of trees) from the prohibition,' while Nâr. thinks that according to another Sm*r*iti another penance, the Pras*r*itiyâvaka, shall be performed for eating the latter.

157. Gaut. XXIII, 4-5; Vas. XXIII, 30; Vi. LI, 3-4. With respect to this verse and the preceding one, see also above, V, 19-21, where other penances are prescribed. Kull. and Râgh. think that this rule refers to an offence committed once, while those given in the fifth chapter apply to a relapse. Regarding the Tapta K*r*i*kkh*ra, see below, verse 215.

158. Vi. LI, 43-44. The commentators state that the term

(home from his teacher's house), eats food, given at a monthly (*S*râddha), he shall fast during three days and pass one day (standing) in water.

159. But a student who on any occasion eats honey or meat, shall perform an ordinary K*rikkh*ra (penance), and afterwards complete his vow (of studentship).

160. He who eats what is left by a cat, by a crow, by a mouse (or rat), by a dog, or by an ichneumon, or (food) into which a hair or an insect has fallen, shall drink (a decoction of) the Brahmasuvar*k*alâ (plant).

161. He who desires to be pure, must not eat forbidden food, and must vomit up such as he has eaten unintentionally, or quickly atone for it by (various) means of purification.

162. The various rules respecting penances for eating forbidden food have been thus declared; hear now the law of those penances which remove the guilt of theft.

---

mâsika, 'a monthly (*S*râddha),' refers to a so-called Ekoddish*t*a *S*râddha. According to Medh., 'others' thought that, because a student is allowed to partake of a *S*râddha by II, 189, the inviter should perform the penance. According to Medh., the student shall on the fourth day stand in water; but according to Gov., Kull., on one of the three fast days; according to Nâr., on the first.

159. Vi. LI, 45; Vas. XXIII, 12; Yâ*gñ*. III, 282. Instead of brahma*k*ârî, 'a student,' Medh., Gov., Nâr., and Nand. read vrata*k*ârî, 'a man performing a vow,' and Nâr. explains it by 'a student, a hermit, a widow, an ascetic and so forth,' while the other commentators refer the term to a student alone.

160. Vi. LI, 46; Vas. XXIII, 11. 'Food into which an insect or a hair has fallen,' i. e. 'without scattering earth on it' (Gov., Kull., Râgh.). Nâr. adds during one day.

161. Gaut. XXIII, 26. 'Means of purification,' i. e. 'penances' (Medh., Gov., Kull., Râgh.), or 'purgative decoctions' ('others,' Medh., Nâr., Nand.).

163. The chief of the twice-born, having voluntarily stolen (valuable) property, grain, or cooked food, from the house of a caste-fellow, is purified by performing K*rikkh*ra (penances) during a whole year.

164. The lunar penance has been declared to be the expiation for stealing men and women, and (for wrongfully appropriating) a field, a house, or the water of wells and cisterns.

165. He who has stolen objects of small value from the house of another man, shall, after restoring the (stolen article), perform a Sâ*m*tapana K*rikkh*ra for his purification.

166. (To swallow) the five products of the cow (pa*ñk*agavya) is the atonement for stealing eatables of various kinds, a vehicle, a bed, a seat, flowers, roots, or fruit.

---

163. Vi. LII, 5. According to Medh. and Nâr. it is meant that others stealing the same articles from caste-fellows must perform the same penance. Medh., Gov., Kull., Nand., and Nâr. think that the verse gives the extreme limit of the penance, and that under special circumstances it may be reduced.

164. Vi. LII, 6. 'Men and women,' i. e. 'slaves' (Medh.). Râgh. mentions a var. lect. ta*d*âgânâm, 'or a tank,' instead of *g*alânâm, 'of the water.' Nâr. and Râgh. think that the penance is intended for an offence committed unintentionally.

165. Vi. LII, 7. 'Objects of small value,' i. e. 'earthen vessels, wooden ones, e. g. a trough, or iron utensils, e. g. a hoe' (Medh.), or 'tin, lead and the like' (Gov., Kull., Râgh.), or 'straw and the like' (Nâr.). K. omits 'after restoring,' and reads tatpâpasya vi*s*uddhaye, 'for the expiation of that sin.'

166. Vi. LII, 8. Medh. says that the penance is to last one day only. Nâr. thinks that the Mahâsâ*m*tapana penance is indicated by the mention of the pa*ñk*agavya, and that this holds good in the case of an unintentional offence only. Nand. adds, 'With this and the following rules the words "after restoring the property" have still their force;' so also Kull. on verse 165.

167. Fasting during three (days and) nights shall be (the penance for stealing) grass, wood, trees, dry food, molasses, clothes, leather, and meat.

168. To subsist during twelve days on (uncooked) grains (is the penance for stealing) gems, pearls, coral, copper, silver, iron, brass, or stone.

169. (For stealing) cotton, silk, wool, an animal with cloven hoofs, or one with uncloven hoofs, a bird, perfumes, medicinal herbs, or a rope (the penance is to subsist) during three days (on) milk.

170. By means of these penances, a twice-born man may remove the guilt of theft; but the guilt of approaching women who ought not to be approached (agamyâ), he may expiate by (the following) penances.

171. He who has had sexual intercourse with sisters by the same mother, with the wives of a friend, or of a son, with unmarried maidens, and with females of the lowest castes, shall perform the penance, prescribed for the violation of a Guru's bed.

167. Vi. LII, 9. According to Nâr. the rule refers to an unintentional offence.

168. Vi. LII, 10. According to Medh. the penance may be shortened according to the special circumstances of the case. Nâr. says, 'This refers to cases when the theft is not committed in times of distress.'

169. Vi. LII, 11. According to Nâr. this rule holds good if the theft is committed in times of distress and very small quantities are taken. Gov. and Kull. observe on this verse and the preceding ones, that the apparent inequality of the penances, which are prescribed equally for great and small things, will disappear if special circumstances, such as the frequency of the offence, time and place, the character of the owner and so forth, are taken into account.

171. Gaut. XXIII, 12–13, 32; Vas. XX, 15–16; Baudh. II, 1, 13; Vi. XXXIV, 2; XXXVI, 7; LIII, 1; Yâ*gñ*. III, 233. See also above, verse 59. According to Medh., Gov., Kull., and Râgh., the penance to be performed is that mentioned above in verse 106, while self-immolation is prescribed for repeated intentional offences only. Nâr. speaks of a twelve years' penance.

172. He who has approached the daughter of his father's sister, (who is almost equal to) a sister, (the daughter) of his mother's sister, or of his mother's full brother, shall perform a lunar penance.

173. A wise man should not take as his wife any of these three; they must not be wedded because they are (Sapi*nd*a-)relatives, he who marries (one of them), sinks low.

174. A man who has committed a bestial crime, or an unnatural crime with a female, or has had intercourse in water, or with a menstruating woman, shall perform a Sâ*m*tapana *Kr*i*kkh*ra.

175. A twice-born man who commits an unnatural offence with a male, or has intercourse with a female in a cart drawn by oxen, in water, or in the day-time, shall bathe, dressed in his clothes.

176. A Brâhma*n*a who unintentionally approaches a woman of the *K*a*nd*âla or of (any other) very low caste, who eats (the food of such persons) and accepts

172. I read with all the commentators and K. in the second line mâtu*s k*a bhrâtur âptasya (âptâ*m k*a, Nand.) instead of mâtu*s k*a bhrâtus tanayâm (editions). According to Kull. and Nâr. the rule refers to an offence committed by mistake and, as the former says, once only.

173. This verse is directed against the custom of the southerners, mentioned by Baudh. I, 2, 3. 'Sinks low,' i. e. 'falls into hell or begets base-born offspring' (Medh.). Gov. and Kull. adopt the former explanation, while Nâr. says 'he becomes an outcast.'

174. Gaut. XXII, 36; XXIII, 34; Vi. LIII, 4, 7; Yâg*ñ*. III, 288. A bestial crime with a cow is excepted, see Vi. LIII, 3. Medh. mentions a var. lect., *g*ale khe *k*a, instead of *g*ale *k*aiva, which agrees with Vish*n*u's text.

175. Vi. LIII, 4; Yâg*ñ*. III, 291. Nâr. says that the verse refers to an unintentional offence.

176. Vas. XXIII, 41; Baudh. II, 4, 13–14; Vi. LIII, 5–6. 'Very low caste,' i. e. 'Mle*kkh*as or barbarians, *S*abaras and so forth' (Medh., Gov., Kull.), or 'Sûtas and the like' (Nâr.), or '*G*avanas

(presents from them) becomes an outcast; but (if he does it) intentionally, he becomes their equal.

177. An exceedingly corrupt wife let her husband confine to one apartment, and compel her to perform the penance which is prescribed for males in cases of adultery.

178. If, being solicited by a man (of) equal (caste), she (afterwards) is again unfaithful, then a K*rikkh*ra and a lunar penance are prescribed as the means of purifying her.

179. The sin which a twice-born man commits by dallying one night with a V*ri*shalî, he removes in three years, by subsisting on alms and daily muttering (sacred texts).

180. The atonement (to be performed) by sinners (of) four (kinds) even, has been thus declared; hear now the penances for those who have intercourse with outcasts.

181. He who associates with an outcast, himself becomes an outcast after a year, not by sacrificing

---

(i. e. Mahommedans) and the like' (Râgh.). In the first case the penance for a Patita must be performed; in the second, no penance can be prescribed.

177. Vas. XXI, 8, 12–13; Vi. LIII, 8. Adultery is an Upapâtaka according to verse 60, and to be expiated, according to verse 118, by a Govrata or a *K*ândrâya*n*a, which latter seems to be here intended. The commentators add that the penance must be lighter or heavier, according to the caste of the male offender.

178. I read with Gov., Nâr. upamantritâ instead of upayantritâ (editions, K., Nand.). Medh. seems to have read anumantritâ.

179. Âp. I, 27, 11; Baudh. II, 2, 11; Vi. LIII, 9. 'A V*ri*shalî,' i. e. a *K*a*nd*âlî (Medh., Kull., Râgh.). But others, mentioned by Medh., Gov., and Nâr., think that a *S*ûdra female is meant. Nand. places this verse before verse 178.

181. Gaut. XXI, 3; Vas. I, 22; Baudh. II, 2, 35; Yâ*gñ*. III, 261; Vi. XXXV, 3–5. Gov. and Nâr. explain the verse differently, 'He who associates with an outcast by sacrificing for him or by forming

for him, teaching him, or forming a matrimonial alliance with him, but by using the same carriage or seat, or by eating with him.

182. He who associates with any one of those outcasts, must perform, in order to atone for (such) intercourse, the penance prescribed for that (sinner).

183. The Sapi*nd*as and Samânodakas of an outcast must offer (a libation of) water (to him, as if he were dead), outside (the village), on an inauspicious day, in the evening and in the presence of the relatives, officiating priests, and teachers.

184. A female slave shall upset with her foot a pot filled with water, as if it were for a dead person; (his Sapi*nd*as) as well as the Samânodakas shall be impure for a day and a night;

185. But thenceforward it shall be forbidden to converse with him, to sit with him, to give him a share of the inheritance, and to hold with him such intercourse as is usual among men;

186. And (if he be the eldest) his right of primogeniture shall be withheld and the additional share,

---

a matrimonial alliance with him, himself becomes an outcast after a year, but not by using the same carriage or seat or eating with him.' In the latter case four years are required. The parallel passage of Vish*n*u shows, however, clearly what is meant.

182. Vi. LIV, 1.

183–186. Gaut. XX, 4–7; Vas. XV, 12–16; Baudh. II, 1, 36; Yâ*gñ*. III, 295.

183. 'In the presence of the relatives, &c.,' i. e. 'of those who perform the ceremony, not of those of the outcast' (Medh.).

184. 'As if it were for a dead person,' i. e. 'saying, "This is for N. N."' (Medh.), 'turning to the south' (Gov., Kull., Nâr., Nand., Râgh.).

185. I prefer K.'s reading nivartera*m*s tatas tasmât. According to Medh. 'others' explained dâyâdya, 'a share of the inheritance,' by 'money,' and thought that all sums due to him were to be given to his heirs.

due to the eldest son; and in his stead a younger brother, excelling in virtue, shall obtain the share of the eldest.

187. But when he has performed his penance, they shall bathe with him in a holy pool and throw down a new pot, filled with water.

188. But he shall throw that pot into water, enter his house and perform, as before, all the duties incumbent on a relative.

189. Let him follow the same rule in the case of female outcasts; but clothes, food, and drink shall be given to them, and they shall live close to the (family-)house.

190. Let him not transact any business with unpurified sinners; but let him in no way reproach those who have made atonement.

191. Let him not dwell together with the murderers of children, with those who have returned evil for good, and with the slayers of suppliants for protection or of women, though they may have been purified according to the sacred law.

192. Those twice-born men who may not have been taught the Sâvitrî (at the time) prescribed by the rule, he shall cause to perform three K*rikkh*ra (penances) and afterwards initiate them in accordance with the law.

187–188. Gaut. XX, 10–14; Vas. XV, 17–21; Baudh. II, 1, 36; Yâ*gñ*. III, 296.

188. Thus Gov., Kull., Râgh., and others quoted by Medh. But the latter commentator himself refers sa tu, 'but he,' to one of the relatives, and Nâr. seems to agree with him.

189. Yâ*gñ*. III, 297.

190–191. Vi. LIV, 32–33; Yâ*gñ*. III, 299.

192. Âp. I, 1, 23–2, 10; Vas. XI, 76–79; Vi. LIV, 26. Regarding the times of the initiation, see above, II, 38.

193. Let him prescribe the same (expiation) when twice-born men, who follow forbidden occupations or have neglected (to learn) the Veda, desire to perform a penance.

194. If Brâhma*n*as acquire property by a reprehensible action, they become pure by relinquishing it, muttering prayers, and (performing) austerities.

195. By muttering with a concentrated mind the Sâvitrî three thousand times, (dwelling) for a month in a cow-house, (and) subsisting on milk, (a man) is freed from (the guilt of) accepting presents from a wicked man.

196. But when he returns from the cow-house, emaciated with his fast, and reverently salutes, (the Brâhma*n*as) shall ask him, 'Friend, dost thou desire to become our equal?'

197. If he answers to the Brâhma*n*as, 'Forsooth, (I will not offend again),' he shall scatter (some) grass for the cows; if the cows hallow that place (by eating the grass) the (Brâhma*n*a) shall re-admit him (into their community).

---

193. Vi. LIV, 27.

194. Vi. LIV, 24, 28; Yâ*gñ*. III, 290. 'By a reprehensible action,' i.e. 'by receiving presents from wicked men or, according to others, by acquiring money in any manner forbidden to him. The latter extend the rule to other Âryans' (Medh.). Gov., Kull., and Nâr. refer the verse to Brâhma*n*as and to their accepting presents from wicked men and similar acts.

195. Medh. remarks that according to some the offender shall daily recite the Gâyatrî three thousand times, according to others three thousand times in the whole month.

196–197. Yâ*gñ*. III, 300.

197. The beginning of the verse is explained differently by Nâr. and Nand.: 'If he tells the truth to the Brâhma*n*as, i.e. with respect to his offence and his penance.' Medh. takes tîrtha in its usual sense, 'a bathing-place,' and connects it with pratigraha*m* kuryu*h*,

198. He who has sacrificed for Vrâtyas, or has performed the obsequies of strangers, or a magic sacrifice (intended to destroy life) or an Ahîna sacrifice, removes (his guilt) by three K*rikkh*ra (penances).

199. A twice-born man who has cast off a suppliant for protection, or has (improperly) divulged the Veda, atones for his offence, if he subsists during a year on barley.

200. He who has been bitten by a dog, a jackal, or a donkey, by a tame carnivorous animal, by a man, a horse, a camel, or a (village-)pig, becomes pure by suppressing his breath (Prâ*n*âyâma).

201. To eat during a month at each sixth mealtime (only), to recite the Sa*m*hitâ (of a Veda), and (to perform) daily the *S*âkala oblations, are the means of purifying those excluded from society at repasts (Apâṅktya).

'they shall re-admit at the bathing-place.' Nâr. says it means vyavahâravartman. The translation follows Gov., Kull., and Râgh.

198. Âp. I, 26, 7; Vi. LIV, 25; Yâ*gñ*. III, 289. Vrâtyas, see above, X, 20. 'A magic rite (intended to destroy life),' i. e. 'a *S*yena sacrifice and the like.' The Ahîna sacrifices are those lasting between two and twelve days; see Weber, Ind. Stud. X, 355. Medh. thinks that the rule refers to the person who offers the sacrifices (ya*g*amâna), while others mentioned by him hold that it applies to the officiating priests.

199. Yâ*gñ*. III, 289. Veda*m* viplâvya, 'having (improperly) divulged the Veda,' i. e. 'having taught people who ought not to be taught' (Medh., Gov., Kull., Nand.), means according to Nâr. 'having improperly interpreted the Veda or perverted its sense by omitting Anusvâras, Visargas, and the like,' according to Râgh. 'having intentionally forgotten it.'

200. Gaut. XXIII, 7; Vas. XXIII, 31; Vi. LIV, 12; Yâ*gñ*. III, 277. 'A tame carnivorous animal,' i. e. 'a cat, an ichneumon, and so forth' (Medh., Gov., Kull., Râgh.). Nâr. reads agrâmyai*h* ('grâmyai*h*) kravyâdbhi*h*, and gives as an instance 'a wolf.'

201. Regarding the Apâṅktyas, elsewhere called Paṅktidûsha*n*as,

202. A Brâhma*n*a who voluntarily rode in a carriage drawn by camels or by asses, and he who bathed naked, become pure by suppressing his breath (Prâ*n*âyâma).

203. He who has relieved the necessities of nature, being greatly pressed, either without (using) water or in water, becomes pure by bathing outside (the village) in his clothes and by touching a cow.

204. Fasting is the penance for omitting the daily rites prescribed by the Veda and for neglecting the special duties of a Snâtaka.

205. He who has said 'Hu*m*' to a Brâhma*n*a, or has addressed one of his betters with 'Thou,' shall bathe, fast during the remaining part of the day, and appease (the person offended) by a reverential salutation.

206. He who has struck (a Brâhma*n*a) even with a blade of grass, tied him by the neck with a cloth, or conquered him in an altercation, shall appease him by a prostration.

'defilers of the company,' see above, III, 151 seq. Nâr. remarks that this penance is to be performed by those only for whom no other expiation is specially prescribed. The *S*âkala-homas are oblations offered with the eight verses Vâ*g*asaneyi-sa*m*hitâ VIII, 13.

202. Vi. LIV, 23; Yâ*gñ*. III, 291. Medh. and Kull. remark that he who rides on the back of camels or donkeys has to perform more than one Prâ*n*âyâma.

203. Vi. LIV, 10. 'Outside the village,' i. e. 'in a river or the like' (Medh., Gov., Kull., Râgh.).

204. Vi. LIV, 29. The rules for a Snâtaka are those given in the fourth chapter. The daily rites are the Agnihotra and so forth. The fasting is to last one day (Medh., Kull., Nâr.).

205. Yâ*gñ*. III, 292. 'One's betters ought to be addressed with "You"' (Medh.).

206. Yâ*gñ*. III, 292. See above, IV, 166. Gov. and Nâr. say, 'a Brâhma*n*a more venerable than himself.'

207. But he who, intending to hurt a Brâhma*n*a, has threatened (him with a stick and the like) shall remain in hell during a hundred years; he who (actually) struck him, during one thousand years.

208. As many particles of dust as the blood of a Brâhma*n*a causes to coagulate, for so many thousand years shall the shedder of that (blood) remain in hell.

209. For threatening a Brâhma*n*a, (the offender) shall perform a K*rikkh*ra, for striking him an Atik*rikkh*ra, for shedding his blood a K*rikkh*ra and an Atik*rikkh*ra.

210. For the expiation of offences for which no atonement has been prescribed, let him fix a penance after considering (the offender's) strength and the (nature of the) offence.

211. I will (now) describe to you those means, adopted by the gods, the sages, and the manes, through which a man may remove his sins.

212. A twice-born man who performs (the K*rikkh*ra penance), revealed by Pra*g*âpati, shall eat during three days in the morning (only), during (the next) three days in the evening (only), during the (following) three days (food given) unasked, and shall fast during another period of three days.

207–208. See above, IV, 165, 167–169, where slightly different versions of these verses occur. I read with all the commentators and K. dvi*g*anmana*h*, 'of a Brâhma*n*a,' instead of mahîtale, 'on the ground' (editions).

209. Vi. LIV, 30; Yâ*gñ*. III, 293. Medh. points out that these offences have already been dealt with above in verses 67 and 125, and thinks that the penance prescribed in the latter verse may be performed optionally instead of those mentioned here.

210. Vi. LIV, 34; Yâ*gñ*. III, 294.

212. Âp. I, 27, 7; Gaut. XXVI, 2–5; Vas. XXI, 20; Baudh. II,

213. (Subsisting on) the urine of cows, cowdung, milk, sour milk, clarified butter, and a decoction of Kusa-grass, and fasting during one (day and) night, (that is) called a Sâmtapana Krikkhra.

214. A twice-born man who performs an Atikrikkhra (penance), must take his food during three periods of three days in the manner described above, (but) one mouthful only at each meal, and fast during the last three days.

215. A Brâhmana who performs a Taptakrikkhra (penance) must drink hot water, hot milk, hot clarified butter and (inhale) hot air, each during three days, and bathe once with a concentrated mind.

216. A fast for twelve days by a man who controls himself and commits no mistakes, is called a Parâka Krikkhra, which removes all guilt.

217. If one diminishes (one's food daily by) one

2, 38; IV, 5, 6–7; Vi. XLVI, 10; Yâgñ. III, 320. According to Medh., food which a wife brings unasked is also 'food given unasked.'

213. Baudh. IV, 5, 13; Vi. XLVI, 19; Yâgñ. III, 313. There are two ways of performing this penance: Either the penitent may eat the six substances during one day and fast on the next, or he may subsist one day on each of the six and fast on the seventh day (Medh., Gov.). The other commentators give the first explanation only.

214. Gaut. XXV, 18–19; Vas. XXIV, 1–2; Baudh. II, 2, 40; IV, 5, 8; Yâgñ. III, 320. 'Above,' i.e. in verse 213.

215. Vas. XXI, 18; Baudh. II, 2, 37; IV, 5, 10; Vi. XLVI, 11; Yâgñ. III, 318.

216. Baudh. IV, 5, 15; Vi. XLVI, 18; Yâgñ. III, 221. 'Commits no mistakes,' i.e. 'with respect to the general rules to be followed during the performance of a Krikkhra,' see Vas. XXIV, 5 (Medh., Nâr.).

217–226. Gaut. XXVII; Vas. XXIV, 45–47; XXVII, 21; Baudh. III, 8; IV, 5, 17–21; Vi. XLVII; Yâgñ. III, 324–327.

217. The form of the lunar penance described in this verse is

mouthful during the dark (half of the month) and increases (it in the same manner) during the bright half, and bathes (daily) at the time of three libations (morning, noon, and evening), that is called a lunar penance (*K*ândrâya*n*a).

218. Let him follow throughout the same rule at the (*K*ândrâya*n*a, called) yavamadhyama (shaped like a barley-corn), (but) let him (in that case) begin the lunar penance, (with a) controlled (mind), on the first day of the bright half (of the month).

219. He who performs the lunar penance of ascetics, shall eat (during a month) daily at midday eight mouthfuls, controlling himself and consuming sacrificial food (only).

220. If a Brâhma*n*a, with concentrated mind, eats (during a month daily) four mouthfuls in a morning and four after sunset, (that is) called the lunar penance of children.

221. He who, concentrating his mind, eats during a month in any way thrice eighty mouthfuls of sacrificial food, dwells (after death) in the world of the moon.

222. The Rudras, likewise the Âdityas, the Vasus and the Maruts, together with the great sages, practised this (rite) in order to remove all evil.

223. Burnt oblations, accompanied by (the recitation of) the Mahâvyâh*ri*tis, must daily be made (by

the so-called pipîlikâmadhya or ant-shaped one, where the fast or lean days lie in the middle.

218. It will be advisable to read with Medh. and Gov., in the second line, *k*aret instead of *k*aran. Gov. has *k*aran in the first line. Nand. reads the last words quite differently, (niyata*s*) *k*ândrâya*n*am athâparam.

221. 'In any way,' i. e. 'without observing any particular limit as to the number of mouthfuls to be eaten on each day' (Nâr.).

the penitent) himself, and he must abstain from injuring (sentient creatures), speak the truth, and keep himself free from anger and from dishonesty.

224. Let him bathe three times each day and thrice each night, dressed in his clothes; let him on no account talk to women, *S*ûdras, and outcasts.

225. Let him pass the time standing (during the day) and sitting (during the night), or if he is unable (to do that) let him lie on the (bare) ground; let him be chaste and observe the vows (of a student) and worship his Gurus, the gods, and Brâhma*n*as.

226. Let him constantly mutter the Sâvitrî and (other) purificatory texts according to his ability; (let him) carefully (act thus) on (the occasion of) all (other) vows (performed) by way of penance.

227. By these expiations twice-born men must be purified whose sins are known, but let him purify those whose sins are not known by (the recitation of) sacred texts and by (the performance of) burnt oblations.

---

224. Medh. remarks that the penitent may however talk to the female members of his household, if an occasion requires it.

225. Vratî syât, 'observe the vows (of a student),' i. e. 'wear the girdle of Mu*ñg*a-grass, a staff and so forth' (Gov., Kull. Nâr.), means according to Medh. 'let him resolve to abstain from that which is not forbidden by good men.'

226. 'Purificatory texts,' i. e. 'the Aghamarsha*n*a, the Pâvamânîs and so forth;' see Vi. LVI. '(Other) vows,' i. e. 'the K*r*ikkh*ras.'

227. Vas. XXV, 3. Penances are usually imposed by a parishad, an assembly of learned Brâhma*n*as. In the case of secret sins the penances shall be settled by the learned in a general way, not with reference to a special case. By this interpretation the commentators get over the difficulty which the reading *s*odhayet, 'let him purify,' offers. But Nâr. reads anâvishk*r*itapâpâ*s* tu mantrair homai*s* *k*a *s*odhanai*h*, 'but those whose sins are not known, by sacred texts and burnt oblations, (declared to be) means of purification.'

228. By confession, by repentance, by austerity, and by reciting (the Veda) a sinner is freed from guilt, and in case no other course is possible, by liberality.

229. In proportion as a man who has done wrong, himself confesses it, even so far he is freed from guilt, as a snake from its slough.

230. In proportion as his heart loathes his evil deed, even so far is his body freed from that guilt.

231. He who has committed a sin and has repented, is freed from that sin, but he is purified only by (the resolution of) ceasing (to sin and thinking) 'I will do so no more.'

232. Having thus considered in his mind what results will arise from his deeds after death, let him always be good in thoughts, speech, and actions.

233. He who, having either unintentionally or intentionally committed a reprehensible deed, desires to be freed from (the guilt of) it, must not commit it a second time.

234. If his mind be uneasy with respect to any act, let him repeat the austerities (prescribed as a penance) for it until they fully satisfy (his conscience).

235. All the bliss of gods and men is declared by the sages to whom the Veda was revealed, to have

---

228. Âpadi, 'in case no other course is possible,' i. e. 'if the offender is unable to perform penances or to recite Vedic texts.'

230. 'His body,' i. e. 'the soul in his body' (Medh., Gov., Kull., Nand.), or 'the subtle body' (Nâr.).

231. Instead of naiva*m*, 'so no (more),' Nâr. reads naina*h* ('I will) not sin (any more),' and K.'s reading naina*m* points to the same var. lect. Gov., Nand., and the best MS. of Medh. read naitat kuryât punar iti, and the translation would then be 'but he is purified (only) by ceasing (to sin), thereby that he does so no more.'

235. 'To have austerity for its root, austerity for its middle, and

austerity for its root, austerity for its middle, and austerity for its end.

236. (The pursuit of sacred) knowledge is the austerity of a Brâhma*n*a, protecting (the people) is the austerity of a Kshatriya, (the pursuit of) his daily business is the austerity of a Vai*s*ya, and service the austerity of a *S*ûdra.

237. The sages who control themselves and subsist on fruit, roots, and air, survey the three worlds together with their moving and immovable (creatures) through their austerities alone.

238. Medicines, good health, learning, and the various divine stations are attained by austerities alone; for austerity is the means of gaining them.

239. Whatever is hard to be traversed, whatever is hard to be attained, whatever is hard to be reached, whatever is hard to be performed, all (this) may be accomplished by austerities; for austerity (possesses a power) which it is difficult to surpass.

240. Both those who have committed mortal sin (Mahâpâtaka) and all other offenders are severally freed from their guilt by means of well-performed austerities.

241. Insects, snakes, moths, bees, birds and beings, bereft of motion, reach heaven by the power of austerities.

austerity for its end,' i. e. 'to be produced, to continue, and to end in consequence of austerities performed' (Medh., Kull., Nâr.).

238. Medh. explains aushadhâni, 'medicines,' by 'elixirs.' Instead of agado (Kull., K., Râgh.) Medh., Gov., Nâr., and Nand. read agadâ*h*, and explain it by 'medicines' (Medh., Nand.), 'remedies or charms against poison' (Gov., Nâr.).

241. Instead of kî*t*â*s* *k*a, 'insects,' Nâr. reads *s*vâna*s* *k*a, 'dogs.' Gov. and Nand. say that the verse refers to the Kî*t*opâkhyâna and the Kapotâkhyâna, told in the Itihâsas (Mahâbhârata XII).

242. Whatever sin men commit by thoughts, words, or deeds, that they speedily burn away by penance, if they keep penance as their only riches.

243. The gods accept the offerings of that Brâhma*n*a alone who has purified himself by austerities, and grant to him all he desires.

244. The lord, Pra*g*âpati, created these Institutes (of the sacred law) by his austerities alone; the sages likewise obtained (the revelation of) the Vedas through their austerities.

245. The gods, discerning that the holy origin of this whole (world) is from austerity, have thus proclaimed the incomparable power of austerity.

246. The daily study of the Veda, the performance of the great sacrifices according to one's ability, (and) patience (in suffering) quickly destroy all guilt, even that caused by mortal sins.

247. As a fire in one moment consumes with its bright flame the fuel that has been placed on it, even so he who knows the Veda destroys all guilt by the fire of knowledge.

248. The penances for sins (made public) have been thus declared according to the law; learn next the penances for secret (sins).

249. Sixteen suppressions of the breath (Prâ*n*âyâma) accompanied by (the recitation of) the Vyâh*ri*tis

245. I read with all the commentators and K. at the end of the verse, udbhavam, instead of uttamam (editions).

246. Vas. XXVII, 7; Yâ*gñ*. III, 311.

247. Vas. XXVII, 1–2.

248. Kull. and Râgh. state that Gov. omits this verse, while Medh. gives it. The accessible MS. of Gov., however, shows it, but without a commentary. Medh. says only that 'some' read it. Nâr. and Nand. omit it.

249. Vas. XXVI, 4; Vi. LV, 5; Baudh. IV, 1, 29. The best

and of the syllable Om, purify, if they are repeated daily, after a month even the murderer of a learned Brâhma*n*a.

250. Even a drinker of (the spirituous liquor called) Surâ becomes pure, if he mutters the hymn (seen) by Kutsa, 'Removing by thy splendour our guilt, O Agni,' &c., (that seen) by Vasish*th*a, 'With their hymns the Vasish*th*as woke the Dawn,' &c., the Mâhitra (hymn) and (the verses called) *S*uddhavatîs.

251. Even he who has stolen gold, instantly becomes free from guilt, if he once mutters (the hymn beginning with the words) 'The middlemost brother of this beautiful, ancient Hot*ri*-priest' and the *S*ivasa*m*kalpa.

252. The violator of a Guru's bed is freed (from sin), if he repeatedly recites the Havishpântîya (hymn), (that beginning) 'Neither anxiety nor misfortune,' (and that beginning) 'Thus, verily, thus,' and mutters the hymn addressed to Purusha.

253. He who desires to expiate sins great or

---

explanation of the words 'accompanied by (the recitation of) the Vyâh*ri*tis and (of) the syllable Om' is Nâr.'s, who asserts that they indicate the necessity of reciting the Gâyatrî with the *S*iras text during the performance of each Prâ*n*âyâma; see Vas. XXV, 13.

250. Vas. XXVI, 5. The hymn seen by Kutsa, i. e. Rig-veda I, 97; that seen by Vasish*th*a, i. e. Rig-veda VII, 80. The Mâhitra hymn, i. e. Rig-veda X, 185. The *S*uddhavatîs, i. e. Rig-veda VIII, 84, 7–9. Medh., Gov., Nâr., and K. read mâhendram for mâhitram, and Nâr. adds that some give the latter reading. The hymns are to be recited during a month sixteen times (Gov., Kull., Râgh.), or 108 times a day (Nâr.).

251. Vas. XXVI, 6. The hymn is found Rig-veda I, 164; the *S*ivasa*m*kalpa, Vâg. Sa*m*h. XXXIV, 1. 'Once,' i. e. 'once daily during a month' (Gov., Kull., Nâr.).

252. Vas. XXVI, 7; Yâg*ñ*. III, 305. The four hymns are Rig-veda X, 88; X, 126; X, 119; and X, 90.

253. The two verses are found Rig-veda I, 24, 14, and VII, 89, 5.

small, must mutter during a year the *Rik*-verse 'May we remove thy anger, O Varu*n*a,' &c., or 'Whatever offence here, O Varu*n*a,' &c.

254. That man who, having accepted presents which ought not to be accepted, or having eaten forbidden food, mutters the Taratsamandîya (*Rik*as), becomes pure after three days.

255. But he who has committed many sins, becomes pure, if he recites during a month the (four verses) addressed to Soma and Rudra, and the three verses (beginning) 'Aryaman, Varu*n*a, and Mitra,' while he bathes in a river.

256. A grievous offender shall mutter the seven verses (beginning with) 'Indra,' for half a year; but he who has committed any blamable act in water, shall subsist during a month on food obtained by begging.

257. A twice-born man removes even very great guilt by offering clarified butter with the sacred texts belonging to the *S*âkala-homas, or by muttering the *Rik*, (beginning) 'Adoration.'

258. He who is stained by mortal sin, becomes pure, if, with a concentrated mind, he attends cows for a year, reciting the Pâvamânî (hymns) and subsisting on alms.

---

254. Gaut. XXIV, 2–3; Baudh. IV, 2, 4–5. The verses are found Rig-veda IX, 58, 1–4.

255. The verses are found Rig-vedá VI, 74, 1–4, and IV, 2, 4–6.

256. The verses are found Rig-veda I, 106, 1–7.

257. The Mantras for the *S*âkala-homas, i. e. Vâ*g*. Sa*m*h. VIII, 13. The verse is found Rig-veda VI, 51, 8. According to Nâr. the Mantras must be muttered 108 times.

258. The Pâvamânî hymns, i. e. the ninth Ma*nd*ala of the Rig-veda.

259. Or if, pure (in mind and in body), he thrice repeats the Sa*m*hitâ of the Veda in a forest, sanctified by three Parâka (penances), he is freed from all crimes causing loss of caste (pâtaka).

260. But if (a man) fasts during three days, bathing thrice a day, and muttering (in the water the hymn seen by) Aghamarsha*n*a, he is (likewise) freed from all sins causing loss of caste.

261. As the horse-sacrifice, the king of sacrifices, removes all sin, even so the Aghamarsha*n*a hymn effaces all guilt.

262. A Brâhma*n*a who retains in his memory the *Ri*g-veda is not stained by guilt, though he may have destroyed these three worlds, though he may eat the food of anybody.

263. He who, with a concentrated mind, thrice recites the *Rik*sa*m*hitâ, or (that of the) Yagur-veda, or (that of the) Sâma-veda together with the secret (texts, the Upanishads), is completely freed from all sins.

264. As a clod of earth, falling into a great lake, is quickly dissolved, even so every sinful act is engulfed in the threefold Veda.

265. The *Rik*as, the Yagus(-formulas) which differ (from the former), the manifold Sâman(-songs), must

259. 'The Sa*m*hitâ,' i. e. the Mantras and Brâhma*n*as (Kull., Râgh.), the former alone (Nâr.). 'Parâka penances,' see above, verse 216. The verse seems to refer to the Ana*s*natpârâya*n*a, fully described by Baudh. III, 9.

260-261. Gaut. XXIV, 10-12; Vas. XXVI, 8; Baudh. III, 5; IV, 2, 15; Vi. LV, 7; Yâ*gñ*. III, 302. The Aghamarsha*n*a is found Rig-veda X, 190.

262. Vas. XXVII, 3. 263. Baudh. IV, 5, 29.

264. I read with Gov., Nand., and K. pr. manu 'kshipram' instead of 'kshiptam' (Medh., K. sec. manu, editions).

265. Medh. and Gov. read âdyâni, 'chief,' instead of anyâni, 'which differ.' Medh. explains it as 'either those found in the

be known (to form) the triple Veda; he who knows them, (is called) learned in the Veda.

266. The initial triliteral Brahman on which the threefold (sacred science) is based, is another triple Veda which must be kept secret; he who knows that, (is called) learned in the Veda.

CHAPTER XII.

1. 'O sinless One, the whole sacred law, (applicable) to the four castes, has been declared by thee; communicate to us (now), according to the truth, the ultimate retribution for (their) deeds.'

2. To the great sages (who addressed him thus) righteous Bh*ri*gu, sprung from Manu, answered, 'Hear the decision concerning this whole connexion with actions.'

3. Action, which springs from the mind, from speech, and from the body, produces either good or evil results; by action are caused the (various) conditions of men, the highest, the middling, and the lowest.

4. Know that the mind is the instigator here

Sa*m*hitâ, not those read in the Brâhma*n*a or those recited according to the Sa*m*hitâpâ*th*a, not those recited according to the Pada or Kramapâ*th*as.' Gov. gives the first explanation only.

266. K. omits this verse, and inserts in its stead the following lines:

esha vo vadita['bhihita]s sarva*h* prâya*s*kittavi*n*ir*n*aya*h* ı
nai*h*sreyasa*m* karmavidhim viprasyaita*m* nibodhata ıı
ata*h* para*m* pravakshyâmi sa*m*sâravidhim uttamam ı

Nand. gives the first two lines after verse 266, reading, however, ityeshâ(?)bhihita*h*.

XII. 1. Râgh. takes tattvata*h* parâm separately and explains the second line as follows: 'communicate to us (now) the retribution for (their) deeds (and) supreme (liberation, which springs) from (the recognition of) truth.'

4. 'Of three kinds,' i.e. 'good, middling, or bad.' 'Has three

below, even to that (action) which is connected with the body, (and) which is of three kinds, has three locations, and falls under ten heads.

5. Coveting the property of others, thinking in one's heart of what is undesirable, and adherence to false (doctrines), are the three kinds of (sinful) mental action.

6. Abusing (others, speaking) untruth, detracting from the merits of all men, and talking idly, shall be the four kinds of (evil) verbal action.

7. Taking what has not been given, injuring (creatures) without the sanction of the law, and holding criminal intercourse with another man's wife, are declared to be the three kinds of (wicked) bodily action.

8. (A man) obtains (the result of) a good or evil mental (act) in his mind, (that of) a verbal (act) in his speech, (that of) a bodily (act) in his body.

9. In consequence of (many) sinful acts committed with his body, a man becomes (in the next birth) something inanimate, in consequence (of sins) com-

---

locations,' i. e. 'the mind, speech, and the body.' 'Falls under ten heads,' i. e. 'those mentioned in verses 5–7.' The mind, which is here called the instigator, is the internal organ, which has the faculty of sa*m*kalpa, 'volition.'

5. 'Thinking in one's heart what is undesirable,' means according to Medh. either 'thinking of or wishing anything that may be injurious to others or what is forbidden.' Gov. and Nâr. give the first explanation, the other commentators the second. Others mentioned by Medh. explained vitathâbhinive*s*am, 'adherence to false doctrines' (i. e. the denial of a future state, of the authority of the Vedas and so forth), by 'a constant deep hatred.' In their remarks on this verse and the next two, the commentators point out that the opposites of the acts mentioned are the different kinds of good actions.

5–9. Yâg*ñ*. III, 131, 134–136.

mitted by speech, a bird, or a beast, and in consequence of mental (sins he is re-born in) a low caste.

10. That man is called a (true) tridandin in whose mind these three, the control over his speech (vâgdanda), the control over his thoughts (manodanda), and the control over his body (kâyadanda), are firmly fixed.

11. That man who keeps this threefold control (over himself) with respect to all created beings and wholly subdues desire and wrath, thereby assuredly gains complete success.

12. Him who impels this (corporeal) Self to action, they call the Kshetragña (the knower of the field); but him who does the acts, the wise name the Bhûtâtman (the Self consisting of the elements).

13. Another internal Self that is generated with all embodied (Kshetragñas) is called *G*îva, through which (the Kshetragña) becomes sensible of all pleasure and pain in (successive) births.

---

10. Usually an ascetic who wears three staves (danda) tied together, is called a tridandin. According to our verse this outward sign avails nothing. That man only deserves the name tridandin who keeps a threefold control (danda) over himself.

11. 'Complete success,' i. e. 'final liberation.'

12. 'This (corporeal) Self,' i. e. 'the body' (Medh., Gov., Kull.), or 'the gross visible body which includes the three sheaths' (Râgh., Nâr.). 'The Kshetragña (the knower of the field),' i. e. 'the individual Soul (*G*îva),' (Medh. on verse 13, Nâr.), the Paramâtman (Nand.); Râgh. quotes, in explanation of the term 'the field,' Bhagavadgîtâ XIII, 5–6. 'The Bhûtâtman (the Self consisting of the elements),' i. e. 'the body which is composed of or a modification of the elements, i. e. of earth and so forth' (Medh., Gov., Kull., Râgh.), 'the Self which has the form of the non-sentient, the elements and so forth' (Nâr.), or 'the *G*îva' (Nand.).

13. According to Medh. 'some' understand by the term *G*îva 'the subtile body (liṅga sarîra) which is overspread by Mahat, the Great One,' because the individual soul, which is usually called

14. These two, the Great One and the Kshetra*gñ*a, who are closely united with the elements, pervade him who resides in the multiform created beings.

---

*G*îva, has been mentioned in verse 12 under the appellation Kshetra*gñ*a. He adds that 'others' explain *G*îva by 'the internal organ, which has the form of mind, intelligence, and egoism.' The former view is adopted by Râgh., while Gov., who paraphrases *G*îva by mana*h*, 'the mind,' and Kull. as well as Nâr., who render it by 'Mahat,' 'the Great One or intelligence,' lean towards the second. Nand. says, '*g*îvasa*m*g*ñ*a*h* means "he who fully knows the *G*îvas," i.e. the omniscient.' Saha*g*a*h*, 'that is generated with,' means according to Medh. and Gov. 'that is associated with until the period of destruction (pralaya) or until final liberation is obtained.'

14. The term mahân, 'the Great One,' is referred by Medh., Gov., Kull., Nâr., Râgh. to the *G*îva mentioned in the preceding verse, and hence is explained by each in accordance with the view expressed on verse 13. Bhûtasa*m*p*ri*ktau, 'closely united with the elements' (Medh., Gov., Kull.), or 'enveloped by the elements' (Râgh.), means according to Nâr. 'united with the Bhûtâtman.' Sthita*m* ta*m* vyâpya tish*th*ata*h*, 'pervade him who resides,' i. e. 'pervade' (Gov.), or 'rest on' (Kull.), or 'conceal through illusion' (Nâr.) him, i. e. 'the Paramâtman, the Supreme Soul' (Gov., Kull., Nâr.), 'who resides in all created beings' (Gov., Nâr.) 'as the witness' (Kull., Nâr.). Gov. adds 'or (the expression vyâpya tish*th*ata*h*) "they pervade" is used because the Supreme Soul pervades everything.' This latter explanation probably refers to Medh.'s rendering, according to which the verse must be translated 'Those two, the Great One and the Knower of the Field, who are closely united, rest on him who resides in the multiform created beings, pervading (them).' Medh. expressly declares that tish*th*ata*h* is to be taken as a transitive verb (sarvakarmatva*m* [sakarmatva*m*] tish*th*ater anekârthatvât). He explains 'him' by 'the Supreme Soul,' and adds that the expression 'rest on' is justified, because the Paramâtman is the cause of the whole world, and the product rests on its cause. Râgh. differs very much, and says, 'Those two, the Great One (i. e. the Intelligence and by implication the subtile body) and the Knower of the Field, i. e. the individual soul enveloped by the five elements (and) pervading him who is found in the manifold created beings, i. e. the gross bodies, and reside, i. e. there, as the enjoyers.' Nand. finally has the following explanation: 'Those two, i. e. the

15. From his body innumerable forms go forth, which constantly impel the multiform creatures to action.

16. Another strong body, formed of particles (of the) five (elements and) destined to suffer the torments (in hell), is produced after death (in the case) of wicked men.

17. When (the evil-doers) by means of that body have suffered there the torments imposed by Yama, (its constituent parts) are united, each according to its class, with those very elements (from which they were taken).

---

individual and the Supreme Soul; united with the elements, i.e. residing in the body; the Great One, i.e. the Supreme Soul and the Knower of the Field; in the manifold, i.e. in the gross and in the subtile; him who is found, i.e. the field (kshetra), pervading they reside. The meaning is that the individual soul pervades the body and the Supreme Soul pervades the individual soul.'

15. 'From his body,' i.e. 'from nature or the form of the Supreme Soul (Paramâtman, Medh., Nâr.) or from the body of Brahman which is endowed with the qualities' (Râgh.), 'like waves from the ocean or sparks from fire, in the manner mentioned in the Vedânta philosophy' (Gov., Kull.). 'Others,' mentioned by Medh., and Nand. explain the expression by 'from the root-evolvent or matter (prak*ri*ti) which is the body of the Supreme Soul.' Mûrtaya*h*, 'forms,' i.e. 'Kshetra*gñ*as' (Gov., Kull., Nâr.), or 'souls limited by subtile bodies' (Râgh.), or 'portions which are the causes of the production of forms' (Nand.).

16. Dhruvam, 'strong,' i.e. 'able to withstand the supernatural torments' (Medh., Kull., Râgh.). Gov. and Nand. read d*ridh*am.

17. The translation follows Medh., Gov., and Râgh., with whom Nâr. seems to agree, and it presupposes that the construction of the verse is ungrammatical. Kull. and Nand., who wish to show that Manu's text does not depart from the ordinary rules of grammar, assume that the subject of both clauses is dushk*ri*tino *g*îvâ*h*, 'the evil-doing souls.' The former says, 'The evil-doing souls that are subtile, having suffered by means of that produced body those torments imposed by Yama, are individually dissolved on the disappearance of the gross body, in those very constituent portions of

18. He, having suffered for his faults, which are produced by attachment to sensual objects, and which result in misery, approaches, free from stains, those two mighty ones.

---

the elements;' the meaning is, 'they remain being united with them.' Nand.'s explanation is more intelligible. According to him the translation must be as follows: '(The individual souls) having suffered by means of that body the torments of Yama, are dissolved (on the termination of their sufferings, as far as that body is concerned), in those very (five) elements according to the proportion of their works' (vibhâgaṡas tatkarmavibhâgânurûpam). But it seems to me that these attempts to save the grammatical reputation of the author are useless.

18. The translation follows the reading of Gov. (comm.), Kull., Nand., and Râgh., anubhûyâsukhodarkân. Medh., Gov. (text), and K. read anubhûya sukhodarkân, '(after the expiation) of which happiness is the result' (Medh.). 'He,' i. e. 'the individual soul' (kshetra*gñ*a, Medh., Gov., Nand.), or 'the individual soul limited by the subtile body' (Kull., Râgh.), refers according to Nâr. to 'the Great One' (Mahân). 'Those two mighty ones,' i. e. 'the Great One and the Supreme Soul' (Medh. 'others,' Gov., Kull.), are according to Medh. and Râgh. 'the Great One and the Kshetra*gñ*a' (mentioned verse 14), according to Nâr. and Nand. (on verse 19) 'the *G*îva and the Paramâtman or Supreme Soul.' Medh. adds that under his explanation the verse looks as if it were self-contradictory, because the end to be attained and the attainer are the same, but that the distinction is merely figurative. For the expression 'he approaches' means 'he becomes nothing else but that' [i. e. after the dissolution of the body, assumed in order to suffer the punishments, he remains purely Kshetra*gñ*a and Mahân]. His words are, ata*h* kshetra*gñ*am abhyetîti prâpta*m* ta*k k*a viruddha*m* sa eva prâpya[*h*] prâpaka*s k*a । satyam aupa*k*âriko bhedo 'bhipreta*h* । abhyetîty ayam artha*h* । etâvanmâtra*s*esho bhavati yad uta kshetra*gñ*atayâ prâptâdisa*m*ghâtmakena mahân iti vyapadish*t*ena phaleshu tâvanmâtra*h* pari*s*ishyate । liṅga*g*îva*s k*a kshetra*gñ*a*h* ॥ Râgh., the only other commentator, who occupies himself with the ulterior meaning of the verse, renders abhyeti, 'he approaches,' by anuga*kkh*ati, 'he follows,' and adds 'in order to produce a new body' (*s*arîrântarârambhâya). He further quotes *S*atapatha-brâhma*n*a XIV, 7, 2, 5, in order to show that according to the Veda the individual soul, united with the subtile body, makes for itself another body.

19. Those two together examine without tiring the merit and the guilt of that (individual soul), united with which it obtains bliss or misery both in this world and the next.

20. If (the soul) chiefly practises virtue and vice to a small degree, it obtains bliss in heaven, clothed with those very elements.

21. But if it chiefly cleaves to vice and to virtue in a small degree, it suffers, deserted by the elements, the torments inflicted by Yama.

22. The individual soul, having endured those torments of Yama, again enters, free from taint, those very five elements, each in due proportion.

23. Let (man), having recognised even by means of his intellect these transitions of the individual soul (which depend) on merit and demerit, always fix his heart on (the acquisition of) merit.

24. Know Goodness (sattva), Activity (ra*g*as), and Darkness (tamas) to be the three qualities of the

---

19. 'Those two,' i. e. 'the Great One and the Supreme Soul' (mahatparamâtmânau, Gov., Kull.), are according to Medh., who modifies the explanation given on the preceding verse, the Mahân and the Paramâtman; according to Râgh., the Mahân and the Kshetra*gñ*a. Pa*s*yata*h*, 'examine,' means according to Râgh. 'by their presence cause to be performed.' 'The guilt,' i.e. 'which remains after the sufferings (in hell,' Kull.). Nand. explains the first line very differently: 'Those two (merit and demerit) watchfully attend him (the Kshetra*gñ*a) who is bent on performing good and evil.' 'United with which,' i. e. 'with merit and guilt' (Medh., Gov., Kull., Nand.), refers in Râgh.'s opinion to the Mahân and the Kshetra*gñ*a.

20. 'With those very elements,' i. e. 'with a gross body consisting of the before-mentioned five elements.'

21. 'Deserted by the elements,' i. e. 'after death' (Kull., Nâr.).

22. Medh. and K. read abhyeti for apyeti.

24. Yâ*gñ*. III, 182. 'Of the Self,' i. e. 'of the Mahat' (Kull.,

Self, with which the Great One always completely pervades all existences.

25. When one of these qualities wholly predominates in a body, then it makes the embodied (soul) eminently distinguished for that quality.

26. Goodness is declared (to have the form of) knowledge, Darkness (of) ignorance, Activity (of) love and hatred; such is the nature of these (three) which is (all-)pervading and clings to everything created.

27. When (man) experiences in his soul a (feeling) full of bliss, a deep calm, as it were, and a pure light, then let him know (that it is) among those three (the quality called) Goodness.

28. What is mixed with pain and does not give satisfaction to the soul one may know (to be the quality of) Activity, which is difficult to conquer, and which ever draws embodied (souls towards sensual objects).

Râgh., Nâr., Nand.), the latter two saying mahattattvasya, 'of the (Sâ*m*khya) principle, called Mahat.' Medh.'s somewhat longer discussion arrives at the same result.

25. 'In a body,' i. e. 'in a subtile body' (Râgh.). Medh. and Gov. add to the first clause 'in consequence of acts done in a former life.'

26. Kull. takes etat, 'such,' in the sense of 'as follows.' Nâr. and Nand. take the last line somewhat differently: 'The nature of these three is pervaded by the (three characteristics just mentioned and) clings to all created beings.'

27. 'A (feeling) full of bliss,' i. e. 'without any particular cause for such a sensation' (Gov.). I take tatra, which Gov. and Kull. explain by tasmin and construe with âtmani, in the sense of teshu, 'among those three.' Râgh. says tatreti tribhi*h*.

28. Medh. has apratipam, which he explains by apratyaksham, 'not perceptible by the senses,' instead of apratigham, 'difficult to conquer.'

29. What is coupled with delusion, what has the character of an undiscernible mass, what cannot be fathomed by reasoning, what cannot be fully known, one must consider (as the quality of) Darkness.

30. I will, moreover, fully describe the results which arise from these three qualities, the excellent ones, the middling ones, and the lowest.

31. The study of the Vedas, austerity, (the pursuit of) knowledge, purity, control over the organs, the performance of meritorious acts and meditation on the Soul, (are) the marks of the quality of Goodness.

32. Delighting in undertakings, want of firmness, commission of sinful acts, and continual indulgence in sensual pleasures, (are) the marks of the quality of Activity.

33. Covetousness, sleepiness, pusillanimity, cruelty, atheism, leading an evil life, a habit of soliciting favours, and inattentiveness, are the marks of the quality of Darkness.

---

29. I follow Gov., Kull., Nâr., Râgh., and K., who read avyaktavishayâtmakam instead of avyakta*m* vishayâtmakam (Nand., editions). Medh.'s reading is doubtful. 'What is coupled with delusion,' i. e. 'where it is impossible to decide if the (thing) is real or unreal' (Gov., Kull., Râgh.). Avyaktavishayâtmakam, 'what has the character of an undiscernible mass' (asphu*t*avishayâkârasvabhâvam, Kull., Râgh.), or 'what has the form of an undiscernible mass and the nature of which is unreal' (aspash*t*avishayâkârâsatsvabhâvam, Gov.), means according to Nâr. 'where the mass and the soul are not luminous' (aprakâ*s*o vishaya âtmâ *k*a yatra).

31. The last words of the verse, which have been translated according to Medh., mean according to Nâr. literally '(are the result) of Goodness (and) the marks of (that) quality' (sâttvika*m* sattva*g*anya*m* gu*n*asya tasyaiva laksha*n*a*m* *k*ihnam).

32. Adhairyam, 'want of firmness,' means according to Nâr. 'want of a contented disposition.'

33. Bhinnav*ri*ttitâ, 'leading an evil life,' i. e. 'omitting to live

34. Know, moreover, the following to be a brief description of the three qualities, each in its order, as they appear in the three (times, the present, past, and future).

35. When a (man), having done, doing, or being about to do any act, feels ashamed, the learned may know that all (such acts bear) the mark of the quality of Darkness.

36. But, when (a man) desires (to gain) by an act much fame in this world and feels no sorrow on failing, know that it (bears the mark of the quality of) Activity.

37. But that (bears) the mark of the quality of Goodness which with his whole (heart) he desires to know, which he is not ashamed to perform, and at which his soul rejoices.

38. The craving after sensual pleasures is declared to be the mark of Darkness, (the pursuit of) wealth (the mark) of Activity, (the desire to gain) spiritual

---

according to the rule of conduct;' pramâda*h*, 'inattentiveness,' i. e. 'to duty.'

34. Instead of trishu, 'in the three (times,' Medh., Gov., Kull., Râgh.), Nand. reads n*ri*shu, 'in men.' Nâr., who reads trishu, explains the words trayâ*n*â*m* gu*n*ânâm, trishu as follows: 'of the three,' i. e. 'of the study of the Veda and so forth;' 'of the gu*n*as, i. e. 'of the three classes of virtues;' 'in the three,' i. e. 'in the three original qualities.'

36. Nand. has *rikkh*ati instead of i*kk*ati. I read with Medh., Gov., Kull., Nâr., Râgh., and Nand., na *k*a *so*kati instead of sa *k*a *so*kati (editions). K. reads naiva. 'And feels no sorrow on failing,' i. e. 'if on failing to accomplish his undertaking he begins another, but does not desist from it out of sorrow, that is the meaning' (Râgh.).

37. Instead of yat sarve*n*a (Gov., Kull.), Medh. and K. read ya*h* sarve*n*a, and Nand. sarva*m* yene°. 'Which with his whole (heart) he desires to know,' i. e. 'the meaning of the Veda and so forth' (Kull., Râgh.).

merit the mark of Goodness; each later (named quality is) better than the preceding one.

39. I will briefly declare in due order what transmigrations in this whole (world a man) obtains through each of these qualities.

40. Those endowed with Goodness reach the state of gods, those endowed with Activity the state of men, and those endowed with Darkness ever sink to the condition of beasts; that is the threefold course of transmigrations.

41. But know this threefold course of transmigrations that depends on the (three) qualities (to be again) threefold, low, middling, and high, according to the particular nature of the acts and of the knowledge (of each man).

42. Immovable (beings), insects, both small and great, fishes, snakes, and tortoises, cattle and wild animals, are the lowest conditions to which (the quality of) Darkness leads.

43. Elephants, horses, *S*ûdras, and despicable barbarians, lions, tigers, and boars (are) the middling states, caused by (the quality of) Darkness.

44. *K*âra*n*as, Supar*n*as and hypocrites, Râkshasas

---

40. Yâ*gñ*. III, 137–139.

41. 'Of the knowledge (of each man),' i. e. 'if the acts were committed intentionally or not' (Medh.).

42. 'Immovable (beings),' i. e. 'trees and so forth.' Pa*s*ava*h*, 'cattle,' i. e. 'cows and so forth' (Nâr.), or 'dogs and so forth' (Râgh.). Instead of saka*kkh*apâ*h* (Gov., Kull., Râgh.), 'and tortoises,' Medh., Nâr., and Nand. read sarîs*ri*pâ*h*, 'creeping things,' i. e. 'scorpions and the like' (Nâr.). Instead of m*ri*gâs *k*aiva (Gov., Kull., Râgh.), 'and wild animals (or deer),' Medh. and Nand. have *s*rigâlâs *k*a, 'and jackals.'

43. Mle*kkh*â*h*, 'barbarians,' i. e. '*S*abaras and so forth' (Nâr.).

44. *K*âra*n*a may denote a caste of men, i. e. 'bards, singers, panders, and the like' (Medh.), or 'rope-dancers' (Nâr.), or 'Na*t*as'

and Pi*s*â*k*as (belong to) the highest (rank of) conditions among those produced by Darkness.

45. *Gh*allas, Mallas, Na*t*as, men who subsist by despicable occupations and those addicted to gambling and drinking (form) the lowest (order of) conditions caused by Activity.

46. Kings and Kshatriyas, the domestic priests of kings, and those who delight in the warfare of disputations (constitute) the middling (rank of the) states caused by Activity.

47. The Gandharvas, the Guhyakas, and the servants of the gods, likewise the Apsarases, (belong all to) the highest (rank of) conditions produced by Activity.

48. Hermits, ascetics, Brâhma*n*as, the crowds of the Vaimânika deities, the lunar mansions, and the Daityas (form) the first (and lowest rank of the) existences caused by Goodness.

(Gov., Kull.); but it may also, with Râgh., be referred to a class of mythological beings. Supar*n*as are the bird-deities, mentioned above, I, 37.

45. *Gh*allas, Mallas, i. e. 'those mentioned above, X, 22 (Kull., Nâr.), who are fencers with sticks or wrestlers and jesters' (Medh., Kull.). Na*t*as, i. e. 'those exhibiting themselves on the stage' (rangâvatârakâ*h*, Medh., Kull.). I read with Medh., Gov., Nâr., and Nand. purushâ*s* *k*a kuv*ri*ttaya*h*, 'men who subsist by despicable occupations,' instead of purushâ*h* *s*astrav*ri*ttaya*h*, 'men living by the trade of arms' (Kull., editions).

46. With respect to the low estimation in which domestic priests are held, see the verse quoted Pa*ñk*atantra II, 63 (Bombay edition). Nand. reads dânayuddhapradhânâ*s* *k*a, 'very liberal men, and those delighting in strife.'

47. Guhyakas, i. e. 'evil spirits who hurt children;' Yakshas, i. e. 'the guardians of treasures' (Nâr.). Both are demigods, servants of Kubera. 'The servants of the gods,' i. e. 'Vidyâdharas and so forth.'

48. Medh. mentions an opinion, held by 'others,' according to

49. Sacrificers, the sages, the gods, the Vedas, the heavenly lights, the years, the manes, and the Sâdhyas (constitute) the second order of existences, caused by Goodness.

50. The sages declare Brahmâ, the creators of the universe, the law, the Great One, and the Undiscernible One (to constitute) the highest order of beings produced by Goodness.

51. Thus (the result) of the threefold action, the whole system of transmigrations which (consists) of three classes, (each) with three subdivisions, and which includes all created beings, has been fully pointed out.

---

which the Yatis, 'ascetics,' are a people living on mount Meru. 'The Vaimânika deities,' i.e. 'those who move in mid-air with their palatial chariots, called vimânas.' Instead of Daityâ*h*, Nâr. mentions as a var. lect. Siddhâ*h*.

49. 'The Vedas,' i.e. 'sounds placed in a certain sequence' (Medh.), or 'the guardian deities or personifications of the Vedas, such as are described in the Itihâsas as belonging to the court of Brahman' (Medh. 'others,' Gov., Kull., Nâr., Râgh.). With respect to the next two terms the commentators vacillate whether the things mentioned or their regents (adhish*th*âtrî devatâ) are intended.

50. Brahmâ, i.e. 'Hira*n*yagarbha' (Gov., Kull., Râgh.). 'The creators of the universe,' i.e. 'Marî*k*i and the rest;' see above, I, 35; 'the law,' i.e. 'either the meaning of the Veda or the incarnate law' (Medh.); according to the other commentators, the latter only. 'The Great One,' i.e. 'the deity presiding over the principle (of the Sâ*m*khya philosophy) called the Great One (or Intellect,' Gov., Kull., Râgh.); 'the Undiscernible One,' i.e. 'the deity presiding over the root-evolvent or chief cause of the Sâ*m*khya philosophy' (Gov., Kull., Râgh.). Medh., who discusses and rejects these explanations of the last two terms, holds that they refer to the Supreme Soul (paramâtman). Nâr. explains 'the Undiscernible' by 'egoism.' Medh., Gov., and K. read avyakta eva *k*a instead of avyaktam eva *k*a.

51. Medh. and K. read esha dharma*h*, 'Thus the law with respect to the threefold action, &c.' Nand. places verse 81 immediately after this.

52. In consequence of attachment to (the objects of) the senses, and in consequence of the non-performance of their duties, fools, the lowest of men, reach the vilest births.

53. What wombs this individual soul enters in this world and in consequence of what actions, learn the particulars of that at large and in due order.

54. Those who committed mortal sins (mahâpâtaka), having passed during large numbers of years through dreadful hells, obtain, after the expiration of (that term of punishment), the following births.

55. The slayer of a Brâhma*n*a enters the womb of a dog, a pig, an ass, a camel, a cow, a goat, a sheep, a deer, a bird, a *K*a*nd*âla, and a Pukkasa.

56. A Brâhma*n*a who drinks (the spirituous liquor called) Surâ shall enter (the bodies) of small and large insects, of moths, of birds, feeding on ordure, and of destructive beasts.

57. A Brâhma*n*a who steals (the gold of a Brâhma*n*a shall pass) a thousand times (through the bodies) of spiders, snakes and lizards, of aquatic animals and of destructive Pi*s*â*k*as.

58. The violator of a Guru's bed (enters) a hundred times (the forms) of grasses, shrubs, and creepers, likewise of carnivorous (animals) and of (beasts) with fangs and of those doing cruel deeds.

---

52. Yâ*gñ*. III, 219. 'Fools,' i. e. 'those who do not perform penances' (Gov., Kull.).

55. Yâ*gñ*. III, 207. Nand. reads Pulkasa, Medh. and Gov. Pu*kh*kasa with a *G*ihvâmûlîya which looks like *sh*.

56. Yâ*gñ*. III, 207.

57. Yâ*gñ*. III, 208. 'Aquatic animals,' i. e. 'crocodiles and so forth' (Gov.). Gov. explains lûta, 'spider,' by 'scorpion.' K. omits this verse.

58. Yâ*gñ*. III, 208. The commentators explain 'carnivorous

59. Men who delight in doing hurt (become) carnivorous (animals); those who eat forbidden food, worms; thieves, creatures consuming their own kind; those who have intercourse with women of the lowest castes, Pretas.

60. He who has associated with outcasts, he who has approached the wives of other men, and he who has stolen the property of a Brâhma*n*a become Brahmarâkshasas.

61. A man who out of greed has stolen gems, pearls or coral, or any of the many other kinds of precious things, is born among the goldsmiths.

62. For stealing grain (a man) becomes a rat, for stealing yellow metal a Ha*m*sa, for stealing water a Plava, for stealing honey a stinging insect, for stealing milk a crow, for stealing condiments a dog, for stealing clarified butter an ichneumon;

63. For stealing meat a vulture, for stealing fat a cormorant, for stealing oil a winged animal (of the

---

(animals)' by 'vultures and the like,' '(beasts) with fangs' by 'lions or tigers and the like.' 'Those doing cruel deeds' are, according to Gov., 'men such as *S*abaras;' according to Kull., 'animals such as tigers.'

59. 'Creatures consuming their own kind,' i. e. 'fish and the like.' Nand. places verse 60 before verse 59.

60. Yâ*gñ*. III, 212. 'A Brahmarâkshasa,' lit. 'a Brâhma*n*ical Râkshasa,' is an evil spirit. K. omits this verse.

61. Yâ*gñ*. III, 213. According to another explanation, which Medh. considers the only admissible one, and which the other commentators mention as an alternative, hemakart*ri*, 'a goldsmith,' is the name of a bird.

62. Yâ*gñ*. III, 214, 215; Vi. XLIV, 15–20. Rasam, 'condiments,' i. e. the juice of sugar-cane, &c. (Kull.), means according to Nâr. 'quicksilver.'

63. Yâ*gñ*. III, 211, 215; Vi. XLIV, 21–25. I read with Medh., Gov., and Nand., vasâm, 'fat,' instead of vapâm (Kull., editions);

kind called) Tailapaka, for stealing salt a cricket, for stealing sour milk a bird (of the kind called) Balâkâ.

64. For stealing silk a partridge, for stealing linen a frog, for stealing cotton-cloth a crane, for stealing a cow an iguana, for stealing molasses a flying-fox;

65. For stealing fine perfumes a musk-rat, for stealing vegetables consisting of leaves a peacock, for stealing cooked food of various kinds a porcupine, for stealing uncooked food a hedgehog.

66. For stealing fire he becomes a heron, for stealing household-utensils a mason-wasp, for stealing dyed clothes a francolin-partridge;

67. For stealing a deer or an elephant a wolf, for stealing a horse a tiger, for stealing fruit and roots a monkey, for stealing a woman a bear, for stealing water a black-white cuckoo, for stealing vehicles a camel, for stealing cattle a he-goat.

68. That man who has forcibly taken away any kind of property belonging to another, or who has eaten sacrificial food (of) which (no portion) had been offered, inevitably becomes an animal.

---

which latter word Nâr. also gives, but explains by meda*h*. The Tailapaka is probably the cockroach. *K*îrîvâka, 'a cricket,' may also mean 'a cicada.' Nand. reads *K*akravâka, 'a Brâhma*n*î duck.'

64. Yâ*gñ*. III, 215; Vi. XLIV, 25–30. Regarding Vâgguda, 'the flying-fox,' see note on Gaut. XVII, 34. Râgh. confirms the explanation given there, as he says that it is a bird flying at night. Medh. and Nand. seem to have had a different reading at the end of the verse. The MSS. of the former have krau*ñk*o godhâ mâ*m*sâshu valguti*h* (?), and that of the latter godhâ gavya*m* dado sallam (?).

65. Yâ*gñ*. III, 213; Vi. XLIV, 31–34.

66. Yâ*gñ*. III, 214–215; Vi. XLIV, 35–37.

67. Yâ*gñ*. III, 214; Vi. XLIV, 38–43.

68. Yâ*gñ*. III, 217; Vi. XLIV, 44.

69. Women, also, who in like manner have committed a theft, shall incur guilt; they will become the females of those same creatures (which have been enumerated above).

70. But (men of the four) castes who have relinquished without the pressure of necessity their proper occupations, will become the servants of Dasyus, after migrating into despicable bodies.

71. A Brâhma*n*a who has fallen off from his duty (becomes) an Ulkâmukha Preta, who feeds on what has been vomited; and a Kshatriya, a Ka*t*apûtana (Preta), who eats impure substances and corpses.

72. A Vai*s*ya who has fallen off from his duty becomes a Maitrâksha*g*yotika Preta, who feeds on pus; and a *S*ûdra, a *K*ailâ*s*aka (Preta, who feeds on moths).

---

69. Vi. XLIV, 45. 'In like manner,' i. e. 'intentionally' (Gov., Kull.).

70. I follow Medh., Gov., Nâr., Nand., Râgh., and K., who read dasyushu instead of *s*atrushu, 'of their enemies' (editions). Gov. explains dasyushu by *s*atrushu, and the same explanation is given by Kull.; while according to Medh., 'thieves and robbers' are meant; and according to Nâr., 'forest-tribes, such as *S*abaras.' Nand. reads pretatâm (MS. prenatâm) for preshyatâm, and explains it by 'will become Pi*s*â*k*as among the Dasyus.' His reading looks like a correction made on account of the next verses.

71. Ulkâmukha, i. e. 'with flaming mouth' (Medh.). Medh. prefers Kû*t*apûtana, 'with a stinking nose,' to Ka*t*apûtana (Kull., Nâr., Râgh., Nand., K.). Gov. reads Ka*th*apûtana.

72. Maitrâksha*g*yotika is, according to Medh., Kull., and Râgh., to be explained as a kind of Preta who has a light in or sees with the anus. Medh. gives another explanation, according to which it simply means 'a Preta,' and adds that 'others' explain it by 'an owl.' *K*ailâ*s*aka, 'a (Preta) who feeds on moths' (Gov.), means according to Kull., 'who feeds on body-lice.' *K*elâ*s*aka is the reading of Gov., Nâr., and Nand.

73. In proportion as sensual men indulge in sensual pleasures, in that same proportion their taste for them grows.

74. By repeating their sinful acts those men of small understanding suffer pain here (below) in various births;

75. (The torture of) being tossed about in dreadful hells, Tâmisra and the rest, (that of) the Forest with sword-leaved trees and the like, and (that of) being bound and mangled;

76. And various torments, the (pain of) being devoured by ravens and owls, the heat of scorching sand, and the (torture of) being boiled in jars, which is hard to bear;

77. And births in the wombs (of) despicable (beings) which cause constant misery, and afflictions from cold and heat and terrors of various kinds,

78. The (pain of) repeatedly lying in various wombs and agonizing births, imprisonment in fetters hard to bear, and the misery of being enslaved by others,

79. And separations from their relatives and dear ones, and the (pain of) dwelling together with the wicked, (labour in) gaining wealth and its loss, (trouble in) making friends and (the appearance of) enemies,

80. Old age against which there is no remedy, the

---

73. I follow Medh. and Gov., who explain ku*s*alatâ, literally 'cleverness' (Kull., Râgh.), by ekarasibhâva*h*.

75–76. See above, IV, 88–89; Yâg*ñ*. III, 206, 221–225.

76. Medh. reads karambhavâlukâs taptâ*h*, and explains karambha*h* by karmada*h* (kardama*h*?), 'heated mud and sand (?)'. The translation follows Kull.'s and Râgh.'s notes. Medh., Gov., Râgh., Nand., and K. read sudu*h*sahân, 'very hard to bear,' which has been given above, instead of dâru*n*ân, 'terrible' (Kull., editions).

pangs of diseases, afflictions of many various kinds, and (finally) unconquerable death.

81. But with whatever disposition of mind (a man) performs any act, he reaps its result in a (future) body endowed with the same quality.

82. All the results, proceeding from actions, have been thus pointed out; learn (next) those acts which secure supreme bliss to a Brâhma*n*a.

83. Studying the Veda, (practising) austerities, (the acquisition of true) knowledge, the subjugation of the organs, abstention from doing injury, and serving the Guru are the best means for attaining supreme bliss.

84. (If you ask) whether among all these virtuous actions, (performed) here below, (there be) one which has been declared more efficacious (than the rest) for securing supreme happiness to man,

85. (The answer is that) the knowledge of the Soul is stated to be the most excellent among all of them; for that is the first of all sciences, because immortality is gained through that.

86. Among those six (kinds of) actions (enumer-

---

81. E.g. if while a man performs an act his disposition is sâttvika, or 'chiefly penetrated by the quality of Goodness,' he will reap its reward in a body produced chiefly by that quality, e.g. that of a god.

83. Yâ*gñ*. III, 190.

84. Medh. omits this verse.

85. Yâ*gñ*. I, 199. 'The knowledge of the Soul,' i.e. not that of the Kshetra*gñ*a, but that of the Supreme Soul, which is taught in the Upanishads (Medh., Gov., Kull., Nand.), means according to Nâr., 'meditation' (dhyânam). Nand. asserts that the genitive sarveshâm, 'among all,' stands in the sense of the ablative. According to him the translation should be, 'is more excellent than all those.'

86. Medh. takes the genitive sha*nn*âm, 'among those six,' in the

ated above, the performance of) the acts taught in the Veda must ever be held to be most efficacious for ensuring happiness in this world and the next.

87. For in the performance of the acts prescribed by the Veda all those (others) are fully comprised, (each) in its turn in the several rules for the rites.

88. The acts prescribed by the Veda are of two kinds, such as procure an increase of happiness and

---

sense of an ablative, and according to him the translation would be, 'The acts taught in the Veda must ever be held to be more efficacious for ensuring happiness in this world and in the next than all those six (kinds of) actions (enumerated above).' He proposes two explanations for karma vaidikam. 'The acts taught in the Veda' may either be 'the *S*rauta rites, such as the *G*yotish*t*oma,' or 'those called further on, in verses 88–89, nivr*i*tta,' i. e. 'rites performed as a matter of duty, without a desire for rewards.' Nand. accepts the first explanation, and so does Gov., who, however, takes the genitive in its usual sense, 'among those six.' Nâr. adopts Medh.'s second explanation, and says, 'acts, taught in the Veda,' i. e. 'sacrifices and so forth, performed without the intention of (gaining) rewards,' and construes the genitives like Gov. The same construction is adopted by Kull., who explains karma vaidikam by 'the knowledge of the Supreme Soul.' Medh.'s second explanation seems to be the best, on account of verses 89 and 90, where 'knowledge,' i. e. 'the knowledge of the Supreme Soul' (see verse 85) and the performance of the nivr*i*ttam karma are said to effect final liberation. The explanation of the genitives sha*nn*âm eteshâm by 'among those six' may perhaps be defended, if vaidika*m* karma is taken to correspond to vedâbhyâsa*h*, 'studying the Veda (and obeying its rules),' in verse 83. But Medh.'s explanation of the construction is quite possible.

87. Kull. alters his explanation of vaidika*m* karma slightly, and interprets it by 'the worship of the Supreme Soul' (paramâtmopâsanâ), and quotes B*ri*hadâra*n*yaka-upanishad IV, 4, 22 in support of his view. The other commentators find no difficulty in showing that both 'the *S*rauta sacrifices' and 'the nivr*i*ttâkhya*m* karma' include all the six points mentioned above, verse 83. I read in the first line with K. hi instead of tu (Medh., Gov., Kull., Nand.).

88. Kull. again changes his explanation of the expression 'acts

cause a continuation (of mundane existence, pravritta), and such as ensure supreme bliss and cause a cessation (of mundane existence, nivritta).

89. Acts which secure (the fulfilment of) wishes in this world or in the next are called pravritta (such as cause a continuation of mundane existence); but acts performed without any desire (for a reward), preceded by (the acquisition) of (true) knowledge, are declared to be nivritta (such as cause the cessation of mundane existence).

90. He who sedulously performs acts leading to future births (pravritta) becomes equal to the gods; but he who is intent on the performance of those causing the cessation (of existence, nivritta) indeed, passes beyond (the reach of) the five elements.

91. He who sacrifices to the Self (alone), equally recognising the Self in all created beings and all created beings in the Self, becomes (independent like) an autocrat and self-luminous.

---

taught in the Veda,' and takes it to mean 'sacrifices like the *G*yotish*t*oma and the worship of images.'

89. Medh. explains *g*ñânapûrvam, 'preceded by (the acquisition of true) knowledge,' to mean 'whereof knowledge is the chief (part,' *g*ñânam âdya*m* mukhya*m* yasya).

90. Kull. remarks that the expression 'becomes equal to the gods' gives only an instance of the rewards attainable by kâmyâni karmâ*n*i. 'Passes beyond (the reach of) the five elements,' i. e. 'casts off the subtile body' (Nâr.), or 'obtains final liberation' (Medh., Gov., Kull.).

91. Îsa-upanishad, 6. 'He who sacrifices to the Self (alone),' i. e. 'who connects himself with the nature of one who consists of all deities, i. e. thinks, "Not Agni, nor Âditya is the deity, I am here the deity"' (âtmânam eva sarvadevatâmayatvena yogayate । manyate nâstir [nâgnir] âdityo vâ devatâ । aham iha *k*a devatâ mati [ihaiva devatâ iti?], Medh., similarly Gov. and Nâr.), means according to Kull., Râgh., and Nand., 'he who performs the *G*yotish*t*oma and the like (sacrifices) in the manner of the Brahmârpa*n*a,' i. e. in such

92. After giving up even the above-mentioned sacrificial rites, a Brâhmana should exert himself in (acquiring) the knowledge of the Soul, in extinguishing his passions, and in studying the Veda.

93. For that secures the attainment of the object of existence, especially in the case of a Brâhmana, because by attaining that, not otherwise, a twice-born man has gained all his ends.

94. The Veda is the eternal eye of the manes, gods, and men; the Veda-ordinance (is) both beyond the sphere of (human) power, and beyond the sphere of (human) comprehension; that is a certain fact.

---

a manner that he understands Brahman to be the object of the worship, and makes over the merit to Brahman. The participial clause means, according to Medh. and Gov., thinking 'I am contained in the whole creation, both the movable and the immovable' (vyavasthitah, Gov.), or 'I am, as it were, the whole world' (aham ivaitaggagat, Medh.) and 'all created beings are contained in me' (mayy avasthitâni, Gov., mayi sthitâni, Medh.). Kull., Râgh., and Nand. (who reads sampasyan) explain it on pure Vedânta principles. The sacrificer is to recognise his identity with the Supreme Soul, and that through this identity he is one with all created beings, and that all created beings are one with him. The double rendering of the term svârâgyam is based on the double meaning of the verb râg, 'to rule' and 'to shine.' Medh. alone points it out. Kull. gives the second meaning alone, and takes the phrase a little differently: 'attains the state of the self-luminous (Brahman).' Gov., Nâr., and Nand. give Medh.'s first meaning only.

92. 'Above-mentioned,' i.e. 'as securing supreme bliss' (Nand.), or 'the Agnihotra and the rest' (Medh., Gov., Kull.). The last three commentators point out that this verse is not intended to authorise an irregular discontinuance of the daily rites.

93. Nand. omits this verse. Kritakrityah, 'has gained all his ends' (Medh.), is taken by Gov. in its other sense, 'has done all he ought to do' (kritakaranîyah).

94. Instead of asakyam, 'beyond (the sphere of human) power,' i.e. 'which cannot have been produced by men' (Gov., Kull.), Nâr. and Nand. read atarkyam, 'beyond (the sphere of human) reasoning' (tarkenânyathâsambhavam, Nâr.; îdrisam ity adhyavasâtum

95. All those traditions (sm*ri*ti) and all those despicable systems of philosophy, which are not based on the Veda, produce no reward after death; for they are declared to be founded on Darkness.

96. All those (doctrines), differing from the (Veda), which spring up and (soon) perish, are worthless and false, because they are of modern date.

97. The four castes, the three worlds, the four orders, the past, the present, and the future are all severally known by means of the Veda.

98. Sound, touch, colour, taste, and fifthly smell are known through the Veda alone, (their) production (is) through the (Vedic rites, which in this respect are) secondary acts.

---

a*s*akyam apaurusheyatvât, Nand.). Aprameyam, 'beyond (the sphere of human) comprehension,' may, according to the commentators, mean either that the Veda can never be fully known, on account of the number of its branches and of the depth of its meaning, or that it cannot be understood by human reasoning alone, but requires the help of grammar of the Mîmâ*m*sâ and so forth.

95. As an example of false traditions Medh. names 'rules such as "Heavenly bliss is attained by worshipping *K*aityas," which occur in the *S*obha and other Siddhântas of the Nirgranthas (Digambara *G*ainas).' 'Despicable systems of philosophy,' e.g. 'that of the *K*ârvâkas' (Kull.). Pretya, 'after death' (paraloke, Gov., Kull.), means according to Medh. prakarsham prâpya, 'after attaining eminence.' Medh. mentions the explanation adopted above as that of 'others,' and adds that it requires the reading prete.

97. Nâr. and Râgh. explain prasidhyati, 'are made known,' by *g*âyate, 'are produced.' Gov. and Kull. point to III, 76.

98. I read with all the commentators prasidhyanti instead of prasûyante (Indian editions). The last words of the verse are extremely doubtful. Medh. reads prasûtir gu*n*akarmata*h*, and Gov. seems to have adopted the same version, though the text of the Pu*n*a MS. has prabhûtagu*n*akarmata*h*. Kull. and Râgh. give prasûtigu*n*akarmata*h*; Nand. prasûtigu*n*akarmabhi*h*, and Nâr. prasûtigu*n*adharmata*h*, with which reading a var. lect., mentioned by Medh., prasûtegu*n*adharmata*h* may have originally agreed. In concluding his note on the

99. The eternal lore of the Veda upholds all created beings; hence I hold that to be supreme,

verse Medh. remarks that many other varr. lectt. exist which he omits, because they are useless (vai*k*itryapâ*th*ântarâ*n*i nishprayoganatvân na likhyante). The explanations differ still more than the readings. The translation follows Medh.'s interpretation. According to him the verse means that 'sound and the rest are known to be enjoyable and means of obtaining pleasure through the Veda, as they are perceived in the form of melodies and so forth at the performance of Vedic rites,' but that 'the Veda is not their material cause, the Vedic rites being secondary actions only with respect to their production' (*s*abdâdînâm bhogyatvena sukhasâdhanânâ*m* vedâd eva prasiddhi*h* । vaidikakarmânush*th*ânâd gîtâdi*s*abdopapatti*h* . . . . na punar veda upâdânakâra*n*am . . . . etad âha prasûtir gu*n*akarmata*h* । prasûti*h* *s*abdâdînâm utpatti*h* । tadartha*m* gu*n*akarma phalârthatvât pradhânakarme [ma] *k*a *k*itrâdishu gu*n*adharma [karme] ty uktam). Gov.'s short note in substance agrees with this view (ye svargâdivipratâ [shayâ] upabhogyatvenâbhimatâ*h* *s*abdâdayo vishayâs te 'bhimatavishayopabhogotpattyartha*m* yad upakâraka*m* karmâgnihotrâdika*m* tadanush*th*ânadvâre*n*a vedâd eva prasidhyanti). According to Kull. the meaning of the compound is, 'through the Vedic rites, (originating from) the (three) qualities (Goodness and so forth, which are) the sources (of sound and so forth).' Râgh. gives two explanations: '(The elements which are the substrata of) sound, touch, colour, taste, and fifthly (of) smell, are known through the Veda according to their origin, their qualities, and their actions.' Afterwards he gives for the last word an alternative version which closely agrees with Kull.'s view. Nand. says, 'Sound and so forth, together with their sources, i. e. ether and so forth, with their qualities, i. e. their manifold subdivisions, e. g. the sha*d*ga (note), and so forth, and with their actions, i. e. attracting the organs of sensation and so forth, are known from the Veda alone.' Nâr. finally interprets his reading as follows: '(Sound and so forth) are produced from the Veda alone, which is characterised—the affix tasi has the meaning of the third and other cases—by the following, (viz.) the origin, i. e. the cause of production, quality, i. e. excessiveness and so forth, property, i. e. fragrance and so forth' (prasûti*h* *g*anmahetu*h* । gu*n*a utka*t*atvâdi । dharma*h* surabhitvâdi*h* । t*ri*tîyâdi tasi*h* । etair upalakshitâd vedât prasidhyanti *g*âyante).

99. In explanation of the first line the commentators point to

which is the means of (securing happiness to) these creatures.

100. Command of armies, royal authority, the office of a judge, and sovereignty over the whole world he (only) deserves who knows the Veda-science.

101. As a fire that has gained strength consumes even trees full of sap, even so he who knows the Veda burns out the taint of his soul which arises from (evil) acts.

102. In whatever order (a man) who knows the true meaning of the Veda-science may dwell, he becomes even while abiding in this world, fit for the union with Brahman.

103. (Even forgetful) students of the (sacred) books are more distinguished than the ignorant, those who remember them surpass the (forgetful) students, those who possess a knowledge (of the meaning) are more distinguished than those who

---

III, 76, and the corresponding Vedic passages. Gov. and Kull. explain asya *g*anto*h*, 'of these creatures,' by 'of men entitled to perform Vedic rites.' Nâr. takes the second line differently: 'Through that, i. e. the Veda alone, I know that highest, i. e. meditation, which is the means, i. e. the means of securing final liberation to these creatures' (yad asya *g*anto*h* sâdhanam apavarga-sâdhanam | para*m* dhyâna*m* dhyeyâdi | tad etasmâd vedâd eva manye *g*âne).

100. Medh. places this verse later. The order in which the remaining verses of the Sa*m*hitâ are read in the MSS. differs very much from that adopted by the other commentators. They stand as follows: 106, 107, 108, 100, 101, 102, 103, 104, 105, 109, 110, 111, 112, 113, 114, 115, 116, 117, 118, 119, 120, 121, 122; next both the text and the commentary of 91, 92, 93 are repeated, and then comes the last verse, 126.

101. Vas. XXVII, 2.

103. Ag*ñ*ebhya*h*, 'than the ignorant,' i. e. 'entirely ignorant'

(only) remember (the words), men who follow (the teaching of the texts) surpass those who (merely) know (their meaning).

104. Austerity and sacred learning are the best means by which a Brâhma*n*a secures supreme bliss; by austerities he destroys guilt, by sacred learning he obtains the cessation of (births and) deaths.

105. The three (kinds of evidence), perception, inference, and the (sacred) Institutes which comprise the tradition (of) many (schools), must be fully understood by him who desires perfect correctness with respect to the sacred law.

106. He alone, and no other man, knows the sacred law, who explores the (utterances) of the sages and the body of the laws, by (modes of) reasoning, not repugnant to the Veda-lore.

(Medh., Nâr.), 'who have not studied the Veda' (Nand.), means according to Gov. and Kull., 'those who have learned a little.' Granthina*h*, '(forgetful) students' (Kull., Nand.), means according to Medh. and Gov., 'students who learn the texts alone, but do not take very great trouble with them;' according to Nâr., 'men who know the text only.' Dhâri*n*a*h*, 'those who remember (the texts)' (Kull., Nand.), are according to Medh. and Gov., 'men who are very persevering in studying;' according to Nâr., 'those who know the meaning of the texts.' Nâr. takes *gñ*ânin, 'he who knows (the meaning of the texts),' in the sense of 'he who knows the Soul or Self.'

104. Yâ*gñ*. I, 200.

105. *S*âstram, 'the (sacred) Institutes,' i. e. 'the Veda, which has many *S*âkhâs' (Gov., Nâr.), or 'the Veda and the Sm*ri*ti' (Medh.), or 'the Sm*ri*ti' (Kull.). Nand. reads siddhim, 'a complete knowledge or accurate performance,' instead of *s*uddhim. The Pu*n*a copy of Nâr. stops with this verse, the remaining leaves being lost.

106. 'The utterances of the sages,' i. e. 'the Veda.' 'The body of the laws,' i. e. 'the Sm*ri*ti.' 'The modes of reasoning' are, according to Medh. and Kull., the Mîmâ*m*sâ of *G*aimini; according to 'others' quoted by Medh., all the philosophical schools, excepting

107. Thus the acts which secure supreme bliss have been exactly and fully described; (now) the secret portion of these Institutes, proclaimed by Manu, will be taught.

108. If it be asked how it should be with respect to (points of) the law which have not been (specially) mentioned, (the answer is), 'that which Brâhma*n*as (who are) *S*ish*t*as propound, shall doubtlessly have legal (force).'

109. Those Brâhma*n*as must be considered as *S*ish*t*as who, in accordance with the sacred law, have studied the Veda together with its appendages, and are able to adduce proofs perceptible by the senses from the revealed texts.

---

those which, like the Bauddhas, Nirgranthas, and Lokâyatikas, deny the authority of the Vedas.

108-115. Âp. II, 29, 13-14; Gaut. XXVIII, 48-51; Vas. III, 20; Baudh. I, 1, 5-13, 16; Yâg*ñ*. I, 9-10.

109. 'In accordance with the sacred law,' i. e. 'while observing the rules prescribed for a student.' The expression *s*rutipratyakshahetava*h*, 'who are able to adduce proofs perceptible by the senses from the revealed texts,' is variously interpreted. According to Medh. it means either 'those who possess the revealed texts, (proof through) perception and argument' (*s*rutipratyakshe hetu*s* *k*a *s*rutipratyakshahetava*h*), or 'those for whom the revealed texts which are perceptible by the senses, are the reason for distinguishing between virtue and sin' (athavâ *s*rute*h* pratyaksha*s*rute*h* ı pratyaksha*s*abda*h* *s*raute pratyaye pratyakshatulyatvât prayukta*h* ı sa *k*a hetur dharmâdharmaparig*ñ*âne kâra*n*a*m* yeshâ*m* ta evam u*k*yante); according to Gov., 'who are the cause of the teaching of the subjects perceptible in the Veda' (vedago*k*arapadârthopade*s*akâra*n*abhûtâ*h*); according to Kull., 'who are the causes of making the revealed texts perceptible, by reciting the revealed texts;' and according to Nand., 'those for whose knowledge and exposition of the law hearing and perception by means of the senses are the causes' (yeshâ*m* *s*rava*n*am pratyaksha*m* *k*a dharmag*ñ*ânava*k*anayor hetus te). 'The appendages,' i. e. 'the Itihâsas and Purâ*n*as' (Medh. according to the Mahâbhârata,

110. Whatever an assembly, consisting either of at least ten, or of at least three persons who follow their prescribed occupations, declares to be law, the legal (force of) that one must not dispute.

111. Three persons who each know one of the three principal Vedas, a logician, a Mîmâmsaka, one who knows the Nirukta, one who recites (the Institutes of) the sacred law, and three men belonging to the first three orders shall constitute a (legal) assembly, consisting of at least ten members.

112. One who knows the *Rig*-veda, one who knows the Yagur-veda, and one who knows the Sâma-veda, shall be known (to form) an assembly consisting of at least three members (and competent) to decide doubtful points of law.

113. Even that which one Brâhmana versed in the Veda declares to be law, must be considered (to have) supreme legal (force, but) not that which is proclaimed by myriads of ignorant men.

114. Even if thousands of Brâhmanas, who have

Nand.), or 'the Aṅgas, Mîmâmsâ, the law-books, the Purânas, and so forth' (Gov., Kull.).

110. Medh. and Gov. read vikârayet instead of vikâlayet (Kull., Nand.).

111. 'Three men belonging to the first three orders,' i. e. 'a student, a householder, and a hermit' (Gov., Kull., Nand.). Medh. says that some think 'a student, a householder, and an ascetic' to be meant, because the hermit must not enter a village, and because Gautama, in the enumeration of the castes, places the ascetic before the hermit, while others refer the words to Manu's first three orders. The reading traividyo, which all the commentaries give, is probably incorrect. It ought to be traividyam, tisrinâm vidyânâm samâhârah; see Yâgñ. I, 9, and compare kâturvidyam, kâturvaidyam, Baudh. I, 1, 1, 8, and Vas. III, 20.

114. Avratânâm, 'who have not fulfilled their sacred duties,' i. e. 'who have not fulfilled the vows incumbent on a student' (Gov., Kull.).

not fulfilled their sacred duties, are unacquainted with the Veda, and subsist only by the name of their caste, meet, they cannot (form) an assembly (for settling the sacred law).

115. The sin of him whom dunces, incarnations of Darkness, and unacquainted with the law, instruct (in his duty), falls, increased a hundredfold, on those who propound it.

116. All that which is most efficacious for securing supreme bliss has been thus declared to you; a Brâhma*n*a who does not fall off from that obtains the most excellent state.

117. Thus did that worshipful deity disclose to me, through a desire of benefiting mankind, this whole most excellent secret of the sacred law.

118. Let (every Brâhma*n*a), concentrating his mind, fully recognise in the Self all things, both the real and the unreal, for he who recognises the universe in the Self, does not give his heart to unrighteousness.

---

115. Nand. gives yad for yam, instead of tamobhûtâ*h*, 'incarnations of Darkness,' the reading of the Dharma-sûtras, tamomû*dh*â*h*, 'perplexed by Darkness or ignorance.'

118. Sampa*s*yet, 'let (every Brâhma*n*a) fully recognise,' i. e. 'let him clearly realise in his mind' (sâkshâtkuryât, Medh., Kull.), through devotional exercises (upâsanâ, Medh.), or through deep meditation (Kull.), or 'let him vow to be solely intent on that one object of knowledge, to the exclusion of the knowledge of all other knowable objects' (*gñ*eyântaravishayanirâkara*n*ena tadeka*gñ*eyanish*th*âm anubrûyât, Medh.). Âtmani, 'in the Self,' i. e. 'in the Supreme Self' (Kull., Nand.), or 'in his own individual Self' (Gov.). Medh. remarks that 'the learned dispute regarding the meaning of the term âtman, and that besides the two explanations already given a third was proposed by some, according to which it meant 'the corporeal Self.' Medh. himself considers the first explanation to be the correct one. Sadasat, 'the real and the unreal,' i. e. either 'the

119. The Self alone is the multitude of the gods, the universe rests on the Self; for the Self produces the connexion of these embodied (spirits) with actions.

120. Let him meditate on the ether as identical with the cavities (of the body), on the wind as identical with the organs of motions and of touch, on the most excellent light as the same with his digestive organs and his sight, on water as the same with the (corporeal) fluids, on the earth as the same with the solid parts (of his body);

121. On the moon as one with the internal organ, on the quarters of the horizon as one with his sense of hearing, on Vish*n*u as one with his (power of) motion, on Hara as the same with his strength, on Agni (Fire) as identical with his speech, on Mitra as identical with his excretions, and on Pra*g*âpati as one with his organ of generation.

122. Let him know the supreme Male (Purusha, to be) the sovereign ruler of them all, smaller even than small, bright like gold, and perceptible by the intellect (only when) in (a state of) sleep(-like abstraction).

123. Some call him Agni (Fire), others Manu, the

---

products and the causes,' or 'the intelligent and the non-intelligent' (Nand.), means according to Gov., 'that which possesses a shape of certain proportions and its opposite' (mûrtam p*ri*thivyâdi ya*kk*âmûrtam âkâ*s*âdi). Medh. proposes two other explanations, 1. 'that which is both existent and non-existent, i.e. comes into existence and perishes;' 2. 'that which like the hare's horn is non-existent, and that which like ether is eternal.' The word samâhita*h*, 'concentrating himself,' may have, as Medh. thinks, a technical meaning, and refer to the Samâdhi, mentioned in the Yoga and Vedânta systems.

119. In this verse Gov., too, explains âtmâ by paramâtmâ.

120. Medh. explains snehe, 'on the (corporeal) fluids,' by 'on the viscous substances,' e.g. 'the brain and so forth.'

Lord of creatures, others Indra, others the vital air, and again others eternal Brahman.

124. He pervades all created beings in the five forms, and constantly makes them, by means of birth, growth and decay, revolve like the wheels (of a chariot).

125. He who thus recognises the Self through the Self in all created beings, becomes equal(-minded) towards all, and enters the highest state, Brahman.

126. A twice-born man who recites these Institutes, revealed by Manu, will be always virtuous in conduct, and will reach whatever condition he desires.

124. The five forms are the five great elements, which produce all bodies (Gov., Kull., Nand.).

125. Instead of param padam, 'the highest state,' Nand. reads sanâtanam, 'the eternal (Brahman).'

APPENDIX.

Quotations from the Institutes of Manu, in the translated Hindu Law-books[1].

I, 101. Col. Dig. II, 4, 42.

II, 96. Mit. II, 1, 22.

140. Sar. Vi. 421, 426, 436–7.

145. Col. Dig. V, 424; Vîram. III, 4, 7.

146. Dây. XI, 4, 3.

172. Col. Dig. V, 123.

III, 4–11. Col. Dig. IV, 185.

5. Datt. Mî. VI, 27.

12. Col. Dig. V, 144; Dây. IX, 2; Mit. I, 8, 7.

14. Col. Dig. V, 147.

15–7. Col. Dig. V, 145; Dây. IX, 9; Vîram. II, 1, 25.

18. Col. Dig. IV, 52.

20–1. Dây. IV, 3, 4.

42. Vîram. III, 1, 2.

49. Sm*ri*. *K*. XI, 2, 4; Sar. Vi. 138, 332, 336, Varad. p. 41.

51. Dây. IV, 3, 24.

55. Col. Dig. IV, 42.

56–9. Col. Dig. IV, 39.

60. Col. Dig. IV, 40, 189, 1; May. IV, 8, 21.

61–2. Col. Dig. IV, 189, 2–3.

81. Dây. XI, 6, 17.

---

[1] Colebrooke's Digest (Col. Dig.); Vyavahâramayûkha, by Borradaile (Vyav.); Dâyabhâga and Mitâksharâ on Inheritance, by Colebrooke (Dây.; Mit.); Mitâksharâ on Vyavahâra, by Macnaghten (M. Mit.); Dâyakramasa*m*graha, by Wynch (Dâyakr.); Dattakamîmâ*m*sâ and Dattaka*k*andrikâ, by Sutherland (Datt. Mî.; Datt. *K*and.); Vivâda*k*intâma*n*i, by Prosonno Koomar Tagore (Viv. *K*int.); Vîramitrodaya on Inheritance, by Golâpchand Sarkâr (Vîram.); Sm*ri*ti*k*andrikâ, by T. Kristnaswamy Iyer (Sm*ri*. *K*.); Sarasvatîvilâsa, by Foulkes (Sar. Vi.); Vyavahâramâdhava and Varadarâ*g*îya on Inheritance, by Burnell (Mâdh.; Varad.).

IV, 162. M. Mit. II, 8, 21.
V, 60. Dây. XI, 1, 42; XI, 6, 17; Datt. Mî. VI, 27.
127. Col. Dig. V, 321.
147–9. Col. Dig. IV, 86.
150. Col. Dig. IV, 89.
153–6. Col. Dig. IV, 103.
157. Col. Dig. IV, 139; Mit. I, 10, 9; Vîram. II, 2, 4; Sar. Vi. 345.
158. Col. Dig. IV, 139; Mit. I, 10, 9; Vîram. II, 2, 4.
159. Col. Dig. IV, 140; Mit. I, 10, 9; Vîram. II, 2, 4.
160. Col. Dig. IV, 141; Mit. I, 10, 9; Datt. Mî. I, 29; Vîram. II, 2, 4.
161. Col. Dig. IV, 142; Mit. I, 10, 9; Vîram. II, 2, 4; Sar. Vi. 345.
162. Col. Dig. IV, 143.
163. Col. Dig. IV, 161.
165. Col. Dig. IV, 105.
VII, 14–28. Viv. *K*int. pp. 320–2.
82. Col. Dig. V, 163; Dây. IX, 20.
85. Col. Dig. II, 4, 63.
127–40. Col. Dig. II, 2, 14, 1–13.
VIII, 1–2. May. I, 1, 5.
4. Col. Dig. II, 1, 2; May. I, 1, 3; Viv. *K*int. p. 4.
5–7. Col. Dig. II, 1, 2; May. I, 1, 3; M. Mit. I, 2, 5.
11. M. Mit. I, 1, 12.
13. M. Mit. I, 1, 15; VI, 1, 59.
27. Col. Dig. V, 449; Viv. *K*int. p. 300.
28. Col. Dig. V, 480, 1.
29. Col. Dig. V, 480, 2; May. IV, 10, 10; Sm*ri*. *K*. IX, 2, 27.
30. Col. Dig. II, 2, 60, 1; May. VII, 8; M. Mit. V, 4.
31–2. Col. Dig. II, 2, 60, 2–3.
33. May. VII, 8; M. Mit. V, 5.
34. Viv. *K*int. p. 180.

(VIII), 35. May. VII, 10; M. Mit. V, 11.
37–8. M. Mit. V, 9.
40. May. VII, 11; M. Mit. V, 12.
43. M. Mit. I, 2, 7.
45. Col. Dig. II, 4, 68.
46. Col. Dig. I, 50, 233.
47. Col. Dig. I, 233.
48. Col Dig. I, 234; Viv. *K*int. p. 43.
49. Col. Dig. I, 235; Viv. *K*int. p. 43.
50. Col. Dig. I, 254.
51. Col. Dig. I, 264.
59. Col. Dig. I, 265; Viv. *K*int. p. 47.
68. M. Mit. VI, 1, 6.
70. May. II, 3, 8.
74. M. Mit. VI, 1, 1.
79–80. May. II, 3, 14.
87. May. II, 3, 4.
102. May. II, 3, 17; M. Mit. VI, 1, 22.
107. M. Mit. VI, 1, 29.
108. May. II, 3, 20; M. Mit. VI, 1, 45.
113. May. II, 3, 17; II, 3; M. Mit. VI, 1, 23; VIII, 20, 1.
115. M. Mit. VIII, 10, 2.
117. M. Mit. VI, 1, 31.
120. M. Mit. VI, 1, 49; Viv. *K*int. p. 221.
121. M. Mit. VI, 1, 49; Viv. *K*int. p. 222.
122. Viv. *K*int. p. 221.
123. M. Mit. III, 4, 9; Viv. *K*int. p. 222.
124–5. M. Mit. III, 4, 4.
128. M. Mit. I, 1, 6.
129. M. Mit. III, 4, 3.
132–4. Col. Dig. III, 1, 77, 1–3.
138. Viv. *K*int. p. 222.
139. Col. Dig. I, 273; Viv. *K*int. pp. 48, 221.
140. Col. Dig. I, 23, 29, 1.
141. Col. Dig. I, 29, 2; Viv. *K*int. p. 7.
143. Col. Dig. I, 91, 117; II, 2, 7; Viv. *K*int. pp. 21, 25.
144. Col. Dig. I, 87; May. V, 2, 3.

(VIII), 146. May. II, 2, 7.
147. M. Mit. III, 2, 6.
150. Col. Dig. I, 78.
151. Col. Dig. I, 43, 61; May. V, 1, 7; Viv. *K*int. p. 17.
152. Col. Dig. I, 42.
153. Col. Dig. I, 41.
154. Col. Dig. I, 48, 257, 1.
155. Col. Dig. I, 257, 2.
156. Col. Dig. I, 258.
157. Col. Dig. I, 33; Viv. *K*int. p. 19.
159-60. Col. Dig. I, 151, 1-2.
161. Col. Dig. I, 154.
162. Col. Dig. I, 155.
163. Col. Dig. II, 2, 11; II, 4, 57.
165. May. IX, 10; Vîram. V, 1, 2.
166. Col. Dig. I, 186.
167. Col. Dig. I, 190; Dâyakr. XII, 1, 1; Viv. *K*int. p. 39.
168. Col. Dig. II, 2, 10.
177. Col. Dig I, 245; May. V, 4, 6.
179. Col. Dig. II, 1, 13; Viv. *K*int. p. 49.
180. Col. Dig. II, 1, 16.
181-4. Col. Dig. II, 1, 47, 1-4.
185. Col. Dig. II, 1, 20.
186. Col. Dig. II, 1, 21; Viv. *K*int. p. 51.
187. Col. Dig. II, 1, 46.
188. Col. Dig. II, 1, 49.
189. Col. Dig. II, 1, 26; Viv. *K*int. p. 51.
191. Col. Dig. II, 1, 37; May. VI, 2.
192. Col. Dig. II, 1, 38; May. VI, 5; Viv. *K*int. p. 54.
193. Col. Dig. II, 1, 39; Viv. *K*int. p. 53.
194. Col. Dig. II, 1, 48.
195. Col. Dig. II, 1, 17.
196. Col. Dig. II, 1, 50.
197. Col. Dig. II, 2, 5; Viv. *K*int. p. 56.
198. Col. Dig. II, 2, 40; Viv. *K*int. pp. 56, 222.
199. Col. Dig. II, 2, 27.

(VIII), 201. Col. Dig. II, 2, 36.
202. Col. Dig. II, 2, 50; May. VII, 5; Viv. *K*int. p. 58.
203. Col. Dig. II, 2, 61; Viv. *K*int. p. 119.
206. Col. Dig. II, 3, 32; Viv. *K*int. p. 65.
207. Col. Dig. II, 3, 33.
208. Col. Dig. II, 3, 35, 1.
209. Col. Dig. II, 3, 35, 2; Viv. *K*int. p. 67.
210. Col. Dig. II, 3, 35, 3; Viv. *K*int. p. 66.
212. Col. Dig. II, 4, 48, 1; Viv. *K*int. pp. 84, 223.
213. Col. Dig. II, 4, 48, 2.
215. Col. Dig. III, 1, 76; May. XI, 4; Viv. *K*int. p. 98.
216. Col. Dig. III, 1, 81; May. XI, 4; Viv. *K*int. p. 99.
217. Col. Dig. III, 1, 78; May. XI, 4; Viv. *K*int. p. 99.
218. Col. Dig. III, 2, 1.
219–20. Col. Dig. III, 2, 15; Viv. *K*int. p. 110.
222. Col. Dig. III, 3, 7; 23, 1; Viv. *K*int. p. 113.
223. Col. Dig. III, 3, 23, 2; Viv. *K*int. p. 113.
224–7. Col. Dig. IV, 166–9.
228. Col. Dig. III, 3, 24; Viv. *K*int. p. 113.
229. Col. Dig. III, 4, 1.
230. Col. Dig. III, 4, 9; Viv. *K*int. p. 105.
231. Col. Dig. III, 4, 2; Viv. *K*int. p. 105.
232. Col. Dig. III, 4, 12; Viv. *K*int. p. 106.
233. Col. Dig. III, 4, 7; Viv. *K*int. p. 106.
234. Col. Dig. III, 4, 18.
235–6. Col. Dig. III, 4, 16.
237. Col. Dig. III, 4, 19; May. XV, 3; Viv. *K*int. p. 132.
238. Col. Dig. III, 4, 25; Viv. *K*int. p. 132.
239. Col. Dig. III, 4, 32.
240. Col. Dig. III, 4, 29; May. XVII, 9.
241. Col. Dig. III, 4, 36; Viv. *K*int. p. 133.
242. Col. Dig. III, 4, 54; Viv. *K*int. p. 136.
244. Col. Dig. III, 4, 59.
245–52. Viv. *K*int. p. 120.

(VIII), 253. Viv. *K*int. p. 121.
257. May. XV, 4.
259–61. Viv. *K*int. p. 121.
262. Viv. *K*int. p. 124.
264. May. XV, 11 ; Viv. *K*int. p. 126.
267. May. XVI, 1, 3 ; Viv. *K*int. p. 140.
268. Viv. *K*int. p. 140.
273. Viv. *K*int. p. 142.
275. May. XVI, 1, 4.
276–7. Viv. *K*int. p. 141.
279. May. XVI, 2, 4 ; Viv. *K*int. p. 150.
280–1. May. XVI, 2, 4 ; Viv. *K*int. pp. 146, 150.
281–2. Viv. *K*int. pp. 146, 150.
283. Viv. *K*int. pp. 147, 150.
284. Viv. *K*int. p. 148.
285. May. XVI, 2, 8 ; Viv. *K*int. p. 155.
286. Viv. *K*int. p. 149.
288–9. Viv. *K*int. p. 183.
296–8. May. XXII (CCXLII).
299. Col. Dig. III, 1, 11, 1 ; Viv. *K*int. p. 151.
300. Col. Dig. III, 1, 11, 2 ; M. Mit. IV, 1, 9 ; Viv. *K*int. p. 151.
302. Col. Dig. II, 1, 59 ; Viv. *K*int. p. 157.
303. Viv. *K*int. p. 157.
304. Col. Dig. II, 2, 19 ; Viv. *K*int. p. 322.
305–6. Viv. *K*int. p. 322.
308. Col. Dig. II, 3, 58.
319. Viv. *K*int. p. 173.
320. May. XVII, 8.
321. May. XVII, 8 ; Viv. *K*int. p. 170.
322. May. XVII, 8 ; Viv. *K*int. p. 171.
323. May. XVII, 8 ; Viv. *K*int. p. 166.
324–5. Viv. *K*int. p. 167.
326–30. Viv. *K*int. p. 172.
331. Viv. *K*int. p. 171.
333. Viv. *K*int. p. 172.
335–6. Viv. *K*int. p. 221.
337–8. Viv. *K*int. p. 176.
339. Viv. *K*int. p. 179.

(VIII), 340. Mit. I, 1, 8; Vîram. I, 14; Viv. *K*int. p. 177; Mâdh. p. 4.
341. Viv. *K*int. p. 179.
342. Viv. *K*int. p. 168.
348–9. M. Mit. II, 8, 20.
350. May. XVIII, 8; M. Mit. II, 8, 19, 20.
352. Viv. *K*int. p. 203.
354. May. XIX, 3; Viv. *K*int. p. 202.
355–6. Viv. *K*int. p. 202.
359. Viv. *K*int. p. 203.
360. Viv. *K*int. p. 200.
361. Viv. *K*int. p. 202.
362. Viv. *K*int. pp. 203–4.
363. Viv. *K*int. p. 203.
364. Viv. *K*int. p. 205.
365. May. XV, 5.
366. Viv. *K*int. p. 205.
367–70. Viv. *K*int. p. 206.
371–2. Viv. *K*int. p. 207.
373. Viv. *K*int. pp. 207–8.
374. May. XIX, 6; Viv. *K*int. p. 209.
375. Viv. *K*int. p. 209.
376. May. XIX, 7; Viv. *K*int. p. 209.
377. May. XIX, 7; Viv. *K*int. p. 210.
378. May. XVIII, 14; XIX, 6; Viv. *K*int. p. 210.
379. Viv. *K*int. p. 210.
380–1. M. Mit. VI, 1, 53; Viv. *K*int. p. 211.
382. May. XIX, 7; Viv. *K*int. p. 211.
383–4. Viv. *K*int p. 211.
385. Viv. *K*int. pp. 207, 211.
386–7. Viv. *K*int. p. 322.
388. Col. Dig. II, 3, 42; Viv. *K*int. pp. 69, 212.
389. Viv. *K*int. pp. 185, 212.
390. May. I, 1, 14.
398. Viv. *K*int. p. 161.
402. Col. Dig. III, 3, 48.
410. Col. Dig. I, 5.
411. Col. Dig. III, 1, 37, 1; May. X, 3; Viv. *K*int. p. 95.

(VIII), 412. Col. Dig. III, 1, 37, 2; Viv. *K*int. p. 95.
413. Col. Dig. III, 1, 38; Viv. *K*int. p. 95.
414. Col. Dig. III, 1, 36; Viv. *K*int. p. 95.
415. Col. Dig. III, 1, 33.
416. Col. Dig. II, 4, 56; III, 1, 52, 1; May. IV, 10, 7; Vîram. I, 12; V, 1, 2; Varad. p. 6.
417. Col. Dig. III, 1, 52, 2.
IX, 1-2. Col. Dig. IV, 2-3.
3. Col. Dig. IV, 5.
4. Col. Dig. IV, 14.
5-7. Col. Dig. IV, 9, 1-3.
8-9. Col. Dig. IV, 19-20.
10-1. Col. Dig. IV, 30, 1-2.
12. Col. Dig. IV, 32.
13. Col. Dig. IV, 99.
14-5. Col. Dig. IV, 22, 1-2.
16. Col. Dig. IV, 23.
17. Col. Dig. IV, 24; Viv. *K*int. p. 220.
18-9. Col. Dig. IV, 25-6.
22-4. Col. Dig. IV, 33, 1-3.
25. Col. Dig. IV, 34.
26-8. Col. Dig. IV, 35, 1-3.
30. Col. Dig. IV, 109.
32-4. Col. Dig. V, 253, 1-3.
35. Col. Dig. V, 254; Dây. XI, 3, 3; Dâyakr. I, 5, 2.
36-7. Col. Dig. V, 255-6.
38-40. Col. Dig. V, 257, 1-3.
42-6. Col. Dig. V, 252, 1-5.
47. Col. Dig. V, 252, 6; Dây. XIII, 5; Dâyakr. VIII, 5; Smr*i*. *K*. XVI, 20; Mâdh. p. 57.
48. Col. Dig. V, 214, 1; 252, 7.
49. Col. Dig. V, 214, 2; 252, 8; Viv. *K*int. p. 131.
50-1. Col. Dig. V, 214, 3-4.
52. Col. Dig. V, 214, 5; Mit. I, 10, 6; Vîram. II, 2, 4; Mâdh. p. 23.
53. Col. Dig. V, 244; Mit. I, 10, 4; Datt. *K*and. II, 35; Vîram. II, 2, 4; Mâdh. p. 53.

(IX), 54. Col. Dig. V, 236; Dâyakr. XII, 2, 15; Viv. *K*int. p. 131.
55. Dâyakr. XII, 2, 15.
59. Col. Dig. IV, 146; V, 229; Mit. I, 10, 8; Datt. Mî. VII, 21; Vîram. II, 2, 4; Sar. Vi. 342.
60. Col. Dig. V, 228; Mit. I, 10, 8; Vîram. II, 2, 4; Sar. Vi. 342; Mâdh. p. 23.
62. Col. Dig. IV, 150.
63. Col. Dig. V, 227.
64–8. Col. Dig. IV, 156, 1–5; Mit. I, 10, 8; Vîram. II, 2, 4; Sar. Vi. 343; Mâdh. p. 23.
69. Col. Dig. IV, 170, 1; Mit. I, 10, 10; Vîram. II, 2, 4; Mâdh. p. 24.
70. Col. Dig. IV, 170, 2; Dây. IX, 28; Mit. I, 10, 10; Vîram. II, 2, 4; Mâdh. p. 24.
71. Col. Dig. IV, 171.
72–3. Col. Dig. IV, 174, 1–2.
74. Col. Dig. IV, 45, 1.
75. Col. Dig. IV, 45, 2; 116.
76. Col. Dig. IV, 154.
77. Col. Dig. IV, 56.
78–9. Col. Dig. IV, 57, 1–2.
80. Col. Dig. IV, 67.
81. Col. Dig. IV, 70.
82. Col. Dig. IV, 73.
83. Col. Dig. IV, 75.
84. Col. Dig. IV, 112.
85. Col. Dig. IV, 46.
86. Col. Dig. IV, 47.
87. Col. Dig. V, 414.
(85–87: Dây. XI, 1, 47; Vîram. III, 1, 10.)
89. Col. Dig. IV, 179.
94. Vîram. II, 1, 2.
95–6. Col. Dig. IV, 188, 1–2.
97. Col. Dig. IV, 172.
98–100. Col. Dig. IV, 173, 1–3.
101–2. Col. Dig. IV, 190, 1–2.
103. Col. Dig. V, 2; Dây. I, 3; Vîram. I, 2; Smr*i*. *K*. I, 1; Sar. Vi. 37.

(IX), 104. Col. Dig. V, 4; Dây. I, 14; II, 8; III, 1; Mit. I, 3, 3; 5, 7; May. IV, 4, 1; Dâyakr. I, 1, 1; VII, 1; Vîram. I, 10–21, 22, 27, 51; II, 1, 1–2; Viv. *K*int. p. 224; Sm*ri*. *K*. I, 12, 18; Sar. Vi. 49; Mâdh. p. 1; Varad. p. 6.

105. Col. Dig. V, 9; Dây. I, 36; III, 15; Mit. I, 3, 3; Vîram. II, 1, 7, 11; Viv. *K*int. p. 226; Sm*ri*. *K*. II, 2, 10; Mâdh. p. 8.

106. Col. Dig. V, 10, 1; Dây. I, 36; XI, 1, 32; Mit. I, 11, 12; Datt. *K*and. I, 5; Vîram. II, 1, 7; Sar. Vi. 369; Mâdh. p. 44.

107. Col. Dig. V, 10, 2; Dây. I, 36; Vîram. II, 1, 7; Mâdh. p. 8.

108. Col. Dig. V, 12; Dây. VI, 1, 54; Vîram. II, 1, 7.

109. Col. Dig. V, 13; Vîram. II, 1, 7.

110. Col. Dig. V, 14; Vîram. II, 1, 7.

111. Col. Dig. V, 18; Dây. I, 27, 37; Vîram. I, 21; II, 1, 7; Viv. *K*int. p. 227; Sm*ri*. *K*. II, 2, 10–11.

112. Col. Dig. V, 34; Dây. II, 37; Mit. I, 2, 4; I, 3, 3; May. IV, 4, 9; Vîram. II, 1, 9, 11; Viv. *K*int. p. 234; Sm*ri*. *K*. II, 1, 25; III, 8; Mâdh. p. 8; Varad. p. 2.

113. Col. Dig. V, 36.

114. Col. Dig. V, 37; Viv. *K*int. p. 234.

115. Col. Dig. V, 38; Dây. II, 45; Sm*ri*. *K*. III, 5.

116. Col. Dig. V, 39, 1; Dây. II, 37; Mit. I, 3, 3; May. IV, 4, 9; Vîram. II, 1, 10; Sm*ri*. *K*. III, 10, 12; Mâdh. p. 8.

117. Col. Dig. V, 39, 2; Dây. II, 37; Mit. I, 3, 3; May. IV, 4, 9; Dâyakr. VII, 18; Vîram. II, 1, 10; Sm*ri*. *K*. III, 12; Mâdh. p. 8.

118. Col. Dig. V, 120; Dây. III, 36; Mit. I, 7, 9; Vîram. II, 1, 21; V, 2, 1; Viv. *K*int. p. 248; Sm*ri*. *K*. IV, 32; Sar. Vi. 126, 133, 287; Varad. p. 10.

119. Col. Dig. V, 70; Mit. I, 4, 18; May. IV, 7, 17.

120. Col. Dig. V, 76, 1; Mit. II, 1, 10; Vîram. II, 2, 18; III, 1, 6.

(IX), 121. Col. Dig. V, 76, 2; Vîram. II, 2, 18.
122-3. Col. Dig. V, 55, 1-2.
124. Col. Dig. V, 56.
125. Col. Dig. V, 57; Dâyakr. VII, 14; Viv. *K*int. p. 233.
126. Col. Dig. V, 64.
127. Col. Dig. V, 212; Dây. X, 2; Datt. Mî. I, 9; Vîram. II, 2, 3; Varad. p. 23.
128. Col. Dig. V, 222, 1; Vîram. II, 2, 3; Varad. p. 23.
129. Col. Dig. V, 222, 2; Vîram. II, 2, 3.
130. Col. Dig. V, 210; Dây. XI, 2, 1; May. IV, 8, 10; Vîram. III, 2, 1; Viv. *K*int. p. 292; Sm*ri*. *K*. XI, 2, 7; Sar. Vi. 543, 552; Varad. pp. 35-6.
131. Col. Dig. V, 209, 491; Dây. IV, 2, 13; May. IV, 10, 17; Vîram. V, 2, 2, 4; Viv. *K*int. p. 267; Sm*ri*. *K*. IX, 3, 12; Sar. Vi. 288; Mâdh. p. 44; Varad. p. 44.
132. Col. Dig. V, 220, 3; Dây. XI, 2, 19; Dâyakr. I, 4, 1; Vîram. III, 3, 2; Viv. *K*int. p. 294.
133. Col. Dig. V, 220, 1; Dây. XI, 2, 19; Varad. pp. 35-6.
134. Col. Dig. V, 206; Dây. II, 39; X, 2; Mit. I, 11, 23; Dây. VII, 16; Vîram. II, 2, 17; Viv. *K*int. p. 286; Sar. Vi. 376, 558; Mâdh. p. 20; Varad. p. 26.
135. Dây. XI, 2, 16; Mâdh. p. 45; Varad. p. 48.
136. Col. Dig. V, 207; 220, 2; Dây. X, 3; XI, 2, 20; Mit. II, 2, 6; Datt. *K*and. I, 22; Vîram. II, 2, 17; III, 3, 1; Sar. Vi. 564, 660, 667; Mâdh. p. 26; Varad. p. 35.
137. Col. Dig. V, 11; Dây. XI, 1, 31; Vîram. III, 1, 11.
138. Col. Dig. V, 302; Dây. V, 6; XI, 1, 31; Vîram. III, 1, 11.
139. Dây. IV, 2, 10; XI, 6, 9, 31; Dâyakr. II, 4, 7; Datt. Mî. VII, 17; Varad. p. 36.
140. Col. Dig. V, 208; Vîram. II, 2, 3.

(IX), 141. Col. Dig. V, 278; Datt. *K*and. V, 20; Vîram. II, 2, 18; Sm*ri*. *K*. X, 13; Varad. p. 23.

142. Col. Dig. V, 181; Mit. I, 11, 32; May. IV, 5, 21; Datt. Mî. II, 8; VI, 6, 47; VIII, 1; Datt. *K*and. II, 18; Vîram. II, 2, 18; Sm*ri*. *K*. X, 15; Sar. Vi. 388; Mâdh. p. 24; Varad. p. 23.

143. Col. Dig. V, 234; Sm*ri*. *K*. V, 12.

144. Col. Dig. V, 226.

145. Col. Dig. V, 235.

146. Col. Dig. V, 232; Mit. II, 1, 10; Datt. Mî. V, 51; Vîram. II, 1, 18; III, 1, 6; Mâdh. p. 31.

147. Col. Dig. V, 233; Mâdh. p. 40.

148. Col. Dig. V, 139, 1.

149. Col. Dig. V, 60, 1; 139, 2; Mâdh. p. 16.

150. Col. Dig. V, 60, 2; 139, 3.

151. Col. Dig. V, 60, 3; 139, 4; Dây. IX, 12; Vîram. II, 1, 25.

152. Col. Dig. V, 140, 1; Dây. IX, 12; Vîram. II, 1, 25; Mâdh. p. 16; Varad. p. 18.

153. Col. Dig. V, 140, 2; Dây. IX, 12; Vîram. II, 1, 25; Viv. *K*int. p. 271; Varad. p. 18.

154. Col. Dig. V, 166; Dây. IX, 27; Mit. I, 11, 41; Dâyakr. VII, 19; Vîram. II, 1, 25; II, 2, 21; Viv. *K*int. p. 273; Sar. Vi. 394; Mâdh. p. 17; Varad. p. 20.

155. Col. Dig. V, 167; Dây. IX, 27; Mit. I, 8, 10; May. IV, 4, 29; Vîram. II, 1, 25; II, 2, 21; Viv. *K*int. p. 273; Sm*ri*. *K*. II, 2, 7; Mâdh. p. 17; Varad. p. 20.

156. Col. Dig. V, 53.

157. Col. Dig. V, 66; Dâyakr. VII, 22; Datt. *K*and. V, 32; Varad. p. 19.

158. Col. Dig. V, 188, 1; Datt. Mî. II, 56; Datt. *K*and. V, 11; Viv. *K*int. p. 279; Varad. p. 25.

159. Col. Dig. V, 188, 2; Mit. I, 11, 30; Datt. *K*and. V, 11; Vîram. II, 2, 19; Viv. *K*int. p. 279; Sar. Vi. 386; Mâdh. p. 22.

(IX), 160. Col. Dig. V, 188, 3; Mit. I, 11, 30; Datt. *K*and. V, 11; Vîram. II, 2, 19; Viv. *K*int. p. 279; Sar. Vi. 386; Mâdh. p. 22; Varad. p. 26.

162. Dây. X, 15; Vîram. II, 2, 18.

163. Dây. X, 13; Mit. I, 11, 28; Vîram. II, 2, 18; Viv. *K*int. p. 286; Sm*ri*. *K*. X, 2; Sar. Vi. 380, 383; Mâdh. p. 21.

164. Dây. X, 11; Mit. I, 11, 29; Vîram. II, 2, 18; Sar. Vi. 385; Mâdh. p. 2; Varad. p. 25.

165. Datt. Mî. II, 57; Datt. *K*and. V, 10.

166. Col. Dig. V, 194; Datt. Mî. I, 68; Vîram. II, 2, 2.

167. Col. Dig. V, 231; Vîram. II, 2, 4; Sm*ri*. *K*. X, 4.

168. Col. Dig. V, 275; Mit. I, 11, 9; May. IV, 5, 1; Datt. Mî. I, 7; II, 23; Datt. *K*and. I, 12; Vîram. II, 2, 8; Sm*ri*. *K*. X, 4; Sar. Vi. 366; Varad. p. 23.

169. Col. Dig. V, 285; Vîram. II, 2, 10; Sm*ri*. *K*. X, 4; Varad. p. 23.

170. Col. Dig. V, 250; Vîram. II, 2, 5; Sm*ri*. *K*. X, 4; Varad. p. 23.

171. Col. Dig. V, 291; Sm*ri*. *K*. X, 4; Varad. p. 23.

172. Col. Dig. V, 263; Mit. I, 11, 7; Vîram. II, 2, 6; Sm*ri*. *K*. X, 4; Varad. p. 23.

173. Col. Dig. V, 288; Vîram. II, 2, 12; Sm*ri*. *K*. X, 4; Varad. p. 23.

174. Col. Dig. V, 282; Mit. I, 11, 16; Datt. Mî. II, 24; Vîram. II, 2, 9; Sm*ri*. *K*. X, 4; Sar. Vi. 372; Varad. p. 23.

175. Col. Dig. V, 269; Vîram. II, 2, 7; Sm*ri*. *K*. X, 4; Varad. p. 25.

177. Col. Dig. V, 287; Vîram. II, 2, 11; Sm*ri*. *K*. X, 4; Varad. p. 23.

178. Col. Dig. V, 187; Dây. IX, 28; Vîram. II, 2, 14; Sm*ri*. *K*. X, 4; Varad. p. 25.

179. Col. Dig. V, 186; Dây. IX, 29; Datt. *K*and. V, 30; Viv. *K*int. p. 274; Varad. p. 21.

(IX), 180. Col. Dig. V, 301; Datt. Mî. I, 33, 42, 56; Datt. *K*and. I, 8; Vîram. II, 2, 15; Varad. p. 25.

181. Col. Dig. V, 271; Datt. Mî. VI, 12.

182. Col. Dig. V, 276; Dây. XI, 5, 7; Mit. I, 11, 36; May. IV, 5, 19; Datt. Mî. II, 29, 65; Datt. *K*and. I, 20; Vîram. II, 2, 8; Sm*ri*. *K*. X, 8; Sar. Vi. 390; Varad. p. 27.

183. Col. Dig. V, 506; Dây. IV, 3, 32; Datt. Mî. II, 69; Datt. *K*and. I, 23; Vîram. II, 2, 8; V, 2, 14.

184. Col. Dig. V, 298; Datt. *K*and. V, 8; Vîram. 2, 2, 19.

185. Col. Dig. V, 223; Dây. XI, 1, 40; XI, 5, 5; Mit. I, 11, 33; II, 1, 7, 9, 35; II, 4, 1; Datt. *K*and. V, 8; Vîram. III, 1, 6; III, 2, 3; III, 4, 7; III, 5, 1; Viv. *K*int. p. 295; Sm*ri*. *K*. X, 1; XI, 1, 1; XI, 3, 6; XI, 4, 10; Sar. Vi. 485, 488, 491, 575; Mâdh. pp. 22, 27, 30; Varad. pp. 38–9.

186. Col. Dig. V, 370; Dây. IV, 3, 36; XI, 1, 40; XI, 6, 7, 10, 14, 17; Dâyakr. I, 10, 5; II, 6, 2; Vîram. III, 1, 11.

187. Col. Dig. V, 434; Dây. XI, 6, 10, 14, 17, 21, 24; Mit. II, 3, 3; II, 4, 5; May. IV, 8, 19; IV, 10, 28; Dâyakr. I, 10, 15, 21, 28; II, 6, 2; III, 4, 2; III, 4, 11; III, 5, 2; III, 7, 5; Viv. *K*int. p. 295; Sm*ri*. *K*. XI, 5, 9; Sar. Vi. 569; Mâdh. p. 27; Varad. p. 34.

188. Col. Dig. V, 442; Dây. XI, 6, 26; Mit. II, 7, 4; Vîram. III, 7, 8; Sm*ri*. *K*. XI, 6, 5; Sar. Vi. 609; Mâdh. p. 29.

189. Col. Dig. II, 3, 23, 1; V, 443; Dây. XI, 6, 34; Mit. II, 4, 4; II, 7, 5–6; Vîram. III, 7–8; Viv. *K*int. p. 298; Sm*ri*. *K*. XI, 6, 6; Sar. Vi. 610, 612.

190. Col. Dig. II, 3, 23, 2; May. IV, 10, 8.

191. Col. Dig. V, 344; Dây. X, 16.

(IX), 192. Col. Dig. V, 485; Dây. IV, 2, 1; Mit. II, 11, 19; Vîram. II, 1, 18; V, 2, 1, 5; Viv. *K*int. pp. 226, 266; Sm*ri*. *K*. IX, 3, 6; Sar. Vi. 309; Mâdh. p. 43; Varad. p. 43.

193. Col. Dig. V, 498; Mit. II, 11, 17; May. IV, 10, 16; Vîram. V, 2, 1; Sm*ri*. *K*. IX, 3, 10; Sar. Vi. 285; Mâdh. p. 43; Varad. p. 43.

194. Col. Dig. V, 462; Dây. IV, 1, 4; Mit. II, 11, 4; May. IV, 10, 1; Vîram. V, 1, 1; Viv. *K*int. p. 256; Sm*ri*. *K*. IX, 1, 1, 3; Sar. Vi. 260; Mâdh. p. 44; Varad. p. 45.

195. May. IV, 10, 13; Vîram. V, 2, 1; Sm*ri*. *K*. IX, 3, 1; Varad. p. 46.

196. Col. Dig. V, 502; Dây. IV, 2, 27; May. IV, 10, 29; Dâyakr. II, 3, 14; II, 4, 10; Vîram. V, 2, 9; Viv. *K*int. p. 269; Sm*ri*. *K*. IX, 3, 28; Sar. Vi. 319; Mâdh. p. 44; Varad. p. 46.

197. Col. Dig. V, 503; Dây. IV, 2, 27; May. IV, 10, 29; Dâyakr. II, 3, 19; Vîram. V, 2, 9; Viv. *K*int. p. 269; Mâdh. p. 44; Varad. p. 47.

198. Col. Dig. V, 495; Dây. IV, 2, 16; IV, 3, 3; Mit. II, 11, 22; May. IV, 10, 19; Dâyakr. II, 5, 3; Vîram. V, 2, 5; Sm*ri*. *K*. IX, 3, 40; Sar. Vi. 307; Mâdh. p. 44; Varad. p. 45.

199. Col. Dig. V, 474; Vîram. V, 1, 5; Sm*ri*. *K*. IX, 1, 14.

200. Col. Dig. V, 473; Mit. I, 4, 19; II, 11, 34; Viv. *K*int. p. 260; Sm*ri*. *K*. IX, 2, 27; Sar. Vi. 201; Mâdh. p. 50; Varad. p. 49.

201. Col. Dig. V, 329, 1; Dây. V, 7; Mit. II, 10, 5; May. IV, 11, 3; Dâyakr. III, 1; Vîram. VIII, 1; Viv. *K*int. p. 243; Sm*ri*. *K*. V, 4; Sar. Vi. 148; Mâdh. p. 39; Varad. p. 13.

202. Col. Dig. V, 329, 2; Mit. II, 10, 5; Vîram. VIII, 2; Viv. *K*int. p. 243; Sm*ri*. *K*. V, 22; Sar. Vi. 159; Varad. p. 13.

203. Col. Dig. V, 329, 3; Vîram. VIII, 9; Viv. *K*int. p. 243; Varad. p. 13.

(IX), 204. Col. Dig. V, 341; Dây. VI, 1, 54; Mit. I, 4, 13; Varad. p. 30.

205. Col. Dig. V, 73; May. IV, 7, 14; Viv. *K*int. p. 254; Varad. p. 30.

206. Col. Dig. V, 345; Dây. VI, 1, 9, 31, 51; May. IV, 7, 1; Dâyakr. IV, 2, 2; Viv. *K*int. p. 249; Sm*ri*. *K*. VII, 26; Varad. p. 28.

207. Col. Dig. V, 107; Dây. III, 28; Vîram. II, 1, 15; Viv. *K*int. p. 237; Sm*ri*. *K*. II, 2, 26; Varad. p. 12.

208. Col. Dig. V, 348; Dây. VI, 1, 3, 31; Mit. I, 4, 10; May. IV, 7, 4; Dâyakr. IV, 2, 5; Vîram. VII, 1; Viv. *K*int. p. 250; Sm*ri*. *K*. VII, 27; Sar. Vi. 173; Varad. p. 29.

209. Col. Dig. V, 91; Dây. II, 21; VI, 2, 32; Mit. I, 5, 11; May. IV, 4, 5; Vîram. II, 1, 17; Viv. *K*int. p. 229; Sar. Vi. 223; Mâdh. p. 13.

210. Col. Dig. V, 35, 406, 1; Dây. XII, 1; Mit. II, 9, 12; May. IV, 9, 2; Vîram. IV, 1, 4; Sm*ri*. *K*. XII, 3; Mâdh. p. 34; Varad. p. 52.

211. Col. Dig. V, 406, 2; Mit. II, 9, 12; May. IV, 9, 13; Vîram. IV, 4; Sm*ri*. *K*. XI, 1, 51; XII, 17; Sar. Vi. 767; Mâdh. pp. 35–6; Varad. p. 52.

212. Col. Dig. V, 406, 3; Dây. XI, 6, 32; Mit. II, 9, 12; May. IV, 9, 13; Vîram. IV, 4, 6; Sm*ri*. *K*. XI, 1, 51; XII, 17; Sar. Vi. 767; Mâdh. pp. 35–6; Varad. p. 52.

213. Col. Dig. V, 52; Mit. I, 9, 5; May. IV, 7, 24; Vîram. II, 1, 7; VI, 2; Viv. *K*int. p. 234; Sar. Vi. 781; Mâdh. p. 52.

214. Col. Dig. V, 317; Dây. V, 6; May. IV, 11, 9; Vîram. VIII, 11; Viv. *K*int. p. 242; Sm*ri*. *K*. V, 19; Varad. p. 12.

215. Col. Dig. V, 29; Dây. II, 86; Vîram. II, 1, 10; Viv. *K*int. p. 235.

216. Col. Dig. V, 101; Dây. I, 46; II, 2; VII, 1;

Mit. I, 6, 4, 7; May. IV, 34; Dây. V, 14; Vîram. II, 1, 24; Viv. *K*int. p. 276, 305; Smri. *K*. XIII, 15; Sar. Vi. 231, 234; Mâdh. p. 14.

(IX), 217. Col. Dig. V, 424; Dây. XI, 3, 2; Mit. II, 1, 7; II, 4, 4; II, 5, 1; May. IV, 8, 18; Dâyakr. I, 10, 4; Vîram. III, 4, 7; III, 5, 1; III, 7, 1; Viv. *K*int. p. 294; Smri. *K*. XI, 4, 10; XI, 5, 6; Sar. Vi. 576, 583, 584, 765; Varad. pp. 36, 40.

218. Col. Dig. V, 375; Dây. XIII, 1; Dâyakr. VIII, 2; Vîram. VI, 1; Smri. *K*. XIV, 1; Sar. Vi. 775; Mâdh. p. 53.

219. Col. Dig. V, 343; Dây. VI, 2, 23; May. IV, 7, 15; Dâyakr. IV, 2, 13; Vîram. VII, 2; Smri. *K*. VII, 39; Sar. Vi. 197; Mâdh. p. 50; Varad. p. 30.

222–3. Viv. *K*int. p. 317.

224. May. XXI, 2; Viv. *K*int. p. 317.

229. Col. Dig. III, 1, 34.

231–2. Viv. *K*int. pp. 190–1.

237. Viv. *K*int. p. 213.

254. Viv. *K*int. p. 157.

262. Viv. *K*int. p. 157.

272–4. Viv. *K*int. p. 178.

275. May. XXII, (CCXLIII); Viv. *K*int. p. 189.

276. Viv. *K*int. p. 166.

277. Viv. *K*int. p. 169.

278. Viv. *K*int. p. 177.

282. May. XV, 9; Viv. *K*int. p. 125.

283. Viv. *K*int. p. 126.

285–6. Viv. *K*int. p. 188.

287. Viv. *K*int. p. 159.

289. Viv. *K*int. p. 189.

290. Viv. *K*int. p. 187.

291. Viv. *K*int. pp. 131, 157.

292. Viv. *K*int. p. 163.

317. Col. Dig. II, 2, 22.

327. Col. Dig. II, 2, 24.

X, 43. Col. Dig. II, 3, 22, 3.
75. Col. Dig. II, 2, 21.
76. Col. Dig. I, 7, 3.
83. Col. Dig. II, 4, 22.
96. Col. Dig. II, 3, 22; Viv. *K*int. p. 188.
97. Col. Dig. I, 74.
115. Col. Dig. II, 4, 20; Mit. I, 1, 16; Viv. *K*int. p. 76; Sar. Vi. 472; Mâdh. p. 5.
116. Col. Dig. II, 4, 21.
117. Col. Dig. I, 35; II, 4, 23.
118. Col. Dig. II, 2, 23.
130. Col. Dig. II, 4, 26.
XI, 16. Vîram. I, 46.
90. M. Mit. II, 8, 19.
111–5. Vîram. I, 44.
177. Col. Dig. IV, 82.
189. Vîram. III, 1, 10; Smr*i*. *K*. XI, 1, 49.
228. Col. Dig. I, 206.

A.

SYNOPSIS

OF

PARALLEL PASSAGES.

By the advice of the editor I add a detailed synopsis of the parallel passages from the six Dharma-sûtras and Smritis, as well as of the wholly or partly identical verses from the Mahâbhârata, Parâsara, Mânava Srâddhakalpa, the Upanishads, and some other works. I trust that, though references to the Smritis have already been given in the notes to the translation, this addition will not be found useless. The principle on which I have worked is a different one, and this synopsis shows much more clearly which rules of Manu's work are represented in the older books and which are not. It also shows at a glance which verses I have been able to trace elsewhere. According to what has been said in the Introduction, both points are of some importance. I have used this opportunity to supply some omissions, and to correct the misprints occurring in the figures of the quotations given in the notes. Wherever the notes and the synopsis differ, the latter alone is to be relied on. The addition of an asterisk (*) to a quotation means that the passage is in verse, and that it is thus intimately connected with Manu's Sloka. The passages quoted from the Mahâbhârata are all cognate verses. Hence no asterisks have been added.

Abbreviations: Ga. = Gautamîya Dharmasâstra; Ba. = Baudhâyanîya Dharmasâstra; Âp. = Âpastambîya Dharma-sûtra; Va. = Vâsishtha Dharmasâstra; Vi. = Vishnu Smriti; Yâ. = Yâgñavalkîya Dharmasâstra; Par. = Parâsara Smriti (Calc. ed.); Mâ. Sr. = Mânava-Srâddhakalpa (Introduction, pp. xl–xliii); Â. Gri. = Âsvalâyana Grihya-sûtra (Calc. ed.); Sâ. Gri. = Sâṅkhâyana Grihya-sûtra; Pâ. Gri. = Pâraskara Grihya-sûtra; Go. Gri. = Gobhilîya Grihya-sûtra (Calc. ed.); Mai. Up. = Maitrâyanîyabrâhmanopanishad; Îsâ. Up. = Îsâvâsyopanishad; Sa. Up. = Samhitopanishad; Nir. = Nirukta; Mah. = Mahâbhârata; V. P. = Vishnu-purâna, Wilson's translation, edited by Dr. F. E. Hall.

Manu I.

1. . . . .
2. . . . .
3. . . . .
4. . . . .
5. . . . .
6. . . . .
7. . . . .
8. . . . .
9. . . . .
10. V.P. I, p. 56; Mah. XII, 342, 40.
11. . . . .
12. . . . .
13. . . . .
14. . . . .
15. . . . .
16. . . . .
17. . . . .
18. Mah. XII, 233, 12[b].
19. . . . .
20. Mah. XII, 233, 8.
21. Mah. XII, 233, 26.
22. . . . .
23. . . . .
24. . . . .
25. . . . .
26. . . . .
27. . . . .
28. Mah. XII, 233, 16.
29. Mah. XII, 233, 17.
30. . . . .
31. . . . .
32. . . . .
33. . . . .
34. . . . .
35. . . . .
36. . . . .
37. . . . .
38. . . . .
39. . . . .
40. . . . .
41. . . . .
42. . . . .
43. . . . .
44. . . . .
45. . . . .
46. . . . .
47. . . . .
48. . . . .
49. . . . .
50. . . . .
51. . . . .
52. . . . .
53. . . . .
54. . . . .
55. . . . .
56. . . . .
57. . . . .
58. . . . .
59. . . . .
60. . . . .
61. . . . .
62. . . . .
63. . . . .
64. Mah. XII, 232, 12–13.
65. Mah. XII, 232, 15.
66. Mah. XII, 232, 16.
67. Mah. XII, 232, 17.
68. Mah. XII, 232, 18–19.
69. Mah. XII, 232, 20.
70. Mah. XII, 232, 21.
71. Mah. XII, 232, 29.
72. Mah. XII, 232, 30.
73. Mah. XII, 232, 31.
74. . . . .
75. Mah. XII, 233, 4.
76. Mah. XII, 233, 5.
77. Mah. XII, 233, 6.

78. Mah. XII, 233, 7.
79. . . . .
80. . . . .
81. Mah. XII, 232, 23.
82. Mah. XII, 232, 24.
83. Mah. XII, 232, 25.
84. Mah. XII, 232, 26; III, 200, 16.
85. Mah. XII, 232, 27.
86. Mah. XII, 232, 28; Par. I, 23*.
87. . . . .
88. . . . .
89. . . . .
90. . . . .
91. . . . .
92. . . . .
93. . . . .
94. Yâ. I, 198–99.
95. . . . .
96. . . . .
97. . . . .
98. . . . .
99. Yâ. I, 198.
100. . . . .
101. . . . .
102. . . . .
103. . . . .
104. . . . .
105. . . . .
106. . . . .
107. . . . .
108. Va. VI, 1a*.
109. Va. VI, 2*, 3–5*.
110. . . . .
111. . . . .
112. . . . .
113. . . . .
114. . . . .
115. . . . .
116. . . . .
117. . . . .
118. . . . .
119. . . . .

Manu II.

1. . . . .
2. . . . .
3. . . . .
4. . . . .
5. . . . .
6. Ba. I, 1, 1–6; Ga. I, 1–3; Âp. I, 1, 1–3; Va. I, 4–6.
7. . . . .
8. . . . .
9. . . . .
10. . . . .
11. . . . .
12. Yâ. I, 7*.
13. . . . .
14. Ga. I, 4; Âp. I, 30, 9.
15. . . . .
16. . . . .
17. . . . .
18. . . . .
19. . . . .
20. . . . .
21. . . . .
22. Ba. I, 2, 9–10; Va. I, 8–9.
23. Ba. I, 2, 12; Va. I, 13–15; Yâ. I, 2.
24. Ba. I, 2, 13–15; Âp. I, 32, 18; Vi. LXXXIV, 2, 4.
25. . . . .
26. Ga. VIII, 14; Yâ. I, 10.
27. Yâ. I, 13a.
28. . . . .
29. Mah. III, 180, 34a; Vi. XXVII, 4; Yâ. I, 11; Â. *Gri.* I, 15, 1–3; *S*â. *Gri.* I, 24, 1–

3; Pâ. Gri. I, 16, 3–4; Go. Gri. II, 7, 21.

30. Vi. XXVII, 5; Yâ. I, 12; Â. Gri. I, 15. 4; Sâ. Gri. I, 24, 4–5; Pâ. Gri. I, 17, 1; Go. Gri. II, 8, 8.

31. Vi. XXVII, 6–9.

32. Pâ. Gri. I, 17, 4.

33. . . . .

34. Vi. XXVII, 10–11; Yâ. I, 12; Â. Gri. I, 16, 1; Sâ. Gri. I, 27, 1; Pâ. Gri. I, 17, 5; I, 19, 1.

35. Vi. XXVII, 12; Yâ. I, 12; Â. Gri. I, 17, 1; Sâ. Gri. I, 28, 1–2; Pâ. Gri. II, 1, 1–2; Go. Gri. II, 9, 1.

36. Ga. I, 5, 7, 11; Ba. I, 3, 7–9; Âp. I, 1, 18; Va. XI, 49–51; Vi. XXVII, 15–17; Yâ. I, 14; Â. Gri. I, 19, 1–4; Sâ. Gri. II, 1, 1, 4–5; Pâ. Gri. II, 2, 1–3; Go. Gri. II, 10, 1–3.

37. Ga. I, 6; Âp. I, 1, 19–20.

38. Vi. XXVII, 26*; Ga. I, 12–14; Ba. I, 3, 12; Âp. I, 1, 21; Va. XI, 71–73; Â. Gri. I, 19, 5–6; Sâ. Gri. II, 1, 6–8; Pâ. Gri. II, 5, 36–38; Go. Gri. II, 10, 4.

39. Vi. XXVII, 27*; Ga. XXI, 11; Va. XI, 74; Â. Gri. I, 19, 6; Sâ. Gri. II, 1, 9–13; Pâ. Gri. II, 5, 39; Go. Gri. II, 10, 5.

40. Âp. I, 1, 28; 2, 6; Va. XI, 75; Â. Gri. I, 19, 7; Pâ. Gri. II, 5, 40; Go. Gri. II, 10, 6.

41. Ga. I, 16–21; Ba. I, 3, 14; Âp. I, 2, 39–3, 9; Va. XI, 61–67; Vi. XXVII, 19–20; Yâ. I, 29; Â. Gri. I, 19, 8; Sâ. Gri. II, 1, 2, 4–5; Pâ. Gri. II, 5, 16–19; Go. Gri. II, 10, 8–9.

42. Ga. I, 15; Ba. I, 3, 13; Âp. I, 2, 33–37; Va. XI, 58–60; Vi. XXVII, 18; Yâ. I, 29; Â. Gri. I, 19, 10–11; Sâ. Gri. II, 1, 15–17; Pâ. Gri. II, 5, 21–23; Go. Gri. II, 10, 10.

43. Pâ. Gri. II, 5, 24.

44. Ba. I, 8, 5; Vi. XXVII, 19; Yâ. I, 29; Go. Gri. II, 10, 12.

45. Ga. I, 22–24; Ba. I, 3, 15; Âp. I, 2, 38; Va. XI, 52–54; Vi. XXVII, 21, 23; Yâ. I, 29; Â. Gri. I, 19, 12–13; Sâ. Gri. II, 1, 18–20; Pâ. Gri. II, 5, 25–28; Go. Gri. II, 10, 11.

46. Ga. I, 26; Ba. I, 3, 15; Va. XI, 55–57; Vi. XXVII, 22; Â. Gri. I, 19, 13; Sâ. Gri. II, 1, 21–24.

47. Ga. I, 25; Vi. XXVII, 24.

48. Ga. II, 8, 35; Âp. I, 3, 25; Â. Gri. I, 22, 5–6; Sâ. Gri. II, 6, 4; Pâ. Gri. II, 5, 1; Go. Gri. II, 10, 41–42.

49. Ga. II, 36; Ba. I, 3, 16–17; Âp. I, 3, 28–30; Va. XI, 68–70; Vi. XXVII, 25; Yâ. I, 30; Â. Gri. I, 22, 8; Pâ. Gri. II, 5, 2–4.

50. Â. Gri. I, 22, 7; Sâ. Gri. II, 6, 5–6; Pâ. Gri. II, 5, 5–7; Go. Gri. II, 10, 43.

51. Ga. II, 39, 40; Âp. I, 3, 31–42; Vi. LXVIII, 40–41; Yâ. I, 31; Â. Gri. I, 22, 9; Sâ. Gri. II, 6, 7; Pâ. Gri. II, 5, 8; Go. Gri. II, 10, 44.

52. Mah. XIII, 104, 57.

53. Ga. II, 41; IX, 59; Ba. II, 5, 21; II, 12, 7; Vi. LXVIII, 34–35.
54. Va. III, 69; Ba. II, 12, 7; Vi. LXVIII, 42–43; Yâ. I, 31.
55. . . . .
56. Ba. II, 12, 9; II, 13, 11; Yâ. I, 112; Âp. II, 1, 2–3; Vi. LXVIII, 48.
57. . . . .
58. Ba. I, 8, 14; Va. III, 26; Vi. LXII, 6; Yâ. I, 18.
59. Ba. I, 8, 15–16; Va. III, 26; Vi. LXII, 1–4; Yâ. I, 19.
60. Ba. I, 8, 19–21; Ga. I, 36; Âp. I, 16, 2–10; Va. III, 27–29; Vi. LXII, 6–8; Yâ. I, 20; Go. *Gri*. I, 2, 5–9.
61. Ba. I, 8, 17; Âp. I, 15, 4–7; Va. III, 31; Vi. LXII, 5; Yâ. I, 18, 20; Go. *Gri*. I, 2, 5, 22–23.
62. Ba. I, 8, 23*; Vi. LXII, 9*; Ga. I, 36; Va. III, 31–34; Yâ. I, 21; Go. *Gri*. I, 2, 29.
63. Ba. I, 8, 5–10; Âp. I, 6, 18–19; Go. *Gri*. II, 2, 1–3.
64. Vi. XXVII, 29*; Ba. I, 6, 6–9.
65. Yâ. I, 36; Ga. II, 9; Â. *Gri*. I, 18, 2; Pâ. *Gri*. II, 1, 3; Go. *Gri*. III, 1, 1.
66. Vi. XXVII, 13; Yâ. I, 13; Â. *Gri*. I, 15, 12; 16, 6; 17, 18.
67. Vi. XXII, 32; XXVII, 14; Yâ. I, 13.
68. . . . .
69. Ga. II, 6, 8, 10; Yâ. I, 15; Â. *Gri*. I, 22, 1–2.
70. . . . .
71. Ba. I, 3, 25–28; Âp. I, 5, 19, 23; Vi. XXX, 32; Yâ. I, 26; *S*â. *Gri*. II, 7, 4–6; IV, 8, 15.
72. Ga. I, 46; Âp. I, 15, 22.
73. Ga. I, 46; *S*â. *Gri*. IV, 8, 12, 16–17.
74. Ga. I, 57; Âp. I, 13, 6–7; Vi. XXX, 33; *S*â. *Gri*. IV, 8, 12–13.
75. Ga. I, 48–50; Ba. II, 7, 5–7.
76. Vi. LV, 10*.
77. Vi. LV, 11*.
78. Vi. LV, 12*; Ba. II, 11, 6.
79. Vi. LV, 13*; Ba. IV, 1, 29; Va. XXVI, 4.
80. Vi. LV, 14*; Ba. II, 7, 15.
81. Vi. LV, 15*.
82. Vi. LV, 16*; Ba. II, 7, 22.
83. Va. X, 5*; Vi. LV, 17*.
84. Vi. LV, 18*; Ba. IV, 1, 26; Va. XXV, 11.
85. Vi. LV, 19*; Va. XXVI, 9*.
86. Vi. LV, 20*; Va. XXVI, 10*.
87. Vi. LV, 21*; Va. XXVI, 11*.
88. . . . .
89. . . . .
90. . . . .
91. . . . .
92. . . . .
93. . . . .
94. . . . .
95. . . . .
96. . . . .
97. . . . .
98. . . . .
99. . . . .
100. . . . .
101. Ga. II, 10–11; Ba. II, 7, 13–14; Âp. I, 30, 8; Va. VII, 16; Vi. XXVIII, 2–3;

Yâ. I, 23–25; *S*â. G*ri*. II, 9, 1–3.
102. Ba. II, 7, 18, 20; Va. XXVI, 2–3.
103. Ba. II, 7, 15.
104. Ba. II, 11, 6.
105. Âp. I, 12, 9; Va. XIII, 7.
106. Âp. I, 12, 3–5.
107. Vi. XXX, 34–38; Yâ. I, 41–46; Â. G*ri*. III, 3, 2–3.
108. Ga. II, 8, 30, 35; Ba. I, 3, 16; 4, 4–8; Âp. I, 4, 16, 23; 5, 25; Va. VII, 9, 15; Vi. XXVIII, 4, 7, 9, 12; Yâ. I, 25.
109. Yâ. I, 28.
110. Ba. I, 4, 2; Âp. I, 32, 22–24; Va. II, 12.
111. Vi. XXIX, 7*.
112. Sa. Up. III* (p. 30, Bur.); Ba. I, 4, 1a*; Vi. XXIX, 8*.
113. Ba. I, 4, 1b*.
114. Nir. II, 4*; Sa. Up. III* (pp. 29–30, Bur.); Va. II, 8*; Vi. XXIX, 9*.
115. Nir. II, 4*; Va. II, 9*; Vi. XXIX, 10*.
116. Vi. XXX, 41–42.
117. Vi. XXX, 43*; Ga. VI, 1–3, 5; Ba. I, 3, 25–28; Âp. I, 5, 19–20; 14, 7–9; Va. XIII, 41–43; Vi. XXVIII, 14–17; Go. G*ri*. III, 1, 27.
118. . . . .
119. Ga. II, 21, 25; Âp. I, 8, 11.
120. Mah. XIII, 104, 64b–65a.
121. Âp. I, 5, 15; Ba. I, 3, 23.
122. Ga. VI, 5; Ba. I, 3, 27; Âp. I, 5, 12; Va. XIII, 44; Vi. XXVIII, 17; Yâ. I, 26; *S*â. G*ri*. IV, 12, 5.
123. Va. XIII, 45.
124. Vi. XXVIII, 17.
125. Âp. I, 5, 18; Va. XIII, 46.
126. . . . .
127. Ga. V, 41; Âp. I, 14, 26–29.
128. Ga. VI, 19.
129. Vi. XXXII, 7.
130. Ga. VI, 9; Ba. I, 3, 45; Âp. I, 14, 11; Va. XIII, 41; Vi. XXXII, 4; *S*â. G*ri*. IV, 12, 1–5.
131. Ga. VI, 7; Âp. I, 14, 6–9; Vi. XXXII, 2.
132. Ga. VI, 7–8; Vi. XXXII, 2.
133. Vi. XXXII, 3.
134. Âp. I, 14, 13*; Ga. VI, 14–17.
135. Mah. XIII, 8, 21; Âp. I, 14, 25*; Vi. XXXII, 17*.
136. Vi. XXXII, 16*; Ga. VI, 20; Va. XIII, 56–57; Yâ. I, 116.
137. Ga. VI, 10; Yâ. I, 116.
138. Ga. VI, 24; Ba. II, 6, 30; Âp. II, 11, 7; Va. XIII, 58, 60; Vi. LXIII, 51; Yâ. I, 117.
139. Ga. VI, 25; Âp. II, 11, 5–6; Va. XIII, 59; Yâ. I, 117.
140. Ga. I, 9–10; Âp. I, 1, 13; Va. III, 21; Vi. XXIX, 1; Yâ. I, 34.
141. Va. III, 22–23; Vi. XXIX, 2; Yâ. I, 35.
142. Yâ. I, 34.
143. Vi. XXIX, 3; Yâ. I, 35.
144. Sa. Up. III* (p. 32, Bur.); Nir. II, 4*; Va. II, 10*; Vi. XXX, 47*; Âp. I, 1, 14.
145. Va. XIII, 48*; Ga. VI, 51; Yâ. I, 35.
146. Vi. XXX, 44*; Ga. VI, 50; Va. II, 3–5.
147. Vi. XXX, 45*; Âp. I, 1, 17.
148. Vi. XXX, 46*; Ga. I, 8; Âp. I, 1, 16.

149. . . . .
150. . . . .
151. Ba. I, 3, 47.
152. . . . .
153. . . . .
154. Mah. III, 133, 12.
155. Vi. XXXII, 18*.
156. Ga. VI, 21–23.
157. Mah. XII, 36, 46; Va. III, 11*; Ba. I, 1, 10*; Par. VIII, 23*.
158. Mah. XII, 36, 47; Par. VIII, 24*.
159. Ga. II, 42; Âp. I, 8, 25–30.
160. . . . .
161. . . . .
162. . . . .
163. . . . .
164. . . . .
165. . . . .
166. Âp. I, 12, 1–2; Yâ. I, 40.
167. Ba. II, 11, 8.
168. Va. III, 2*; Vi. XXVIII, 36.
169. Va. II, 3*; Vi. XXVIII, 37; Yâ. I, 39.
170. Mah. III, 180, 34b; Va. II, 3*; Vi. XXVIII, 38.
171. Va. II, 6a*; Ga. I, 10; Va. II, 4–5; Ba. I, 3, 6a; Âp. II, 15, 19.
172. Mah. III, 180, 35a; Va. II, 6b*; Ba. I, 3, 6b*; Ga. II, 4–5.
173. . . . .
174. Vi. XXVII, 28*.
175. . . . .
176. Ga. II, 8; Va. VII, 17; Vi. XXVIII, 4–5; Yâ. I, 22.
177. Ga. II, 13; Ba. I, 3, 23–24; Âp. I, 2, 23, 25–26; Yâ. I, 33; Pâ. *Gri.* II, 5, 12; Go. *Gri.* III, 1, 17, 19, 23.
178. Ga. II, 13; Ba. I, 3, 24; Âp. I, 3, 11, 17–24; 7, 5; Va. VII, 15; Vi. XXVIII, 11; Yâ. I, 33; Go. *Gri.* III, 1, 16, 19, 25–26.
179. Ga. II, 13, 16, 17; Ba. I, 3, 20; Âp. I, 3, 12–13; 7, 3, 8–10; Vi. XXVIII, 11; Yâ. I, 33; Pâ. *Gri.* II, 5, 12; Go. *Gri.* III, 1, 16.
180. Vi. XXVIII, 48.
181. Vi. XXVIII, 51*.
182. Ba. I, 3, 19; Âp. I, 4, 13–14; Â. *Gri.* I, 22, 5; *S*â. *Gri.* II, 6, 8; Pâ. *Gri.* II, 5, 11; Go. *Gri.* III, 1, 27.
183. Ga. II, 35; Ba. I, 3, 18; Âp. I, 3, 25; Vi. XXVIII, 9; Yâ. I, 29.
184. Ga. II, 37–38.
185. . . . .
186. Ba. I, 3, 19; Âp. I, 4, 16; Vi. XXVIII, 4; Â. *Gri.* I, 22, 6; *S*â. *Gri.* II, 6, 8; Pâ. *Gri.* II, 5, 9, 11; Go. *Gri.* III, 1, 27.
187. Vi. XXVIII, 52*; Yâ. III, 281.
188. Yâ. I, 32.
189. Yâ. I, 32.
190. Yâ. I, 32.
191. Ga. II, 29–30; Âp. I, 5, 24–27; Va. VII, 13; Vi. XXVIII, 6–7; Yâ. I, 27; *S*â. *Gri.* II, 6, 8; Pâ. *Gri.* II, 5, 11; Go. *Gri.* III, 1, 15.
192. Ga. II, 22; Âp. I, 5, 17.
193. Âp. I, 6, 18–20.
194. Ga. II, 21; Ba. I, 3, 21; Âp. I, 4, 22, 28; Vi. XXVIII, 13.
195. Ga. II, 25; Âp. I, 6, 5; Vi. XXVIII, 18.

196. Vi. XXVIII, 19*; Ga. II, 28; Ba. I, 3, 38; Va. VII, 12; Âp. I, 6, 6–9; Pâ. Gri. II, 5, 30.
197. Vi. XXVIII, 20–22.
198. Ga. II, 14–15, 21; Âp. I, 2, 21; 3, 15; 6, 13–17; 8, 8–10; Vi. XXVIII, 23; Sâ. Gri. IV, 8, 5, 7–11.
199. Ga. II, 18, 23; Âp. I, 8, 15; Vi. XXVIII, 24–25.
200. Vi. XXVIII, 26.
201. . . . .
202. . . . .
203. Âp. I, 6, 15, 23.
204. Ba. I, 3, 34; Âp. I, 8, 12–13; Vi. XXVIII, 27–28.
205. Va. XIII, 54[a]*; Ga. VI, 3–4; Âp. I, 6, 29–30; 8, 19–20; Vi. XXVIII, 29–30.
206. Âp. I, 7, 28–29.
207. Ga. II, 31; Ba. I, 3, 44; Âp. I, 7, 29–30; Va. XIII, 54; Vi. XXXII, 1.
208. Vi. XXVIII, 31.
209. Ga. II, 32; Ba. I, 3, 36; Âp. I, 7, 30; Vi. XXVIII, 32–33.
210. Ga. II, 31; Ba. I, 3, 37; Âp. I, 7, 27; Vi. XXXII, 2, 5.
211. Ga. II, 32; Ba. I, 3, 37; Âp. I, 7, 27; Vi. XXXII, 6.
212. Vi. XXXII, 13*; Ga. II, 34; Ba. I, 3, 33.
213. Mah. XIII, 48, 38.
214. Mah. XIII, 48, 37.
215. . . . .
216. Vi. XXXII, 14*.
217. Vi. XXXII, 15*; Ga. VI, 2; Âp. I, 14, 8.
218. . . . .
219. Ga. I, 27; II, 10; Âp. I, 2, 31–32; 30, 8; Va. VII, 11; Vi. XXVIII, 41.
220. Vi. XXVIII, 53*; Ga. XXIII, 21; Ba. II, 7, 16; Âp. II, 12, 13–14; Va. XX, 4.
221. Va. I, 18; Âp. II, 12, 22.
222. Ga. II, 11; Ba. II, 7, 2; Vi. XXVIII, 2.
223. Mah. XIII, 105, 13; Âp. II, 29, 11.
224. . . . .
225. Ga. XXI, 15; Âp. I, 14, 6; Vi. XXXI, 1–3.
226. . . . .
227. . . . .
228. Vi. XXXI, 5.
229. Mah. XII, 108, 5[b].
230. Mah. XII, 108, 6; Vi. XXXI, 7*.
231. Mah. XII, 108, 7; Vi. XXXI, 8; Âp. I, 3, 44.
232. Mah. XII, 108, 8[a].
233. Mah. XII, 108, 8[b]–9; Vi. XXXI, 10*.
234. Mah. XII, 108, 12; Vi. XXXI, 9*.
235. Vi. XXXI, 6.
236. . . . .
237. . . . .
238. Mah. XII, 165, 31[a], 32[a]; Âp. II, 29, 11.
239. Mah. XII, 165, 31[b], 32[a].
240. . . . .
241. Ga. VII, 1–3; Ba. I, 3, 41–43; Âp. II, 4, 25.
242. . . . .
243. Ga. III, 5, 6; Ba. II, 11, 13; Âp. II, 21, 6; Va. VII, 4; Vi. XXVIII, 43; Yâ. I, 49.
244. Ga. III, 9; Yâ. I, 50.
245. Ga. II, 48–49; Âp. I, 7, 19; Vi. XXVIII, 42; Yâ. I, 51; Â. Gri. III, 9, 4; Go. Gri. III, 4, 1–2.

246. *S*â. G*ri*. III, 1, 18.
247. Ga. III, 7; Vi. XXVIII, 44–45; Yâ. I, 49.
248. Ga. III, 8; Va. VII, 5–6; Vi. XXVIII, 46; Yâ. I, 49.
249. Vi. XXVIII, 47*.

MANU III.

1. Ga. II, 45–47; Ba. I, 3, 1–4; Âp. I, 2, 12–16; Yâ. I, 36; Â. G*ri*. I, 22, 3–4; Pâ. G*ri*. II, 5, 13–15; II, 6, 2–3.
2. Va. VIII, 1; Yâ. I, 52.
3. *S*â. G*ri*. III, 1, 5, 17; Go. G*ri*. III, 4, 30–34.
4. Ga. IV, 1; Va. VIII, 1; Yâ. I, 52; Â. G*ri*. I, 5, 3–6; III, 9, 4; *S*â. G*ri*. I, 5, 6–10; Pâ. G*ri*. II, 6, 1, 4; Go. G*ri*. II, 1, 2.
5. Ga. IV, 2–5; Va. VIII, 1–2; Ba. II, 1, 37–38; Vi. XXIV, 9–10; Yâ. I, 53; Go. G*ri*. III, 4, 4–5.
6. Â. G*ri*. I, 5, 1.
7. Yâ. I, 54.
8. Vi. XXIV, 12–16; Yâ. I, 53.
9. . . . .
10. . . . .
11. Yâ. I, 53.
12. . . . .
13. Ba. I, 16, 2–5; Va. I, 24–25; Vi. XXIV, 1–4; Yâ. I, 57; Pâ. G*ri*. I, 4, 8–11.
14. Va. I, 26; Yâ. I, 56.
15. Vi. XXVI, 6*; Va. I, 27.
16. Ba. II, 2, 7.
17. Va. I, 27.
18. Vi. XXVI, 7*; Va. XIV, 11.
19. . . . .
20. Mah. I, 73, 8.
21. Mah. I, 73, 8–9; Ba. I, 20, 1; Va. I, 29; Vi. XXIV, 18.
22. . . . .
23. Mah. I, 73, 10; Ga. IV, 15.
24. Mah. I, 73, 10–11; Ga. IV, 14; Ba. I, 20, 10; Âp. II, 12, 3; Vi. XXIV, 27–28.
25. Mah. I, 73, 11–12.
26. Mah. I, 73, 13; Ba. I, 20, 12.
27. Ga. IV, 6; Ba. I, 20, 2; Âp. II, 11, 17; Va. I, 30; Vi. XXIV, 19; Yâ. I, 58; Â. G*ri*. I, 6.
28. Ga. IV, 9; Ba. I, 20, 5; Âp. II, 11, 19; Va. I, 31; Vi. XXIV, 20; Yâ. I, 59; Â. G*ri*. I, 6.
29. Ga. IV, 8; Ba. I, 20, 4; Âp. II, 11, 18; Va. I, 32; Vi. XXIV, 21; Yâ. I, 59; Â. G*ri*. I, 6.
30. Ga. IV, 7; Ba. I, 20, 3; Vi. XXIV, 22; Yâ. I, 60; Â. G*ri*. I, 6.
31. Ga. IV, 11; Ba. I, 20, 6[1]; Âp. II, 12, 1; Va. I, 35; Vi. XXIV, 24; Yâ. I, 61; Â. G*ri*. I, 6.
32. Ga. IV, 10; Ba. I, 20, 7[1]; Âp. II, 11, 20; Va. I, 33; Vi. XXIV, 23; Yâ. I, 61; Â. G*ri*. I, 6.

[1] The order of the Sûtras followed here is that adopted by Dr. Hultzsch in his edition of the text.

33. Ga. IV, 12; Ba. I, 20, 8; Âp. II, 12, 2; Va. I, 34; Vi. XXIV, 25; Yâ. I, 61; Â. *Gri.* I, 6.
34. Ga. IV, 13; Ba. I, 20, 9; Vi. XXIV, 26; Yâ. I, 61; Â. *Gri.* I, 6.
35. . . . .
36. . . . .
37. Ga. IV, 33; Vi. XXIV, 29; Yâ. I, 58; Â. *Gri.* I, 6.
38. Ga. IV, 29–32; Vi. XXIV, 30–32; Yâ. I, 59–60; Â. *Gri.* I, 6.
39. . . . .
40. . . . .
41. . . . .
42. Ba. I, 21, 1; Âp. II, 12, 4.
43. Vi. XXIV, 5; Yâ. I, 62.
44. Vi. XXIV, 6–8; Yâ. I, 62.
45. Ga. V, 1–2; Ba. IV, 1, 18–19; Âp. II, 1, 17–18; Va. XII, 21–24; Vi. LXIX, 1; Yâ. I, 79–81; *S*â. *Gri.* IV, 11, 16; Pâ. *Gri.* I, 11, 7–8.
46. Yâ. I, 79.
47. Yâ. I, 79.
48. Yâ. I, 79.
49. . . . . . , . . .
50. Yâ. I, 79.
51. Ba. I, 21, 2–3; II, 2, 27; Âp. II, 13, 11; Va. I, 37–38.
52. . . . .
53. Mah. XIII, 45, 20; Âp. II, 13, 12; Va. I, 36.
54. Mah. XIII, 46, 1^b–2^a.
55. Mah. XIII, 46, 3; Yâ. I, 82.
56. Mah. XIII, 46, 5^b–6^a.
57. Mah. XIII, 46, 6^b.
58. Mah. XIII, 46, 7.
59. . . . .
60. . . . .
61. Mah. XIII, 46, 4.
62. . . . .
63. Ba. I, 10, 26*.
64. Ba. I, 10, 28^a*.
65. Ba. I, 10, 28^b*.
66. Ba. I, 10, 29.
67. Ga. V, 7–8; Ba. II, 4, 22; Vi. LIX, 1–2; Yâ. I, 97.
68. Par. II, 11*; Vi. LIX, 19.
69. Vi. LIX, 20.
70. Ga. V, 3–4, 9; Ba. II, 5, 11; II, 11, 1; Vi. LIX, 20–25; Yâ. I, 102; Â. *Gri.* III, 1, 1–4.
71. . . . .
72. Vi. LIX, 26*.
73. *S*â. *Gri.* I, 5, 1; Pâ. *Gri.* I, 4, 1.
74. Â. *Gri.* I, 1, 3; *S*â. *Gri.* I, 10, 6.
75. Â. *Gri.* III, 2, 2.
76. Mah. XII, 264, 11; Mai. Up. VI, 37; Va. XI, 13.
77. . . . .
78. Va. VIII, 14–16; Vi. LIX, 27–28.
79. . . . .
80. Vi. LIX, 29*; *S*â. *Gri.* II, 16, 6.
81. Yâ. I, 23, 104.
82. Mah. XIII, 97, 8^b–9^a; Mâ. *S*r. IV*; Vi. LXVII, 23–25.

83.–86. Ga. V, 10; Ba. II, 5, 11; Âp. II, 3, 12, 16–17; Va. XI, 3; Vi. LXVII, 1–3; Â. *Gri.* I, 2, 1–2; *S*â. *Gri.* II, 14, 1–4; Pâ. *Gri.* II, 9, 1–12.

87.–91. Ga. V, 11–17; Âp. II, 3, 12, 15, 18–23; II, 4, 1–8; Va. XI, 4; Vi. LXVII, 4–22; Â. *Gri.* I, 2, 3–10; *S*â. *Gri.* II, 14, 5–17; Pâ. *Gri.* II, 9, 3–10; Go. *Gri.* I, 4, 8–12.

92. Âp. II, 9, 5–6; Vi. LXVII, 26; Yâ. I, 103; *S*â. G*ri*. II, 14, 22.
93. Âp. II, 4, 9; Vi. LXVII, 28, 32, 44, 46.
94. Ba. II, 5, 15; Âp. II, 4, 10–11; Va. XI, 5; Vi. LIX, 14; LXVII, 27; Yâ. I, 108; *S*â. G*ri*. II, 14, 20; Pâ. G*ri*. II, 9, 11–12.
95. . . . .
96. Ga. V, 18; Yâ. I, 108; *S*â. G*ri*. II, 14, 19.
97. Va. III, 8.
98. . . . .
99. Ga. V, 31–34; Va. VIII, 12; Âp. II, 4, 13, 16; II, 6, 7–14; Vi. LXVII, 45; Yâ. I, 107.
100. *S*â. G*ri*. II, 17, 1*; Vi. LXVII, 33.
101. Âp. II, 4, 14*; Ga. V, 35–36; Yâ. I, 107.
102. Va. VIII, 7*; Vi. LXVII, 34*; Ga. V, 40.
103. Va. VIII, 8[a]*; Vi. LXVII, 35*; Par. I, 43*; *S*â. G*ri*. II, 16, 3*; Ga. V, 40; Âp. II, 6, 5.
104. Yâ. I, 112.
105. Va. VIII, 8[b]*; Ga. V, 40; Va. VIII, 4–5; Vi. LXVII, 29–30; Yâ. 107.
106. Ga. V, 38–39; Âp. II, 8, 2–4; Yâ. I, 104.
107. Yâ. I, 107.
108. Âp. II, 6, 16–17; Va. XI, 12.
109. . . . .
110. Ga. V, 43.
111. Vi. LXVII, 36*; Ga. V, 44.
112. Vi. LXVII, 37*; Ga. V, 45; Ba. II, 5, 14; Âp. II, 4, 18–20.
113. Vi. LXVII, 38*; Yâ. I, 108.
114. Vi. LXVII, 39*; Ga. V, 25; Ba. II, 13, 5[a–b]; Âp. II, 4, 12; Yâ. I, 105; *S*â. G*ri*. II, 14, 21; Pâ. G*ri*. II, 9, 13.
115. Ba. II, 13, 5[c–d]*; Vi. LXVII, 40*; Ba. II, 5, 18.
116. Vi. LXVII, 41*; Âp. II, 8, 2; Yâ. I, 105; Pâ. G*ri*. II, 9, 14.
117. Vi. LXVII, 42*; Ba. II, 13, 6.
118. Vi. LXVII, 43*; Ba. II, 13, 2.
119. Ga. V, 27–28; Ba. II, 6, 36–38; Âp. II, 8, 5–9; Va. XI, 1–2; Yâ. I, 109–10; Â. G*ri*. I, 24, 1–4; *S*â. G*ri*. II, 15, 1–9; Pâ. G*ri*. I, 3, 1–3; Go. G*ri*. IV, 10, 24–26.
120. Ga. V, 29–30; Ba. II, 6, 37; Yâ. I, 110; *S*â. G*ri*. II, 15, 10.
121. Go. G*ri*. I, 4, 19.
122. Ga. XV, 2; Yâ. I, 217.
123. . . . .
124. . . . .
125. Ba. II, 15, 10*; Va. XI, 27*; Mâ. *S*r. IV*; Ga. XV, 21; Vi. LXXIII, 3–4; Yâ. I, 228; Â. G*ri*. IV, 7, 2; *S*â. G*ri*. IV, 1, 2.
126. Ba. II, 15, 11*; Va. XI, 28*; Mâ. *S*r. IV*.
127. . . . .
128. Va. III, 8[a]*; Â. G*ri*. IV, 7, 2.
129. Ga. XV, 21; Va. XI, 29.
130. Vi. LXXXII, 2.
131. . . . .

132. . . . .
133. . . . .
134. Mah. XIII, 90, 50; Va. VI, 26; Vi. LXXXIII, 9–13; Yâ. I, 221.
135. Mah. XIII, 90, 51[a].
136. . . . .
137. . . . .
138. Ga. XV, 12; Ba. II, 14, 6; Âp. II, 17, 4; Va. XI, 17.
139. Âp. II, 17, 9.
140. Mah. XIII, 90, 42.
141. Mah. XIII, 90, 46; Âp. II, 17, 8*.
142. Mah. XIII, 90, 44.
143. . . . .
144. Ba. II, 14, 4; Âp. II, 17, 5–6; Va. XI, 18.
145. Mâ. *S*r. IV*; Ba. II, 14, 4.
146. . . . .
147. . . . .
148. Mâ. *S*r. IV*; Ga. XV, 20; Vi. LXXXIII, 17–18; Yâ. I, 220.
149. Vi. LXXXII, 1–2.
150. Ga. XV, 16; Va. XI, 19; Yâ. I, 223–224.
151. Ga. XV, 16, 18; Vi. LXXXII, 13.
152. Ga. XV, 18; Vi. LXXXII, 8–9.
153. Ga. XV, 16, 18; Va. XI, 19; Vi. LXXXII, 26; Yâ. I, 222.
154. Ga. XV, 16, 18; Va. XI, 19; Yâ. I, 223.
155. Ga. XV, 17–18; Yâ. I, 222.
156. Vi. LXXXII, 20–21; Yâ. I, 222, 223.
157. Vi. LXXXII, 23, 29; Yâ. I, 224.
158. Mah. XIII, 90, 7; Ga. XV, 18; Yâ. I, 223–224.
159. Mah. XIII, 90, 8; Ga. XV, 19; Vi. LXXXII, 5, 28; Yâ. I, 222, 223.
160. Ga. XV, 18; Vi. LXXXII, 18; Yâ. I, 223.
161. Ga. XV, 18; Âp. II, 17, 21; Va. XI, 19; Vi. LXXXII, 19; Yâ. I, 222.
162. Âp. II, 17, 21; Vi. LXXXII, 7.
163. . . . .
164. Ga. XV, 18; Vi. LXXXII, 22; Yâ. I, 223.
165. Yâ. I, 223.
166. Ga. XV, 16; Yâ. I, 224.
167. . . . .
168. . . . .
169. . . . .
170. Mah. XIII, 90, 11[b]–12[a].
171. Par. IV, 20.
172. Mah. XII, 165, 68[a]; Ba. II, 1, 39*; Par. IV, 19*.
173. . . . .
174. Par. IV, 17*.
175. . . . .
176. . . . .
177. . . . .
178. . . . .
179. . . . .
180. Mah. XIII, 90, 13[b]–14[a].
181. Mah. XIII, 90, 14[b]–15[a].
182. . . . .
183. . . . .
184. Mah. XIII, 90, 36; Ga. XV, 9, 28; Âp. II, 17, 22; Vi. LXXXIII, 5; Yâ. I, 219.
185. Mah. XIII, 90, 26[b]–27[a]; Mâ. *S*r. IV*; Ga. XV, 28; Ba. II, 14, 2; Âp. II, 17, 22; Vi.

LXXXIII, 2–4, 15, 16; Yâ. I, 219–221.
186. Mâ. *S*r. IV*; Yâ. I, 219.
187. Ba. II, 14, 6; Âp. II, 17, 11–15; Va. XI, 17; Vi. LXXIII, 2; Yâ. I, 225.
188. Ga. XV, 23; Yâ. I, 225.
189. Mâ. *S*r. IV.
190. . . . .
191. Ga. XV, 22.
192. . . . .
193. . . . .
194. . . . .
195. . . . .
196. . . . .
197. . . . .
198. . . . .
199. . . . .
200. . . . .
201. . . . .
202. Mâ. *S*r. II; Âp. II, 19, 3–5; Vi. LXXIX, 24; Yâ. I, 236.
203. . . . .
204. . . . .
205. Vi. LXXIII, 27; Yâ. I, 244.
206. Ga. XV, 25; Âp. II, 18, 6; Yâ. I, 227; Vi. LXXXV, 62.
207. Vi. LXXXV, 54–61.
208. Vi. LXXIII, 2; Yâ. I, 226; Â. G*ri*. IV, 7, 2.
209. Ba. II, 14, 7; Vi. LXXIII, 12; Yâ. I, 231; Â. G*ri*. IV, 8, 1; *S*â. G*ri*. IV, 1, 5.
210. Ba. II, 14, 7; Âp. II, 17, 17–19; Vi. LXXIII, 12; Yâ. I, 235; Â. G*ri*. IV, 7, 5–7; *S*â. G*ri*. IV, 1, 2–3.
211. Ba. II, 14, 7; Â. G*ri*. IV, 8, 4; *S*â. G*ri*. IV, 1, 6.
212. Â. G*ri*. IV, 8, 5–6.
213. . . . .
214. Â. G*ri*. IV, 7, 9.
215. Vi. LXXIII, 17–19; Yâ. I, 241; *S*â. G*ri*. IV, 1, 10.
216. Vi. LXXIII, 22.
217. . . . .
218. Vi. LXXIII, 23.
219. . . . .
220. Vi. LXXV, 1.
221. Vi. LXXV, 4.
222. . . . .
223. . . . .
224. Âp. II, 19, 9; Va. XI, 26.
225. Ba. II, 15, 3*; Va. XI, 25*.
226.
227. } Âp. II, 16, 23–24; II, 19, 19–22; Vi. LXXIII, 21, 23–24.
228. Âp. II, 17, 4.
229. Âp. II, 18, 3; Vi. LXXIX, 19–21; LXXXI, 2.
230. . . . .
231. Ba. II, 14, 5; Vi. LXXIX, 5–15; Yâ. I, 239.
232. Vi. LXXIII, 16; Â. G*ri*. IV, 8, 10; *S*â. G*ri*. IV, 1, 8.
233. . . . .
234. Vi. LXXIX, 16; LXXXIII, 18.
235. Va. XI, 35*, 36; Yâ. I, 235.
236. Vi. LXXXI, 11, 19.
237. Va. XI, 32*; Vi. LXXXI, 20*.
238. Mah. XIII, 90, 19; Vi. LXXXI, 12–13.
239. Ga. XV, 24; Âp. II, 17, 20; Vi. LXXXI, 6–9.
240. . . . .
241. . . . .
242. Vi. LXXXI, 15.
243. Vi. LXXXI, 18.
244. Vi. LXXXI, 21*; Yâ. I, 240; Â. G*ri*. IV, 8, 14.

245. Vi. LXXXI, 22*; Va. XI, 23*.
246. Vi. LXXXI, 23*; Va. XI, 24*.
247. Vi. XXI, 2–3; Yâ. II, 250; *S*â. G*ri*. IV, 2, 1–4.
248. . . . .
249. . . . .
250. Mah. XIII, 90, 12b–13a; Va. XI, 37*.
251. Vi. LXXIII, 26; Yâ. I, 240; Â. G*ri*. IV, 8, 11; *S*â. G*ri*. IV, 2, 5–7.
252. Yâ. I, 243; Â. G*ri*. IV, 8, 15.
253. Â. G*ri*. IV, 8, 11; *S*â. G*ri*. IV, 1, 12; Yâ. I, 240.
254. Va. III, 69–71; *S*â. G*ri*. IV, 2, 5; IV, 4, 14.
255. . . . .
256. . . . .
257. . . . .
258. Vi. LXXIII, 27.
259. Vi. LXXIII, 28*; Yâ. I, 245*.
260. Yâ. I, 256; Go. G*ri*. IV, 3, 31–34.
261. Ba. II, 14, 9; Â. G*ri*. IV, 8, 12–13; *S*â. G*ri*. IV, 1, 9.
262. Go. G*ri*. IV, 3, 27.
263. . . . .
264. . . . .
265. Va. XI, 21–22; Yâ. I, 256.
266. . . . .
267. Mah. XIII, 88, 3; Ga. XV, 15; Vi. LXXX, 1; Yâ. I, 257.
268. Mah. XIII, 88, 5; Ga. XV, 15; Vi. LXXX, 2–5; Yâ. I, 257.
269. Mah. XIII, 88, 7; Ga. XV, 15; Vi. LXXX, 6–9; Yâ. I, 257–258.
270. Ga. XV, 15; Âp. II, 16, 27; Vi. LXXX, 10; Yâ. I, 258.
271. Mah. XIII, 88, 9b; Ga. XV, 15; Âp. II, 16, 26; Vi. LXXX, 11–12; Yâ. I, 257.
272. Ga. XV, 15; Âp. II, 17, 1–3; Vi. LXXX, 14; Yâ. I, 259.
273. Mah. XIII, 88, 15; Âp. II, 19, 22; Yâ. I, 260.
274. Mah. XIII, 88, 12a; Mâ. *S*r. II; Va. XI, 40*; Vi. LXXVIII, 52–53.
275. . . . .
276. Ga. XV, 3; Âp. II, 16, 6; Va. XI, 16.
277. Ga. XV, 4; Âp. II, 16, 8–22; Vi. LXXVIII, 8–49; Yâ. I, 261–267.
278. Âp. II, 16, 5; Va. XI, 36; Vi. LXXIII, 2.
279. Yâ. I, 232.
280. Âp. II, 17, 23; Vi. LXXVII, 8.
281. . . . .
282. . . . .
283. Mâ. *S*r. II; Ba. II, 11, 3; Âp. I, 13, 1.
284. Yâ. I, 268.
285. Mah. III, 2, 60; XII, 244, 12a–13b.
286. . . . .

Manu IV.

1. Mah. XII, 244, 1.
2. Mah. XII, 263, 6.
3. . . . .
4. . . . .
5. *S*â. Gri. IV, 11, 13.
6. *S*â. Gri. IV, 11, 15.
7. Yâ. I, 128.
8. Yâ. I, 128.
9. Mah. XII, 244, 4.
10. . . . .
11. . . . .
12. Yâ. I, 129.
13. . . . .
14. Va. XXVII, 8*; *S*â. Gri. IV, 11, 16.
15. Yâ. I, 129.
16. . . . .
17. Ba. I, 10, 30; Vi. LXXI, 4; Yâ. I, 129.
18. Vi. LXXI, 5–6; Yâ. I, 123.
19. Vi. LXXI, 8; Yâ. I, 99.
20. . . . .
21. Ga. V, 3.
22. . . . .
23. . . . .
24. . . . .
25. Ba. II, 4, 23; Va. XI, 46; Vi. LIX, 4; Yâ. I, 124.
26. Ba. II, 4, 23; Va. XI, 46; Vi. LIX, 5–7, 9; Yâ. I, 125; *S*â. Gri. III, 8, 1.
27. . . . .
28. . . . .
29. . . . .
30. Yâ. I, 130.
31. *S*â. Gri. I, 2.
32. Ga. V, 22; Ba. II, 5, 19–20; Âp. II, 4, 13.
33. Ga. IX, 63–64; Va. XII, 2; Vi. LXIII, 1; Yâ. I, 130.
34. Ga. IX, 3; Âp. I, 30, 13; Va. XII, 4; Vi. LXXI, 9.
35. Ga. IX, 4, 6, 7, 71–72; Ba. I, 5, 7; Âp. I, 30, 10–12; Yâ. I, 131.
36. Ba. I, 5, 3–5; I, 6, 1; II, 6, 7; Va. XII, 14, 37–38; Âp. I, 8, 2; Vi. LXXI, 13–16; Yâ. I, 133; *S*â. Gri. IV, 11, 21–22; Go. Gri. III, 4, 25–27.
37. Mah. XIII, 104, 17b–18a; Ba. II, 6, 10; Âp. I, 31, 20; Va. XII, 10; Vi. LXXI, 17–21; Yâ. I, 135; *S*â. Gri. IV, 11, 2; Pâ. Gri. II, 7, 6.
38. Ga. IX, 52; Ba. II, 6, 15; Âp. I, 31, 15; Va. XII, 9; Vi. LXXI, 23; LXIII, 42–43; Â. Gri. III, 9, 6; Pâ. Gri. II, 7, 8; Go. Gri. III, 5, 11.
39. Ga. IX, 66; Vi. LXIII, 26–30; Yâ. I, 133; *S*â. Gri. IV, 12, 15.
40. Ga. IX, 29–30; Va. XII, 6; Vi. LXIX, 11; Go. Gri. III, 5, 5.
41. . . . .
42. . . . .
43. Vi. LXVIII, 46*; Ga. IX, 32; Va. XII, 31; Vi. LXXI, 25; Yâ. I, 131; *S*â. Gri. IV, 11, 10.
44. Ga. IX, 32, 48; Vi. LXXI, 26; Yâ. I, 135.
45. Ga. IX, 40, 61; Va. VI, 12; XII, 11; Ba. II, 6, 24;

Âp. I, 30, 18; Vi. LX, 11, 16, 19; LXIV, 5; LXVIII, 14; Yâ. I, 131, 134; Â. *Gri*. III, 9, 6; Pâ. *Gri*. II, 7. 6.
46. Va. VI, 12*; Ga. IX, 40; Âp. I, 30, 18; Vi. LX, 4, 10, 21; Yâ. I, 134; Pâ. *Gri*. II, 7, 15.
47. Vi. LX, 8–9, 15; Yâ. I, 134.
48. Ga. IX, 12; Âp. I, 30, 20; Vi. LX, 22; Yâ. I, 134; *S*â. *Gri*. IV, 12, 23.
49. Ga. IX, 37–38, 41–43; Ba. I, 10, 10; Âp. I, 30, 14–15; Va. XII, 13; Vi. LX, 1, 3, 23; Yâ. I, 16; Pâ. *Gri*. II, 7, 15; *S*â. *Gri*. IV, 12, 20–22.
50. Va. VI, 10*; Ba. I, 10, 10; Âp. I, 31, 1; Vi. LX, 2; Yâ. I, 16; *S*â. *Gri*. IV, 12, 25.
51. Va. VI, 13*.
52. Va. VI, 11*.
53. Ga. IX, 32; Âp. I, 15, 20; I, 30, 22; Va. XII, 27; Vi. LXXI, 26, 32–34, 37; Yâ. I, 135, 137; Â. *Gri*. III, 9, 6; *S*â. *Gri*. IV, 11, 1.
54. Ga. IX, 73; Âp. I, 15, 21; II, 12, 6; Vi. LXXI, 36; Yâ. I, 137.
55. Vi. LXIII, 8; LXVIII, 12; LXXI, 41, 55; see above, II, IV, 220–221.
56. Âp. I, 30, 19; Vi. LXXI, 32–35; Yâ. I, 137; *S*â. *Gri*. IV, 12, 26.
57. Ga. IX, 54–55; Va. XII, 42; Vi. LXX, 13; LXXI, 56, 58; Yâ. I, 138; *S*â. *Gri*. IV, 11, 6; IV, 12, 7.
58. Mah. XII, 193, 20; XIII, 163, 50[a]; Ba. II, 6, 38*; Vi. LXXI, 60; *S*â. *Gri*. IV, 7, 48.
59. Ga. IX, 22–23; Ba. II, 6, 11, 17; Âp. I, 31, 10, 18; Va. XII, 32–33; Vi. LXXI, 62; Yâ. I, 140.
60., 61. Ga. IX, 65; Ba. II, 6, 21, 31; Âp. I, 15, 22; I, 32, 18; Vi. LXIII, 2; LXXI, 64–68.
62. Ga. IX, 58; Vi. LXVIII. 27; see above, II, 56–57; *S*â. *Gri*. IV, 11, 8.
63. Ga. IX, 9, 50, 56; Ba. II, 6, 5; Vi. LXVIII, 21; LXXI, 69.
64. Ga. IX, 51; Âp. II, 20, 13; Vi. LXXI, 70–71; Pâ. *Gri*. II, 7, 3–4.
65. Vi. LXVIII, 20; LXXI, 39.
66. Ga. IX, 4; Vi. LXXI, 47; *S*â. *Gri*. IV, 11, 9.
67. Vi. LXIII, 13–15, 17.
68. . . . .
69. Vi. LXXI, 44, 46; Yâ. I, 139.
70. Ga. IX, 51; Âp. I, 32, 28; Vi. LXXI, 42–43.
71. Mah. XIII, 104, 15[a].
72. Ga. IX, 32; Ba. II, 6, 9; Âp. I, 32, 5; Vi. LXIII, 16; *S*â. *Gri*. IV, 12, 11.
73. Ga. IX, 32; Ba. II, 6, 13; Âp. I, 31, 23; Yâ. I, 140; Pâ. *Gri*. II, 7, 6; Go. *Gri*. III, 5, 35.
74. Ga. IX, 32; Ba. II, 6, 6; Va. XII, 36; Vi. LXVIII, 19, 23; LXXI, 45; Yâ. I, 138; Go. *Gri*. III, 5, 12.
75. Ga. IX, 60; Vi. LXVIII, 29; LXX, 3; Â. *Gri*. III, 9, 6.
76. Mah. XIII, 104, 61[b]–62[a]; Vi. LXVIII, 34; LXX, 1.
77. Ga. IX, 32; Ba. II, 6, 26;

Va. XII, 45; Vi. LXIII, 46; Yâ. I, 135; Â. Gri. III, 9, 7; Sâ. Gri. IV, 12, 19; Pâ. Gri. II, 7, 6.
78. Ga. IX, 15; Ba. II, 6, 16; Âp. II, 20, 11; Vi. LXIII, 24–25; Yâ. I, 139.
79. . . . .
80. Va. XVIII, 14*; Âp. I, 31, 24; Vi. LXXI, 48–52.
81. Va. XVIII, 15*.
82. Mah. XIII, 104, 69; Vi. LXVIII, 38; LXXI, 53.
83. Vi. LXIV, 12.
84. Yâ. I, 140.
85. Yâ. I, 141.
86. . . . .
87. . . . .
88. Vi. XLIII, 2–7.
89. Vi. XLIII, 8–15.
90. Vi. XLIII, 16–22.
91. . . . .
92. Mah. XIII, 104, 16[a]; Va. XII, 47; Vi. LX, 1; Sâ. Gri. IV, 11, 19.
93. Vi. LXXI, 77.
94. Mah. XIII, 104, 18[b].
95. Ga. XVI, 1–2; Ba. I, 12, 16; Âp. I, 9, 1, 3; Va. XIII, 1–5; Vi. XXX, 1; Yâ. I, 142; Â. Gri. III, 5, 2–3, 14; Sâ. Gri. IV, 5, 1–2; Pâ. Gri. II, 10, 1–2; II, 11, 10–11; Go. Gri. III, 3, 1, 13.
96. Ba. I, 12, 16; Âp. I, 9, 2; Vi. XXX, 2; Yâ. I, 143; Sâ. Gri. IV, 6, 1; Pâ. Gri. II, 12, 1; Go. Gri. III, 3, 14.
97. Ga. XVI, 40; Vi. XXX, 4; Sâ. Gri. IV, 6, 9.
98. Va. XIII, 6–7; Vi. XXX, 3.
99. Ga. XVI, 19; Ba. I, 21, 15; Âp. I, 9, 9–11; Va. XVIII, 12–13; Vi. XXX, 14, 27; Yâ. I, 148; Sâ. Gri. IV, 7, 20.
100. . . . .
101. Va. XIII, 8.
102. Ga. XVI, 5–6.
103. Ga. XVI, 22; Ba. I, 21, 6; Va. XIII, 36–37; Vi. XXX, 8, 9; Yâ. I, 145, 149; Sâ. Gri. IV, 7, 4; Pâ. Gri. II, 11, 2; Go. Gri. III, 3, 17, 19.
104. Ga. XVI, 10, 23; Âp. I, 11, 8, 27–28, 31.
105. Ga. XVI, 15–16, 22; Ba. I, 21, 4; Âp. I, 11, 30–31; Va. XIII, 32–33, 35; Vi. XXX, 9; Yâ. I, 145; Pâ. Gri. II, 11, 2–3; Go. Gri. III, 3, 18–19.
106. Ba. I, 21, 7; Âp. I, 9, 2c–24; I, 11, 29; Va. XIII, 9; Yâ. 145.
107. Ga. XVI, 19, 45; Ba. I, 21, 4; II, 6, 33–34; Âp. I, 10, 22; I, 11, 31; Va. XIII, 17; Yâ. I, 150; Sâ. Gri. IV, 7, 27.
108. Ga. XVI, 7, 19; Ba. I, 21, 5; Âp. I, 9, 14; I, 10, 17; Va. XIII, 11; Vi. XXX, 10; Yâ. I, 148; Sâ. Gri. IV, 7, 24, 37; Pâ. Gri. II, 11, 4, 6; Go. Gri. III, 3, 28.
109. Ga. XVI, 11, 12, 18, 34, 46; Ba. I, 21, 8, 21; Âp. I, 10, 25–26; I, 11, 17, 25–26; I, 32, 12; Vi. XXX, 16; Yâ. I, 149; Sâ. Gri. IV, 7, 5, 36; Pâ. Gri. II, 11, 2, 4.
110. Ga. XVI, 22; Âp. I, 11, 30; Va. XIII, 34; Vi. XXX, 5; Yâ. I, 146; Go. Gri. III, 3, 25.
111. Âp. I, 10, 26; I, 11, 25; Yâ. I, 146.

112. Ga. XVI, 17, 34; Va. XIII, 14, 23; Vi. XXX. 17; *S*â. Gri. IV, 7, 45.
113. Ga. XVI, 7, 12, 35; Ba. I, 21, 4, 5, 17, 22; Âp. I, 9, 28; I, 11, 15, 25, 31; Va. XIII, 10, 21–22; Vi. XXX, 4; Yâ. I, 146, 148, 150; *S*â. Gri. IV, 7, 7–8, 17, 31; Pâ. Gri. II, 11, 1, 4, 6; Go. Gri. III, 3, 20–21.
114. Ba. I, 21, 22*.
115. Ga. XVI, 8; Ba. I, 21, 16; Âp. I, 10, 17; I, 11, 33; Va. XIII, 35; Vi. XXX, 9, 12; Yâ. I, 148, 150; Pâ. Gri. II, 11, 6.
116. Ga. I, 61; XVI, 18; Ba. I, 21, 8; Âp. I, 9, 6; I, 11, 9; Va. XIII, 13, 26–27; Vi. XXX, 15; Yâ. I, 146, 148; *S*â. Gri. IV, 7, 12, 22, 50; Pâ. Gri. II, 11, 6.
117. Ga. XVI, 48; Va. XIII, 16*; *S*â. Gri. IV, 7, 55*; Ba. I, 21, 10–11.
118. Ga. XVI, 34; Ba. I, 21, 20; *S*â. Gri. IV, 7, 2–3; Pâ. Gri. II, 11, 2, 5.
119. *S*â. Gri. IV, 5, 17*; Âp. I, 10, 1–2; Ga. XVI, 36, 38; Vi. XXX, 5, 24–25; Yâ. I, 144, 146; Pâ. Gri. II, 10, 23; II, 11, 2; Go. Gri. III, 3, 22.
120. Ga. XVI, 17; Âp. I, 9, 27; I, 11, 16; Va. XIII, 17–19; Vi. XXX, 18–21; Yâ. I, 151; *S*â. Gri. IV, 7, 23, 32, 34.
121. Ga. XVI, 20, 34; Âp. I, 10, 20; Va. XIII, 20, 28, 31; Vi. XXX, 11, 19–21; Yâ. I, 149; *S*â. Gri. IV, 7, 40, 48; Pâ. Gri. II, 11, 4.
122. Âp. I, 11, 8; Vi. XXX, 7; Yâ. I, 149; *S*â. Gri. IV, 7, 28, 38; Pâ. Gri. II, 11, 1; Go. Gri. III, 3, 28.
123. Ga. XVI, 21; Ba. I, 21, 5; Âp. I, 10, 17–18; Va. XIII, 30; Vi. XXX, 26; Yâ. I, 145, 148; *S*â. Gri. IV, 7, 21; Pâ. Gri. II, 11, 6.
124. . . . .
125. . . . .
126. Ga. I, 59; Vi. XXX, 22; Yâ. I, 147; *S*â. Gri. IV, 7, 33.
127. Yâ. I, 149; Â. Gri. III, 4, 7; *S*â. Gri. IV, 7, 6, 9–11, 13–14; Pâ. Gri. II, 11, 7–9; Go. Gri. III, 3, 24–27.
128. Mah. XIII, 104, 29; Ba. I, 21, 18; Âp. I, 31, 21; Va. XII, 21; Vi. LXIX, 1; Yâ. I, 79.
129. Ba. II, 6, 25; Âp. I, 32, 8; Vi. LXIV, 3–4, 6; Â. Gri. III, 9, 6.
130. Vi. LXIII, 40; Yâ. I, 152.
131. Mah. XIII, 104, 27[b]–28[a]; Vi. LXIII, 19.
132. Vi. LXIII, 41; Yâ. I, 152.
133. . . . .
134. Mah. XIII, 104, 21.
135. Yâ. I, 153.
136. . . . .
137. Vi. LXXI, 76; Yâ. I, 153.
138. Ga. IX, 68; Vi. LXXI, 73–74; Yâ. I, 132.
139. Ga. IX, 20, 32; Âp. I, 31, 13–14; Vi. LXXI, 57; Yâ. I, 132; Go. Gri. III, 5, 19–20.
140. Mah. XIII, 104, 24[b]–25[a]; Ba. II, 6, 21–23; Va. XII,

43; Vi. LXIII, 4, 6–7, 9; *Sâ. Gri.* IV, 12, 12; Go. *Gri.* III, 5, 32–34.
141. Mah. XIII, 104, 35; Vi. LXXI, 2.
142. Âp. I, 15, 18; Yâ. I, 155.
143. Âp. I, 16, 14.
144. Vi. LXXI, 79.
145. . . . .
146. Va. XXVI, 14*.
147. . . . .
148. . . . .
149. . . . .
150. Vi. LXXI, 86; LXXVI, 1; Yâ. I, 217.
151. Mah. XIII, 104, 82; Ga. IX, 39; Âp. I, 31, 2; Yâ. I, 154.
152. Mah. XIII, 104, 23.
153. Âp. I, 31, 21–22.
154. Mah. XIII, 104, 65b–66a; Ba. II, 6, 35; Âp. II, 7, 7–11.
155. Vi. LXXI, 90*; Yâ. I, 154.
156. Mah. XIII, 104, 6; Vi. LXXI, 91*; Va. VI, 7*.
157. Va. VI, 6*.
158. Mah. XIII, 104, 13; Va. VI, 8*; Vi. LXXI, 92*.
159. . . . .
160. . . . .
161. . . . .
162. Âp. I, 1, 14; Ga. XXI, 15.
163. Mah. XIII, 104, 36; Âp. I, 31, 25; Va. XII, 41; Vi. LXXI, 83.
164. Mah. XIII, 104, 37; Vi. LXXI, 80–82.
165. Ga. XXI, 20.
166. Ga. XXI, 21.
167., 168. Ga. XXI, 22.
169. . . . .
170. . . . .
171. . . . .
172. . . . .
173. . . . .
174. Mah. III, 94, 4.
175. Ga. IX, 50, 68–70.
176. Ga. IX, 47, 73; Vi. LXXI. 84–85; Yâ. I, 156.
177. Va. VI, 42*.
178. . . . .
179. Mah. XII, 244, 14b–15a; Yâ. I, 157.
180. Mah. XII, 244, 15b–16a; Yâ. I, 158.
181. Mah. XII, 244, 16b–17a.
182. Mah. XII, 244, 17b–18a.
183. Mah. XII, 244, 18b–19a.
184. Mah. XII, 244, 19b–20a.
185. Mah. XII, 244, 20b–21a.
186. Vi. LVII, 6–7.
187. Vi. LVII, 8.
188. Va. VI, 32*; Yâ. I, 201–202.
189. . . . .
190. . . . .
191. Yâ. I, 202.
192. Vi. XCIII, 7*.
193. . . . .
194. . . . .
195. Vi. XCIII, 8*.
196. Vi. XCIII, 9*.
197. Vi. XCIII, 10*.
198. Vi. XCIII, 11*.
199. Vi. XCIII, 12*.
200. Vi. XCIII, 13*.
201. Ba. II, 5, 6; Vi. LXIV, 1; Yâ. I, 159.
202. Ba. II, 6, 29; Yâ. I, 160.
203. Vi. LXIV, 16; Yâ. I, 159.
204. Yâ. III, 313–314.
205. Ga. XVII, 18; Âp. I, 18, 27.
206. . . . .
207. Ga. XVII, 9–10; Âp. I, 16,

23–27; I, 19, 1; Va. XIV, 3, 22–23; Vi. LI, 19; Yâ. I, 162, 167, 168.
208. Ga. XVII, 10–11; Âp. I, 16, 29; Vi. LI, 17–18; Yâ. I, 167, 168.
209. Ga. XVII, 12, 17; Âp. I, 18, 16–17; Va. XIV, 9–10; Vi. LI, 7, 9, 17; Yâ. I, 161, 168.
210. Mah. XII, 36, 29[a]; Ga. XVII, 17–18; Âp. I, 18, 18, 22–26; I, 19, 1; Va. XIV, 2–3; Vi. LI, 7–9; Yâ. I, 161.
211. Ga. XVII, 14, 16, 17; Âp. I, 17, 17–20; I, 18, 13; I, 19, 15; Va. XIV, 2, 4, 20, 28–29; Vi. LI, 9, 10; Yâ. I, 161–162, 167; *S*â. *Gri*. IV, 11, 11; Go. *Gri*. III, 5, 9.
212. Âp. I, 19, 15[a]*; Va. XIV, 19[a]*; Ga. XVII, 17, 19; Âp. I, 16, 19; I, 17, 3; I, 18, 21; Va. XIV, 2; Vi. LI, 10; Yâ. I, 162.
213. Ga. XVII, 17–19, 20; Âp. I, 17, 4; II, 6, 19–20; Va. XIV, 2; Vi. LI, 11, 18, 20; Yâ. I, 162–164, 167.
214. Ga. XVII, 18; Âp. I, 18, 30; Va. XIV, 3; Vi. LI, 12; Yâ. I, 161, 164, 165.
215. Âp. I, 18, 19; Va. XIV, 5; Vi. LI, 14; Yâ. I, 161, 163.
216. Ga. XVII, 18; Va. XIV, 3, 11; Vi. LI, 15–16; Yâ. I, 163, 164.
217. Mah. XII, 36, 28[b]; Ga. XVII, 18; Âp. I, 16, 18; Va. XIV, 6, 11; Yâ. I, 163.
218. Mah. XII, 36, 27; Va. XIV, 2; Vi. LI, 8.
219. . . . .
220. Mah. XII, 36, 28[a].
221. . . . .
222. Ga. XXIII, 23–24.
223. Âp. I, 18, 3–8, 14.
224. Mah. XII, 265, 11[b]–12[a]; Ba. I, 10, 5*; Va. XIV, 17.
225. Mah. XII, 265, 12[b]–13[a]; Ba. I, 10, 5*; Va. XIV, 17.
226. . . . .
227. Vi. XCII, 32; Yâ. I, 201.
228. Yâ. I, 203.
229. Va. XXIX, 8; Vi. XCI, 3, 15, 16; XCII, 21, 23; Yâ. I, 210.
230. Vi. XCII, 13, 14; Yâ. I, 210.
231. Vi. XCII, 5, 11, 12; Yâ. I, 204–206, 210.
232. Va. XXIX, 12; Vi. XCII, 22, 27; Yâ. I, 211.
233. Va. XXIX, 19; Yâ. I, 212.
234. . . . .
235. . . . .
236. . . . .
237. . . . .
238. . . . .
239. . . . .
240. Mah. XIII, 111, 11[b]–12[a].
241. Mah. XIII, 111, 10[b], 13[b], 14.
242. Mah. XIII, 111, 15[a].
243. . . . .
244. . . . .
245. . . . .
246. . . . .
247. Ga. XVII, 3; Âp. I, 18, 1; Va. XIV, 12; Vi. LVII, 10; Yâ. I, 214.
248. Va. XIV, 16*; Âp. I, 19, 14*; Vi. LVII, 11*; Yâ. I, 215.

249. Va. XIV, 18*; Âp. I, 19, 14*; Vi. LVII, 12*.
250. Ga. XVII, 3; Ba. I, 9, 8; Âp. I, 18, 1; Va. XIV, 12; Vi. LVII, 10; Yâ. I, 214.
251. Va. XIV, 13*; Vi. LVII, 13*; Ga. XVII, 4; Âp. I, 7, 20; Yâ. I, 216.
252. Vi. LVII, 15*.
253. Vi. LVII, 16*; Ga. XVII, 5-6; Âp. I, 17, 14; Yâ. I, 166.
254. . . . .
255. . . . .
256. . . . .
257. . . . .
258. . . . .
259. . . . .
260. Ga. IX, 74; Ba. II, 3, 1; Va. VIII, 17.

Manu V.

1. . . . .
2. . . . .
3. . . . .
4. . . . .
5. Ga. XVII, 32; Âp. I, 17, 26, 28; Va. XIV, 33; Vi. LI, 3, 34, 36; Yâ. I, 171.
6. Ga. XVII, 32, 33; Va. XIV, 33; Vi. LI, 36; Yâ. I, 171.
7. Ga. XVII, 31; Vi. LI, 37; Yâ. I, 171, 173.
8. Ga. XVII, 22-26; Ba. I, 12, 9-11; Âp. I, 17, 22-24; Va. XIV, 34-35; Vi. LI, 38-40; Yâ. I, 170.
9. Ga. XVII, 14; Ba. I, 12, 15; Âp. I, 17, 18; Va. XIV, 37-38; Vi. LI, 38, 42; Yâ. I, 167, 170.
10. Ga. XVII, 14; Ba. I, 12, 14; Âp. I, 17, 19; Vi. LI, 42; Yâ. I, 169.
11. Ga. XVII, 28-29; Ba. I, 12, 1-2; Âp. I, 17, 29, 34; Va. XIV, 48; Vi. LI, 28, 29, 30; Yâ. I, 172.
12. Ga. XVII, 28-29; Ba. I, 12, 3; Âp. I, 17, 32-33, 35; Va. XIV, 48; Vi. LI, 3, 29; Yâ. I, 172, 173, 174.
13. Ga. XVII, 35; Va. XIV, 48; Vi. LI, 27; Yâ. I, 172, 174, 175.
14. Ga. XVII, 29, 34; Ba. I, 12, 3, 8; Va. XIV, 48; Vi. LI, 21, 29; Yâ. I, 173, 174, 175.
15. . . . .
16. Ga. XVII, 36-37; Ba. I, 12, 8; Vi. LI, 21; Yâ. I, 177-178.
17. Ga. XVII, 27; Ba. I, 12, 5; Âp. I, 17, 37; Va. XIV, 39, 44; Vi. LI, 6, 27; Yâ. I, 174.
18. Ga. XVII, 27; Ba. I, 12, 4-5; Âp. I, 17, 37; Va. XIV, 39, 40, 47; Vi. LI, 6, 26; Yâ. I, 177.
19. Ga. XXIII, 5; Vi. LI, 3-4; Yâ. I, 176.
20. Yâ. I, 176.
21. . . . .
22. Va. XIV, 15.
23. . . . .
24. Vi. LI, 35; Yâ. I, 169.
25. Vi. LI, 35; Yâ. I, 169.
26. Yâ. I, 178.
27. Yâ. I, 179.
28. Mah. XII, 10, 6.

29. Mah. XII, 99, 15.
30. . . . .
31. . . . .
32. . . . .
33. . . . .
34. Vi. LI, 62*.
35. Va. XI, 34*.
36. Vi. LI, 59*.
37. . . . .
38. Vi. LI, 60*; Yâ. I, 180.
39. Vi. LI, 61*.
40. Vi. LI, 63*.
41. Va. IV, 6*; Vi. LI, 64*; *S*â. G*ri*. II, 16, 1*.
42. Vi. LI, 65*.
43. Vi. LI, 66*.
44. Vi. LI, 67*.
45. Vi. LI, 68*.
46. Vi. LI, 69*.
47. Vi. LI, 70*; Yâ. I, 181.
48. Vi. LI, 71*; Va. IV, 7*.
49. Vi. LI, 72*.
50. Vi. LI, 73*.
51. Vi. LI, 74*.
52. Mah. XIII, 115, 14[a], 36[a]; 116, 11[a]; Vi. LI, 75*.
53. Mah. XIII, 115, 10, 16; Vi. LI, 76*; Yâ. I, 181.
54. Vi. LI, 77*.
55. Vi. LI, 78*.
56. . . . .
57. . . . .
58. Par. III, 21*; Âp. II, 15, 4–5; Vi. XXII, 26–27; Yâ. III, 18, 23.
59. Ga. XIV, 1; Ba. I, 11, 1; Va. IV, 16; Vi. XXII, 1; Yâ. III, 18; Â. G*ri*. IV, 4, 18; *S*â. G*ri*. IV, 7, 6.
60. Ga. XIV, 13; Ba. I, 11, 2; Âp. II, 15, 2–3; Va. IV, 17–18; Vi. XXII, 5.
61. Va. XIV, 20*; Ga. XIV, 14; Ba. I, 11, 1.
62. Par. III, 31*; Ga. XIV, 15–16; Ba. I, 11, 19–23; Va. IV, 21–22; Yâ. III, 19.
63. . . . .
64. Ga. XIV, 23, 25, 27.
65. Vi. XXII, 85*; Â. G*ri*. IV, 4, 19.
66. Ga. XIV, 17; Ba. I, 11, 31; Vi. XXII, 72; Yâ. III, 20.
67. Vi. XXII, 29–30; Yâ. III, 23.
68. Ba. I, 11, 4; Yâ. III, 1.
69. Ba. I, 11, 4; Âp. II, 15, 6–7; Va. IV, 34; Vi. XXII, 28; Yâ. III, 1; Â. G*ri*. IV, 4, 24; Pâ. G*ri*. III, 10, 4–7.
70. . . . .
71. Ga. XIV, 20; Ba. I, 11, 30; Â. G*ri*. IV, 4, 26; *S*â. G*ri*. IV, 7, 13; Pâ. G*ri*. II, 11, 8; Go. G*ri*. III, 3, 24.
72. Ba. I, 11, 8*; Â. G*ri*. IV, 4, 23.
73. Ga. XIV, 37–39; Ba. I, 11, 24; Âp. II, 15, 9–10; Yâ. III, 16; Â. G*ri*. IV, 4, 16.
74. . . . .
75. Vi. XXII, 39; Yâ. III, 21; Pâ. G*ri*. III, 10, 44.
76. Ga. XIV, 44; Va. IV, 36; Vi. XXII, 40–41; Yâ. III, 21; Pâ. G*ri*. III, 10, 45.
77. Yâ. III, 21.
78. Ga. XIV, 19, 44.
79. Ga. XIV, 6; Ba. I, 11, 17–18; Va. IV, 24; Vi. XXII, 35; Yâ. III, 20.
80. Ga. XIV, 28; Ba. I, 11, 28; Vi. XXII, 42–44; Yâ. III, 24; Â. G*ri*. IV, 4, 21; *S*â.

Gri. IV, 7, 9–10; Pâ. Gri. II, 11, 7; Go. Gri. III, 3, 26.
81. Ga. XIV, 20, 22; Ba. I, 11, 29–30; Vi. XXII, 44; Yâ. III, 24.
82. Vi. XXII, 45–46; Yâ. III, 24–25; Go. Gri. III, 3, 25.
83. Ga. XIV, 2–5; Va. IV, 27–30; Vi. XXII, 1–4; Yâ. III, 22.
84. . . . .
85. Ga. XIV, 30; Ba. I, 9, 5; I, 11, 36; Va. IV, 38; Vi. XXII, 69; Yâ. III, 30.
86. Ba. I, 15, 31.
87. . . . .
88. Vi. XXII, 87 *; Yâ. III, 5.
89. Vi. XXII, 56; Yâ. III, 6.
90. Yâ. III, 6.
91. Vi. XXII, 86 *; Yâ. III, 15.
92. . . . .
93. Va. XIX, 48 *; Ga. XIV, 1, 45–46; Ba. I, 11, 1; Vi. XXII, 48–50; Yâ. III, 27, 28.
94. Va. XIX, 47 *.
95. Ga. XIV, 9–11; Vi. XXII, 47, 52; Yâ. III, 21, 27.
96. . . . .
97. . . . .
98. Yâ. III, 29.
99. . . . .
100. . . . .
101. Ba. I, 11, 33.
102. Vi. XXII, 8; Yâ. III, 15.
103. Par. III, 48 *; Ga. XIV, 31; Vi. XXII, 64; Yâ. III, 26.
104. . . . .
105. Vi. XXII, 88 *; Ba. I, 8, 52; Yâ. I, 194; III, 31.
106. Vi. XXII, 89 *.
107. Vi. XXII, 90 *; Yâ. III, 32, 33.
108. Va. III, 58 *; Vi. XXII, 91 *; Par. VII, 4 *; Yâ. III, 32.
109. Ba. I, 8, 2 *; III, 1, 27 *; Va. III, 60 *; Vi. XXII, 92 *; Yâ. III, 33–34.
110. Vi. XXII, 93 *.
111. Ga. I, 29–30; Ba. I, 8, 32, 46–47; I, 14, 4; Âp. I, 17, 11; Va. III, 49, 50.
112. Ba. I, 8, 33, 46–47; Va. III, 61–62; Vi. XXIII, 7; Yâ. I, 182.
113. . . . .
114. Ba. I, 8, 33; Va. III, 58, 63; Vi. XXIII, 25, 26; Yâ. I, 190.
115. Ga. I, 29; Ba. I, 8, 35; I, 13, 27; I, 14, 16–17; Âp. I, 17, 12; Va. III, 49; Vi. XXIII, 27, 29–30; Yâ. I, 190.
116. Par. VII, 2 *; Ba. I, 8, 50–51; I, 13, 26, 29–32; Âp. I, 17, 13; Vi. XXIII, 8, 10; Yâ. I, 182–183.
117. Par. VII, 3 a *; Vi. XXIII, 9, 11; Yâ. I, 183–184.
118. Par. VII, 28 b–29 a *; Ga. I, 29; Ba. I, 8, 42; I, 13, 11; I, 14, 11–12; Va. III, 49; Vi. XXIII, 13–14, 18; Yâ. I, 184.
119. Ga. I, 33; Ba. I, 8, 36, 38, 43; I, 13, 13; Va. III, 53; Vi. XXIII, 14–15, 18; Yâ. I, 182.

120. Ba. I, 8, 39–42; Va. III, 55; Vi. XXIII, 19–22; Yâ. I, 186–187.
121. Ga. I, 30–31; Ba. I, 8, 45–47; Va. III, 51–52; Vi. XXIII, 23; Yâ. I, 185.
122. Vi. XXIII, 56*; Ga. I, 29; Ba. I, 8, 34; I, 13, 21–25; I, 14, 2; Âp. I, 17, 10; Va. III, 49, 58; Vi. XXIII, 16, 18, 33; Yâ. I, 187–188.
123. Va. III, 59*; Ga. I, 34; Ba. I, 8, 49; I, 14, 3; Vi. XXIII, 5.
124. Va. III, 57*; Ga. I, 31–32; Ba. I, 9, 11; I, 13, 16–20; Va. III, 56; Yâ. I, 188.
125. Vi. XXIII, 38*; Va. XIV, 23; Yâ. I, 189.
126. Ga. I, 42; Va. III, 48; Yâ. I, 191.
127. Mah. XIII, 104, 40; Ba. I, 9, 9*; Va. XIV, 24*; Vi. XXIII, 47*; Yâ. I, 191.
128. Ba. I, 9, 10*; Va. III, 35–36, 47*; Vi. XXIII, 43; Yâ. I, 192.
129. Ba. I, 9, 1*; Vi. XXIII, 48*; Va. III, 46; Yâ. I, 187.
130. Ba. I, 9, 2*; Va. XXVIII, 8*; Vi. XXIII, 49*; Va. III, 45–46; Yâ. I, 187, 193.
131. Vi. XXIII, 50*; Va. III, 45; Yâ. I, 192.
132. Vi. XXIII, 51*; Yâ. I, 194.
133. Vi. XXIII, 52*; Yâ. I, 193.
134. Ga. I, 43; Ba. I, 10, 11–15; Âp. I, 16, 15; Va. VI, 14; Vi. LX, 24; Yâ. I, 17.
135. Vi. XXII, 81*.
136. Va. VI, 18*; Vi. LX, 23; Ba. I, 10, 12–14.
137. Va. VI, 19*; Vi. LX, 26*.
138. Ga. I, 36, 44–45; Ba. I, 8, 26; Âp. I, 16, 7; Va. III, 28; Vi. XXII, 75; LXII, 8.
139. Ga. I, 36; Ba. I, 8, 19–22; Âp. I, 16, 2–6; Va. III, 26–27; Vi. LXII, 6–7; Yâ. I, 20; see also above, II, 60.
140. Âp. II, 3, 4–8.
141. Vi. XXIII, 53*; Ga. I, 38–41; Ba. I, 8, 24–25; Âp. I, 16, 11–13; Va. III, 37; Yâ. I, 195.
142. Ba. I, 10, 34*; Va. III, 42*; Vi. XXIII, 54*; Yâ. I, 195.
143. Vi. XXIII, 55*; Ga. I, 28; Ba. I, 8, 27–29; Va. III, 43.
144. Âp. II, 1, 23; Vi. XXII, 67.
145. Ga. I, 37; Âp. I, 16, 14; Va. III, 38; Vi. XXII, 75; Yâ. I, 196; Go. *Gri.* I, 2, 32.
146. . . . .
147. Ga. XVIII, 1; Ba. II, 3, 44; Va. V, 1; Vi. XXV, 12; see also below, IX, 2.
148. Ba. II, 3, 45; Va. V, 3; Vi. XXV, 13; Yâ. I, 85; see also below, IX, 3.
149. Yâ. I, 86.
150. Vi. XXV, 4–6; Yâ. I, 83.
151. Vi. XXV, 13–14; Yâ. I, 75, 83.
152. . . . .
153. . . . .
154. Yâ. I, 77.
155. Vi. XXV, 15*; Yâ. I, 77.
156. } Yâ. I, 75.
157. }
158. . . . .

159. Âp. II, 23, 5.
160. Vi. XXV, 17*; Par. IV, 26*; Yâ. I, 75.
161. . . . .
162. . . . .
163. . . . .
164. Va. XXI, 14[b].
165. . . . .
166. Yâ. I, 87.
167. } Yâ. I, 89.
168. }
169. . . . .

Manu VI.

1. } Ga. III, 1; Ba. II, 17, 2–5; Âp. II, 21, 1–5, 19; II, 22, 6–7; Vi. XCIV, 1–2; Yâ. III, 45.
2. }
3. Ga. III, 28; Ba. II, 11, 15; Âp. II, 21, 8–9; Vi. XCIV, 3; Yâ. III, 45.
4. Ga. III, 27; Ba. II, 11, 15; Va. IX, 9; Vi. XC, 4; Yâ. III, 45.
5. Ga. III, 29; Ba. II, 11, 15; Va. IX, 12; Vi. XCIV, 5; Yâ. III, 46.
6. Ga. III, 34; Ba. II, 11, 15; III, 3, 19; Âp. II, 22, 1, 13–14, 17; Va. IX, 1; Vi. XCIV, 8–10; Yâ. III, 46.
7. Ga. III, 29, 30; Ba. II, 11, 15; III, 3, 5–7, 20; Âp. II, 22, 7; Va. IX, 7.
8. Ba. III, 3, 19; Âp. II, 21, 21; II, 22, 11; Va. IX, 8; Vi. XCIV, 6; Yâ. III, 48.
9. Ba. III, 3, 5–7, 20; Âp. II, 22, 12; Va. IX, 10.
10. . . . .
11. Âp. II, 22, 17–18.
12. . . . .
13. Ga. III, 26; Ba. II, 11, 15; Âp. II, 22, 2, 17; II, 23, 2; Va. IX, 4; Vi. XCV, 7–11; Yâ. III, 49.
14. . . . .
15. Âp. II, 22, 24; Vi. XCIV, 12; Yâ. III, 47.
16. Va. IX, 4; Yâ. III, 46.
17. Ba. III, 3, 2, 9–12; Vi. XCV, 14–15; Yâ. III, 49.
18. Ga. III, 35; Ba. II, 11, 15; III, 2, 11; Âp. II, 23, 1; Vi. XCIV, 11; Yâ. III, 47.
19. Vi. XCV, 5–6; Yâ. III, 50.
20. Vi. XCV, 12–13; Yâ. III, 50.
21. Ba. III, 2, 9, 11; Âp. II, 23, 2.
22. Ga. III, 26; Ba. II, 11, 15; Va. IX, 9; Vi. XCIV, 10; Yâ. III, 48, 51.
23. Vi. XCV, 1–4; Yâ. III, 52.
24. . . . .
25. Âp. II, 21, 21; Va. IX, 11; Yâ. III, 54.
26. Va. IX, 5, 11; Vi. XCIV, 7; Yâ. III, 45, 51, 54.
27. Yâ. III, 54.
28. Vi. XCIV, 13*; Yâ. III, 55.
29. . . . .
30. . . . .
31. Ba. III, 3, 9, 13–14; Âp. II, 23, 4; II, 23, 2; Yâ. III, 55.
32. . . . .
33. Ba. II, 17, 1–6; Vi. XCVI, 1.

34. Ba. II, 17, 16*; II, 17, 15.
35.
36.
37. } Ba. II, 11, 34; Âp. II, 24, 8; Yâ. III, 57.
38. Ba. II, 17, 18–28; Vi. XCVI, 1–2; Yâ. III, 56.
39. Mah. XII, 245, 28; 279, 22; Ba. II, 17, 29; Va. X, 1.
40. Ba. II, 17, 30; Va. X, 2–3.
41. Ga. III, 16; Ba. II, 11, 24; II, 17, 31; Va. X, 12, 28.
42. Mah. XII, 246, 4[b]–5[a].
43. Mah. XII, 246, 5[b]; Ga. III, 11, 14; Ba. II, 11, 16; Âp. II, 21, 10; Va. X, 6; Vi. XCVI, 2.
44. Mah. XII, 246, 7; Ga. III, 18–19, 25; Ba. II, 11, 19, 21; II, 17, 44; Âp. II, 21, 11; Va. X, 9–10, 13, 27; Vi. XCVI, 10–11.
45. Mah. XII, 246, 15; Vi. XCVI, 18.
46. Ba. II, 11, 25; II, 17, 43; II, 18, 2; Vi. XCVI, 14–17.
47. Mah. XII, 279, 6[a]; Ga. III, 24; Ba. II, 11, 23; Va. X, 29; Vi. XCVI, 19–20, 23.
48. Mah. XII, 279, 6[b]; Ba. II, 18, 3.
49. Mah. XII, 331, 30; Âp. II, 21, 13; Va. X, 17, 20.
50. Va. X, 21*.
51. Vi. XCVI, 5; Yâ. III, 59.
52. Ga. III, 22; Ba. II, 11, 18; II, 17, 10–11; Va. X, 6; Yâ. III, 58.
53. Vi. XCVI, 8; Yâ. III, 60.
54. Vi. XCVI, 7; Yâ. III, 60.
55. Ba. II, 18, 12; Va. X, 24–25; Vi. XCVI, 3; Yâ. III, 59.
56. Ga. III, 15; Ba. II, 11, 22; II, 18, 4–6; Va. X, 7–8; Vi. XCVI, 6; Yâ. III, 59.
57. Mah. XII, 279, 10; Va. X, 22*; Vi. XCVI, 4.
58. Mah. XII, 279, 11[b]; Vi. XCVI, 9.
59. Ba. II, 18, 10–13; Va. X, 25.
60. Ba. II, 18, 2–3; Yâ. III, 61.
61. Vi. XCVI, 36, 38; Yâ. III, 63–64.
62. Vi. XCVI, 27–29, 37; Yâ. III, 63–64.
63. Vi. XCVI, 39; Yâ. III, 63–64.
64. Vi. XCVI, 40–42; Yâ. III, 63–64.
65. Va. X, 14; Yâ. III, 63–64.
66. Va. X, 18; Yâ. III, 65.
67. . . . .
68. . . . .
69. . . . .
70. Va. X, 5.
71. Va. XXV, 6; Ba. IV, 1, 24.
72. Vi. XCVI, 24.
73. Vi. XCVI, 25.
74. . . . .
75. Âp. II, 21, 14–16.
76. Mah. XII, 330, 42; Mai. Up. III, 4; Vi. XCVI, 43–53.
77. Mah. XII, 330, 43; Mai. Up. III, 4; Vi. XCVI, 43–53.
78. . . . .
79. . . . .
80. . . . .
81. . . . .
82. . . . .
83. Ba. II, 18, 20–27; Âp. II, 21, 4; Va. X, 4.
84. . . . .
85. . . . .

86. . . . .
87. Ga. III, 2–3; Ba. II, 11, 12; Âp. II, 21, 1.
88. Ga. III, 1; Âp. II, 21, 2.
89. Ga. III, 36; Va. VIII, 14; Vi. LIX, 27–29.
90. Va. VIII, 15*; VIII, 16.
91. . . . .
92. Va. X, 30; Yâ. III, 66.
93. . . . .
94. . . . .
95. Va. X, 26.
96. . . . .
97. . . . .

Manu VII.

1. . . . .
2. . . . .
3. . . . .
4. . . . .
5. . . . .
6. . . . .
7. . . . .
8. . . . .
9. . . . .
10. . . . .
11. . . . .
12. . . . .
13. . . . .
14. Yâ. I, 353.
15. . . . .
16. Ga. XII, 51; Va. XIX, 9; Vi. III, 91; Yâ. I, 367.
17. . . . .
18. Mah. XII, 15, 2.
19. Yâ. I, 355.
20. . . . .
21. . . . .
22. Mah. XII, 15, 34.
23. . . . .
24. . . . .
25. Mah. XII, 15, 11; Vi. IV, 95*.
26. Ga. XI, 2; Yâ. I, 308–309.
27. . . . .
28. . . . .
29. . . . .
30. . . . .
31. Ga. XI, 4.
32. Vi. IV, 96*; Yâ. I, 333.
33. Vi. IV, 97*.
34. . . . .
35. . . . .
36. . . . .
37. Vi. III, 76.
38. Vi. III, 77.
39. . . . .
40. . . . .
41. . . . .
42. . . . .
43. Ga. XI, 3; Yâ. I, 310.
44. . . . .
45. . . . .
46. } Vi. III, 50.
47. }
48. Vi. III, 51–52.
49. . . . .
50. . . . .
51. . . . .
52. . . . .
53. . . . .
54. Vi. III, 71; Yâ. I, 311.
55. . . . .
56. Yâ. I, 311.
57. . . . .
58. Yâ. I, 311.
59. . . . .

60. . . . .
61., 62. Vi. III, 16-21.
63. . . . .
64. . . . .
65. . . . .
66. . . . .
67. . . . .
68. . . . .
69. Vi. III, 4-5; Yâ. I, 320.
70. Mah. XII, 86, 5; Vi. III, 6.
71. . . . .
72. . . . .
73. . . . .
74. . . . .
75. . . . .
76. Âp. II, 25, 2-3.
77. . . . .
78. Ga. XI, 12-18; Ba. I, 18, 7-8; Va. XIX, 3-6; Vi. III, 70; Yâ. I, 312-313.
79. Âp. II, 26, 1; Vi. III, 78, 81, 84; Yâ. I, 313.
80. Yâ. I, 321.
81. . . . .
82., 83. Yâ. I, 314.
84. Va. XXX. 7*; Yâ. I, 315.
85. Ga. V, 20; Vi. XCIII, 1-4.
86. . . . .
87. Ga. X, 16; Ba. I, 18, 9; Vi. III, 43.
88. Vi. III, 44; Yâ. I, 322.
89. Âp. II, 26, 2-3; Vi. III, 45; Yâ. I, 323.
90. Ba. I, 18, 10; Yâ. I, 323.
91., 92., 93. Ga. X, 18; Ba. I, 18, 11; Âp. II, 10, 11; Yâ. I, 325.
94. Âp. II, 26, 3; Yâ. I, 324.
95. Yâ. I, 324.
96., 97. Ga. X, 20-23.
98. . . . .
99. Va. XVI, 6; Yâ. I, 316.
100. . . . .
101. . . . .
102. Mah. XII, 140, 7.
103. Mah. XII, 140, 8.
104. . . . .
105. Mah. XII, 83, 49; 140, 24.
106. Mah. XII, 140, 25.
107. . . . .
108. . . . .
109. . . . .
110. . . . .
111. . . . .
112. . . . .
113. . . . .
114. . . . .
115. Mah. XII, 87, 3; Âp. II, 26, 4-5; Vi. III, 7-10.
116. Mah. XII, 87, 4; Vi. III, 11-12.
117. Mah. XII, 87, 5; Vi. III, 13-15.
118. Mah. XII, 87, 6a.
119. Mah. XII, 87, 6b-8a.
120. Mah. XII, 87, 9b-10a.
121. Mah. XII, 87, 10b-11a; Âp. II, 26, 4.
122. Mah. XII, 87, 11b-12a; Yâ. I, 337.
123. Mah. XII, 87, 12b-13a; Yâ. I, 337.
124. Yâ. I, 337.
125. . . . .
126. . . . .
127. Mah. XII, 87, 13b-14a.
128. Ba. I, 18, 15; Âp. II, 26, 9.
129. . . . .
130. Ga. X, 24-25; Ba. I, 18, 1; Va. I, 42; Vi. III, 22, 24.

131. Ga. X, 27; Va. I, 42; Vi. III, 25.
132. Ga. X, 27; Vi. III, 23, 25.
133. Ga. X, 11; Âp. II, 26, 10; Va. I, 43; XIX, 23; Vi. III, 26.
134. Mah. XIII, 61, 30; Ga. X, 9; Âp. II, 25, 11; Vi. III, 79.
135. Yâ. III, 44.
136. Va. I, 44; Vi. III, 27.
137. Va. XIX, 26–27.
138. Ga. X, 31–32; Va. XIX, 28; Vi. III, 32.
139. Mah. XII, 87, 18b.
140. . . . .
141. Vi. III, 73; Yâ. II, 3.
142. Ga. X, 7–8; Ba. I, 18, 1; Âp. II, 10, 6; Va. XIX, 1; Vi. III, 2; Yâ. I, 334.
143. Mah. XIII, 61, 31.
144. . . . .
145. . . . .
146. . . . .
147., 148. Yâ. I, 343.
149. . . . .
150. . . . .
151. . . . .
152. . . . .
153. . . . .
154. . . . .
155., 156., 157., 158. Vi. III, 38; Yâ. I, 344.
159. Vi. III, 38; Yâ. I, 345.
160. Vi. III, 39; Yâ. I, 346.
161. . . . .
162. . . . .
163. . . . .
164. . . . .
165. . . . .
166. . . . .
167. . . . .
168. . . . .
169. . . . .
170. . . . .
171. Yâ. I, 347.
172. . . . .
173. . . . .
174. . . . .
175. . . . .
176. . . . .
177. . . . .
178. . . . .
179. . . . .
180. . . . .
181. . . . .
182. Vi. III, 40; Yâ. I, 347.
183. Vi. III, 41.
184. . . . .
185. . . . .
186. . . . .
187. . . . .
188. . . . .
189. . . . .
190. . . . .
191. Mah. XII, 100, 47.
192. . . . .
193. . . . .
194. . . . .
195. . . . .
196. . . . .
197. . . . .
198. . . . .
199. . . . .
200. . . . .
201. . . . .
202. Vi. III, 47.
203. Vi. III, 42; Yâ. I, 342.
204. . . . .
205. Yâ. I, 348.

206. . . . .
207. . . . .
208. Yâ. I, 351.
209. . . . .
210. . . . .
211. . . . .
212. . . . .
213. . . . .
214. . . . .
215. . . . .
216. Yâ. I, 326.
217. . . . .
218. Vi. III, 87.
219. Vi. III, 88.
220. Vi. III, 85.
221. Yâ. I, 328.
222. Yâ. I, 328.
223. } Yâ. I, 329.
224. }
225. Yâ. I, 330.
226. . . . .

Manu VIII.

1. Ga. XIII, 26; Va. XVI, 2; Vi. III, 72; Yâ. I, 359; II, 1.
2. . . . .
3. Ga. XI, 19–24; Va. I, 17; XVI, 4–5.
4. . . . .
5. . . . .
6. . . . .
7. . . . .
8. . . . .
9. Ga. XIII, 26; Va. XVI, 2; Vi. III, 73; Yâ. II, 3.
10. . . . .
11. . . . .
12. . . . .
13. . . . .
14. . . . .
15. Mah. III, 313, 28; XII, 90, 15b–c.
16. . . . .
17. . . . .
18. Ba. I, 19, 8*; Ga. XIII, 11.
19. Ba. I, 19, 8*.
20. . . . .
21. . . . .
22. . . . .
23. . . . .
24. . . . .
25. } Yâ. II, 13–15.
26. }
27. Ga. X, 48; Va. XVI, 8–9; Vi. III, 65.
28. Vi. III, 65.
29. . . . .
30. Ga. X, 36–38; Va. XVI, 19–20; Yâ. II, 33.
31. Yâ. II, 33.
32. Yâ. II, 33.
33. . . . .
34. . . . .
35. Vi. III, 63; Yâ. II, 35.
36. Vi. III, 64; Yâ. II, 35.
37. Ga. X, 44; Va. III, 14; Vi. III, 58; Yâ. II, 34.
38. Ga. X, 43; Vi. III, 56–57; Yâ. II, 34.
39. Ga. X, 45; Va. III, 13; Vi. III, 58–62; Yâ. II, 35.
40. Ga. X, 46–47; Âp. II, 26, 8; Vi. III, 66–67; Yâ. II, 36.
41. Ga. XI, 11, 20; Ba. I, 2, 1–8; Âp. II, 15, 1; Va. I, 17; XIX, 7; Vi. III, 3; Yâ. I, 360.
42. . . . .

43. Ga. XIII, 27.
44. Ga. XI, 23–24; Âp. II, 29, 6; Va. XVI, 4–5.
45. . . . .
46. . . . .
47. . . . .
48. . . . .
49. . . . .
50. Vi. VI, 18; Yâ. II, 40.
51. . . . .
52. . . . .
53.–56. Yâ. II, 16.
57. . . . .
58. . . . .
59. Yâ. II, 11.
60. . . . .
61. Ga. XIII, 1.
62. Ba. I, 19, 13; Vi. VIII, 8; Yâ. II, 68.
63. Ga. XIII, 2; Âp. II, 29, 7; Va. XVI, 28; Vi. VIII, 8; Yâ. II, 68.
64. Ga. XIII, 2; Vi. VIII, 3; Yâ. II, 70–71.
65. Ba. I, 19, 13; Vi. VIII, 2; Yâ. II, 70.
66. Ba. I, 19, 13; Vi. VIII, 2, 3; Yâ. II, 70–71.
67. Ba. I, 19, 13; Vi. VIII, 2; Yâ. II, 70.
68. Va. XVI, 30*.
69. Va. XVI, 29; Yâ. II, 69.
70. . . . .
71. . . . .
72. Ga. XIII, 9; Vi. VIII, 6; Yâ. II, 72.
73. Vi. VIII, 39*; Yâ. II, 78, 80.
74. Ba. I, 19, 7; Vi. VIII, 13–14.
75. Ga. XIII, 7; Ba. I, 19, 14–15; Âp. II, 29, 9–10.
76. Vi. VIII, 12.
77. Yâ. II, 72.
78. . . . .
79. Ga. XIII, 5; Âp. II, 29, 7; Vi. VIII, 24; Yâ. II, 73.
80. . . . .
81. . . . .
82. . . . .
83. . . . .
84. . . . .
85. . . . .
86. . . . .
87. Âp. II, 29, 7; Vi. VIII, 19.
88. Vi. VIII, 20–23.
89. Vi. VIII, 25; Yâ. II, 73–74.
90. Ba. I, 19, 10; Vi. VIII, 26; Yâ. II, 75.
91. . . . .
92. . . . .
93. Va. XVI, 33*.
94. . . . .
95. . . . .
96. . . . .
97. . . . .
98. Ba. I, 19, 12 b-c*; Va. XVI, 34*; Ga. XIII, 14–15.
99. Ba. I, 19, 12 d*; Ga. XIII, 16.
100. Ga. XIII, 18–19.
101. . . . .
102. Ba. I, 10, 24*.
103. . . . .
104. Ga. XIII, 24–25; Va. XVI, 36; Vi. VIII, 15; Yâ. II, 83.
105. Yâ. II, 83.
106. Ba. I, 19, 16; Vi. VIII, 16.
107. Ga. XIII, 6; Yâ. II, 76.
108. Yâ. II, 113.
109. Ga. XIII, 12–13; Vi. VIII, 19.

110. . . . .
111. . . . .
112. Va. XVI, 36*; Ga. XXIII, 29.
113. Vi. VIII, 22–23.
114.–115. Vi. XI–XII; Yâ. II, 103–109.
116. . . . .
117. Vi. VIII, 40*.
118. . . . .
119.–123. Yâ. II, 81.
124. Ga. XII, 46–47; Vi. V, 2–8.
125. . . . .
126. Ga. XII, 51; Yâ. I, 367.
127.–128. Va. XIX, 43; Yâ. I, 356.
129.–130. Yâ. I, 366.
131.–137. Vi. IV, 1–13; Yâ. I, 361–364.
138. Vi. IV, 14*; Yâ. I, 365.
139. Vi. VI, 20–21; Yâ. II, 42.
140. Ga. XII, 29; Va. II, 51; Yâ. II, 37.
141. Yâ. II, 37.
142. Va. II, 48*; Vi. VI, 2; Yâ. II, 37.
143. Ga. XII, 32; Vi. VI, 5.
144. Vi. VI, 6; Yâ. II, 59.
145. Vi. VI, 7–8; Yâ. II, 58.
146. . . . .
147.–148. Ga. XII, 37; Va. XVI, 16–17; Yâ. II, 24.
149. Va. XVI, 18*; Ga. XII, 38–39; Yâ. II, 25.
150. . . . .
151. Ga. XII, 31, 36; Vi. VI, 11–14, 16–17; Yâ. II, 39.
152. . . . .
153. Ga. XII, 30, 34–35.
154. . . . .
155. . . . .
156. . . . .
157. . . . .
158. Vi. VI, 41; Yâ. II, 53.
159. Va. XVI, 31*; Ga. XII, 41; Vi. VI, 41; Yâ. II, 47, 53.
160. Vi. VI, 41; Yâ. II, 54.
161. . . . .
162. . . . .
163. Yâ. II, 32.
164. Vi. VII, 11.
165. Vi. VII, 7; Yâ. II, 89.
166. Vi. VI, 39; Yâ. II, 45.
167. . . . .
168. Vi. VII, 6; Yâ. II, 89.
169. . . . .
170. Va. XIX, 14–15.
171. . . . .
172. . . . .
173. . . . .
174. . . . .
175. . . . .
176. Vi. VI, 19; Yâ. II, 40.
177. . . . .
178. . . . .
179. . . . .
180. Yâ. II, 65.
181. . . . .
182. . . . .
183. . . . .
184. . . . .
185. . . . .
186. . . . .

187. . . . .
188. . . . .
189. Yâ. II, 66.
190. . . . .
191. Vi. V, 169–171.
192. . . . .
193. . . . .
194. . . . .
195. . . . .
196. . . . .
197. . . . .
198. . . . .
199. Yâ. II, 168.
200. . . . .
201. . . . .
202. Vi. V, 164–165; Yâ. II, 169–170.
203. Yâ. II, 245.
204. Yâ. I, 66.
205. . . . .
206. . . . .
207. Yâ. II, 265.
208. . . . .
209. . . . .
210. . . . .
211. Yâ. II, 259.
212. . . . .
213. . . . .
214. . . . .
215. 216. 217. Âp. II, 28, 2–3; Vi. V, 153–154; Yâ. II, 193.
218. . . . .
219. Vi. V, 168; Yâ. II, 192.
220. . . . .
221. . . . .
222. Yâ. II, 177.
223. . . . .
224. 225. Yâ. I, 66.
226. . . . .
227. . . . .
228. . . . .
229. . . . .
230. Vi. V, 137; Yâ. II, 164.
231. Vi. V, 139.
232. Vi. V, 138; Yâ. II, 164.
233. . . . .
234. . . . .
235. Vi. V, 137–138.
236. . . . .
237. Yâ. II, 167.
238. . . . .
239. . . . .
240. Ga. XII, 19–20; Âp. II, 28, 5; Vi. V, 140–146; Yâ. II, 162.
241. Ga. XII, 21–26; Vi. V, 147–149; Yâ. II, 161.
242. Vi. V, 150; Yâ. II, 163.
243. Âp. II, 28, 1.
244. . . . .
245. . . . .
246. 247. Yâ. II, 151.
248. . . . .
249. . . . .
250. Yâ. II, 151.
251. . . . .
252. . . . .
253. . . . .
254. . . . .
255. . . . .
256. Yâ. II, 152.
257. Yâ. II, 153.
258. . . . .
259. . . . .
260. . . . .
261. . . . .
262. Va. XVI, 13–15; Yâ. II, 154.
263. Yâ. II, 153.
264. . . . .
265. Yâ. II, 153.

266. . . . .
267. Ga. XII, 1, 8, 10; Yâ. II, 207.
268. Ga. XII, 11–13; Yâ. II, 207.
269. Vi. V, 33–35, 37–38; Yâ. II, 205–206.
270. Ga. XII, 1; Âp. II, 27, 14; Vi. V, 23.
271. Vi. V, 25.
272. Vi. V, 24.
273. Vi. V, 26.
274. Vi. V, 27; Yâ. II, 204.
275. Vi. V, 28.
276. . . . .
277. . . . .
278. . . . .
279. Ga. XII, 1; Vi. V, 19; Yâ. II, 215.
280. Yâ. II, 215.
281. Ga. XII, 7; Âp. II, 27, 15; Vi. V, 20.
282. Vi. V, 21–22.
283. Vi. V, 65.
284. Vi. V, 66–72; Yâ. II, 218–220.
285. Vi. V, 55–59.
286. Vi. V, 75–76.
287. Vi. V, 75–76; Yâ. II, 222.
288. . . . .
289. . . . .
290. . . . .
291. Yâ. II, 299.
292. Yâ. II, 298–299.
293. . . . .
294. . . . .
295. . . . .
296. . . . .
297.–298. } Vi. V, 50–54.
299.–300. } Ga. II, 43–44; Âp. I, 8, 30.
301. . . . .
302. Âp. II, 25, 15; Vi. V, 196; Yâ. I, 335.
303. . . . .
304. Yâ. I, 334.
305. Mah. XII, 75, 7; Va. I, 44.
306. Yâ. I, 334.
307. . . . .
308. Yâ. I, 336.
309. . . . .
310. . . . .
311. . . . .
312. . . . .
313. . . . .
314. Ga. XII, 43; Ba. II, 1, 16; Âp. I, 25, 4; Va. XX, 41; Vi. LII, 1; Yâ. III, 257.
315. Ba. II, 1, 17; Va. XX, 41.
316. Ba. II, 1, 17*; Ga. XII, 44–45; Âp. I, 25, 4–5; Va. XX, 41; Vi. LII, 2; Yâ. III, 257.
317. Va. XIX, 44*; Âp. I, 19, 16*.
318. Va. XIX, 45*.
319. . . . .
320. Vi. V, 12.
321. Vi. V, 13.
322. Vi. V, 81–82.
323. . . . .
324.–325. } Vi. V, 77–78.
326.–331. } Vi. V, 83–86.
332. Yâ. II, 230.
333. . . . .
334. . . . .
335. Mah. XII, 121, 60; Yâ. I, 357*.
336. . . . .

337. } Ga. XII, 15-17.
338. }
339. Ga. XII, 28; Âp. I, 28, 3; Yâ. II, 166.
340. Ga. XII, 49-50.
341. . . . .
342. . . . .
343. . . . .
344. . . . .
345. . . . .
346. . . . .
347. . . . .
348. Ba. II, 4, 18; Va. III, 24.
349. Ga. VII, 25; Ba. II, 4, 18; Va. III, 24.
350. Va. III, 17*; Ba. I, 18, 12-13; Va. III, 15-16; Vi. V, 191-192; V, 189*.
351. Va. III, 18*; Ba. I, 18, 13; Va. III, 17; Vi. V, 190*.
352. . . . .
353. . . . .
354. Âp. II, 26, 19; Yâ. II, 285.
355. Âp. II, 26, 18.
356. . . . .
357. } Yâ. II, 284.
358. }
359. Ba. II, 4, 2*; II, 4, 1; Âp. II, 26, 20.
360. . . . .
361. Yâ. II, 285.
362. Ba. II, 4, 3*.
363. Yâ. II, 293.
364. }
365. } Yâ. II, 288.
366. }
367. }
368. . . . .
369. . . . .
370. . . . .
371. Mah. XII, 165, 64; Ga. XXIII, 14; Vi. V, 18.
372. Mah. XII, 165, 65; Ga. XXIII, 15; Va. XXI, 1-3.
373. Mah. XII, 165, 66[b].
374. Ga. XII, 2; Ba. II, 3, 52; Âp. II, 27, 9; Va. XXI, 1, 5; Yâ. II, 286, 294.
375. . . . .
376. . . . .
377. Âp. II, 26, 20; Va. XXI, 2-3; Yâ. II, 286.
378. Vi. V, 40; Yâ. II, 286.
379. . . . .
380. Ga. VIII, 13; Ba. I, 18, 17; Vi. V, 2.
381. . . . .
382. . . . .
383. . . . .
384. . . . .
385. Vi. V, 41, 43; Yâ. II, 294.
386. Vi. V, 196*.
387. . . . .
388. . . . .
389. Vi. V, 163; Yâ. II, 237.
390. . . . .
391. . . . .
392. Vi. V, 94; Yâ. II, 263.
393. . . . .
394. Âp. II, 26, 16-17.
395. . . . .
396. Yâ. II, 238.
397. Yâ. II, 179.
398. Yâ. II, 261.
399. Vi. V, 130; Yâ. II, 261.
400. Yâ. II, 262.
401. Yâ. II, 252.
402. Yâ. II, 251.
403. Va. XIX, 13.
404. . . . .
405. . . . .
406. . . . .
407. Vi. V, 132-133.
408. . . . .

409. . . . .
410. . . . .
411. . . . .
412. . . . .
413. . . . .
414. . . . .
415. . . . .
416. . . . .
417. . . . .
418. . . . .
419. . . . .
420. . . . .

Manu IX.

1. . . . .
2. Ga. XVIII, 1; Ba. II, 3, 44; Va. V, 1; Vi. XXV, 12–13; Yâ. I, 85; see also above, V, 147–148.
3. Mah. XIII, 46, 14; Ba. II, 3, 45*; Va. V, 3*.
4. Ga. XVIII, 22; Ba. IV, 1, 12, 17–19; Va. XVII, 69–70; Yâ. I, 64.
5. . . . .
6. Mah. III, 12, 68.
7. . . . .
8. Yâ. I, 56.
9. Yâ. I, 81.
10. . . . .
11. . . . .
12. . . . .
13. . . . .
14. . . . .
15. . . . .
16. . . . .
17. Mah. XIII, 40, 12[b]–13[a].
18. Mah. XIII, 40, 11[b]–12[a]; Ba. I, 11, 7; see also above, II, 66.
19. . . . .
20. *S*â. G*ri*. III, 13, 5; Âp. *S*r. I, 9, 9.
21. . . . .
22. . . . .
23. . . . .
24. . . . .
25. . . . .
26. . . . .
27. Mah. XIII, 46, 11.
28. . . . .
29. See above, V, 165.
30. Va. XXI, 14; see above, V, 164.
31. . . . .
32. Ga. XVIII, 9–14; Âp. II, 13, 6–7; Va. XVII, 6–9, 63–64.
33. . . . .
34. . . . .
35. . . . .
36. . . . .
37. . . . .
38. . . . .
39. . . . .
40. . . . .
41. . . . .
42. . . . .
43. . . . .
44. . . . .
45. Âp. II, 14, 16.
46. . . . .
47. Vi. V, 160; Yâ. I, 65.
48. . . . .
49. . . . .
50. Va. XVII, 8*.
51. . . . .
52. . . . .
53. . . . .

54. Par. IV, 16*.
55. . . . .
56. . . . .
57. . . . .
58. . . . .
59. Ga. XVIII, 4–5; Ba. II, 4, 9–10; Va. XVII, 56; Yâ. I, 68.
60. Va. XVII, 61; Yâ. I, 68.
61. Ga. XVIII, 8.
62.–63. Yâ. I, 69.
64. . . . .
65. . . . .
66. . . . .
67. . . . .
68. . . . .
69. . . . .
70. . . . .
71. Vi. V, 160–161; Yâ. I, 65.
72.–73. Vi. V, 162; Yâ. I, 66.
74. . . . .
75. Vi. XXV, 9–10; Yâ. I, 84.
76. Ga. XVIII, 15, 17; Va. XVII, 75–80.
77. . . . .
78. . . . .
79. . . . .
80. Yâ. I, 73.
81. Ba. II, 4, 6*.
82. . . . .
83. . . . .
84. . . . .
85. . . . .
86. Vi. XXVI, 1; Yâ. I, 88.
87. Mah. XIII, 46, 36[b]; Vi. XXVI, 2–3.
88. Ga. XVIII, 21; Va. XVII, 70; Ba. IV, 1, 11.
89. . . . .
90. Mah. XIII, 44, 16; Ba. IV, 1, 14[a-b]*; Ga. XVIII, 20; Va. XVII, 67–68; Vi. XXIV, 40; Yâ. I, 64.
91. . . . .
92. Ga. XVIII, 20.
93. Vi. XXIV, 41.
94. Mah. XIII, 44, 14[a].
95. Mah. XIII, 44, 27[a].
96. . . . .
97. . . . .
98. Âp. II, 13, 11.
99. . . . .
100. . . . .
101. . . . .
102. . . . .
103. . . . .
104. Ga. XXVIII, 1; Ba. II, 3, 3, 8; Vi. XVIII, 36; Yâ. II, 117.
105. Ga. XXVIII, 3; Ba. II, 3, 13; Âp. II, 14, 6.
106. . . . .
107. Va. XVII, 1; Vi. XV, 45.
108. . . . .
109. Mah. XIII, 105, 6[a].
110. . . . .
111. Ga. XXVIII, 4.
112. Ga. XXVIII, 5–7; Ba. II, 3, 4; Vi. XVIII, 37; Yâ. II, 114.
113. . . . .
114. Ga. XXVIII, 11–13; Ba. II, 3, 6; Va. XVII, 43; Yâ. II, 114.
115. Âp. II, 13, 13.
116. Ga. XXVIII, 8.
117. Ga. XXVIII, 9–10; Va. XVII, 42.
118. Vi. XVIII, 35; Yâ. II, 124.
119. Ba. II, 3, 9.
120. . . . .

121. . . . .
122. . . . .
123. Ga. XXVIII, 14.
124. Ga. XXVIII, 15.
125. Ga. XXVIII, 16.
126. . . . .
127. Ga. XXVIII, 18; Ba. II, 3, 15; Va. XVII, 15–17; Vi. XV, 5.
128. . . . .
129. . . . .
130. Mah. XIII, 45, 11; Ba. II, 3, 14.
131. Mah. XIII, 45, 12; Ga. XXVIII, 24; Ba. II, 3, 43; Va. XVII, 46; Vi. XVII, 21.
132. . . . .
133. Mah. XIII, 45, 13 b; Yâ. II, 128.
134. . . . .
135. . . . .
136. Ga. XXVIII, 19.
137. Ba. II, 16, 6*; Va. XVII, 5*; Vi. XV, 46*; Yâ. I, 78.
138. Vi. XV, 44*.
139. Vi. XV, 47*.
140. Ba. II, 3, 16*.
141. Va. XV, 9–10; Ba. Par. 16.
142. . . . .
143.
144. } Ga. XXVIII, 23.
145. . . . .
146. . . . .
147. . . . .
148. . . . .
149. Va. XVII, 47.
150. Mah. XIII, 47, 11.
151. . . . .
152. Vi. XVIII, 1.
153. Ba. II, 3, 10; Va. XVII, 48–50; Vi. XVIII, 2–5; Yâ. II, 125.
154. Vi. XVIII, 32.
155. Ga. XXVIII, 39.
156. Vi. XVIII, 28–30, 36–37.
157. Mah. XIII, 47, 56; Vi. XVIII, 31.
158. Vi. XV, 1.
159. Ba. II, 3, 31*; Ga. XXVIII, 32; Va. XVII, 25.
160. Ba. II, 3, 32*; Ga. XXVIII, 33; Va. XVII, 38.
161. . . . .
162. Vi. XVII, 23*.
163. Vi. XV, 28–30.
164. Ba. II, 3, 11.
165. Ga. XXVIII, 34; Yâ. II, 132.
166. Ba. II, 3, 14; Âp. II, 13, 1; Va. XVII, 13; Vi. XV, 2; Yâ. II, 128.
167. Ba. II, 3, 17–18; Va. XVII, 14; Vi. XV, 3; Yâ. I, 69; II, 127–128.
168. Ba. II, 3, 20; Va. XVII, 29; Vi. XV, 18–19; Yâ. II, 130.
169. Ba. II, 3, 21; Yâ. II, 131.
170. Ba. II, 3, 22; Va. XVII, 24; Vi. XV, 13–14; Yâ. II, 129.
171. Ba. II, 3, 23; Va. XVII, 37; Vi. XV, 24–25; Yâ. II, 132.
172. Ba. II, 3, 24; Va. XVII, 22–23; Vi. XV, 10–11; Yâ. II, 129.
173. Ba. II, 3, 25; Va. XVII, 26–27; Vi. XV, 15–16; Yâ. II, 131.
174. Ba. II, 3, 26; Va. XVII, 30–32; Vi. XV, 20–21; Yâ. II, 131.
175. Ba. II, 3, 27; Va. XVII, 18–19; Vi. XV, 7–9; Yâ. II, 130.
176. Ba. IV, 1, 16 b–c*; Va. XVII, 74; Vi. XV, 8.

177. Ba. II, 3, 28; Va. XVII, 33–35; Vi. XV, 22–23; Yâ. II, 131.
178. Ba. II, 3, 30; Va. XVII, 38; Vi. XV, 27.
179. Yâ. II, 133.
180. . . . .
181. Ba. II, 3, 33–35; Âp. II, 13, 6–10.
182. Va. XVII, 10*; Vi. XV, 42.
183. Va. XVII, 11*; Vi. XV, 41.
184. Va. XVII, 39, 81; Vi. XV, 28–29.
185. Vi. XVII, 6, 8; Yâ. II, 135.
186. Mâ. *Sr*. III*; Ba. I, 11, 9.
187. Ga. XXVIII, 21; Ba. I, 11, 10–13; Âp. II, 14, 2–3; Va. XVII, 81–82; Vi. XVII, 11; Yâ. II, 135.
188. Ga. XXVIII, 41; Ba. I, 11, 14; Va. XVII, 84–86; Vi. XVII, 14.
189. Ga. XXVIII, 42; Ba. I, 11, 15–16; Âp. II, 14, 5; Va. XVII, 83; Vi. XVII, 13.
190. . . . .
191. . . . .
192.
193. } Yâ. II, 117.
194. Vi. XVII, 18; Yâ. II, 143.
195. . . . .
196. Vi. XVII, 19; Yâ. II, 145.
197. Vi. XVII, 20; Yâ. II, 145.
198. Mah. XIII, 47, 25.
199. Mah. XIII, 47, 24b.
200. Vi. XVII, 22*.
201. Ga. XXVIII, 43; Ba. II, 3, 37–40; Âp. II, 14, 1; Va. XVII, 52–53; Vi. XV, 32; Yâ. II, 140.
202. Ga. XXVIII, 43; Ba. II, 3, 37–40; Va. XVII, 54; Vi. XV, 33; Yâ. II, 140.
203. Ga. XXVIII, 44; Vi. XV, 34–36; Yâ. II, 141.
204. . . . .
205. Ga. XXVIII, 31.
206. Ga. XXVIII, 30; Yâ. II, 118–119.
207. Yâ. II, 116.
208. Mah. XIII, 105, 11; Vi. XVIII, 42*.
209. Vi. XVIII, 43*; Yâ. II, 119.
210. Vi. XVIII, 41*; Yâ. II, 120.
211. . . . .
212. Vi. XVII, 17; Yâ. II, 138.
213. Mah. XIII, 105, 7.
214. Mah. XIII, 105, 10; Ga. XXVIII, 40; Ba. II, 3, 38; Âp. II, 14, 15.
215. Mah. XIII, 105, 12; Yâ. II, 120.
216. Ga. XXVIII, 29; Vi. XVII, 3; Yâ. II, 122.
217. Vi. XVII, 7; Yâ. II, 135.
218. Yâ. II, 126.
219. Vi. XVIII, 44*; Ga. XXVIII, 46–47.
220. . . . .
221. . . . .
222. . . . .
223. . . . .
224. Yâ. II, 304.
225. . . . .
226. . . . .
227. . . . .
228. . . . .
229. Yâ. II, 43.
230. . . . .
231. Vi. V, 180.
232. Vi. V, 9, 11; Yâ. II, 240.
233. . . . .

234. Yâ. II, 305.
235. . . . .
236. . . . .
237. Ba. I, 18, 18; Vi. V, 3–7.
238. . . . .
239. . . . .
240. . . . .
241. . . . .
242. . . . .
243. . . . .
244. . . . .
245. . . . .
246. . . . .
247. . . . .
248. . . . .
249. . . . .
250. . . . .
251. . . . .
252. . . . .
253. . . . .
254. . . . .
255. . . . .
256. . . . .
257. . . . .
258. . . . .
259. . . . .
260. . . . .
261. . . . .
262. . . . .
263. . . . .
264. . . . .
265. . . . .
266. . . . .
267. . . . .
268. . . . .
269. . . . .
270. . . . .
271. . . . .
272. . . . .
273. . . . .
274. Vi. V, 74.
275. . . . .
276. Yâ. II, 273.
277. Vi. V, 136.
278. Yâ. II, 276.
279. Yâ. II, 279.
280. Yâ. II, 273.
281. . . . .
282. Vi. V, 106–107.
283. . . . .
284. Vi. V, 175–177.
285. Vi. V, 174.
286. Vi. V, 124; Yâ. II, 245–246.
287. . . . .
288. . . . .
289. . . . .
290. . . . .
291. . . . .
292. Yâ. II, 297.
293. . . . .
294. Yâ. I, 352.
295. . . . .
296. . . . .
297. . . . .
298. . . . .
299. . . . .
300. . . . .
301. . . . .
302. . . . .
303. . . . .
304. . . . .
305. . . . .
306. . . . .
307. . . . .
308. . . . .
309. . . . .
310. . . . .
311. . . . .
312. . . . .
313. . . . .
314. . . . .
315. Mah. XIII, 152, 16.
316. . . . .

317. Mah. XIII, 152, 21.
318. Mah. XIII, 152, 22.
319. Mah. XIII, 152, 23.
320. Mah. XII, 78, 21.
321. Mah. XII, 56, 24; 78, 22.
322. Ga. XI, 14; Va. XIX, 4.
323. . . . .
324. . . . .
325. . . . .
326. . . . .
327. Mah. XII, 60, 23[b]–24[a].
328. Mah. XII, 60, 26[b]–27[a].
329. . . . .
330. . . . .
331. . . . .
332. . . . .
333. . . . .
334. . . . .
335. . . . .
336. . . . .

MANU X.

1. . . . .
2. . . . .
3. . . . .
4. Mah. XIII, 46, 18[a]; Âp. I, 1, 3–5; Ba. I, 16, 1; Va. II, 1–2; Yâ. I, 10.
5. Âp. I, 13, 1; Vi. XVI, 1; Yâ. I, 90.
6. Ba. I, 16, 6; Âp. II, 13, 4–5.
7. Ga. IV, 16; Ba. I, 16, 7; Va. XVIII, 8.
8. Ga. IV, 16; Ba. I, 16, 7; I, 17, 3; Va. XVIII, 8; Yâ. I, 91.
9. Ga. IV, 16; Ba. I, 16, 7; I, 17, 4; Va. XVIII, 8; Yâ. I, 92.
10. . . . .
11. Ga. IV, 17; Ba. I, 16, 8; I, 17, 7–8; Va. XVIII, 6; Vi. XVI, 5–6; Yâ. I, 93–94.
12. Ga. IV, 17; Ba. I, 16, 8; Vi. XVI, 4, 6; Yâ. I, 93–94.
13. . . . .
14. . . . .
15. . . . .
16. Ba. I, 17, 7; Va. XVIII, 1–3; Vi. XVI, 4; Yâ. I, 93–94.
17. Ba. I, 17, 8; Vi. XVI, 5–6; Yâ. I, 93–94.
18. Ga. IV, 19; Ba. I, 16, 8, 11–12; I, 17, 13–14; Va. XVIII, 5; Vi. XVI, 5.
19. Ba. I, 16, 8, 9–10; I, 17, 11–12; Va. XVIII, 2.
20. Ba. I, 16, 16 *.
21. Ga. IV, 20.
22. Ga. IV, 21.
23. . . . .
24. Yâ. I, 96.
25. . . . .
26. . . . .
27. Mah. XIII, 48, 14.
28. Mah. XIII, 48, 15.
29. Mah. XIII, 48, 16; Vi. XVI, 7.
30. Mah. XIII, 48, 17.
31. Mah. XIII, 48, 18.
32. Mah. XIII, 48, 19[c]–20[a].
33. Mah. XIII, 48, 20[b].
34. Mah. XIII, 48, 21[a].
35. Mah. XIII, 48, 24[b]–25[a].
36. Mah. XIII, 48, 25[b]–26[a].
37. Mah. XIII, 48, 26[b]–27[a].
38. Mah. XIII, 48, 27[b].

39. Mah. XIII, 48, 28 b; Va. XVIII, 3.
40. Mah. XIII, 48, 29; Vi. XVI, 17*.
41. . . . .
42. . . . .
43. Mah. XIII, 33, 21; 35, 17.
44. Mah. XIII, 33, 22; 35, 18.
45. . . . .
46. . . . .
47. Vi. XVI, 10, 12–13.
48. Vi. XVI, 8.
49. Vi. XVI, 9.
50. Mah. XIII, 48, 32 a, 33 a.
51. Vi. XVI, 14.
52. Mah. XIII, 48, 32 b; Vi. XVI, 14.
53. . . . .
54. . . . .
55. . . . .
56. Vi. XVI, 11.
57. Va. XVIII, 7; Vi. XVI, 17.
58. Mah. XIII, 48, 41.
59. Mah. XIII, 48, 42.
60. Mah. XIII, 48, 44.
61. . . . .
62. Mah. XIII, 48, 34 a, 35 a; Vi. XVI, 18*.
63. Yâ. I, 122*; Ga. VIII, 23; Âp. I, 23, 6; Vi. II, 16–17.
64. Ga. IV, 22; Yâ. I, 96.
65. . . . .
66. . . . .
67. . . . .
68. . . . .
69. . . . .
70. . . . .
71. . . . .
72. . . . .
73. . . . .
74. Va. II, 13.
75. Ga. X, 1–2; Ba. I, 18, 2; Âp. II, 10, 4; Va. II, 13–14; Vi. II, 5, 9, 11; Yâ. I, 118.
76. Vi. II, 11.
77. Ga. X, 1; Ba. I, 18, 3; Âp. II, 10, 6; Va. II, 15–16; Vi. II, 9; Yâ. I, 118.
78. Ga. X, 1; Ba. I, 18, 4; Âp. II, 10, 7; Va. II, 18; Vi. II, 9.
79. Ga. X, 7, 15, 49; Ba. I, 18, 3–4; Âp. II, 10, 6–7; Va. II, 17, 19; Vi. II, 6–7, 12–13; Yâ. I, 119.
80. . . . .
81. Ga. VII, 6; Ba. II, 4, 16; Va. II, 22; Vi. II, 15; Yâ. III, 35.
82. Ga. VII, 7; Ba. II, 4, 19–21; Va. II, 24, 32–36; Yâ. III, 35; *Sâ. Gri.* IV, 11, 15.
83. . . . .
84. Mah. III, 208, 23; XII, 263, 45 b–46 a; Ba. II, 4, 20–21; Va. II, 32–36.
85. Ga. VII, 8; Âp. I, 20, 10–11; Yâ. III, 39.
86. Ga. VII, 9, 14–15; Ba. II, 2, 27; Âp. I, 20, 12–13; Va. II, 24, 26, 29; Vi. LIV, 18, 21; Yâ. III, 36, 38.
87. Ga. VII, 9, 10; Va. II, 24–26; Vi. LIV, 18, 20; Yâ. III, 36–38.
88. Ga. VII, 9, 11–12; Âp. I, 20, 12–13; Va. II, 26; Vi. LIV, 18–19, 21; Yâ. III, 36–38.
89. Ga. VII, 13–15; Âp. I, 20, 12; Va. II, 28; Vi. LIV, 21; Yâ. III, 37–38.
90. Va. II, 31; Yâ. III, 39.

91. Ba. II, 2, 26*; Va. II, 30*.
92. Va. II, 27*; Yâ. III, 40.
93. Yâ. III, 40.
94. Ga. VII, 16–17, 21; Âp. I, 20, 15; Va. II, 37–39.
95. Ga. VII, 26; Vi. II, 15.
96. Va. II, 23.
97. . . . .
98. Va. II, 23; Vi. II, 15.
99. } Ga. X, 57, 60; Vi. II, 14;
100. } Yâ. I, 120.
101. . . . .
102. Ga. VII, 4; Âp. I, 18, 5–8, 14–15.
103. Va. XXVII, 9.
104. Yâ. III, 41.
105. . . . .
106. . . . .
107. . . . .
108. . . . .
109. . . . .
110. . . . .
111. Âp. I, 28, 11; Va. XX, 45–46; Vi. LIV, 28; see below, XI, 194.
112. . . . .
113. . . . .
114. Va. XII, 3.
115. Ga. X, 39–42.
116. Yâ. III, 42.
117. Va. II, 40–43.
118. . . . .
119. Ga. X, 16, 41; see also above, VII, 88.
120. Va. XIX, 37.
121. Ga. X, 56; Yâ. I, 120.
122. . . . .
123. . . . .
124. Ga. X, 61.
125. Ga. X, 58–59.
126. } Ga. X, 64–65; Yâ. I, 121,
127. } 262.
128. . . . .
129. Ga. X, 63.
130. . . . .
131. . . . .

Manu XI.

1. Mah. XII, 165, 1; Ga. V, 21; Ba. II, 5, 19; Âp. II, 10, 1–2.
2. Mah. XII, 165, 2[b].
3. Mah. XII, 165, 3[b]; Ga. V, 22; Ba. II, 5, 20.
4. Mah. XII, 165, 4.
5. Âp. II, 10, 3.
6. . . . .
7. Mah. XII, 165, 5[b-c]; Va. VIII, 10; Vi. LIX, 8–9; Yâ. I, 124.
8. . . . .
9. . . . .
10. . . . .
11. Mah. XII, 165, 6.
12. Mah. XII, 165, 7; Ga. XVIII, 25.
13. Mah. XII, 165, 8; Ga. XVIII, 24.
14. Mah. XII, 165, 9; Ga. XVIII, 26–27.
15. Mah. XII, 165, 10.
16. Mah. XII, 165, 11; Ga. XVIII, 28–29; Yâ. III, 43.
17. Mah. XII, 165, 12; Ga. XVIII, 30; Yâ. III, 43.
18. . . . .
19. . . . .
20. . . . .
21. Mah. XII, 165, 13; Ga. XVIII, 32.

22. Mah. XII, 165, 14ᵃ; Ga. XVIII, 31; Yâ. III, 44.
23. Mah. XII, 165, 14ᵇ.
24. Vi. LIX, 11; Yâ. I, 127.
25. Yâ. I, 127.
26. . . . .
27. Mah. XII, 165, 15ᵃ; Vi. LIX, 10; Yâ. I, 126.
28. Mah. XII, 165, 15ᵇ.
29. Mah. XII, 165, 16.
30. Mah. XII, 165, 17.
31. Mah. XII, 165, 18.
32. . . . .
33. . . . .
34. Mah. XII, 165, 20ᵇ–21ᵃ; Va. XXVI, 16.
35. Mah. XII, 165, 19ᵇ–20ᵃ.
36. Mah. XII, 165, 21ᵇ–22ᵃ; Ga. II, 4; Âp. II, 15, 18–19; Va. II, 6.
37. Mah. XII, 165, 22ᵇ–22ᶜ.
38. Mah. XII, 165, 23.
39. Mah. XII, 165, 24.
40. Mah. XII, 165, 25.
41. Ga. XXII, 34; Va. I. 18; XXI, 27; Vi. LIV, 13.
42. . . . .
43. . . . .
44. Mah. XII, 34, 2; Ga. XIX, 2; Ba. III, 10, 2; Va. XXII, 1; Yâ. III, 219–220.
45. Ga. XIX, 3–6; Va. XX, 1–2; Ba. III, 10, 3–5; Va. XXII, 3–5; Yâ. III, 226.
46. Yâ. III, 226.
47. . . . .
48. Va. XX, 43; Vi. XLV, 1.
49. Va. I, 18; XX, 6; XX, 44; Vi. XLV, 3–6; Yâ. III, 209.
50. Vi. XLV, 7–10; Yâ. III, 211.
51. Vi. XLV, 11–14; Yâ. III, 210.
52. Vi. XLV, 20–21, 31.
53. Vi. XLV, 32*.
54. Yâ. III, 220.
55. Ga. XXI, 1; Âp. I, 21, 8; Va. I, 19–21; Vi. XXXV, 1–2; Yâ. III, 227.
56. Ga. XXI, 10; Vi. XXXVI, 1; XXXVII, 1–3; Yâ. III, 228.
57. Ga. XXI, 1; Âp. I, 21, 8; Vi. XXXVI, 2; XXXVII, 4–5; Yâ. III, 228–229.
58. Ba. II, 2, 3–4; Vi. XXXVI, 3; Yâ. III, 230.
59. Ga. XXI, 1; Ba. II, 2, 13; Âp. I, 21, 8–9, 17–18; Vi. XXXVI, 4–7; Yâ. III, 231.
60. Ga. XXI, 1, 11; Âp. I, 21, 9–10; Va. I, 23; Vi. XXXVII, 6, 9–10, 13; Yâ. III, 234, 235, 237, 239–240.
61. Ga. XXI, 11; Vi. XXXVII, 15–18; Yâ. III, 234–235, 238.
62. Ga. XXI, 11; Ba. II, 2, 13; Yâ. III, 236–238.
63. Ga. XXI, 11; Ba. II, 2, 5; Vi. XXXVII, 14, 19–21; Yâ. III, 234–235.
64. Ga. XXI, 11; Vi. XXXVII, 22–26; Yâ. III, 240, 242.
65. Ga. XXI, 11; Âp. I, 21, 14–15; Vi. XXXVII, 7, 24, 27; Yâ. III, 239–240.
66. Ga. XXI, 11; Ba. II, 2, 13; Vi. XXXVII, 28–30, 32; Yâ. III, 234, 242.
67. Ga. XXI, 1, 11; Va. I, 23; Vi. XXXVII, 13, 31, 33; Yâ. III, 236–237, 239.
68. Vi. XXXVIII, 1–6.

69. Vi. XXXIX, 1.
70. Ba. II, 2, 6 ; Vi. XL, 1.
71. Ba. II, 2, 15–16 ; Âp. I, 21, 12–17 ; Vi. XLI, 1–4.
72. Ga. XXII, 1 ; Ba. II, 1, 1.
73. Ga. XXII, 4–6 ; Ba. II, 1, 2–3 ; Âp. I, 24, 11–20 ; I, 28, 21–29, 1 ; Vi. L, 1–6, 15 ; Yâ. III, 243.
74. Mah. XII, 35, 4 ; Ga. XXII, 2–3 ; Âp. I, 25, 11 ; Yâ. III, 248.
75. Ga. XXII, 10 ; Ba. II, 1, 4.
76. Mah. XII, 35, 5^{a}.
77. Mah. XII, 35, 5^{b}–6^{a} ; Yâ. III, 250.
78. Yâ. III, 249.
79. Âp. I, 24, 18.
80. Par. VIII, 42* ; Ga. XXII, 7 ; Va. XX, 27 ; Yâ. III, 244–245.
81. Ga. XXII, 8 ; Âp. I, 24, 21 ; Va. XX, 28 ; Yâ. III, 246.
82. . . . .
83. Ga. XXII, 9 ; Ba. II, 1, 5 ; Âp. I, 24, 22 ; Vi. XXXV, 6 ; Yâ. III, 244.
84. . . . .
85. See above, IX, 317 ; I, 93–95.
86. See below, XII, 112.
87. . . . .
88. Ga. XXII, 12–13 ; Ba. II, 1, 12 ; Âp. I, 24, 6–9 ; Va. XX, 23–24, 34–36 ; Vi. L, 7–9 ; Yâ. III, 251.
89. Vi. L, 10.
90. Ga. XXI, 7 ; Ba. II, 1, 6.
91. Mah. XII, 165, 48^{a} ; Ga. XXIII, 1 ; Ba. II, 1, 18 ; Âp. I, 25, 3 ; Va. XX, 22 ; Yâ. III, 253.
92. Yâ. III, 253.
93. Vi. LI, 1 ; Yâ. III, 254.
94. . . . .
95. Vi. XXII, 82*.
96. . . . .
97. . . . .
98. . . . .
99. . . . .
100., 101. See above, VIII, 314–316.
102. Âp. I, 25, 10 ; Vi. LII, 3 ; Yâ. III, 258.
103. . . . .
104. Ga. XXIII, 8–9 ; Ba. II, 1, 13–14 ; Âp. I, 25, 2 ; Va. XX, 14 ; Vi. XXXIV, 2 ; Yâ. III, 259.
105. Mah. XII, 165, 50^{b}–51^{a} ; Ga. XXIII, 10–11 ; Ba. II, 1, 15 ; Âp. I, 25, 1 ; Va. XX, 13 ; Yâ. III, 259.
106. Vi. LIII, 1 ; Yâ. III, 260.
107. Vi. LIII, 6 ; Yâ. III, 260.
108. . . . .
109. Ga. XXII, 18 ; Âp. I, 26, 1 ; Va. XXI, 18 ; Vi. L, 16 ; Yâ. III, 263.
110. Vi. L, 22.
111. Vi. L, 16 ; Yâ. III, 263.
112. Vi. L, 17–18.
113. Par. VIII, 41* ; Vi. L, 19–20.
114. Par. VIII, 39* ; Vi. L, 21.
115. Par. VIII, 40*.
116. Vi. L, 24.
117. Yâ. III, 263.
118. Vi. XXXVII, 35.
119. Ga. XXIII, 17 ; Ba. II, 1, 31–33 ; Âp. I, 26, 8–9 ; Va. XXIII, 1–3 ; Yâ. III, 280 ; Pâ. *Gri.* III, 12, 1–3.
120. Ga. XXV, 4 ; Ba. II, 1, 35.
121. Vi. XXVIII, 48* ; Ba. II, 1, 30 ; Va. XXIII, 4.
122. Ga. XXV, 1–2.

123. Vi. XXVIII, 49*; Ga. XXIII, 18; Pâ. Gri. III, 12, 6-8.
124. Vi. XXVIII, 50*; Ga. XXIII, 19; Pâ. Gri. III, 12, 8.
125. Vi. XXXVIII, 7*.
126. Vi. XXXIX, 2; XL, 2; XLI, 5.
127. Ga. XXII, 14-16; Ba. II, 1, 8-10; Va. XX, 31-33; Vi. L, 12-15; Yâ. III, 266-267.
128. Ga. XXII, 14; Ba. I, 19, 1; Âp. I, 24, 1, 4; Yâ. III, 266.
129. Yâ. III, 266.
130. Ga. XXII, 15; Ba. I, 19, 2; Âp. I, 24, 2, 4; Yâ. III, 267.
131. Ga. XXII, 16; Ba. I, 19, 2; Âp. I, 24, 3-4; Yâ. III, 267.
132. Ga. XXII, 19; Ba. I, 19, 6; Âp. I, 25, 13; Va. XXI, 24; Vi. L, 30-32; Yâ. III, 270.
133. Yâ. III, 270.
134. Ga. XXII, 23, 25; Vi. L, 34-35; Yâ. III, 273.
135. Ga. XXII, 24; Vi. L, 36-39; Yâ. III, 271, 273-274.
136. Ba. I, 19, 6; Vi. L, 33; Yâ. III, 272.
137. Ba. I, 19, 4; Vi. L, 25-28; Yâ. III, 271.
138. Vi. L, 29, 40-41; Yâ. III, 272-273.
139. Ga. XXII, 26; Yâ. III, 268.
140. Va. XXI, 26; Yâ. III, 274.
141. Vi. L, 46*; Ga. XXII, 20-21; Âp. I, 26, 2; Va. XXI, 25; Yâ. III, 269.
142. Vi. L, 47*; Ga. XXII, 22; Yâ. III, 275.
143. Vi. L, 48*; Yâ. III, 276.
144. Vi. L, 49*; Yâ. III, 275.
145. Vi. L, 50*; Yâ. III, 276.
146. . . . .
147. Ga. XXIII, 2; Ba. II, 1, 19, 21; Va. XX, 19; Vi. LI, 4; Yâ. III, 255.
148. Ba. II, 1, 22*; Va. XX, 21; Vi. LI, 23-24.
149. . . . .
150. Mah. XII, 165, 76[b]; Ga. XXIII, 6; Vi. LI, 25.
151. Ga. XXIII, 3; Va. XX, 20; Vi. LI, 2; Yâ. III, 255.
152. Va. XX, 18*; Par. XII, 3*; Ba. II, 1, 20; Vi. LI, 5.
153. Va. XIV, 33; Vi. LI, 50, 54, 56; see above, IV, 222.
154. . . . .
155. . . . .
156. Vi. LI, 27, 34.
157. Ga. XXIII, 4-5; Va. XXIII, 30; Vi. LI, 3-4.
158. Va. XXIII, 12; Vi. LI, 43-44.
159. Va. XXIII, 11; Vi. LI, 45; Yâ. III, 282.
160. Va. XXIII, 11; Vi. LI, 46-47.
161. Ga. XXIII, 26.
162. . . . .
163. Âp. I, 25, 10; Vi. LII, 5.
164. Vi. LII, 6.
165. Vi. LII, 7.
166. Vi. LII, 8.
167. Vi. LII, 9.
168. Vi. LII, 10.
169. Vi. LII, 11, 13.
170. . . . .
171. Ga. XXIII, 12-13, 32; Ba. II, 2, 13-14; Va. XX, 15-16; Vi. XXXIV, 2; LIII, 1; Yâ. III, 233.
172. . . . .
173. Ba. II, 1, 37-38.
174. Ga. XXII, 36; XXIII, 34; Âp. I, 26, 7; Vi. LIII, 4, 7; Yâ. III, 288.

175. Vi. LIII, 4; Yâ. III, 291.
176. Ba. II, 4, 14*; II, 4, 13; Va. XXIII, 41; Vi. LIII, 5–6.
177. Mah. XII, 165, 63 b; Vi. LIII, 8.
178. . . . .
179. Vi. LIII, 9*; Âp. I, 27, 11*; Ba. II, 2, 11*; Par. VII, 10*.
180. . . . .
181. Mah. XII, 165, 37; Ba. II, 2, 35*; Va. I, 22*; Ga. XXI, 3; Vi. XXXV, 3–5; Yâ. III, 261.
182. Vi. LIV, 1.
183. Ga. XX, 4–6; Ba. II, 1, 36; Va. XV, 12–13; Yâ. III, 295.
184. Ga. XX, 4, 7; Va. XV, 12, 14; Vi. XXII, 57.
185. Ga. XX, 8–9; Va. XV, 15–16; Yâ. III, 295; see above, IX, 201.
186. See above, IX, 201.
187. Ga. XX, 10; Ba. II, 1, 36; Va. XV, 17–21; Yâ. III, 296.
188. Ga. XX, 11–14; Ba. II, 1, 36; Yâ. III, 296.
189. Yâ. III, 297.
190. Vi. LIV, 31*.
191. Vi. LIV, 32*; Yâ. III, 299.
192. Vi. LIV, 26*; Âp. I, 1, 23–2, 10; Va. XI, 76–79.
193. Vi. LIV, 27*.
194. Vi. LIV, 28*.
195. Vi. LIV, 24*; Yâ. III, 290.
196. } Ba. II, 1, 36; Yâ. III, 300.
197. }
198. Vi. LIV, 25*; Âp. I, 26, 7; Yâ. III, 289.
199. Yâ. III, 289.
200. Ga. XXIII, 7; Va. XXIII, 31; Vi. LIV, 12; Yâ. III, 277.
201. . . . . .
202. Yâ. III, 291.
203. . . . .
204. Vi. LIV, 29*.
205. Par. XI, 49*; Yâ. III, 292.
206. Par. XI, 50*; Yâ. III, 292.
207. . . . .
208. Mah. XII, 165, 45 b–46 a.
209. Ba. II, 1, 7*; Vi. LIV, 30*; Par. XI, 51*; Yâ. III, 293.
210. Vi. LIV, 34*; Yâ. III, 294.
211. . . . .
212. Ga. XXVI, 2–5; Ba. II, 2, 38; IV, 5, 6–7; Âp. I, 27, 7; Va. XXI, 20; Vi. XLVI, 10; Yâ. III, 320.
213. Ba. IV, 5, 11*; Va. XXVII, 13*; Par. X, 29*; Vi. LIV, 19; Yâ. III, 315.
214. Ba. IV, 5, 8*; Ga. XXVI, 18–19; Ba. II, 2, 40; Va. XXIV, 1–2; Yâ. III, 320.
215. Ba. II, 2, 37; IV, 5, 10; Va. XXI, 21; Vi. XLVI, 11; Yâ. III, 318.
216. Ba. IV, 5, 15*; Vi. XLVI, 18; Yâ. III, 321.
217. Va. XXVII, 21*; Par. X, 2*; Ga. XXVII, 12–13; Ba. III, 8, 10, 19–23; Va. XXIII, 45; Vi. XLVII, 4–5; Yâ. III, 324.
218. Ga. XXVII, 14; Ba. III, 8, 26; IV, 5, 17; Va. XXVII, 21; Vi. XLVII, 3, 6.
219. Ba. IV, 5, 19*; Vi. XLVII, 7.
220. Ba. IV, 5, 18*; Vi. XLVII, 8.
221. Ba. IV, 5, 20*; Ga. XXVII, 18; Ba. III, 8, 31; Vi. XLVII, 9; Yâ. III, 325, 327.
222. Ba. III, 8, 30; Vi. XLVII, 10.

223. Ga. XXVI, 1-6; XXVII, 2; Ba. III, 8, 3, 7-9, 12-13.
224. Ba. III, 8, 17; Yâ. III, 326.
225. Ba. III, 8, 14-16.
226. Va. XXIV, 46; Yâ. III, 309.
227. Va. XXV, 3.
228. . . . .
229. . . . .
230. Mah. XIII, 112, 5.
231. . . . .
232. . . . .
233. . . . .
234. . . . .
235. . . . .
236. . . . .
237. . . . .
238. . . . .
239. Vi. XCV, 17*.
240. . . . .
241. . . . .
242. . . . .
243. . . . .
244. . . . .
245. . . . .
246. Va. XXVII, 7*; Yâ. III, 311.
247. Va. XXVII, 1-2.
248. . . . .
249. Ba. IV, 1, 29*; Va. XXVI. 4*; Vi. LV, 2.
250. Va. XXVI, 5*; Vi. LV, 4; Yâ. III, 304.
251. Va. XXVI, 6*; Yâ. III, 304.
252. Va. XXVI, 7*; Vi. LV, 6; Yâ. III, 305.
253. . . . .
254. Ga. XXIV, 2-3; Ba. IV, 2, 4-5.
255. . . . .
256. . . . .
257. . . . .
258. . . . .
259. . . . .
260. Ga. XXIV, 10, 12; Ba. III, 5, 2-5; Va. XXVI, 8; Yâ. III, 302.
261. Vi. LV, 7*; Ba. IV, 2, 15.
262. Va. XXVII, 3*.
263. Ba. III, 9, 1-21; IV, 5, 29.
264. . . . .
265. . . . .
266. . . . .

MANU XII.

1. . . . .
2. . . . .
3. . . . .
4. . . . .
5. Yâ. III, 134.
6. Yâ. III, 135.
7. Yâ. III, 136.
8. . . . .
9. Yâ. III, 131, 134-136.
10. . . . .
11. . . . .
12. Maitr. Up. III, 3.
13. . . . .
14. . . . .
15. . . . .
16. . . . .
17. . . . .
18. . . . .
19. . . . .
20. . . . .
21. . . . .
22. . . . .
23. . . . .
24. Yâ. III, 182.
25. . . . .
26. . . . .

27. Mah. XII, 194, 31; 219, 29.
28. Mah. XII, 194, 32; 219, 30.
29. Mah. XII, 194, 33; 219, 31.
30. . . . .
31. Yâ. III, 137.
32. Maitr. Up. III, 5; Yâ. III, 138.
33. Yâ. III, 139.
34. . . . .
35. . . . .
36. . . . .
37. . . . .
38. . . . .
39. . . . .
40. Yâ. III, 137–139.
41. . . . .
42. . . . .
43. . . . .
44. . . . .
45. . . . .
46. . . . .
47. . . . .
48. . . . .
49. . . . .
50. . . . .
51. . . . .
52. Yâ. III, 219.
53. . . . .
54. . . . .
55. Yâ. III, 207.
56. Yâ. III, 207.
57. Yâ. III, 208.
58. Yâ. III, 208.
59. . . . .
60. Yâ. III, 212.
61. Yâ. III, 213.
62. Vi. XLIV, 14–20; Yâ. III, 214–215.
63. Vi. XLIV, 21–25; Yâ. III, 211, 215.
64. Vi. XLIV, 26–30; Yâ. III, 215.
65. Vi. XLIV, 31–34; Yâ. III, 213.
66. Vi. XLIV, 35–37; Yâ. III, 214–215.
67. Vi. XLIV, 38–43; Yâ. III. 214.
68. Vi. XLIV, 44*; Yâ. III, 217.
69. Mah. XIII, 111, 130; Vi. XLIV, 45*.
70. . . . .
71. . . . .
72. . . . .
73. . . . .
74. . . . .
75. } Yâ. III, 206; see above,
76. } IV, 88–89.
77. . . . .
78. . . . .
79. . . . .
80. . . . .
81. . . . .
82. . . . .
83. Yâ. III, 190.
84. . . . .
85. . . . .
86. . . . .
87. . . . .
88. . . . .
89. . . . .
90. . . . .
91. Îsâ. Up. 6; Âp. I, 23, 1.
92. . . . .
93. . . . .
94. . . . .
95. . . . .
96. . . . .
97. . . . .
98. . . . .
99. . . . .
100. . . . .
101. Va. XXVII, 2*.
102. . . . .
103. . . . .
104. . . . .

105. . . . .
106. . . . .
107. . . . .
108. Ga. XXVIII, 48.
109. Va. VI, 43* ; Ba. I, 1, 5–6 ; Âp. II, 29, 13–14 ; Va. I, 6–7.
110. Ga. XXVIII, 49; Ba. I, 1, 7, 9.
111. Ba. I, 1, 8* ; Va. III, 20* ; Par. VIII, 34*.
112. Yâ. I, 9.
113. Ga. XXVIII, 50.
114. Ba. I, 1, 16* ; Va. III, 5* ; Par. VIII, 12*.
115. Ba. I, 1, 11 * ; Va. III, 6* ; Par. VIII, 13*.
116. . . . .
117. . . . .
118. . . . .
119. . . . .
120. . . . .
121. . . . .
122. . . . .
123. . . . .
124. . . . .
125. . . . .
126. . . . .

INDEX.

INDEX.

ADDITIONS AND CORRECTIONS.

Page xx, ll. 26-33. The tradition which asserts that the Gautamîya and Vâsishtha Dharmasâstras originally were the property of Vedic schools, studying the Sâma-veda and the Rig-veda, has already been mentioned by Colebrooke in his Essay on the Mîmâmsâ. It goes back to Kumârila, who adduces it in his Vârttika on Mîmâmsâ-sûtra, I, 3, 11 (Tantra-vârttika, p. 179, Benares Sanskrit Series). The same author states there that the Dharmasâstra of Sankha and Likhita belonged to the Vâgasaneyins.

P. xxxix, *add at the end of note* 3: 'It is, however, found in some other Grihya-sûtras.'

P. lvii, *add at the end of note* 4: 'The copy of the Munich MS. No. 83 has मनः.'

P. cxii, l. 1. More important is the fact that Kumârila, who, as I hold with Professor Max Müller, cannot be placed later than 700 A.D., knew our Manu-smriti. In the portions of the Tantra-vârttika, published in the Benares Sanskrit Series, I find the following verses quoted, i, 21b (p. 203, l. 14); ii, 140 (p. 178, l. 8); iv, 178 (p. 138, l. 17); v, 56 (p. 111, l. 11); viii, 57 (p. 199, l. 23); ix, 182 (p. 135, l. 2); xi, 30 (p. 110, l. 19); xi, 93 (p. 136, l. 19); xi, 94 (p. 136, l. 24); xi, 96b (p. 137, l. 7); xii, 95 (p. 117, l. 20); xii, 105, 106b (p. 80, l. 18). Most of these quotations show some variae lectiones, which, however, are not very important, and possibly, nay probably, are due to inaccuracy on Kumârila's part. One verse, quoted p. 241, l. 22, is not traceable in our Manu. Kumârila names Manu throughout as the first and most venerable authority on the sacred law. His predecessor, the author of the metrical Tîkâ, on the Mîmâmsâ-sûtra, which he quotes at great length, holds the same opinion, and clearly and frequently alludes to our Manu-smriti.

P. 11, ch. I, ver. 19, *add at the end of the note:* 'The idea that seven Purushas make up man, occurs Satapatha-brâhmana VI, 1, 1, 3, and 6.'

P. 32, ch. II, v. 15, *add at the end of the note:* 'The passages referred to in the text are quoted in the Sabarabhâshya on Mîmâmsâ-sûtra, II, 4, 8.'

P. 33, ch. II, v. 21, *for* 'to the east of Prayâga and to the west of Vinasana' *read* 'to the west of Prayâga and to the east of Vinasana.'

P. 39, ch. II, v. 52, *for* 'truthfulness, if he faces the east' *read* 'truthfulness, if he faces the north.'

P. 58, ch. II, v. 151, *for* 'old enough to be) fathers' *read* 'old enough to be his) fathers.'

P. 94, ch. III, v. 103 note, *read at the end:* 'âgatam apy atithi*m* na vidyât.'

P. 101, ch. III, v. 141 note, *for* 'paisak*î*' *read* 'Pai*s*â*k*î.'

P. 105, ch. III, v. 159, *for* 'substances used for flavouring' *read* 'condiments.'

P. 112, ch. III, v. 202 note, *for* 'akshayâyakalpate' *read* 'akshayâyopak.'

P. 121, ch. III, v. 251, *for* 'Rest either (here or at home)' *read* 'Take rest.'

P. 126, ch. III, v. 274 note. The passage quoted by Vi*gñ*âne*s*vara on Yâ*gñ*. I, 217, is to the following effect: 'When the moon stands in the (asterism) sacred to the manes (Maghâ*h*) and the sun in the (asterism) Hasta, that lunar day is sacred to Yama; it is called the elephant's shadow.' Another explanation of the same term from the Malamâsatattva, quoted in the Petersburg Dictionary, asserts that it means an eclipse of the sun.

P. 137, ch. IV, v. 55, *after* 'let him not take off his garland' *add* '(with his own hands).'

P. 141, ch. IV, v. 80 note, *add* 'Regarding the consequences of giving spiritual advice to a *S*ûdra, see also Mah. XIII, 10, 55.'

P. 144, ch. IV, note to vv. 95-97, *for* 'The Pushya-day is the sixth lunar day of each month' *read* 'The Pushya-day of the month of Pausha is the day of the full moon; see Bâpudeva *S*âstrî, note on Sûryasiddhânta, p. 94, s. 16.'

P. 147, ch. IV, v. 113 note, *add* 'Some parallel passages make the latter meaning more probable.'

P. 172, ch. V, v. 16 note, *add* 'For Sa*s*alkas on all (occasions,' Medh., Gov.) Ku. proposes 'Sa*s*alkas of all (kinds).'

P. 182, ch. V, v. 82 note, *for* 'such a one who is mentioned' *read* 'such a one as is mentioned.'

P. 189, ch. V, v. 115, *for* 'for solid things' *read* 'for things piled up.' The commentators give as examples 'couches, beds, and the like,' and apparently refer to the cushions and mattresses used for such purposes.

P. 199, ch. VI, v. 6. The translation 'a dress made of bark or grass' ought to be placed in the text, instead of 'a tattered garment.'

P. 206, ch. VI, v. 43 note, *for the first* 'asa*m*kasuka*h*' *read* 'asa*m*kusuka*h*.'

P. 222, ch. VII, v. 43. In accordance with the explanation of Medh., 'the science of dialectics, (which gives) self-knowledge' ought to be inserted in the text, instead of 'the science of dialectics and the knowledge of the (supreme) Soul;' see Introduction, p. xxxvii.

P. 234, ch. VII, v. 118 note, *insert* 'or Mahattara' *after* 'Grâmakû*t*a,' *and* 'are' *before* 'the so-called haks.'

P. 241, ch. VII, v. 157, *for* 'consists)' *read* '(consists).'

Pages 253, 255, superscription, *for* 'ceremonial' *read* 'criminal.'

P. 253, ch. VIII, v. 4 note, *insert at beginning* '*Ri*nasyâdânam.'

P. 257, ch. VIII, v. 25 note, *for* 'âkâra' *read* 'â*k*âra' (twice).

P. 263, ch. VIII, v. 53 note, *for* 'apadesam' *read* 'adesam.'

P. 265, ch. VIII, v. 65 note, *for* 'includes according to Nâr., Gov., Nand., Medh. also ascetics,' *read* 'includes according to Nâr., Gov., Medh. also ascetics, or, refers to the latter alone, Nand.'

P. 288, ch. VIII, v. 192 note, *for* 'Nâr. takes' *read* 'Nâr. and Nand. take.'

P. 292, ch. VIII, v. 210 note. Add after the quotation from Âsv. Srauta-sûtra, 'Âp. Srauta-sûtra XIII, 5, 12.'

P. 295, ch. VIII, v. 227 note, *dele* 'Nand. omits this verse and the next.'

P. 295, ch. VIII, v. 228 note, *add* 'Nand. omits this verse.'

P. 296, ch. VIII, v. 237 note, *add after* 'The samyâ is,' 'either the wedge at the yoke, or.'

P. 308, ch. VIII, v. 309 note, *for* 'who takes the goods of Brâhmanas or injures them' *read* 'who takes the goods of Brâhmanas, injures, or abandons them.'

P. 331, ch. IX, v. 20 note, *add* 'The Pratîka of this verse is quoted by Vi. LXXIII, 12; see also Âp. Srauta-sûtra I, 9, 9, where a somewhat different version occurs.'

P. 339, ch. IX, vv. 64-68 note, *for* 'Aupagandhani' *read* 'Aupagaṅghani,' which latter is the correct form of the name.

P. 352, ch. IX, v. 128 note, *add* 'The story agrees exactly with Mah. XII, 343, 57; see also Vishnu-purâna, vol. ii, p. 10 (ed. Hall).'

P. 362, ch. IX, v. 170, *for* 'Gûdhotpanna' *read* 'Gûdhotpanna.'

P. 398, ch. IX, v. 315 note, *add at end*, 'see also Mah. XIII, 33, 17.'

P. 399, ch. IX, v. 323. Mah. XII, 65, 1 seq. recommend âhave dehatyâgam, 'death in battle,' for a king.

P. 405, ch. X, v. 19 note, *for* 'the name of caste' *read* 'the name of the caste.'

P. 406, ch. X, v. 22. The form Likkhivi for Likkhavi actually occurs.

P. 407, ibid., *for* 'waters' *read* 'water.'

P. 416, ch. X, v. 64 note, *for* 'Sacred Books of the East, II,' *read* 'S. B. E. XIV.'

P. 425, ch. X, v. 111, *for* 'offering sacrifices for teaching' *read* 'offering sacrifices for, or, teaching.'

P. 443, ch. XI, v. 64 note, *add* 'Yâ. III, 240 favours Nâr.'s explanation of mahâyantrapravartana.'

P. 457, ch. XI, v. 134, *for* 'a spade of black iron' *read* 'a mattock of black iron.'

P. 479, ch. XI, v. 242, *for* 'penance' *read* 'austerity' (twice).

P. 480, ch. XI, v. 250, *for* '(that seen) by Vasishtha' *read* 'the three verses (seen) by Vasishtha.' *Make the same correction in the note, and add,* 'the correct reading in the text is prati tryrikam.'

P. 481, ch. XI, v. 253, *add at the end*, or, 'Thus, verily thus.'

P. 512, ch. XII, v. 120 note, *add* 'Compare for this verse and the next, Rig-veda X, 90, 13-14.'

TRANSLITERATION OF ORIENTAL ALPHABETS ADOPTED FOR THE TRANSLATIONS OF THE SACRED BOOKS OF THE EAST.

CONSONANTS.	MISSIONARY ALPHABET.			Sanskrit.	Zend.	Pehlevi.	Persian.	Arabic.	Hebrew.	Chinese.
	I Class.	II Class.	III Class.							
Gutturales.										
1 Tenuis	k	...	....	क	𐬐	[illegible]	ک	ك	כּ	k
2 „ aspirata	kh	...	....	ख	𐬑	[illegible]	...	...	כ	kh
3 Media	g	...	....	ग	𐬔	[illegible]	گ	...	גּ	...
4 „ aspirata	gh	...	....	घ	𐬖	[illegible]	...	...	ג	...
5 Gutturo-labialis	q	...	....	...	....	...	ق	ق	ק	...
6 Nasalis	ṅ (ng)	...	....	ङ	{𐬧 (ng) / 𐬣 (N)}	...	...	...	...	...
7 Spiritus asper	h	...	....	ह	𐬵 (𐬺 *hv*)	[illegible]	ه	ه	ה	h, hs
8 „ lenis	’	...	....	...	....	...	ا	ا	א	...
9 „ asper faucalis	‘h	...	....	...	....	...	ح	ح	ח	...
10 „ lenis faucalis	’h	...	....	...	....	...	ع	ع	ע	...
11 „ asper fricatus	...	*‘h*	....	...	....	...	خ	خ	ח	...
12 „ lenis fricatus	...	*’h*	....	...	....	...	...	...	...	...
Gutturales modificatae (palatales, &c.)										
13 Tenuis	...	*k*	....	च	𐬗	[illegible]	چ	...	...	*k*
14 „ aspirata	...	*kh*	....	छ	....	...	...	...	...	*kh*
15 Media	...	*g*	....	ज	𐬘	[illegible]	ج	ج	...	...
16 „ aspirata	...	*gh*	....	झ	....	...	غ	غ	...	...
17 „ Nasalis	...	*ñ*	....	ञ	....	...	...	...	...	...

CONSONANTS (*continued*).	MISSIONARY ALPHABET. I Class.	II Class.	III Class.	Sanskrit.	Zend.	Pehlevi.	Persian.	Arabic.	Hebrew.	Chinese.
18 Semivocalis	y	. . .	. . . .	य	𐬌𐬌, 𐬫 init.	[illegible]	ي	ي	י	y
19 Spiritus asper	. . .	(ẏ)	. . . .	. . .	. . . .	. . .	. . .	. . .	. . .	. . .
20 ,, lenis	. . .	(ẏ̓)	. . . .	. . .	. . . .	. . .	. . .	. . .	. . .	. . .
21 ,, asper assibilatus	. . .	*s*	. . . .	श	𐬱	[illegible]	ش	ش	. . .	. . .
22 ,, lenis assibilatus	. . .	*z*	. . . .	. . .	𐬲	[illegible]	ژ	. . .	. . .	*z*
Dentales.										
23 Tenuis	t	. . .	. . . .	त	𐬙	[illegible]	ت	ت	תּ	t
24 ,, aspirata	th	. . .	. . . .	थ	𐬚	. . .	. . .	. . .	ת	th
25 ,, assibilata	. . .	. . .	TH	. . .	. . . .	. . .	ث	ث	. . .	. . .
26 Media	d	. . .	. . . .	द	𐬛	[illegible]	د	د	דּ	. . .
27 ,, aspirata	dh	. . .	. . . .	ध	𐬜	. . .	. . .	. . .	ד	. . .
28 ,, assibilata	. . .	. . .	DH	. . .	. . . .	. . .	ذ	ذ	. . .	. . .
29 Nasalis	n	. . .	. . . .	न	𐬥	[illegible]	ن	ن	נ	n
30 Semivocalis	l	. . .	. . . .	ल	. . . .	[illegible]	ل	ل	ל	l
31 ,, mollis 1	. . .	*l*	. . . .	ळ	. . . .	. . .	. . .	. . .	. . .	. . .
32 ,, mollis 2	. . .	. . .	L	. . .	. . . .	. . .	. . .	. . .	. . .	. . .
33 Spiritus asper 1	s	. . .	. . . .	स	𐬯	[illegible]	س (ث)	س	שׂ	s
34 ,, asper 2	. . .	. . .	s (ʃ)	. . .	. . . .	. . .	. . .	. . .	ס	. . .
35 ,, lenis	z	. . .	. . . .	. . .	𐬰	[illegible]	ز (ذ)	ز	ז	z
36 ,, asperrimus 1	. .	. . .	z (ȝ)	. . .	. . . .	. . .	ص	ص	צ	ȝ, ȝh
37 ,, asperrimus 2	. . .	. . .	ẓ (ȝ)	. . .	. . . .	. . .	ض	. . .	. . .	. . .

Dentales modificatae (linguales, &c.)										
38 Tenuis	...	*t*	....	ट	....	...	ط	ط	ט	...
39 „ aspirata	...	*th*	....	ठ	....	...	ط	ط	...	...
40 Media	...	*d*	....	ड	𐬜	[illegible]	...	...	...	...
41 „ aspirata	...	*dh*	....	ढ	....	...	...	ض	...	...
42 Nasalis	...	*n*	....	ण	𐬣	...	...	...	...	...
43 Semivocalis	r	...	....	र	𐬭	[illegible]	ر	ر	ר	...
44 „ fricata	...	*r*	....	....	....	...	...	...	...	*r*
45 „ diacritica	...	...	R	....	....	...	...	...	...	...
46 Spiritus asper	sh	...	....	ष	𐬴	[illegible]	...	...	...	sh
47 „ lenis	zh	...	....	....	....	...	...	...	...	...
Labiales.										
48 Tenuis	p	...	....	प	𐬞	[illegible]	پ	...	פּ	p
49 „ aspirata	ph	...	....	फ	....	...	...	...	פ	ph
50 Media	b	...	....	ब	𐬠	[illegible]	ب	ب	בּ	...
51 „ aspirata	bh	...	....	भ	....	...	...	...	ב	...
52 Tenuissima	...	*p*	....	....	....	...	...	...	...	...
53 Nasalis	m	...	....	म	𐬨	[illegible]	م	م	מ	m
54 Semivocalis	w	...	....	....	𐬡	...	...	...	...	w
55 „ aspirata	hw	...	....	....	....	...	...	...	...	...
56 Spiritus asper	f	...	....	....	𐬟	[illegible]	ف	ف	...	f
57 „ lenis	v	...	....	व	»	[illegible]	و	و	ו	...
58 Anusvâra	...	*m*	....	ं	𐬥 ã	...	...	...	...	...
59 Visarga	...	*h*	....	ः	....	...	...	...	...	...

VOWELS.	MISSIONARY ALPHABET. I Class.	II Class.	III Class.	Sanskrit.	Zend.	Pehlevi.	Persian.	Arabic.	Hebrew.	Chinese.
1 Neutralis	0	...	...	...	...	...	...	...	אְ	ă
2 Laryngo-palatalis	ĕ	...	...	...	...	...	...	...	...	...
3 „ labialis	ŏ	...	...	...	...	𐭠 fin.	...	...	...	...
4 Gutturalis brevis	a	...	...	अ	𐬀	𐭠 init.	َ	َ	אַ	a
5 „ longa	â	(a)	...	आ	𐬁	𐭠	ـَا	ـَا	אָ	â
6 Palatalis brevis	i	...	...	इ	𐬌	...	ِ	ِ	אִ	i
7 „ longa	î	(i)	...	ई	𐬍	𐭩	ـِي	ـِي	אִי	î
8 Dentalis brevis	li	...	...	ऌ	...	...	...	...	...	...
9 „ longa	lî	...	...	ॡ	...	...	...	...	...	...
10 Lingualis brevis	ri	...	...	ऋ	...	...	...	...	...	...
11 „ longa	rî	...	...	ॠ	...	...	...	...	...	...
12 Labialis brevis	u	...	...	उ	𐬎	...	ُ	ُ	אֻ	u
13 „ longa	û	(u)	...	ऊ	𐬏	𐭥	ـُو	ـُو	וּ	û
14 Gutturo-palatalis brevis	e	...	...	...	𐬈 (e) 𐬉 (e)	...	...	...	אֶ	e
15 „ longa	ê (ai)	(e)	...	ए	𐬉, 𐬈	𐭩	ـَيْ	ـَيْ	אֵ	ê
16 Diphthongus gutturo-palatalis	âi	(ai)	...	ऐ	...	...	...	...	...	âi
17 „ „	ei (ĕi)	...	...	...	...	...	...	...	...	ei, êi
18 „ „	oi (ŏu)	...	...	...	...	...	...	...	...	...
19 Gutturo-labialis brevis	o	...	...	...	𐬊	...	...	...	אָ	o
20 „ longa	ô (au)	(o)	...	ओ	𐬋	𐭥	ـَوْ	ـَوْ	וֹ	...
21 Diphthongus gutturo-labialis	âu	(au)	...	औ	𐬃 (au)	...	...	...	...	âu
22 „ „	eu (ĕu)	...	...	...	...	...	...	...	...	...
23 „ „	ou (ŏu)	...	...	...	...	...	...	...	...	...
24 Gutturalis fracta	ä	...	...	...	...	...	...	...	...	...
25 Palatalis fracta	ï	...	...	...	...	...	...	...	...	...
26 Labialis fracta	ü	...	...	...	...	...	...	...	...	ü
27 Gutturo-labialis fracta	ö	...	...	...	...	...	...	...	...	...

Clarendon Press, Oxford.

A SELECTION OF

BOOKS

PUBLISHED FOR THE UNIVERSITY BY

HENRY FROWDE,

AT THE OXFORD UNIVERSITY PRESS WAREHOUSE,

AMEN CORNER, LONDON.

ALSO TO BE HAD AT THE

CLARENDON PRESS DEPOSITORY, OXFORD.

[*Every book is bound in cloth, unless otherwise described.*]

LEXICONS, GRAMMARS, ORIENTAL WORKS, &c.

ANGLO-SAXON.—*An Anglo-Saxon Dictionary*, based on the MS. Collections of the late Joseph Bosworth, D.D., Professor of Anglo-Saxon, Oxford. Edited and enlarged by Prof. T. N. Toller, M.A. (To be completed in four parts.) Parts I-III. A—SAR. 4to. 15*s.* each.

ARABIC.—*A Practical Arabic Grammar.* Part I. Compiled by A. O. Green, Brigade Major, Royal Engineers, Author of 'Modern Arabic Stories.' Second Edition, Enlarged and Revised. Crown 8vo. 7*s.* 6*d.*

CHINESE.—*A Handbook of the Chinese Language.* By James Summers. 1863. 8vo. half bound, 1*l.* 8*s.*

—— *A Record of Buddhistic Kingdoms*, by the Chinese Monk FÂ-HIEN. Translated and annotated by James Legge, M.A., LL.D. Crown 4to. cloth back, 10*s.* 6*d.*

ENGLISH.—*A New English Dictionary, on Historical Principles:* founded mainly on the materials collected by the Philological Society. Edited by James A. H. Murray, LL.D., with the assistance of many Scholars and men of Science. Vol. I. A and B. Imperial 4to. half Morocco, 2*l.* 12*s.* 6*d.*

Part IV, Section II, C—CASS. Beginning of Vol. II, 5*s.*

B

ENGLISH.—*An Etymological Dictionary of the English Language.* By W. W. Skeat, Litt.D. *Second Edition.* 1884. 4to. 2*l.* 4*s.*

——Supplement to the First Edition of the above. 4to. 2*s.* 6*d.*

—— *A Concise Etymological Dictionary of the English Language.* By W. W. Skeat, Litt.D. *Third Edition.* 1887. Crown 8vo. 5*s.* 6*d.*

GREEK.—*A Greek-English Lexicon*, by Henry George Liddell, D.D., and Robert Scott, D.D. Seventh Edition, Revised and Augmented throughout. 1883. 4to. 1*l.* 16*s.*

—— *A Greek-English Lexicon*, abridged from Liddell and Scott's 4to. edition, chiefly for the use of Schools. Twenty-first Edition. 1884. Square 12mo. 7*s.* 6*d.*

—— *A copious Greek-English Vocabulary*, compiled from the best authorities. 1850. 24mo. 3*s.*

—— *A Practical Introduction to Greek Accentuation*, by H. W. Chandler, M.A. Second Edition. 1881. 8vo. 10*s.* 6*d.*

HEBREW.—*The Book of Hebrew Roots*, by Abu 'l-Walîd Marwân ibn Janâh, otherwise called Rabbî Yônâh. Now first edited, with an Appendix, by Ad. Neubauer. 1875. 4to. 2*l.* 7*s.* 6*d.*

—— *A Treatise on the use of the Tenses in Hebrew.* By S. R. Driver, D.D. Second Edition. 1881. Extra fcap. 8vo. 7*s.* 6*d.*

—— *Hebrew Accentuation of Psalms, Proverbs, and Job.* By William Wickes, D.D. 1881. Demy 8vo. 5*s.*

—— *A Treatise on the Accentuation of the twenty-one so-called Prose Books of the Old Testament.* By William Wickes, D.D. 1887. Demy 8vo. 10*s.* 6*d.*

ICELANDIC.—*An Icelandic-English Dictionary*, based on the MS. collections of the late Richard Cleasby. Enlarged and completed by G. Vigfússon, M.A. With an Introduction, and Life of Richard Cleasby, by G. Webbe Dasent, D.C.L. 1874. 4to. 3*l.* 7*s.*

—— *A List of English Words the Etymology of which is illustrated by comparison with Icelandic.* Prepared in the form of an APPENDIX to the above. By W. W. Skeat, Litt.D. 1876. stitched, 2*s.*

—— *An Icelandic Primer*, with Grammar, Notes, and Glossary. By Henry Sweet, M.A. Extra fcap. 8vo. 3*s.* 6*d.*

—— *An Icelandic Prose Reader*, with Notes, Grammar and Glossary, by Dr. Gudbrand Vigfússon and F. York Powell, M.A. 1879. Extra fcap. 8vo. 10*s.* 6*d.*

LATIN.—*A Latin Dictionary*, founded on Andrews' edition of Freund's Latin Dictionary, revised, enlarged, and in great part rewritten by Charlton T. Lewis, Ph.D., and Charles Short, LL.D. 1879. 4to. 1*l.* 5*s.*

MELANESIAN.—*The Melanesian Languages.* By R. H. Codrington, D.D., of the Melanesian Mission. 8vo. 18*s.*

SANSKRIT.—*A Practical Grammar of the Sanskrit Language*, arranged with reference to the Classical Languages of Europe, for the use of English Students, by Sir M. Monier-Williams, M.A. Fourth Edition. 8vo. 15*s.*

—— *A Sanskrit-English Dictionary*, Etymologically and Philologically arranged, with special reference to Greek, Latin, German, Anglo-Saxon, English, and other cognate Indo-European Languages. By Sir M. Monier-Williams, M.A. 1888. 4to. 4*l.* 14*s.* 6*d.*

—— *Nalopákhyánam.* Story of Nala, an Episode of the Mahá-Bhárata: the Sanskrit text, with a copious Vocabulary, and an improved version of Dean Milman's Translation, by Sir M. Monier-Williams, M.A. Second Edition, Revised and Improved. 1879. 8vo. 15*s.*

—— *Sakuntalā.* A Sanskrit Drama, in Seven Acts. Edited by Sir M. Monier-Williams, M.A. Second Edition, 1876. 8vo. 21*s.*

SYRIAC.—*Thesaurus Syriacus:* collegerunt Quatremère, Bernstein, Lorsbach, Arnoldi, Agrell, Field, Roediger: edidit R. Payne Smith, S.T.P. Fasc. I-VI. 1868-83. sm. fol. each, 1*l.* 1*s.* Fasc. VII. 1*l.* 11*s.* 6*d.*

Vol. I, containing Fasc. I-V, sm. fol. 5*l.* 5*s.*

—— *The Book of Kalīlah and Dimnah.* Translated from Arabic into Syriac. Edited by W. Wright, LL.D. 1884. 8vo. 21*s.*

GREEK CLASSICS, &c.

Aristophanes: A Complete Concordance to the Comedies and Fragments. By Henry Dunbar, M.D. 4to. 1*l.* 1*s.*

Aristotle: The Politics, with Introductions, Notes, etc., by W. L. Newman, M.A., Fellow of Balliol College, Oxford. Vols. I. and II. Medium 8vo. 28*s.*

Aristotle: The Politics, translated into English, with Introduction, Marginal Analysis, Notes, and Indices, by B. Jowett, M.A. Medium 8vo. 2 vols. 21*s.*

Catalogus Codicum Graecorum Sinaiticorum. Scripsit V. Gardthausen Lipsiensis. With six pages of Facsimiles. 8vo. *linen*, 25*s.*

Heracliti Ephesii Reliquiae. Recensuit I. Bywater, M.A. Appendicis loco additae sunt Diogenis Laertii Vita Heracliti, Particulae Hippocratei De Diaeta Libri Primi, Epistolae Heracliteae. 1877. 8vo. 6*s.*

Herculanensium Voluminum Partes II. 1824. 8vo. 10*s.*

Fragmenta Herculanensia. A Descriptive Catalogue of the Oxford copies of the Herculanean Rolls, together with the texts of several papyri, accompanied by facsimiles. Edited by Walter Scott, M.A., Fellow of Merton College, Oxford. Royal 8vo. *cloth*, 21*s.*

Homer: A Complete Concordance to the Odyssey and Hymns of Homer; to which is added a Concordance to the Parallel Passages in the Iliad, Odyssey, and Hymns. By Henry Dunbar, M.D. 1880. 4to. 1*l.* 1*s.*

—— *Scholia Graeca in Iliadem.* Edited by Professor W. Dindorf, after a new collation of the Venetian MSS. by D. B. Monro, M.A., Provost of Oriel College. 4 vols. 8vo. 2*l.* 10*s.* Vols. V and VI. *In the Press.*

—— *Scholia Graeca in Odysseam.* Edidit Guil. Dindorfius. Tomi II. 1855. 8vo. 15*s.* 6*d.*

Plato: Apology, with a revised Text and English Notes, and a Digest of Platonic Idioms, by James Riddell, M.A. 1878. 8vo. 8*s.* 6*d.*

—— *Philebus,* with a revised Text and English Notes, by Edward Poste, M.A. 1860. 8vo. 7*s.* 6*d.*

—— *Sophistes and Politicus,* with a revised Text and English Notes, by L. Campbell, M.A. 1867. 8vo. 18*s.*

—— *Theaetetus,* with a revised Text and English Notes, by L. Campbell, M.A. Second Edition. 8vo. 10*s.* 6*d.*

—— *The Dialogues,* translated into English, with Analyses and Introductions, by B. Jowett, M.A. A new Edition in 5 volumes, medium 8vo. 1875. 3*l.* 10*s.*

—— *The Republic,* translated into English, with an Analysis and Introduction, by B. Jowett, M.A. Medium 8vo. 12*s.* 6*d.*

Thucydides: Translated into English, with Introduction, Marginal Analysis, Notes, and Indices. By B. Jowett, M.A. 2 vols. 1881. Medium 8vo. 1*l.* 12*s.*

THE HOLY SCRIPTURES, &c.

STUDIA BIBLICA.—Essays in Biblical Archæology and Criticism, and kindred subjects. By Members of the University of Oxford. 8vo. 10*s.* 6*d.*

ENGLISH.—*The Holy Bible in the earliest English Versions,* made from the Latin Vulgate by John Wycliffe and his followers: edited by the Rev. J. Forshall and Sir F. Madden. 4 vols. 1850. Royal 4to. 3*l.* 3*s.*

[**Also reprinted from the above, with Introduction and Glossary by W. W. Skeat, Litt. D.**

ENGLISH.—*The Books of Job, Psalms, Proverbs, Ecclesiastes, and the Song of Solomon:* according to the Wycliffite Version made by Nicholas de Hereford, about A.D. 1381, and Revised by John Purvey, about A.D. 1388. Extra fcap. 8vo. 3*s*. 6*d*.

—— *The New Testament in English*, according to the Version by John Wycliffe, about A.D. 1380, and Revised by John Purvey, about A.D. 1388. Extra fcap. 8vo. 6*s*.]

—— *The Holy Bible:* an exact reprint, page for page, of the Authorised Version published in the year 1611. Demy 4to. half bound, 1*l*. 1*s*.

—— *The Psalter, or Psalms of David, and certain Canticles*, with a Translation and Exposition in English, by Richard Rolle of Hampole. Edited by H. R. Bramley, M.A., Fellow of S. M. Magdalen College, Oxford. With an Introduction and Glossary. Demy 8vo. 1*l*. 1*s*.

—— *Lectures on the Book of Job.* Delivered in Westminster Abbey by the Very Rev. George Granville Bradley, D.D., Dean of Westminster. Crown 8vo. 7*s*. 6*d*.

—— *Lectures on Ecclesiastes.* By the same Author. Crown 8vo. 4*s*. 6*d*.

GOTHIC.—*The Gospel of St. Mark in Gothic*, according to the translation made by Wulfila in the Fourth Century. Edited with a Grammatical Introduction and Glossarial Index by W. W. Skeat, Litt. D. Extra fcap. 8vo. 4*s*.

GREEK.—*Vetus Testamentum* ex Versione Septuaginta Interpretum secundum exemplar Vaticanum Romae editum. Accedit potior varietas Codicis Alexandrini. Tomi III. Editio Altera. 18mo. 18*s*. The volumes may be had separately, price 6*s*. each.

—— *Origenis Hexaplorum* quae supersunt; sive, Veterum Interpretum Graecorum in totum Vetus Testamentum Fragmenta. Edidit Fridericus Field, A.M. 2 vols. 1875. 4to. 5*l*. 5*s*.

—— *The Book of Wisdom:* the Greek Text, the Latin Vulgate, and the Authorised English Version; with an Introduction, Critical Apparatus, and a Commentary. By William J. Deane, M.A. Small 4to. 12*s*. 6*d*.

—— *Novum Testamentum Graece.* Antiquissimorum Codicum Textus in ordine parallelo dispositi. Accedit collatio Codicis Sinaitici. Edidit E. H. Hansell, S.T.B. Tomi III. 1864. 8vo. 24*s*.

—— *Novum Testamentum Graece.* Accedunt parallela S. Scripturae loca, etc. Edidit Carolus Lloyd, S.T.P.R. 18mo. 3*s*.

On writing paper, with wide margin, 10*s*.

GREEK.—*Novum Testamentum Graece* juxta Exemplar Millianum. 18mo. 2*s.* 6*d.* **On writing paper, with wide margin, 9*s.***

—— *Evangelia Sacra Graece.* Fcap. 8vo. limp, 1*s.* 6*d.*

—— *The Greek Testament*, with the Readings adopted by the Revisers of the Authorised Version:—

(1) Pica type, with Marginal References. Demy 8vo. 10*s.* 6*d.*
(2) Long Primer type. Fcap. 8vo. 4*s.* 6*d.*
(3) The same, on writing paper, with wide margin, 15*s.*

—— *The Parallel New Testament*, Greek and English; being the Authorised Version, 1611; the Revised Version, 1881; and the Greek Text followed in the Revised Version. 8vo. 12*s.* 6*d.*

The Revised Version is the joint property of the Universities of Oxford and Cambridge.

—— *Canon Muratorianus:* the earliest Catalogue of the Books of the New Testament. Edited with Notes and a Facsimile of the MS. in the Ambrosian Library at Milan, by S. P. Tregelles, LL.D. 1867. 4to. 10*s.* 6*d.*

—— *Outlines of Textual Criticism applied to the New Testament.* By C. E. Hammond, M.A. Fourth Edition. Extra fcap. 8vo. 3*s.* 6*d.*

HEBREW, etc.—*Notes on the Hebrew Text of the Book of Genesis.* With Two Appendices. By G. J. Spurrell, M.A. Crown 8vo. 10*s.* 6*d.*

—— *The Psalms in Hebrew without points.* 1879. Crown 8vo. Price reduced to 2*s.*, in stiff cover.

—— *A Commentary on the Book of Proverbs.* Attributed to Abraham Ibn Ezra. Edited from a MS. in the Bodleian Library by S. R. Driver, M.A. Crown 8vo. paper covers, 3*s.* 6*d.*

—— *The Book of Tobit.* A Chaldee Text, from a unique MS. in the Bodleian Library; with other Rabbinical Texts, English Translations, and the Itala. Edited by Ad. Neubauer, M.A. 1878. Crown 8vo. 6*s.*

—— *Horae Hebraicae et Talmudicae*, a J. Lightfoot. A new Edition, by R. Gandell, M.A. 4 vols. 1859. 8vo. 1*l.* 1*s.*

LATIN.—*Libri Psalmorum* Versio antiqua Latina, cum Paraphrasi Anglo-Saxonica. Edidit B. Thorpe, F.A.S. 1835. 8vo. 10*s.* 6*d.*

—— *Old-Latin Biblical Texts: No. I.* The Gospel according to St. Matthew from the St. Germain MS. (g_1). Edited with Introduction and Appendices by John Wordsworth, D.D. Small 4to., stiff covers, 6*s.*

—— *Old-Latin Biblical Texts: No. II.* Portions of the Gospels according to St. Mark and St. Matthew, from the Bobbio MS. (k), &c. Edited by John Wordsworth, D.D., W. Sanday, M.A., D.D., and H. J. White, M.A. Small 4to., stiff covers, 21*s.*

LATIN.—*Old-Latin Biblical Texts: No. III.* The Four Gospels, from the Munich MS. (q), now numbered Lat. 6224 in the Royal Library at Munich. With a Fragment from St. John in the Hof-Bibliothek at Vienna (Cod. Lat. 502). Edited, with the aid of Tischendorf's transcript (under the direction of the Bishop of Salisbury), by H. J. White, M.A. Small 4to. stiff covers, 12*s.* 6*d.*

OLD-FRENCH.—*Libri Psalmorum* Versio antiqua Gallica e Cod. MS. in Bibl. Bodleiana adservato, una cum Versione Metrica aliisque Monumentis pervetustis. Nunc primum descripsit et edidit Franciscus Michel, Phil. Doc. 1860. 8vo. 10*s.* 6*d.*

FATHERS OF THE CHURCH, &c.

St. Athanasius: Historical Writings, according to the Benedictine Text. With an Introduction by William Bright, D.D. 1881. Crown 8vo. 10*s.* 6*d.*

—— *Orations against the Arians.* With an Account of his Life by William Bright, D.D. 1873. Crown 8vo. 9*s.*

St. Augustine: Select Anti-Pelagian Treatises, and the Acts of the Second Council of Orange. With an Introduction by William Bright, D.D. Crown 8vo. 9*s.*

Canons of the First Four General Councils of Nicaea, Constantinople, Ephesus, and Chalcedon. 1877. Crown 8vo. 2*s.* 6*d.*

—— *Notes on the Canons of the First Four General Councils.* By William Bright, D.D. 1882. Crown 8vo. 5*s.* 6*d.*

Cyrilli Archiepiscopi Alexandrini in XII Prophetas. Edidit P. E. Pusey, A.M. Tomi II. 1868. 8vo. cloth, 2*l.* 2*s.*

—— *in D. Joannis Evangelium.* Accedunt Fragmenta varia necnon Tractatus ad Tiberium Diaconum duo. Edidit post Aubertum P. E. Pusey, A.M. Tomi III. 1872. 8vo. 2*l.* 5*s.*

—— *Commentarii in Lucae Evangelium* quae supersunt Syriace. E MSS. apud Mus. Britan. edidit R. Payne Smith, A.M. 1858. 4to. 1*l.* 2*s.*

—— Translated by R. Payne Smith, M.A. 2 vols. 1859. 8vo. 14*s.*

Ephraemi Syri, Rabulae Episcopi Edesseni, Balaei, aliorumque Opera Selecta. E Codd. Syriacis MSS. in Museo Britannico et Bibliotheca Bodleiana asservatis primus edidit J. J. Overbeck. 1865. 8vo. 1*l.* 1*s.*

Eusebius' Ecclesiastical History, according to the text of Burton, with an Introduction by William Bright, D.D. 1881. Crown 8vo. 8*s*. 6*d*.

Irenaeus: The Third Book of St. Irenaeus, Bishop of Lyons, against Heresies. With short Notes and a Glossary by H. Deane, B.D. 1874. Crown 8vo. 5*s*. 6*d*.

Patrum Apostolicorum, S. Clementis Romani, S. Ignatii, S. Polycarpi, quae supersunt. Edidit Guil. Jacobson, S.T.P.R. Tomi II. Fourth Edition, 1863. 8vo. 1*l*. 1*s*.

Socrates' Ecclesiastical History, according to the Text of Hussey, with an Introduction by William Bright, D.D. 1878. Crown 8vo. 7*s*. 6*d*.

ECCLESIASTICAL HISTORY, BIOGRAPHY, &c.

Ancient Liturgy of the Church of England, according to the uses of Sarum, York, Hereford, and Bangor, and the Roman Liturgy arranged in parallel columns, with preface and notes. By William Maskell, M.A. Third Edition. 1882. 8vo. 15*s*.

Baedae Historia Ecclesiastica. Edited, with English Notes, by G. H. Moberly, M.A. 1881. Crown 8vo. 10*s*. 6*d*.

Bright (W.). Chapters of Early English Church History. 1878. 8vo. 12*s*.

Burnet's History of the Reformation of the Church of England. A new Edition. Carefully revised, and the Records collated with the originals, by N. Pocock, M.A. 7 vols. 1865. 8vo. *Price reduced to* 1*l*. 10*s*.

Councils and Ecclesiastical Documents relating to Great Britain and Ireland. Edited, after Spelman and Wilkins, by A. W. Haddan, B.D., and W. Stubbs, M.A. Vols. I. and III. 1869–71. Medium 8vo. each 1*l*. 1*s*.

Vol. II. Part I. 1873. Medium 8vo. 10*s*. 6*d*.

Vol. II. Part II. 1878. Church of Ireland; Memorials of St. Patrick. Stiff covers, 3*s*. 6*d*.

Hamilton (John, Archbishop of St. Andrews), The Catechism of. Edited, with Introduction and Glossary, by Thomas Graves Law. With a Preface by the Right Hon. W. E. Gladstone. 8vo. 12*s*. 6*d*.

Hammond (C. E.). Liturgies, Eastern and Western. Edited, with Introduction, Notes, and Liturgical Glossary. 1878. Crown 8vo. 10*s*. 6*d*.

An Appendix to the above. 1879. Crown 8vo. paper covers, 1*s*. 6*d*.

John, Bishop of Ephesus. The Third Part of his Ecclesiastical History. [In Syriac.] Now first edited by William Cureton, M.A. 1853. 4to. 1*l*. 12*s*.

—— Translated by R. Payne Smith, M.A. 1860. 8vo. 10*s*.

Leofric Missal, The, as used in the Cathedral of Exeter during the Episcopate of its first Bishop, A.D. 1050–1072; together with some Account of the Red Book of Derby, the Missal of Robert of Jumièges, and a few other early MS. Service Books of the English Church. Edited, with Introduction and Notes, by F. E. Warren, B.D. 4to. half morocco, 35*s*.

Monumenta Ritualia Ecclesiae Anglicanae. The occasional Offices of the Church of England according to the old use of Salisbury, the Prymer in English, and other prayers and forms, with dissertations and notes. By William Maskell, M.A. Second Edition. 1882. 3 vols. 8vo. 2*l*. 10*s*.

Records of the Reformation. The Divorce, 1527–1533. Mostly now for the first time printed from MSS. in the British Museum and other libraries. Collected and arranged by N. Pocock, M.A. 1870. 2 vols. 8vo. 1*l*. 16*s*.

Shirley (W. W.). Some Account of the Church in the Apostolic Age. Second Edition, 1874. Fcap. 8vo. 3*s*. 6*d*.

Stubbs (W.). Registrum Sacrum Anglicanum. An attempt to exhibit the course of Episcopal Succession in England. 1858. Small 4to. 8*s*. 6*d*.

Warren (F. E.). Liturgy and Ritual of the Celtic Church. 1881. 8vo. 14*s*.

ENGLISH THEOLOGY.

Bampton Lectures, 1886. *The Christian Platonists of Alexandria.* By Charles Bigg, D.D. 8vo. 10*s*. 6*d*.

Butler's Works, with an Index to the Analogy. 2 vols. 1874. 8vo. 11*s*.

Also separately,

Sermons, 5*s*. 6*d*. *Analogy of Religion*, 5*s*. 6*d*.

Greswell's Harmonia Evangelica. Fifth Edition. 8vo. 9*s*. 6*d*.

Heurtley's Harmonia Symbolica: Creeds of the Western Church. 1858. 8vo. 6*s*. 6*d*.

Homilies appointed to be read in Churches. Edited by J. Griffiths, M.A. 1859. 8vo. 7*s*. 6*d*.

Hooker's Works, with his life by Walton, arranged by John Keble, M.A. Seventh Edition. *Revised by R. W. Church, M.A., D.C.L., Dean of St. Paul's, and F. Paget, D.D.* 3 vols. medium 8vo. 36*s*.

Hooker's Works, the text as arranged by John Keble, M.A. 2 vols. 1875. 8vo. 11*s*.

Jewel's Works. Edited by R. W. Jelf, D.D. 8 vols. 1848. 8vo. 1*l*. 10*s*.

Pearson's Exposition of the Creed. Revised and corrected by E. Burton, D.D. Sixth Edition, 1877. 8vo. 10*s.* 6*d.*

Waterland's Review of the Doctrine of the Eucharist, with a Preface by the late Bishop of London. Crown 8vo. 6*s.* 6*d.*

—— *Works,* with Life, by Bp. Van Mildert. A new Edition, with copious Indexes. 6 vols. 1856. 8vo. 2*l.* 11*s.*

Wheatly's Illustration of the Book of Common Prayer. A new Edition, 1846. 8vo. 5*s.*

Wyclif. A Catalogue of the Original Works of John Wyclif, by W. W. Shirley, D.D. 1865. 8vo. 3*s.* 6*d.*

—— *Select English Works.* By T. Arnold, M.A. 3 vols. 1869–1871. 8vo. 1*l.* 1*s.*

—— *Trialogus.* With the Supplement now first edited. By Gotthard Lechler. 1869. 8vo. 7*s.*

HISTORICAL AND DOCUMENTARY WORKS.

British Barrows, a Record of the Examination of Sepulchral Mounds in various parts of England. By William Greenwell, M.A., F.S.A. Together with Description of Figures of Skulls, General Remarks on Prehistoric Crania, and an Appendix by George Rolleston, M.D., F.R.S. 1877. Medium 8vo. 25*s.*

Clarendon's History of the Rebellion and Civil Wars in England. Re-edited from a fresh Collation of the Original MS. in the Bodleian Library, with Marginal Dates, and Occasional Notes, by W. Dunn Macray, M.A., F.S.A. In six volumes, crown 8vo. *cloth,* 2*l.* 5*s.*

Clarendon's History of the Rebellion and Civil Wars in England. Also his Life, written by himself, in which is included a Continuation of his History of the Grand Rebellion. With copious Indexes. In one volume, royal 8vo. 1842. 1*l.* 2*s.*

Clinton's Epitome of the Fasti Hellenici. 1851. 8vo. 6*s.* 6*d.*

—— *Epitome of the Fasti Romani.* 1854. 8vo. 7*s.*

Corpvs Poeticvm Boreale. The Poetry of the Old Northern Tongue, from the Earliest Times to the Thirteenth Century. Edited, classified, and translated, with Introduction, Excursus, and Notes, by Gudbrand Vigfússon, M.A., and F. York Powell, M.A. 2 vols. 1883. 8vo. 42*s.*

Earle (J., M.A.). A Handbook to the Land-Charters, and other Saxonic Documents. Crown 8vo. *cloth,* 16*s.*

Freeman (E. A.). History of the Norman Conquest of England; its Causes and Results. In Six Volumes. 8vo. 5*l.* 9*s.* 6*d.*

—— *The Reign of William Rufus and the Accession of* Henry the First. 2 vols. 8vo. 1*l.* 16*s.*

Gascoigne's Theological Dictionary ("Liber Veritatum"): Selected Passages, illustrating the condition of Church and State, 1403–1458. With an Introduction by James E. Thorold Rogers, M.A. Small 4to. 10*s.* 6*d.*

Johnson (Samuel, LL.D.), Boswell's Life of; including Boswell's Journal of a Tour to the Hebrides, and Johnson's Diary of a Journey into North Wales. Edited by G. Birkbeck Hill, D.C.L. In six volumes, medium 8vo. With Portraits and Facsimiles of Handwriting. Half bound, 3*l.* 3*s.* (See p. 21.)

Magna Carta, a careful Reprint. Edited by W. Stubbs, D.D. 1879. 4to. stitched, 1*s.*

Passio et Miracula Beati Olaui. Edited from a Twelfth-Century MS. in the Library of Corpus Christi College, Oxford, by Frederick Metcalfe, M.A. Small 4to. stiff covers, 6*s.*

Protests of the Lords, including those which have been expunged, from 1624 to 1874; with Historical Introductions. Edited by James E. Thorold Rogers, M.A. 1875. 3 vols. 8vo. 2*l.* 2*s.*

Rogers (J. E. T.). History of Agriculture and Prices in England, A D. 1259–1793.

Vols. I—VI (1259–1702). 8vo. 7*l.* 2*s.*

—— *The First Nine Years of the Bank of England.* 8vo. 8*s.* 6*d.*

Stubbs (W., D.D.). Seventeen Lectures on the Study of Medieval and Modern History, &c., delivered at Oxford 1867–1884. Crown 8vo. 8*s.* 6*d.*

Sturlunga Saga, including the Islendinga Saga of Lawman Sturla Thordsson and other works. Edited by Dr. Gudbrand Vigfússon. In 2 vols. 1878. 8vo. 2*l.* 2*s.*

York Plays. The Plays performed by the Crafts or Mysteries of York on the day of Corpus Christi in the 14th, 15th, and 16th centuries. Now first printed from the unique MS. in the Library of Lord Ashburnham. Edited with Introduction and Glossary by Lucy Toulmin Smith. 8vo. 21*s.*

Manuscript Materials relating to the History of Oxford. Arranged by F. Madan, M.A. 8vo. 7*s.* 6*d.*

Statutes of the University of Oxford, codified in the year 1636 under the authority of Archbishop Laud. Edited by the late J. Griffiths, D.D., with an Introduction on the History of the Laudian Code, by C. L. Shadwell, M.A., B.C.L. 4to. 1*l.* 1*s.*

Statutes made for the University of Oxford, and for the Colleges and Halls therein, by the University of Oxford Commissioners. 1882. 8vo. 12*s*. 6*d*.

Statutes supplementary to the above, approved by the Queen in Council, 1882–1888. 8vo. 2*s*. 6*d*.

Statuta Universitatis Oxoniensis. 1888. 8vo. 5*s*.

The Oxford University Calendar for the year 1888. Crown 8vo. 4*s*. 6*d*.

The present Edition includes all Class Lists and other University distinctions for the eight years ending with 1887.

Also, supplementary to the above, price 5s. (pp. 606),

The Honours Register of the University of Oxford. A complete Record of University Honours, Officers, Distinctions, and Class Lists; of the Heads of Colleges, &c., &c., from the Thirteenth Century to 1883.

The Examination Statutes for the Degrees of B.A., B. Mus., B.C.L., and B.M. Revised to the end of Michaelmas Term, 1887. 8vo. sewed, 1*s*.

The Student's Handbook to the University and Colleges of Oxford. Ninth Edition. Crown 8vo. 2*s*. 6*d*.

MATHEMATICS, PHYSICAL SCIENCE, &c.

Acland (H. W., M.D., F.R.S.). Synopsis of the Pathological Series in the Oxford Museum. 1867. 8vo. 2*s*. 6*d*.

Annals of Botany. Edited by Isaac Bayley Balfour, M.A., M.D., F.R.S., Sydney H. Vines, D.Sc., F.R.S., and William Gilson Farlow, M.D., Professor of Cryptogamic Botany in Harvard University, Cambridge, Mass., U.S.A., and other Botanists. Royal 8vo. Vol. I., half morocco, 1*l*. 16*s*.

Vol. II. No. 1. *Just Published.*

Burdon-Sanderson (J., M.D., F.R.SS. L. and E.). Translations of Foreign Biological Memoirs. I. Memoirs on the Physiology of Nerve, of Muscle, and of the Electrical Organ. Medium 8vo. 21*s*.

De Bary (Dr. A.). Comparative Anatomy of the Vegetative Organs of the Phanerogams and Ferns. Translated and Annotated by F. O. Bower, M.A., F.L.S., and D. H. Scott, M.A., Ph.D., F.L.S. With 241 woodcuts and an Index. Royal 8vo., half morocco, 1*l*. 2*s*. 6*d*.

De Bary (Dr. A.) Comparative Morphology and Biology of the Fungi Mycetozoa and Bacteria. Authorised English Translation by Henry E. F. Garnsey, M.A. Revised by Isaac Bayley Balfour, M.A., M.D., F.R.S. With 198 Woodcuts. Royal 8vo., half morocco, *1l. 2s. 6d.*

—— *Lectures on Bacteria.* Second improved edition. Authorised translation by H. E. F. Garnsey, M.A. Revised by Isaac Bayley Balfour, M.A., M.D., F.R.S. With 20 Woodcuts. Crown 8vo. *6s.*

Goebel (Dr. K.). Outlines of Classification and Special Morphology of Plants. A New Edition of Sachs' Text Book of Botany, Book II. English Translation by H. E. F. Garnsey, M.A. Revised by I. Bayley Balfour, M.A., M.D., F.R.S. With 407 Woodcuts. Royal 8vo. half morocco, *21s.*

Müller (J.). On certain Variations in the Vocal Organs of the Passeres that have hitherto escaped notice. Translated by F. J. Bell, B.A., and edited, with an Appendix, by A. H. Garrod, M.A., F.R.S. With Plates. 1878. 4to. paper covers, *7s. 6d.*

Price (Bartholomew, M.A., F.R.S.). Treatise on Infinitesimal Calculus.

Vol. I. Differential Calculus. Second Edition. 8vo. *14s. 6d.*

Vol. II. Integral Calculus, Calculus of Variations, and Differential Equations. Second Edition, 1865. 8vo. *18s.*

Vol. III. Statics, including Attractions; Dynamics of a Material Particle. Second Edition, 1868. 8vo. *16s.*

Vol. IV. Dynamics of Material Systems; together with a chapter on Theoretical Dynamics, by W. F. Donkin, M.A., F.R.S. 1862. 8vo. *16s.*

Pritchard (C., D.D., F.R.S.). Uranometria Nova Oxoniensis. A Photometric determination of the magnitudes of all Stars visible to the naked eye, from the Pole to ten degrees south of the Equator. 1885. Royal 8vo. *s. 6d.*

—— *Astronomical Observations* made at the University Observatory, Oxford, under the direction of C. Pritchard, D.D. No. 1. 1878. Royal 8vo. paper covers, *3s. 6d.*

Rigaud's Correspondence of Scientific Men of the 17th Century, with Table of Contents by A. de Morgan, and Index by the Rev. J. Rigaud, M.A. 2 vols. 1841–1862. 8vo. *18s. 6d.*

Rolleston (George, M.D., F.R.S.). Forms of Animal Life. A Manual of Comparative Anatomy, with descriptions of selected types. Second Edition. Revised and enlarged by W. Hatchett Jackson, M.A. Medium, 8vo. cloth extra, *1l. 16s.*

—— *Scientific Papers and Addresses.* Arranged and Edited by William Turner, M.B., F.R.S. With a Biographical Sketch by Edward Tylor, F.R.S. With Portrait, Plates, and Woodcuts. 2 vols. 8vo. *1l. 4s.*

Sachs (Julius von). Lectures on the Physiology of Plants. Translated by H. Marshall Ward, M.A. With 445 Woodcuts. Royal 8vo. half morocco, *1l. 11s. 6d.*

Westwood (J. O., M.A., F.R.S.). *Thesaurus Entomologicus Hopeianus*, or a Description of the rarest Insects in the Collection given to the University by the Rev. William Hope. With 40 Plates. 1874. Small folio, half morocco, *7l. 10s.*

The Sacred Books of the East.

TRANSLATED BY VARIOUS ORIENTAL SCHOLARS, AND EDITED BY F. MAX MÜLLER.

[Demy 8vo. cloth.]

Vol. I. The Upanishads. Translated by F. Max Müller. Part I. The *Kh*ândogya-upanishad, The Talavakâra-upanishad, The Aitareya-âra*n*yaka, The Kaushîtaki-brâhma*n*a-upanishad, and The Vâ*g*asaneyi-sa*m*hitâ-upanishad. *10s. 6d.*

Vol. II. The Sacred Laws of the Âryas, as taught in the Schools of Âpastamba, Gautama, Vâsish*th*a, and Baudhâyana. Translated by Prof. Georg Bühler. Part I. Âpastamba and Gautama. *10s. 6d.*

Vol. III. The Sacred Books of China. The Texts of Confucianism. Translated by James Legge. Part I. The Shû King, The Religious portions of the Shih King, and The Hsiâo King. *12s. 6d.*

Vol. IV. The Zend-Avesta. Translated by James Darmesteter. Part I. The Vendîdâd. *10s. 6d.*

Vol. V. The Pahlavi Texts. Translated by E. W. West. Part I. The Bundahi*s*, Bahman Ya*s*t, and Shâyast lâ-shâyast. *12s. 6d.*

Vols. VI and IX. The Qur'ân. Parts I and II. Translated by E. H. Palmer. *21s.*

Vol. VII. The Institutes of Vish*n*u. Translated by Julius Jolly. *10s. 6d.*

Vol. VIII. The Bhagavadgîtâ, with The Sanatsu*g*âtîya, and The Anugîtâ. Translated by Kâshinâth Trimbak Telang. *10s. 6d.*

Vol. X. The Dhammapada, translated from Pâli by F. Max Müller; and The Sutta-Nipâta, translated from Pâli by V. Fausböll; being Canonical Books of the Buddhists. *10s. 6d.*

Vol. XI. Buddhist Suttas. Translated from Pâli by T. W. Rhys Davids. 1. The Mahâparinibbâna Suttanta; 2. The Dhamma-*k*akka-ppavattana Sutta; 3. The Tevigga Suttanta; 4. The Akaṅkheyya Sutta; 5. The *K*etokhila Sutta; 6. The Mahâ-sudassana Suttanta; 7. The Sabbâsava Sutta. 10*s*. 6*d*.

Vol. XII. The *S*atapatha-Brâhma*n*a, according to the Text of the Mâdhyandina School. Translated by Julius Eggeling. Part I. Books I and II. 12*s*. 6*d*.

Vol. XIII. Vinaya Texts. Translated from the Pâli by T. W. Rhys Davids and Hermann Oldenberg. Part I. The Pâtimokkha. The Mahâvagga, I-IV. 10*s*. 6*d*.

Vol. XIV. The Sacred Laws of the Âryas, as taught in the Schools of Âpastamba, Gautama, Vâsish*th*a and Baudhâyana. Translated by Georg Bühler. Part II. Vâsish*th*a and Baudhâyana. 10*s*. 6*d*.

Vol. XV. The Upanishads. Translated by F. Max Müller. Part II. The Ka*th*a-upanishad, The Mu*nd*aka-upanishad, The Taittirîyaka-upanishad, The B*ri*hadâra*n*yaka-upanishad, The *S*veta*s*vatara-upanishad, The Pra*s*ña-upanishad, and The Maitrâya*n*a-Brâhma*n*a-upanishad. 10*s*. 6*d*.

Vol. XVI. The Sacred Books of China. The Texts of Confucianism. Translated by James Legge. Part II. The Yî King. 10*s*. 6*d*.

Vol. XVII. Vinaya Texts. Translated from the Pâli by T. W. Rhys Davids and Hermann Oldenberg. Part II. The Mahâvagga, V-X. The *K*ullavagga, I-III. 10*s*. 6*d*.

Vol. XVIII. Pahlavi Texts. Translated by E. W. West. Part II. The Dâ*d*istân-î Dînîk and The Epistles of Mânû*sk*îhar. 12*s*. 6*d*.

Vol. XIX. The Fo-sho-hing-tsan-king. A Life of Buddha by A*s*vaghosha Bodhisattva, translated from Sanskrit into Chinese by Dharmaraksha, A.D. 420, and from Chinese into English by Samuel Beal. 10*s*. 6*d*.

Vol. XX. Vinaya Texts. Translated from the Pâli by T. W. Rhys Davids and Hermann Oldenberg. Part III. The *K*ullavagga, IV-XII. 10*s*. 6*d*.

Vol. XXI. The Saddharma-pu*nd*arîka; or, the Lotus of the True Law. Translated by H. Kern. 12*s*. 6*d*.

Vol. XXII. *G*aina-Sûtras. Translated from Prâkrit by Hermann Jacobi. Part I. The Â*k*ârâṅga-Sûtra. The Kalpa-Sûtra. 10*s*. 6*d*.

Vol. XXIII. The Zend-Avesta. Translated by James Darmesteter. Part II. The Sîrôzahs, Yasts, and Nyâyis. 10*s*. 6*d*.

Vol. XXIV. Pahlavi Texts. Translated by E. W. West. Part III. Dînâ-î Maînôg-î Khirad, *S*ikand-gûmânîk, and Sad-Dar. 10*s*. 6*d*.

Second Series.

Vol. XXV. Manu. Translated by Georg Bühler. 21*s*.

Vol. XXVI. The *S*atapatha-Brâhma*n*a. Translated by Julius Eggeling. Part II. 12*s*. 6*d*.

Vols. XXVII and XXVIII. The Sacred Books of China. The Texts of Confucianism. Translated by James Legge. Parts III and IV. The Lî *K*î, or Collection of Treatises on the Rules of Propriety, or Ceremonial Usages. 25*s*.

Vols. XXIX and XXX. The G*ri*hya-Sûtras, Rules of Vedic Domestic Ceremonies. Translated by Hermann Oldenberg.

Part I (Vol. XXIX), 12*s*. 6*d*. *Just Published.*
Part II (Vol. XXX). *In the Press.*

Vol. XXXI. The Zend-Avesta. Part III. The Yasna, Visparad, Âfrînagân, and Gâhs. Translated by L. H. Mills. 12*s*. 6*d*.

The following Volumes are in the Press:—

Vol. XXXII. Vedic Hymns. Translated by F. Max Müller. Part I.

Vol. XXXIII. Nârada, and some Minor Law-books. Translated by Julius Jolly. [*Preparing.*]

Vol. XXXIV. The Vedânta-Sûtras, with *S*aṅkara's Commentary. Translated by G. Thibaut. [*Preparing.*]

*** *The Second Series will consist of Twenty-Four Volumes.*

Clarendon Press Series.

I. ENGLISH, &c.

An Elementary English Grammar and Exercise Book. By O. W. Tancock, M.A. Second Edition. Extra fcap. 8vo. 1*s*. 6*d*.

An English Grammar and Reading Book, for Lower Forms in Classical Schools. By O. W. Tancock, M.A. Fourth Edition. Extra fcap. 8vo. 3*s*. 6*d*.

Typical Selections from the best English Writers, with Introductory Notices. Second Edition. In 2 vols. Extra fcap. 8vo. 3*s*. 6*d*. each.
Vol. I. Latimer to Berkeley. Vol. II. Pope to Macaulay.

Shairp (J. C., LL.D.). Aspects of Poetry; being Lectures delivered at Oxford. Crown 8vo. 10*s*. 6*d*.

A Book for the Beginner in Anglo-Saxon. By John Earle, M.A. Third Edition. Extra fcap. 8vo. 2*s*. 6*d*.

An Anglo-Saxon Reader. In Prose and Verse. With Grammatical Introduction, Notes, and Glossary. By Henry Sweet, M.A. Fourth Edition, Revised and Enlarged. Extra fcap. 8vo. 8*s*. 6*d*.

A Second Anglo-Saxon Reader. By the same Author. Extra fcap. 8vo. 4*s*. 6*d*.

An Anglo-Saxon Primer, with Grammar, Notes, and Glossary. By the same Author. Second Edition. Extra fcap. 8vo. 2*s*. 6*d*.

Old English Reading Primers; edited by Henry Sweet, M.A.
I. Selected Homilies of Ælfric. Extra fcap. 8vo., stiff covers, 1*s*. 6*d*.
II. Extracts from Alfred's Orosius. Extra fcap. 8vo., stiff covers, 1*s*. 6*d*.

First Middle English Primer, with Grammar and Glossary. By the same Author. Extra fcap. 8vo. 2*s*.

Second Middle English Primer. Extracts from Chaucer, with Grammar and Glossary. By the same Author. Extra fcap. 8vo. 2*s*.

A Concise Dictionary of Middle English, from A.D. 1150 to 1580. By A. L. Mayhew, M.A., and W. W. Skeat, Litt.D. Crown 8vo. half roan, 7*s*. 6*d*.

A Handbook of Phonetics, including a Popular Exposition of the Principles of Spelling Reform. By H. Sweet, M.A. Ext. fcap. 8vo. 4*s*. 6*d*.

C

Elementarbuch des Gesprochenen Englisch. Grammatik, Texte und Glossar. Von Henry Sweet. *Second Edition.* Extra fcap. 8vo., stiff covers, 2*s.* 6*d.*

History of English Sounds from the earliest Period. With full Word-Lists. By Henry Sweet, M.A. Demy 8vo. 14*s.*

Principles of English Etymology. First Series. *The Native Element.* By W. W. Skeat, Litt.D. Crown 8vo. 9*s.*

The Philology of the English Tongue. By J. Earle, M.A. Fourth Edition. Extra fcap. 8vo. 7*s.* 6*d.*

An Icelandic Primer, with Grammar, Notes, and Glossary. By Henry Sweet, M.A. Extra fcap. 8vo. 3*s.* 6*d.*

An Icelandic Prose Reader, with Notes, Grammar, and Glossary. By G. Vigfússon, M.A., and F. York Powell, M.A. Ext. fcap. 8vo. 10*s.* 6*d.*

The Ormulum; with the Notes and Glossary of Dr. R. M. White. Edited by R. Holt, M.A. 1878. 2 vols. Extra fcap. 8vo. 21*s.*

Specimens of Early English. A New and Revised Edition. With Introduction, Notes, and Glossarial Index.

Part I. By R. Morris, LL.D. From Old English Homilies to King Horn (A.D. 1150 to A.D. 1300). Second Edition. Extra fcap. 8vo. 9*s.*

Part II. By R. Morris, LL.D., and W. W. Skeat, Litt.D. From Robert of Gloucester to Gower (A.D. 1298 to A.D. 1393). Third Edition. Extra fcap. 8vo. 7*s.* 6*d.*

Specimens of English Literature, from the 'Ploughmans Crede' to the 'Shepheardes Calender' (A.D. 1394 to A.D. 1579). With Introduction, Notes, and Glossarial Index. By W. W. Skeat, Litt.D. Fourth Edition. Extra fcap. 8vo. 7*s.* 6*d.*

The Vision of William concerning Piers the Plowman, in three Parallel Texts; together with *Richard the Redeless.* By William Langland (about 1362–1399 A.D.). Edited from numerous Manuscripts, with Preface, Notes, and a Glossary, by W. W. Skeat, Litt.D. 2 vols. 8vo. 31*s.* 6*d.*

The Vision of William concerning Piers the Plowman, by William Langland. Edited, with Notes, by W. W. Skeat, Litt.D. Fourth Edition Extra fcap. 8vo. 4*s.* 6*d.*

Chaucer. I. *The Prologue to the Canterbury Tales;* the Knightes Tale; The Nonne Prestes Tale. Edited by R. Morris, LL.D. Sixty-sixth thousand. Extra fcap. 8vo. 2*s.* 6*d.*

—— II. *The Prioresses Tale; Sir Thopas; The Monkes Tale; The Clerkes Tale; The Squieres Tale,* &c. Edited by W. W. Skeat, Litt.D. Third Edition. Extra fcap. 8vo. 4*s.* 6*d.*

Chaucer. III. *The Tale of the Man of Lawe;* The Pardoneres Tale; The Second Nonnes Tale; The Chanouns Yemannes Tale. By the same Editor. *New Edition, Revised*. Extra fcap. 8vo. 4*s*. 6*d*.

—— IV. *Minor Poems*. By the same Editor. Extra fcap. 8vo. *Just ready*.

Gamelyn, The Tale of. Edited with Notes, Glossary, &c., by W. W. Skeat, Litt.D. Extra fcap. 8vo. Stiff covers, 1*s*. 6*d*.

Minot (Laurence). Poems. Edited, with Introduction and Notes, by Joseph Hall, M.A., Head Master of the Hulme Grammar School, Manchester. Extra fcap. 8vo. 4*s*. 6*d*.

Spenser's Faery Queene. Books I and II. Designed chiefly for the use of Schools. With Introduction and Notes by G. W. Kitchin, D.D., and Glossary by A. L. Mayhew, M.A. Extra fcap. 8vo. 2*s*. 6*d*. each.

Hooker. Ecclesiastical Polity, Book I. Edited by R. W. Church, M.A. Second Edition. Extra fcap. 8vo. 2*s*.

OLD ENGLISH DRAMA.

The Pilgrimage to Parnassus with *The Two Parts of the Return from Parnassus*. Three Comedies performed in St. John's College, Cambridge, A.D. MDXCVII–MDCI. Edited from MSS. by the Rev. W. D. Macray, M.A., F.S.A. Medium 8vo. Bevelled Boards, Gilt top, 8*s*. 6*d*.

Marlowe and Greene. Marlowe's Tragical History of Dr. Faustus, and *Greene's Honourable History of Friar Bacon and Friar Bungay*. Edited by A. W. Ward, M.A. *New and Enlarged Edition*. Extra fcap. 8vo. 6*s*. 6*d*.

Marlowe. Edward II. With Introduction, Notes, &c. By O. W. Tancock, M.A. Extra fcap. 8vo. Paper covers, 2*s*. Cloth 3*s*.

SHAKESPEARE.

Shakespeare. Select Plays. Edited by W. G. Clark, M.A., and W. Aldis Wright, M.A. Extra fcap. 8vo. stiff covers.

The Merchant of Venice. 1*s*.
Richard the Second. 1*s*. 6*d*.
Macbeth. 1*s*. 6*d*.
Hamlet. 2*s*.

Edited by W. Aldis Wright, M.A.

The Tempest. 1*s*. 6*d*.
As You Like It. 1*s*. 6*d*.
Julius Cæsar. 2*s*.
Richard the Third. 2*s*. 6*d*.
King Lear. 1*s*. 6*d*.
Midsummer Night's Dream. 1*s*. 6*d*.
Coriolanus. 2*s*. 6*d*.
Henry the Fifth. 2*s*.
Twelfth Night. 1*s*. 6*d*.
King John. 1*s*. 6*d*.

Shakespeare as a Dramatic Artist; a popular Illustration of the Principles of Scientific Criticism. By R. G. Moulton, M.A. Crown 8vo. 5*s*.

C 2

Bacon. I. *Advancement of Learning.* Edited by W. Aldis Wright, M.A. Third Edition. Extra fcap. 8vo. 4*s*. 6*d*.

—— II. *The Essays.* With Introduction and Notes. By S. H. Reynolds, M.A., late Fellow of Brasenose College. *In Preparation.*

Milton. I. *Areopagitica.* With Introduction and Notes. By John W. Hales, M.A. Third Edition. Extra fcap. 8vo. 3*s*.

—— II. *Poems.* Edited by R. C. Browne, M.A. 2 vols. Fifth Edition. Extra fcap. 8vo. 6*s*. 6*d*. Sold separately, Vol. I. 4*s*.; Vol. II. 3*s*.

In paper covers:—

Lycidas, 3*d*. L'Allegro, 3*d*. Il Penseroso, 4*d*. Comus, 6*d*.

—— III. *Paradise Lost.* Book I. Edited by H. C. Beeching. Extra fcap. 8vo. stiff cover, 1*s*. 6*d*.; in white Parchment, 3*s*. 6*d*.

—— IV. *Samson Agonistes.* Edited with Introduction and Notes by John Churton Collins. Extra fcap. 8vo. stiff covers, 1*s*.

Bunyan. I. *The Pilgrim's Progress, Grace Abounding, Relation of the Imprisonment of Mr. John Bunyan.* Edited, with Biographical Introduction and Notes, by E. Venables, M.A. 1879. Extra fcap. 8vo. 5*s*. In ornamental Parchment, 6*s*.

—— II. *Holy War, &c.* Edited by E. Venables, M.A. In the Press.

Clarendon. History of the Rebellion. Book VI. Edited by T. Arnold, M.A. Extra fcap. 8vo. 4*s*. 6*d*.

Dryden. Select Poems. Stanzas on the Death of Oliver Cromwell; Astræa Redux; Annus Mirabilis; Absalom and Achitophel; Religio Laici; The Hind and the Panther. Edited by W. D. Christie, M.A. Second Edition. Extra fcap. 8vo. 3*s*. 6*d*.

Locke's Conduct of the Understanding. Edited, with Introduction, Notes, &c., by T. Fowler, D.D. Second Edition. Extra fcap. 8vo. 2*s*.

Addison. Selections from Papers in the Spectator. With Notes. By T. Arnold, M.A. Extra fcap. 8vo. 4*s*. 6*d*. In ornamental Parchment, 6*s*.

Steele. Selections from the Tatler, Spectator, and Guardian. Edited by Austin Dobson. Extra fcap. 8vo. 4*s*. 6*d*. In white Parchment, 7*s*. 6*d*.

Pope. With Introduction and Notes. By Mark Pattison, B.D.

—— I. *Essay on Man.* Extra fcap. 8vo. 1*s*. 6*d*.

—— II. *Satires and Epistles.* Extra fcap. 8vo. 2*s*.

Parnell. The Hermit. Paper covers, 2*d*.

Gray. Selected Poems. Edited by Edmund Gosse. Extra fcap. 8vo. Stiff covers, 1*s*. 6*d*. In white Parchment, 3*s*.

—— *Elegy and Ode on Eton College.* Paper covers, 2*d*.

Goldsmith. Selected Poems. Edited, with Introduction and Notes, by Austin Dobson. Extra fcap. 8vo. 3*s.* 6*d.* In white Parchment, 4*s.* 6*d.*

—— *The Traveller.* With Notes by G. Birkbeck Hill, D.C.L. Extra fcap. 8vo. Paper covers, 1*s.*

—— *The Deserted Village.* Paper covers, 2*d.*

Johnson. I. *Rasselas.* Edited, with Introduction and Notes, by G. Birkbeck Hill, D.C.L. Extra fcap. 8vo. Bevelled boards, 3*s.* 6*d.* In white Parchment, 4*s.* 6*d.*

—— II. *Rasselas; Lives of Dryden and Pope.* Edited by Alfred Milnes, M.A. (London). Extra fcap. 8vo. 4*s.* 6*d.*

Lives of Dryden and Pope. Stiff covers, 2*s.* 6*d.*

—— III. *Life of Milton.* Edited, with Notes, etc., by C. H. Firth, M.A. Extra fcap. 8vo. *cloth*, 2*s.* 6*d.* *Stiff cover*, 1*s.* 6*d.*

—— IV. *Vanity of Human Wishes.* With Notes, by E. J. Payne, M.A. Paper covers, 4*d.*

—— V. *Wit and Wisdom of Samuel Johnson.* Edited by G. Birkbeck Hill, D.C.L. Crown 8vo. 7*s.* 6*d.*

—— VI. *Boswell's Life of Johnson. With the Journal of a Tour to the Hebrides.* Edited, with copious Notes, Appendices, and Index, by G. Birkbeck Hill, D.C.L., Pembroke College. With Portraits and Facsimiles. 6 vols. Medium 8vo. *Half bound*, 3*l.* 3*s.*

Cowper. Edited, with Life, Introductions, and Notes, by H. T. Griffith, B.A.

—— I. *The Didactic Poems of* 1782, with Selections from the Minor Pieces, A.D. 1779–1783. Extra fcap. 8vo. 3*s.*

—— II. *The Task, with Tirocinium*, and Selections from the Minor Poems, A.D. 1784–1799. Second Edition. Extra fcap. 8vo. 3*s.*

Burke. Select Works. Edited, with Introduction and Notes, by E. J. Payne, M.A.

—— I. *Thoughts on the Present Discontents; the two Speeches on America.* Second Edition. Extra fcap. 8vo. 4*s.* 6*d.*

—— II. *Reflections on the French Revolution.* Second Edition. Extra fcap. 8vo. 5*s.*

—— III. *Four Letters on the Proposals for Peace with the* Regicide Directory of France. Second Edition. Extra fcap. 8vo. 5*s.*

Keats. Hyperion, Book I. With Notes by W. T. Arnold, B.A. Paper covers, 4*d.*

Byron. Childe Harold. Edited, with Introduction and Notes, by H. F. Tozer, M.A. Extra fcap. 8vo. 3*s.* 6*d.* In white Parchment, 5*s.*

Scott. Lay of the Last Minstrel. Edited with Preface and Notes by W. Minto, M.A. With Map. Extra fcap. 8vo. Stiff covers, 2*s.* Ornamental Parchment, 3*s.* 6*d.*

—— *Lay of the Last Minstrel.* Introduction and Canto I, with Preface and Notes, by the same Editor. 6*d.*

II. LATIN.

Rudimenta Latina. Comprising Accidence, and Exercises of a very Elementary Character, for the use of Beginners. By John Barrow Allen, M.A. Extra fcap. 8vo. 2*s.*

An Elementary Latin Grammar. By the same Author. Fifty-Seventh Thousand. Extra fcap. 8vo. 2*s.* 6*d.*

A First Latin Exercise Book. By the same Author. Fourth Edition. Extra fcap. 8vo. 2*s.* 6*d.*

A Second Latin Exercise Book. By the same Author. Extra fcap. 8vo. 3*s.* 6*d.*

A Key to First and Second Latin Exercise Books, in one volume, price 5*s.* Supplied to *Teachers only* on application to the Secretary of the Clarendon Press.

Reddenda Minora, or Easy Passages, Latin and Greek, for Unseen Translation. For the use of Lower Forms. Composed and selected by C. S. Jerram, M.A. Extra fcap. 8vo. 1*s.* 6*d.*

Anglice Reddenda, or Extracts, Latin and Greek, for Unseen Translation. By C. S. Jerram, M.A. Third Edition, Revised and Enlarged. Extra fcap. 8vo. 2*s.* 6*d.*

Anglice Reddenda. Second Series. By the same Author. Extra fcap. 8vo. 3*s.*

Passages for Translation into Latin. For the use of Passmen and others. Selected by J. Y. Sargent, M.A. Seventh Edition. Extra fcap. 8vo. 2*s.* 6*d.*

Exercises in Latin Prose Composition; with Introduction, Notes, and Passages of Graduated Difficulty for Translation into Latin. By G. G. Ramsay, M.A., LL.D. Second Edition. Extra fcap. 8vo. 4*s.* 6*d.*

Hints and Helps for Latin Elegiacs. By H. Lee-Warner, M.A. Extra fcap. 8vo. 3*s.* 6*d.*

First Latin Reader. By T. J. Nunns, M.A. Third Edition. Extra fcap. 8vo. 2*s.*

Caesar. The Commentaries (for Schools). With Notes and Maps. By Charles E. Moberly, M.A.

The Gallic War. Second Edition. Extra fcap. 8vo. 4*s.* 6*d.*
The Gallic War. Books I, II. Extra fcap. 8vo. 2*s.*
The Civil War. Extra fcap. 8vo. 3*s.* 6*d.*
The Civil War. Book I. Second Edition. Extra fcap. 8vo. 2*s.*

Cicero. Speeches against Catilina. By E. A. Upcott, M.A., Assistant Master in Wellington College. In one or two Parts. Extra fcap. 8vo. 2*s.* 6*d.*

—— *Selection of interesting and descriptive passages.* With Notes. By Henry Walford, M.A. In three Parts. Extra fcap. 8vo. 4*s.* 6*d.*

Each Part separately, limp, 1*s.* 6*d.*

Part I. Anecdotes from Grecian and Roman History. Third Edition.
Part II. Omens and Dreams: Beauties of Nature. Third Edition.
Part III. Rome's Rule of her Provinces. Third Edition.

—— *De Senectute.* Edited, with Introduction and Notes, by L. Huxley, M.A. In one or two Parts. Extra fcap. 8vo. 2*s.*

—— *Selected Letters* (for Schools). With Notes. By the late C. E. Prichard, M.A., and E. R. Bernard, M.A. Second Edition. Extra fcap. 8vo. 3*s.*

—— *Select Orations* (for Schools). In Verrem I. De Imperio Gn. Pompeii. Pro Archia. Philippica IX. With Introduction and Notes by J. R. King, M.A. Second Edition. Extra fcap. 8vo. 2*s.* 6*d.*

—— *In Q. Caecilium Divinatio,* and *In C. Verrem Actio Prima.* With Introduction and Notes, by J. R. King, M.A. Extra fcap. 8vo. limp, 1*s.* 6*d.*

—— *Speeches against Catilina.* With Introduction and Notes, by E. A. Upcott, M.A. In one or two Parts. Extra fcap. 8vo. 2*s.* 6*d.*

Cornelius Nepos. With English Notes. By Oscar Browning, M.A. Third Edition. Revised by W. R. Inge, M.A. (In one or two Parts.) Extra fcap. 8vo. 3*s.*

Horace. Selected Odes. With Notes for the use of a Fifth Form. By E. C. Wickham, M.A. In one or two Parts. Extra fcap. 8vo. *cloth,* 2*s.*

Livy. Selections (for Schools). With Notes and Maps. By H. Lee-Warner, M.A. Extra fcap. 8vo. In Parts, limp, each 1*s.* 6*d.*

Part I. The Caudine Disaster. Part II. Hannibal's Campaign in Italy. Part III. The Macedonian War.

—— Books V–VII. With Introduction and Notes. By A. R. Cluer, B.A. Second Edition. Revised by P. E. Matheson, M.A. (In one or two Parts.) Extra fcap. 8vo. 5*s.*

—— Books XXI, XXII, and XXIII. With Introduction and Notes. By M. T. Tatham, M.A. Extra fcap. 8vo. 4*s.* 6*d.*

—— Book XXII. By the same Editor. Extra fcap. 8vo. 2*s.* 6*d.*

Ovid. Selections for the use of Schools. With Introductions and Notes, and an Appendix on the Roman Calendar. By W. Ramsay, M.A. Edited by G. G. Ramsay, M.A. Third Edition. Extra fcap. 8vo. 5*s.* 6*d.*

Ovid. Tristia. Book I. The Text revised, with an Introduction and Notes. By S. G. Owen, B.A. Extra fcap. 8vo. 3*s*. 6*d*.

Plautus. Captivi. Edited by W. M. Lindsay, M.A. Extra fcap. 8vo. (In one or two Parts.) 2*s*. 6*d*.

—— *The Trinummus.* With Notes and Introductions. (Intended for the Higher Forms of Public Schools.) By C. E. Freeman, M.A., and A. Sloman, M.A. Extra fcap. 8vo. 3*s*.

Pliny. Selected Letters (for Schools). With Notes. By the late C. E. Prichard, M.A., and E. R. Bernard, M.A. Extra fcap. 8vo. 3*s*.

Sallust. With Introduction and Notes. By W. W. Capes, M.A. Extra fcap. 8vo. 4*s*. 6*d*.

Tacitus. The Annals. Books I–IV. Edited, with Introduction and Notes (for the use of Schools and Junior Students), by H. Furneaux, M.A. Extra fcap. 8vo. 5*s*.

—— *The Annals.* Book I. With Introduction and Notes, by the same Editor. Extra fcap. 8vo. limp, 2*s*.

Terence. Andria. With Notes and Introductions. By C. E. Freeman, M.A., and A. Sloman, M.A. Extra fcap. 8vo. 3*s*.

—— *Adelphi.* With Notes and Introductions. (Intended for the Higher Forms of Public Schools.) By A. Sloman, M.A. Extra fcap. 8vo. 3*s*.

—— *Phormio.* With Notes and Introductions. By A. Sloman, M.A. Extra fcap. 8vo. 3*s*.

Tibullus and Propertius. Selections. Edited by G. G. Ramsay, M.A. Extra fcap. 8vo. (In one or two vols.) 6*s*.

Virgil. With Introduction and Notes. By T. L. Papillon, M.A. Two vols. Crown 8vo. 10*s*. 6*d*. The Text separately, 4*s*. 6*d*.

—— *Bucolics.* Edited by C. S. Jerram, M.A. In one or two Parts. Extra fcap. 8vo. 2*s*. 6*d*.

—— *Aeneid* I. With Introduction and Notes, by C. S. Jerram, M.A. Extra fcap. 8vo. limp, 1*s*. 6*d*.

—— *Aeneid* IX. Edited, with Introduction and Notes, by A. E. Haigh, M.A., late Fellow of Hertford College, Oxford. Extra fcap. 8vo. limp, 1*s*. 6*d*. In two Parts, 2*s*.

Avianus, The Fables of. Edited, with Prolegomena, Critical Apparatus, Commentary, etc. By Robinson Ellis, M.A., LL.D. Demy 8vo. 8*s*. 6*d*.

Catulli Veronensis Liber. Iterum recognovit, apparatum criticum prolegomena appendices addidit, Robinson Ellis, A.M. 1878. Demy 8vo. 16*s*.

—— *A Commentary on Catullus.* By Robinson Ellis, M.A. 1876. Demy 8vo. 16*s*.

Catulli Veronensis Carmina Selecta, secundum recognitionem Robinson Ellis, A.M. Extra fcap. 8vo. 3*s*. 6*d*.

Cicero de Oratore. With Introduction and Notes. By A. S. Wilkins, Litt. D.
Book I. Second Edition. 1888. 8vo. 7*s*. 6*d*. Book II. 1881. 8vo. 5*s*.

—— *Philippic Orations.* With Notes. By J. R. King, M.A. Second Edition. 1879. 8vo. 10*s*. 6*d*.

—— *Select Letters.* With English Introductions, Notes, and Appendices. By Albert Watson, M.A. Third Edition. Demy 8vo. 18*s*.

—— *Select Letters.* Text. By the same Editor. Second Edition. Extra fcap. 8vo. 4*s*.

—— *pro Cluentio.* With Introduction and Notes. By W. Ramsay, M.A. Edited by G. G. Ramsay, M.A. 2nd Ed. Ext. fcap. 8vo. 3*s*. 6*d*.

Horace. With a Commentary. Volume I. The Odes, Carmen Seculare, and Epodes. By Edward C. Wickham, M.A. Second Edition. 1877. Demy 8vo. 12*s*.

—— A reprint of the above, in a size suitable for the use of Schools. In one or two Parts. Extra fcap. 8vo. 6*s*.

Livy, Book I. With Introduction, Historical Examination, and Notes. By J. R. Seeley, M.A. Second Edition. 1881. 8vo. 6*s*.

Ovid. P. Ovidii Nasonis Ibis. Ex Novis Codicibus edidit, Scholia Vetera Commentarium cum Prolegomenis Appendice Indice addidit, R. Ellis, A.M. 8vo. 10*s*. 6*d*.

Persius. The Satires. With a Translation and Commentary. By John Conington, M.A. Edited by Henry Nettleship, M.A. Second Edition. 1874. 8vo. 7*s*. 6*d*.

Juvenal. XIII Satires. Edited, with Introduction and Notes, by C. H. Pearson, M.A., and Herbert A. Strong, M.A., LL.D., Professor of Latin in Liverpool University College, Victoria University. In two Parts. Crown 8vo. Complete, 6*s*.

Also separately, Part I. Introduction, Text, etc., 3*s*. Part II. Notes, 3*s*. 6*d*.

Tacitus. The Annals. Books I–VI. Edited, with Introduction and Notes, by H. Furneaux, M.A. 8vo. 18*s*.

King (J. E., M.A.) and C. Cookson, M.A. The Principles of Sound and Inflexion, as illustrated in the Greek and Latin Languages. 1888. 8vo. 18*s*.

Nettleship (H., M.A.). Lectures and Essays on Subjects connected with Latin Scholarship and Literature. Crown 8vo. 7*s*. 6*d*.

—— *The Roman Satura.* 8vo. sewed, 1*s*.

—— *Ancient Lives of Vergil.* 8vo. sewed, 2*s*.

Papillon (*T. L., M.A.*). *A Manual of Comparative Philology.* Third Edition, Revised and Corrected. 1882. Crown 8vo. 6*s.*

Pinder (*North, M.A.*). *Selections from the less known Latin* Poets. 1869. 8vo. 15*s.*

Sellar (*W. Y., M.A.*). *Roman Poets of the Augustan Age.* VIRGIL. New Edition. 1883. Crown 8vo. 9*s.*

—— *Roman Poets of the Republic.* New Edition, Revised and Enlarged. 1881. 8vo. 14*s.*

Wordsworth (*J., M.A.*). *Fragments and Specimens of Early* Latin. With Introductions and Notes. 1874. 8vo. 18*s.*

III. GREEK.

A Greek Primer, for the use of beginners in that Language. By Charles Wordsworth, D.C.L. Seventh Edition. Extra fcap. 8vo. 1*s.* 6*d.*

A Greek Testament Primer. An Easy Grammar and Reading Book for the use of Students beginning Greek. By the Rev. E. Miller, M.A. Extra fcap. 8vo. 3*s.* 6*d.*

Easy Greek Reader. By Evelyn Abbott, M.A. In one or two Parts. Extra fcap. 8vo. 3*s.*

Graecae Grammaticae Rudimenta in usum Scholarum. Auctore Carolo Wordsworth, D.C.L. Nineteenth Edition, 1882. 12mo. 4*s.*

A Greek-English Lexicon, abridged from Liddell and Scott's 4to. edition, chiefly for the use of Schools. Twenty-first Edition. 1886. Square 12mo. 7*s.* 6*d.*

Greek Verbs, Irregular and Defective. By W. Veitch. Fourth Edition. Crown 8vo. 10*s.* 6*d.*

The Elements of Greek Accentuation (for Schools): abridged from his larger work by H. W. Chandler, M.A. Extra fcap. 8vo. 2*s.* 6*d.*

A SERIES OF GRADUATED GREEK READERS:—

First Greek Reader. By W. G. Rushbrooke, M.L. Second Edition. Extra fcap. 8vo. 2*s.* 6*d.*

Second Greek Reader. By A. M. Bell, M.A. Extra fcap. 8vo. 3*s.* 6*d.*

Fourth Greek Reader; being Specimens of Greek Dialects. With Introductions, etc. By W. W. Merry, D.D. Extra fcap. 8vo. 4*s.* 6*d.*

Fifth Greek Reader. Selections from Greek Epic and Dramatic Poetry, with Introductions and Notes. By Evelyn Abbott, M.A. Extra fcap. 8vo. 4*s.* 6*d.*

The Golden Treasury of Ancient Greek Poetry: being a Collection of the finest passages in the Greek Classic Poets, with Introductory Notices and Notes. By R. S. Wright, M.A. Extra fcap. 8vo. 8*s.* 6*d.*

A Golden Treasury of Greek Prose, being a Collection of the finest passages in the principal Greek Prose Writers, with Introductory Notices and Notes. By R. S. Wright, M.A., and J. E. L. Shadwell, M.A. Extra fcap. 8vo. 4*s*. 6*d*.

Aeschylus. Prometheus Bound (for Schools). With Introduction and Notes, by A. O. Prickard, M.A. Second Edition. Extra fcap. 8vo. 2*s*.

—— *Agamemnon.* With Introduction and Notes, by Arthur Sidgwick, M.A. Third Edition. In one or two parts. Extra fcap. 8vo. 3*s*.

—— *Choephoroi.* With Introduction and Notes by the same Editor. Extra fcap. 8vo. 3*s*.

—— *Eumenides.* With Introduction and Notes, by the same Editor. In one or two Parts. Extra fcap. 8vo. 3*s*.

Aristophanes. In Single Plays. Edited, with English Notes, Introductions, &c., by W. W. Merry, D.D. Extra fcap. 8vo.

I. The Clouds, Second Edition, 2*s*.
II. The Acharnians, Third Edition. In one or two parts, 3*s*.
III. The Frogs, Second Edition. In one or two parts, 3*s*.
IV. The Knights. In one or two parts, 3*s*.

Cebes. Tabula. With Introduction and Notes. By C. S. Jerram, M.A. Extra fcap. 8vo. 2*s*. 6*d*.

Demosthenes. Orations against Philip. With Introduction and Notes, by Evelyn Abbott, M.A., and P. E. Matheson, M.A. Vol. I. Philippic I. Olynthiacs I–III. In one or two Parts. Extra fcap. 8vo. 3*s*.

Euripides. Alcestis (for Schools). By C. S. Jerram, M.A. Extra fcap. 8vo. 2*s*. 6*d*.

—— *Hecuba.* With Notes by C. H. Russell. *In the Press.*

—— *Helena.* Edited, with Introduction, Notes, etc., for Upper and Middle Forms. By C. S. Jerram, M.A. Extra fcap. 8vo. 3*s*.

—— *Heracleidae.* Edited with Introduction and Notes by C. S. Jerram, M.A. Extra fcap. 8vo. 3*s*.

—— *Iphigenia in Tauris.* Edited, with Introduction, Notes, etc., for Upper and Middle Forms. By C. S. Jerram, M.A. Extra fcap. 8vo. cloth, 3*s*.

—— *Medea.* By C. B. Heberden, M.A. In one or two Parts. Extra fcap. 8vo. 2*s*.

Herodotus, Book IX. Edited, with Notes, by Evelyn Abbott, M.A. In one or two Parts. Extra fcap. 8vo. 3*s*.

Herodotus, Selections from. Edited, with Introduction, Notes, and a Map, by W. W. Merry, D.D. Extra fcap. 8vo. 2*s*. 6*d*.

Homer. Odyssey, Books I–XII (for Schools). By W. W. Merry, D.D. Fortieth Thousand. (In one or two Parts.) Extra fcap. 8vo. 5*s*.

Books I, and II, *separately*, each 1*s*. 6*d*.

—— *Odyssey*, Books XIII–XXIV (for Schools). By the same Editor. Second Edition. Extra fcap. 8vo. 5*s*.

—— *Iliad*, Book I (for Schools). By D. B. Monro, M.A. Second Edition. Extra fcap. 8vo. 2*s*.

—— *Iliad*, Books I–XII (for Schools). With an Introduction, a brief Homeric Grammar, and Notes. By D. B. Monro, M.A. Second Edition. Extra fcap. 8vo. 6*s*.

—— *Iliad*, Books VI and XXI. With Introduction and Notes. By Herbert Hailstone, M.A. Extra fcap. 8vo. 1*s*. 6*d*. each.

Lucian. Vera Historia (for Schools). By C. S. Jerram, M.A. Second Edition. Extra fcap. 8vo. 1*s*. 6*d*.

Lysias. Epitaphios. Edited, with Introduction and Notes, by F. J. Snell, B.A. (In one or two Parts.) Extra fcap. 8vo. 2*s*.

Plato. Meno. With Introduction and Notes. By St. George Stock, M.A., Pembroke College. (In one or two Parts.) Extra fcap. 8vo. 2*s*. 6*d*.

Plato. The Apology. With Introduction and Notes. By St. George Stock, M.A. (In one or two Parts.) Extra fcap. 8vo. 2*s*. 6*d*.

Sophocles. For the use of Schools. Edited with Introductions and English Notes By Lewis Campbell, M.A., and Evelyn Abbott, M.A. *New and Revised Edition*. 2 Vols. Extra fcap. 8vo. 10*s*. 6*d*.

Sold separately, Vol. I, Text, 4*s*. 6*d*.; Vol. II, Explanatory Notes, 6*s*.

Sophocles. In Single Plays, with English Notes, &c. By Lewis Campbell, M.A., and Evelyn Abbott, M.A. Extra fcap. 8vo. limp.

Oedipus Tyrannus, Philoctetes. New and Revised Edition, 2*s*. each.
Oedipus Coloneus, Antigone, 1*s*. 9*d*. each.
Ajax, Electra, Trachiniae, 2*s*. each.

—— *Oedipus Rex*: Dindorf's Text, with Notes by the present Bishop of St. David's. Extra fcap. 8vo. limp, 1*s*. 6*d*.

Theocritus (for Schools). With Notes. By H. Kynaston, D.D. (late Snow). Third Edition. Extra fcap. 8vo. 4*s*. 6*d*.

Xenophon. Easy Selections (for Junior Classes). With a Vocabulary, Notes, and Map. By J. S. Phillpotts, B.C.L., and C. S. Jerram, M.A. Third Edition. Extra fcap. 8vo. 3*s*. 6*d*.

—— *Selections* (for Schools). With Notes and Maps. By J. S. Phillpotts, B.C.L. Fourth Edition. Extra fcap. 8vo. 3*s*. 6*d*.

—— *Anabasis*, Book I. Edited for the use of Junior Classes and Private Students. With Introduction, Notes, etc. By J. Marshall, M.A., Rector of the Royal High School, Edinburgh. Extra fcap. 8vo. 2*s*. 6*d*.

Xenophon. Anabasis, Book II. With Notes and Map. By C. S. Jerram, M.A. Extra fcap. 8vo. 2*s*.

—— *Anabasis*, Book III. Edited with Introduction, Analysis, Notes, etc., by J. Marshall, M.A. Extra fcap. 8vo. 2*s*. 6*d*.

—— *Cyropaedia*, Book I. With Introduction and Notes by C. Bigg, D.D. Extra fcap. 8vo. 2*s*.

—— *Cyropaedia*, Books IV and V. With Introduction and Notes by C. Bigg, D.D. Extra fcap. 8vo. 2*s*. 6*d*.

—— *Hellenica*, Books I, II. With Introductions and Notes by G. E. Underhill, M.A., Fellow and Tutor of Magdalen College. Extra fcap. 8vo. *cloth*, 3*s*.

Aristotle's Politics. With an Introduction, Essays, and Notes. By W. L. Newman, M.A., Fellow of Balliol College. Vols. I and II. Medium 8vo. 28*s*.

Aristotle. On the History of the Process by which the Aristotelian Writings arrived at their present form. An Essay by Richard Shute, M.A., late Student of Christ Church; with a Brief Memoir of the Author. 8vo. 7*s*. 6*d*.

Aristotelian Studies. I. On the Structure of the Seventh Book of the Nicomachean Ethics. By J. C. Wilson, M.A. 8vo. stiff, 5*s*.

Aristotelis Ethica Nicomachea, ex recensione Immanuelis Bekkeri. Crown 8vo. 5*s*.

Demosthenes and Aeschines. The Orations of Demosthenes and Æschines on the Crown. With Introductory Essays and Notes. By G. A. Simcox, M.A., and W. H. Simcox, M.A. 1872. 8vo. 12*s*.

Head (Barclay V.). Historia Numorum: A Manual of Greek Numismatics. Royal 8vo. half-bound. 2*l*. 2*s*.

Hicks (E. L., M.A.). A Manual of Greek Historical Inscriptions. Demy 8vo. 10*s*. 6*d*.

Homer. Odyssey, Books I–XII. Edited with English Notes, Appendices, etc. By W. W. Merry, D.D., and the late James Riddell, M.A. 1886. Second Edition. Demy 8vo. 16*s*.

Homer. A Grammar of the Homeric Dialect. By D. B. Monro, M.A. Demy 8vo. 10*s*. 6*d*.

Polybius. Selections from Polybius. Edited by J. L. Strachan-Davidson, M.A., Fellow and Tutor of Balliol College. With three Maps. Medium 8vo. buckram, 21*s*.

Sophocles. The Plays and Fragments. With English Notes and Introductions, by Lewis Campbell, M.A. 2 vols.

Vol. I. Oedipus Tyrannus. Oedipus Coloneus. Antigone. 8vo. 16*s*.
Vol. II. Ajax. Electra. Trachiniae. Philoctetes. Fragments. 8vo. 16*s*.

IV. FRENCH AND ITALIAN.

Brachet's Etymological Dictionary of the French Language. Translated by G. W. Kitchin, D.D. Third Edition. Crown 8vo. 7*s.* 6*d.*

—— *Historical Grammar of the French Language.* Translated by G. W. Kitchin. D.D. Fourth Edition. Extra fcap. 8vo. 3*s.* 6*d.*

Works by GEORGE SAINTSBURY, M.A.

Primer of French Literature. Extra fcap. 8vo. 2*s.*

Short History of French Literature. Crown 8vo. 10*s.* 6*d.*

Specimens of French Literature, from Villon to Hugo. Crown 8vo. 9*s.*

MASTERPIECES OF THE FRENCH DRAMA.

Corneille's Horace. Edited, with Introduction and Notes, by George Saintsbury, M.A. Extra fcap. 8vo. 2*s.* 6*d.*

Molière's Les Précieuses Ridicules. Edited, with Introduction and Notes, by Andrew Lang, M.A. Extra fcap. 8vo. 1*s.* 6*d.*

Racine's Esther. Edited, with Introduction and Notes, by George Saintsbury, M.A. Extra fcap. 8vo. 2*s.*

Beaumarchais' Le Barbier de Séville. Edited, with Introduction and Notes, by Austin Dobson. Extra fcap. 8vo. 2*s.* 6*d.*

Voltaire's Mérope. Edited, with Introduction and Notes, by George Saintsbury. Extra fcap. 8vo. cloth, 2*s.*

Musset's On ne badine pas avec l'Amour, and *Fantasio.* Edited, with Prolegomena, Notes, etc., by Walter Herries Pollock. Extra fcap. 8vo. 2*s.*

The above six Plays may be had in ornamental case, and bound in Imitation Parchment, price 12*s.* 6*d.*

Perrault's Popular Tales. Edited from the Original Editions, with Introduction, etc., by Andrew Lang, M.A. Extra fcap. 8vo., paper boards, 5*s.* 6*d.*

Sainte-Beuve. Selections from the Causeries du Lundi. Edited by George Saintsbury, M.A. Extra fcap. 8vo. 2*s.*

Quinet's Lettres à sa Mère. Selected and edited by George Saintsbury, M.A. Extra fcap. 8vo. 2*s.*

Gautier, Théophile. Scenes of Travel. Selected and Edited by George Saintsbury, M.A. Extra fcap. 8vo. 2*s.*

L'Éloquence de la Chaire et de la Tribune Françaises. Edited by Paul Blouët, B.A. Vol. I. Sacred Oratory. Extra fcap. 8vo. 2*s.* 6*d.*

Edited by **GUSTAVE MASSON, B.A.**

Corneille's Cinna. With Notes, Glossary, etc. Extra fcap. 8vo. *cloth,* 2*s.* Stiff covers, 1*s.* 6*d.*

Louis XIV and his Contemporaries; as described in Extracts from the best Memoirs of the Seventeenth Century. With English Notes, Genealogical Tables, &c. Extra fcap. 8vo. 2*s.* 6*d.*

Maistre, Xavier de. Voyage autour de ma Chambre. Ourika, by *Madame de Duras;* Le Vieux Tailleur, by *MM. Erckmann–Chatrian;* La Veillée de Vincennes, by *Alfred de Vigny;* Les Jumeaux de l'Hôtel Corneille, by *Edmond About;* Mésaventures d'un Écolier, by *Rodolphe Töpffer.* Third Edition, Revised and Corrected. Extra fcap. 8vo. 2*s.* 6*d.*

—— *Voyage autour de ma Chambre.* Limp, 1*s.* 6*d.*

Molière's Les Fourberies de Scapin, and *Racine's Athalie.* With Voltaire's Life of Molière. Extra fcap. 8vo. 2*s.* 6*d.*

Molière's Les Fourberies de Scapin. With Voltaire's Life of Molière. Extra fcap. 8vo. stiff covers, 1*s.* 6*d.*

Molière's Les Femmes Savantes. With Notes, Glossary, etc. Extra fcap. 8vo. *cloth,* 2*s.*. Stiff covers, 1*s.* 6*d.*

Racine's Andromaque, and *Corneille's Le Menteur.* With Louis Racine's Life of his Father. Extra fcap. 8vo. 2*s.* 6*d.*

Regnard's Le Joueur, and *Brueys and Palaprat's Le Grondeur.* Extra fcap. 8vo. 2*s.* 6*d.*

Sévigné, Madame de, and her chief Contemporaries, Selections from the Correspondence of. Intended more especially for Girls' Schools. Extra fcap. 8vo. 3*s.*

Dante. Selections from the Inferno. With Introduction and Notes. By H. B. Cotterill, B.A. Extra fcap. 8vo. 4*s.* 6*d.*

Tasso. La Gerusalemme Liberata. Cantos i, ii. With Introduction and Notes. By the same Editor. Extra fcap. 8vo. 2*s.* 6*d.*

V. GERMAN.

Scherer (W.). A History of German Literature. Translated from the Third German Edition by Mrs. F. Conybeare. Edited by F. Max Müller. 2 vols. 8vo. 21*s.*

Max Müller. The German Classics, from the Fourth to the Nineteenth Century. With Biographical Notices, Translations into Modern German, and Notes. By F. Max Müller, M.A. A New Edition, Revised, Enlarged, and Adapted to Wilhelm Scherer's 'History of German Literature,' by F. Lichtenstein. 2 vols. crown 8vo. 21*s.*

GERMAN COURSE. By HERMANN LANGE.

The Germans at Home; a Practical Introduction to German Conversation, with an Appendix containing the Essentials of German Grammar. Third Edition. 8vo. 2*s.* 6*d.*

The German Manual; a German Grammar, Reading Book, and a Handbook of German Conversation. 8vo. 7*s.* 6*d.*

Grammar of the German Language. 8vo. 3*s.* 6*d.*

German Composition; A Theoretical and Practical Guide to the Art of Translating English Prose into German. Ed. 2. 8vo. 4*s.* 6*d.*

German Spelling; A Synopsis of the Changes which it has undergone through the Government Regulations of 1880. Paper covers, 6*d.*

Lessing's Laokoon. With Introduction, English Notes, etc. By A. Hamann, Phil. Doc., M.A. Extra fcap. 8vo. 4*s.* 6*d.*

Schiller's Wilhelm Tell. Translated into English Verse by E. Massie, M.A. Extra fcap. 8vo. 5*s.*

GERMAN CLASSICS.

With Biographical, Historical, and Critical Introductions, Arguments (to the Dramas), and Complete Commentaries.

Edited by C. A. BUCHHEIM, Phil. Doc. Professor in King's College, London.

Lessing:
- (*a*) *Nathan der Weise.* A Dramatic Poem. 4*s.* 6*d.*
- (*b*) *Minna von Barnhelm.* A Comedy. 3*s.* 6*d.*

Goethe:
- (*a*) *Egmont.* A Tragedy. 3*s.*
- (*b*) *Iphigenie auf Tauris.* A Drama. 3*s.*

Schiller:
- (*a*) *Wilhelm Tell.* A Drama. Large Edition. With a Map. 3*s.* 6*d.*
- (*b*) *Wilhelm Tell.* School Edition. With a Map. 2*s.*
- (*c*) *Historische Skizzen.* With a Map. 2*s.* 6*d.*

Heine:
- (*a*) *Prosa:* being Selections from his Prose Writings. 4*s.* 6*d.*
- (*b*) *Harzreise.* Cloth, 2*s.* 6*d.*; paper covers, 1*s.* 6*d.*

Modern German Reader. A Graduated Collection of Extracts from Modern German Authors:—

Part I. Prose Extracts. With English Notes, a Grammatical Appendix, and a Complete Vocabulary. Fourth Edition. 2*s.* 6*d.*

Part II. Extracts in Prose and Poetry. With English Notes and an Index. Second Edition. 2*s.* 6*d.*

Becker (the Historian):

Friedrich der Grosse. Edited, with Notes, an Historical Introduction, and a Map. 3*s.* 6*d.*

Niebuhr:

Griechische Heroen-Geschichten (Tales of Greek Heroes). Edited, with English Notes and a Vocabulary, by Emma S. Buchheim. Second, Revised Edition. *cloth,* 2*s.*

An Old High German Primer. With Grammar, Notes, and Glossary. By Joseph Wright, Ph.D. Extra fcap. 8vo. 3*s.* 6*d.*

A Middle High German Primer. With Grammar, Notes, and Glossary. By Joseph Wright, Ph.D. Extra fcap. 8vo. 3*s.* 6*d.*

VI. MATHEMATICS, PHYSICAL SCIENCE, &c.

By LEWIS HENSLEY, M.A.

Figures made Easy: a first Arithmetic Book. Crown 8vo. 6*d.*

Answers to the Examples in Figures made Easy, together with two thousand additional Examples, with Answers. Crown 8vo. 1*s.*

The Scholar's Arithmetic. Crown 8vo. 2*s.* 6*d.*

Answers to the Examples in the Scholar's Arithmetic. 1*s.* 6*d.*

The Scholar's Algebra. Crown 8vo. 2*s.* 6*d.*

Aldis (W. S., M.A.). A Text-Book of Algebra: with Answers to the Examples. Crown 8vo. 7*s.* 6*d.*

Baynes (R. E., M.A.). Lessons on Thermodynamics. 1878. Crown 8vo. 7*s.* 6*d.*

Chambers (G. F., F.R.A.S.). A Handbook of Descriptive Astronomy. Third Edition. 1877. Demy 8vo. 28*s.*

Clarke (Col. A. R., C.B., R.E.). Geodesy. 1880. 8vo. 12*s.* 6*d.*

Cremona (Luigi). Elements of Projective Geometry. Translated by C. Leudesdorf, M.A. 8vo. 12*s.* 6*d.*

Donkin. Acoustics. Second Edition. Crown 8vo. 7*s.* 6*d.*

Etheridge (R.). Fossils of the British Islands, Stratigraphically arranged. Part I. PALAEOZOIC. 4to. 1*l.* 10*s.* *Just ready.*

Euclid Revised. Containing the Essentials of the Elements of Plane Geometry as given by Euclid in his first Six Books. Edited by R. C. J. Nixon, M.A. Crown 8vo.

Sold separately as follows,

Book I. 1*s.* | Books I, II. 1*s.* 6*d.*

Books I–IV. 3*s.* 6*d.* | Books V, VI. 3*s.*

D

Euclid.—Geometry in Space. Containing parts of Euclid's Eleventh and Twelfth Books. By the same Editor. Crown 8vo. 3*s.* 6*d.*

Galton (Douglas, C.B., F.R.S.). The Construction of Healthy Dwellings. Demy 8vo. 10*s.* 6*d.*

Hamilton (Sir R. G. C.), and J. Ball. Book-keeping. New and enlarged Edition. Extra fcap. 8vo. limp cloth, 2*s.*

Ruled Exercise books adapted to the above may be had, price 2*s.*

Harcourt (A. G. Vernon, M.A.), and *H. G. Madan, M.A. Exercises in Practical Chemistry.* Vol. I. Elementary Exercises. Fourth Edition. Crown 8vo. 10*s.* 6*d.*

Maclaren (Archibald). A System of Physical Education: Theoretical and Practical. Extra fcap. 8vo. 7*s.* 6*d.*

Madan (H. G., M.A.). Tables of Qualitative Analysis. Large 4to. paper, 4*s.* 6*d.*

Maxwell (J. Clerk, M.A., F.R.S.). A Treatise on Electricity and Magnetism. Second Edition. 2 vols. Demy 8vo. 1*l.* 11*s.* 6*d.*

—— *An Elementary Treatise on Electricity.* Edited by William Garnett, M.A. Demy 8vo. 7*s.* 6*d.*

Minchin (G. M., M.A.). A Treatise on Statics with Applications to Physics. Third Edition, Corrected and Enlarged. Vol. I. *Equilibrium of Coplanar Forces.* 8vo. 9*s.* Vol. II. *Statics.* 8vo. 16*s.*

—— *Uniplanar Kinematics of Solids and Fluids.* Crown 8vo. 7*s.* 6*d.*

Phillips (John, M.A., F.R.S.). Geology of Oxford and the Valley of the Thames. 1871. 8vo. 21*s.*

—— *Vesuvius.* 1869. Crown 8vo. 10*s.* 6*d.*

Prestwich (Joseph, M.A., F.R.S.). Geology, Chemical, Physical, and Stratigraphical. In two Volumes.

Vol. I. Chemical and Physical. Royal 8vo. 25*s.*

Vol. II. Stratigraphical and Physical. With a new Geographical Map of Europe. Royal 8vo. 36*s.*

Rolleston (George, M.D., F.R.S.). Forms of Animal Life. A Manual of Comparative Anatomy, with descriptions of selected types. Second Edition. Revised and enlarged by W. Hatchett Jackson, M.A. Medium, 8vo. cloth extra, 1*l.* 16*s.*

Smyth. A Cycle of Celestial Objects. Observed, Reduced, and Discussed by Admiral W. H. Smyth, R.N. Revised, condensed, and greatly enlarged by G. F. Chambers, F.R.A.S. 1881. 8vo. 12*s.*

Stewart (Balfour, LL.D., F.R.S.). An Elementary Treatise on Heat, with numerous Woodcuts and Diagrams. Fifth Edition. Extra fcap. 8vo. 7*s.* 6*d.*

Vernon-Harcourt (L. F., M.A.). A Treatise on Rivers and Canals, relating to the Control and Improvement of Rivers, and the Design, Construction, and Development of Canals. 2 vols. (Vol. I, Text. Vol. II, Plates.) 8vo. 21*s.*

—— *Harbours and Docks;* their Physical Features, History, Construction, Equipment, and Maintenance; with Statistics as to their Commercial Development. 2 vols. 8vo. 25*s.*

Walker (James, M.A.). The Theory of a Physical Balance. 8vo. stiff cover, 3*s.* 6*d.*

Watson (H. W., M.A.). A Treatise on the Kinetic Theory of Gases. 1876. 8vo. 3*s.* 6*d.*

Watson (H. W., D. Sc., F.R.S.), and S. H. Burbury, M.A.

I. *A Treatise on the Application of Generalised Coordinates to the Kinetics of a Material System.* 1879. 8vo. 6*s.*

II. *The Mathematical Theory of Electricity and Magnetism.* Vol. I. Electrostatics. 8vo. 10*s.* 6*d.*

Williamson (A. W., Phil. Doc., F.R.S.). Chemistry for Students. A new Edition, with Solutions. 1873. Extra fcap. 8vo. 8*s.* 6*d.*

VII. HISTORY.

Bluntschli (J. K.). The Theory of the State. By J. K. Bluntschli, late Professor of Political Sciences in the University of Heidelberg. Authorised English Translation from the Sixth German Edition. Demy 8vo. half bound, 12*s.* 6*d.*

Finlay (George, LL.D.). A History of Greece from its Conquest by the Romans to the present time, B.C. 146 to A.D. 1864. A new Edition, revised throughout, and in part re-written, with considerable additions, by the Author, and edited by H. F. Tozer, M.A. 7 vols. 8vo. 3*l.* 10*s.*

Fortescue (Sir John, Kt.). The Governance of England: otherwise called The Difference between an Absolute and a Limited Monarchy. A Revised Text. Edited, with Introduction, Notes, and Appendices, by Charles Plummer, M.A. 8vo. half bound, 12*s.* 6*d.*

Freeman (E.A., D.C.L.). A Short History of the Norman Conquest of England. Second Edition. Extra fcap. 8vo. 2*s.* 6*d.*

George (H. B., M.A.). Genealogical Tables illustrative of Modern History. Third Edition, Revised and Enlarged. Small 4to. 12*s.*

Hodgkin (T.). Italy and her Invaders. Illustrated with Plates and Maps. Vols. I—IV, A.D. 376–553. 8vo. 3*l.* 8*s.*

D 2

Hughes (*Alfred*). *Geography for Schools.* With Diagrams. Part I. Practical Geography. Crown 8vo. 2*s*. 6*d*.

Part II. General Geography. *In preparation.*

Kitchin (*G. W., D.D.*). *A History of France.* With numerous Maps, Plans, and Tables. In Three Volumes. *Second Edition.* Crown 8vo. each 10*s*. 6*d*.

Vol. I. Down to the Year 1453.

Vol. II. From 1453–1624. Vol. III. From 1624–1793.

Lucas (*C. P.*). *Introduction to a Historical Geography of the British Colonies.* With Eight Maps. Crown 8vo. 4*s*. 6*d*.

Payne (*E. J., M.A.*). *A History of the United States of America.* In the Press.

Ranke (*L. von*). *A History of England*, principally in the Seventeenth Century. Translated by Resident Members of the University of Oxford, under the superintendence of G. W. Kitchin, D.D., and C. W. Boase, M.A. 1875. 6 vols. 8vo. 3*l*. 3*s*.

Rawlinson (*George, M.A.*). *A Manual of Ancient History.* Second Edition. Demy 8vo. 14*s*.

Ricardo. Letters of David Ricardo to Thomas Robert Malthus (1810–1823). Edited by James Bonar, M.A. Demy 8vo. 10*s*. 6*d*.

Rogers (*J. E. Thorold, M.A.*). *The First Nine Years of the Bank of England.* 8vo. 8*s*. 6*d*.

Select Charters and other Illustrations of English Constitutional History, from the Earliest Times to the Reign of Edward I. Arranged and edited by W. Stubbs, D.D. Fifth Edition. 1883. Crown 8vo. 8*s*. 6*d*.

Stubbs (*W., D.D.*). *The Constitutional History of England,* in its Origin and Development. Library Edition. 3 vols. demy 8vo. 2*l*. 8*s*.

Also in 3 vols. crown 8vo. price 12*s*. each.

—— *Seventeen Lectures on the Study of Medieval and Modern History*, &c., delivered at Oxford 1867–1884. Crown 8vo. 8*s*. 6*d*.

Wellesley. A Selection from the Despatches, Treaties, and other Papers of the Marquess Wellesley, K.G., during his Government of India. Edited by S. J. Owen, M.A. 1877. 8vo. 1*l*. 4*s*.

Wellington. A Selection from the Despatches, Treaties, and other Papers relating to India of Field-Marshal the Duke of Wellington, K.G. Edited by S. J. Owen, M.A. 1880. 8vo. 24*s*.

A History of British India. By S. J. Owen, M.A., Reader in Indian History in the University of Oxford. In preparation.

VIII. LAW.

Alberici Gentilis, I.C.D., I.C., De Iure Belli Libri Tres. Edidit T. E. Holland, I.C.D. 1877. Small 4to. half morocco, 21*s*.

Anson (Sir William R., Bart., D.C.L.). Principles of the English Law of Contract, and of Agency in its Relation to Contract. Fifth Edition. Demy 8vo. 10*s*. 6*d*.

—— *Law and Custom of the Constitution.* Part I. Parliament. Demy 8vo. 10*s*. 6*d*.

Bentham (Jeremy). An Introduction to the Principles of Morals and Legislation. Crown 8vo. 6*s*. 6*d*.

Digby (Kenelm E., M.A.). An Introduction to the History of the Law of Real Property. Third Edition. Demy 8vo. 10*s*. 6*d*.

Gaii Institutionum Juris Civilis Commentarii Quattuor; or, Elements of Roman Law by Gaius. With a Translation and Commentary by Edward Poste, M.A. Second Edition. 1875. 8vo. 18*s*.

Hall (W. E., M.A.). International Law. Second Ed. 8vo. 21*s*.

Holland (T. E., D.C.L.). The Elements of Jurisprudence. Fourth Edition. Demy 8vo. 10*s*. 6*d*.

—— *The European Concert in the Eastern Question*, a Collection of Treaties and other Public Acts. Edited, with Introductions and Notes, by Thomas Erskine Holland, D.C.L. 8vo. 12*s*. 6*d*.

Imperatoris Iustiniani Institutionum Libri Quattuor; with Introductions, Commentary, Excursus and Translation. By J. B. Moyle, B.C.L., M.A. 2 vols. Demy 8vo. 21*s*.

Justinian, The Institutes of, edited as a recension of the Institutes of Gaius, by Thomas Erskine Holland, D.C.L. Second Edition, 1881. Extra fcap. 8vo. 5*s*.

Justinian, Select Titles from the Digest of. By T. E. Holland, D.C.L., and C. L. Shadwell, B.C.L. 8vo. 14*s*.

Also sold in Parts, in paper covers, as follows:—

Part I. Introductory Titles. 2*s*. 6*d*. Part II. Family Law. 1*s*.
Part III. Property Law. 2*s*. 6*d*. Part IV. Law of Obligations (No. 1). 3*s*. 6*d*.
Part IV. Law of Obligations (No. 2). 4*s*. 6*d*.

Lex Aquilia. The Roman Law of Damage to Property: being a Commentary on the Title of the Digest 'Ad Legem Aquiliam' (ix. 2). With an Introduction to the Study of the Corpus Iuris Civilis. By Erwin Grueber, Dr. Jur., M.A. Demy 8vo. 10*s*. 6*d*.

Markby (*W., D.C.L.*). *Elements of Law* considered with reference to Principles of General Jurisprudence. Third Edition. Demy 8vo. 12*s*. 6*d*.

Stokes (*Whitley, D.C.L.*). The Anglo-Indian Codes.
Vol. I. *Substantive Law*. 8vo. 30*s*.
Vol. II. *Adjective Law*. In the Press.

Twiss (*Sir Travers, D.C.L.*). The Law of Nations considered as Independent Political Communities.

Part I. On the Rights and Duties of Nations in time of Peace. A new Edition, Revised and Enlarged. 1884. Demy 8vo. 15*s*.

Part II. On the Rights and Duties of Nations in Time of War. Second Edition, Revised. 1875. Demy 8vo. 21*s*.

IX. MENTAL AND MORAL PHILOSOPHY, &c.

Bacon's Novum Organum. Edited, with English Notes, by G. W. Kitchin, D.D. 1855. 8vo. 9*s*. 6*d*.

—— Translated by G. W. Kitchin, D.D. 1855. 8vo. 9*s*. 6*d*.

Berkeley. *The Works of George Berkeley, D.D.*, formerly Bishop of Cloyne; including many of his writings hitherto unpublished. With Prefaces, Annotations, and an Account of his Life and Philosophy, by Alexander Campbell Fraser, M.A. 4 vols. 1871. 8vo. 2*l*. 18*s*.

The Life, Letters, &c. 1 vol. 16*s*.

—— *Selections from*. With an Introduction and Notes. For the use of Students in the Universities. By Alexander Campbell Fraser, LL.D. Third Edition. Crown 8vo. 7*s*. 6*d*.

Fowler (*T., D.D.*). *The Elements of Deductive Logic*, designed mainly for the use of Junior Students in the Universities. Ninth Edition, with a Collection of Examples. Extra fcap. 8vo. 3*s*. 6*d*.

—— *The Elements of Inductive Logic*, designed mainly for the use of Students in the Universities. Fourth Edition. Extra fcap. 8vo. 6*s*.

—— *and Wilson* (*J. M., B.D.*). *The Principles of Morals* (Introductory Chapters). 8vo. *boards*, 3*s*. 6*d*.

—— *The Principles of Morals*. Part II. (Being the Body of the Work.) 8vo. 10*s*. 6*d*.

Edited by T. FOWLER, D.D.

Bacon. *Novum Organum*. With Introduction, Notes, &c. 1878. 8vo. 14*s*.

Locke's Conduct of the Understanding. Second Edition. Extra fcap. 8vo. 2*s*.

Danson (J. T.). The Wealth of Households. Crown 8vo. 5*s.*

Green (T. H., M.A.). Prolegomena to Ethics. Edited by A. C. Bradley, M.A. Demy 8vo. 12*s.* 6*d.*

Hegel. The Logic of Hegel; translated from the Encyclopaedia of the Philosophical Sciences. With Prolegomena by William Wallace, M.A. 1874. 8vo. 14*s.*

Hume's Treatise of Human Nature; reprinted from the Original Edition, and edited by L. A. Selby-Bigge, M.A., Fellow and Lecturer of University College. Crown 8vo. 9*s.*

Lotze's Logic, in Three Books; of Thought, of Investigation, and of Knowledge. English Translation; Edited by B. Bosanquet, M.A., Fellow of University College, Oxford. Second Edition. 2 vols. Crown 8vo. 12*s.*

—— *Metaphysic*, in Three Books; Ontology, Cosmology, and Psychology. English Translation; Edited by B. Bosanquet, M.A. Second Edition. 2 vols. Crown 8vo. 12*s.*

Martineau (James, D.D.). Types of Ethical Theory. Second Edition. 2 vols. Crown 8vo. 15*s.*

—— *A Study of Religion: its Sources and Contents.* 2 vols. 8vo. 24*s.*

Rogers (J. E. Thorold, M.A.). A Manual of Political Economy, for the use of Schools. Third Edition. Extra fcap. 8vo. 4*s.* 6*d.*

Smith's Wealth of Nations. A new Edition, with Notes, by J. E. Thorold Rogers, M.A. 2 vols. 8vo. 1880. 21*s.*

X. FINE ART.

Butler (A. J., M.A., F.S.A.) The Ancient Coptic Churches of Egypt. 2 vols. 8vo. 30*s.*

Head (Barclay V.). Historia Numorum. A Manual of Greek Numismatics. Royal 8vo. *half morocco*, 42*s.*

Hullah (John). The Cultivation of the Speaking Voice. Second Edition. Extra fcap. 8vo. 2*s.* 6*d.*

Jackson (T. G., M.A.). Dalmatia, the Quarnero and Istria; with Cettigne in Montenegro and the Island of Grado. By T. G. Jackson, M.A., Author of 'Modern Gothic Architecture.' In 3 vols. 8vo. With many Plates and Illustrations. *Half bound*, 42*s.*

Ouseley (Sir F. A. Gore, Bart.). A Treatise on Harmony. Third Edition. 4to. 10*s.*

—— *A Treatise on Counterpoint, Canon, and Fugue,* based upon that of Cherubini. Second Edition. 4to. 16*s.*

—— *A Treatise on Musical Form and General Composition.* Second Edition. 4to. 10*s.*

Robinson (J. C., F.S.A.). A Critical Account of the Drawings by Michel Angelo and Raffaello in the University Galleries, Oxford. 1870. Crown 8vo. 4*s.*

Troutbeck (J., M.A.) and R. F. Dale, M.A. A Music Primer (for Schools). Second Edition. Crown 8vo. 1*s.* 6*d.*

Tyrwhitt (R. St. J., M.A.). A Handbook of Pictorial Art. With coloured Illustrations, Photographs, and a chapter on Perspective by A. Macdonald. Second Edition. 1875. 8vo. half morocco, 18*s.*

Upcott (L. E., M.A.). An Introduction to Greek Sculpture. Crown 8vo. 4*s.* 6*d.*

Vaux (W. S. W., M.A.). Catalogue of the Castellani Collection of Antiquities in the University Galleries, Oxford. Crown 8vo. 1*s.*

The Oxford Bible for Teachers, containing Supplementary HELPS TO THE STUDY OF THE BIBLE, including Summaries of the several Books, with copious Explanatory Notes and Tables illustrative of Scripture History and the characteristics of Bible Lands; with a complete Index of Subjects, a Concordance, a Dictionary of Proper Names, and a series of Maps. Prices in various sizes and bindings from 3*s.* to 2*l.* 5*s.*

Helps to the Study of the Bible, taken from the OXFORD BIBLE FOR TEACHERS, comprising Summaries of the several Books, with copious Explanatory Notes and Tables illustrative of Scripture History and the Characteristics of Bible Lands; with a complete Index of Subjects, a Concordance, a Dictionary of Proper Names, and a series of Maps. Crown 8vo. *cloth,* 3*s.* 6*d.*; 16mo. *cloth,* 1*s.*